MONEY,
FINANCIAL INSTITUTIONS,
AND THE ECONOMY

A Book of Readings

MONEY,
FINANCIAL INSTITUTIONS,
AND THE ECONOMY

A Book of Readings

JAMES A. CRUTCHFIELD

Professor of Economics
University of Washington

CHARLES N. HENNING

Professor of Finance
and Director of B. A. Faculty Publications
University of Washington

WILLIAM PIGOTT

Associate Professor of Finance
University of Washington

PRENTICE-HALL, INC., Englewood Cliffs, N. J.

PRENTICE-HALL INTERNATIONAL, INC., *London*
PRENTICE-HALL OF AUSTRALIA PTY., LTD., *Sydney*
PRENTICE-HALL OF CANADA,, LTD., *Toronto*
PRENTICE-HALL OF INDIA (PRIVATE) LTD., *New Delhi*
PRENTICE-HALL OF JAPAN, INC., *Tokyo*

Current printing (last digit):
12 11 10 9 8 7 6 5 4 3

Printed in the United States of America
60060-C

Preface

NO FIELD IN ECONOMICS HAS SEEN MORE EXCITING
developments during the postwar years than money and banking.
In the United States, as in most other nations of the free world,
there has been a remarkable upsurge of interest in the use of
monetary policy as a device for maintaining economic stability,
and with it a significant broadening of the monetary aspects of
macroeconomic theory. An equally important development was
the growing recognition that monetary analysis and public policy
could no longer ignore the impact of various nonbank financial
institutions which have come to play an increasingly important
role in American financial markets.

All of this involves much more than an updating of existing
facts and theory. In a very real sense, the Federal Reserve
System, the Treasury, and the various segments of the financial
community were all feeling their way in the new financial
environment of the early postwar years. The full significance of
these changes in the operations of financial institutions and in
concepts and techniques of economic stabilization policy has not
yet been fully integrated into accepted economic doctrine.

These developments provide the basic justification for a
new book of readings in the field of money, banking, and financial institutions. It has become increasingly difficult to include
in a conventional text the necessary breadth of empirical in-

formation and an adequate sampling of conflicting views on vital matters of economic theory and policy in the field of money and credit. This book is designed to fill both needs.

We have also tried to provide readings that will stimulate the interest and test the abilities of both graduate and undergraduate students with a particular interest in the field. The best of textbooks can provide no satisfactory substitute for original writing in conveying to the serious student the importance of the lively discussions of monetary issues that have characterized the last two decades.

The editors have intentionally included selections in their entirety, generally, or in only slightly abridged form, because they believe that only thus does the reader gain the flavor of the arguments advanced by particular authors. Abridgments have been made where necessary, but it is believed that a slightly smaller number of articles with only minor abridgments is preferable to a larger number of articles abridged so extensively that the flavor of the original presentations may be lost.

The editors very much appreciate the helpful comments of Paul M. Horvitz, Senior Economist, Office of the Comptroller of the Currency, who reviewed the selections. Responsibility for final selection and editing rests, of course, with the editors.

JAMES A. CRUTCHFIELD
CHARLES N. HENNING
WILLIAM PIGOTT

Table of Contents

Part Three: FINANCIAL INSTITUTIONS
AND THE MONEY MARKET

3 he supports Friedman's view.

Part Six: INTERNATIONAL FINANCE

MONEY,
FINANCIAL INSTITUTIONS,
AND THE ECONOMY

A Book of Readings

Part One

MONEY AND CREDIT
IN A BUSINESS
ENTERPRISE ECONOMY

1

Money, Debt, and Liquid Assets

ECONOMICS IS PRIMARILY CONCERNED WITH THE PRODUC-
tion of real goods and services and with the mechanisms designed
to insure that we produce as much of the right kinds of economic
goods as our resources and technical knowledge permit. Markets
for final products include markets for goods used by consumers
and markets for goods destined for service in further production
—the markets for capital goods. In the highly specialized American economy, division of labor has extended further to the
fields of financial services as well as to physical production and
marketing. There are, then, important markets for financial
assets—in the broad sense, representing claims on physical goods
and services—whose orderly functioning is an inseparable part of
an efficient private enterprise economy.

The readings in Chapter 1 emphasize the fact that money
is one of a group of financial assets, all of which are substitutable
in some degree. Money stands at one extreme as the perfectly
liquid asset usable without delay or penalty to settle any transaction, but modern monetary theory regards money as more
than a simple medium of exchange; in its capacity as a store
of value, it must compete with a host of other financial claims,
many of which are virtually as safe and convenient to hold as
money and which offer the added attraction of interest return.
These range from very close substitutes, that might be termed

3

"near monies" that are convertible into cash virtually on demand, to less liquid claims, usually bearing higher rates of interest or a higher rate of return including both dividends and capital gains, that can be converted only at some risk of capital loss. In Chapter 1 we are concerned with the definition of money and with its proper setting among the array of liquid assets available to meet the special needs of financial institutions, other types of business firms, and households. Definitional matters are peculiarly important relative to money, since few concepts in the whole field of economics are more elusive. There is still disagreement among monetary economists as to what should be included in a definition of the money supply. Similar confusion surrounds the term "credit" —a common word that means many different things to people who nevertheless use it freely.

Selection 1

MONEY, INCOME, AND EXPENDITURE
GEORGE N. HALM

> *This selection provides a broad view of the role of money in income and expenditure flows; of the effects of increases and decreases in the rate of flow of money; of the manner in which saving and investment, through credit markets and the production of capital goods, affect the flow of money; and how this in turn affects the levels of income and of output. Professor Halm makes it clear that spending depends on both the size of the money supply and the velocity of circulation of money. Beginning with a two-sector economy (consumers and business firms) and two types of assets (money and consumer goods), he introduces another sector (financial institutions) and two other types of assets (financial assets other than money and real capital assets). The acquisition and holding of different proportions of these assets by different sectors of the economy constitutes the core of "money and banking," or "Money, Financial Institutions, and the Economy," the title we have used.*

THE CIRCULAR FLOW OF MONEY

We turn now to a brief introductory study of the circular flow of money through the economy. Money has often been referred to as the blood circulating in the economic body or as the oil which lubricates the economic machine. Our discussion of the flow of money will show that these metaphors are not badly chosen, that money is indeed of basic importance for a healthy economy, and that a disease which affects the bloodstream of the economy may become very dangerous. . . .

Looking at our economy as a whole, we see the breadwinners of family households earn their personal income by contributing, in one way or another, to the productive activities which go on in business firms, that is, in the farms,

• From George N. Halm, *Economics of Money and Banking,* revised ed., pp. 11–20. Copyright 1961 by Richard D. Irwin, Inc., Homewood, Ill. Reprinted by permission of Richard D. Irwin, Inc., and the author.

factories, offices, and stores of the nation. Personal income may be earned as wages, salaries, rents, interest, or dividends.

We can watch a flow of personal income, consisting of repeated payments of money by business firms to family households. Where does the money come from which firms pay, at weekly or other intervals, to family households? The answer is obvious: firms sell their products (which we assume at first to consist exclusively of consumers' goods) to family households which purchase them by spending their income on consumption.

Thus consumption expenditure by families leads to a return flow of money to business firms.

Figure 1 shows in a very simplified way how personal income, earned by family households through the sale of productive services to business firms, is spent on the purchase of consumers' goods which are the products of these business firms. The money paid out by the firms flows back to the firms, so that the firms again can make these payments upon which the steady flow of personal income depends. In this way money circulates through the economy.

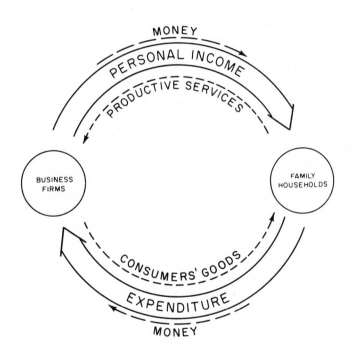

Figure 1

Income and money are not identical, of course, but income is received in the form of money, is used up by spending money, and is expressed as a total amount for some period, say a year, in terms of money.

It is perfectly proper to speak, as we have done, of a circular flow of money. Yet, as we watch carefully, we see this difference between the income flow and expenditure flow, on the one hand, and the flow of money, on the other.

A picture of the income flow and expenditure flow can be taken, as it were, only with a movie camera. Money, on the other hand, can be the object of both a snapshot and a moving picture. The snapshot shows most of the money resting in the money reserves of families and firms; only a relatively insignificant part is caught in the act of transfer from one reserve to another. Thus we can visualize a given total supply or stock of money as the sum of all money reserves. A moving picture, however, would reveal movements of the individual units of money from hand to hand and from account to account, and this movement is essentially circular in the sense described above.

Here we can add one more distinction between money and commodities: commodities pass through the market; they are produced, sold, consumed, and replaced through continuous production. By contrast money stays in the market and is used over and over again.

Since the total amount of money (revealed by our snapshot) is limited and smaller than annual personal income, we see that total expenditure per year depends not only on the supply of money but also on the speed with which money circulates. This velocity of circulation of money is measured by the number of times money is transferred from one owner to another during a period such as a year or a month.

A DECREASE IN THE FLOW OF MONEY

Our discussion according to Figure 1 revealed a flow of income and expenditure which could maintain itself indefinitely. At the end of each week workers and others are paid and they buy, during the following week, what they produced the week before, and the firms accumulate during the week the money needed for the next payday. Since our example was full of identities (income equals expenditure, which equals the value of production, which equals the cost of production, which equals income), we did not meet with any difficulties. Difficulties, however, may easily occur.

Suppose, for instance, that many people decide to hold larger money reserves than before. If the total supply of money is not increased, they will, as a group, not be able to achieve their aim. We saw that the total supply of money is equal to the sum of all money reserves. Thus if A wants to hold a larger reserve of money, somebody else must necessarily get along with a smaller one. If there is a general tendency to hold more money, the consequences may be serious because those who want to increase their money reserves can do so only by spending less than before.

Figure 2, which illustrates this process, is divided into two pictures referring to two consecutive rounds of the money flow. Assume that the first round starts at the firms. The firms pay out the same amount of personal income as in Figure 1 and employ all persons previously employed, for they sold all the consumers' goods produced in the preceding period at prices which covered the cost of production. As in Figure 1, the flow of money from firms to families is marked by an arrow *Personal Income,* whose width indicates the size of this income flow. Some families now decide to keep part of the income formerly spent on consumption. Their money reserve increases but their expenditure decreases. This is indicated by a split in the *Expenditure* arrow of Figure 2. The part of the arrow reaching the firms is narrower than it used to be and is also narrower than the arrow which left the firms. The firms' receipts are smaller than anticipated. As far as consumers' goods are concerned, two assumptions are possible: (a) consumers' goods remain unsold and/or (b) consumers' goods will be sold at lower prices than anticipated. Disappointed, the managers of the firms decide to produce less during the next round and to employ fewer men. Having received less money, the firms have less money to spend on productive services.

In the second round the firms' income payments are reduced, a fact that

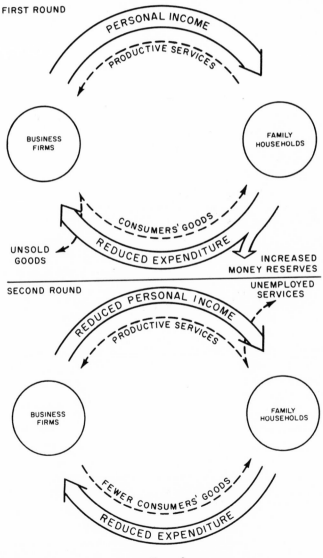

Figure 2

is illustrated by the narrower *Personal Income* arrow leading from firms to families. Families, earning less income than before, spend less than before and the *Expenditure* remains as narrow as in the first round. This is so not because of a desire to increase money reserves still further but simply because the personal income of families is decreased.

Families which find their income decreased and firms which have reduced their production will hold less money than before. We had to expect this result since we knew already that, with a fixed supply of money, the higher money reserves of A had somehow to lead to lower reserves of B.

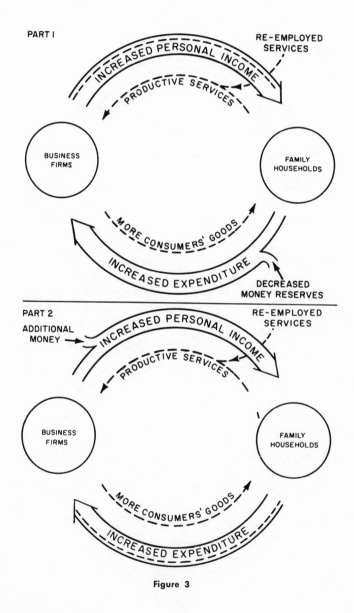

Figure 3

AN INCREASE IN THE FLOW OF MONEY

The opposite case of that shown in Figure 2 would be an increase in the flow of money. Such an increase could be caused either by a release of money reserves (Figure 3, Part 1) or by the borrowing of additional money by firms (Figure 3, Part 2). Either case might result in expanded production and an increase in the personal income flow.

Let us follow the second suggestion. The producer of a new product, which is sure to sell, borrows from the bank. The loan consists of additional money. If unused resources and unemployed labor are available, our manufacturer will meet no difficulties in expanding production. He will pay out additional income to family households and will produce additional products which can be sold because personal income and expenditure will have increased. If, on the other hand, the economy was fully employed before our new production process started, the effects of a creation of additional money will be different. Then personal income will have increased not because of the hiring of unemployed workers but because of the hiring away of employed workers from other occupations. Wage rates and wage payments will increase, but since there will not be more goods for sale, the prices of consumers' goods will rise so that the total value of goods sold will correspond to the increased flow of expenditure and also to the increased cost of production.

When this process takes place on a large scale, we have before us the well-known picture of price inflation. Incidentally, with higher personal income and with increased cost of production, families and firms will tend to hold larger reserves of money. Since we assumed the creation of additional money, and since the supply of money is equal to all money reserves, we see how this demand for larger reserves will be satisfied and where the additional money goes.

SAVINGS, INVESTMENT, AND THE FLOW OF MONEY

Our discussion of the circular flow of money was oversimplified. Investment goods production was left out of consideration because our firms were assumed to produce only consumers' goods. Furthermore, we left out of account the process called "savings," or we considered it only in connection with increased money reserves. How do investment goods production and saving change our picture of the circular flow of money?

We define investment as the purchase or production of new capital goods by business firms. Capital or investment goods are goods which serve production purposes. They are bought with the intention of making a profit and not for the direct satisfaction of human wants. Capital goods (such as machines, tools, materials, factory buildings) are bought by firms from other firms which specialize in their production.[1]

---

[1] This treatment of investment is an oversimplification. It does not allow for inventory accumulation, for government investment, for investment in residential housing by the owner, etc.

Where do the funds come from which business firms spend on these capital goods? This question leads us to the problem of saving. A man is said to save when he does not spend all his income on consumers' goods. Suppose that a worker receives $100 on payday. Instead of spending the whole $100 the following week on consumption he spends only $90. He has saved $10. For the economy as a whole we can say that total saving per period amounts to the total income earned in one period (Y) minus the money spent on consumption (C) in the succeeding period. S equals Y minus C.

If we stopped here we could be tempted to assume that the act of saving interrupts the flow of money because income received by the families does not return to the firms. However, this is by no means necessary. If we assume that savings are eagerly borrowed by business firms for investment purposes, if we assume that what is not spent by families on consumers' goods is spent by firms on capital goods, no interruption of our money flow need occur.

In Figure 4 we see how the saved portion of personal income is used to purchase credit instruments.[2] This act of purchasing securities, incidentally, is also often referred to as "investment." In order to distinguish this concept of investment from the one used above (the purchase or production of new capital

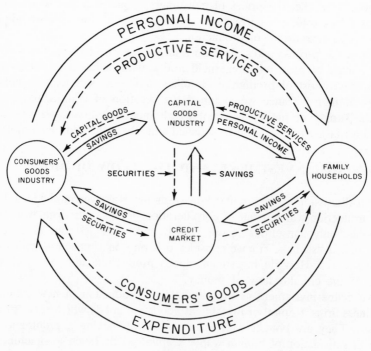

Figure 4

---

[2] We assume that these securities are newly issued. The purchase of existing securities which constitutes merely a transfer for one owner to another is not matched by physical investment.

goods), we can speak of financial investment if we want to indicate the purchase of credit instruments. These securities permit the temporary transfer of money from the creditor to the debtor, from the man who saves (consumes less than he is entitled to) to the manager of the firm who has entrepreneurial initiative.

The firms spend the money which they receive through the sale of securities on capital goods of all kinds. Capital goods are produced by firms in the capital goods industry. These firms employ workers and make income payments to family households just like firms in the consumers' goods industry. The only difference is that their products are bought by other firms rather than by consumers.[3]

Following Figure 4 we can see how the circular flow of money has been changed, but not interrupted, by the inclusion of saving and investment in our model. Starting at the family households we notice how part of the personal income earned is spent, as before, on consumers' goods. But the saved portion of personal income is used to purchase securities sold by business firms. The saving public and the business firms are brought together by a variety of credit institutions (commercial banks, savings banks, and investment banks) which operate on the credit market. Through this credit market the saved portion of personal income flows to firms and is used to purchase capital goods or productive services for the production of capital goods. It is important to notice that through these investment expenditures the circular flow of money is maintained in spite of the reduction of consumption which is implied in the very concept of saving. The saved portion of the personal income finds its way back to family households as income payments to those who work in the capital goods industry.

Were it not for the fact that families save part of their income, the total expenditure on consumers' goods would tend to be greater than the supply of consumers' goods at stable prices. This is because the families' income is now earned in producing both consumers' and capital goods and therefore larger than the value of the consumers' goods. We see that, far from being necessarily harmful, the process of saving has made it possible to increase the productivity of the economy through the creation of more and better productive equipment. Productive resources which would have been devoted to consumers' goods production had the families insisted on spending their whole income on consumption are freed through the process of saving, thus permitting the production of additional capital goods, which will turn out more and better consumers' goods in the future. This also explains why in debt contracts the borrower is able to promise more future money for a given amount of present money.

These beneficial effects of saving depend on investment. If we should not be able to find investment outlets for additional savings, the consequences would be those shown in Figure 2. Income which is saved would fail to be spent on capital goods, total expenditure would decrease, and total income would fall. This contractionist spiral would continue until, at lower income levels, saving

---

[3] Again it must be kept in mind that we are here working with a simplified model which does not do justice to such cases as the purchase of a newly built home by the owner.

would decrease far enough to match investment or until, for one reason or another, investment would sufficiently increase to match saving.

As saving can exceed investment, so can investment exceed saving.[4] We have already discussed the case of a creation of additional money which causes a broadening of the income-expenditure flow. New investment can be financed by the creation of additional money. In this case additional saving is not a precondition of an increased production of capital goods. The economic consequences will depend, in part, on the existence or non-existence of unemployed productive resources and unemployed men (as already discussed in connection with Figure 3, Part 2).

Selection 2

WHY HOLD CASH BALANCES?

GEORGE GARVY

> *George Garvy here analyzes some of the reasons for holding money. The flow of money, discussed in the first selection, may be speeded up if individuals and business firms hold smaller cash balances, or it may be retarded if they hold larger cash balances. Because demand deposits constitute the major portion of the money supply (currency constitutes only a small part of the money supply in a modern economy), turnover or velocity of money may be measured by turnover or velocity of demand deposits. Velocity of deposits is an indication of the "transactions velocity" of money—the number of times money is used, during a given period, for all transactions involving money. This measure of velocity is much larger than "income velocity," a measure more commonly used in recent years. Income velocity means the number of times the money supply would have to be transferred during a given period to purchase the total national income, or GNP, produced during that period. Money is, of course, exchanged in many transactions which do not involve final purchases of goods and services produced during the period—loans, gifts, intermediate purchases, such as purchases of flour by a bakery, and purchases of existing assets, such as houses built during previous periods, or securities purchased on one of the securities exchanges. Analysis of transactions velocity represents one approach to monetary theory; this approach has been less used in recent years than the income velocity approach because the income-expenditure approach has regarded GNP and its components as important variables.*

Monetary theory has always recognized that in modern society money performs several basic functions. There is, however, a diversity of views as to the best way of classifying uses of money and as to the rationale underlying such classifications. The distinction between money as a means of payment and as a

---

[4] Modern theory often assumes an accounting identity of saving and investment according to which any increases in investment will be matched automatically by an increase in saving.

• From George Garvy, *Deposit Velocity and Its Significance*, Federal Reserve Bank of New York, 1959, pp. 26–37. Reprinted by the courtesy of the Federal Reserve Bank of New York and the author.

store of value is familiar from the older writings of monetary economists. In more recent monetary theory, the motives for holding liquid funds for other-than-transactions purposes are variously rationalized. In the literature, in accordance with the analytical framework first developed by Keynes, precautionary and speculative motives are imputed. Holdings of money have been termed defensive in periods of fluctuating equity values. A distinction has been made between "current" and "capital" balances. In other types of analysis, both similar and different terminology or rationalizations are encountered. The analysis has been gradually widened to include a whole spectrum of liquidity instruments in addition to money.

Without choosing between alternative theoretical models or lines of reasoning, it is sufficient to recognize that there are several motives for holding demand deposit balances other than the need for maintaining cash balances proportionate to the volume of anticipated payments. The rate of turnover of demand deposits may, therefore, change for two main reasons:

1. Because the cash balances required to make a given amount of payments may vary (as a result of changes in the composition and timing of the payments flow, in the speed of check collection, in requirements as to compensating balances, etc.), and

2. Because the amount of balances maintained for reasons other than to serve as a basis for meeting payments requirements may vary absolutely as well as in relation to transactions balances.

It is sufficient to recognize that fluctuations in the level of both business activity and prices of goods and services and in the volume of trading in intangible assets, the irregularities in the flow of income and expenditure, the requirements of growth, and many of the uncertainties of modern life make it desirable to own liquid reserves in addition to cash balances held to meet normal payments flows. The need for liquidity is basic to the operation of our economic system. But any attempt merely to enumerate the various factors that come into play in determining the liquidity requirements of each transactor group and to distinguish such needs from transactions requirements would immediately reveal numerous difficulties. For instance, does an oil company, which regularly bids for oil leases, keep "speculative" balances, or are funds kept in readiness to make such bids part of ordinary transactions balances? Or how should funds being accumulated by institutional investors in order to participate in an anticipated private placement be classified? Indeed, in many cases, reasons for holding money are overlapping rather than additive. For our subsequent discussion it is sufficient to recognize that in the case of business firms there will be, at times, in addition to planned liquidity reserves, some temporarily redundant funds that are also kept in liquid form pending their use in current operations, investment in real or in financial assets, or for repayment of debt.

HOW ARE LIQUIDITY NEEDS MET?

Money is a liquidity instrument "par excellence." Yet, as there are alternatives to money in discharging obligations, there are also substitute sources of liquidity. Money has a preferred place in the spectrum of liquidity instruments but the level of demand for money as an instrument of liquidity depends on its competitive position in relation to alternative instruments. The range of liquidity instruments available to, or preferred by, the various categories of economic units is not the same. Furthermore, the liquidity instruments available and the prevailing views as to their moneyness have varied over time.

Thus, most people would consider time deposits, postal savings deposits, and shares in savings and loan associations (even though theoretically these shares are merely claims on realizable assets) as near substitutes for cash. . . .

The growth of savings and other time deposits in commercial and savings banks and of holdings of shares in savings and loan associations reflects primarily the demand for such liquidity instruments on the part of consumers (in part offset by the declining popularity of postal savings accounts). The various types of time deposits constitute the most important type of asset holdings for individuals; individual spending units hold more of their liquid assets in savings accounts than in checking accounts and United States savings bonds combined. Savings institutions are fully aware of the fact that their attractiveness depends to an appreciable extent upon their ability to endow their liabilities with the characteristics of near money. To maintain this attitude in the minds of their depositors, they normally waive any legal requirements with respect to prior withdrawal notice that may exist, and make passbook loans almost automatically. Some of these institutions go so far as to issue checks or money orders and, in general, try to emphasize not only security and income but also the ready availability of funds entrusted to them. Another important source of liquidity for individuals is federal government securities. Savings bonds are widely held by all, including the lower income groups; some individuals in the upper income groups also use short-term marketable securities as a source of liquidity.

Corporations usually hold their liquid reserves in the form of demand deposits and open market securities. In contrast to individuals, they do not normally maintain currency reserves and make relatively little use of time deposits; they do not hold savings and loan shares or deposits in mutual savings banks to any extent. In the twenties, call loans, Treasury certificates of indebtedness, bankers' acceptances, and commercial paper provided the most convenient instruments for holding corporate reserves, but since the thirties Treasury bills (first introduced in 1929) have come to occupy a position of predominance. Since the end of World War II, several types of short-term securities of government agencies were added to the range of liquidity instruments used by corporations. Among private obligations, finance company paper rose rapidly in importance after World War II. It has an important advantage arising from the ability of the issuer to tailor the size and maturity of each obligation to the specific needs of corporations (or of other investors) anxious to find employment for temporarily idle funds. Similarly, some corporations have utilized repurchase agreements with government securities dealers to obtain short-term investments that would fit their needs.

The liquidity instruments that are used by various kinds of economic units overlap to a large extent. The preference for various categories depends upon the ease and cost of conversion into money (in itself a function of the size, organization, and activity of the market for each security), the comparative earnings available on competing instruments, tax consideration, etc. Over time, and most markedly since World War II, there has been a substantial increase in the variety of instruments and of institutional arrangements available. At the same time, the need periodically to accumulate large reserves has been intensified by the rise both in income taxes and in other forms of taxation.

Numerous other developments have had important and, in part, contradictory influences upon the need for bank balances and their rate of use. Growing urbanization, the decline of agriculture as a source of income, the rise in average family income, the simultaneous decrease in the importance of income paid in kind, the decline in the proportion of the foreign born (unfamiliar with or distrustful of banking operations), the general increase in levels of education, and the growing importance of the corporate form of doing business are some of the influences tending to increase the demand for deposit balances. Important factors in the opposite direction include the increased share of government in income and expenditures, the expansion of consumer credit, and the use of charge-account facilities.

Demand for liquidity reserves is in the main related to uncertainty. Important institutional developments that have taken place since the thirties have increased the ability of the individual to meet contingencies without immediate recourse to cash; similarly, the growth of consumer credit facilities and, more generally, the greater availability of bank credit to individuals have tended to reduce the need to carry protective balances. All forms of government and private compulsory or voluntary insurance tend to obviate the need to accumulate a backlog for the proverbial rainy day and to keep at least part of it liquid. A large and increasing proportion of the population is protected against (at least the first) impact of unemployment, sickness, and accidents on the job and on the road, so that the proper identification card is often a substitute for cash.

Currency is the main competitor of checking accounts in performing the payments function and, to a limited extent, also as a liquidity reserve. Indeed, with increased per capita income, currency in the hands of the public now is much larger in relation to GNP than in the twenties. There are, furthermore, additional ways of making payments, together with various factors affecting the efficiency with which deposit balances are used.

BALANCES HELD TO COMPENSATE BANKS

It is usually assumed that the size of the average balance held by each economic unit (family, business firm, or governmental unit) is regulated by its transactions and liquidity requirements. Insufficient attention is paid, however, to the fact that a very large part of total demand deposit balances serves to compensate banks for services performed in handling payments and in providing credit facilities.

Individuals as well as businesses usually have an option to pay an *explicit* service charge for the handling of their accounts or to compensate their banks *implicitly* by holding balances on which the banks can earn an income equivalent to the service charge.[1] A substantial part of banking services is paid for by keeping appropriate compensating balances and such balances are a large proportion of total demand deposits. The significance of the compensating balance has grown in recent decades (it should be recalled that before 1933 the holder of demand deposits, instead of being charged for services, was paid interest) as the use of account analysis for determining charges has been generalized. . . .

Banks, particularly large institutions, also ordinarily require or expect their customers to maintain appropriate balances in return for the extension of credit lines.[2] Such balances are usually referred to as compensating or commensurate balances; we shall use below the latter term to distinguish them from balances maintained at banks for checking and similar services. A recent survey of approximately 100 of the largest banks indicates that more than 70 per cent of these banks require commensurate balances; other banks require such balances usually, but not always, or only from certain categories of borrowers, such as finance companies. An equally large proportion of banks require commensurate balances for term loans as well. More than half of the responding banks also require commensurate balances for specific loans.[3] Such balances are determined as a certain percentage (usually 15 to 20 per cent) of the amount of borrowing outstanding or (about 10 to 20 per cent) of credit lines granted. Frequently, corporations which do not establish formal credit lines maintain sufficiently large balances with their main banks in order to facilitate access to credit in the case of need. Indeed, most of the banks which have no formal minimum balance requirements would, nevertheless, take the customer's usual deposit balance into account in providing loan accommodations and in setting the interest rate on loans.

The amount of compensating (or commensurate) balances is determined by the primary functions which they perform: to compensate banks for costs incurred in rendering a wide range of services and to assure adequate access to credit. Yet, at the same time, they may satisfy part or all of the liquidity requirements of their owners. Indeed, compensating balances are not completely immobilized and can be withdrawn in case of need, usually at the cost of incurring service charges. Since compensating balances are normally based on average rather than on minimum balances, they can be drawn down temporarily to meet unexpected drains of funds. Bank policies with respect to compensating balances are quite flexible (but not necessarily in periods of tight money), and many

---

[1] The United States Government also compensates commercial banks for certain services by keeping appropriate balances (see H. J. Cooke, "Managing the Treasury's Cash Balances," in *The Treasury and the Money Market,* Federal Reserve Bank of New York, 1954, p. 8). However, neither debits nor deposits currently used to compute the index of deposit turnover include United States government accounts (although they were included prior to 1943).

[2] Roughly one-third of all member banks with total deposits between $20 million and $50 million require such balances, and for the largest institutions (with deposits of $500 million and over) this percentage rises to 93. See "Credit Lines and Minimum Balances Requirements," *Federal Reserve Bulletin,* June, 1956, pp. 573–9, for data based on the October, 1955, survey of commercial and industrial loans at member banks. See also, D. P. Jacobs, "Sources and Costs of Funds of Large Sales Finance Companies," *Consumer Instalment Credit,* Part II, Vol. 1, Board of Governors of the Federal Reserve System (Washington, D. C., 1957), pp. 341–52.

[3] F. P. Gallot, "Why Compensating Balances?—Part II," *Bulletin of the Robert Morris Associates,* August, 1958, pp. 309–319.

business customers rightly consider such balances as part of their liquid reserves.

Neither consumer nor mortgage loans involve commensurate balances, nor do most types of financial loans such as loans to brokers. The share of commensurate balances in the total deposits of a given bank will thus depend on the composition of its loan portfolio. This is significant when comparing turnover ratios among individual banks or localities and where assessing long-run changes in transactions velocity in the light of changes in the composition of assets of the banking system as a whole.

Prior to 1933 commercial banks paid interest on demand deposits, no compensating balances in the current sense were held, and the practice of requiring commensurate balances was less prevalent than now. This is an important and perhaps even one of the major reasons why the transactions velocity of demand deposits in the fifties is considerably lower than in the twenties in spite of the great progress that has been made in collecting and managing funds by large holders of demand balances.

The lodgment in the deposit structure of a large volume of compensating balances has the effect of dampening cyclical swings in velocity. Their aggregate volume tends to be related to the activity of an account; any increase in activity calls for a corresponding increase in balances. Compensating balances are sensitive to interest rates only to a limited extent. The earnings credit, on the basis of which the size of required balances is computed, moves with the general level of interest rates, but rates used for computing earnings credit are adjusted only when major changes in interest levels take place, and even then with a lag.[4] Compensating and "goodwill" balances are, on the whole, rather insensitive to fluctuations in interest rates, although in times of monetary stringency corporations will tend to reduce them. Furthermore, under the pressure of high or rising interest rates some depositors maintaining a large number of accounts will tend to eliminate certain low-activity accounts. Bankers, however, will place more emphasis on commensurate balances when loan demand is strong. It is, indeed, generally believed that commensurate balances are used as a credit-rationing device and that bankers raise their requirements in times of tight money; one of their effects is to increase effective yields on loans. In the 1958 Robert Morris Associates survey, about as many bankers indicated that the general availability of funds did not influence balance requirements as the number replying in the affirmative. Although the split of views was about the same in 1954, the general and significant tightening of requirements revealed by comparing survey results on the two dates suggests that commensurate balances are used to ration credit. And, indeed, in the 1958 survey, bankers declared, by a margin of more than two to one, that the "tight money" climate of the past few years focused attention on commensurate balances. Experience in these years indicates that, when money becomes more plentiful, banks tend to maintain but are ready to reduce the balances required against credit lines.

This fact that commensurate balances are related to activity acts as a kind of automatic brake, tending to counteract any sharp rise or fall in velocity, even

---

[4] If, in a period of expansion, reserve requirements are raised, higher earnings credit may be offset, in part or entirely, since required reserves are deducted from compensating balances on which the earnings credit is based.

though it cannot be assumed that compensating and commensurate balances rise and fall in direct proportion to the level of business activity or of aggregate deposits. On the other hand, the volume of such deposits is clearly considerably less sensitive to changes in interest rates than funds which are held exclusively for liquidity or speculative purposes.

The relationship between compensating and commensurate balances, on the one hand, and the level of business activity and of interest rates, on the other, is sufficiently complex to suggest that a simplification of the analysis by treating them as part of transaction balances is inadequate. This is particularly true when analysis of transactions velocity is extended to the twenties.

ACTIVATION OF IDLE BALANCES

It is frequently said that in periods of expanding business activity "idle balances are drawn into circulation." The distinction between "active" and "idle" balances (distinguished frequently in academic literature as M_1 and M_2) is, indeed, essentially an expository device. While there are some demand deposit accounts that are virtually dormant for prolonged periods of time (or that are occasionally increased, but not drawn against), nearly all accounts show some degree of activity. What is meant by reference to idle balances is the excess over amounts normally required to meet smoothly an anticipated flow of payments. For each business firm, individual, or other spending unit, the amount of idle balances depends on a number of factors, such as the nature of the business of the account owner, the geographic and time pattern of payments, and the requirements of the bank as to minimum or compensating balances, to name only the most important. All these factors may be subject to long-run as well as to cyclical influences.

When business activity expands, business firms require larger balances to support a larger volume of production and distribution. Some firms will have ample cash resources to meet increased needs (and what earlier appeared as idle or redundant balances will now be drawn into active use), while others will replenish their cash balance through borrowing. Currency requirements also tend to increase in periods of business expansion, and since additional currency is normally obtained by drawing against deposit balances, the initial impact is a reduction in such balances. During a period of business contraction, the reverse process takes place, as funds obtained from the liquidation of inventories and other business funds not needed for transacting a reduced volume of business are banked at a time when reduced yields on alternative liquidity instruments reduce their attractiveness. Those who hold cash for speculative purposes may change their expectations as to the future of prices of goods and/or securities or of yields on various types of securities; or they may use balances built up earlier to acquire goods or securities as the favorable situations which they anticipated materialize. Balances withdrawn to purchase income-yielding liquidity instruments are of course not lost to the banking system, unless these instruments are acquired from a bank. They may reappear as demand deposits of other holders who need to increase their transactions balances and for this purpose are willing to part with other types of liquidity instruments (or with investments that do not possess a high degree of liquidity), or in other ways.

Economic units which distribute their liquid reserves among cash and securities (including time deposits in various forms) will normally alter this distribution in response to changing liquidity needs and to the relative returns available on different types of securities. Any change in the proportion of demand deposits held for transactions and for all other purposes combined tends to be reflected statistically in the rate of deposit turnover. There is, of course, no way of ascertaining to what extent a rise or fall in this rate is due to a changed composition of demand deposits resulting from a shift in the purposes for which they are held, and to what extent is due to a more or less efficient use of deposits in making payments.

The volume and composition of credit outstanding is bound to have an influence on cyclical changes in the rate of deposit turnover. If a large volume of credit is used by firms which experience a decline in activity, the accompanying contraction of working capital (for instance, as a result of inventory liquidation) will most likely result in loan repayments or retirement of callable or maturing long-term debt. Such firms are likely to be in a better position to bring their bank balances into a better relationship with payments than businesses that do not use outside funds. Firms or individuals who cannot (or choose not to) reduce their balances by repaying bank loans or retiring longer term indebtedness will attempt to make the best possible use of redundant funds by investing them; when such funds are allocated among various types of liquid investments, some part is likely to be kept in the form of demand deposits.

It is frequently said that balances created through loan extension are particularly active, since their very creation attests to the need for additional transactions balances. This may or may not be so, depending on the subsequent use made of the additional balances. When borrowed funds are drawn down rapidly to pay for materials or services, they immediately enter the payments stream and, from the second round on, are indistinguishable from other checkbook money. All that can be said is that the deposits created through additional loan extension probably increase transactions balances initially and, by reducing the relative share of other balances, contribute to the increase in over-all velocity. But if the borrowed money is used to provide a more comfortable cash margin and to relieve the comptroller from worries about keeping a close check on the cash flow, the net result may be a slowing-down, rather than an acceleration, of turnover. In any case, however, the volume and structure of bank loans and of other borrowing in relation to the level of demand deposits have to be considered as one of the elements determining velocity.

The process which is frequently referred to as the activation of idle balances is best looked upon as a reshuffling in the ownership distribution of checkbook money (in part as a result of the expansion of the money supply) and, more generally, in liquid-asset holdings as interest rates rise. As the volume of payments rises with business activity, existing accounts become more active. Some balances are ample enough to support additional transactions and their turnover rates accordingly rise; other accounts that have been kept close to minimum needs include no margin of idle funds and have to be built up by borrowing or by conversion of liquid assets into cash. Their rates of turnover may not change much as balances and transactions rise more or less in step, but the growth of such balances will increase the share of active accounts in total demand balances.

In addition to the more active use of balances to transact a larger volume of business, several additional developments tend to influence the cyclical increase of velocity. One is the relative growth of trading in private securities. Since capital formation is more volatile than the flow of national income, rising activity is accompanied by a more-than-proportionate increase in capital expenditures and in the various activities related to their financing. Availability of new securities tends to give rise to a chain reaction in portfolio adjustments, and activity in outstanding securities generally increases as profits expectations rise, but not uniformly, thus offering additional inducements for switches. Additional opportunities for portfolio adjustments arise from changes in the relationship of long- and short-term rates and among various long-term rates. There are sufficient data to show that trading in existing assets tends to rise more rapidly than physical activity.

Rising interest rates which typically accompany an improvement in business activity make holdings of reserves in money market instruments increasingly attractive. As a result, temporarily redundant funds are invested in income yielding securities, frequently even when funds can be invested for only a few days. The amount of debits arising from the purchase and quick resale (or redemption) of securities or from repurchase agreements in periods of rising market rates of interest is very large. On the other hand, when rates are low, the return available on such short-term investments is not worth the effort since the brokerage fees and other costs are relatively inflexible, being related to the amounts involved rather than to the yields expected.[5] In periods of low money market rates, the cost involved in investing such funds for a few days or weeks may be prohibitive, but this hurdle is overcome when rates rise.

The activation of balances is thus a complex process, involving an increased use of balances owned by the same economic unit, shifts of deposit balances among units which rearrange their holdings of liquidity instruments, and loan expansion. It would appear that the influence of rising interest rates on velocity operates primarily not through a reduction of idle funds (included in the denominator of the turnover ratio), but through the considerable volume of debits generated by the endeavor of corporate treasurers and also of state and municipal financial officers to earn income on the last dollar of temporarily redundant funds (which increases the numerator). To a considerable extent, statistical data showing rising turnover velocity reflect the churning-over of funds rather than the cyclical reduction of hoards.

The size and use of demand deposit accounts maintained by various depositor groups and the mode and frequency of their use have been undergoing

---

[5] For a theoretical model discussing the effect of cost on investment of excess funds, see W. J. Baumol, "The Transactions Demand for Cash: An Inventory Theoretic Approach," *Quarterly Journal of Economics,* November, 1952, pp. 545–56.

long-run changes which are as yet insufficiently explored. These involve in part changes in attitudes on the part of various depositor groups with respect to their transactions and liquidity needs, and in part changes in banking techniques which affect the size of balances required to meet a given flow of payments and to assure related banking services. Transactions velocity of demand deposits can thus be viewed as the statistical reflection of at least two sets of forces: one is the extent to which demand deposits are used in preference to other means of payments and liquidity instruments; the other is the "efficiency" with which demand deposits are used, which in turn represents prevailing payments procedures of individuals or business firms as well as banking practices.

Selection 3

MONEY AND THE STREAM OF PAYMENTS: THE CASH BALANCES APPROACH

ALBERT G. HART AND PETER B. KENEN

In this selection Albert G. Hart and Peter B. Kenen provide further analysis of motives for holding money: the transactions, precautionary, investment, and speculative motives. All except the transactions motive arise out of the existence of uncertainty; the demand for money depends on the probability *of certain changes that cannot be foreseen with certainty. Thus uncertainty is central in a theory of the role of money in the economy.*

Hart and Kenen also introduce the reader to the concept of money substitutes—financial assets that serve as well as money or nearly as well as money for several of the purposes for which money is held. As long as an individual can quickly convert such assets into money—as long as they possess liquidity—they may be held instead of money. Moreover, they have the additional advantage of providing an interest income.

An attempt by those who hold money—the public—to reduce money holdings cannot directly cause a reduction in the total money supply; an individual may reduce his money holdings and acquire money substitutes (or other financial or real assets), but as long as certain things are accepted as money they must be held by someone. Hence, interest rate and other changes that induce individuals to hold money substitutes increase such holdings without reducing the money supply. Transactions velocity of money tends to increase, and income velocity may *increase. For example, if $1 million is transferred from commercial banks to savings and loan associations, these associations acquire title to bank deposits, and then lend or invest most of the amount (all but a small reserve). Borrowers then hold title to the deposits, and presumably make purchases or repay debt; sellers or creditors then hold title to the deposits. Bank loans and investments are not reduced, but loans and investments of savings and loan associations increase. Conse-*

• From Albert G. Hart and Peter B. Kenen, *Money, Debt and Economic Activity,* 3rd ed., pp. 230–244. Copyright 1961 by Prentice-Hall, Inc., Englewood Cliffs, New Jersey. Reprinted by permission of Prentice-Hall, Inc., and the authors.

quently, transactions velocity of money tends to increase. If the additional loans and investments result in additional real output, income velocity of money also increases. Thus the existence of money substitutes makes it possible for an increase in the money supply to have greater effect, because of the accompanying increase in velocity.

MOTIVES FOR HOLDING CASH

Introduction

While Keynes himself made an enormous contribution to our understanding of the demand for cash,[1] most simple Keynesian models do not give sufficient attention to people's motives for holding money. This is why Keynesian models attach too little importance to money and monetary policy. In order that we may fully appreciate the influence of money, we must look much more closely at the demand for money.

Who holds the cash?

To survey the motives for holding cash, we must have some idea of the way in which cash is distributed. Is the typical holder of cash a wage earner? An old lady on an annuity? A big corporation? We know from bank statistics (Table 1) that the lion's share of demand deposits is held in very large accounts. Financial and nonfinancial corporations held 45.2 per cent of adjusted demand deposits at the beginning of 1960; the former had average balances of $38,500, the latter average balances of $22,000. A vast number of individuals have checking accounts, but most of these cash balances are relatively small and they account for only 29.5 per cent of total demand deposits.

Even now a large number of families do not have checking accounts. Fewer than a third of spending units with incomes below $3,000 were reported as having checking accounts in 1959 (Table 2), while a mere 17 per cent of the households surveys reported checking balances above $500 (Table 3). These data on personal balances and the large average size of corporate accounts suggest that we should regard the checking-deposit component of total cash assets as mainly administered by business firms and persons of large affairs.

It would seem that time deposits are held mainly by households, although foreign holdings of dollars are sometimes placed on time deposit at commercial banks. Once again, however, savings accounts are not uniformly distributed among consuming units. Fewer than half of the households with incomes below $5,000 were reported as having savings accounts in 1959 (Table 2), and better than half of the households that had time deposits had accounts smaller than $1,000 (Table 3). There is considerable concentration even in the holdings of this component of total cash, though probably less than in respect of checking

---

[1] The argument of this chapter, indeed, rests largely on the work of Keynes, *General Theory of Employment, Interest, and Money* (New York: Harcourt, Brace, and World, Inc., 1936) and J. R. Hicks, "Suggestion for Simplifying the Theory of Money," *Economica,* February 1935; *Value and Capital* (Oxford: Clarendon Press, 1939). But it will go a good way beyond their position, especially in handling uncertainty.

Table 1

THE OWNERSHIP OF DEMAND DEPOSITS, JANUARY, 1960

	Average size	Per cent of total accounts	
	of account	By number of	By amount
Type of owner	(in dollars)	accounts	on deposit
All owners[1]	$ 1,918	100.0	100.0
Nonfinancial business			
Corporate	22,000	3.4	38.2
Noncorporate	3,541	6.5	11.9
Financial business			
Corporate	38,500	0.4	7.0
Noncorporate	4,800	0.4	1.7
Farm operators	1,467	5.3	4.0
Individuals (personal)	719	78.7	29.5
Nonprofit organizations	1,793	5.1	4.8
All other owners[2]	10,000	0.2	2.9

SOURCE: *Federal Reserve Bulletin*, April, 1960.
Detail may not add to total because of rounding.
[1] Excludes government and interbank deposits.
[2] Trust departments of banks and foreign owners.

Table 2

CONSUMERS' HOLDINGS OF CASH, EARLY 1959

Size of spending units—1958	Percentage of spending units holding		
Income (dollars)	Some liquid assets[1]	Checking accounts	Savings accounts
All income classes	75	55	50
Under $1,000	39	23	22
$1,000-$1,999	50	29	32
$2,000-$2,999	56	36	34
$3,000-$3,999	72	46	46
$4,000-$4,999	79	55	48
$5,000-$5,999	86	66	54
$6,000-$7,499	93	72	65
$7,500-$9,999	96	81	71
$10,000 and over	98	91	73

SOURCE: *Federal Reserve Bulletin*, July, 1959.
[1] Includes checking accounts, savings accounts, U.S. government savings bonds, shares in savings and loan associations and in credit unions. Excludes currency.

Table 3

THE SIZE OF CONSUMERS' CASH HOLDINGS, EARLY 1959[1]

	Per cent of spending units with		
	Any	Checking	Savings
Size of holding	liquid assets[2]	accounts	accounts
Zero	25	45	50
$1-$199	18	24	13
$200-$499	13	15	7
$500-$999	12	8	8
$1,000-$1,999	10	5	7
$2,000 or over	22	4	15

SOURCE: Same as Table 2.
[1] This table is merely a rearrangement of the data in Table 2 by size of holding rather than income group.
[2] See note to Table 2.

accounts. We should assume that time deposits are held mainly by individuals, but that these individuals are largely drawn from the middle and upper income groups.

Evidence on holdings of paper currency is fragmentary. Incomplete surveys of business cash suggest that most of the currency belongs to households, but the fact that more than a quarter of the currency outstanding is in denominations of $50 or over—denominations that are not too common in the average person's wallet—does suggest that currency is also concentrated. The concentration must be less than with bank deposits, but is still important enough to warrant our attention.

Putting the evidence together is not easy. As checking deposits are more than half of the total cash supply, we can be sure that business and wealthy individuals hold a large slice of that total. Our theories about motives for holding cash can therefore assume businesslike behavior in cash management, along with a connection between cash holdings and the markets in stocks and bonds. Our theories about the consumers' transactions demand for cash are apt to be less relevant to an explanation of total cash holdings, yet theories that connect cash management to consumers' saving patterns must be taken seriously in view of the rather wide distribution of total time deposits.

A list of motives for holding cash

At first glance, there would seem to be little reason for households and firms to hold a cash balance day after day. Cash cannot be eaten, worn, slept in, or used to keep off the weather. Since it is valued only because it can be used to buy other things, why should cash be kept unspent?

One might reply that when one person spends cash, somebody else gets it; *using* cash does not *use it up*. The total amount of cash in existence arises from bank loans to private parties, from government deficits, importation and mining of gold, and so forth. The sum of individual holdings is simply the total of cash that is brought into existence by these transactions. But this explanation does not get us far—it would only be adequate if everyone always passed cash on at the earliest possible moment, and each dollar was owned by its present holder only because he had not yet had time to spend it. This would imply a velocity up to the mechanical maximum, which can only happen in hyperinflation.

Economists use a more or less standardized list of motives for holding cash. These motives can be classified as follows:

> 1. *Transactions Motive.* Holding enough cash to carry the holder past some foreseen trough in his holdings—to absorb the excess of cash outlays over cash receipts until the arrival of a foreseen substantial receipt.
> 2. *Margin-of-Safety* (or *Precautionary*) *Motive.* Holding enough cash to cushion the ill effects of an unexpected outlay or of a failure of receipts, and to safeguard financial respectability.
> 3. *Investment Motive.* Holding cash as the embodiment of wealth because the holder cannot see his way clear to put his wealth into any other form.
> 4. *Speculative Motive.* Holding cash because the holder is waiting for something he wants to buy to come down in price.

We cannot divide the cash balance of a given holder into definite parts representing each of these motives. The same cash balance may "double in brass." If, for example, a holder has accumulated cash for speculative purposes, he also has a margin of safety, so that his needs under the second motive are swallowed up in those under the fourth. Besides, the different motives shade into one another. In analyzing them, it is less important to keep them distinct than to keep track of the common element that binds them all together—*the adaptation of business dealings to uncertainty.*

The transactions motive

The transactions motive is a matter of avoiding the inconveniences, expenses, and annoyances that occur when we run out of cash. Every household or firm has lean periods "when everything goes out and nothing comes in." When we have cash on hand or cash coming in, and can foresee such a lean period coming, we make sure that we will enter that lean period with enough cash to see us through.

The working of the transactions motive depends on the factors listed by Fisher in his discussion of velocity. People who are paid weekly need less cash for transactions purposes than people with the same income who are paid monthly. People who run up a bill at the grocer's and settle the bill on payday need less cash (as of two days after payday, for example) than those who buy exclusively at cash-and-carry stores. People who are able to borrow, and do not mind doing so, need less cash than those who feel that borrowing is a sin.

The size of an individual's transactions needs depends on how far that person looks ahead, and which future receipts and expenditures he assumes to be beyond his control. It also depends on whether he has any reason for holding a minimum transactions balance. A cash-holder may be subject to bank service charges if his balance dips below a certain level; then he has a transactions motive to keep his balance equal to this minimum *plus* any excess of outlays over receipts that he anticipates.

The particular assets that can serve transactions needs depend on the nature of those needs. If a man is about to take a trip during which he will deal entirely with strangers, he will need coin and paper money. If he is about to make a number of payments to people by mail, he will need a bank balance subject to check. But if he plans an elaborate vacation next summer and has plenty of time beforehand to change his banking arrangements, a savings account can fill his needs just as well as a checking account or a roll of bills. For fairly remote requirements, non-cash assets may serve in lieu of cash.

The margin-of-safety motive and the principle of linkage of risks

Future transactions are *uncertain.* Few of us could make a precise estimate of all our receipts and disbursements. Reliable advance estimates can be made for selected items, but the uncertain items are more numerous and usually more important.

Suppose that a business gauges its present cash needs by the *most probable* course of receipts and expenditures for the next two months. If one or two items get out of control, the whole plan is thrown out of gear. A customer who has bought a lot on credit may not pay when expected; the price of some essential material may prove higher than forecast; or, on the optimistic side, some unexpected bargain that the firm cannot afford to neglect may appear. Firms and households must buttress their estimates by maintaining a margin of safety in their cash balances.

As cash is not ordinarily an income-yielding asset, it might seem that income prospects would be maximized by cutting cash holdings to a minimum. But a margin of safety in cash holdings is not a luxury, paid for by accepting reduced income prospects. A margin of safety makes income prospects better rather than worse. The reason for this is called the

Principle of linkage of risks

An old proverb says, "Misfortunes never come singly." Our affairs are often arranged so that if one thing goes wrong, many others will go wrong in consequence. A motorist on a long trip may make a close estimate of his cash requirements and take just enough currency with him to pay for gasoline and meals. If he is unlucky enough to be arrested for speeding, misfortunes pile up at a great rate. He not only has to pay the fine, but also suffers a night in jail, the ignominy and expense of having to wire his friends for funds, and perhaps substantial loss by not arriving in time to attend to his business. A similar chain of misfortunes would be set off if his car were to be crippled and need emergency repairs.

The same kind of thing can happen in business. Suppose that a small firm has made large sales on credit to a customer who goes bankrupt. This means that certain cash receipts will not come in when expected, if at all. If the firm has figured its cash position closely, the customer's bankruptcy creates a need to push sales harder than intended, to dun other customers into paying up more quickly, get more credit from suppliers, borrow more at the bank, and so forth. The loss will start a chain of consequences that work the wrong way. Price cuts to push sales may induce customers to postpone purchases in the hope of further price cuts. Pressure on customers to pay more promptly may lose good will and interfere with sales; it may start gossip that will hurt our firm's credit rating. Suppliers are likely to wonder whether our firm is still a good credit risk; to apply for increased credit may be just the way to persuade them that they should be reducing their advances. A loan application at the bank that arises from the firm's loss will not necessarily be rejected, but the applicant for a "distress loan" must expect the banker to probe into his affairs with embarrassing closeness. If gossip begins to spread that our firm has asked for a bank loan and been refused, the firm's credit rating with suppliers will suffer and its other troubles will be compounded. A loss of receipts threatens to strip the firm of its working capital, might force it to liquidate some of its physical assets at a forced sale, and could even drive it into bankruptcy. The "going-concern value" of the assets of a competently managed firm exceeds their "break-up value" at forced sale;

if the firm has to sell some of its assets to meet a shortage of cash, this excess of going-concern value evaporates.

These chain reactions can be avoided by allowing a margin of safety in the cash position. Had our motorist carried enough cash to pay his fine, his troubles would never have compounded. Had our firm held enough cash to take its loss in stride, its earning power would not have been impaired. A *stronger cash position weakens the linkage of risks,* so that one misfortune will not bring another in its wake.

In more pleasant directions, a stronger cash position also guarantees the ability to seize opportunities. Our motorist might have found for sale the puppy his daughter wanted for her birthday. With extra cash, he could have taken it along. Our firm might have been offered a large batch of materials at a very good price—a chance to lower its costs for several months ahead. Without extra cash, it could not buy ahead except by cutting down its purchases of other materials or of the labor needed to use the materials, so that the bargain offer would not be useful.[2] Here again, a strong cash position is not a luxury bought at the expense of reduced income prospects, but is itself a way to improve income prospects.

The margin-of-safety motive can be served by "near-moneys," although these are not usable for making payments. If our motorist carried savings bonds with him, he could get cash at any bank in case of need, but could hold onto his bonds if no emergency developed. Our firm could use marketable securities for the same purpose. These assets must not be essential to the holder's operations, and must promise to yield almost as much on quick sale as they would if the holder took plenty of time to market them. Our motorist, for example, could get cash for his tires or for the watch on his wrist. But if he sold the tires, he would have to stop his trip, and if he sold the watch he would get much less than it would cost him to replace it. To provide a margin of safety, noncash assets must be "liquid."

The margin-of-safety motive and financial respectability

Some households or businesses may not feel the need for a margin of safety in response to the uncertainty of their forecasts. But nearly everyone is affected by social pressure to allow such a margin for the sake of financial respectability.

A strong credit rating is one of the most important intangible assets a firm or household can have. To be known as one who sails too close to the wind is bad for credit. Our firm or household may never actually get into trouble by carrying a low cash balance, but those who know that its cash is low are apt to suspect rash management.

It has been remarked that the surest way to get a bank loan is to show that you don't need it. Borrowers who always allow a margin of safety can count on getting loans at low interest. Borrowers who keep their cash balances low are

---

[2] Where the need for cash arises from a stroke of good luck rather than bad, the prospects of a bank loan are brighter. Borrowing power at the bank is a more useful substitute for cash when seizing opportunities than when trying to cover losses.

usually looked on with skepticism by the low-interest lenders, particularly commercial banks. They will be shunted over to lenders who make heavier charges, or loaded with inconvenient and humiliating collateral requirements. In terms of interest costs, it may pay the borrower to forego present profitable uses of funds in order to get low-interest loans later on.

Many firms and households in a country like the United States probably manage their affairs by rule of thumb rather than by precise calculations of probable gain and loss. The tradition of financial conservatism, built up partly by the example of successful firms and households and partly by the "educational" campaigns of banks, gives a prominent place to the principle of a safety margin in cash holdings. During the 1920's, many firms adopted a financial policy that allowed them to avoid bank borrowing in all circumstances. The sad experience of the firms that did not do so (and of individuals who had borrowed to buy securities) during the contraction of bank loans which started in 1929 caused even more vigorous efforts by business to gain emancipation from a dependence on banks. Those who sought emancipation during the interwar period may have acted on their own analysis of the needed margin of safety or on revised rules of thumb that were coming to be accepted as financial respectability. In either case, the "margin-of-safety motive" was at work.

Prolonged prosperity since World War II may have somewhat weakened the margin-of-safety motive. Businesses and individuals have shown an increased willingness to borrow, and appear to be carrying smaller cash balances in relation to transactions requirements, for velocity has increased sharply in the 1950's. But margin-of-safety considerations still affect cash-management decisions and could reappear strongly in the event of a sharp business downturn.

Credit rationing and the demand for cash assets

Our discussion of the margin-of-safety motive and the linkage of risks brings out a fact: the demand for cash assets or, more broadly, for liquidity, is sharply affected by *credit rationing*.[3]

The linkage of risks would not exist, and there would be no margin-of-safety motive, if everyone could borrow all he honestly believed he could repay at a market rate of interest. Anyone threatened with business losses because of a shortage of cash could get out of trouble by using his borrowing power.

But the loan market cannot be like that. Lenders cannot be sure of the honesty, good judgment, or business prospects of would-be borrowers. An exhaustive investigation of a borrower's credit standing is too expensive. Lenders take refuge in rules of thumb that relate borrowing power to the supply of collateral, or to the borrower's ratio of current assets to current liabilities, or of net worth to debt, or both.

This rationing of would-be borrowers affects their affairs in several ways.

---

[3] In a broader view, what is at issue is *capital rationing*. On capital rationing as an influence on business planning and upon the working of interest, see A. G. Hart, *Anticipations, Uncertainty and Dynamic Planning* (Chicago: University of Chicago Press, 1940; reprint, New York: Augustus Kelley, 1951), pp. 39–50, 67–74.

1. Some borrowers (probably the majority by number, but not usually the largest firms or the richest households) would like to borrow more at the interest rates they now pay, but credit rationing prevents them from borrowing all they want.

2. Most borrowers are conscious of limits to their lines of credit, and have to scale down their operations to correspond to those limits.

3. Most borrowers have to allow for the danger that their lines of credit may shrink, and make their margins of safety large enough to cover this possibility.

4. To reduce this danger, or to expand their lines of credit, most borrowers have incentives to show financial prudence.

These effects of credit rationing explain why an increase of liquidity for a firm or household weakens the linkage of risks and increases the range of expenditures that can safely be undertaken. The effect of money on expenditures other than through changes in interest rates hinges on this relationship between liquidity and the linkage of risks.

The investment motive

Some holders of cash choose to hold it simply because they see no income-yielding alternative.

There is a deep-seated tradition in our middle-class society of "keeping capital intact." Some people are spendthrifts who cannot hang on to cash or property of any kind, but most—including the majority of those who save or inherit—feel that to "dissipate capital" is a sin, and will avoid doing so if they can.

Most wealth belongs to people who probably know of various ways to invest it for income. But a good many who own a little capital and struggle to keep it intact do not see any practical way to keep it except in cash. They may hold paper money, but are more apt to have savings bonds or a savings account at a bank.

People like this will succeed in saving when they are in full health and jobs are easy to get. They may have to use up their savings when they are caught by ill health or unemployment, when they have young people to educate, or when they reach retirement. On balance, this group of savers-in-cash are likely to gain ground in times of high employment. It is likely that they accounted for a good part of the growth in currency, time deposits, and United States savings bonds during World War II.

In the early postwar years, many people who had been steady savers used their wartime savings to finance new cars, furniture, and appliances, to move to California, or to travel in Europe. But net liquid savings continued to rise.

The speculative motive

A large proportion of the total money stock is held by households and firms actively interested in owning noncash assets—stock-exchange securities, real estate, inventories, and productive equipment. Some of the cash requirements related to dealings in these assets are straightforward transactions requirements.

A man who has decided to buy a house, for instance, has to build up cash for his down payment. The greater part of cash holdings that relate to these asset dealings must be viewed as *speculative*—linked with purchases that will only be made after the price has dropped or news comes in that makes the asset in question more attractive.

In some instances the cash-holder's interest in the asset market is *purely* speculative; he is waiting for a chance to buy an asset in order to sell it on the same market later, at a higher price. More often, the cash-holder wants the asset for use—to contribute direct services, as does a house; to contribute to production, as does a machine; to yield cash income, as does a bond or a dividend-paying stock. Even when the buyer wants assets for use, he cannot entirely avoid speculation. A holder who expects to use an asset himself may also be on the lookout for a favorable chance to sell it. Anyone who wants to own assets has to make guesses about the best time to buy. If he can postpone his purchase, he will not knowingly buy something whose price will soon fall sharply.

When someone deliberately sells a noncash asset or foregoes its purchase because he thinks its price is likely to fall, he is described in speculative lingo as a "bear." A bear hopes to gain by holding cash until the price decline has occurred. If he operates on a two-way market, he is able not only to postpone purchases, but also to sell his present holdings and increase his cash. If facilities exist, as on stock and organized commodity exchanges, he may go even further and sell short, collecting cash now or later in exchange for a promise to deliver noncash assets at an agreed future date. The bear who sells short is gambling on "covering" his contract by buying the asset cheap before he has to deliver.

Very often, one who is a "bear" on asset A is a "bull" on another asset B. He thinks he can gain by selling asset A and holding cash, but he thinks he can gain even more by selling asset A and investing the proceeds in asset B. If a bear holds cash, he must be bearish not only on asset A but also bearish (or, at least, not bullish) on all of the other assets in which he is interested.

This list of other assets need not include all the assets in the economic system. Most holders of cash are not prepared to commit themselves to a limitless range of assets, but rather operate within a restricted list. If a stock-market speculator takes a bear position and holds cash, we can infer that he forecasts a general fall in stock prices. But it does not follow that he is forecasting a fall in other prices—in real estate, foreign currencies, or commodities. He may simply be refusing to bet on any forecast of those other prices. If the list of assets that a person will consider becomes very short, the speculative motive for holding cash merges with the investment motive already discussed.[4]

This limitation of interests to a restricted field applies especially to managers of "other people's money." The administrator of a trust fund, for example, is commonly limited to bonds and mortgages. If he cannot find investment opportunities of this sort, he will let cash accumulate in the trust account as its present portfolio of bonds matures. He may be *almost* sure of price increases

---

[4] In many discussions, the investment motive is not handled separately. There is nothing logically wrong with treating it as a limiting case of the speculative motive, but treating the two separately makes the situations we are discussing easier to recognize.

in stocks, real estate, or commodities, but he cannot—or will not—move onto these markets with the money entrusted to him. Corporation managers may also pile up cash because they lack appropriate ways to spend it. A corporation is ordinarily organized to carry on a stated line of business. An oil company will deal in oil lands, refining and distributing facilities, or the securities of other oil companies it might want to control. If it is not prepared to buy such assets at a given moment, the company may pile up cash far beyond transactions and precautionary requirements. The officers of the company may feel certain that houses, wheat, or railway shares are going to rise in price, but may not feel free to put the company's cash into such assets.

Uncertainty in the speculative motive

You cannot be a bear unless someone else is a bull. If everyone agrees that a certain railroad share will soon be worth only 80 per cent of what it sold for yesterday, today's quotation must quickly fall to 80 per cent of yesterday's. If at today's price someone is bearish, someone else must hold a *different opinion*. The bear cannot place his bet on a price decline unless somebody else is sufficiently optimistic to place a bet against that price decline. . . .[5]

Just as different people forecast asset prices differently, a single individual is likely to make forecasts that are not entirely clear-cut. Uncertainty may be described as a difference of opinion *within* a person's mind, so a person's judgment on a particular price may take a compound form: (1) that the price is more likely to rise than to fall over the next few months; but (2) that a fall is possible over the next few months; *and* (3) that the price is quite likely to go lower before it rises. The speculator's best policy is quite different under such a compound guess than it would be if he knew that the price would rise steadily on a stated timetable, for several months ahead.

Speculators rarely put all their eggs in one basket. Now and then, "plungers" stake everything on a bullish or bearish forecast about a particular price, but most speculators mix bullish and bearish behavior. They *differentiate* their portfolios of property held so as to include different kinds and different degrees of risk.[6] As uncertainty grows, speculators will seek to add cash to their portfolios. The speculative and margin-of-safety motives converge at this point, for a risky speculative position intensifies the linkage of risks. A bull speculator who has stretched his cash position to the limit and has bought stock "on margin" is vulnerable to a chain of calamities. If the price of his stock falls, his broker may call upon him to put up more cash, and the bull must either disrupt his other operations or sell his stocks at just the moment when he is more than ever convinced that the stock is bound to go up.

The speculative demand for cash is probably intensified by the interplay

---

[5] This argument relates to future prices of durable assets like securities and storable commodities. Everybody may agree that strawberries will cost less next year without lowering this year's price.

[6] The speculator's problem in differentiating his portfolio is much the same as that which a banker faces in deciding how to balance his portfolio of assets, except that the range of assets from which the banker has to choose consists almost entirely of debts receivable.

of taxes and "selective credit controls." The tax rates on capital gains from securities held more than six months are much lower than the rates that apply to the ordinary income of upper-bracket taxpayers. These taxpayers are thereby attracted to speculative operations, but the Federal Reserve sets minimum cash margins on the purchase of stock-exchange securities. These margin requirements have recently ranged from 50 per cent to 100 per cent of the securities' purchase price. Because of these requirements, it now takes much more cash to swing a speculative operation than it did in the 1920's.

Near-moneys in the demand for cash

The concept of cash used thus far includes money and time deposits, and matches the usage generally followed in accounting. But *cash* might have been defined more narrowly to omit deposits not subject to check, or more widely to include short-term government securities and savings and loan shares.

Had a narrower concept of cash been adopted, we would have had to talk differently about several topics, but the substance of the argument would have been the same. The importance of time deposits as a substitute for checking deposits would have needed recognition regardless of definitions. Nor can we ignore the monetary importance of life insurance cash values, savings and loan association shares, and Treasury securities merely because these and similar claims are not included in our notion of cash.

Whether a claim can actually be used for payment is only important in relation to the transactions motive. If cash is wanted for margin-of-safety or speculative reasons, direct use in payment does not come in question. An asset can be a substitute for cash if it is *liquid* (if it has moneyness), and is a *nonoperating asset*.

Liquid, you will recall, means the holder is confident that he can get a stated price for the asset on short notice. Because price certainty and the speed with which it can be realized are both matters of degree, moneyness itself is a matter of degree. With cash, moneyness is complete, but all debts receivable have some degree of moneyness that shades off as the date of repayment recedes and as the debtor's credit standing becomes more doubtful. Debts payable have *negative moneyness,* varying with the date of maturity and the probability of being able to renew.

An asset is nonoperating if the owner can part with it without upsetting his affairs. Many highly liquid assets, such as inventories and debts receivable from customers, are operating assets because an effort to cash in on them would cut into a firm's ability to sell its products.

Another way of ranking assets as money substitutes is to ask whether the owner will consider selling them. Assets of varying moneyness may be priced so low that the holder would prefer to keep them either for use or for speculation. In some instances, holders set up taboos around certain assets. Many holders of life insurance refuse to borrow on their policies and plan their affairs so that they can avoid doing so. In other instances, as with bonds, owners may consider selling at high prices, but will refuse to sell them at a discount unless, of course, they come to expect a default on interest or principal.

There is room for debate as to the degree to which assets are regarded as money substitutes. Most observers think that short-term government securities are prized chiefly as money substitutes, but life insurance cash values, though a contractual claim that is very liquid, are held chiefly by policyholders who refuse to draw on them.

An effective money substitute can only be defined in the light of the way people feel and behave. We may be sure that the list of substitutes is quite long, and that the makeup of the list varies continually.

Selection 4

USE OF THE WORD "MONEY"

FEDERAL RESERVE BANK OF ST. LOUIS

We found in the preceding selection that a number of other financial assets constitute money substitutes; they may be held instead of money. As a matter of fact, as this selection indicates, the term "money" is often used to mean a broad range of financial assets. When the term "money" is used in this sense, money is often referred to as being "tight" in periods of prosperity, because there is not enough of these financial assets to meet the demand; at the same time, "money" in the narrow sense of the assets used for spending (currency and demand deposits) is normally in excess supply in prosperity: money balances actually held are usually greater than the balances people desire to hold. In fact, because actual money balances exceed desired money balances, people are willing to increase spending—both velocity and the level of business activity increase. The double usage of the term "money" creates confusion unless terms are clearly understood; the purpose of this selection is to clarify these points.

In discussions of monetary conditions, the word "money" is often used in more than one sense. For instance, in one manner of speaking, money may be judged to be tight in times of economic boom or expansion, the demand being great relative to supply. In this context, *money* means loan or investment funds, and the term *credit* could apply equally well. According to this way of speaking, money (credit) usually becomes easy during recessions, the demand being small relative to supply.

In another context, changes in business conditions may be described as reflecting changes in the amount of money people wish to hold relative to its supply. What is important, according to this view, is the discrepancy between *actual* and *desired* money balances. According to this view, during expansionary phases, the public's actual money balances are greater than desired money; in an attempt to reduce its money balances, the public steps up its rate of spending on goods and services or financial assets. During recessions actual balances are less than desired balances; accordingly, in an attempt to hold larger money

---

• From Federal Reserve Bank of St. Louis, *Review,* October, 1963, p. 7. Reprinted by permission of the Federal Reserve Bank of St. Louis.

balances the public reduces its rate of spending. Used in this way *money* means particular highly-liquid assets, and the words "demand deposits and currency" or "cash" could be substituted.[1]

Proper monetary action, according to this view, is to provide the public with the amount of money that it desires to hold at high employment levels of economic activity consistent with avoidance of inflation. By injecting more demand deposits and currency into the economy when the demand for these assets rises relative to the demand for other goods, monetary action can satisfy the public's desire to increase cash balances without a decline in total spending. If the increase in money supply is adequate, the public will be encouraged to maintain its expenditures, and total economic activity will be supported. Conversely, as an anti-inflationary measure, the central bank can reduce the supply of demand deposits and currency or increase them less rapidly, the process working in reverse.

When both viewpoints are considered, it becomes evident that during a business contraction when money (credit) appears to be in relatively plentiful supply, it may be appropriate for money (demand deposits and currency) to be expanded rapidly. This, in turn, tends to make credit still more abundant. Conversely, in a boom or an inflation, when money (credit) is in great demand, it may be desirable for the monetary authorities to make money (demand deposits and currency) available less rapidly. Credit will tend to become even scarcer relative to demand.

If the distinction between these different meanings of the word "money" is kept in mind, discussions of monetary conditions and actions may be clarified. During times of economic slack and underemployment of resources, some say that money, meaning loan and investment funds, is relatively available and that since monetary conditions are very easy, the monetary authorities are doing all that they can desirably or usefully do. For those who think that the quantity of cash relative to the amount of cash which would be desired at full employment is a significant way of judging monetary conditions, a quite different view of the situation may be justified.

It is not intended here to prove that one or the other of the two major concepts of money is the more useful or significant. It is only intended to suggest that in a discussion of monetary conditions or actions, it would probably be desirable to distinguish between the two meanings of the word "money."

---

[1] Some analysts prefer to include other liquid assets, such as time deposits in commercial banks.

2

Monetary Standards
in the United States

THE READINGS IN CHAPTER 2 ARE DESIGNED TO CLARIFY
the elusive tie between gold and money in the American economy. Myths die hard, and the myth of convertibility of money
into gold as an essential requirement for a stable economic system is one of the hardiest. Much of the monetary history of the
United States could be described as a search for some automatic
relationship between the money stock and the one or more
monetary metals that would provide, automatically, the proper
amount of money for continued economic development with a
minimum of cyclical instability. Much of the story of the gold
standard is now history, but the persistent minority arguments
for a return to some form of the gold standard make it desirable
to acquaint the student with the monetary functions of gold and
with its past and present relations to our money supply. The
more interesting and significant use of gold as a means of international settlement of balances involves some different questions,
and is discussed in detail in the readings in Chapter 12.

For a careful review of current proposals for reform of the
international monetary system—including the Triffin plan and
the proposal for flexible exchange rates—see Fritz Machlup,
"Proposals for Reform of the International Monetary System,"
in *Factors Affecting the United States Balance of Payments*,
Compilation of Studies prepared for the Subcommittee on In-

ternational Exchange and Payments, Joint Economic Committee, 87th Cong., 2nd Sess. (Washington: Government Printing Office, 1962), pp. 209–237. A part of Professor Machlup's presentation is reprinted in the present volume of readings, as Selection 45.

Selection 5

GOLD AS A DOMESTIC STANDARD IN THE UNITED STATES
FEDERAL RESERVE BANK OF SAN FRANCISCO

> *This selection recounts some historical factors in the adoption of gold as a domestic monetary standard in the United States, and some of the reasons why the gold standard was abandoned when crises occurred because of war or financial panics. Desire for a gold standard reflects a desire for stability of relationships. In an uncertain world, stability is not easily obtained through any specific legal arrangements.*

THE DEVELOPMENT OF THE UNITED STATES MONETARY SYSTEM

It was in the late 18th century that the United States became an independent nation and added even more colorful and turbulent chapters to the history of money and banking. The legal provisions in our Constitution pertaining to a monetary standard reflect the reaction against the chaotic situation that existed under the Articles of Confederation when each state issued its own coin and currency, augmenting the already wide range of bank notes, foreign coin, and paper currency in circulation. The Constitution reserved to Congress the "power to coin money, regulate the value thereof, and of foreign coin . . ." and specified that "No State shall . . . coin money, emit bills of credit, make anything but gold and silver coin a tender in payment of debt. . . ." The Coinage Act of 1792 provided for the establishment of a mint and a bimetallic standard with the mint ratio of 15 fine grains of silver to 1 of gold. The United States monetary unit became the dollar because the Spanish milled dollar (the fabled "pieces of eight") was the coin most widely used and most uniform in value in comparison with the great variety of shillings which had been issued by the individual states. All coins were full-bodied because of continued distrust of credit money, but foreign coins remained in circulation and as legal tender until 1856 because of the scarcity of domestic coins.

Although the United States was officially on a bimetallic standard, its operation was not entirely successful. Until 1834 gold tended to leave the country, partly because gold was valued at a 15.5 to 1 ratio in France and partly because England was on a gold standard after 1821. In an attempt to arrest the outflow of gold, the mint ratio was changed in 1834 to 16 to 1, which over-

---

• From *The Search for Certainty in an Uncertain World,* Federal Reserve Bank of San Francisco. Reprinted by permission of the Federal Reserve Bank of San Francisco.

valued gold and caused a return flow to the United States. Silver in turn tended to drop out of circulation. During periods of crisis, moreover, bank notes were often not kept redeemable in specie. The disappearance of silver coins, especially the fractional coins, also handicapped business, and "shinplasters" (fractional paper issued by banks) and other private token money were poor substitutes. Finally, in 1853, Congress converted fractional silver into token coins (coins with metal content less than the face value of the coin), but the reduction in metal content was not large enough so that these coins also disappeared from circulation during the Civil War inflation. As a result, bank notes eventually formed the major part of the circulating medium of the period.

During the Civil War, the United States was on an inconvertible paper standard because of the heavy requirements of war financing. State and national bank notes, Treasury greenbacks, and bank-created checking deposits in favor of the Treasury constituted the principal circulating media in place of gold, silver, and fractional coins, the value of which as metal rose above their mint prices. For fourteen years after the end of the Civil War, the United States remained on a inconvertible paper standard, primarily because of inability to agree on the metallic content of the dollar since United States prices had doubled over prewar levels. Finally, in 1878, Congress restored the prewar gold content of the dollar, necessitating a sharp deflation which adversely affected the economy and severely penalized debtors. The return to the prewar standard was accomplished in a series of steps taken over a number of years. In 1873, free and unlimited coinage of silver was discontinued—the so-called "Crime of '73." In 1875, the Gold Resumption Act provided for the return to a gold-based dollar. In 1879, the dollar was actually made convertible into gold, and greenbacks became redeemable in gold. Thereafter, the role of silver in the United States monetary system deteriorated rapidly. Under legislation passed in 1878 and 1890 the Treasury was authorized to purchase silver for monetary use but not for use as standard money. There is clearly apparent in the history of the United States a division between the creditor and the debtor. As long as they remained readily identifiable groups—such as the Eastern seaboard and the frontier, the city dweller and the farmer—the "money issue" was in the forefront of American politics, with one group or area favoring "sound money" while the other opposed limitations on the money supply which were attributed to Wall Street control. The defeat of William Jennings Bryan in 1896 effectively ended the agitation in favor of silver although it certainly did not settle the more basic issue involved. The act of March 14, 1900 officially placed the United States on a single gold standard.

THE RISE OF THE UNITED STATES BANKING SYSTEM

Paralleling the development of the United States monetary system was the rise of the banking system. The first modern bank—Bank of North America— was incorporated in Philadelphia in 1782 to aid in financing the Revolutionary War. Similar institutions were founded in Massachusetts and New York. The only other banks were unincorporated private banks. In 1791 the first federally chartered bank—The First Bank of the United States—was set up. Its conservative policies, especially in regard to redemption of state bank notes, were attacked as hindering the development of the nation, and questions about the constitutionality of Congress action in awarding federal bank charters led to its demise in 1811. The ensuing five years were characterized by rapid proliferation of state bank notes, many of which soon became worthless. Consequently, The Second Bank of the United States was chartered by Congress in 1816 to counteract the abuses of state banking, but it encountered many of the same problems faced by its predecessor. In addition, its central banking functions—such as control of currency issues—did not accord with its private ownership and commercial banking business. Frontier philosophy contributed to the refusal by Congress to extend the charter of the bank in 1836.

Incorporated and unincorporated state banks then took over most of the banking business; their record was checkered—some were good but many were bad. By 1863, it became evident that a national banking system was necessary to replace the unsound and unsafe state system and to help finance the Civil War. The National Banking Act required national banks to maintain reserves against their outstanding notes (until 1874) and against their deposits. Noteholders were further protected by various provisions regulating note issues. Additional legislation in 1865 placed a 10 per cent tax on the circulating notes of state banks as a means of encouraging them to apply for federal charters. In the first few years after the tax was put into effect, the number of state banks dropped sharply. State banking revived thereafter as notes became a relatively unimportant part of a bank's business, and also because state banking regulations were generally less restrictive than those of the federal government.

The national banking system, however, had its share of shortcomings. The supply of national bank notes tended to be inflexible and unresponsive to seasonal needs and emergencies since their volume depended primarily on the supply of government bonds which constituted the collateral behind the notes. The pyramiding of reserves through concentration of interbank balances in the leading cities and the rigidity of the reserve requirements were other sources of weakness. The defects of the system were mirrored in the frequency of banking panics—in1873, 1884, 1893, and 1907—and more numerous periods of serious credit stringencies. In 1907, the National Monetary Commission was created to study the United States banking system, and its recommendations served as the basis for the legislation setting up the Federal Reserve System.

The Federal Reserve Act was designed to correct the deficiencies of the national banking system and the monetary structure. It provided for a more flexible supply of credit and for greater control by the monetary authorities. A gold requirement of 40 per cent against notes and 35 per cent against deposits of the Federal Reserve Banks was set up primarily to ensure the convertibility of notes and deposits. Eligible paper and later government securities constituted the remainder of the collateral behind Federal Reserve notes. The gold requirement, which has taken the form of gold certificates since 1934, was unchanged until 1945 when it was reduced by Congress to its present level of 25 per cent against both Federal Reserve note and deposit liabilities. A bill has recently been introduced into Congress which would abolish the present 25 per cent gold requirement.

WIDESPREAD ADOPTION OF THE GOLD STANDARD

In adopting a *de facto* gold standard in 1879, the United States was in step with the major countries of western Europe, almost all of which had adopted gold as their monetary standard of value by the second half of the 19th century. There were a number of factors which were responsible for this general return to gold. The disastrous inflationary effects of overissue of bank notes led an increasing number of countries to restrict by law the issuance of currency to the amount of gold coin or bullion held by the bank. In England, the Peel Act of 1844 drastically limited the note issue of the Bank of England to a fiduciary issue of £14 million, backed by government securities, with any amount in excess to be fully backed by gold. In Germany, the Reichsbank was also required to keep a gold cover for its notes. Thus gold assumed increased importance as a backing or cover for the issuance of paper currency since the gold requirements tended to limit the money supply.

One of the principal reasons inducing countries to join England on the gold standard bandwagon was their equating of England's prosperity and economic strength with the gold standard system. It was not realized that the successful operation of the gold standard in England rested on England's resources and not the other way around. The extensive use of sterling drafts in international trade and the indebtedness of many countries to England also encouraged expansion of the list of gold standard countries. A further push toward gold occurred in 1871 when the German Empire switched from a silver to a gold standard. Prior to this time, countries on a bimetallic standard were able to maintain bimetallism and stable exchange rates with sterling because of large, new supplies of gold from California and Australia in the 1840's, which replenished gold drains from England. After 1870, however, the flood of silver from Germany, from Asia (especially India), and from new deposits in Nevada led to a concerted shift towards the gold standard. The table on page 40 gives the dates on which the major nations went on the gold standard during the latter part of the nineteenth century and the first few years of the twentieth century. In the United States, silver producers, debtors, and those who feared the gold standard would limit the supply of credit needed for economic expansion continued to protest the abandonment of silver as a monetary standard.

THE GOLD STANDARD IN THE TWENTIETH CENTURY

From 1870 to World War I almost all major countries of the world were on a gold specie (or coin) standard. Their currencies were convertible into gold, in either large or small amounts, at the initiative of any holder, and exports and imports of gold were unrestricted. This was the period known as the "golden age of the gold standard." In the United States, the complaints of the silver advocates were lost in the general prosperity which prevailed. In addition, the money supply tripled as the supply of gold was increased by use of the newly developed cyanide process and by new gold discoveries in the Yukon region of

Alaska and in the Rand district of the Transvaal in South Africa, and as the rapid growth of banks expanded demand deposits.

The outbreak of World War I resulted in the suspension of the gold standard by most western nations, and gold coin and bullion were further concentrated in the hands of governments and central banks as these countries refused to redeem their money in gold or permit gold exports. At the conclusion of the war in 1919, the United States terminated restrictions on gold exports and on convertibility of currency into gold, thereby fully restoring the gold coin standard without altering the dollar's prewar gold content. Other countries recovered more slowly from the inflationary effects of war financing and did not return to a gold standard until later—Britain in 1925 and France in 1928. Most western European countries which did reestablish a gold standard adopted a gold bullion standard, under which coinage of gold was discontinued and other types of money were not necessarily convertible into gold. Under a bullion standard, gold is bought and sold by the government or central bank at a fixed price and in unlimited quantities and serves as a monetary reserve and medium for foreign payments. A number of countries at this time went on a gold

DATES OF ADOPTING GOLD STANDARDS

Great Britain	1816	Holland	1875
Germany	1871	Uruguay	1876
Sweden		United States	1879
Norway	1873	Austria	1892
Denmark		Chile	1895
France		Japan	1897
Belgium		Russia	1898
Switzerland	1874	Dominican Republic	1901
Italy		Panama	1904
Greece		Mexico	1905

SOURCE: Chandler, Lester V., *The Economics of Money and Banking*, rev. ed. (New York: Harper & Row, Publishers, 1953), p. 122.

exchange standard, under which the monetary unit is defined not in gold but in the currency of some country which is on the gold standard. Both the gold bullion and gold exchange standards economized the use of gold. Since most countries were no longer on a gold coin standard, gold lost its former importance as a domestic medium of exchange; its monetary significance was as a reserve backing the money supply in the form of currency and demand deposits and as a means of settling international payments balances. This concentration of gold in the hands of governments and central banks gave them increased discretionary powers in monetary management, both domestically and internationally.

The international gold standard that was restored after World War I differed in important respects from the prewar model. The environment in which it operated and its institutions had changed significantly. The prewar exchange relationships and the highly efficient and centralized international banking system had been disturbed, and international capital and gold flows were often disruptive.

The collapse of the stock market in the United States in 1929, coupled with bank failures there and elsewhere in the world, was enough to upset the highly precarious international monetary balance that had been achieved. As the depression spread, various countries abandoned gold as a monetary standard in an effort to insulate themselves from external deflationary pressures. . . .

The United States legally abandoned the gold coin standard in March, 1933, and in January, 1934, established a gold bullion standard and reduced the gold value of the dollar. Gold coinage was ended and existing coins were melted down into bars, and gold bullion was held domestically only under license for industry or the arts and sold for export only under Treasury regulations. The gold clauses existing in debt contracts were abrogated, and all coins and currencies of the United States were declared to be legal tender for payment of debt. At the outbreak of World War II, only the United States and a few other countries were on a limited form of gold standard. Most nations were on inconvertible paper standards under which the various types of money within a country were kept at a parity with each other but not at a constant value in terms of any metal. During the war, practically the whole world went off the gold standard, including the United States in the sense that it placed restrictions on the use of gold in international payments. Since World War II, only the United States and a few other countries have adhered to a monetary standard based on gold.

Gold, nevertheless, is still of significance on both the domestic and international scene. Under the rules of the International Monetary Fund, the par value of member country currencies must be expressed in terms of gold or United States dollars of the weight and fineness in effect in 1944. Relatively few countries today, on the other hand, have in effect legal requirements for the holding of gold against notes or other sight liabilities issued by their central banks. In western Europe, for instance, only five countries have gold cover requirements against notes and/or certain other liabilities, four others permit gold *or* foreign exchange to be held as cover, while nine countries have no prescribed minimum legal requirements or the requirements have been suspended. The trend in the past several years has been towards the liberalization of required minimum holdings. This does not mean, of course, that central banks do not continue to hold gold and/or foreign exchange, either against their note and deposit liabilities or as international reserves. A great deal of variation also exists in the degree to which individuals may hold, transfer, and buy and sell gold. Major areas today where private gold ownership is prohibited are the United States, the United Kingdom and certain sterling area countries, and Scandinavia. There are many countries, including Belgium, Canada, Germany, and Switzerland, which allow their nationals to hold, transfer, buy and sell gold domestically and generally export or import gold freely. Another group of countries permits their citizens to carry on the same types of gold transactions except for export and import; the outstanding example in this category is France. In the over-all total of gold transactions, private transactions are generally not very substantial although at times their influence on gold prices is discernible. The primary function of gold at the present time is in the settlement of international payments.

The domestic importance of gold has declined, and managed paper currencies are more the rule than the exception.

THE DOMESTIC VIRTUES OF GOLD

What were the reasons for the popularity of gold as a domestic monetary standard? In the first place, it was felt that under a gold specie standard the money supply would be relatively stable since the monetary authorities could not increase the money supply unless gold supplies increased. This restraint was also viewed as a direct check upon the ability of central governments to engage in excessive expenditure. Under a system of fractional gold reserve requirements, these constraints were weakened somewhat but would still tend to operate along similar lines.

Another advantage claimed for the domestic gold standard was that gold production tended to increase when the general price level was low and to decrease when prices rose, providing a more or less automatic response to economic conditions. When the economy needed an injection of money, gold output expanded; when prices rose unduly, output fell. Thus the gold standard was viewed as serving as an automatic check on the expansion of money and as a protection against inflation. The necessity of relying on changes in the gold stock for changes in the money supply, however, often resulted in a shortage of money during seasonal peaks of activity or for longer run economic development. Further, the deflationary impact of limited gold supplies was liable to occur at inopportune moments of history. Finally, gold discoveries and improvement in mining techniques or changes in the industrial demand for gold bear no clear relation to the need for funds.

SUMMARY

The basic function of money as a medium of exchange and measure of value for the purchase of goods and services and payment of debt has remained constant over history. The forms of money, however, have changed radically over time and will undoubtedly continue to evolve. The direction of monetary development will vary from country to country and will be dependent upon the preferences of individuals and governments, the state of economic and financial advancement, the type of government, and the degree of national and international control over money and economic activity. As exchange of goods and services contributed to specialization and thereby to more efficient production and higher living standards, the means of exchange also became more specialized as efforts were directed towards increasing the efficiency of the exchange mechanism. This evolution has been expressed in the movement from commodity money to representative coinage, from coins to paper currency, and from paper currency to deposits.

The preceding brief historical survey of gold in the monetary system has stressed several points. One is that gold shared the domestic stage with silver through much of history and only emerged supreme in the relatively recent past although it always was preferred as an international means of payment.

Second, it was not until the second half of the nineteenth century that most countries attained monetary sovereignty with national currencies of their own. Prior to that time, domestic monetary conditions were often influenced by the internal circulation of foreign coins. The experience of individual nations with their own national monetary systems therefore covers a relatively short span of time. Similarly, the use of gold as a currency standard has been a comparatively recent development. Third, the gold standard has been associated throughout history with economically strong countries with large stakes in international trade, for example, the Byzantine and Moslem empires, the Italian cities, and England. As a consequence, there developed a strong tendency to attribute economic strength to the existence of the gold standard. Last, although the gold standard was lauded for its contributions to stability and economic growth, it generally was abandoned in favor of an inconvertible paper standard whenever a crisis—such as war or financial panics—occurred because the governments or monetary authorities wanted greater flexibility in monetary management at such times.

Gold thus has lost its former importance as a domestic medium of exchange, and managed currencies represent the prevailing monetary system. Gold, however, remains as a part of the monetary reserves of governments and central banks. As a standard of value for international payments, gold has lost little of its luster.

Selection 6

THE CASE FOR GOING BACK TO GOLD

MICHAEL A. HEILPERIN

> *This selection provides a view not commonly found in current textbooks and other readily available materials. Most writers today do not suggest a return to a domestic gold standard, although they may recognize the role of gold in international payments. The viewpoint presented by Michael Heilperin is in all probability one that is held by a rather small minority; but for this reason it is desirable that it be included in a book of readings. Mr. Heilperin, although he obviously disagrees with them quite vigorously, indicates the nature of the plans advocated by those who, like Robert Triffin, believe that an International Monetary Fund with greater powers than those now possessed should be able to issue international currency, but to limit its issue in order to prevent inflation; he also indicates the viewpoint of those who, like Milton Friedman, believe in flexible exchange rates.*

This summer [1962] the gathering doubts about the strength of the United States economy, reflected in the stock-market plunge and the flagging of business

---

• From Michael A. Heilperin, "The Case for Going Back to Gold," *Fortune*, September, 1962, pp. 108–112, 144–159. Copyright 1962 by Time, Inc. Reprinted by permission of *Fortune* and the author.

enthusiasm, were accompanied—and indeed reinforced—by renewed uneasiness about the strength of the dollar. To be sure, as Washington spokesmen have been emphasizing, the balance-of-payments deficit has been running at a lower rate than last year. But there is still a considerable deficit, and the cumulative effect of deficits in ten out of the last eleven years has given foreigners a $16.9-billion claim against United States gold reserves. And although the outflow of gold itself has somewhat abated, memories of the frightening 1960 run on gold are still fresh, and its causes are still with us.

Politicians as well as monetary authorities seem deeply impressed with the perils of the situation. The Kennedy Administration professes its determination to bring the balance-of-payments deficit to an end, and in considering ways to speed up the domestic economy it is painfully aware of the need to keep up the appearance of fiscal integrity. The Federal Reserve and the central banks of Western Europe have taken steps to cooperate in meeting any speculative movement that might threaten the dollar.

Such defensive measures are reassuring, but the fear of crisis will persist and can be banished only by a positive policy that leads to a profound reform of the international monetary system. The aim of such reform must be to establish order in the monetary relations of the United States and its trading partners in the Atlantic family of nations.

The essentials of monetary order can be summed up in three conditions:

First, the guarantee of unqualified freedom in international payments—i.e., no controls or threat of controls on the exchange of one currency for another.

Second, a fixed relationship among the various currencies so that businessmen can plan their trade and investment operations ahead without fear that their money will suddenly change in value.

Third, a means of bringing the balance of payments of every country quickly into equilibrium so that some countries do not go on suffering chronic deficits while others keep building up embarrassing surpluses.

My contention is that these conditions of order can be brought about only by a restoration of the gold standard—in its classic sense, with currencies unconditionally redeemable in gold at home and abroad, and with the settlements of international accounts made in gold and gold only. In my judgment, this move will have to be accompanied by a revaluation of gold.

The return of gold to its once preeminent position as the base of money and credit is the only way of insuring against wide fluctuations in the values of currencies and restrictions on free exchange. And the sensitive response of the money supply to the flow of gold in and out of a country would be the most effective discipline on national economic policies.

The steps back to the gold standard should be taken in unison by all the advanced industrial nations of the West, but it is fitting and proper that the initiative should come from the United States. A bold and imaginative approach to monetary order would be a natural companion policy to President Kennedy's trade program, for free trade cannot flourish on weak and uncertain financial underpinnings.

A CRISIS OF CONFIDENCE

I am aware that this propsal is highly controversial, and that it will strike some readers as preposterously anachronistic: *"Go back* to the gold standard? Haven't you noticed that Queen Victoria has been dead for a long time?" An eminent New York banker has gone so far as to suggest that restoring the gold standard would be "like repealing the twentieth century." I am tempted to reply that the twentieth century, with its record of wars, tyrannies, and depressions, might be well worth repealing. But a more serious answer is to paraphrase a remark Winston Churchill once made about democracy: "It has been said that democracy is the worst form of government except all those other forms that have been tried from time to time." So it might be said that the gold standard is the worst form of monetary system—except all other forms.

The monetary arrangement under which the Western world has been transacting its business for most of the past half-century is intrinsically unstable and disorderly. Monetary experts call this arrangement the gold exchange standard; it is, in fact, an adulterated version of the gold standard. Its main characteristic is that only two major currencies, the British pound sterling and the United States dollar, are backed by gold. Other countries base their currencies partly on the reserves they hold in pounds or dollars—on the assumption that these "key currencies" are "as good as gold." The deficiencies of this arrangement were admirably described in *Fortune* by the eminent French economist, Jacques Rueff ("The West is Risking a Credit Collapse," July, 1961).

As Rueff pointed out, the fact that other countries use dollars as reserves for their money means that they are ready to accept dollars, in lieu of gold, in settlement of United States balance-of-payments deficits. This in turn allows the United States to go on running deficits without losing a commensurate amount of gold; thus the deficits do not have the effect they should have in diminishing the United States' own money supply and setting in train the retrenchment that would bring its international accounts back into balance. Moreover, foreign central banks have been basing an ever expanding supply of money and credit on the ever expanding dollar reserves they are accepting as payment from the United States. In effect, two pyramids of money and credit have been built on the straining back of the United States gold reserve.

The great danger is that a crisis of confidence—a sudden fear that the dollar was no longer "as good as gold"—would cause a disastrous credit collapse not only in the United States but through the non-Communist world. The precautions taken by central bankers to avert speculative movements would be of little avail against such a general crisis of confidence. The very countermeasures governments would be likely to take in an emergency—for example, stringent exchange controls—would only worsen the catastrophe.

Even if the situation is viewed in less dire terms, the danger is still apparent. Essentially, the gold exchange standard introduces a volatile component into monetary reserves. The dollar is volatile because it can be converted into gold at any time (not by American citizens, but by foreigners); that is why dollars are held as reserves in the first place. Once dollar reserves are so converted, they disappear. But the rate at which foreigners exchange their dollars for gold is not based on any tangible, predictable economic circumstances; it depends on confidence. As we have seen in the past couple of years, the United States gold loss comes in flurries, each creating waves of anxiety that build into long-term uncertainty. By reducing the volume of currency reserves available to finance world trade, any sustained conversion of large amounts of dollars into gold could lead to a sudden and acute shortage of international liquidity, with deflationary effects on trade and business activity generally.

The gold standard would, above all, take this volatile component out of money. Once mined, gold remains in being, even if it is occasionally hoarded. It would provide a firm, secure reserve for money and credit and give international trade and investment much greater protection from the vagaries of confidence.

THE SIGNALING SYSTEM

Over the years, an economic mythology, built of misrepresentation and oversimplification, has grown up around the gold standard. To begin with, it was an interlocking system of national managed currencies: The price of gold was fixed by statute, bank notes were fully convertible into gold, and there was absolute freedom of gold imports and exports. Central banks had a far greater management function than is usually admitted by textbook writers; much judgment had to be exercised, and errors were not infrequent. There were, however, certain important limitations on the freedom of action of monetary managers; these were imposed by the obligation to keep notes fully convertible into gold. Thus the gold standard made it impossible, in practice, for the various countries to carry on "independent" national policies of either inflation or deflation. As an empirical fact, prices "moved in step" throughout the whole gold-standard area.

The gold standard also contained within it a mechanism to keep international payments in balance, operating through an international "signaling system." When a country had a deficit in its external payments, it lost gold, which caused its economy to contract. When it had a surplus it gained gold, which caused an expansion. This loss or gain of gold acted as a signal for monetary authorities to undertake measures to bring external payments into balance: Generally these measures amounted to changes in the official discount rate (up in deficit countries, down in surplus countries), accompanied by open-market operations that would lead, in deficit countries, to credit contraction, and, in surplus countries, to credit expansion.

The timing and extent of these measures were the major responsibility of central banks (and it is here that we find management and exercise of judgment). The important thing is that the signals were followed by appropriate policies, i.e., those that would reinforce the effect of gold movements. In practice, international payments were kept in balance by movements of short-term capital from surplus to deficit countries, induced by the differential in interest rates.

A TESTIMONIAL FROM G.B.S.

It should be noted that under the old gold standard there was full convertibility—i.e., convertibility into gold coin. The merit of this was well put in an essay by Oxford economist Sir Roy Harrod, who comments from the vantage point of British experience (Britain, as is well known, was the center of the nineteenth-century gold-standard system). Wrote Harrod: "The British doctrine, held with great emphasis and often repeated, was that if you wanted to discourage individuals from hoarding gold as a store of value, the sovereign recipe was to make sterling absolutely freely convertible by individuals . . . into gold. By establishing free convertibility, you caused gold hoarding propensity to wither and die."

Though it did not prevent occasional local panics and depressions, the gold standard satisfied the requirements of long-term international monetary order. For about two hundred years, ending in 1914—i.e., during the entire period that Britain was *de facto* or legally on the gold standard—the "secular trend" of prices, expressed in sterling, was level: This means that such price movements as took place over that long stretch of years were invariably reversed, thus preserving the value of money for the saver and investor.

George Bernard Shaw, who could be very shrewd, especially where money was concerned, wrote in *The Intelligent Woman's Guide to Socialism, Capitalism, Sovietism and Fascism:*

> The most important thing about money is to maintain its stability, so that a pound will buy as much a year hence or ten years hence or fifty years hence as today, and no more. With paper money this stability has to be maintained by the government. With a gold currency it tends to maintain itself even when the natural supply of gold is increased by discoveries of new deposits, because of the curious fact that the demand for gold in the world is practically infinite. You have to choose (as a voter) between trusting to the natural stability of gold and the natural stability of the honesty and intelligence of the members of the Government. And, with due respect for these gentlemen, I advise you, as long as the Capitalist system lasts, to vote for gold.

In the heyday of the gold standard, most people would have considered this advice beyond argument, and only a shrill minority of American Greenbackers and Free Silverites would have raised their voices in dissent. Why then did a monetary system that worked so well for so long fall into such wide disrepute?

WRONG DIAGNOSIS, BAD SEMANTICS

World War I, by disrupting the sensitive network of finance, trade, and investment in Europe, dealt the gold standard a blow from which it really never recovered. During the war, with all fiscal and monetary disciplines necessarily cast to the winds, the gold standard was honored only in the breach. By the early 1920's the price level as expressed in currencies at their prewar parity had risen 60 to 100 per cent. But the price of gold itself remained the same, and since the cost of producing the metal had increased along with other prices, production of new gold declined. Consequently, monetary authorities began to worry about a shortage of gold.

It was then that they came up with an arrangement that would, in the language of the 1922 Genoa Economic Agreement, "economize on the monetary uses of gold." The Genoa Conference originated the gold exchange standard as we know it today. The theory was that gold could be "economized" if countries were not required to base their currencies on gold itself but could use as reserves those few "key" currencies that were backed by gold. The adoption of the gold exchange standard wrought an unwholesome change in the monetary rules of the game, for it weakened the signaling system and the whole delicate mechanism that had brought equilibrium under the gold standard. Yet the experts of that time (and even most experts today) failed to make a sharp enough contrast between the two systems. The old system came to be blamed for the faulty functioning of the new one—wrong economic diagnosis, compounded by bad semantics.

At the time of the Genoa Conference, the only nation that was actually on gold was the United States. In 1925, Britain went back to the gold standard in a modified form called the "gold bullion standard"—i.e., anyone could convert pounds into gold bullion but there was no gold coinage. Thus the pound joined the dollar as a "key" currency. But the mistake the British made was to re-establish the 1914 sterling price of gold. This automatically put the pound back to its pre-World War I parity with the dollar (4.86 dollars to the pound). In terms of the price levels in the two countries, this was unrealistic; the pound was overvalued by about 10 per cent.

As a result, British exports became, at least in part, non-competitive, and there ensued a period of high and chronic unemployment, aggravated in 1929 by the onset of the worldwide depression. The gold standard was blamed *as a system* for what amounted to two wrong decisions: (1) a mistake in fixing the parity of the pound, and (2) a mistaken belief that gold could be held at its prewar value.

As financial chaos spread throughout Europe, central banks began converting their sterling reserves, causing a run on Britain's gold when, in September, 1931, the gold standard was suspended. The pound was devalued in relation both to gold and to the dollar, British exports expanded, and unemployment declined. The abandonment of the gold standard was given credit for what was, in effect, a long-needed correction of the currency's overvaluation.

HOW F.D.R. SET THE GOLD PRICE

The crisis spread in 1932 to the dollar. United States bank failures undermined international confidence in the dollar, and there were large, though by no means dangerous, withdrawals of gold from the country just as Franklin D. Roosevelt took office. One of his first steps was to suspend gold shipment abroad and to order private owners of gold in the United States to deliver up their gold coin or bullion against bank notes. Thereupon, from the end of October, 1933, until January, 1934, Roosevelt progressively raised the dollar price of gold (which had long been fixed at $20.67 an ounce) as a matter of policy, because he was assured by his economic adviser, Professor George F. Warren, a Cornell agricultural economist, that this was the way to raise the general price level. In *The Coming of the New Deal,* Arthur Schlesinger, Jr., recalls the capriciousness with which this policy was carried out:

> Starting on October 25, Henry Morgenthau and Jesse Jones met in the President's bedroom every morning to set the price of gold. Jones was there as head of the RFC, which did the buying; Morgenthau, because of his recent experience in helping maintain wheat prices through a government purchase program. . . . While Roosevelt ate his eggs and drank his coffee, the group discussed what the day's price was to be. . . . One day Morgenthau came in, more worried than usual, and suggested an increase from 19 to 22 cents. Roosevelt took one look at Morgenthau's anxious face and proposed 21 cents. "It's a lucky number," he said with a laugh, "because it's three times seven." . . .

Little wonder that "tinkering with the price of gold" today makes bankers shudder.

In January, 1934, the price of gold was finally stabilized at $35 an ounce of fine gold. It has stayed there ever since. The Gold Reserve Act ruled out gold coinage and declared that "no currency of the United States shall be redeemed in gold." No private individual or bank in the United States is permitted to own gold except for industrial, professional, or artistic use (in 1961 the prohibition was extended to American citizens residing abroad). The Treasury, using the Federal Reserve as its banker, was authorized to sell gold to foreign governments and central banks in settlement of United States balances abroad. The dollar at home became an inconvertible paper currency, though backed by gold to the extent of 25 per cent of outstanding Federal Reserve notes and demand liabilities. This "anchorage to gold" is the last safeguard against "printing press" inflation.

The coup de grace to the gold standard, so far as the United States was concerned, was delivered by the United States Supreme Court's celebrated "gold clause" verdicts on February 18, 1935. The gold clause, written into certain contracts, specified payment in gold dollars. The purpose was to protect lenders against currency devaluation, and it was obviously incompatible with New Deal monetary policy. In two five-to-four decisions the Court ruled that the authority of Congress to regulate the value of money was paramount and the gold clause was therefore void in private contracts. The effect of this ruling by the highest court of the land was to make people wonder how much any tie to gold was worth in practice.

FIRST-AID STATION FOR CURRENCIES

World War II threw the international monetary system once again into chaos. The United States came out of the war with most of the world's effective productive capacity—and about 60 per cent of its gold. During this period of "dollar shortage," most nations struggled to conserve foreign exchange by imposing strict controls on monetary transactions. But the effort to restore normal conditions began early, with the Bretton Woods agreement in 1944, which provided that the currencies of participating nations should be given a fixed gold value; it allowed gold a minor role in the settlement of international accounts. Essentially, Bretton Woods revived the gold exchange standard as it had originated at Genoa twenty-two years before—i.e., currencies could be backed not only by gold itself but by reserves of "key" currencies that were fully backed by gold. Once again, the pound and the dollar became the "key" currencies.

The great innovation of Bretton Woods was the establishment of the International Monetary Fund as a sort of first-aid station for temporarily disabled currencies. By drawing on the fund, countries confronted by drains on their reserves could gain a breathtaking spell and put their houses in order before panic developed. Eventually, under the firm and expert guidance of Dr. Per Jacobsson, the Swedish economist who was appointed managing director in 1956, the IMF became an important influence for monetary stability. Gradually, the nations of Europe were emboldened to begin dismantling their exchange controls. In 1954 the London gold market was reopened, and in 1958, by formal agreement, European authorities adopted "nonresident convertibility"—i.e., a person who does not officially reside in a country has the unrestricted right to convert the currency of that country into any other. By then, the dollar shortage had passed into history, and, ironically, it was the United States that was beginning to worry about its gold reserves.

THE DOCTORS DISAGREE

Many leading monetary authorities, Dr. Jacobsson included, insist that there is nothing wrong with the present situation that cannot be corrected by more effective use of the IMF and the exercise of stronger self-discipline by individual governments. Their assumption is that the dollar and other vulnerable currencies can be defended, in the short run, by the deployment of IMF resources to curb speculation, and, in the long run, by voluntary efforts to end balance-of-payments deficits. This optimistic reliance on voluntary policies seems to me delusory. It is precisely because the United States and other nations have felt insufficient compulsion to put their houses in order that we are in our present fix. And the reason why this compulsion is lacking is that the gold exchange standard actually encourages procrastination.

A number of American and European experts agree that improvisation and stopgap measures won't work. But a brief look at some of their recommendations for monetary reform shows that they differ as sharply in their diagnosis as they do in the cures they offer.

One widely publicized group of money doctors considers the problem to be entirely one of insufficient liquidity, by which they mean that insufficient means of payment are available for settling international accounts. The contention is that there is sufficient liquidity only so long as the United States has a payments deficit and keeps pouring out dollars; if the United States deficit were to disappear, liquidity would dry up. The cure this group proposes is to establish an entirely new international currency, to be issued by the IMF against reserves of gold and key currencies that the fund would acquire from national central banks. The latter would be required to deposit a set fraction (say 20 per cent) of their own reserves with the IMF in exchange for an equivalent amount of the international currency. In addition, the IMF would engage in credit and open-market operations that would enable it to issue more of its currency as growing international trade created the need for it.

THE TRIFFIN PLAN AND OTHERS

The best-known advocate of this approach is Professor Robert Triffin of Yale, whose "Triffin Plan" has been making the international rounds since 1959. The grandfather of the idea was Lord Keynes, who proposed an international currency and "clearing union" in 1943, a year before the IMF was born. Keynes called the international currency unit "bancor," a concept used, with variations, by Triffin.

Logically, this scheme, which would erect a vast structure of IMF credit on a very inadequate gold base, would lead eventually to the demonetization of gold. This is hardly surprising, considering that Keynes called gold "a barbarous relic," and Triffin makes no bones about referring to the monetary uses of gold as "absurd." If gold ceased to be of any importance, what would keep the international currency from expanding indefinitely into a runaway inflation? In Triffin's view, the board of directors of the IMF would have the sole power to issue "bancor," and this power would be strictly limited so as to avoid inflation. But it is not clear how this safeguard would work in practice, or how the vaguely defined open-market and credit operations of the IMF would affect monetary conditions in individual countries. Perhaps the most telling criticism of the Triffin Plan was made not long ago by Under Secretary of the Treasury Robert V. Roosa, when he derided "the often proposed types of action that basically involve an oath of allegiance by all governments and central banks to a synthetic currency device, created by an extranational authority bearing neither the responsibility nor the disciplines of sovereignty."

A second school of monetary reformers shares the Keynes-Triffin disrespect for gold but comes to very different conclusions. The so-called "floating rates" approach, advocated by Professor Milton Friedman of Chicago University, among others, would abandon gold reserves and fixed exchange rates and allow the market place to determine what a currency was worth. Currencies would be fully convertible with each other, and would fluctuate the way stocks do in response to the play of supply and demand. If a country were running a balance-of-payment deficit, the "market" for its currency would be poor and its rate of exchange would fall. This would have the effect of boosting exports and eventually erasing the payments deficit. Conversely, a country running a payments surplus would find its currency in great demand and quoted at a high exchange rate; its exports would decrease, and the surplus would disappear. The great appeal of the "floating rates" system is that, in theory, it would automatically keep the balance of payments of all nations in equilibrium and thus remove that problem from the realm of practical preoccupation. In practice, however, movements of exchange rates would not have a corrective effect on the balance of payments unless accompanied by appropriate government fiscal and credit policy.

A country bent on inflating its economy would feel far less restraint than at present. Moreover, floating rates would cause intolerable confusion. World business is made up of thousands of individual decisions that must be based on the ability to anticipate future conditions. The absence of fixed exchange rates would remove the stability that is an essential of monetary order.

TO GOLD IN TWO PHASES

Only a return to the gold standard can satisfy the need for monetary order. I do not pretend that the path to this fundamental reform will be easy. It will require the closest international cooperation, the sure hand of monetary authorities, and the most enlightened and courageous statesmanship.

There is an organization already in being through which the advanced nations of the West can work together to construct a new monetary framework. Its mouth-twisting title is the Monetary Subcommittee of the Economic Planning Committee of the Organization for Economic Cooperation and Development. Represented in it are the United States, Canada, Britain, France, West Germany, Italy, the Netherlands, Sweden (as delegate for the Scandinavian countries), Switzerland, and Austria. The chairman is Emil van Lennep, the able Treasurer General of the Netherlands. The van Lennep group is already engaged in creating a more favorable monetary environment for durable monetary order. It is exploring, in particular, ways of coordinating national fiscal and credit policies for countering cyclical recessions. At present its scope is limited to encouraging voluntary cooperation, but it could easily be converted into an instrument for formal commitments.

As I envision it, the return to the gold standard would be accomplished in two phases. Phase I would be an agreement by all the nations in the van Lennep group—meaning, in effect, the whole Atlantic Community—henceforth to pay off all balance-of-payments deficits in gold and gold only. Countries that based their currencies in part on reserves of dollars or sterling would continue to do so for the time being, but further accumulation of such reserves would be halted. This step would bring to a halt the perniciously deceptive spread of dollar holdings abroad under the gold exchange standard. The United States would be compelled to get its payments into balance in a hurry—or face immediate and continuing losses of gold. This transition would give the participating nations a chance to get used to the new discipline, and to begin synchronizing their monetary and interest-rate policies.

Phase II would comprise three separate simultaneous moves:

1. A decision by the United States to pay off in gold all short-term dollar obligations held by foreigners. This would finally get rid of the gold exchange standard and put the dollar once again on firm footing. No longer would an uncertain threat hang over United States gold, encouraging speculation and threatening financial crisis.

2. An agreement by the nations in the van Lennep group to make all their currencies fully convertible into gold. Convertibility is, of course, the essence of the gold standard. The United States would have to repeal the New Deal monetary legislation and restore private ownership of gold. Quite apart from

other considerations, this would be a welcome reaffirmation of a property right that has been denied Americans for a quarter of a century.[1]

3. Joint action, again by the van Lennep group, to double the price of gold in terms of all currencies. For the United States, this would mean raising the price from $35 to $70 an ounce. My motive is not, I must emphasize, to get the United States out of its present scrape. Nor do I share the view of economists such as Sir Roy Harrod that a rise in the gold price, by itself, would solve our monetary problems by increasing international liquidity; the root of these problems is not shortage of liquidity but disorder. My reason for revaluing gold is that, otherwise, the transition to a true gold standard would be impossible. For one thing, if the United States were to pay off immediately its dollar debts abroad at $35 an ounce, it would lose so much of its reserve that none would be left to support the domestic currency.

For another thing, though there is no real liquidity shortage in the world today, one might eventually develop when the expansion of money and credit became tightly linked to gold. Just as it did after World War I, the price of gold has remained unchanged while the prices of everything else have risen sharply. As a result, gold production has been discouraged, and additions to the world gold supply have lagged far behind the expansion in world trade. Over the past decade, newly mined gold provided only about one-third—and since 1958 one-fourth—of the annual increase in currency reserves (not including those of United States). The difference was made up by gold from United States reserves (which dwindled from $23.2 billion worth in 1952 to $16.4 billion worth in 1962) and by increased dollar holdings abroad.

MANY PEOPLE WILL BE PROVOKED

When the gold standard is re-established, nations will no longer be able to augment their reserves by increasing their dollar holdings. When gold becomes the exclusive means of international payment and the exclusive backing for currency, therefore, it will become crucially important that the supply of new metal keep pace with the growth of trade. The present price of gold is inadequate to ensure such a supply.

The proposal to revalue gold will provoke a number of objections. Some people will see it merely as a devaluation of the dollar. This is such an explosive issue that hardly anyone in a responsible government position will even admit that it is being considered. But a careful distinction must be made between a unilateral devaluation of the dollar, undertaken in panic, and a readjustment of the gold price, accomplished by international agreement as part of a plan to restore monetary order.

A second objection that will be raised is that revaluation will have a great inflationary effect because, rightly or wrongly, people associate any jiggering of

---

[1] A number of advocates of the gold standard, notably Professor Walter Spahr of New York University, urge a return to gold coinage. Gold-bullion convertibility—i.e., the right of individuals to exchange sizable sums of money for gold-bullion bars—would serve the purpose of the gold standard without introducing the complications that the issue of coins might entail.

the gold price with inflationary finance. But this danger will be averted under my proposal because revaluation will be accompanied by full gold convertibility of the dollar, the best possible safeguard for stable money.

Finally, critics will point out that any change in the gold price will have to be approved by Congress, which might spend many months in debating the matter; meanwhile there would be such a mighty run on United States gold reserves as to precipitate the very crisis of confidence we have been so fearful of. This is a telling objection, but it is not insurmountable. If all the countries in the Atlantic Community undertake these reforms in the proper international spirit, it should be possible for central banks to take the joint action needed to stem a run on gold during the time revaluation is under public discussion. This will require considerable ingenuity and skill, but the stakes of lasting monetary reform surely justify the effort.

FREEDOM OF ACTION

The most serious objection to the whole idea of reviving the gold standard is that it would deprive governments of their freedom of action in dealing with cyclical unemployment and recession. In fact, however, the gold standard would allow governments considerable leeway in fiscal policy. For example, the United States could run a deficit to counter a recession if it met the deficit by borrowing at high enough rates of interest to tap genuine savings—and not, as has been the case in the past, at such low rates that it was in effect pumping inflation into the economy. The gold-standard discipline would not prevent the United States from coping efficiently with domestic problems; it would merely narrow the choice of methods used.

Those who believe that the United States should be free to inflate its way out of recessions will doubtless feel frustrated; perhaps it is high time they were. Americans still suffer, as a nation, from a hangover of economic nationalism from the days when we were a much less important economic and political influence on the world scene. We have learned a great deal about our international role in the past forty years. This is one more lesson.

Once these reforms have been carried out, the great edifice of free trade can at last be completed—on a foundation of stable money. The United States will play its role as the world's greatest creditor nation with a currency that inspires universal confidence. The whole non-Communist community of nations will take on greater political and economic strength with which to protect its freedom and assist the backward countries to improve their lot. By reinstating gold as the heart of the international monetary system we shall be drawing upon successful past experiences, rather than taking a hazardous flight into the unknown. We shall have built a bridge over the half-century of disorder.

Part Two

COMMERCIAL BANKING: THEORY AND PRACTICE

3

Commercial Banks
and Bank Asset Management

IN THE UNITED STATES AND IN MOST OTHER HIGHLY DE-
veloped economies, a very large proportion of all final payments
is made through checks on demand deposits in banks. Commercial banks create demand deposits when they make loans and
investments, thus increasing the money supply. At the same
time, commercial banks hold time deposits and in this activity
they compete with other financial institutions that have liabilities
in the form of fixed-value redeemable claims—e.g., savings and
loan associations, mutual savings banks, and credit unions.

Commercial banks add to (and at times reduce) the size
of the money supply by changing the amounts that they hold
in the form of three major asset categories—cash, loans, and
investments. By making loans and investments, and sometimes
reducing their cash holdings when these are above minimum
requirements, banks satisfy asset portfolio preferences of borrowers who create liabilities. Business firms that wish to acquire
capital assets and consumers who wish to acquire capital assets
such as houses or to purchase consumer goods create liabilities
in the form of promissory notes and mortgages; banks acquire
these financial assets and create liabilities in the form of demand
deposits.

As creators of demand deposits, banks help to satisfy portfolio preferences of consumers and business firms (and the gov-

ernment); these sectors desire to hold financial assets in various forms—demand deposits, time deposits, life insurance and pension claims, bonds, stocks, etc. Their demands for such assets depend both on the stock of assets already held and on the flow of payments to each sector.

Because liabilities created by the banks constitute the major part of the money supply, bank asset management is especially important. Thus the environment in which banks operate and their asset management problems merit close attention. By acquiring earning assets, banks concurrently increase the money supply; if this results in more money than the public wishes to hold, people will attempt to reduce money holdings by acquiring other assets. This cannot be done; other assets can be acquired, but someone must hold all money created. However, the acquisition of other assets tends to force down yields on such assets, and eventually the public may be satisfied to hold the existing money supply. The fall in yields tends to reduce the attractiveness of loans and investments for banks, thus limiting (at some point) further creation of money.

Selection 7

THE ECONOMIC ENVIRONMENT OF THE BANKING SYSTEM
ROLAND I. ROBINSON

This selection deals with environmental factors that affect commercial banking asset management and with the over-all problems of management of funds. Roland Robinson outlines basic environmental factors that affect bank management; the changing needs for financial services, the volatility of the money markets, the effects of Federal Reserve policy and of fiscal and debt management policy all influence the supply and demand for credit. Because of these environmental changes, banks must maintain adequate liquidity to meet varying conditions, and must adapt loan and investment policy to forces concerning which they are not completely informed.

The banking system of the United States operates in an economic environment of strength, growth, and dynamic change. Change gives strong underlying support to financial development. An active and even aggressive financial system is important because a high rate of saving is needed. Change means that obsolescence becomes more important than depreciation; new methods mean new machines which, in turn, require saving. When functioning properly our banking system also assures the employment of savings in some productive form. . . .

Because economic instability is wasteful of resources and demoralizing for people, the principle of government intervention to reduce its severity has been widely accepted by persons of all political persuasions. It is now accepted, by

• From Roland I. Robinson, *The Management of Bank Funds,* 2nd ed., pp. 20–34. Copyright 1962 by McGraw-Hill Book Company, New York. Reprinted by permission of McGraw-Hill Book Company and the author.

all but a handful of dissidents, that governmental fiscal and monetary powers should be exercised in the interest of producing economic stability, or at least of avoiding the excesses of instability. . . .

THE FINANCIAL ENVIRONMENT

Apart from the general economic characteristics of the economy of the United States, a number of its special financial characteristics should be noted.

An evolutionary financial system

The financial system of the United States is an evolutionary one, changing constantly in response to new needs and new demands. New financial institutions appear, but more often existing institutions change their character to be able to meet new needs. The relative importance of various financial institutions constantly changes. Occasionally, a type of financial institution disappears; the fixed investment trust is one of the rare examples. The important conclusion for commercial banking to be drawn from this historical generalization is that competition frequently arises from quite unexpected and new sources. To survive, commercial banks must be adaptable in the provision of services. If older credit forms preferred by banks do not meet the changed needs of customers, it will be the banks—not the customers—who must adapt themselves. A complex economy demands a wide variety of economic and financial services. Unless existing institutions adapt to change quickly and adequately they will inevitably tend to lose their share of the total market. . . .

The market for money is not simple; it is complex. Part is open and well advertised; part is concealed in a multitude of individual and private transactions. Economists have long defined a "market" as any recognized arrangement or area for bringing buyers and sellers together. The more striking illustrations are the highly organized and centralized markets: the stock market, the grain market, and the various commodity markets. But any arena in which buying and selling takes place is a market. In that sense, a money market exists wherever a borrower and a lender get together: in the securities markets, where bonds are bought and sold; on the platform of a small country bank, where an ill-at-ease farmer sits and chats with the cashier until he finally admits that "he'd like to get a little money." Thus part of this market is an open, centralized, explicit market with promptly available quotations. Anyone sitting by a telephone can, without too much trouble, find out just what United States government securities are yielding in terms of effective interest income based on market transactions of the past few minutes. Another part of the market is dispersed, without published quotations, and cloaked in secrecy.

To some extent all open and free competitive markets are characterized by a fairly great degree of volatility. Only where prices are administered by a few price leaders can short-run price fluctuations be avoided. The financial markets, however, are unusually volatile for a wide variety of reasons.

It is customary to speak of markets as being dominated by supply and demand; this is a truism of elementary economics. This trite observation, however, does not supply an adequate reason for the considerable volatility of financial markets. In financial markets demand is for credit, and supply ultimately comes from saving. Both factors are characterized historically by large variations. Furthermore, these markets are extraordinarily sensitive to expectations of the future: expectations as to changes in general business developments as well as expectations as to developments in the areas of public policy. This means, in effect, that commercial banks frequently operate in a market subject to extraordinarily sharp and quick price fluctuations. The highest ability of a bank manager is that of being able to change policy quickly when the economic climate of markets changes. The commercial banker who is unable to adapt himself to varying market conditions usually fails to take advantage of all of the opportunities open to him.

Federal Reserve policy

Of all the factors influencing the financial environment in which commercial banks operate, Federal Reserve policy is the most important. The influence of the Federal Reserve System is partly direct and well publicized. However, it is also felt through channels that are not always immediately evident in the markets.

The reason the Federal Reserve operates so directly on the commercial banks is that it is the branch of government that manages money. Since commercial-bank demand deposits have come to be the most important kind of money in our economic order, management of them is a clearly recognized governmental function. This function is exercised by the Federal Reserve as the central bank for the nation. The central banking responsibility has sometimes been complicated by exercise of other and related kinds of authority, such as banking supervision and the provision of a number of important banking services, among them the clearing and collection of checks. These matters, however, are never more than incidental to the System's basic obligations.

The Federal Reserve, as the manager of money in the United States, is expected to limit the creation of new money when the economy generates more demand than can be accommodated by existing resources. On the other hand, when economic activity slackens, the Federal Reserve attempts to stimulate it by liberal dosages of newly created money. In other words, the Federal Reserve tends to operate almost directly counter to the changes in demands for credit likely to be encountered by commercial banks. Specifically, it makes banking reserves expensive and scarce at times when the demand for bank credit tends to be very high. On the opposite side of the business cycle it lowers the cost and increases the availability of reserves at the very times when the demand for bank credit tends to slacken. . . .

The way in which Federal Reserve policy is expressed may not always be immediately evident to bankers. A change in the discount rates of the Federal Reserve banks is a well-publicized fact known to all commercial banks. A more subtle and silent way of adjustment used by the Federal Reserve System is through open-market operations which take directions that may not be immediately evident to commercial banks. Even the most sophisticated money-market banks are sometimes in doubt as to the nature of prevailing policy. The net effect of open-market operations, however, is to change the volume of reserves available to the banking system as a whole. While shifts of funds among individual banks may explain either favorable or unfavorable experiences at the clearinghouse, when the Federal Reserve holds the supply of reserves in check, banks will tend to find adverse balances at the clearinghouse and in mail collections. On the other hand, when Federal Reserve policy is one of ease, banks will tend to find both mail clearings and clearinghouse balances favorable.

The initial impact of Federal Reserve credit action is either on the bank that buys from or sells to the open-market account of the System or on the bank that is depositary for the person or nonbanking institution that buys from or sells to the open-market account. When the bank feeling the initial impact adjusts its reserve position, this action shifts the impact to other banks within the banking system. As they take corrective action, the full effect is spread throughout the monetary system. This is the familiar "multiple expansion" process elaborated in all textbooks on money and banking.

Fiscal policy and debt management

Fiscal policy, the other part of the public weapon for economic stabilization, has less immediate effects on banks. A great many commercial banks (all the leading ones) maintain tax and loan deposit accounts for the Treasury. The rate at which funds are called from these accounts is often a factor of considerable significance in short-term planning of a bank's cash position. Many banks subscribe to new Treasury issues when offered even though they do not expect to hold them for long; it is a kind of underwriting activity. Banks naturally favor issues which they can pay for by a credit to their tax and loan account; the giving of this privilege is used by the Treasury Department as a way of inviting underwriting support from banks. These activities appear to be the principal contacts of fiscal activities on banks. In fact, however, the actual points of influence and contact are somewhat broader.

The general fiscal policy of the federal government is expressed in the balance between its receipts and expenditures. An excess of expenditures over receipts tends to stimulate business. Such an excess is financed by an expansion of the public debt. This expansion of the public debt sometimes has a contractive influence but not enough to offset the spending stimulation. An excess of receipts over expenditures, which produces a budget surplus, tends to restrict private expenditures. The resulting surplus, when used to reduce the public debt, tends to have a slightly stimulative effect. The banking system may become quite aware of the shifts of funds through tax and loan accounts which tighten their reserve positions. On the other hand, it is by no means so evident to the individual bank when Treasury expenditures tend to put deposits into banks. . . .

Banks are also concerned about the tax liabilities of their customers; deposits generally show a sharp seasonal drop around each quarterly tax payment date.

HOW THE ECONOMIC AND FINANCIAL ENVIRONMENT AFFECTS THE BANKING SYSTEM

The determinants of money market conditions follow the traditional classification of market factors: those bearing on the demand for money and those bearing on the supply of money. Because this is a field in which the causal factors get intertwined, an exact separation of what is a supply and what is a demand factor is not always possible. For example, Treasury finance and Federal Reserve policy have elements of both. With allowance for this ambiguity, the supply-demand classification will help to classify money market determinants.

The demand for money (or credit)

The major demand for money comes from business firms; therefore, one of the leading factors of money market study is current business finance. What are the current plans for capital outlays? How are inventories growing or declining? What are the changes in current cash position of business concerns? Are their retained earnings likely to be adequate for capital outlays? Will prices advance so as to increase working capital needs?

The study of business finance has many ramifications; sorting out cause and effect is always difficult, often impossible. For example, suppose there is an observed increase in business inventories. An increase in physical volume may have been the cause but not necessarily; the increase in dollar amount may only reflect higher prices. But which caused which? Did the higher prices cause the larger inventories, or did the buying in an effort to maintain or increase inventories drive up the prices of goods? We thus find that a study of the money markets is not so much a purely financial survey as one that goes back to basic economic analysis. The study of general business conditions is necessarily the root and foundation of money market study.

Governmental units, both federal and state, are often important demand elements in the money markets, dominant ones in time of war. The demand for consumer credit, in both installment and noninstallment form, is an important though far from leading money market factor. Although in recent years private foreign borrowing in our money markets has been moderate, there are times when it is an important demand factor.

Variations in credit demand

Bank borrowing is basically a marginal source of credit to a great many business concerns; consequently, business demand for bank credit tends to vary widely. Short-term business borrowing is frequently used to carry either inventories or receivables, both of which tend to fluctuate parallel to changes in the level of economic activity. Such borrowing, however, may fluctuate because of special circumstances not directly related to the level of business activity. For example, business borrowing may be used either to delay long-term borrowing, if interest rates are currently felt to be high, or possibly to anticipate later long-term borrowing. Such demands for bank credit, while not directly related to the level of economic activity, are certainly strongly influenced by it.

In recent years many large corporations have found that their smaller customers depend on the trade credit they extend to them (frequently with rather generous terms) as a vital part of their financing. This may require the larger companies to draw down their cash balances or to undertake larger bank borrowing. Since the amounts of accounts receivable outstanding tend to fluctuate with business conditions, such variations likewise tend to increase the already variable or fluctuating pattern of demand for bank credit.

Variations in the demand for credit may also be observed in the area of consumer credit. This is evident in the direct bank loans to consumers but it is even more sharply expressed in the indirect loans to consumers made through credits to sales finance concerns. The rather sharp movements in demand for credit of sales finance concerns is also expressed in their policies of maintaining lines of credit to cover the sales finance paper that they market directly in the commercial paper market.

Variations in the demand for bank credit pose particularly awkward problems of bank management because in periods of tight or inaccesible funds customers are likely to fall back on banks after failing to cover their requirements by other means. This is particularly true of the small and moderate-sized businesses that frequently are such an important part of the clientele of banks. To some extent small businesses appear to be more sensitive to fluctuations in economic conditions than large businesses. Wider swings in their activity seem to occur, and these create wider variations in their demand for bank credit.

Variations in funds available

The most important long-term supply element on the money markets is private saving: saving by individuals and the retention of earnings by business concerns. (The second seldom comes to the open capital markets.) It is rather artificial to speak of savings as a supply of money or credit, since it means that income has been diverted from consumption and made available for capital outlays. But, in the usual individual savings transaction, the saver builds up his savings in money and then turns the money over to someone who uses it. . . .

Variations in the supply of bank reserves often come at awkward moments. Central banking policy tends to vary the supply of funds available in a direction opposite to the variation in credit demand. Deposit growth tends to be curbed by the Federal Reserve during periods of boom so that the balances available to the individual banks no longer are growing. On the other hand, credit ease which is the policy of the Federal Reserve during times of slower business has the net effect of increasing deposits when the demand for credit is relatively slack. This conflict of tendencies is particularly important in the analysis of specific loan and investment policies.

Variations in interest rates

Bankers have one economic characteristic in common with farmers: the principal sales product of banks, which is short-term credit, has one of the most volatile prices in the entire economic spectrum. . . . The effect of variations in open-market interest rates is not fully reflected in the rate that affects banks most since the prime loan rate does not move as widely nor as promptly as open-market rates. Nevertheless, the connection between the two is relatively strong. A banker must recognize not only the direct connection between investment earnings and these open-market rates but the indirect influence of the rates on the bargains that he can appropriately make with customers.

The variations in interest rates not only affect the current earnings of banks but also have considerable effect on the value of securities held in bank portfolios. One of the principal objects of investment management, indeed, is to follow protective policies that will avoid the extreme risks implicit in fluctuations in interest rates and, if possible, to turn these fluctuations to their advantage.

Variations in quality of credit

Relatively short-term and quickly reversed fluctuations in business conditions do not have profound effects on the quality of credit. It could be said, for example, that since World War II variations in business conditions have had only slight effects on the over-all quality of credit. A longer historical view, however, shows that the quality of credit has been influenced by variations in business conditions and that these variations at times can have considerable curbing or dampening effect on banking activity. Unrealized losses or threats of losses in either loans or investments cannot help but limit a banker's room for maneuver.

MANAGERIAL PROBLEMS CAUSED BY EXTERNAL ECONOMIC ENVIRONMENT

All these aspects of the external economic environment in which the banking system operates find their expression in a variety of ways. . . .

Liquidity management

Sizable changes in business conditions mean that a bank must maintain liquidity adequate to meet a wide range of contingencies. Liquidity requirements may become particularly compelling under two different types of circumstances which are at opposite ends of the scale of economic developments. A low level of economic activity normally means that liquidity tends to accumulate. In periods of great adversity it is possible, even if not likely, that some individual banks may be subject to sizable deposit drains. For example, an extreme drop in economic activity might cause banks in some areas to lose funds to the rest of the country and so lose liquidity. If times are so bad as to raise questions about the solvency of a bank, the pressure for liquidity can become even greater.

The opposite circumstance is the need to provide liquidity so that a bank can meet the loan demands of favored customers. This circumstance arises when a high level of economic activity prevails. This is the more real and more pressing type of liquidity requirement normally met in managerial operations.

Loan policy

In one way or another many of the points that might be made with respect to the effects of external economic influences on loan policy have already been anticipated: the fluctuations in loan demands and the liquidity provision that must be made to meet them. It is worth noting, however, that loan policy may be influenced in other ways by the anticipation of likely fluctuations in external economic development. For example, if a bank tends to have customers of a given type or customers concentrated in particular industries, it may be wise to make extraordinary efforts to promote business in lines that either offset or minimize the risks implicit in areas of concentration that naturally appear in their institutions.

Loan policy may require the prudent banker to establish in good times quality standards which can be maintained in other periods. It is doubtful whether loans should be granted in periods of prosperity to customers who would be unwelcome in times of adversity. Even more specifically, it may be dubious wisdom to seek the business customers in lines that are likely to be unduly subject to unfavorable external economic developments.

Influence on investment policy

The influence of external economic events on investment policy is felt mainly in the nature of interest rate developments. A specific example will show the way in which interest rate relationships influence investment policy. As is well known . . . , short-term interest rates fluctuate through a wider range than long-term interest rates. On the other hand, the prices of short-term securities fluctuate far less than those of long-term securities.

Not so well observed, but of considerable significance, however, is the fact that intermediate-term interest rates have recently fluctuated a great deal. They have fluctuated through so wide a range as to make variations in their prices almost as great as those of long-term securities. This fact could and probably should have a great influence on bank investment policy. In recent periods intermediate-term securities have sometimes been almost as risky to buy as long-term securities. By the same token, however, they sometimes offer considerably more promise of capital gains profits for a given degree of risk than is true of long-term securities. . . . The even spacing of maturities, a policy long widely recommended for banks, may not, in fact, prove to be as profitable as a more flexible investment policy. The potential improvement of return from the investment portfolio without extending maturity by taking advantage of variations in intermediate-term interest rates may be considerable.

The reasons that have accounted for these sizable fluctuations in intermediate-term interest rates lie outside the discussion at this stage. It is worth observing, however, that they have been an important expression of the variations in the supply of funds in the capital markets as well as variations in demand for such funds.

The discussion of variations in loan demand also has a bearing on investment policy. Since, as has already been made clear, investment policy is definitely subsidiary to loan policy, this means that, in effect, one objective of investment policy is to provide the liquidity needed to support appropriate loan policy. External events, in the form of changes in quality of credit as well as in interest rates, thus have a bearing on the formation of investment policy.

Earnings management

Because of variations in the cycle of prosperity and recession, banks naturally must expect some variations in earnings. These variations in real earnings may also be complicated by variations in the time at which earnings are realized and reported. Some of these variations grow out of tax factors. For purposes of good stockholder relations, banks may be hesitant to encourage any sizable variations in earnings that might be produced by this combination of external economic developments and tax factors. Unfortunately, a bank that wishes to stabilize its earnings may fail to maximize them. A compromise that serves both objectives is not always possible to achieve in a fully satisfactory way.

Assurance of solvency

A basic managerial problem created by the external economic environment is that banks must take precautions to assure their solvency, not only in periods of prosperity but also in periods of adversity. This is primarily a matter of the policy with respect to capital funds, but it also involves the policies with respect to liquidity and the control of quality in investment accounts.

Selection 8

THE PROBLEM OF MANAGING BANK FUNDS
CHARLES T. TAYLOR

> *This selection outlines some of the problems of management of assets by banks. Unlike some types of business, banks have only relatively small amounts of fixed assets; most of their assets consist of cash, loans, and investments. (Cash is rather broadly interpreted to include items in process of collection as well as cash in vault and deposit balances in other banks, including the Federal Reserve Bank of the district if the bank is a member of the Federal Reserve System.) Banks must maintain adequate liquidity in the form of cash and secondary reserve assets that can quickly be converted into cash without significant loss. Having provided sufficient liquidity, they normally wish to use as much funds as possible for loans, because income from loans is usually greater than income from investments; moreover, they must be in a position to "accommodate" regular borrowers, who rely on banks to meet short-term needs for funds. The problem of bank asset management exists at all times, but it is highlighted when seasonal shifts in deposits and in loan demand create pressures on bank management. Thus the selection by Charles T. Taylor shows the nature of the problem with clarity by examining bank asset management as it is affected by seasonal shifts.*
>
> *As Taylor indicates, elasticity of the total money supply, envisaged in the original Federal Reserve Act, may or may not be necessary; but elasticity in the supply of credit in particular communities is needed as long as seasonal fluctuations in many lines of business activity are a "fact of life."*

• From Charles T. Taylor, "Meeting Seasonal Loan Demands," Federal Reserve Bank of Atlanta, *Monthly Review*, November, 1963, pp. 1–5. Reprinted by permission of the Federal Reserve Bank of Atlanta and the author.

Frequently, because of seasonal forces, banks in an area may lose deposits when loan demands are high and gain deposits when loan demands are low. Such alternate periods of "tightness" and "ease" create a problem for an individual bank in managing its funds, regardless of how well Federal Reserve policy reduces the seasonal pressures on the entire banking system. This difficulty occurs because seasonal patterns in local areas frequently differ from those of the entire banking system. This is so because commercial banks make most of their loans to local borrowers and because the economic structures underlying the seasonal loan demands of these borrowers differ from area to area.

Every banker knows on the basis of past experience that more of his customers will be requesting loans in certain months than in others and that these months are the same year after year. Thus, the seasonal patterns that are derived from data based on banking reports merely formalize what bankers already know. Applying statistical techniques to monthly loan data for recent years, we have developed measures of seasonal movements, technically called seasonal adjustment factors. These factors tell us the typical increase or decrease from month to month, assuming the levels of outstanding loans were influenced solely by seasonal influences and not by general economic conditions, long-term growth or decline, or irregular forces.

THE LOAN MIX

The figure for total loans outstanding is a composite of the loans a bank has made to a wide variety of borrowers with different credit needs. The borrowings of some of these persons have a seasonal pattern; those of others do not. The borrowings that show a seasonal pattern are quite likely to do so because of customers' needs for more short-term working capital during certain months of the year, rather than from their needs for longer-term funds. In this respect, the seasonal loan demands of farmers and businessmen are similar. A farmer needs funds to buy seed and fertilizer, pay hired labor, and cover living expenses until his crops are harvested and sold. The retail merchant needs working capital to accumulate inventories prior to his heaviest selling months and to carry the accounts receivable of his customers after the goods are sold. The home builder needs construction funds to pay for labor and materials used during the good building months, before the houses are ready for sale. The mortgage banker may need funds while mortgages acquired during the peak home-buying months are being "seasoned." These and other types of borrowers may differ in their specific seasonal needs, but they all have a greater need for short-term working capital in some months than in others and they receive some of these funds from banks.

With so many different kinds of borrowers, the seasonal lending patterns of total loans outstanding naturally differ from bank to bank and from area to area merely because of the "loan mix." In addition, banks with a high proportion of borrowers whose primary need is for long-term credit are less likely to have a marked seasonal lending pattern than banks with a high proportion of short-term borrowers. For example, although consumers tend to concentrate their car buying in the first half of the year, which causes new automobile instalment loans by banks to be highest then, changes in loans outstanding show less seasonal response than new loans. This may be explained by saying that the new credit granted for comparatively long terms is only a small part of the total outstandings and, in some cases, repayments are heavy in the same months in which new loans are highest.

THE BANKER'S PROBLEM

This tendency for loans to rise and fall during the year in a regular recurring pattern is of more than casual interest to the banker. Unless he plans and prepares for these seasonal peaks in lending, he may find himself either unable to meet the usual credit demands of his customers or discover at the same time year after year that he is in an uncomfortably tight "cash position." The very same forces that are determining the seasonal pattern of his loans may also be drawing funds out of his bank when he most needs them and vice versa.

Bankers tend to regard the amount of their deposits as imposing a limit on their loans or investments, even though they may know that the banking system as a whole "creates" deposits when it extends credit on the basis of available reserves. This is so because a bank is likely to gain reserves during a deposit expansion and lose them during a contraction. How much an individual bank can lend or invest, therefore, depends upon its ability to attract or retain deposits. Since both the inflow and withdrawal of deposits are influenced by seasonal forces, the banker must take them into consideration when he formulates his loan and investment policies.

In some farming communities, for example, income is derived principally from the sale of a few specific crops in the late summer and early autumn, and deposits build up during these months. During this period, the banker has ample funds to lend. The demand for loans, however, is then at a seasonal low because farming activity is at a low ebb. After that, deposit declines begin to drain reserves month by month well into the following year until the crops are harvested and sold. Beginning in the spring, money must be spent for seed, fertilizer, and other production expenses; some of this money travels outside the local banking area, thus adding to the bank deposit drains. This is the time, however, when loan demands are high. The banker in such an area finds that when he needs funds most he has a shortage of loanable funds and when loanable funds are abundant he needs them least. Thus, conflicting seasonal deposit and loan patterns may pose serious problems in the management of a bank's funds. Not all banks have identical problems, but most of them have seasonal problems of some sort. Since bankers know with some confidence when there will be "tight" and "easy" periods each year, they plan their operations accordingly to keep available funds fully employed and earning profits and also to meet seasonal drains on their reserves when they occur.

MEETING THE PROBLEM

Bankers meet these seasonal problems by properly managing their secondary reserves, which are, in the words of the money and banking textbooks, those

earning assets that may be quickly converted to cash at all times without appreciable loss. Instead of leaving their funds idle during slack periods, they invest
them in earning assets that can readily be converted into cash without loss. Since
short-term securities of the United States government are subject to fewer price
fluctuations than long-term securities, they are the chief components of secondary reserves. Skillful management spaces the maturities of these issues so that
securities will mature as funds are needed. Although higher earnings could be
obtained from a portfolio consisting entirely of long-term securities, there is the
risk that, with a rise in yields and a consequent decline in prices, a loss would
be incurred if the securities were sold before maturity.

The management of a bank's cash position is a special art. First of all, some
knowledge of seasonal changes in loans and deposits is needed. It also requires
a man with a "sharp pencil" who will watch his bank's cash position from day
to day or even from hour to hour. He checks by phone with his Federal Reserve
Bank to determine his reserve position; he checks within his own bank on any
expected large deposit changes; and he knows if large blocks of securities are
maturing. He must be able to estimate not only today's position, but also what
it will likely be in the future. Only then can he decide whether he should use
any existing excess funds in the Federal funds market, buy short-term securities
or commercial paper, or whether the bank could prudently earn higher yields
on intermediate- or longer-term government or municipal securities. When he
discovers that the bank is likely to be deficient in reserves, he must decide how
to erase the deficiency. Because of the special skills required and the time involved, a money-position specialist is frequently found only at the larger city
banks.

For many banks, especially the smaller ones, managing the bank's money
position may be only one of the numerous tasks performed by a bank officer.
Paying such close attention to the bank's daily cash position, however, may not
be compensated by an additional gain in earnings. Some banks, therefore, prefer
to keep a cushion of excess reserves and correspondent balances that will meet
most emergencies. Sometimes, if not carried to an extreme, such a policy may
be the most economical one to follow.

BORROWING FOR SEASONAL NEEDS

Why, then, if a banker by planning can manage his bank's funds to provide
for seasonal needs, do some banks occasionally borrow from the district Federal
Reserve Bank or from other banks for seasonal needs? There are two general
reasons: the imprecision inherent in forecasting and mistakes in bank management.

Changes in the demand for bank loans and in the level of bank deposits
are caused, of course, by changes in general economic conditions, the long-term
growth of a community, and by other not completely predictable events, as well
as by seasonal forces. At times, these forces may push up loan demands or
drain off deposits beyond a banker's prudent expectations. Moreover, the seasonal pattern of lending may change as the economic character of the community the bank serves changes. For any such reason, plans for meeting seasonal

problems may prove inadequate. Furthermore, the "sharper" the banker's "pencil" and the greater his attempts to remain fully invested at all times, the more likely it is that he will find himself faced with special seasonal problems. Thus, large banks are more frequent borrowers than smaller ones.

A banker may find, for example, that deposit withdrawals are greater than he can meet by liquidating short-term securities. To raise funds by selling his long-term securities on a falling market might incur losses. Sometimes such emergency seasonal needs can be met by borrowing from other banks through the Federal funds market. At other times, member banks exercise their privilege of borrowing from the Federal Reserve Banks.

"Access to the Federal Reserve discount facilities," we are told in *Regulation A* of the Board of Governors, "is granted as a privilege of membership. . . . Federal Reserve credit is generally extended on a short-term basis to a member bank in order to enable it to adjust its asset position when necessary because of a sudden withdrawal of deposits or seasonal requirements beyond those that can be reasonably met from the bank's own resources."

Not all seasonal borrowing by member banks can be traced to the fallibility of forecasting and planning for seasonal needs that are to be expected. For example, there is the banker who is surprised year after year to find a seasonal pattern at his bank. He ties up all his funds in long-term securities to take advantage of their yield or income. When confronted by declining deposits, he may find himself in the position of having to replenish his reserves by selling his securities at a loss if money market interest rates have been rising. Or, there is the banker who tries to achieve the seemingly impossible feat of increasing both his loans and investments while his deposits are declining. Circumstances such as these, even though they can be traced to lack of foresight and should have been avoided, can be met temporarily by borrowing at the Federal Reserve Bank's discount window, since assisting banks to maintain a liquid position is one of the primary concerns of the Federal Reserve authorities. However, in such cases, the Federal Reserve Bank authorities take steps to help the member bank avoid such borrowing in the future.

Most banks are able to meet seasonal pressures on their cash positions by properly managing their funds and use the privilege of borrowing from the Federal Reserve Banks only occasionally, if at all. For example, even in the so-called "tight money" year of 1959, only 115 out of about 450 member banks in one district resorted to borrowing from the Federal Reserve Bank.

The burden of serving the needs of the public, therefore, falls upon both the Federal Reserve and the privately owned and operated commercial banks. Neither can do the job alone. Thus, the Federal Reserve System helps this nation's banks meet seasonal needs for money and credit in two ways. By providing the banking system with reserves in accordance with seasonal needs, it helps avoid periods of general seasonal credit stringency; by extending the discount privilege to member banks, it helps the individual bank solve its problem of meeting seasonal credit demands in its own community.

On the other hand, the Federal Reserve System must have the help of local bank management in meeting the seasonal credit needs of individual communities. Together, the Federal Reserve System and individual banks operate to provide that seasonal elasticity in the supply of money and credit envisioned by those who wrote the Federal Reserve Act fifty years ago. If one measure of the success of Federal Reserve policy is the avoidance of periods of general seasonal credit stringency, one measure of commercial bank management is how well it meets the peculiar seasonal needs of its own customers.

Selection 9

RESERVES: DEFINITIONS

FEDERAL RESERVE BANK OF ST. LOUIS

This selection (and the four that follow) discuss some specific aspects of bank asset management. Bank asset management is a matter of establishing priorities: the first priority is the maintenance of sufficient (but not excessive) reserves to meet requirements. Available funds in excess of such needs should then be placed, in sufficient amounts, in secondary reserve assets; secondary reserve needs depend upon the variability or volatility of deposits and of loan demand. If banks have wide seasonal or other fluctuations in deposits and in loan demand, they may need large amounts of secondary reserve assets, such as short-term government securities, which can be sold quickly with little loss. Only after sufficient provision has been made for adequate amounts of secondary reserve assets should a bank use funds for the basic purpose of making business, consumer, and other loans. Yet it is important that a bank be able to meet loan demand in its area, and some secondary reserves may be held for the purpose of sale to meet loan demand when this is necessary. Finally, in fourth priority is the investment of other funds— if any—in securities to provide income. Such funds are usually invested in longer-term government securities and in tax-exempt municipal securities, in order to secure more income than could be obtained by investing in short-term securities.

This selection deals with definitions of terms related to reserves. Current readings often refer to excess reserves, "net free reserves," and other terms; unless these are understood, the reader is not in a position to understand more advanced articles that deal with policy and policy guides.

Various measures of member bank reserves are frequently referred to; following are brief definitions of the more commonly used concepts of bank reserves.

Reserve Measure	*Definition*
Required reserves	Member banks are required to maintain as reserves an amount equal to a prescribed portion of their deposits. Currently, reserve requirements are 4 per cent of total time deposits plus 16.5 and

• From the Federal Reserve Bank of St. Louis, *Review,* September, 1963. Reprinted by permission of the Federal Reserve Bank of St. Louis.

Reserve Measure (Cont'd)	*Definition* (Cont'd)
	12 per cent, respectively, of reserve city and country bank net demand deposits. (Net demand deposits are gross demand deposits less cash items in the process of collection and demand balances due from domestic banks.)
Excess reserves	Total reserves less required reserves.
Total reserves	Member bank deposits with Federal Reserve Banks plus member bank vault cash. The sum of required and excess reserves.
Total reserves, adjusted for reserve requirement changes	In order to present a comparable total reserves time series, taking into consideration changes in reserve requirements, certain adjustments are necessary. The required reserve series is recomputed on the basis of current reserve requirements. Required reserves so adjusted are combined with actual excess reserves. The resulting series is sometimes referred to as "effective reserves."
Reserves available for private deposits	Total reserves less required reserves against United States Treasury deposits based on current reserve requirements applicable to these deposits for each class of bank.
Reserves available for private demand deposits	Reserves available for private deposits less required reserves against time and savings deposits based on current reserve requirements.
Borrowed reserves	Discounts and advances from Federal Reserve Banks, mainly advances secured by United States government securities or eligible paper.
Net free or net borrowed reserves	Excess reserves less member bank borrowings from Federal Reserve Banks. The resulting difference is called net free when positive and net borrowed when negative.
Nonborrowed reserves	Total reserves less member bank borrowings from Reserve Banks.

Selection 10

THE PROBLEMS OF COMMERCIAL BANK LIQUIDITY

A SPECIAL REPORT BY THE ECONOMIC POLICY COMMISSION OF THE AMERICAN BANKERS ASSOCIATION

All economic units are confronted by the problem of the need for liquidity—the need for sufficient money, or assets that can be converted into money with little delay and no significant loss, to meet

anticipated and unanticipated payments. (Money is defined to mean whatever is generally accepted in payment for goods and services and in settlement of debts.) Banks have an especially important liquidity problem, because one of their functions is to meet the demand for currency by the public, and another function is to meet the demand for credit that comes from borrowers. Although bank demand deposits are a form of money, the public may choose to hold more money in the form of currency and less in the form of bank deposits; banks must meet withdrawal requests or close their doors. At the same time, borrowers may demand more credit, and banks must try, in general, to meet the loan demand of their regular customers. If currency withdrawals cause deposits to decline at the same time that loan demand causes them to increase, both factors result in a drain on bank reserves. The problem of bank liquidity is examined in some detail in the following selection. During World War II, many banks acquired such a large volume of government securities that they had more than sufficient liquidity. The postwar period was at first, as indicated in this selection, a period of reduction of excess liquidity; by the time of publication of this selection (1957), the problem of liquidity had again emerged as a significant banking problem. The consequences of this problem for monetary policy, for debt management by the government, and for the provision of adequate long-run liquidity to permit growth of the money supply and expansion in business activity are explored in the last paragraphs of this selection.

For more than two decades the commercial banks of this country experienced superabundant liquidity. Recently, this situation has substantially changed. Today, many bank executives and directors, for the first time in their own experience, are confronted with the age-old problems of bank liquidity. . . .

More and more banks have approached what they regard as a "loaned up" position, in the sense that they are unwilling to increase loans further at the expense of their liquid assets. In a recent survey conducted by the Department of Monetary Policy of the A.B.A., "decline in liquidity" was cited more often than any other factor as a reason for the adoption of more selective lending policies.

The decline in bank liquidity poses extremely important questions for bank managements. Bankers are naturally concerned as to how they can continue to meet their customers' legitimate credit needs without reducing secondary reserves below the minimum deemed essential for safety. What factors should be considered in determining what this minimum is? Should loan portfolios be regarded as an additional source of liquidity to meet possible deposit losses? How would banks be affected if a recession should come? Would they have an opportunity to replenish their secondary reserves, or would there be a danger of heavy deposit shrinkages and a drain of cash from the banks, as has happened in some past periods?

Experience does not provide ready answers to these questions. The de-

---

• From "The Problems of Commercial Bank Liquidity," *Banking,* November, 1957, pp. 40–43, 128–129. Copyright 1957 by the American Bankers Association. Reprinted by permission of *Banking.*

velopments of the postwar period afford little indication as to what pressures might be expected if a major business downturn should occur. Nor can we generalize very confidently from the experience of earlier years. Modern banking differs in many important respects from that of a quarter-century ago, and the broader institutional environment has also undergone significant changes.

DECLINE IN LIQUIDITY SINCE 1945

The accompanying charts show the trends in average loan-deposit and liquidity ratios for the commercial banks as a group and the three classes of Federal Reserve member banks. Of course, the averages conceal important differences among individual banks.

From the end of 1945 to mid-1957, loans of all commercial banks rose $67 billion. However, largely as a result of a reduction of $34 billion in banks' holdings of governments, the increase in deposits amounted to only $38.5 billion. Hence, . . . the average ratio of loans to deposits rose from 17.4 per cent to nearly 50 per cent. As indicated by Figure 1, loan-deposit ratios are highest at the central reserve city banks.* This reflects the extremely heavy loan demands

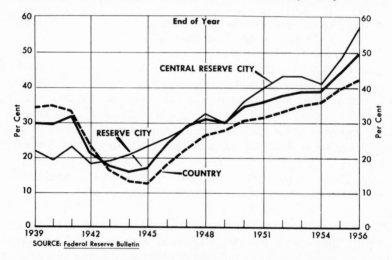

SOURCE: Federal Reserve Bulletin

Figure 1. LOAN-DEPOSIT RATIOS, 1939-1956—ALL MEMBER BANKS, BY RESERVE STATUS (Source: Federal Reserve Bulletin).

in the money centers and the fact that banks in these centers have suffered a relative loss of deposits to other places.

Figure 2 shows the decline in insured commercial banks' holdings of governments due within five years. By mid-1957, these holdings were down about $10 billion from their 1950 peak. The decline is even more striking when measured in terms of a percentage of deposits. As of the June 6, 1957, call date,

* *Editor's note:* the classification of banks as central reserve city banks was discontinued in 1962, but loan-deposit ratios tend to be high at the banks in the largest cities. New York and Chicago were the central reserve cities in the classification used until 1962.

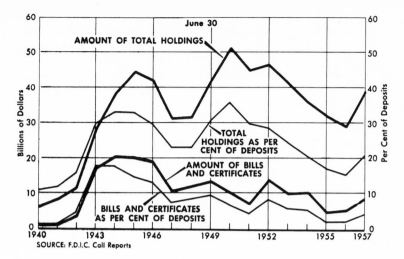

Figure 2. BANK HOLDINGS OF GOVERNMENTS DUE WITHIN FIVE YEARS, 1940-1957—INSURED COMMERCIAL BANKS (Source: F.D.I.C. Call Reports).

they amounted to 21 per cent of total deposits, while holdings of bills and certificates came to only 4.5 per cent . . . .

Comparing the three classes of member banks (Figure 3), we note that the decline in liquidity ratios has been especially marked in the central reserve cities. By contrast, country member banks have experienced a relatively moderate decline over the postwar period as a whole, although the average ratio for this class of banks has declined quite sharply since 1950.

The change in loan-deposit and liquidity ratios takes on greater significance

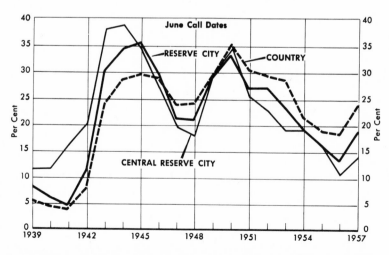

Figure 3. RATIO OF GOVERNMENTS DUE WITHIN FIVE YEARS TO DEPOSITS ALL MEMBER BANKS, BY RESERVE STATUS, 1939-1957 (Source: Member Bank Call Reports).

in the light of what has happened in the government bond market. Medium-
and long-term Treasury obligations are now quoted at substantial discounts from
par and the market for these obligations has become very thin. Clearly, banks'
remaining holdings cannot be regarded as being anywhere near as liquid as they
were only a few years ago and had been for many years.*

TWO REASONS WHY BANKS NEED LIQUIDITY

The problems of bank liquidity must be approached from two viewpoints:
(1) the need for what might be termed "protective" liquidity to meet deposit
losses, and (2) availability of funds for meeting loan demands.

A going bank must be prepared to meet deposit losses without undue disturbance of its loan portfolio, without incurring inordinate losses from the sale
of long-term investments prior to maturity, and without excessive resort to borrowing from outside sources. To meet such losses, banks rely mainly on their
secondary reserves of short-dated governments carrying little or no market risk.

There are no cut-and-dried rules which can tell a bank how large a secondary reserve it needs. In general, bankers try to be prepared to meet reasonably foreseeable deposit losses and, in addition, to have some extra margin of
protection against contingencies which they cannot foresee. Protective liquidity
needs depend not only on the probable or possible behavior of the bank's deposits under various conditions, but on various internal factors as well. For
example, a bank with a thin capital position may need a higher degree of liquidity than one with a higher ratio of capital to deposits, since it must be extra
careful to avoid substantial capital losses.

In addition to being able to meet deposit losses with a minimum of internal
strain, banks need liquidity to enable them to accommodate new loan demands
which may develop. Repayments on old loans provide funds for making new
loans, and, in addition, banks may hold secondary reserve assets which can be
disposed of in order to accommodate an expected upturn in loans. In recession
periods, banks normally add to their holdings of governments, and in so doing
they will endeavor to put enough of their funds into short-term issues so that
they will be able to expand loans readily when business turns upward.

During booms, it may be expected that this extra liquidity will be worked
off. . . .

As liquidity declines to the "safety" minimum, the bank's ability to make
new loans comes to depend increasingly on the flow of repayments on old ones
—unless the bank is willing to incur capital losses on longer-term investments
or unless the Federal Reserve supplies additional cash reserves.

The suggestion has been advanced in some quarters that bankers should
give thought in the future to some precautionary selling of long bonds in an early

---

* *Editor's note:* It should be evident that what is a "liquid asset" depends upon the
situation. When the Federal Reserve System was buying government securities from
the banks at pegged yields (during World War II and until 1951), all such securities were
completely liquid. Under some conditions even short-term government securities may not
be as liquid as cash, and long-term government securities may be quite illiquid—that is,
they may *not* be immediately marketable without significant loss.

phase of business recovery and rising loan demands. Certainly, it may be said in retrospect that complete reliance on avoiding any sale of long bonds in the early stages of the current upswing has not worked well for many banks. However, we should not underestimate the difficulty of predicting future credit demand and what is an "early phase."

LOAN PORTFOLIO AS SOURCE OF LIQUIDITY

Loans provide liquidity in the sense that repayments bring in cash periodically. It is difficult to compare the degree of liquidity in modern loan portfolios with that of years back. Years ago, banks relied for liquidity mainly on security loans and short-term business loans. However, security loans were never a very reliable source of liquidity in periods of general stress, and some short-term business loans were essentially term loans for "capital" purposes and were repeatedly renewed. Today, long-term loans to home-buyers, consumers, and business borrowers are generally amortized, and this assures a steady inflow of cash so long as borrowers can meet the payments. The quality of loans is also better, probably, than it was a quarter-century or so ago, and this has reduced the danger of loan delinquencies.

A fair degree of liquidity in the loan portfolio may be important from the standpoint of the bank's ability to meet day-to-day requests for new loans. The longer a bank's loan maturities, the slower its loan turnover, even though the loans are amortized, and the less flexibility it has to take on new lending business which may develop. . . .

The significance of this point may be seen from the experience with government-backed mortgages. Stretching out of repayment periods has tended to reduce the cash run-off from repayments and has thus tended to reduce lenders' capacity to handle new loan applications. In this way, it has contributed to some extent to tightening the market for today's home-buyer who desires financing. Similar considerations apply in the case of consumer instalment credit and business loans.

It will be recognized, of course, that the make-up of loan portfolios and the length of repayment periods are influenced by many factors beyond the control of bank managements. Nevertheless, banks should not lose sight of the fact that a certain amount of liquidity in the loan portfolio is essential to sound, serviceable banking, and that heavy concentration on long-term loans may reduce the bank's liquidity unduly unless it is offset by extra liquidity in the securities portfolio.

While loans provide liquidity in the sense just described, they should not be regarded as an important source of *protective* liquidity for meeting deposit losses. It is true, of course, that *in periods of declining loan demands,* loan repayments would release funds which could be used to meet a cash drain if the need arose. Normally, however, funds from this source will be needed for making new loans, and they should be available for this purpose. Except under highly unusual conditions, it should never be necessary for a bank to curtail its loan volume in order to meet deposit losses. In fact, a main reason for maintaining secondary reserves is to avoid disturbances of the loan portfolio when cash pressures come.

Experience has shown that heavy reliance on loan repayments to meet deposit losses is questionable banking practice. If a bank has adequate secondary reserves, its ability to cope with a cash drain should be practically independent of its ability to secure loan repayments. This independence is important at all times, but it is particularly important in bad times, when loan refusals and forced loan liquidation could have serious effects on borrowers and on the general community in addition to producing heavy losses for lenders.

NEED FOR PROTECTIVE LIQUIDITY IN RECESSIONS

Bank liquidity typically declines in boom periods as loans rise. At such times, determination of the minimum protective requirements assumes special importance, because of the danger that many banks may be exposed to cash drains when business turns down.

Certainly it can be said that lack of adequate liquidity has been a troublesome factor in past periods of sharply declining business. Studies of the experience of 1920–21 and the early 1930's have shown illiquidity to be the chief *immediate* cause of the banking difficulties of those periods. The liquidity problem was particularly acute in farm areas, because debt repayments and other transactions tended to result in a net drain of bank deposits out of those areas. In an attempt to cope with deposit losses, banks engaged in a frantic scramble for liquidity through wholesale dumping of investments and curtailment of lending operations. Larger holdings of secondary reserve assets would have enabled them to avoid heavy capital losses and given them more time to work out of poorer-grade assets. Also banks could have continued to meet the sound credit needs of their communities.

Obviously, there are important differences between the banking situation today and that of the early 1930's. For one thing, the quality of bank investments is unquestionably much higher, and the same thing is probably true of loans. Also, institutional changes have occurred which should operate to reduce the magnitude of cash losses which banks might expect to suffer in a period of declining business.

However, it should not be assumed that banks would not face liquidity problems in a future recession. A greater awareness of the uncertainties that beset the future would contribute to the chances of avoiding serious difficulties over the years ahead.

POSSIBLE FUTURE LIQUIDITY NEEDS

It is often said that banks do not need to be as much concerned as formerly about liquidity needs in recession periods because cyclical declines will be held within much narrower limits than in the past. There can be no assurance, however, that future recessions will be of the extremely mild variety experienced in 1949 and 1953–54. In fact, it would be safer to base policies on the assumption that they will be of somewhat greater magnitude. Certainly, the possibility of a sharp setback cannot be discounted as beyond the realm of probability.

It is often observed that total deposits of the banking system appear to be much less vulnerable to contraction in recession periods than they formerly were. In the mild recessions of 1949 and 1953–54, total deposits of all commercial banks actually increased. One reason for this was that loans increased in both periods. Also, the legal reserve percentages were cut, and this enabled banks to add to their holdings of governments.

This situation contrasted sharply with 1929–33. In that period, loans declined $19 billion, or 54 per cent, while investments rose only $300,000,000. As a result, commercial bank deposits dropped $17 billion, or nearly 35 per cent.

Loan volume is probably much less susceptible to recession shrinkage than it was 25 years ago. But even if loans were to drop off sharply in a future recession, deposits of the *banking system as a whole* would probably be little affected —barring currency hoarding or gold losses. This is true because most banks could be expected to use excess reserves acquired through loan repayments to add to their holdings of Treasury and other securities.* If the Federal Reserve were to release additional cash reserves, or if the Treasury were to run deficits and finance them through the banking system, total bank credit and deposits could even increase.

However, this does not mean that *individual* banks might not face liquidity problems. The important thing, as far as a particular bank is concerned, is how its clearings with other banks would be affected in a period of declining business and loan contraction. While deposits of the banks as a group might be little affected, important *shifts* of deposits could occur. Some banks would be bound to lose deposits and cash reserves to others having a more rapid rate of loan liquidation. That is to say, funds on deposit with some banks would be used to pay down loans at other banks.

Also, we could expect *regional shifts* of deposits to take place as a result of shifts in the "balance of payments" among different communities and sections. This could result from various economic factors, but the most obvious reason would be flows of funds resulting from debt repayments. The effects on the geographical distribution of deposits could be quite different from those experienced during boom times. . . .

A third factor affecting protective liquidity needs is the reduced danger of runs. Certainly, federal deposit insurance has greatly reduced the danger of widespread currency withdrawals. It should be recognized, however, that the realization on the part of large depositors that their deposits are not fully covered might cause them in a time of uncertainty to shift some of their deposits. In this connection, it may be noted that while the proportion of *accounts* fully

* *Editor's note:* Thus the existence of a sizable national debt may prevent the decline in the money supply which occurred in 1929–1933, and thus may prevent recessions from becoming serious depressions—especially if, as some economists have found, the decline in the money supply is closely correlated with fluctuations in business activity in major depressions.

protected by deposit insurance is about the same (98 per cent) for all size classes of banks, the proportion of *dollar totals* covered by insurance varies greatly, ranging from about 90 per cent in the smallest-size banks to roughly a third in the very large ones.

Equally difficult to evaluate, insofar as their effects on protective liquidity are concerned, are the broadened powers of the Federal Reserve and the likelihood that these powers would be used much more energetically to combat deflation than they were in the early 1930's. Then, the System's open-market powers were used belatedly and on a relatively modest scale to ease pressure on bank reserves due to gold outflows and currency hoarding, and the Reserve Board did not have statutory authority to lower the reserve percentages. In future recessions, the Federal Reserve will serve much more effectively as a tower of strength to aid the banks that it did at that time.

This, however, is more applicable to the *banking system as a whole* in its influence on liquidity needs. Central banking actions designed to guard the banks as a group against a liquidity crisis will not necessarily assure that *individual banks* will be free from pressure. The liquidity of every bank must be *primarily* the responsibility of the management of that bank, and the management should determine liquidity needs in the light of the bank's own situation and its position in the banking system.

Similarly, banks should not rely with excessive heaviness on borrowing from the Federal as a source of funds for meeting a cash drain. True, the Federal's powers to grant advances have been greatly broadened since the early 1930's. The borrowing privilege is useful for effecting routine adjustments in a bank's cash position, and it also affords a handy stopgap in emergencies when the bank may need time to effect suitable asset adjustments. But borrowing is at best a temporary expedient, and access to the discount window does not obviate the need for holding adequate secondary reserves.

From what has been said, it can be seen that while future business declines are not likely to present a danger of heavy and widespread liquidity pressures, there is still a strong possibility that individual banks could experience substantial cash drains in a period of deteriorating economic conditions.

Banks must be careful, therefore, not to revise their liquidity standards too far downward in boom periods. The temptation to do so may be hard to resist when loan demands are insistent and break-even points are being pushed upward by higher wages and salaries and rising interest rates on time deposits. While it seems likely that the great majority of banks have continued to follow sound liquidity practices in recent years, and that many may even be overcautious in assessing their protective liquidity needs, it is well not to lose sight of the fact that past downturns have caught many banks poorly prepared to face cash drains.

BANK LIQUIDITY AND MONETARY POLICY

From the standpoint of the monetary authorities, the reduction in bank liquidity over the postwar period may be regarded as a healthy development. In the early postwar years, as during the late 1930's, banks and other financial institutions were extremely liquid, and this made it difficult for the Federal Reserve to exert a really effective influence on lending. This difficulty was greatly enhanced by the pre-accord policy of par-support of government bonds, which made these obligations almost as liquid as Treasury bills.

With the abandonment of the support policy and the gradual decline in bank liquidity ratios, the Federal Reserve has been able to keep the banking system on a taut leash. It is true, of course, that banks have continued to liquidate securities in order to expand loans, and that they have tended to scale down their liquidity standards and to adopt progressively higher loan-deposit ratios as a guide to their lending policies. However, the restraint policy has unquestionably operated to moderate the rate of expansion of bank loans, while not halting the expansion directly. And it has tended to become increasingly effective as secondary reserve assets declined and portfolio depreciation increased. Furthermore, the shift of government securities from bank portfolios into the hands of non-bank investors has permitted loan expansion to take place without much effect on the money supply.

This shifting process cannot go on indefinitely. Banks in the larger centers have already gone about as far as they can in the direction of exchanging secondary reserve assets for loans. And many banks are now locked into their remaining holdings of securities by substantial market depreciation.

Of course, if we should have a moderate recession and loan demands turned down, most banks would have an opportunity to rebuild their liquidity and would doubtless do so. But if the boom continues, bank liquidity could become an increasingly critical consideration. Unless the Federal Reserve were to supply additional cash reserves, increasing numbers of banks would face a choice between adopting progressively more selective lending policies and taking capital losses on their long bonds. Under these circumstances, it could become necessary for the Federal Reserve to permit a faster increase in bank credit in order to prevent too abrupt and drastic a tightening.

LONG-RANGE NEED FOR ADDITIONAL LIQUID ASSETS

Even if banks should be able to improve their liquidity ratios in the near future, this would not mean that we shall have heard the last of the liquidity problem. A long-range problem may remain. Over the years, bank operations and deposits may be expected to increase in line with the long-run growth of the economy, and this will mean that banks will require a gradually increasing volume of liquid assets. Unless these are supplied, banks could find themselves running low on liquidity at progressively earlier stages of future cyclical upswings.

It may be expected that the private section of the economy will generate additional supplies of commercial paper and other types of short-term money market instruments suitable for use as secondary reserves. However, it appears highly unlikely that the growing need for liquid assets can be fully met from this source.

Fundamentally, the best paper for banks' secondary reserves is short-dated

Treasury obligations. Yet, at the end of 1956, insured commercial banks held less than $8 billion of the over $44 billion of outstanding Treasury bills and certificates. Twelve years earlier, they held $21.5 billion out of a total of $55 billion. This is an extraordinary upset in the ownership pattern of this type of obligation. It reflects mainly a great shift in the habits of corporations and other non-bank institutions with respect to the distribution of their liquid assets as between bank deposits and interest-bearing investments. In recent years, the amount of such liquid holdings seeking remunerative investment has grown prodigiously. Whether this is in large part a temporary phenomenon, resulting from the relatively high level of short money rates in today's market, or whether it marks a fundamental change in financial practices, only time will tell.

Should it prove to be a lasting change, it may be expected that the Treasury will be under increasing pressure over the years ahead to accommodate the form of its borrowing to the rising liquidity needs of both banks and non-banks utilizing short-term governments as the foremost liquidity vehicle. We may thus have the anomalous situation where the Treasury might "unfund" even more of its outstanding debt in order to meet the liquidity requirements of the banking system and the rest of the economy.

The problem could become particularly acute if the Treasury were to run surpluses and use these to pay down its debt, thus further curtailing the supply of short-dated government paper available to investors. In this connection, it may be noted that purchases of public issues by the government's trust accounts have steadily whittled away at the market supply of government obligations, and that this attrition will continue for some years to come as the cash intake of these accounts continues to exceed their outpayments.

A possible long-range solution to the bank liquidity problem is suggested by the Commission's . . . report, *A Plan for Member Bank Reserve Requirements*. Briefly, if the Reserve authorities were gradually to reduce the reserve percentages and simultaneously sell off governments from the System's huge portfolio, it should be possible, over a period of years, to shift some of the Reserve banks' excessive holdings into the hands of the commercial banks. As the Commission's study shows, the Reserve banks now have far larger holdings of governments than they need for either earnings or credit-control purposes. If reserve reductions were carefully timed, they could be accomplished without inflationary effects on bank credit and the money supply, and the utilization of the newly released reserves to build up secondary reserves would contribute to the strength and flexibility of the banking system.

Selection 11

LIQUIDITY—CONCEPTS AND INSTRUMENTS
HOWARD D. CROSSE

The preceding selection dealt largely with liquidity problems of the banking system as a whole. This selection provides an introduction to concepts of liquidity for the individual bank, and to the nature of the instruments used for liquidity purposes. Liquidity is a concept that may refer to several different things: it may refer to the characteristics of particular credit instruments, it may refer to the situation existing for a particular institution, or it may refer to the situation existing for the economy as a whole. Thus we may refer to the liquidity of money or the liquidity of short-term government securities, the liquidity of a bank, or the liquidity of the economy. The selection that follows discusses some of the complexities of measuring the liquidity of a financial institution, and then discusses the nature of some of the instruments used to provide liquidity.

The problem of liquidity for commercial banks is essentially that of having available at all times sufficient funds to meet the demands for money that may be made upon them. Liquidity is the protection against the risk that losses may develop if banks are forced to sell or liquidate credit-worthy assets in an adverse market. In this sense liquidity is protective. In a more positive sense, liquidity can be defined as a bank's (or the banking system's) ability to meet not only possible withdrawals of deposits but to provide for the legitimate credit needs of the community (or the economy) as well. It is in the latter sense that bank liquidity has been most sharply questioned in recent years.[1]

The liquidity of the banking system as a whole, the ability of all banks, or groups of banks, to meet the credit demands that may be made upon them, is the aspect of bank liquidity that has been most measured and discussed. For the individual bank, however, the problem of liquidity can become even more acute because transfers of deposits between banks, which do not affect the aggregate liquidity of the banking system, may be of major concern to the individual bank from which the deposits are withdrawn. It is the purpose of this discussion to examine the concept of bank liquidity both from the viewpoint of the commercial banking system in its entirety, and from that of the individual commercial bank, and to review the instruments of liquidity available to the banking system.

GENERAL MEASURES OF LIQUIDITY

Liquidity is most frequently measured in terms of certain balance sheet ratios. The ratio of loans to deposits, for example, is often used to demonstrate the degree to which banks have already used up their available resources to accommodate the credit needs of their customers. The presumption is that the higher the ratio of loans to deposits, the less able a bank (or all banks) will be to make additional loans.

The loan-deposit ratio undoubtedly has a psychological effect on bank

[1] Alfred Hayes, President of Federal Reserve Bank of New York, in an address to the New Jersey Bankers Association in Atlantic City, May, 1960, said ". . . at some point, banks and their customers quite naturally feel a bit uneasy with their high loan deposit ratios, raising questions as to whether their banks can contribute their share toward further needed growth in the economy."

management. As the ratio rises management may tend to become more cautious and selective in its lending policies and, quite obviously, the total of funds available, roughly measured by deposits, sets an upper limit to a bank's ability to make additional loans without recourse to more or less continuous borrowing. Loan-deposit ratios for member banks in the three reserve categories for selected years are shown in Table 1.

Table 1
LOAN-DEPOSIT RATIOS—SELECTED YEARS
Member Banks by Reserve Classes
(Year-end figures)

Year	Central Reserve City Banks	Reserve City Banks	Country Banks
1920	81.0	83.4	77.8
1928	60.0	67.0	65.4
1934	31.6	35.0	40.7
1945	23.3	17.3	12.9
1954	42.2	39.3	36.3
1958	52.8	48.4	43.7
1959	56.0	51.8	46.0
1960	58.9	55.2	49.6

SOURCE: *Federal Reserve Bulletins.*

The ratio of loans to deposits has been rising steeply in recent years in all categories of banks. Historically, however, if one goes back forty years or more, present-day ratios do not appear unduly high and history may well repeat itself in this respect.

The mere ratio of loans to deposits, however, reveals little about the banks' other assets available for conversion into funds with which to meet deposit withdrawals or to make additional loans. A more significant ratio for the latter purpose is the ratio of short-term assets [2] to deposits. This ratio, for four recent years, is shown in Table 2.

Table 2
SHORT-TERM LIQUID ASSETS RATIO
All Weekly Reporting Member Banks in the United States
(Dollar Figures in Millions)

Liquid assets	1961	1960	1959	1958
Vault cash	$ 1,417	$ 1,240	$ 1,103	$ 996
Balances with other commercial banks	2,956	2,830	2,634	2,570
Loans to banks	2,008	2,067	1,789	1,540
Loans to brokers and dealers	2,432	1,916	2,109	2,179
Treasury bills and certificates	6,279	3,294	4,324	4,446
Treasury notes and bonds maturing within 1 year	5,028	1,433	1,252	3,125
Less borrowings	1,749	2,316	1,966	1,170
Net liquid assets	18,371	10,464	11,245	13,686
Short-term liabilities				
Total deposits	$105,342	$95,233	$91,725	$86,135
(Less cash items in process of collection and required reserves)				
Ratio of net liquid assets to net short-term liabilities	17.4%	11.0%	12.3%	15.9%

SOURCE: *Federal Reserve Bank of New York.*

[2] Defined as assets of the highest quality maturing within one year.

The ratio of liquid assets to deposits is a more accurate indicator of the amount of funds still readily available to a bank than is the ratio of loans to deposits. However, both measures leave out of consideration the flow of funds from loan repayments as well as the *demand* side of the equation; i.e., the amount of funds that a bank or banks may be called upon to supply. The liquidity position of a bank is like a reservoir. It may be adequate, although nearly depleted, just before the season of heavy rains. Or it may be inadequate, although three-quarters full, just before the summer drought. To appraise the liquidity requirements of the individual bank one needs to know more than either of these ratios shows.

DECLINE IN LIQUIDITY AND ITS CAUSES

Table 1 shows that bank liquidity, measured by loan-deposit ratios, has been declining steadily since the end of World War II. During the depression of the 1930's and continuing through the war years, the Federal Reserve System supplied sufficient reserves to the market so that banks seldom had to worry about the availability of funds. Excess reserves, in fact, piled up in the banking system beyond the ability of banks to invest them. With the prices and yields of government securities effectively stabilized by Federal Reserve action, government bonds of any maturity were, for all practical purposes, "liquid" in the sense that they could be readily sold without loss. Bankers literally forgot that a liquidity problem could exist.

Effect of loan expansion

With the return to more or less free markets after the Treasury-Federal Reserve "accord" in 1951,[3] and as the result of the rapid expansion in the private sector of the economy, the demand for bank loans began to rise very sharply. In view of the inflationary potential of rapid credit expansion, the Federal Reserve System supplied reserves to the banks sparingly. Bank loans were expanding at a more rapid rate than the economy as a whole, as measured by GNP, because of the shift from government to private economic activity. Meanwhile deposits, particularly demand deposits, lagged behind the rise in GNP.[4]

To make the loans that were sought, therefore, banks had to reduce their holdings of United States government securities. These sales resulted in falling prices (rising yields) for such securities. By 1953 the liquidity problem in the form of substantial depreciation in United States holdings was clearly in evidence. It subsided temporarily in the recession of 1954 but, with the upsurge in loan demand in 1956 and in 1957, the need for more effective liquidity provisions came directly into the limelight.

---

[3] An agreement which freed the Federal Reserve from its obligation to support fixed prices for government securities. Board of Governors, *Annual Report for 1951*, p. 4.

[4] Between 1945 and 1960 loans at all commercial banks increased from 10.5 per cent of GNP to 22.9 per cent, while total deposits declined from 68.6 per cent of GNP to 42.5 per cent. Most of this relative decline took place before 1951. Since then, time deposits have just about kept pace with economic growth.

Effect of increased deposit velocity

In addition to the fact that bank deposits had not grown as rapidly as the demand for bank credit, bank liquidity was adversely affected by the increase in demand deposit velocity or turnover. As interest rates rose in the face of expanding demands for funds, the use of money acquired a rising value and, since banks could not pay interest on demand deposits and were limited in what they could pay on time and savings deposits, there came into being, outside the commercial banking system, a vast market for liquid credit instruments, which assumed the character of near money.

Traditionally, commerical bank deposits have been the form in which the liquid assets of the economy were held. In recent years, however, a large portion of the liquid assets of individuals and corporations came to be held outside the commercial banking system. . . . Corporations, at the same time, have invested the major portion of their temporarily excess funds in various money-market instruments.

When the holder of a bank deposit elects to use his money to acquire some other form of liquid asset or money substitute, the effect is to transfer deposits and not to extinguish them (if he acquires such assets from someone other than a bank). When a corporate treasurer, for example, draws a check on his bank to purchase Treasury bills from another non-bank holder, the existing deposit is merely credited to the account of a new owner, in all likelihood on the books of another bank. When an individual decides to save some of his money (whether currency or demand deposits) by placing it in a mutual savings bank, he is transferring to the savings institution, temporarily, the *use* of existing money. The first result will be an increase in "due from banks" on the books of the savings institution.

On the other hand if a holder of money uses it to purchase liquid or other assets from a commercial bank, or to repay existing loans, the immediate effect is to reduce bank deposits. When deposits decline, however, a portion of the bank's reserves become "excess," and, in the absence of offsetting action by the Federal Reserve System, these excess reserves can be (and in times of high credit demand quickly will be) used by the commercial banking system to re-create substantially the "lost" deposits by the making of new loans and investments. When credit demand is strong the banking system tends to use all available reserves promptly and fully. That this is true is evidenced by the fact that the sizable growth in near money took place with no net decrease in the aggregate demand deposits in commercial banks.

However, when holders of demand deposits use them actively and invest them fully, the velocity of turnover of deposits rises. With increased velocity the level of deposits in each individual bank tends to fluctuate both more rapidly and more widely. Surplus deposits, not needed for working balance purposes, are quickly withdrawn for investment in other liquidity instruments and the bank is unable to use these funds to make even short-term loans or investments. At best a bank may sell the funds for a day or two in the Federal funds market. Increased deposit velocity, therefore, has had an adverse effect on bank liquidity that is not fully reflected by loan-deposit ratios or the ratio of short-term assets to deposits.

If this point seems belabored it is because its understanding is so essential to comprehending not only the role of money transfers within the banking system but also the nature of the competition for liquidity instruments (near money) and real savings funds between commercial banks, the money market, and other financial institutions.

EFFECT OF CHANGES IN LOAN CHARACTERISTICS

Loan repayments are often considered to be a factor in a bank's liquidity position.[5] Over time they constitute an important source of funds with which to make new loans (to the extent that total loans do not increase) and loan repayments can be used to repay deposits (to the extent that the total of outstanding loans decreases). If the rate of loan repayments is reduced, that is if the loan turnover diminishes, then this source of liquidity is also reduced. Loan turnover tends to decline when the terms of repayment are extended.[6]

It has been many years since short-term, self-liquidating paper made up the bulk of commercial bank loan portfolios. The integration of industry and commerce into larger and more extensive business organizations has long since eliminated much of the need for the kind of short-term credit that historically financed, in separate stages, the transfer of goods from raw material pproducer, to fabricator, to wholesaler, to retailer, and to consumer. Moreover, the increasing importance of time and savings deposits has resulted in the availability of at least theoretically longer-term funds. In any event, capital loans and other longer-term loans have assumed a position of considerable prominence in the vast growth of commercial bank lending since World War II. More than half of the business loans in the New York City banks, for example, have original maturities of more than one year.[7] In smaller banks the growth of mortgage loans and consumer credit, and particularly the tendency to lengthen the terms of such loans, has raised questions concerning the banks' ability to meet short-term credit needs in their communities in the event of a further upsurge in loan demand.

The fact of the matter is that commercial bank loans today are probably more "liquid" than they appear. The regular amortization of term loans, mortgage loans, and consumer credit provides a steady flow of funds for re-lending. While half of the New York City banks' business loans had original maturities of more than one year, it has been estimated that at least a third of the loans outstanding at any time fall due within a year. Mortgage officers know "how hard they have to run in order to stand still" in the matter of just maintaining

[5] Cf. Milton J. Drake, Presentation before National Credit Conference, American Bankers Association, Chicago, January, 1961, "Some Concepts of Bank Liquidity." Reprinted in *Bulletin of the Robert Morris Associates,* Vol. 43, No. 6, February, 1961.

[6] Cf. Federal Reserve Bank of Chicago, "Liquidity of Business Loans," *Business Conditions,* March, 1961, pp. 9–10. Also, Federal Reserve Bank of New York, "Turnover of Business Loans at New York City Banks," *Monthly Review,* Vol. 44, No. 1 (January, 1962), p. 10.

[7] Federal Reserve Bank of New York, "Term Lending by New York City Banks," *Monthly Review,* Vol. 43, No. 2 (February, 1961), pp. 27-31.

an amortizing mortgage portfolio, and experience shows that the average actual life of a twenty-five year mortgage is something under twelve years. Few banks have tried to determine what percentage of their loans will in all probability be repaid in given periods of time.[8]

It is also probable that many of the so-called short-term loans which historically graced commercial bank loan portfolios were short term in name only. Ninety-day notes were all too frequently renewed over and over again with little or no payment. The "demand" mortgages of the 1920's all too often were not reduced until they were foreclosed in the depths of the subsequent depression. Experienced lending officers will freely admit that demand loans, generally, are among the slowest loans on their books.

One may conclude therefore that loan liquidity has not diminished perceptibly in recent years. It should be emphasized, however, that loan repayments do not supply funds for increasing the total of a bank's loan account or to meet the short-term deposit swings at times when loan demands are pressing on the bank's liquidity position. Loan repayments constitute an important source of "protective liquidity" over time, but affect the current liquidity position only to the extent that *net* loan increases or decreases are predictable.

LIQUIDITY NEEDS

The discussion above has been concerned with liquidity needs in general. More specifically, the liquidity needs of individual banks must be related to the demands made upon them for funds over periods of time. Some funds may be called for tomorrow; some may not be needed for a year or more; and additional liquidity may be needed for unforeseen or unpredictable demands as a margin of safety.

A bank obviously would not be operating efficiently if it held in cash today the funds needed to make loans two years later. Therefore, just as the amount of liquidity is related to the potential size of the demand for funds, the form and maturity in which liquid assets are held should be related to the times at which demands for funds are likely to occur.

Liquidity and the money position

Every bank is required by law to maintain a portion of its deposits in the form of cash on hand or demand balances due from specified banks. For banks which are not members of the Federal Reserve System, reserve requirements are established by the laws of the various states and differ widely. A member bank must maintain a minimum percentage of its demand and time deposits in the form of cash in vault or on deposit with the Federal Reserve Bank of its district.[9]

[8] One fairly typical bank with loans of about $25 million and deposits of about $45 million made such an analysis and found that 47 per cent of total loans would be converted into cash within one year. This represented 20 per cent of mortgages, 58 per cent of consumer loans, and 61 per cent of other loans. Citizens Bank of Sheboygan, Michigan, letter to the author, dated February 10, 1961.

[9] Board of Governors of the Federal Reserve System, *Regulation D,* "Reserves of Member Banks" (Fed. Res. Act, Section 19).

Required reserves may be averaged over reserve computation periods; weekly for reserve and central reserve city banks,[10] and biweekly for others, designated as "country banks."

A bank's legal reserve, however, does serve as a temporary buffer between the demand for funds being made upon it and its true liquidity position. When depositors' checks are presented for payment the immediate effect is to reduce the bank's reserve account or correspondent balances. When loans are made the proceeds are usually credited to a deposit account against which checks will be drawn. Thus, as loan proceeds are drawn down, the bank's reserve account or correspondent balance is reduced in exactly the same way as when other deposits are withdrawn. In the absence of offsetting credits, a bank must look to its liquid assets for funds with which to restore its reserve to the required amount within the reserve computation period.[11] Thus a bank's money position immediately reflects the major portion of the demands for funds that may be made upon it. The management of the money position is closely related to, but not a part of, the management of the liquidity position.

Short-term liquidity needs

The short-term liquidity needs of a bank are largely determined by the prospective actions of its larger customers. The holders of sizable deposit balances and the customers who borrow in substantial amounts influence the liquidity position of an individual bank to a degree that is directly related to their size. The needs of important customers for funds, intermittent, constant, or seasonal, will impinge directly and substantially on their banks' liquidity requirements.

Much of the management of a bank's liquidity position, therefore, will revolve around a knowledge of the needs and intentions of large customers and a preparation to cope with them. Alert bank management will endeavor to keep in close touch with those customers whose deposit swings or borrowing needs can substantially affect the bank's own liquidity position in order to learn of their plans as early as possible. This is one important reason for bank officers to visit their customers and to understand the nature of their businesses.

Short-term liquidity needs are also influenced by seasonal factors which may affect the entire level of deposit supply or loan demand. Farm communities, for example, exhibit clear recurrent seasonal patterns of demand and supply of funds that are distinctly different from those, let us say, of suburban communities. Some seasonality of loan demand and deposit flow is found in nearly every community. Certain industries borrow seasonally and corporate needs for funds build up at tax dates.

Most seasonal fluctuations can be quite accurately timed and appropriate liquidity provided on the basis of past experience. In planning for seasonal liquidity needs, the maturity of the liquidity assets can often be closely tailored to the probable time of the demand for funds.

[10] The designation of New York and Chicago as "central reserve city" banks expired July 28, 1962.
[11] Some states require that reserves be maintained on a daily basis and Federal Reserve banks expect that their members will make an effort to avoid large deficiences on any one day, despite the averaging privilege.

Other liquidity needs

In addition to providing funds for the known and generally foreseeable short-term demands, banks require a margin of liquidity for demands that can be predicted over the longer range or which may be unforeseen altogether. These may be designated as longer-term liquidity needs. They are generally related to the secular trends of the community or markets which a bank serves. In rapidly expanding areas loan demand grows at a more rapid pace than deposits are accumulated. Funds must be provided for loan expansion or other ways found for coping with these demands. This is one function of longer-term liquidity.

In stable communities, on the other hand, deposits may show a steady rise while loan demand remains virtually unchanged. In such cases the longer view of liquidity requirements may enable the bank to keep currently more closely invested than it would otherwise. In either case, to gauge its needs for longer-term liquidity bank management must attempt some long-range economic forecasting on the basis of which it can reasonably estimate loan and deposit levels for perhaps five years ahead.

Economic forecasting, however, is at best an inexact science and conservative bank management will maintain some amount of readily available funds to provide for a margin of error. These funds, too, will be included in the bank's longer-term liquidity requirements.

To summarize the foregoing, it should be evident that the management of a bank's liquidity position transcends the simple yardsticks provided by balance sheet ratios. The latter are useful as measures of over-all change, but the position and the need are not always measurable in the same terms. Liquidity needs must be considered both in terms of amount and of the time at which the demands for funds may be made upon the bank (or the banking system). In consequence a bank's portfolio of liquid assets will not be uniform either in its makeup at any given moment, or in its amount over time.

PRIMARY, SECONDARY, AND OTHER LIQUIDITY RESERVES

Writers on the subject of bank liquidity have long recognized the diverse nature of banks' liquidity needs and usually divide a bank's liquidity position into "primary reserves," "secondary reserves," and something variously designated as "tertiary reserves," "Secondary Reserve II" [12] or "Investment Reserve." [13] The latter, whatever it is called, represents the "longer-term" liquidity needs discussed above. These categorical separations are perhaps too confining and the term "investment" reserve may tend to confuse the essential difference in purpose between liquidity assets and the "investment portfolio." The separation between

[12] Roland I. Robinson, *The Management of Bank Funds* (New York: McGraw-Hill Book Company, 1951).

[13] Robert G. Rodkey, *Sound Policies for Bank Management* (New York: The Ronald Press Company, 1944). This term is also adopted by Roger A. Lyon in his recent book *Investment Portfolio Management in the Commercial Bank* (New Brunswick, N. J.: Rutgers University Press, 1960).

shorter-and longer-term liquidity needs and instruments is a fluid and flexible one; what all sections of the liquidity position have in common is the fact that these assets are held to meet estimated needs of funds for other purposes.

Primary reserves are usually defined as cash on hand and demand balances due from banks, or legal reserves plus any excess holdings of non-interest-earning forms of money. They are more readily identifiable than secondary or tertiary reserves, but to a large measure are not part of the liquidity position. To maximize income, excess holdings of money should be held to a minimum. While it is not always possible to attain this ideal fully, especially in small banks where some of the large deposit accounts are of such a temporary nature that they cannot be effectively invested even through the sale of Federal funds, such banks (if members of the Federal Reserve System) can at least see to it that their excess legal reserves are transferred to their correspondents in the money centers. There the funds will be employed and at least will earn for the small bank, "credit" in terms of expanded correspondent banking services.

True liquidity reserves of both short-term and longer-term nature consist of interest-earning liquid assets which under all foreseeable circumstances can be converted into cash with little or no loss when the needs for which they were provided arise.

INSTRUMENTS OF LIQUIDITY

Before attempting to explore the ways in which banks can estimate and provide for their liquidity needs, it will be useful to examine briefly some of the instruments of liquidity which are available. These consist in the first place of assets in which excess funds can be temporarily invested with the assurance that either the liquidity instruments will mature and be paid when the funds are needed, or which can be readily sold, without material loss, in advance of maturity. In the second place, liquidity instruments include the ways in which banks can borrow funds or obtain them in other ways, such as though the sale or participation of assets.

Most of the instruments of bank liquidity are available through the money market which has been defined as ". . . the active market for money and close money substitutes which financial institutions and others rely on to provide the liquidity needed in the usual course of their operations." [14] Money itself, in the form of excess currency and demand deposits due from banks in excess of minimum working balance needs, is a primary form of short-term liquidity. But money is not an earning asset and is therefore not, in any real sense, a money-market instrument.

Federal funds

Money, in the form of excess balances, may be converted into an earning asset by lending it, usually for one day at a time, as "Federal funds." Federal

---

[14] Robert V. Roosa, *Federal Reserve Operations in the Money and Government Securities Markets,* Federal Reserve Bank of New York, July, 1956.

funds transactions represent a loan of reserve balances by one bank to another.[15] Such loans are often unsecured and, within the same city, may be arranged by an exchange of checks; the borrowing bank's check payable through the clearings on the next business day in exchange for the lending bank's check on its reserve account available on the day of the loan. Between cities (and even within some cities) Federal funds transactions are arranged by telephone and effectuated by transfers of reserve balances through the Federal Reserve wire transfer system under an agreement to reverse the transaction on the following day.

When the transaction is entered into for more than one day, or when the amount exceeds the lending bank's unsecured loan limit, a Federal funds transaction may be secured through the device of a repurchase agreement or "buy-back." [16] Under such an arrangement the bank acquiring funds sells securities (usually short-term government securities) to the bank supplying funds under an agreement to repurchase them at a specified time and at a price representing cost plus an agreed upon rate of interest.

Federal funds transactions between banks represent a liquidity instrument technically classified as a loan by the selling bank (even when it purchases securities under a resale agreement).* At the same time it is a form of borrowing for the bank acquiring funds. Because of their very short duration, Federal funds transactions are characteristically used for the shortest-term liquidity needs and especially for the temporary adjustment of a bank's money position or reserve requirements.

Most purchasers of Federal funds like to acquire them in amounts of $1 million or more and will seldom bother with amounts under $500 thousand.[17] This effectively precludes the use of the Federal funds market to the vast majority of banks with aggregate deposits under approximately $20 million,[18] except as occasional sellers of excess reserves derived from unusually large short-term deposits.

[15] Any transfer of bank balances which is effected by entries on the books of a Federal Reserve Bank in the reserve accounts of a member bank and is available on the same day is a Federal funds transaction. Thus a corporation large and important enough to command this service may instruct its bank to pay Federal funds to a government securities dealer against delivery of government securities to be held in custody. By this device the corporation is, in effect, selling Federal funds to the dealer on a secured basis.

[16] "The Repurchase Agreement in the Government Securities Market," *Treasury-Federal Reserve Study of the Government Securities Market,* Part III (Preliminary) 1959, p. C-20.

[17] Smaller amounts are occasionally purchased by the larger banks as an accommodation for valued correspondents, but such transactions are hardly worth while unless entered into for several days.

[18] If $20 million of deposits were evenly divided between time and demand, the reserve requirement for a member bank would be only $850,000, part of which would be held as vault cash. There would be few occasions when such a bank could sell as much as $500,000 without seriously depleting its reserve account.

* *Editor's note:* In 1963 the Comptroller of the Currency ruled that Federal funds transactions were to be regarded as purchases and sales, but the Board of Governors of the Federal Reserve System continued to regard them as loans.

Short-term government securities

Short-term government securities, which have a range of maturities suitable for any liquidity needs, are the most widely used money-market instrument. For short-term and seasonal liquidity, Treasury bills have many advantages. Their availability in weekly auctions and their active secondary market at narrow spreads make them, in some ways, the ideal liquidity instrument. Treasury bills are now issued in 91-day, 182-day and one-year original maturities and, along with other short-dated Treasury obligations, can generally be acquired in the market with maturities that can be specifically tailored to a bank's expected need for funds.

Other securities

Longer-term government securities with maturities from two to five years are ideal liquidity instruments for longer-term liquidity requirements such as projected future increases in net loan demand or longer-range protective liquidity. Government agency securities, high-grade short-term municipal securities and railroad equipment trust notes are also sometimes used for these purposes because of their higher yields or, in the case of municipals, their tax-exemption.

Commercial paper and bankers acceptances

Commercial paper and bankers acceptances [19] are liquidity instruments which are frequently available at yields somewhat above government securities of comparable maturity. Both are obligations of private borrowers which are sold through dealers in the money market. Bankers acceptances are obligations of recognized banks as well. Both instruments in recent years have enjoyed virtually unblemished records for safety of principal. Although they lack some of the flexibility of Treasury issues and do not enjoy as extensive a secondary market, these instruments serve many liquidity purposes admirably and are deserving of careful consideration for at least a part of a bank's liquidity portfolio.

Broker's loan participations

In recent years, primarily to relieve their own credit stringency, the large New York City banks have made available to their correspondents participations in their own loans to brokers. These participations are sold "without recourse" and are not legal obligations of the selling bank. It is understood, however, that the selling bank will ordinarily repurchase the participation, virtually on demand, since it would adversely affect the New York bank's relationship with its broker-customer to have the participating bank call the loan.

---

[19] *Cf.* Goldman Sachs & Co., "Commercial Paper—An Attractive Short-Term Investment," *Brochure* (undated). Also Federal Reserve Bank of Cleveland, *Monthly Business Review,* "Use of Commercial Paper to the Fore," October, 1960, and "Rebound in Use of Bankers Acceptances," January, 1961.

When available, these participations are very attractive liquidity instruments as the rate is usually at or close to the prime rate, less a ¼ per cent or ½ per cent retained by the selling bank for servicing the loan. At times of relative credit ease, however, such participations are parcelled out sparingly by the New York City banks to those correspondents which maintain substantial balances.

Brokers' loans made directly by banks to the brokers for their own account and for the account of others were once an important and highly liquid money-market instrument.[20] Today, for New York City banks, brokers' loans are no more liquid than any other well-secured loan which a bank makes to a valued customer and hesitates to call for fear of disturbing a customer relationship. An exception, of course, are the day-loans to dealers in government securities and acceptances made by the money-market banks at a posted rate. These loans are renewable daily and are a highly specialized form of liquid asset used, like Federal funds, to adjust the money position of the banks in the money centers.

Other liquid assets

Any credit-worthy loan or investment may be included in a bank's port-folio of liquid assets if its maturity conforms with liquidity needs and if the bank will have no compunction about collecting it at maturity. Among such assets will occasionally be found well-secured notes of nondepositors acquired through so-called money brokers. Such loans are usually secured by cash value of life insurance or marketable securities.

Short-term or bond-anticipation notes of municipalities may also be included in the category of liquid assets, as may other customers' notes of a short-term, self-liquidating nature. Banks which grant lines to national finance companies can sometimes arrange for those lines to be used during periods of seasonal excess of funds and paid off when the local credit needs are at a peak. In such event, these loans, too, may be considered part of the bank's liquidity position.

BORROWING ARRANGEMENTS

A bank's ability to borrow or to dispose of assets either temporarily or permanently is a part of its liquidity arrangements. In this sense a bank's own note discounted with its Reserve bank or correspondent is a prime instrument of liquidity. For the longer term, commitments held from other banks to purchase blocks of mortgages or consumer loans constitute a means of providing additional funds to meet the credit demands of a community.

Direct borrowing

Short-term borrowing from a Federal Reserve bank or correspondent, to-gether with the purchase of Federal funds or the sale of securities under a re-purchase agreement, are methods of acquiring funds for relatively short periods

[20] Brokers' loans for the account of others were made illegal by amendment of the Federal Reserve Act in 1933 (48 Stat. 181). This provision is contained in Section 19, Paragraph 8.

of time to restore to required levels reserve balances temporarily depleted by deposit withdrawals. It is not considered sound commercial bank policy to borrow for long periods, or even very frequently, for the purpose of carrying loans or investments or to meet known and predictable recurring seasonal demands for funds. Federal Reserve policy, in this regard, is set forth in the Foreword of Regulation A of the Board of Governors which states:

> Federal Reserve credit is generally extended on a short-term basis to a member bank to enable it to adjust its asset position when necessary because of developments such as a sudden withdrawal of deposits or seasonal requirements for credit beyond those which can reasonably be met by the use of the bank's own resources.[21]

The discount officers of a Federal Reserve bank will question a bank's need for borrowing if it remains in debt for more than about 60 days or if it borrows repeatedly in six or seven reserve computation periods. Correspondent banks may be more lenient but bank examiners will question the need for substantial or prolonged borrowing for purposes other than short-term reserve adjustment. It is not considered appropriate for banks to borrow merely to take advantage of a spread in rates such as usually exists between the discount rate and the rate on brokers' loan participations acquired from a correspondent bank.

These comments, of course, do not pertain to situations in which a bank finds itself with the need to help carry its community through a period of unexpectedly adverse economic circumstances such as crop failures, sharp drops in economic activity caused by natural disasters, strikes in major industries, or other comparable and unpredictable circumstances. Under such conditions the Federal Reserve System is designed to function as the "lender of last resort" and to supply liquidity to the banks serving a community in need.

Sale of assets

For banks operating in areas where the demand for credit chronically exceeds the supply of funds, the sale or participation of assets to other banks offers a convenient method of meeting local loan demands. The practice of originating and selling mortgage loans, for example, has become a business in itself for some banks. The servicing of such loans is usually retained, preserving local customer relationships and providing a source of additional income as well. Banks specializing in mortgage origination often finance home construction while holding commitments from savings banks or others to acquire the permanent mortgages. Additional interim financing or liquidity may be obtained by entering into a "warehousing"[22] arrangement with another commercial bank which

[21] Board of Governors of the Federal Reserve System, "Advances and Discounts by Federal Reserve Banks," *Regulation A,* Revised February 15, 1955.

Cf. Federal Reserve Bank of Philadelphia, "Borrowing From the Federal Reserve Bank —Some Basic Principles," *Business Review,* June, 1958, pp. 3–9.

[22] A financial arrangement whereby one bank holds mortgages originated by another pending their delivery to the permanent holder (usually a savings bank) which is committed to acquire them.

will finance the mortgages pending their acquisition by the ultimate investor. Such warehousing agreements represent a source of additional funds to the originating bank and a liquidity instrument, or short-term investment, to the warehousing institution.

The sale of blocks of consumer paper, particularly home-improvement loans, has also been widely practiced. Such sales are sometimes made "without recourse"; more often a portion of the proceeds is held as a margin or guarantee fund so that the major portion of the risk remains with the originating bank. Agreements to repurchase delinquent items constitute an effective guarantee so that, in essence, what purports to be a sale of assets may be, in effect, a borrowing arrangement.

The participation of loans to correspondent banks is a method of making loans in excess of the originating bank's legal lending limit and also a method of bringing additional funds into the community.

Frequently small and moderate-sized banks have failed to take advantage of these devices for obtaining additional funds for their communities. They have simply closed their loan or mortgage windows rather than take the trouble to make arrangements for placing a portion of the local loans elsewhere. To maintain such sources of additional funds may, at times, require selling assets which a bank might otherwise hold, but long-range considerations and predictable excess loan demand in the future may well dictate keeping open such channels even at the cost of temporary excess liquidity.

Selection 12

SOURCES OF BUSINESS LOAN REPAYMENT

EDWARD F. GEE

When a bank makes loans, the banker's first question should be, how can these loans be repaid? Sometimes it is erroneously believed that the availability of collateral should be the first consideration; but collateral is only a secondary source of repayment, and bankers prefer to make unsecured loans if this is possible—less cost is involved, and thus more net profit can be obtained. A high proportion of business loans are unsecured loans. But a banker must always consider how a loan can be repaid. The following selection presents a slightly different analysis from that commonly presented; the more common classification is that of self-liquidating, shiftable, and anticipated income loans. Yet both classifications hinge on the means of repayment: self-liquidating loans are those that can be repaid from gross income obtained from sale of the assets purchased with the loan proceeds; shiftable loans are those that can be repaid by borrowing from some other source; and anticipated income loans are those that can be repaid from net income plus depreciation charges in future periods. In most loans, the banker is concerned with appraising the prospects that the borrower can obtain income with which to repay the loan. Bank lending (in contrast to investing, which is based on the desire for liquidity or for income from other-wise idle funds) is thus predicated largely on forecasting of income and cash flow. Can the business borrower sell the inventory that he wishes to acquire? Can the consumer earn enough to repay the consumer loan? These are the key questions in bank lending, and they are significant because bank lending is one means through which a possible increase in business activity and income is translated into actuality.

There are only three sources or means by which a loan to a business enterprise can be repaid: (1) turning an asset into cash; (2) acquiring additional capital; (3) borrowing elsewhere. Let us take a fresh look at the meaning and significance of each source.

SOURCES OF BUSINESS LOAN REPAYMENT

Conversion of assets to cash

A loan can be repaid from the conversion of inventory or receivables or other assets to cash. The conversion may take place through the sale of inventory for cash, or through the collection of accounts or notes receivable. The funds thus released become available for the retirement of debt.

A typical conversion cycle might involve the following steps. A bank loan is obtained by a manufacturer for the purpose of purchasing raw materials. Labor is employed and other costs are incurred to convert the raw materials to finished goods. The finished goods are converted into accounts receivable (normally including a profit element) as sales are made. The receivables are collected in due course, and the cycle is completed as the cash thus obtained is used for the retirement of the bank loan.

Two observations may be made. First, it is not at all essential to the repayment of the bank loan that the cycle be completed at a profit to the manufacturer. As long as the manufacturer recovers his costs (raw materials, labor, and manufacturing and operating overhead) the funds returned to him through the collection of receivables will be sufficient to retire the bank debt. The lending banker would wish the manufacturer to enjoy a profit, but this is not essential for loan repayment.

Second, the cycle must involve a relatively *temporary* accretion to inventory, then to receivables (when sales are made on credit), then to cash, if the bank loan is to be paid upon completion of the cycle. If anywhere along the line the funds are diverted to purchase other inventory, to carry other receivables, or to any other purpose, then the conversion cycle is destroyed or retarded and payment of the bank loan must be deferred or made dependent upon some other source.

In addition to the normal conversion of inventories and receivables to cash, other assets may, of course, be converted to cash to enable the retirement of bank debt. Temporary investments in stocks or bonds may be sold or col-

• From B. H. Beckhart, ed., *Business Loans of American Commercial Banks,* Chap. 6, by Edward F. Gee, pp. 115–119. Copyright 1959 by The Ronald Press Company, New York. Reprinted by permission of The Ronald Press Company, the editor, and the author.

lected; land, buildings, machinery, or equipment not essential to the continued conduct of the business may be disposed of for cash; other assets, rights, or claims may be converted into cash. These, however, are not ordinary, continuing sources of loan repayment for a going concern. The normal seasonal or cyclical contraction of inventories or receivables or both is the major source of loan payment funds through the conversion of assets to cash.

Addition to equity capital

The equity capital or net worth of a business is the aggregate of the funds of the owner or owners that are employed in the conduct of the business. This equity capital may be increased in only two ways: (1) through profits that are earned and retained in the business; (2) through additional investments of capital by the existing owner or owners or by an additional owner or owners. A bank loan can be repaid from the additional capital derived from either source.

Inventories and receivables may show no seasonal or cyclical contraction over a period, but if a business produces and retains a net operating profit for the period, that profit will be available for the reduction or payment of a bank loan. In the determination of profit, charges for depreciation, amortization, or depletion may be made against gross income. Such charges involve no expenditures of funds; they are merely an accounting device for allocating the initial cost of fixed and other noncurrent assets over the operating periods of their actual or tax-approved usefulness. In effect, they result in periodical partial conversions of fixed and other noncurrent assets to cash. Hence, the aggregate of such charges, plus the remaining net profit reported for a period, should be available for the repayment of bank debt if the funds thus generated are not otherwise applied.

In a proprietorship or a partnership, the proprietor or the partners may make additional investments of capital from outside resources or one or more new partners may bring added capital into the firm. In a corporation, additional capital stock may be sold privately to existing or new stockholders or publicly in the market. In either instance, the new funds coming into the business become available for the payment of bank debt.

Borrowing directly or indirectly from some other source

This third and final source of a bank loan repayment involves simply the replacement of one debt with another. One bank may be paid completely if, simultaneously, a loan of an equal or a larger amount can be obtained from another bank. A current bank loan may also be retired from the funds derived from the issuance and sale of long-term debentures or first mortgage bonds. Trade accounts payable may be permitted to accumulate at a time when all available funds are applied to the reduction or payment of bank debt. The principals in a business may advance funds to the enterprise to enable the payment of a bank loan. Funds generated for the payment of income taxes and other accrued liabilities may be applied temporarily to the payment of bank debt, pending the time these accruals must be disbursed. In all such instances, the aggregate of all the debts of the business remains unchanged or is increased. One form of debt is merely substituted for another.

REPAYMENT SOURCES AND RISK APPRAISAL

Importance of determining repayment source

From the foregoing review it should be apparent that a consideration of the likely source of repayment is essential to a consideration of the degree of risk involved in a given loan extension. A loan for the purpose of acquiring inventory to be paid from the normal conversion of inventory to receivables to cash in the ordinary course of business, whether or not at a profit, obviously involves less risk to the lender than a loan that can be repaid only from the profits that may or may not be realized from period to period through continuous repetitions of the conversion process. A loan for the purpose of purchasing labor-saving machinery as a means of further improving a profitable operating history, to be paid from conservative projections of future earnings, obviously carries less risk than a loan that can be repaid only if some other creditor is willing and able to step in and take over the risk. For these reasons, a bank must invariably determine the purpose of a loan, in order that it may ascertain the likely source of repayment, before it can evaluate the degree of risk involved in the extension of the loan.

Seasonal loan

In a so-called seasonal loan, the risk evaluation process assumes its simplest order. Here funds from the proceeds of the loan go into working or trading assets, inventories, and receivables, at one point in the borrower's fiscal year, and come out at another point when the period of peak need is past. In appraising the risk, the problem of the lending bank is largely that of determining whether the quality of the inventories and receivables is such that they are capable of being contracted, and whether the likelihood is that they will be contracted, sufficiently in the aggregate, through the normal pattern of fluctuating seasonal needs, to enable the retirement of the loan at its anticipated payment date.

If a comparison, over past periods, of the monthly balance sheets of the business shows a steady or increasing aggregate of trading assets as a result of sales growth or for other reasons, or if there has not been and is not likely to be a significant seasonal variation in the aggregate of receivables and inventories, then the bank must obviously look to other sources for the payment of its loan.

Term loan

A term loan is a loan that is payable, usually from future earnings, over a period running into two or more years. The proceeds may be used for increasing the working or trading assets, for fixed asset expenditures or other non-current purposes, or partly for one and partly for the other, but repayment is always definitely deferred over a specified future period in excess of one year. The loan risk is heightened, as contrasted with that involved in a temporary seasonal loan, through the extended exposure of the loan funds to the operating hazards of the business and through the dependence for normal repayment on all the uncertainties of future earnings.

In considering a term loan, or any loan dependent for repayment on future earnings, the problem of the lending bank is largely that of determining, from the past operating record of the borrowing business and from its future prospects, whether its future earnings are likely to be sufficiently large and sufficiently well-maintained to enable the orderly retirement of the loan in accordance with its scheduled payment terms. Obviously, the risk appraisal process here is a far more difficult one than that ordinarily involved in considering a short-term seasonal loan to be repaid through the seasonal ebb and flow of inventories and receivables.

"Take-out loan"

By what may be called, for want of a better term, a "take-out loan," is meant a loan that has, at its inception, no likely source of repayment other than through funds supplied by some other creditor. A case in point would be a loan to a finance company or a small loan company which might continuously employ, year in and year out, substantial amounts of bank credit, perhaps in a steady or increasing aggregate, under revolving lines of credit. Such loans under a line of credit extended by any one bank are normally repaid only by a simultaneous borrowing under a line of credit extended by some other bank.

Another typical example of a take-out loan is that of a public utility which may borrow from a bank on a current basis for capital improvements, increasing its loans as improvements are made until its financing needs have increased to a point that warrants the flotation of a new capital stock issue or warrants long-term mortgage or debenture financing in the capital markets. From such capital financing the current bank loans are repaid, and the cycle may subsequently start anew. Or a project builder may obtain construction loans from a bank on the strength of a commitment from an insurance company to place a long-term mortgage loan on the project when the construction work is completed. Upon completion, the mortgage loan is arranged and the current bank loans retired.

In these and all other instances of take-out loans, the problem of the lending bank, in appraising the risk involved, is to project the acceptability and eligibility of the borrower, and the willingness and ability of the lender, for the proposed take-out financing over the term of the proposed bank loan. It must assure itself that the borrower will remain acceptable and eligible for financing elsewhere, and that any proposed take-out lender will remain willing and able to take over such financing at the close of some future period. In some such instances, particularly where a firm take-out commitment exists, the process of risk appraisal may be comparatively simple; in others, it may present the most difficult credit decision with which a bank can be faced.

Selection 13

TYPES OF LOANS

HOWARD D. CROSSE

Banks make many types of loans, but a large proportion of all bank loans consists of business loans, mortgage loans, and consumer loans. Application of basic credit principles varies, because of special problems arising in particular fields of lending. For some time it was believed that only loans repayable from gross income—self-liquidating loans—should be made by commercial banks; this was the so-called commercial loan or "real bills" theory of bank lending. Banks were presumed to finance commerce. In early days of United States history, there was some degree of accuracy in such a presumption; the first incorporated banks made loans chiefly for the purpose of financing such commerce as purchase of goods arriving on vessels and the resale of such goods to retail stores and consumers. Banks now chiefly make loans that are expected to be repaid from net income plus depreciation charges, as is evident from the following selection. However, banks are still significant in financing seasonal peaks in business activity. When seasonal loans are made, it can be expected that gross income from sales of the products purchased or manufactured will provide for loan repayment; as activity declines from a seasonal peak, goods produced and inventory acquired can be sold, providing funds for repayment of loans.

The following selection indicates the continuing importance of this function of banking, but it also indicates the different problems encountered in other types of bank lending. The selection concludes with comments on the desirability of some effort by banks for loan development; only if this is done can banks play the part that they should play in encouraging business enterprise. Kenneth Boulding concluded in a recent book that United States banks have had a worse failure record than banks in other countries, but that they have been more active in promoting enterprise, and that "the greater dynamism of the American economy may be in part a result of the high degree of local autonomy in the banking system"; and Paul B. Trescott suggests that it was "no accident that the century of free banking coincides with the most rapid and revolutionary period of the nation's economic development" (Financing American Enterprise (New York: Harper & Row, Publishers, 1963), p. 265).

COMMERCIAL LOANS

Traditionally and practically, the foremost obligation of a commercial bank is to supply the credit needs of business enterprises, including farm operations, in its community. Loans which accomplish this general purpose, whatever

---

form they take, are essentially commercial loans. In terms of purpose and payment, they range from short-term self-liquidating loans to finance the manufacture, storage, or shipment of commodities, through loans to supply working
capital over varying periods of time, to loans to finance the acquisition of capital
assets.[1] Whatever the nature or term of the loan, repayment should be closely
related to purpose and, in the light of both, appropriate provisions for protection
established.

One relatively small bank, in its formal Statement of Policy, makes an
interesting and valid distinction between business loans which are repayable from
gross income and those which are repayable from net profits.[2] The first category
consists of short-term advances for the purpose of furnishing working capital in
excess of normal needs. Such loans can generally be made on an unsecured basis.
These are the traditional commercial loans conceived of as eligible paper under
the Federal Reserve Act. Loans to be repaid out of net profits, on the other
hands, represent extensions of credit for the purpose of financing more or less
continuous needs for working capital as well as term loans for longer-term
capital or equipment financing. Loans of this character usually require some protective arrangement. Such loans make up the bulk of commercial lending today.

Short-term lending

Lending for seasonal or short-term working capital purposes presents
few serious policy questions beyond the need for careful credit analysis. Principal
emphasis is placed on the borrower's liquidity or excess of current assets over
current liabilities. Ordinarily banks actively seek short-term loans, offering
favorable rates and established lines of credit as inducements to prospective
seasonal borrowers.

Lines of credit, however, can present some special policy problems. A line
of credit is not a legal commitment to lend, but a bank would suffer great
embarrassment if it could not supply funds virtually on demand under an established line. If lines are too freely granted, or granted with too little concern
for the borrower's actual needs, they may remain unused until, in a period
of credit stringency, their sudden activation may put considerable pressure on the
bank's own liquidity position. It is sound policy, therefore, to grant credit lines
realistically. Lines of credit are usually approved by the Board of Directors, who
would be well advised to approve them only on the basis of information obtained
from a discussion with the borrower concerning his probable needs.

Longer-term working capital loans

Many business enterprises have need of working capital over periods longer
than a season. Although the amount of credit needed may fluctuate over seasonal
periods, its employment in some amount tends to be prolonged or virtually continuous. Such credit is sound in the sense used here because the loans are related
to a constant flow of transactions each of which, by itself, is of relatively short

---

[1] Space does not permit more than a cursory discussion of commercial lending. For
an exhaustive study of this subject, see *Business Loans of American Commercial Banks*
B. H. Beckhart, editor (New York: The Ronald Press Company, 1959).

[2] The Sullivan County Trust Company, Monticello, New York.

duration but which succeed each other so rapidly that no sooner has one been liquidated than another takes its place. Any business which must carry a relatively large and varied inventory throughout the year, or a business which sells in volume on credit, is likely to be a user of longer-term working capital loans.

In reviewing such loans bank directors should be concerned not only with the current asset position of the borrower but also with his net worth and profitability. Unless the borrower shows a substantial equity in a profitable business the bank will usually require additional protection in the form of pledged receivables or inventory.

Lending to small concerns on any but a short-term seasonal basis often presents special problems. Many of these are closely-held corporations, which as a matter of tax policy, show minimum profits and operate with a nominal net worth. Salaries paid to the principal stockholders are often larger than net profits, and the real net worth is represented either by loans made to the company by its principals, or by the net worth of the principals themselves. In such cases sound policy requires that debt to stockholders be subordinated formally to bank debt and that the bank obtain the endorsement or guarantee of the principals (and their wives) as additional protection. Where quality of management is a vital consideration in the extension of credit, banks may require the assignment of life insurance on the lives of the principals as well.

One specialized form of the longer-term working capital loan is called the revolving credit. Under such an arrangement the bank grants a firm commitment to lend up to a stated amount over a period of a year or more. The outstanding loan ordinarily rises and falls within the commitment and the borrower may, in fact, be out of debt for extended periods. Under a revolving credit the borrower pays a small commitment fee on the unused portion of his line in addition to the agreed-upon rate of interest on the amounts availed of. This fee compensates the bank for holding money available and assures the borrower that he may use the funds when he needs them.

Revolving credit agreements, like term loans (below), often contain restrictive provisions requiring the borrower to maintain certain agreed-upon balance sheet ratios or to limit dividend and salary payments. Many lending arrangements now handled on a 90-day renewable note basis would better conform to the principles of "purpose and payment" if they were written as revolving credits. Not only should banks be entitled to a modest fee for holding money available, but the writing of a revolving credit agreement would necessitate a closer look at the borrower's financial condition and thus result in sounder lending generally.

Term loans

Term loans are usually defined for statistical purposes as loans with an original maturity of more than one year. Functionally, a term loan is one which, regardless of its specific maturity, will be repaid out of the net cash income of the business over a considerable period of time. The proceeds of term loans are typically used to acquire capital assets such as plant and equipment, subsidiary companies, or income-yielding properties such as oil and gas leases.

In considering the granting of loans for purposes such as these, bank officers and directors are concerned not only with the net worth and profitability of the borrower but, primarily, with his "cash flow" projections. Cash flow is a measure of the borrower's ability to repay debt. Depreciation charges, which are deducted from gross income to determine net profits, do not affect cash flow and, in fact, are often the main source of funds for repaying loans made to purchase depreciable assets. On the other hand, scheduled loan repayments, which do not affect net profits, do reduce cash flow.

Term lending has assumed increasing importance in recent years. More than half of the commercial loans of New York City banks, for example, are designated as term loans.[3] Such loans probably account for at least a third of the business loans of the country's larger banks and small banks also commonly make term loans although they may not be specifically designated as such. Loans to business secured by chattel mortgage on equipment (a common form of small bank lending both to business and to farmers) are a form of "term" lending even though they are made on a 90-day renewable note basis. Many commercial mortgage loans are term loans in actuality.

Despite the fact that some doubts have been raised about the appropriateness of commercial bank term lending, the term loan represents a clear case of banks meeting the credit needs of their customers by relating purpose to payment. As for protection, in addition to the collateral usually obtained, and to the provisions for regular amortization, term loans typically contain covenants establishing, among other things, minimum working capital levels and minimum net worth-to-debt ratios, as well as limiting dividends or withdrawals from the business during the term of the loan. Such agreements provide a continuing control over the obligor which is not always possible with respect to the market securities of corporations which term loans have replaced in bank portfolios.

Large enterprises traditionally have financed their capital needs primarily in the capital markets or by direct placement with institutional investors. Many needs for capital financing are still so accommodated. Frequently, however, the amount of a particular acquisition will not be large enough to justify a market flotation, or the cash flow will be sufficiently large to enable the borrower to repay all or part of the obligation in a shorter period of time than would be acceptable to an institutional investor.[4] Rate differentials or anticipated rate changes also play a role in the decision of a large borrower to use his bank or to go to the market.

MORTGAGE LOANS

The true purpose of a mortgage loan is to finance the acquisition or substantial improvement of real property. Liens on real estate are often pledged to secure obligations incurred for other purposes but, in such cases, the real purposes, rather than the form of collateral, should determine the terms of repayment and dictate any other protective features that may be called for.

[3] Federal Reserve Bank of New York, "Term Lending by New York City Banks," *Monthly Review*, Vol. 43, No. 2 (February, 1961), pp. 27–31. The statistics reported here include some revolving credits written for more than one year.

[4] Arrangements are often made for a bank to take the early maturities of a term loan and for an insurance company to take the longer-term obligations.

Mortgage loans in commercial banks are first liens on residential or business properties.[5] Residential mortgages are generally considered more desirable because dwellings, unless of unusual size or design, have a broader market than business properties which are often limited to specialized uses. Commercial mortgages, as noted above, are often term loans in disguise, in which case they should be treated as such.

Residential mortgage lending

The basic policies required in residential mortgage lending are (1) to limit the amount of the loan to a reasonable percentage of the true value of the property, and (2) to require repayment at a rate which will maintain or improve the mortgagor's original equity during the life of the loan. Value is established by an appraisal made by a committee of the directors or by a professional appraiser under their direction. The basis for such valuations is a keystone of mortgage policy. Conservatism will call for some discounting of peak prices which may reflect an inflated demand. Values, however, will vary in each community since growth prospects strongly affect them. Past trends as well as future prospects need to be taken into consideration and a concept of "fair value" developed to fit each bank's particular circumstances. Competition in appraisals, sometimes indulged in, is obviously a dangerous practice.

Regardless of real estate values, however, the principal consideration of residential mortgage lending should be the borrower's ability to repay the loan in conformity with the scheduled payments. No mortgage loan should be made without a knowledge of the mortgagor's income and other financial obligations. Obvious as this may appear it is information which is lacking in too many mortgage files. If it appears, as it may, on the mortgage application, there is no follow-up to show that ability to repay is being maintained. The good experience of the past twenty years during which real estate prices have increased steadily is no excuse for carelessness in mortgage lending.

The maximum term for residential mortgage lending is generally established by law. For national banks the maximum term is twenty years.* Mortgages insured under the National Housing Act of 1934 (FHA) or guaranteed under the Servicemen's Readjustment Act of 1944 (GI) are exempt from these provisions. Recently proposals have been made in Congress to extend mortgage terms under the National Housing Act to forty years. In theory the life of a mortgage should not exceed the useful life of the property, but condition, not age, is the crucial factor, and the quality of the neighborhood may have more to do with sale values than the durability of the structure.

Even though some houses may be maintained in excellent condition and retain their value long beyond twenty years, both the bank and the borrower should be interested in having the debt reduced. Sound lending policy requires that bank credit flow through the economy and not become stagnant; loan repayments are a principal source of new loans to promote further building and

---

[5] National banks may not lend on unimproved property nor may they directly acquire second mortgages (Section 24, Federal Reserve Act).

* *Editor's note:* Under the Housing Act of 1964, the maximum term was extended to 25 years.

growth. From the mortgagor's viewpoint, the burden of additional interest cost on long-term mortgages is considerable. For most homeowners there is no better or more profitable method of regular saving than to increase the monthly payments on their mortgages. Five or 6 percent saved is just as much income as 5 or 6 per cent earned.

As stated above, the condition of a property is as important as its age. Another vital element in the protective arrangements which should safeguard mortgage lending, therefore, is a policy of requiring adequate maintenance. All mortgaged properties should be periodically reappraised,[6] and if deficiencies in maintenance are revealed, the bank should make every effort, including the offer of financing, to encourage the mortgagor to make necessary repairs. If a bank has been reasonably selective as to the character of its mortgagors, the borrower will recognize that adequate maintenance benefits him as much as the bank.

Construction mortgage financing

The origination of mortgage loans through the financing of building construction is a specialized field deserving of comment. All banks occasionally finance the construction of a home or business building for a valued customer with the expectation that they will acquire and hold the mortgage on the completed premises. Such loans require special attention because of the ever-present possibility that construction costs may exceed the original estimates and the bank may find itself more deeply committed than it planned.

The bulk of construction financing, however, is done by banks which sell the permanent mortgages to other institutions. The origination and sale of mortgages is a banking business which has its own risks and specialized techniques for minimizing them. However, either directly or in participation with correspondent banks, it can be a very profitable form of essentially short-term lending.[7] If the originating bank retains the servicing of the mortgages, this type of financing is not only a source of additional revenue but provides valuable customer contacts. The origination and sale of mortgage loans is also one way in which banks in rapidly growing areas can serve their communities beyond the limits of their own resources.

Commercial mortgage lending

In true commercial mortgage lending the primary consideration of policy is the relationship of the income derived from the property to the cost of maintaining it, paying taxes, and servicing the loan. In some cases the income may be derived from an operating business although such loans are likely to be true business loans. More often, the income from the property is the product of a lease or leases to tenants with whom the bank does not deal directly (except as they may be customers for other banking services).

A complete description and appraisal of the property should, of course, be

---

[6] Most authorities suggest reappraisal every three years.

[7] Cf. James F. Schneider, *Construction Loans for Your Short-Term Portfolio*, thesis for Graduate School of Banking, Rutgers University (A.B.A. Library).

on file, but the cost or replacement value of a commercial property is distinctly secondary to its yield as an investment; it is the latter that effectively establishes its resale value. As a matter of policy, therefore, it is important that the bank not only know the amount of the income from the property but assure itself of its continuance and availability for servicing the mortgage during its life. Sound policy dictates that banks not only obtain assignment of the leases but know the credit standing of the lessees as well.

CONSUMER LENDING

As far as commercial banking is concerned, consumer lending has come of age in the past 20 years.[8] Long looked upon with suspicion by bankers, many of whom felt that it was somehow immoral for a person to buy something before he had earned and saved the money, consumer credit has become a way of life for millions of Americans. Buy now and pay later—with bank credit bridging the gap.

Much has been written about the economic implications of the vast growth of consumer credit.[9] The pros and cons of its effect on the business cycle have been hotly debated. Twice in recent years it has been subjected to federal regulation and some still advocate at least stand-by authority to regulate it again. This book is not immediately concerned with these issues. It suffices to note that banks have found lending to consumers to be both safe and profitable if sound policies are followed, and it is with such policies that this discussion is primarily concerned. Consumer loans are an important element of the community's total demand for credit, and the bank which does not reasonably meet this need is, to that extent, failing in its obligations.

In broad usage consumer credit includes both installment credit and non-installment credit. The latter consists of charge accounts granted by merchants, service credit (such as unpaid doctors' bills), and the occasional single payment loans granted by banks to individuals for consumption purposes. Although in recent years a few banks have entered the charge-account field by purchasing accounts from merchants, installment lending is still by far the more important part of consumer lending in point of volume.

Installment credit, in turn, can be subdivided into that group of loans made to meet previously incurred or extraordinary expenses (the typical personal loan) and loans to finance specifically the purchase of goods or services; the "buy now, pay later" concept. In terms of volume the later is of much greater significance.

Personal installment loans to individuals are almost all made on the basis of direct negotiation between the bank and the borrower. Installment sales credit may be handled either on a direct or indirect basis. In the latter case installment sales contracts are purchased by the bank from the seller of the goods or

---

[8] Commercial banks held, on the average, about $17 billion of installment credit during 1961 (*Federal Reserve Bulletin*).

[9] *Cf.* Board of Governors, *Consumer Installment Credit* (four parts in seven volumes), 1957.

services. Indirect lending is almost necessarily engaged in by banks which are seeking a large volume of consumer loans. Many banks do both a direct and indirect business, although some bankers find an inherent conflict of interest between direct automobile financing, for example, and their relationships with the dealers from whom they purchase paper.[10]

Consumer credit principles

Whether a bank lends on a direct or indirect basis, the credit principles of consumer lending are essentially uniform. Unlike commercial lending, the net worth of the borrower is of relatively little importance. The essential ingredients of sound consumer credit are the borrower's ability and willingness to pay. These ingredients are roughly measurable in terms of the borrower's character, his income, and its stability. Character and reputation are usually synonymous and the applicant's previous record for repayment, at the bank or elsewhere, is usually the best credit guide. Volume lending in the consumer credit field is likely to be unduly risky if the bank does not have access to a credit bureau in which all, or most of the local consumer lenders, including merchants, participate and pool their knowledge of the credit records of consumers. Without such a central record duplicate and excess borrowings are an ever-present danger.

Consumer loans are generally made on the basis of a fairly simple application form on which the borrower is asked to state his income, its source, the purpose of the loan, and his other debts. It is essential to verify all such statements because a borrower who misrepresents any of these vital facts is probably a poor risk.

As in any other form of lending the relationship of purpose to payment is of great importance. The purpose should be a reasonable one in the light of the borrower's capacity to repay. While consumer lenders usually take a broader view of capacity than an officer reared in the commercial lending tradition, and while it is not necessary to make a moral judgment as to whether the applicant *ought* to spend the money for a particular purpose, loans to finance extravagances are seldom good risks. In other words, banks err in financing Cadillacs for borrowers who need transportation but can at best afford a second-hand Chevrolet. Loans to refinance outstanding debt, while sometimes appropriate, are also likely to be a sign of overextension.

It can be firmly stated that the longer the terms of the loan the greater the risk. Too often terms are set by competition (especially in indirect lending), but sound policy should stand firm against undue lengthening of terms. If it does not, delinquencies will mount, collection costs will eat up profits, and losses will be substantial.

Direct and indirect lending

Whether to confine a bank's consumer lending to direct loans or to purchase loans from dealers is a key matter of bank policy. About the only virtue of indirect lending is the volume it generates. To obtain and keep the business of important dealers a bank usually has to accept the average run

---

[10] Dealers look to the profit from the differential between the finance charges they assess and the lower rates at which banks discount their paper.

of his credit risks even though it formally reserves the right to be selective. It will also have to finance the dealer's inventory which entails its own risks and expensive procedures. As a result, indirect financing is generally more expensive; it may result in higher collection costs; and the rate of net income is generally lower than on direct lending because of the keen competition for dealer business. However, large volume can be generated and the business is profitable if carefully handled; witness the success of the major finance companies which specialize in this field.

In connection with indirect lending, sound policy requires, in the first place, a careful selection of dealers having both moral and financial responsibility. A second vital principle involves making certain that an obligor actually exists on all paper purchased. This can usually be done by mailing forms directly to the bank. Finally, the financing arrangement with the dealer should place at least a portion of the credit risk on his shoulders. This can be accomplished either by purchasing the paper with full recourse (the usual procedure in the purchase of service or appliance-sales paper) or by the establishment of dealers' reserves. The latter is the usual procedure with respect to automobile financing. The customers' notes are purchased from the dealer on a nonrecourse basis at a discount less than that charged by the dealer to the obligor. All or part of the differential is held by the bank as a reserve against which delinquent loans may be charged. The collection of delinquent loans, including the repossession of the chattel, is thus the dealer's responsibility. To the extent that the reserve at the end of a stated period exceeds an agreed-upon percentage of outstanding loans, it is returned to the dealer thus giving him a financial stake in the collectibility of the paper.

Where dealers require inventory financing on a "floor plan" basis, the bank's protection is no better than the dealer's moral responsibility and the bank's periodic, thorough, and surprise checking of the chattels. Sales "out of trust" are an all too common occurrence. In used car and appliance financing a bank can find itself pitted against some of the shrewdest and least principled business operators on the modern scene and losses can be sudden and substantial if the bank relaxes for a moment.[11]

Another important policy aspect of floor-plan financing is that with respect to curtailment. This refers to the reduction of the loans against unsold merchandise. Competitive pressures have often caused banks to relax what they know are sound policies: requirements for monthly payments on unsold cars or other chattels.

Lending directly to the bank's own customers is, by constrast, a safer and less expensive form of extending consumer credit. Mistakes involve no more than a single borrower here and there, and most of the applicants for loans will be already known to the bank. Direct lending promotes customer relationships and brings in other business. For these reasons many banks, which can obtain a satisfactory volume of consumer loans without purchasing them from dealers,

---

[11] An example of the dangers involved was reported in the *New York Times,* February 27, 1960. Losses of $500,000 were estimated for two savings and loan associations and a commercial bank which had failed to investigate sufficiently home improvement loans which proved to be fraudulent.

have learned that they can afford to offer lower rates to selected borrowers on a direct basis and still earn more net on comparable volume.[12]

Consumer loan delinquencies

The best measure of the soundness of the consumer lending policies of an individual bank is the relative volume of loans on which payments are delinquent. Loans are generally considered "delinquent" when a scheduled monthly payment remains unpaid for thirty days or more, although the operating officers will institute special collection procedures when payments are only a few days past due. Notes ninety days or more past due are seriously delinquent and are usually classified as "loss" by bank examiners.

Delinquencies should be regularly reported to the directors by class of loan and, where indirect financing is involved, by individual dealer account. The American Bankers Association [13] and some state bankers associations and local credit bureaus regularly publish average consumer loan delinquency rates for various localities and different classes of loans. Comparison of the individual bank's figures with these published statistics will give the directors a clear indication of the relative success of their own bank's operations. Any increase in the rate of delinquencies either absolute or in comparison with other banks is a danger signal which may indicate that credit policies or collection techniques need tightening. Individual dealers whose paper shows an abnormally high rate of delinquency should be carefully investigated and perhaps dropped.

On the other hand, if a bank's delinquency rates are consistently below average, its credit policies may be too strict and it could be turning away some acceptable business.

LOAN DEVELOPMENT

A discussion of lending practices would be incomplete without some comment on the spirit with which banks approach lending. To many banks and bankers the negotiation of a loan still appears to represent a situation in which the bank is on the defensive: protecting itself against the onslaughts of potential borrowers behind barricades of minimum ratios and standardized lending procedures. Other banks appear to regard lending as a challenging opportunity and go out seeking loans, some perhaps a little too aggressively. This book's viewpoint concerning bank policy has been that local lending is the primary function of a commercial bank; that a bank should make all the sound local loans it can. If this viewpoint is valid, no well-run bank can take a passive attitude toward lending.

In recent years demands for all kinds of loans have sometimes pressed hard against the funds which many banks have had available for lending. Loan-deposit ratios have been rising steadily and few banks have felt the need to go

[12] Figures furnished to the author by a large suburban bank clearly substantiate its own policy decision to withdraw from dealer financing and concentrate heavily on advertising for direct loans which, it concluded, were considerably more profitable.

[13] American Bankers Association, Instalment Credit Committee, "Delinquency Rates on Bank Instalment Loans" (Monthly Bulletin).

out and look for loans. Yet now, as in the past, the outstandingly successful banks in all parts of the country are those which have found the means to make more loans than their neighbors, and to make some loans which their neighbors do not make at all. Even today there are still many banks with relatively low ratios of loans to deposits. This may be the result, at least in part, of their failure to seek out and service all of the potentially worthy users of credit in their communities.

The essence of loan development lies, first, in a willingness to examine carefully every request for credit and to try conscientiously to make it "bankable," and second, to search actively for opportunities to promote the growth of the community and the individual businesses therein with sound credit. The two go hand in hand and the bank which has an established reputation for constructive lending will not have to do as much searching. Nevertheless, a major objective of visits by bank officers to their customers' places of business, be it farm or factory, should be to find new ways or additional productive purposes for the customer's use of credit.

Those banks which have done an outstanding job of loan development are usually managed by outstanding and imaginative men. It is doubtful if directors can establish loan development as a policy objective without full confidence in the high quality of the bank's operating management. But even in the most conservatively managed bank there is room, if not for broad loan promotion, at least for a limited amount of "promotional lending." The directors could well afford to set aside a modest percentage of the bank's capital and surplus as a revolving fund from which loans they consider to be marginal credits might be made. Such lending, if successful, can contribute materially to the growth and welfare of the community. As the president of a relatively small bank which has aggressively followed such a policy points out:

> Every one of our town's industries grew up here from small-scale beginnings. Not one of them was "attracted" from elsewhere. Our bank financed each one through its early stages, sometimes employing considerable ingenuity to find ways of keeping the loans bankable. For example, today's largest local employer started with one assistant in a basement garage. He financed his entire business expansion, above that permited by plowed-back profits, on credit obtained from this bank.[14]

Opportunities for promotional lending do not present themselves regularly. Each one is different, yet experienced lending officers will recognize promising situations when they arise. They present banks with a challenging opportunity not to deny credit automatically but rather to "use considerable ingenuity," to assess ideas imaginatively, and within reasonable and previously established limits, to take considered risks. Many of an aggressive bank's most valuable and loyal customers will be those who initially were something of a credit gamble, a greater-than-average risk, deliberately taken. Good bank examiners will continue to list such loans in reports of examination, but good bankers will continue to make them.

[14] James A. Maurice, President, The Monticello State Bank, Monticello, Iowa, *Burroughs Clearing House,* January, 1962, pp. 37, 82.

4

Competition for Savings

THE READINGS IN THIS CHAPTER DEAL WITH THE SPECTAC-
ular rise of other types of financial institutions whose operations
are directly competitive with those of the banks. The struggle
for savings deposits has significant longer-run implications for
the structure of American credit markets and the relative importance of different kinds of savings and lending agencies. It
has also raised fundamental questions about the avenues through
which central bank operations affect the availability of credit
and the effectiveness of those operations.

Among the group of institutions that may be termed "de-
posit-type financial institutions"—commercial banks, mutual
savings banks, savings and loan associations, and credit
unions*—there is competition for time deposits; among commercial banks there is competition for demand deposits. Only
commercial banks hold both time and demand deposits. This
fact complicates somewhat the analysis of competition and the
analysis of effects of changes in the money supply. A basic
premise of modern monetary theory, as formulated by some, is
that holders of money cannot, directly, reduce the money supply.
But if time deposits are not counted as money, then they can do

---

* *Editor's note:* Government savings bonds and postal savings deposits may also be
included since they have the same characteristics as deposits and share accounts in the
institutions mentioned above.

so, by shifting demand deposits to time deposits in commercial banks. Thus an increase in the money supply, caused or permitted by the monetary authorities, may be offset by such a shift. However, the effect of the shift may itself be offset by an increase in velocity of money, as is indicated in subsequent selections.

Selection 14

COMPETITION AMONG FINANCIAL INSTITUTIONS FOR DEMAND AND THRIFT DEPOSITS

MARVIN ROZEN

> *In this selection Marvin Rozen describes the nature of the competition for demand deposits and the competition for time deposits. Because of space limitations, only the competition for time deposits between commercial banks and savings and loan associations is discussed. The rapid growth of savings and loan associations is especially important because, although it does not result in any increase in the money supply, it results in an increase in the velocity of money. Banks have the same total of deposits, and can make the same amount of loans and investments, provided the monetary authorities do not take action to restrict this. At the same time, as savings and loan associations grow, they have additional share accounts (deposits), and can make loans and investments. Presumably these tend to permit an increase in business activity, and a rise in the income velocity of money as well as in the transactions velocity of money.*
>
> *In this selection, page references appear after numbers, in many cases, in both text and footnotes; the numbers refer to items listed under "References" at the conclusion of this article.*

COMPETITION FOR DEMAND DEPOSITS

Commercial banks face no interinstitutional competition in satisfying the public's demand for a means of payment; they compete only among themselves.[1]

---

[1] This statement must be qualified in three respects: (a) The public will hold demand deposits to satisfy an asset demand as well as a need for a means of payment. To the extent that demand deposits are held for this reason, commercial banks will encounter competition from other institutions providing liquid and safe assets. (b) To some slight, but unknown, extent, people use their thrift accounts as checking accounts by making banks in New York City, for instance, offer their depositers a limited number of "free" frequent withdrawals in the form of cashier's checks or bank money orders. Savings banks in New York City, for instance, offer their depositors a limited number of "free" bank money orders. (c) The public can also hold currency instead of demand deposits, but this is of greater historical, than current, significance.

• From Marvin Rozen, "Competition Among Financial Institutions for Demand and Thrift Deposits," *Journal of Finance,* May, 1962, pp. 323–331. Copyright 1962 by the American Finance Association, Chicago, Illinois. Reprinted by permission of the *Journal of Finance* and the author. This article is based on a study by Professor Rozen and his late colleague, L. L. Werboff, for the Commission on Money and Credit. Professor Rozen wished to express his indebtedness to his late colleague for many stimulating discussions of the subject matter of this article.

Except for the 200 or so larger banks competing for deposits on a regional or national basis, this competition is highly geographically localized.

Because of the prohibition of explicit interest payments, competition perforce takes a non-price form. Banks compete in their local markets, for instance, by varying the range of services performed (in-plant banking, payroll accounting, automatic savings plans, single billing, credit information, etc.) and the charges thereon (special checking accounts, deposit allowances, account activity costs, etc.),[2] by providing more convenient factilities (new bank buildings, drive-in tellers, free parking, civic and community rooms, etc.) and by attempting to establish product differentiation through advertising. Competition can also take other forms more closely approximating actual price competition. One way is by varying the terms and conditions relating to the maintenance of compensating or commensurate balances by those seeking loans or lines of credit; another is by adjusting actual loan terms to take into consideration the behavior of the prospective borrower's account over some period prior to the loan application.

On the whole, in the kind of local competition marked by service innovation and increased convenience, the innovator is usually quickly followed, and little lasting advantage seems to be derived. The economic feasibility of many of these services, however, is dependent on the attainment of a minimum critical size, because the required equipment is both costly and indivisible and larger size permits specialization. There tends to be a strong correlation between bank size and range of services offered.[3] This means that, as service competition proliferates, the small bank is likely to become more and more disadvantaged. Competition through adjusting compensating balance requirements and varying loan terms in response to past account activity and deposit history is more subtle and therefore difficult to imitate. Furthermore, since actions of this kind tend to be the uniform and nearly simultaneous reaction of all bankers to variations in general monetary ease or stringency, observation of their use as a competitive tactic is likely to be obscured. Thus, although this kind of competiton is exceedingly important, information about its nature and extent is scanty.

The 200 or so larger banks which compete over more geographically distant areas focus their efforts on two major sources of funds: large corporate and interbank balances. As of January 28, 1959, 102,000 accounts of $100,000 or over held 37.2 per cent of all demand deposits of individuals, partnerships, and corporations; and accounts of $25,000 and over, although numbering less than 1 per cent of all accounts, held over 50 per cent of the dollar value

---

[2] With reference to the intensity of this competition, it has been contended that "bank service charges have been exempt from antitrust legislation by a 1918 ruling permitting a local banker's association to call on its members to use a uniform service charge" (see p. 386 of Ref. 1 listed below). The Department of Justice, however, recently (December, 1961) filed a civil antitrust suit, under Section 1 of the Sherman Act, against three New Jersey banks for conspiring to impose uniform charges for financial services.

[3] "In general, the larger the bank, the wider the range of services offered. This applies not only to the basic banking services . . . but to the new ideas that the industry has been pioneering in the last few years" (Ref. 2, p. 17).

of all accounts.[4] As of December 31, 1960, interbank balances were about $17 billion.

Competition in the market for large corporate balances tends to be keener because holders of large balances are economically powerful and financially sophisticated and therefore perfectly willing and able to exploit their advantage of numerous alternatives.[5] Accordingly, competition in services, adjusting compensating and commensurate balances, and setting terms to reflect past account activity play a more important role. But, as shown below, the large corporation usually presses its bargaining advantage through obtaining terms as favorable as possible within the framework of its old banking connections rather than by hopping from bank to bank for, say, a small differential in interest charges. Furthermore, as a matter of policy, firms hold accounts in many banks, and competition is revealed by shifts in relative importance among the several banks rather than by adding new, or breaking off old, connections.[6] Account splitting however, cannot be attributed solely to competitive pressures. It reflects a natural response to the problems associated with increased size and geographical spread of firms,[7] as well as a strategy of using deposit relationships with numerous banks as a bargaining lever to secure preferential treatment.

The stability of banking connections should be emphasized: "One of the most radical decisions a business firm may make is the decision to change its banking connection" (Ref. 4, p. 110). Katona found in his study that more than two-thirds of the firms in his sample have not changed their primary banking connection in the decade following the Second World War. Furthermore, of those that changed, the majority did so by adding more primary banks or reshuffling the relative order of importance of their several banking con-

[4] See Ref. 3, p. 42. The totals exclude deposits of non-profit organizations, trust departments of banks, and foreigners.

[5] "The smaller the business firm the more frequent is the opinion that there is not much competition among banks, and the greater is the concern about absence of sufficient competition" (Ref. 4, p. 30). This is a study based on extensive field interviews with top executives of a representative sample of medium- and large-sized firms.

[6] See Ref. 5, p. 369; see also Ref. 4, Table 21, p. 83, where it is shown that more than 90 per cent of the firms in the sample having a net worth of $9,000,000 or more deal with five or more banks, and roughly two-thirds of the firms having a net worth between $1,000,000 and $9,000,000 deal with three or more banks.

[7] "The growing complexity of corporate structures, resulting from the diversification of output, from mergers, from the tendency to decentralize operations, and from other causes, leads to the multiplication of separate bank accounts. The trend seems to have been toward separating disbursement accounts from collection accounts; special purpose disbursement accounts are usually established mainly for accounting convenience and to facilitate reporting and auditing. . . . Usually the bulk of receipts is concentrated in the principal treasury account which is the focal point of cash management policies of the corporation. This account *may be split among several large banks* located in New York City and perhaps some of the other principal money centers in cases where the head office of the business concern is not in New York City. . . . National corporations (which account for the bulk of corporate sales) usually maintain collection and/or disbursement accounts in most or all localities in which they do business. It is not infrequent for individual corporations to maintain several hundreds of individual accounts; for national retail organizations, the number of accounts may run into the thousands" (Ref. 3, pp. 48–49). (Italics added by Marvin Rozen).

nections rather than by dropping some primary banks and adding others (Ref. 4, p. 112).

The reasons for such stability in banking connections largely reflect the building-up over time of an exceedingly close network of relationships between bank and borrower which make change difficult. Disclosure of intimate financial detail, familiarity with specific problems, financial counseling, the growth of specialized services, personal loyalties, a history of satisfactory dealings, and the potent forces of inertia and tradition—all tend to create indissoluble bonds that can be broken only by radical changes in the condition of either the banker or his borrower. As an executive of one of the firms in Katona's sample put it:

> There is plenty of competition between banks. But you see, there is no incentive to a firm to change banks. There is no advantage to be had. You'll pay the same fees, get the same interest (if any) and you may not be as satisfied with the personal attention you get as you were in your own bank. In your old bank where you have dealt for years you know the men who are specialists in your line. They know you, and know your business. They've probably grown up with you over many years. They understand the problem and your situation. No new man, who hadn't that contact, would be as satisfactory to you.[8]

New accounts would seem to be much fairer game for the play of competitive forces, and the growth of new firms and the spread of existing firms open up the possibility of competing for a new account. One form that obviously suggests itself is the raising of a bank which formerly held only secondary accounts to a principal or primary status.[9] Another example would be a firm switching its principal banker because a major change in its orientation— say an increased emphasis on export markets—would require specialized services that its present connection could not provide. When a new firm is being formed, special efforts are made to win the new account. Developments in banking will mirror changes in the pattern and structure of economic activity, and, at the frontier of change, the most virgorous competition is likely to take place.

Changes in banking connections can thus be caused by factors largely unrelated to aggressive competition and reflect the structural evolution of borrowing firms in size, space, or economic function. To the extent that competition plays a role, it is mainly through dissatisfaction causing firms to look elsewhere— a loan turned down, inadequate services, etc.—rather than a response to the positive inducement of a competitive offer. To a lesser extent, inevitable and

[8] See Ref. 4, p. 116. Note also the following quotation (p. 118): "We would only use a bank with which we have had considerable experience in the past. Many other banks call on us and tell us we have X number of dollars' credit. But it's easier to give the information to the bank who knows our personnel intimately and who knows all our finances inside out and has known them through the years. This way it is the least amount of work to get the loan, and why should we start with any other bank and disclose all our personal figures."

[9] ". . . Apparently expansion in banking begins by establishing weak secondary connections with a firm and then inducing it gradually to shift the emphasis in its banking practices" (Ref. 4, p. 148).

natural differences in outlook, ability, and capability of banks will determine the making or breaking of banking connections.

Competition for interbank deposits is broadly similar to competition for large corporate balances but with some significant differences. On the whole, a closer connection exists between the value of balances maintained and services rendered, and therefore a more precise calculation can be made by both parties of whether arrangements are mutually advantageous. This greater ability to make sharper calculations should lead to greater switching of balances because differences in treatment would be more obvious. Furthermore, correspondents keep balances because they believe the services which they receive—check clearing, financial counseling and intermediation, joint ventures and loan participations, managerial assistance, etc.—are worth it; businesses keep balances, *inter alia,* because they want to improve their borrowing status. Thus, correspondents' balances are kept in return for something; corporate balances in the hope of getting something. This would suggest that correspondent balances that depend on actual performance tend to be more footloose than corporate balances, which are in the nature of a bribe for preferred treatment in the future. Unfortunately, no data are available to substantiate this hypothesis.

Competition for funds can also take the important route of merger and branching policy. Indeed, where allowed by the regulatory authorities, this has probably been a more dramatic source of growth as aggressive banks have written their success in a record of expansion.[10] A very rough indication of the effect of merger and branching on competition for deposits may be obtained from a recent study (Ref. 6, Tables 28 and 29, pp. 54–57) which shows changes in the share of total deposits (including, unfortunately, time deposits) within a banking area of the largest and the five largest commercial banks.

Thus between 1940 and 1958, the percentage of all deposits held by the five largest banks within a state increased in 13 states and declined in 1 for those 14 states with state-wide branch-banking prevalent; increased in 5 and declined in 11 for those 16 states with limited area branch-banking prevalent; and increased in 2 and declined in 16 for those 18 states with unit banking prevalent. Similarly, between 1934 and 1958, in the 31 metropolitan areas in states with limited area branch-banking prevalent, the share of total deposits held by the five largest banks rose in 22 areas and fell in 9 areas; in the 17 metropolitan areas in states with unit banking prevalent, the share of the five largest declined in all but one area. These data provide some fragile support for the broad inference that deposit growth is greatly helped by geographical mobility.

There is also reason to believe that those banks in the forefront of a merger and branching movement are the very ones pioneering in the new services and innovations to attract deposits and increase loans. Likewise, they are most likely to be the first to adopt new mechanization and electronic data-processing devices. It certainly is not strange to find all these characteristics exhibited by a single bank because they are, of course, mutually supporting

---

[10] This is a good illustration of the general point that striving for favorable regulatory treatment is a significant part of competitive activity.

and together explain why such banks are usually the most successful competitors.[11]

One final point to be noted about competition for both correspondent balances and large corporate balances is that important regional shifts have occurred. New York City banks, for instance, have declined in relative deposit importance as a result of the more rapid economic growth of other regions, combined with a generally aggressive policy followed by strategically placed regional banks.[12] This outward drain of deposits has, however, not been matched by an equivalent falling-off in loan demand, so that New York City banks are under great pressure to moderate and reverse this drain, if they can. Recent changes in state banking legislation, permitting New York City banks to expand into surrounding areas, should help to support deposit growth.

COMPETITION FOR THRIFT DEPOSITS

The results of competition for thrift deposits in the postwar period are widely known.[13] The share of savings and loan associations has shown a more than threefold increase, and credit union savings, although much smaller in total amount, have grown by an even greater proportion. The great decline has been in the share of savings held by the federal government. Commercial and mutual savings banks have increased their share slightly. The shares of commercial and mutual savings banks have shown slight fluctuations; all the rest have shown consistent trends. Interest-rate differentials have been broadly consistent with the behavior of market shares.[14] Because of space limitations, only

[11] See Ref. 7 for some indications of the correlation between these various attributes which emerge from a study on mechanization among Third Federal Reserve District banks. Compare the following summary: "Growth is a thread running through most of the other mechanization-related characteristics. The retail bank, the lending bank, the checking-account bank are likely to be the banks that have grown the fastest. Growth is also tied with branch banking. Many branches are acquired through mergers which give substantial, one-shot boosts to deposits. . . . Growth, branches, high loan ratios, etc., generally seem to signify aggressiveness" (p. 4).

[12] On the decline of New York banks, see Ref. 8, chap. 2, and Ref. 9, pp. 74–81. For an example of the growth of a strong regional bank, see Ref. 10 on the expansion of the Wachovia Bank and Trust Company in the Southeast. Regional shifts may also be inferred from a recent study (Ref. 6), which shows that, since 1940, the share of total deposits held by the largest bank, 10 banks, 100 banks, and ½ and 1/10 of 1 per cent of all banks has in each case declined.

[13] Only thrift deposits held by consumers and nonprofit organizations are considered. Other economic units hold relatively small amounts; the major items excluded are corporate and local government time deposits, both of which more properly belong to the category of yield-liquidity assets. Savings associated with life insurance are also omitted.

[14] It is inadequately appreciated that the average interest rates paid by commercial banks, as normally computed, are biased downward because the commercial bank population includes banks which pay merely nominal or non-competitive rates either as a deliberate decision not to compete or by virtue of their spatial isolation. Fundamentally, this can occur because banks are more numerous and more geographically dispersed than other thrift institutions; thus savings and loan associations will always face some local bank competition, but the converse is not true. Interest-rate differentials, therefore, uncorrected for this bias (and sufficient data are not available to make this correction), tend to understate the competitive position of commercial banks.

competition between commercial banks and savings and loan associations will be discussed.

The explanation for these changes in commercial bank and savings and loan associations (SLA) shares is extremely simple. SLA offer, in the public's mind, approximately equivalent safety, liquidity, and convenience and, in addition, a higher rate. This common-sense explanation would appear, to be sure, somewhat obvious, except that a very stimulating and important recent article (Ref. 11) offers a much more complicated explanation of share behavior in the savings market in which the interest-rate factor is submerged, if not eliminated. In addition to stressing the operation of other factors (increase in average size of savings account, the advent of new savers to whom the SLA loss experience of the depression was less important, the increased familiarity of the public with SLA because of their mortgage activities, and aggressive salesmanship) whose importance I would not deny, it is also argued that changes in consumers' preferences, caused by higher incomes, greater savings, and increased liquid-asset holdings, have led to an increased willingness to bear risk. Since SLA deposits are somewhat higher-risk assets than bank savings deposits, their faster growth is attributed to these changes.

The difficulty with this argument can perhaps be expressed in the question: Is it the amount of risk people are *willing* to assume or the amount of risk they *think* they are assuming that has changed? Surely it is a strange point to find in a discussion of thrift that people are willing to shoulder greater risk, because for this type of financial asset there is likely to be an absolute threshold of risk minimality. That is to say, since safety plays such a great role in this decision, it does not seem likely that willingness to assume greater risk plays an important role in explaining SLA growth. If people are more willing to assume risk, other outlets for their funds give ample scope for realization of this shift in their preferences. Contrariwise, people have more likely come to believe that funds in SLA are becoming as safe as funds in commercial banks. Hence it is not a constant risk differential and a changing attitude toward risk but a narrowing risk differential (based on favorable experience) and an unchanging attitude that explain the shift in the savings flow. SLA deposits are insured by a government instrumentality, as are commercial bank deposits, and the small differences in coverage and recovery procedure are not generally perceived by savers. If, indeed, FDIC coverage and procedure are superior, banks cannot make much of this because to do so would reflect adversely on all savings institutions, and public controversy over small points of detail on the relative merits of FDIC-FSLIC would be mutually unprofitable, as well as unedifying.

It is further argued, in the article cited, that interest-rate differentials cannot possibly explain SLA success because commercial bank savings rates have risen proportionately more than SLA rates. (The absolute differential, in the period covered in the article, remained virtually constant.) Therefore, since the relative interest-rate differential was moving against SLA (or remaining the same if the absolute differential is taken), "The interest rate difference is discredited as the explanation for the relative decline of commercial bank savings"

(Ref. 11, p. 5). Is not the belief in instantaneous causation misplaced in this instance? Surely, the growth in SLA share represents the fruits of *maintaining* a persistently favorable differential. Public acceptance takes time; the realization of equivalent safety sinks in only over the years. Thus, even though relative (and absolute) interest-rate differentials may narrow, time and experience are working on the side of the higher rate. Especially where safety and liquidity are such important considerations, allowance for the passage of time before total consequences are felt is essential. This is simply an important illustration of the general significance of distributed lags in the explanation of economic phenomena.[15]

A final point to support the hypothesis that interest-rate differentials are important is the fact that a recent sample survey of the characteristics of SLA in two metropolitan areas reveals that accounts over $5,000, although only 16.6 per cent of total accounts, nevertheless held 63.2 per cent of total savings deposits. If we make the reasonable assumption that holders of large balances are more interest-sensitive than holders of small balances, this would further indicate the importance of rate differentials.[16]

If interest differentials explain in large part the behavior of savings flows, why have not banks competed more vigorously by raising their interest rates further? One obvious explanation is Regulation Q, the legal prohibition embodied in the Banking Acts of 1933 and 1935, which sets a ceiling (now 4 per cent) on the commercial bank savings rate. But this is certainly not the whole story. To put it bluntly, banks feel ambivalent about the role of their savings department: Why pay for funds at one time that can be obtained at little or no cost by the grace of the monetary authorities at other times? Banks, moreover, need saving funds only inermittently when loan demand is intense and the degree of tightness in financial markets makes inadvisable any further liquidation of their holdings of governments.[17] Contrariwise, savings money is needed at all times by other thrift depositories. Therefore, banks are reluctant to maintain savings deposit rates at continuously high levels in order to fill this intermittent gap. Secularly rising ratios of loans to deposits, however, will be a factor overcoming bank reluctance in this connection.

In addition, rates tend to be somewhat inflexible in the sense both that rates are announced in advance and maintained for a minimum time period and

---

[15] A completely analogous phenomenon can be seen in non-financial corporation participation in the short-term money market. Although the proportionately greater rise in the Treasury bill rate has narrowed the relative differential between it and the yield on directly placed commercial paper, the share of non-Treasury short-term securities in corporate portfolios has risen. The explanation is also similar: the growing sophistication of corporate short-term investment portfolio managers (Ref. 12, pp. 350–52).

[16] See Ref. 13, Tables 11 and 12, p. 24. It would be nice to have a similar breakdown of commercial bank savings accounts by size distribution. A more recent survey of savers at 77 associations, located in 27 states and 46 cities, who added or withdrew $1,000 during January, 1961, showed that the higher return was by far the most frequently mentioned reason for saving at a savings and loan association (Ref. 14, Table 4, p. 78).

[17] ". . . Commercial banks, as an industry—and there are many exceptions—are not too much interested in savings accounts as a steady diet. When they need the money because loan demand is heavy and interest rates are high, they go after savings; when there is a surplus of funds seeking investment, they lose the desire for savings accounts" (Ref. 15, p. 153).

that banks would feel somewhat constrained in allowing rates to move flexibly, especially downward, because of the resulting adverse public relations. The public does not expect savings rates to bob up and down like open-market rates. Especially if SLA hold their rate steady (as they are more likely to do for short swings because of longer lags and greater stability in mortgage rates), banks would look extremely bad if they lowered rates in such circumstances. Furthermore, many banks may take the attitude that the game is not worth the candle; that if they cannot engage in unfettered competition with SLA on rates, why chase them at all? Instead they choose to concentrate on the advantages of one-stop banking and other selling efforts. A recent survey of New York State banking shows that banks facing only savings institution competition in the same town pay *lower* rates than banks in one-bank towns, thus indicating that they have given up the struggle on this score.[18]

Bank reluctance to compete on savings rates can also be explained on the grounds that no opportunity to discriminate is provided—the intramarginal savers receive a "free ride" as all savers benefit from higher rates. Of course, this affects SLA too, as is evidenced by the numerous ingenious schemes for giving the long-term saver some preferential reward and utilizing premiums to attract marginal savers without disturbing overmuch those already holding accounts. But the essential difference is that the superiority of banks over SLA in offering a more complete range of services permits them to rely less heavily on interest rates, whereas SLA must employ their best and most effective weapon—the higher rate of return offered on savings. Furthermore, banks might be content as long as their savings accounts show no decline, even though their rate of growth was not so high as SLA. They would be willing to forego rapid growth because they felt that the marginal savings gained thereby were not worth the effort, as long as they did not lose accounts currently held. In a sense they are discriminating by holding onto the non-rate-conscious savers and letting the rate-conscious savers go.

Apart from the question of whether bankers would *want* to pay a higher savings rate, there is the further question of their *ability* to do so. Banks have higher operating costs and lower over-all gross operating returns per dollar of non-cash assets than SLA.[19] Thus the margin available for raising savings rates is squeezed from both sides. Furthermore, the trend in bank operating expenses has been upward, while SLA operating expenses have moved downward. This has been offset so far by the much sharper upward movement in gross

[18] See Ref. 16, Table 25, p. 31. The median savings rates, based on 1955 data, were as follows: banks in one-bank towns—1.71; banks facing savings institution competition only—1.34; and banks facing commercial bank competition—1.78. See also Table 22, p. 28, where the median ratio of time deposits to total assets was the lowest for banks which faced only savings institution competition. These and other data suggest that a much finer breakdown of our bank population would be very helpful. Banks, unlike specialist thrift institutions, exhibit great variation in their willingness to compete for thrift deposits.

[19] Non-cash assets have been used as a base instead of total assets because of the significant difference in bank and SLA ratios of cash assets to total assets. It should also be noted that both non-operating income (mainly capital gains and losses on security transactions) and tax liabilities are excluded from these calculations, although they affect banks to a much greater extent. Operating data are taken from the FDIC *Annual Report* and the FHLB *Combined Financial Statements*.

returns for banks. Should loan rates and security yields fall, however, the probable rigidity of operating expenses, combined with the greater stability of mortgage rates, would make conditions more difficult for banks than for SLA.

One cause for the higher cost of bank operations is the greater number of employees per dollar of assets and per deposit account. In 1959 banks employed roughly 2½ persons for every one employed by SLA per dollar of assets. Likewise, banks employed more than twice as many persons per deposit account as did SLA. And again, whereas the SLA figures show downward trends in the use of labor per dollar of assets and per account, indicating increased labor efficiency, bank figures show either stability or an upward trend. Partly, the more efficient performance of SLA can be traced to the beneficial effect of rapid growth on productivity; partly, the figures are simply an indication of the more complicated nature of banking. Banks provide, of course, more diversified and more numerous services than SLA, and to some extent their larger unit labor requirements reflect this fact, Because of this, the trend comparisons may be more appropriate than absolute comparisions of unit labor requirements.

The lower over-all return received by banks reflects their holdings of lower-yielding investments, whereas SLA earning assets are almost completely in mortgages. In addition, until 1957, average mortgage rates (exclusive of commissions, fees, and premiums) received by SLA were higher than average returns per dollar of loans received by banks. SLA gross mortgage returns (i.e., inclusive of commissions, fees, and premiums), however, have always been higher than the average return on bank loans. Of course, these figures must be interpreted with some care. Bank holdings of state and local government obligations may carry a relatively low yield, but the after-tax yield would be substantially higher. SLA receive a higher return on their mortgage portfolios because they have a higher proportion of conventional mortgages. Banks, on the other hand, place some value on the greater liquidity of federally underwritten mortgages. In addition, the more stringent regulations of permissible bank loan-to-value ratios and maturities acts as a risk screen, giving lower mortgage rates to those who can qualify under the more restrictive terms and forcing those who cannot to pay more for their mortgage money elsewhere. Furthermore, both liquidity needs and the customer orientation of banks lead to the maintenance of a formidable secondary reserve, capable of being run up and down as loan demand falls and rises. Branching limitations also tend to restrict the growth of loans by making it more difficult for banks to reach potential loan customers. Finally, supervisory attitudes toward appropriate risk assets-capital ratios, reinforces, the natural conservatism of bankers on the subject of liquidity, and both together inhibit a more rapid growth of loan assets.

There are other differences between banks and SLA which bankers stress in explaining why they feel hobbled in this competition. Banks, it is argued, face more stringent reserve requirements, and the Federal Home Loan Banks are more accommodating than a stern and unyielding central bank. Thus SLA never have to face as severe a liquidity problem as do banks. On the whole, these statements are true, but the difficult question is to determine how much weight to place on them as determinants of competitive weakness. The over-all impact of these conditions, I believe, has been slight relative to previously mentioned considerations. In any case, is it preferential regulatory treatment or the quickness of their respective liabilities which shapes portfolios? Two other points might be made on this subject: (1) the favorable position of SLA is a direct result of legislation, so that the banks' quarrel with SLA rests on balancing the effect on competitive positions against the clear legislative intent to favor specialist home-financing institutions; (2) it would further seem that banks cannot continuously bemoan their liquidity and reserve requirements but rather must look upon them as something which the state may legitimately claim as a rough *quid pro quo* for the delegation to the banking system of its sovereign right over money creation. Banks profit by this delegation of money-creating power; they must accept the incumbent duties.

Finally, there is the much discussed issue of the relative taxation of banks and SLA. Here again this issue has probably been singled out more for its apparent simplicity than for its impact. The charge of preferential taxation for SLA rests on the provision of the relevant tax statute, which states that mutual organizations can accumulate out of net income, reserves (consisting of surplus, undivided profit, and a bad-debt fund) up to 12 per cent of their savings deposits before they are subject to taxation. The average ratio of reserves to deposits is considerably less than 12 per cent, so that the tax liabilities of SLA are exceedingly modest.[20] Banks are also permitted to build up a loss reserve on a tax-free basis, i.e., amounts credited to reserve are deductible from taxable income but are subject to a maximum limit on reserve accumulation based on their past loss experience. This limit, however, is much lower (averaging 2.4 per cent of eligible loans) than the 12 per cent permitted mutuals, and, as a result, banks are more heavily taxed.* Banks argue that the reserve allowance permitted mutuals is too generous, theirs too skimpy, and that banks and SLA should be treated equally with respect to loss provision. There is no doubt that banks are disadvantaged by the different tax treatment, but again a conflict of principles must be resolved rather than a simple and exclusive issue of equal tax treatment. Namely, mutual institutions by their very nature have no equity cushion as a protection against insolvency, and the tax treatment of mutuals reflects this by enabling them to build up such a cushion unhindered by the long arm of the tax collector. Thus the tax issue is primarily one of deciding what treatment is fair for mutuals vis-a-vis stock corporations, although subsidiary argument over the size of the reserve funds is certainly a proper matter of dispute, as long as a reserve basis is adopted.[21]

[20] For a comparison of taxes paid by different financial institutions in recent years, see Ref. 17, p. 1797.

[21] Perhaps the resolution of this vexing taxation problem might be to abolish loss reserves altogether. Instead, permit financial institutions to borrow from a government agency to cover extraordinary losses and adopt the option, which banks currently have, of charging off ordinary losses against current income with perhaps some carry-back and carry-forward provisions to permit averaging. The main purpose would be to insure against the effect of losses on the stability of the financial system without at the same time getting into arguments over the proper size reserve against unknown loss contingency in the future —that is, to provide a cover for losses after they occur instead of trying to predict the magnitude of the need before they occur.

* *Editor's note:* Tax legislation of 1962 reduced, but did not eliminate, this tax differential.

Another area of competition, apart from rate setting, is selling effort. Opinion is unanimous that in this SLA have been more aggressive and proficient. Advertising outlays have been proportionately greater, and the fact that the FHLB had to establish a maximum figure on premium give-aways is impressive testimony to SLA propensities in this direction. But it is one thing to point to relative expenditure; it is quite another to measure results achieved. To what extent can SLA success be attributed to more vigorous salesmanship? The answer to this question is not certain, but SLA did successfully hurdle the assurance-of-safety threshold;[22] there is no doubt that the message that SLA accounts enjoy an insured status was put across, and, given the importance of safety to savers, this was crucial. Once this was achieved, the public then had to be made aware of the rate differential. Just as with any new and untried product, a disproportionate sales effort is necessary initially to overcome public apathy and ignorance. Looked at from this point of view, the recent growth performance of SLA represents a delayed dividend to capital long ago spent in public education on the virtues of SLA.

The final component of the savings package—convenience—is also an area where SLA have probably made some gains. There are two measures of performance that can be identified in this respect—location and services. With regard to location, the number of SLA head offices has expanded, while the number of bank head offices decreased, and the rate of expansion of branches has been faster for SLA than for banks. With respect to services, SLA have improved their position somewhat, mainly by virtue of the fact that they have been able to take on many bank-type services—traveler's checks, safe-deposit vaults, passbook loans, etc.—which, of course, banks were already performing.

REFERENCES

1. Seiden, M. H. "Pricing a Banking Service—the Special Checking Account," *Journal of Finance,* XV (September, 1960), pp. 371–86.
2. Federal Reserve Bank of Philadelphia. "How Business Tames Its Paper Tiger. Part II," *Business Review,* June, 1960, pp. 11–22.
3. Garvy, George. *Deposit Velocity and Its Significance.* New York: Federal Reserve Bank of New York, 1959.
4. Katona, G. *Business Looks at Banks.* Ann Arbor: University of Michigan Press, 1957.
5. *Federal Reserve Bulletin,* April, 1960.
6. Federal Deposit Insurance Corporation. *Annual Report, 1960.* Washington: Federal Deposit Insurance Corporation, 1961.
7. Federal Reserve Bank of Philadelphia. "How Business Tames Its Paper Tiger. Part III," *Business Review,* July, 1960, pp. 2–8.
8. Finney, K. *Interbank Deposits.* New York: Columbia University Press, 1958.
9. Robbins, S., and N. Terleckyj, *Money Metropolis.* Cambridge: Harvard University Press, 1960.
10. *Business Week,* September 24, 1960.

[22] Between 1945 and 1959 commercial bank savings accounts increased in number by 99.5 per cent; SLA accounts increased by 229 per cent (see Ref. 18, Table 5, p. 10).

11. Alhadeff, D. A. and C. P. "The Struggle for Commercial Bank Savings," *Quarterly Journal of Economics*, LXXII (February, 1958), pp. 1–22.

12. Jacobs, D. P. "The Marketable Security Portfolios of Non-financial Corporations: Investment Practices and Trends," *Journal of Finance*, XV (September, 1960), pp. 341–52.

13. United States Savings and Loan League. *Fact Book, 1960*. Chicago: United States Savings and Loan League, 1960.

14. Kendall, L. T. "Savings in the American Economy," *Conference on Savings and Residential Financing, 1961, Proceedings*, pp. 66–82. Chicago: United States Savings and Loan League, 1961.

15. Bogen, J. "Trends in the Institutionalization of Savings," *Conference on Savings and Residential Financing, 1958, Proceedings*, pp. 146–58. Chicago: United States Savings and Loan League, 1958.

16. New York State Banking Department. *Postwar Banking Developments in New York State*. Albany: New York State Banking Department, *ca.* 1959.

17. Gurley, J. G. and Y. E. "Federal Income Taxation of Mutual Savings Banks and Savings and Loan Associations," Committee on Ways and Means, Tax Revision Compendium, Vol. III. Washington: Government Printing Office, 1959.

18. American Bankers Association. *Statistics on the Savings Market, 1960 Edition*. New York: American Bankers Association, 1960.

Selection 15

PROFIT OR LOSS FROM TIME DEPOSIT BANKING [1]

LELAND J. PRITCHARD

The growth of competition for time deposits has resulted in attention to the question whether such competition is of benefit to the commercial banking system and to the economy in general. Leland Pritchard argues that the source of time deposits is demand deposits; hence, fundamentally, the banks, in seeking and obtaining time deposits, are obtaining something on which they must pay interest, in exchange for something on which they pay no interest. Professor Pritchard also argues that, since the payments velocity (transactions velocity) of time deposits is zero, their expansion means that unless velocity of demand deposits increases sufficiently to compensate for this, aggregate demand declines when funds are transferred from demand deposit to time deposit accounts. He suggests that it is unlikely that a precisely compensating change in velocity occurs, but admits that both this change and the response of the monetary authorities are indeterminate.

There has been a vast and unprecedented growth in the volume of time deposits in the commercial banks during the past two decades and in recent

---

[1] The term "time deposits" is used in an all-inclusive sense to include all types of savings deposits held in the commercial banks as well as time certificates of deposit issued by such banks.

• From Deane Carson, ed., *Banking and Monetary Studies* (Homewood, Ill.: Richard D. Irwin, 1963), pp. 369–386. Reprinted by permission of Richard D. Irwin, Inc., and the author.

years time deposit growth has accelerated resulting in a marked increase in the proportion time deposits are of total bank deposits.[2]

Accompanying this absolute and relative growth there has been a pronounced increase in interest rates paid on time deposits.[3]

The higher rates, combined with the larger volume of time deposits, have not only increased the absolute amount of interest expense, but this item now constitutes a much larger proportion of total bank expenses.[4]

The policies for both higher rates and a larger volume of time deposits have been vigorously fostered by bankers and their organizations.[5]

Without the cooperation of the Board of Governors and the Federal Deposit Insurance Corporation in raising the maximum permissible rates which the member and nonmember insured banks could pay their time deposit customers, the continued uptrend in rates would not, however, have been possible.[6]

The basic premise on which this support for bigger and more costly time deposit rests is the belief that the savings-investment process of the commercial banks is comparable to, if not actually identical with, that of the financial intermediaries.

Innumerable citations of both official government and banker opinion could be documented to the effect that, insofar as their time deposit business is concerned, the commercial banks act as intermediaries between savers and borrowers; that in this respect they perform the same basic functions as savings banks and other thrift institutions.[7]

Confusion concerning the role (and profitability) of time deposit banking apparently stems from the failure to recognize that savings held in the commercial banks originate within the banking system; that the source of time deposits is demand deposits, either directly, or indirectly *via* the currency route.[8]

---

[2] From a figure of $15.7 billion as of the end of 1942, time deposits reached a total of $97.0 billion as of the end of 1962. The proportion of time to total deposits (excluding interbank demand and time deposits) has increased from 21.1 per cent to approximately 41 per cent during this period. Note: Unless otherwise designated, data quoted are from the *Federal Reserve Bulletin*.

[3] As recently as 1956, the member banks were paying an average rate of only 1.5 per cent on their time deposits. This compares with a figure of 2.73 per cent in 1961 and 3.18 per cent in 1962.

[4] Thus, for member banks, the interest expense on time deposits as a percentage of total operating expense (before taxes on net income) increased from about 17 per cent in 1955 to approximately 28 per cent in 1961, and to 33 per cent in 1962.

[5] The evidence for this statement is so widespread as not to warrant documentation.

[6] After remaining at 2½ per cent from January 1, 1936 to December 31, 1956, the maximum rate was raised to 3 per cent effective January 1, 1957 and to 4 per cent effective January 1, 1962. One of the principal reasons motivating the monetary authorities to increase the rates was to enable the commercial banks to meet the competition of other institutions for savings. See, *Federal Reserve Bulletin,* December, 1956, p. 1301, and February, 1962, pp. 136–137; and *1956 Annual Report,* Federal Deposit Insurance Corporation, pp. 83–84.

[7] See, for example, the statement of William McChesney Martin, Jr., Chairman, Board of Governors of the Federal Reserve System before the Joint Economic Committee, January 30, 1962, *Federal Reserve Bulletin,* February, 1962, pp. 136–137. For examples of officially expressed banker opinion of this nature see, *Member Bank Reserve Requirements,* Economic Policy Commission, American Bankers Association, 1957, esp. pp. 127–151.

[8] Cf. Savings and Mortgage Division, American Bankers Association, *Plan for the Determination of Profit or Loss of Savings Accounts in Commercial Banks,* New York,

In contrast to the savings-investment process of the commercial banks, all savings placed at the disposal of savings and loan associations, mutual savings banks and other financial intermediaries originate outside these institutions. This is true both with regard to the individual institution and intermediaries as a group.[9]

Therefore, unlike the intermediaries, where the same methodology may be applied to the group as to a single institution, formulation of estimates of time deposit profitability for the commercial banks requires that we distinguish system operations from individual bank operations. Even in making estimates for individual banks it is necessary to distinguish those instances in which time deposits originate outside the bank from those instances where time deposits are traceable to transfers from demand deposits in the same institution.

A range of estimates of profitability or unprofitability is encompassed in the four models set forth below. Two of these relate to individual bank operations and two relate to system operations.

In the first individual bank model it is assumed that: (1) the increment in time deposits is primary to the given bank; (2) the bank had the opportunity to make bankable loans and fully exploited these opportunities to the extent permitted by the time deposit related expansion of its excess reserves; and (3) all deposits created as a consequence of these loans were checked out and flowed to other banks in the system.

These assumptions are incorporated in the following equation:

$$P = T\,(l-t) \left[\, n - \left(\frac{r+e_t}{l-t}\right)\, \right]$$

Where:

P = amount of profit or loss attributable to the influx of time deposits,
T = volume of primary time deposits,

1951. By matching time deposits against a presumed derived volume of loans on the opposite side of the balance sheet, that is, by treating the commercial banks as intermediaries, the ABA study concluded that time deposit banking was profitable. In effect, the ABA study asked this question: Was the net interest income on loans derived from time deposits greater than the interest paid on these deposits plus other direct and indirect operating expenses chargeable to time deposits? The implicit, and false, premise in this question is that time deposits are a *source* of loan funds to the banking system.

The question the ABA should have asked and based its study on was this: Does a shift from demand to time deposits result in a sufficient modification of monetary policy toward greater ease or less restraint as to allow the banks to acquire earning assets of a volume sufficient to offset the increased costs associated with this shift?

[9] For the intermediaries, either individually or collectively, the savings-investment process, in a mechanical sense, merely involves the transfer of the ownership of existing demand deposits (which have been saved) within the commercial banking system. The deposit of currency, rather than checks drawn on demand deposits, with the intermediaries does not invalidate this conclusion, since currency comes into possession of the public through the "cashing" of demand deposits and is almost entirely returned by the intermediaries to the banking system in exchange for demand deposits.

For a summary of the salient differences of the savings-investment process of the commercial banks *vis-à-vis* the financial intermediaries, see Leland J. Pritchard, "Should Commercial Banks Accept Savings Deposits?" *1961 Proceedings, Conference on Savings and Residential Financing,* Chicago, Illinois, pp. 17, 18.

t = reserve ratio applicable to time deposits,
n = net rate of return on incremental earning assets,
r = average rate of interest paid on time deposits, and
e_t = operating expenses associated with the time deposit function expressed in ratio form.

In effect this model seeks to answer the following question: "To what extent is the net interest income on loans derived from time deposits greater than the interest paid on these deposits plus other direct and indirect operating expenses chargeable to time deposits?"

The actual estimate of the profit (or loss) attributable to the time deposit function is based upon the following assigned values:[10] $T = \$1000$; $t = .05$; $n = .0376$; $r = .0236$; $e_t = .0057$.

Substituting:

$$P = 1000\,(1 - .05)\left[\ .0376 - \left(\frac{.0236 + .0057}{1 - .05}\right)\ \right]$$

$$= \$6.42$$

the estimated profit per annum per $1000 of time deposits *where these deposits are assumed to originate outside the given bank.*

The "T" account proof for the above computation is as follows:

Given Bank			
+ Reserves	1000	+ TD	1000
+ Loans	950	+ DD	950
− Reserves	950	− DD	950
(Consolidated)			
+ Reserves	50	+ TD	1000
+ Loans	950		

Reserve proof:

Increased total reserves = $50
Increased required reserves = (1000) .05 = $50

Profit proof:

Increase in net earnings = (950) .0376 = $37.72
Increase in costs = 1000(.0236 + .0057) = $29.30
Increase in net profits = 35.72 − 29.30 = $6.42

Since, under the above assumptions, the commercial bank is analyzed as if it were an intermediary, it is not surprising to discover that a bank, operating as a separate intermediary financial institution, profits from its time deposit

[10] All interest, income, and expense ratios used are based upon average 1959 functional cost and revenue data compiled from the records of 80 member banks in the first Federal Reserve District. See *1959 Functional Cost Analysis,* Federal Reserve Bank of Boston (mimeographed). A summarization of this study was published in their *Monthly Review,* January, 1961, "What Makes for a More Profitable Bank?"

business.[11] Other studies in which the commercial bank has been treated as an intermediary in the savings-investment process have come to a similar conclusion.[12]

In the second individual bank model it is assumed that: (1) the increment in time deposits is attributable to a transfer from demand deposits in the same institution; (2) the bank had the opportunity to make bankable loans and fully exploited these opportunities to the extent permitted by the time deposit related expansion of its excess reserves; and (3) all deposits created as a consequence of these loans were checked out and flowed to other banks in the system.

These assumptions are incorporated in the following equation:

$$P = T \ (d - t) \left[n - \frac{(r + e_t) - (e_d - a)}{d \quad - \quad t} \right]$$

Where:

d = reserve ratio applicable to demand deposits,

e_d = operating expenses associated with the demand deposit function expressed in ratio form, and

a = activity charge income derived from the demand deposit function, expressed in ratio form.[13]

Values assigned are as follows:[14]

$d = .12; t = .05; n = .0376; r = .0236; e_t = .0057;$
$a_d = .0231; a = .00779; T = \$1000.$

Substituting:

$$P = 1000 \ (.12 - .05) \left[.0376 - \frac{(.0236 + .0057) - (.0231 - .0079)}{.12 - .05} \right]$$

$$= - \$11.36 \ (\text{approx.})$$

the estimated *loss* per annum per $1000 of time deposits *where these deposits originate in the given bank.*

---

[11] Financial intermediaries, such as savings and loan associations and mutual savings banks, have had a phenomenal growth and earnings record since 1945, yet these institutions uniformly pay higher rates on share accounts and savings deposits than is paid by commercial banks on time deposits.

It seems advisable to note that even in the situation depicted by the above model, the gain to the individual bank was accompanied by a net loss to the banking system, if it is assumed that the growth of time deposits in the given bank resulted in a net expansion of time deposits in the banking system. This conclusion derives from the fact that: (1) the growth of time deposits in a particular bank is necessarily at the expense of deposits in other banks (there being nothing in such an individual bank situation to justify any change in assumptions concerning the currency holdings of the public); and (2) time deposits are, dollar for dollar, more costly to hold than are demand deposits.

[12] The 1951 study sponsored by the Savings and Mortgage Division of the American Bankers Association, *supra,* arrived at a median figure of $11.10 profit per annum per $1000 of time deposits.

[13] All other symbols in the above equation were used in the equation for the first model and are defined in the same manner.

[14] With the exception of values assigned to *d, t,* and *T,* ratios were computed from data compiled by the Federal Reserve Bank of Boston, *supra.*

The "T" account proof is as follows:

		Given Bank	
		− DD	1000
		+ TD	1000
+ Loans	70	+ DD	70
− Reserves	70	− DD	70
		(Consolidated)	
− Reserves	70	− DD	1000
+ Loans	70	+ TD	1000

Reserve proof:

Decrease in total reserves = $70
Decrease in required reserves = 1000 (.12 − .12 − .05) = $70

Proof of Loss:

Increase in net earnings = (70) .0376 = $2.632
Increase in costs = 1000 (.0236 + .0057) − 1000 (.0231 − .00779)
$$= 29.30 − 15.31 = 13.99$$
Net loss = 2.632 − 13.99 = $11.358

If the individual bank stands to lose, where time deposits originate consequent to a shift from demand deposits in the same institution, the *a priori* conclusion would seem to be justified that the commercial banks, as a system, are incurring a loss on their time deposit business since, from the standpoint of the banking system, the source of time deposits is demand deposits.[15]

From a system standpoint, however, two factors must be taken into account which are not pertinent to a single bank approach, *viz.*, (1) the influence of time deposit induced changes in demand deposits on the currency holdings of the public; and (2) the response of the monetary authorities to time deposit induced changes in excess reserves.[16]

---

[15] Statistical analyses uniformly indicate an adverse associative relationship between the volume of time deposits and bank profits. The universal conclusion has been that the higher the ratio of time deposits to total deposits, the lower the profit ratios of the banks, irrespective of size. Cf., Horace Secrist, *Banking Ratios,* Stanford University Press, 1930, pp. 154–55; Joseph Aschheim, "Commercial Banks and Financial Intermediaries: Fallacies and Policy Implications," *Journal of Political Economy,* February 1959, pp. 59–71; Deane Carson, "Bank Earnings and the Competition for Savings Deposits," *Journal of Political Economy,* December, 1959, pp. 580–88; Board of Governors, "Member Bank Operating Ratios," *Federal Reserve Bulletin,* July, 1960, p. 811.

Drawing upon this evidence Deane Carson suggests that bankers should look with favor on the growth of "competing" savings institutions: "In general, a shift of savings deposits from commercial banks to SLA (savings and loan associations) will improve the net earnings of the former. . . ." *ibid,* p. 583. A study made by the New York State Banking Department would seem to confirm his recommendations. On the basis of returns from all the banks in New York State it was found that commercial banks located in communities having mutual savings banks and savings and loans associations had higher profit ratios on the average than did banks lacking such "competition." Conceivably this may only be an associative relationship, but the absence of other pertinent differentiating factors (e.g., size of bank) gives a strong presumption that the presence of these financial intermediaries in a community is a causal factor enhancing the earnings of the commercial banks. See *Postwar Banking Developments in New York State,* 1958, Chapter 3, "Impact of Savings Institutions on Commercial Banks."

[16] Time deposit induced effects on interest rates, average and marginal costs and port-

The first of these two factors is referred to as the cash drain factor, which simply expresses in ratio form, the observable statistical fact that the nonbank public chooses to hold a fairly constant proportion of its means-of-payment money in the form of currency.[17]

A system approach to an analysis of the time deposit function must also, as indicated by the second factor above, be cognizant of the response of the monetary authorities to any change in bank excess reserves, whether induced by changes in time deposits or any other factor capable of affecting bank excess reserves independently of Federal Reserve action.

In the first system model it is assumed that the period involved is long enough to allow the nonbank public to adjust its currency holdings to the time deposit induced alteration of its demand deposit holdings, but too short to warrant the assumption that there has been any change in monetary policy. That is to say, neither the return flow of currency effect on total, required, and excess reserves, nor the differential reserve ratio effect on excess reserves, both of which are induced (*ceteris paribus*) by a shift from demand to time deposits, are allowed by the monetary authorities to generate any increase in excess reserves in the system.

The techniques by which monetary policy is executed provide a solid administrative basis to justify the assumption, that for a limited period at least, a shift from demand to time deposits is not allowed to bring about an increase in excess reserves in the banking system, and therefore an increase in bank lending capacity.

The primary criteria on which the monetary authorities rely, in their endeavor to create the desired condition of "ease" or "tightness" in the money markets, are the size and components of the excess reserve position of the member banks rather than the absolute size and direction of movement of the money supply.

In more specific terms, any factor which is capable of altering the over-all lending capacity of the commercial banks is a matter of direct concern to the

folio composition are also of some, though probably minor, significance. (See footnote 25 for a discussion of portfolio adaptations.) Interest effects are excluded from the subsequent model analysis because there seemed to be no justifiable rationale for any particular assumption concerning the rate effects of growth in time deposits. The growth of time deposits has the initial effect of reducing the supply of loan-funds, principally for two reasons: (1) funds held in the form of time deposits are lost to investment, and (2) monetary policy will automatically eliminate the excess reserves created in the banking system consequent to a shift from demand to time deposits. (Further exploration of these two points is given subsequently in the paper.) While the initial effects would tend to push rates up, the stoppage in the flow of monetary savings, which is an inexorable part of time deposit banking, would tend to have a longer-term debilitating effect on demands, particularly the demands for capital goods. Contrary forces are therefore operative and we are left with no rational basis to conjecture even the direction of a time deposit induced change in rates.

Time deposit induced cost effects, other than those directly related to the administration of time deposits, have been excluded, both because they are probably of minor consequence and because no pertinent data are available.

[17] Since 1951 the percentage of currency to demand deposits which the nonbank public has chosen to hold has varied from 27.8 to 25.5. Computations based upon data from the *Federal Reserve Bulletin*.

Manager of the Open Market Account. In executing the general directives of the Open Market Committee the people at the "trading desk" at the Federal Reserve Bank of New York react to the totality of all factors which alter the excess reserve position of the banks (including a switch to time deposits). Thus, for the short run, it is logical to assume that any time deposit induced effects on excess reserves are "washed out." [18]

A theoretical explanation has also been advanced to support the above conclusion. It is based upon the following assumptions:[19] (1) that monetary policy has as an objective a certain level of spending for GNP, and that a growth in time deposits will not, *per se,* alter this objective; (2) that a shift from demand to time deposits involves a decrease in the demand for money balances and that this shift will be reflected in an offsetting increase in the velocity of money;[20] (3) to prevent the increase in velocity from altering the desired level of spending for GNP it is necessary for the Federal Reserve to prevent the diminished money supply brought about by the shift from demand to time deposits from being replenished through an expansion of bank credit; and (4)

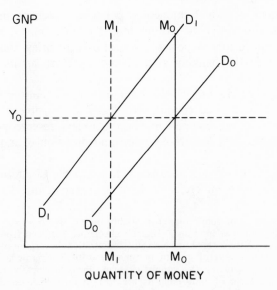

Figure 1

[18] See Robert V. Roosa, *Federal Reserve Operations in the Money and Government Securities Markets,* Federal Reserve Bank of New York, 1956, esp. pp. 64 ff. Also, Paul Meek, *Open Market Operations,* Federal Reserve Bank of New York, 1963.

[19] I am indebted to Professor Lester V. Chandler for the main body of this analysis. See "Should Commercial Banks Accept Savings Deposits?" *Conference on Savings and Residential Financing* (1961 Proceedings), United States Savings and Loan League, Chicago, 1961, pp. 42, 43. This is reprinted in the present volume as selection 17.

[20] I seriously doubt the premise that a shift from demand to time deposits does not *per se* decrease aggregate demand, and I prefer to rest the case (that the banking system is not allowed to expand consequent to a growth in time deposits) on administrative grounds alone.

to prevent the expansion of bank credit requires that the Federal Reserve "mop up" all excess reserves created by the shift from demand to time deposits.

The graphical representation of these assumptions is depicted in the foregoing illustration where:

Y_o = Federal Reserve's desired level of spending for GNP,

M_oM_o = volume of money before the shift from demand to time deposits,

M_1M_1 = volume of money after the shift from demand to time deposits,

D_oD_o = demand for money before the shift from demand to time deposits, and

D_1D_1 = demand for money after the shift from demand to time deposits.

If any expansion of bank credit is allowed by the monetary authorities, the line M_1M_1 will shift to the right and will intersect the new demand curve D_1D_1 at a level higher than Y_0. Therefore, to prevent an undesirable expansion in spending it is necessary for the Reserve authorities to remove all excess reserves created by the growth of time deposits.

Assuming no over-all growth in the banking system is permitted by the monetary authorities, consequent to a growth in time deposits, the estimated profit (or loss) from a given transfer of funds from demand to time deposits is computed as follows:

$$P = \left[T\left(\frac{c}{1+c}\right)(1-d) + T\,(d-t) \right]g + T\left(1 - \frac{c}{1+c}\right)(e_d - a) - T\,(r + e_t)$$

Where:

c = cash drain expressed as a ratio of currency to demand deposits, and

g = average rate of return obtained by member banks on United States obligations in 1959.[21]

All other symbols used in the above equation have been previously defined. Values assigned are as follows:[22]

$$T = \$1000; \; c = .25; \; d = .14; \; t = .05; \; g = .0279;$$
$$e_t = .0057; \; e_d = .0231; \; a = .00779; \; r = .0236$$

Substituting:

$$P = \left[1000\left(\frac{.25}{1.25}\right)(1 - .14) + 1000\,(.14 - .05) \right].0279 + 1000$$

$$\left(1 - \frac{.25}{1.25}\right)(.0231 - .00779) - 1000\,(.0236 + .0057)$$

$$= (7.3098 + 12.248) - 29.30 = \$6.7422,$$

the estimated loss per annum per $1000 *where the shift from demand to time*

[21] On the assumption that the Reserve authorities mop up time deposit induced excess reserves by the sale of governments to the banks through the open market. They do this by selling $T\,(d-t)$ volume of securities to the banks. In order to counteract the effect on excess reserves of a return flow of currency due to a shift from demand to time deposits they sell an additional volume, $T\left(\dfrac{c}{1+c}\right)(1-d)$, of governments to the banks.

[22] The value of .14 was assigned to d, rather than .12 as previously, since the average reserve ratio applicable to demand deposits for the banking system closely approximates .14.

deposits is assumed to have caused no alteration in monetary policy.[23] The "T" account proof is as follows:

BANKING SYSTEM

+ Currency (Reserves)	200	— DD	1000
— Reserves	172	+ TD	1000
+ U. S. Oblig.	172	+ DD	200
— Reserves	90		
+ U. S. Oblig.	90		
(Consolidated)			
— Reserves	62	— DD	800
+ U. S. Oblig.	262	+ TD	1000

Reserve proof:

Decrease in total reserves $= 62$
Decrease in required reserves $= (800) .14 - (1000) .05 = 112 - 50 = 62$

Proof of loss:

Increase in net earnings $= (262) .0279 = \$7.3098$
Decreased (demand deposit) costs $= (800) .01531 = \$12.248$
Increased (time deposit) costs $= (1000) .0293 = \$29.30$
Net loss $= (7.3098 + 12.248) - 29.30 = \$6.74$

Cash drain proof:

Decrease in nonbank public's holdings of currency $= 200$
Decrease in nonbank public's holdings of demand deposits $= 800$
Since $c = .25$ the absolute amount of the cash drain should be $(800) .25$ or $\$200$.

While there may be ample short-term justification for assuming that the Federal Reserve will "mop up" all increases in excess reserves (whether related to the growth of time deposits, return flows of currency or other causes), over the long run it seems quite probable that growth in time deposits will induce the Reserve authorities to follow a somewhat easier, or less restrictive monetary policy than would otherwise have prevailed.

This hypothesis rests upon the fact that the payments velocity of funds shifted into time deposits becomes zero, and remains at zero so long as funds are held in this form. The stoppage of the flow of these funds generates adverse effects in our highly interdependent pecuniary economy, as would any stoppage in the flow of funds however induced.[24] Furthermore it seems highly improbable

[23] The events which have occurred since 1959–60, particularly the sharp rise in interest rates paid on time deposits combined with the virtual sidewise movement of mortgage and other long-term rates would indicate a much larger loss than the above of funds currently being shifted into time deposits.

[24] Time deposit banking arrests the flow of monetary savings into investment because in their time deposit function the commercial banks are neither intermediaries nor creators of loan funds; they are simply custodians of stagnant money. The commercial banks do not loan out time deposits, nor the "proceeds" of time deposits; they do not even loan out reserves or excess legal reserves, although their lending capacity is determined by their excess legal reserve position. When the banks acquire earning assets, that is, when the banks make loans to, or buy securities from, the nonbank public, they pay for these earning assets (from a system standpoint) with newly created money. This newly created money initially takes the form of demand deposits. Of course, monetary savings held in the form of time deposits are not irrevocably lost to investment until destroyed. But on the other

(and in contradiction to Professor Chandler's theoretical analysis presented above) that the stoppage in the flow of these funds is entirely compensated for by an increased velocity of the remaining demand deposits. It is quite probable that the growth of time deposits shrinks aggregate demand and therefore produces adverse effects on GNP, the level of employment, and on other indicators of the state of our economic health. If this is true in any significant degree it would be foolish to contend that a growth in time deposits has no long-run effects on monetary policy. But the extent of these effects, consequent to any given expansion of time deposits, is indeterminate, as is the response of the monetary authorities to these developments.

It is indeed a moot question whether these adverse effects have heretofore been of such a magnitude as to induce the Reserve authorities to follow a sufficiently less restrictive (or easier) monetary policy (than they otherwise would have pursued) as to provide the banks with the added excess reserves requisite to enable them to expand their earnings assets, and thereby their net earnings, by an amount sufficient to more than offset the increased costs associated with the growth of time deposits.

In this fourth and last model, the monetary policy parameter selected allows the banking system to grow approximately *pari passu* with the growth of time deposits. By assuming such a monetary policy the banking system is, in effect, placed in a situation equivalent from a profit standpoint to an intermediary; for as rapidly as demand deposits are shifted into time deposits the banking system is allowed by monetary policy to expand credit and replace the depleted demand deposits. I shall therefore make the quite arbitrary (and I think, un-realistic) assumption that the excess reserves created in the banking system consequent to the shift from demand to time deposits are allowed by the monetary authorities to remain intact, i.e., that monetary policy is altered sufficiently toward greater ease (or less restraint) so that it is "neutral" with respect to this reserve factor. It is also assumed that the banks have the opportunity to exploit these additional excess reserves and that they expand their earning assets to the legally permissible limit.

The incremental amount of earning assets which the banks are able to acquire under the above assumptions for any given expansion of time deposits is indicated by the following equation:

$$L = \left[\frac{T\left(\frac{c}{1+c}\right)(1-D) + T(d-t)}{d+c} \right](1+c)$$

Where:

L = net expansion of bank-held earning assets consequent to a shift of T dollars from demand to time deposits.

Definitions for all other items in the equation are the same as in the previous model.

---

hand they cannot be used to finance investment until their owners (the nonbank public) so decide, and so long as the nonbank public chooses to hold savings in the form of time deposits, the means-of-payment velocity of these funds is zero and the funds are lost to investment, to consumption and indeed to any type of payment.

Substituting the values previously used:

$$L = \left[\frac{1000 \left(\frac{.25}{1.25}\right) (1 - .14) + 1000 \,(.14 - .05)}{.14 + .25} \right] 1.25$$

$$= (671.745)\ 1.24$$
$$= \$839.681,$$

the net expansion in earning assets in the banking system consequent to a shift of 1,000 from demand to time deposits under the above assumptions.

The actual net profit (or loss) is equal to:

$$P = L\,(n - y)$$

Where:

> $P =$ amount of profit (or loss) per annum per X amount transferred from demand to time deposits,
> $n =$ net rate of return on incremental earning assets,[25] and
> $y =$ minimum net average yield which must be earned on incremental earning assets in order to break even.

In equation form:

$$Y = \frac{(r + e_t) - \Delta D\,(e_d - a)}{L'}$$

Where:

> $L' = L$ expressed in ratio form, or .839681 under our present assumptions, and $\Delta D =$ ratio of net decrease in demand deposits to the increase in time deposits.

The equation for ΔD is as follows:

$$\Delta D = \left[\frac{\left(\frac{c}{1 + c}\right) (1 - d) + (d - t)}{d + c} \right] + \left(\frac{c}{1 + c}\right) - 1$$

Substituting:

$$\Delta D = \left[\frac{\left(\frac{.25}{1.25}\right) (1 - .14) + (.14 - .05)}{.14 + .25} \right] + \left(\frac{.25}{1.25}\right) - 1$$

$$= -.128255.$$

[25] The value here assigned to n is .0376, obtained from the income and functional cost study made by the Federal Reserve Bank of Boston, *op. cit.* This value represents the average net rate of return on both loans and investments, and was selected on the assumption that the expanded earning assets are distributed according to the prevailing portfolio pattern.

It is by no means certain, even if credit expansion is allowed and does take place, consequent to a time deposit related expansion in excess reserves, that the newly created funds will only, or even preponderantly, be the consequence of the acquisition of the highest yielding types of earning assets. While legal sanctions tend to encourage such offsets, e.g., relating the maximum permissible volume of mortgage lending to the volume of time deposits, it does not follow that such portfolio adaptations will take place. See David A. Alhadeff and Charlotte P. Alhadeff, "A Note on Bank Earnings and Savings Deposit Rate Policy," *The Journal of Finance,* September, 1959, p. 407, footnote.

That is to say, the decrease in the volume of demand deposits (under the above assumption) tends to be about 12.8 per cent of the increase in the volume of time deposits.

Using this value for ΔD and values previously assigned to r, e_t, e_d, and a, we have:

$$Y = \frac{.0236 + .0057 - .128255\,(.0231 - .00779)}{.839681}$$

$$= .032555, \text{ or approximately 3.26 per cent, the break-even rate of return.}$$

The estimated profit (or loss) under the above assumptions, and using the above computed values for L, n, and y is therefore:

$$P = 839.681\,(.0376 - .03256)$$
$$= 4.2312, \text{ or a profit per annum per \$1,000 transferred to time deposits of}$$
approximately \$4.23.[26]

The "T" account proof for the above computation is as follows:

BANKING SYSTEM

		— DD	1000.
		+ TD	1000.
+ Currency (Reserves)	200.	+ DD	200.
+ Loans and investments	839.681	+ DD	839.681
— Currency (Reserves)	167.936	— DD	167.936
	(Consolidated)		
+ Currency (Reserves)	32.064	+ TD	1000.
+ Loans and investments	839.255	— DD	128.255

Cash drain proof:

Decrease in nonbank public's holdings of currency = \$32.064
Decrease in nonbank public's holdings of demand deposits = \$128.255
Since $c = .25$ the absolute amount of the return flow of currency should be
(128.255) .25 or \$32.064.

Reserve proof:

Net increase in total reserves = \$32.064
Net increase in required reserves = (1000) .05 — (128.255) .14 = 32.044.[27]

Profit proof:

Increase in net earnings = (839.681) .0376 = \$31.572
Decrease in (demand deposit) costs = (128.255) .01531 = \$1.96358
Increase in (time deposit) costs = (1000) .0293 = \$29.30
Net profits = (31.572 + 1.964) — 29.30 = 4.236.[28]

CONCLUSIONS AND RECOMMENDATIONS

If time deposit banking is to add to the aggregate profits of the commercial

[26] If 1962 data were used in connection with the same monetary policy assumptions, a much smaller net profit figure would be obtained, even though the 4 per cent reserve ratio for member bank time deposits (effective October 25, November 1, 1963) were used. See explanation in footnote 25.

[27] Discrepancy due to rounding.

[28] Slight discrepancy between this and previously quoted profit figure due to rounding.

banks, it is necessary to assume that the expansion of time deposits induces the monetary authorities to follow an easier (or less restrictive) monetary policy than they otherwise would pursue.

The following institutional relationships in our present monetary and banking system provide the basis for this conclusion:

(1) From the standpoint of the banking system the source of time deposits is demand deposits. Consequently the expansion of time deposits *per se* adds nothing to total bank liabilities, assets or earning assets. (2) The cost of maintaining time deposit accounts is greater, dollar for dollar, than the cost of maintaining demand deposit accounts.[29] (3) The permissible limits of bank credit expansion, and consequently the aggregate volume of bank earning assets, are controlled by the Federal Reserve authorities.

Not only is it necessary to assume that the growth of time deposits causes a change in monetary policy, but the monetary authorities must be willing to supply the banking system with an additional volume of excess reserves adequate enough to enable the banks to expand their earnings assets, and thereby their net earnings, by an amount sufficient to more than offset the over-all increase in costs associated with the growth of time deposits.

It is indeed a moot question whether the growth of time deposits causes a reorientation of monetary policy to this extent.

It seems probable, therefore, that the fourth model depicted above (which assumes a pronounced reorientation of monetary policy in response to an expansion of time deposits) presents a far too sanguine profit projection for the time deposit function of the commercial banks.[30]

Monetary policy seeks the attainment of our national economic objectives —a high and sustainable rate of economic growth, high employment and reasonable price level stability, and the avoidance of chronic deficits (or surpluses) in our balance of payments—principally through the open market device. Through this device the day to day fluctuations in the volume of excess bank reserves are smoothed out at the level deemed appropriate by the authorities. Neither in the short-run nor over the longer term is the objective to achieve or maintain the volume of our means-of-payment money at any given level. We may assume, therefore, that the initial response of the monetary authorities to a shift from demand to time deposits, *ceteris paribus,* is to effect a volume of sales in the open market sufficient to extinguish the excess reserves brought into being by this shift. If in due course it is decided to maintain excess reserves at a higher level, that is, to follow an easier (or less restrictive) monetary policy, this is presumably undertaken to counteract recessionary tendencies in the economy. This being so, it must be presumed that the growth of time deposits could not induce a shift

---

[29] The much lower costs of administration of time deposits as compared to demand deposits, per dollar of deposits, are more than offset by the interest cost on time deposits and the loss of activity (service charge) revenue derived from demand deposits. See Federal Reserve Bank of Boston and American Banking Association cost studies cited, *supra.*

[30] This conclusion seems to be corroborated by a recent study by Professor Paul F. Smith. See "Optimum Rate on Time Deposits," *The Journal of Finance,* December, 1962, pp. 622–633. His conclusion (based on 1959–60 cost and earnings data): "Rates on time deposits currently being paid by banks are above the optimum rate and may be above the break-even rate."

toward a relaxation of monetary restraints unless such growth has a dampening effect on the economy, a not unlikely possibility since savings held in the form of time deposits are lost to investment (and to any other type expenditure) so long as they are so held. Such a cessation of the circuit income and transactions velocity of funds, funds which constitute a prior cost of production, cannot but have deleterious effects in our highly interdependent pecuniary economy.

The extent of these effects and the exact reaction of the monetary authorities to them are, of course, indeterminate. But we know this: if bank profits are insulated against encroachment by sharply rising costs of time deposit banking, a by-product must be a large dosage of new money in the economy. The propriety of further diluting our money supply in order to overcome the economic handicap presented by a remediable institutional arrangement is certainly open to question.

The much larger question with which we should be concerned, therefore, is the *raison d'etre* of an institutional arrangement whose benefits to the banks are dubious and which undoubtedly exerts deleterious effects on the financial intermediaries and on the economy.

This would seem to be one of those rare instances in which public policy could simultaneously serve the welfare interests of the community and the profit interests of the specific groups immediately affected. Rather than encourage time deposit banking by raising interest ceilings on, and lowering reserve ratios against, time deposits as the bankers and their associations have advocated, and as has been done by our monetary authorities; Congress, the state legislatures, and our national and state monetary authorities—in the interest of the commercial banks, the financial intermediaries and above all in the interest of the community—should pursue every possible means for promoting the orderly and continuous flow of monetary savings into real investment.

The retention of the present ban on interest payments on demand deposits, and the elimination of time deposit banking from the structure of our commercial banking system, will contribute to a realization of this objective.

Selection 16

SHOULD COMMERCIAL BANKS ACCEPT SAVINGS DEPOSITS?

EDWARD E. EDWARDS

Professor Edwards argues that commercial banks must seek time deposits in order to maintain their relative position as financial institutions, that they can profitably accept time deposits, and that their continued importance as a financial institution serving almost all segments of the economy—in contrast to other financial institutions, many of which serve in general only one major sector of the economy—is in the public interest.

• From Edward E. Edwards, "Should Commercial Banks Accept Savings Deposits?" Part II, *Proceedings of the 1961 Conference on Savings and Residential Financing,* May 11 and 12, 1961, pp. 29–38. Reprinted by permission of the United States Savings and Loan League and the author.

Should commercial banks accept savings deposits? I have broken this up into what seemed to me to be two logical parts: First, should banks as a matter of their own management policy accept savings deposits? Second, should banks as a matter of public policy be encouraged to accept savings deposits? This approach seemed to offer the best means of identifying and clarifying any issue of conflict between the self-interest of individual banks and the public interest.

In looking into the reasons why banks, as a matter of management policy, should accept—and promote—savings deposits, the most overpowering reason seems to be that this is absolutely necessary for most banks if they expect to maintain their relative position as financial institutions in the communities they serve. With the possible exception of a few large money centers, no community can provide demand deposits in adequate volume to serve as the sole source of funds for an ambitious bank, much less two or more competing banks. While demand deposit banking might still be profitable, not many bankers are going to be satisfied in a situation in which one after another savings and loan association or other specialized financial institution passes the banks in size.

In many cities the largest financial institution today is a savings and loan association that a decade or so ago was "dwarfed" by the leading bank. In other cities the emergence of an association as the leading institution has been delayed by one or more mergers of competing banks, but quite obviously there is a limit to this means of preventing the inevitable. Thus, ambitious bankers must aggressively build deposits; and, as we shall see, savings deposits offer the best opportunity for deposit building.

BANKS NEED MORE FUNDS TO MEET LOAN DEMANDS

Ambition is not the only reason that banks need to expand their savings deposits. Banks need more funds to meet loan demands. For many years loans have been increasing more rapidly than demand deposits. For example, bank loans increased $56 billion between 1947 and 1957, a decade in which demand deposits increased by only $30 billion. Between 1957 and 1960, loans increased by $24 billion and demand deposits by only $5 billion. Banks have made up these differences in various ways, including selling governments, reducing their primary reserves, investing new capital, retaining earnings, and increasing time and savings deposits.

Bank loans for all banks combined at the end of 1960 exceeded 90 per cent of demand deposits, as compared with less than 60 per cent in 1950 and approximately 30 per cent at the end of World War II. For many individual banks, loans have long since exceeded demand deposits. This situation has not come about from any lack of competitive effort in deposit building. It has resulted from the following simple, basic fact: the combined borrowing (or credit) needs of a bank's customers exceed their combined ability or willingness to hold cash.

Actually, this disparity is far greater than the banking statistics suggest. Despite the great increase in bank loans, borrowing needs that might have been filled by banks have been met to a large extent outside the banking system, with funds provided by the banks' own customers who preferred to hold commercial or finance paper, share accounts, or other financial assets or near monies rather than demand deposits.

Bankers have become all too familiar with corporate treasurers who want to earn something on their "idle" cash balances and with individual depositors who have the ability to carry large deposit balances but want to earn something on their liquid funds. Money, whether in currency or demand deposits, is no longer such a desirable asset that the demand for it is unlimited. Except for a necessary minimum balance, almost any other asset seems to be more desirable than cash.

The individual bank cannot concern itself with concepts such as the idea that banks create the money they loan. The individual bank can only loan (or invest) what it has received from its depositors. Thus, when loan demand increases and investment portfolios have been shrunk to minimum liquidity needs, the only hope is increased deposits.

How can a bank increase its deposits? By getting more depositors and by getting present depositors to keep larger balances. Neither is easy if the bank can offer only demand deposit service. People already have all the checking accounts they want, and all the money they want in them. Thus, a bank which grows only through demand deposits seems doomed to a rate of growth no greater, probably less, than the over-all economic growth of its community. And even to achieve this, it must compete aggressively with other banks.

If banks could pay interest on demand deposits, perhaps they could induce their depositors to carry larger balances. That is another argument, however, as is also the desirability of competing more aggressively for time deposits of corporations.

In this paper I have rather arbitrarily assumed that the term "savings deposits" means the interest-bearing deposits of individuals, thus leaving for the term "time deposits" the interest-bearing deposits of corporations. Most of the arguments for promoting savings deposits also apply to time deposits. The prospects for building up corporate holdings of time deposits do not seem very bright for most banks, however, even including the large, money-market banks that serve large corporations. To compete with commercial paper, Treasury bills, short-term paper in foreign markets and the like, banks certainly would need more freedom than they now have in adjusting interest rates and maturities to changing conditions in the money markets.

Of course, banks could raise additional capital funds, but any substantial increase in capital would quickly drive down earnings per share to a level that would prohibit further sale of stock. Capital funds can never be more than a cushion to protect deposits; and unless capital can be matched by many times its amount in deposits, it will not be forthcoming.

THE ALTERNATIVE TO SAVINGS DEPOSIT GROWTH

With dim prospects for growth from other sources—demand deposits, time deposits of corporations, capital—it would seem rather obvious that promotion of personal savings is absolutely necessary for the ambitious bank. This conclusion becomes even more obvious when we consider what happens when banks fail to promote savings aggressively.

When banks fail to expand their savings deposits to meet growing loan demand, they encourage the growth of the nonbanking intermediaries. The willing but unsatisfied borrowers offer the opportunity, and the willing but unrewarded and unsolicited savers offer the means, for savings and loan associations and other nonbanking intermediaries to flourish. While this might not be too bitter a pill for the bankers to swallow if nothing else happened, the bankers sooner or later begin to realize that the growth of the nonbanking intermediaries makes it unnecessary for the banking system to expand and that the monetary authorities, with an eye on credit needs, are refusing to make additional reserves available to the banks. Under such conditions, competition of banks for additional demand deposits cannot possibly increase their total size. Meanwhile, competition among nonbanking intermediaries further accelerates their growth; and the greater their success, apparently, the more doomed the banks are to remain at existing levels.

Even this might not be too bad, since there will always be wars and depressions during which easy money policies will again give the banks a chance to grow. The trouble here is that, unless the banks can convert the newly created money into something people want (for example, savings deposits), depositors will, when the war or depression is over, transfer their funds into the near monies, since these serve liquidity needs and also pay interest. Then the rapid growth of the nonbanking intermediaries and the resulting credit expansion will again bring back restrictive monetary policies, and the banks will cease to grow.

Somewhere along the way the nonbanking intermediaries, which originally had only limited powers, will begin seeking broader investment powers, insurance of their obligations, expansion of their markets and other favors, no doubt including the right to offer checking account services. They may succeed, too, since they can show how necessary their continued growth is in terms of meeting credit needs.

What a colossal blow it will be to the banker who refused to promote savings deposits in order to be a commercial banker, to find that the "upstairs building and loan association" or the "Friday night credit union" or the "fly-by-night finance company" is now the biggest commercial bank!

Yes, ambition alone is sufficient reason why banks should promote savings deposits. But there is at least one other reason. Savings deposits can be profitable.

TIME DEPOSITS CAN BE PROFITABLE

Professor Pritchard has referred to studies of the profitability of savings deposits, all of which suggested to him that such deposits are not profitable. I have seen these studies, too, but do not reach the same conclusion. What the studies show, primarily, is that savings deposits are not as profitable as demand deposits or, rather, that banks with a high percentage of demand to total deposits are generally more profitable than banks with a high percentage of savings to total deposits. This should have been rather obvious without any studies, but this conclusion does not answer the question: Are savings deposits profitable?

To digress for a moment and take a look at the statistical evidence, what we see is that banks that have no trouble reaching a satisfactory size with demand deposits do not need to promote savings. They are like married men whose incomes are so large their wives do not have to work. On the average, their single income probably exceeds the combined income of husbands and wives who both work and who both have to work because the husband's income is so small. If so, would this prove that it is not profitable for wives to work?

The same data that show that the most profitable banks have the highest percentage of demand deposits will also show that the most profitable banks paid the most taxes. Should we conclude that the road to profit is to pay more taxes? The most profitable banks may contribute most to local colleges and universities, too; but I, for one, would not tell an unprofitable bank that the way to make a profit would be to endow a chair in banking.

To return to the argument, the banker's question should be this: Are savings deposits sufficiently profitable to justify the promotion of savings business?

Since each bank must answer this question for itself, we might first classify all banks into three broad groups. The first group includes those banks that have more than adequate deposits to meet loan demand. Until recently many, perhaps most, banks were in this group, and had been for many years. Quite obviously the promotion of savings deposits might not seem to be profitable to them in the short run. But not too many banks remain in this group.

More banks are in a second group, which may be described as those that are fully loaned up in terms of deposits but not in terms of capital structure. Quite obviously it would be profitable for these banks to promote savings deposits if this did not reduce demand deposits and if the net earnings on the new money exceeded its cost.

Will promotion of savings deposits by banks in this group decrease their demand deposits? Probably so; but if so, the banks are eventually going to lose this part of their demand deposits anyway, through competition from nonbanking intermediaries. Will the net earnings on the new money exceed its cost? Yes, as we shall see.

Finally, there is a third group of banks, those that are fully loaned up in terms of both capital structure and deposits. Is it profitable for them to promote savings when, if they suceed, they must raise additional capital?

Let us assume that such banks will be required by supervisory authorities to raise $1 in capital for each $10 increase in savings. If they use the capital funds for necessary cash reserves and highly liquid assets, with a net return on the total of only 1 per cent, and invest the deposit funds in an equal mixture of home mortgage loans and consumer credit paper, what will be the result?

Judging from the gross earnings, the expenses and the allowances for bad debts on this kind of portfolio in banks, and from the experience of nonbanking intermediaries, savings thus invested should earn a minimum of 4 per cent, and more likely 4½ per cent. This would permit a 3 per cent to 3½ per cent rate on savings, and earnings before taxes of from 11 per cent to 16 per cent on capital, or after tax earnings from 5½ per cent to 8 per cent on capital. If from 20 per cent to 30 per cent of the savings were invested in municipal bonds, the before tax earnings on capital would be cut somewhat, but there would be little tax to pay, and net profit after taxes might run to 10 per cent or better.

REGULATORY CHANGES NEEDED

While these rates of return are not fabulous, they would seem to be more than adequate to justify additional investment of capital, whether through retention of earnings or sale of additional stock. However, savings deposits would be even more profitable if certain unnecessary and undesirable legal restrictions could be removed from our laws and regulatory codes or could be modified.

The first of these is the 5 per cent non-income-producing legal service.* There is no longer any need for such a requirement. I should be glad to argue the point if necessary, but at the moment I wish merely to point out that the cost of maintaining this reserve falls heavily on bank stockholders. If we assume a 10-to-one deposit-capital ratio, the reserve requirement in effect requires one-half of the capital investment to be tied up in nonearning assets. My estimate would be that elimination of the reserve requirement would, without any deterioration in liquidity, increase the return on capital (that is, that part of a bank's capital supporting its savings) by a full 2 per cent before taxes, 1 per cent or more after taxes. This would be an increase in rate of return of as much as one-fifth, or more than enough to justify aggressive promotion of savings by quite a few bankers who now believe that savings are unprofitable.

A second restriction that makes the savings business less profitable than it might be, and which should be liberalized or removed, is the legal language that keeps banks from competing effectively in the home mortgage markets. I refer to the limitations on amount of loan as percentage of appraised value, limits on maturities, rigid requirements as to amortization and finally limits on total size of portfolio. Why is it that banks are free to use their own judgment when they finance cars, boats, trailers, college educations, vacations, funerals and other personal needs, but must abide by some unproved, probably false, standards when financing people's homes? What sense does it make for the federal government to permit mutual savings and loan associations, without any capital base, but whose savings the government is insuring, to make loans under terms which the government forbids to commercial banks, whose savings are also insured, and which have a capital base over and above their reserves for losses? Rather, what sense does it make to prohibit the banks, which have risk capital to fall back on, from making loans under terms that the government approves for insured savings associations, which have no risk capital?

* *Editor's note:* This requirement may be varied between 3 and 6 per cent; it was changed to 4 per cent in 1962.

Of course, banks do not have to invest savings deposits in home mortgages, and this is one of the important advantages they have over most of the non-banking intermediaries. Home mortgages probably never were as profitable as consumer paper, and frequently are less profitable than corporate bonds. In periods of tight money, business loans, with their compensatory balances, probably have a better yield than mortgages. However, for most communities a bank that wants to build savings probably will have to compete aggressively in the home mortgage market.

Two other restrictions on savings growth are closely related but greatly misunderstood. I refer to the traditional capital requirements enforced on banks and the difference in provisions for tax-free loss reserves for banks and for mutual savings institutions. Of the two, the capital requirement is by far the more serious, although quite a few bankers mistakenly believe the tax difference is more important.

Let us assume, first, that there is no such thing as federal income tax but that we do have federal insurance of savings. Can commercial banks and mutual savings institutions compete fairly? Unless the commercial banks have substantially better investment opportunities or lower cost, they cannot possibly pay as high a return on savings as the mutuals. Since bank capital cannot on its own earn a return adequate to attract equity funds, the commercial banks must take out something from the return on savings to add to the return on capital funds in order to pay stockholders a satisfactory return. Thus, if savings earn 4 per cent for both banks and mutuals, and the mutuals pay 4 per cent, a bank may not be able to pay more than 3½ per cent.

Now let us assume a federal income tax on corporations, but with identical provisions for tax-free reserves for all types of financial institutions. With a 50 per cent tax on corporate earnings, and a one-to-10 capital requirement, commercial banks would be squeezed down to a 3 per cent rate of interest to depositors even though their savings earned 4 per cent. This would place them at a distinct disadvantage, even though they had the same formula as the mutuals for tax-free loss reserves.

When we allow mutual institutions to accumulate relatively larger tax-free loss reserves, they have an additional slight advantage; but the really important competitive disadvantage of the banks is their capital requirement. In other words, banks are expected to have a substantial net sound capital over and above loss reserves, and mutual institutions are not. Since both are insured, it would seem that what is adequate for the one would be adequate for the other.

What banks should seek, rather than changes in the way mutuals are taxed, would, in my opinion, be one or both of the following:

1. A change in bank capital requirement formulas which in effect would eliminate or greatly reduce the need for capital behind savings deposits. Counting loss reserves as a part of capital in the formula, and permitting larger tax-free reserves, would be a logical step forward.

2. Legislation or regulatory changes that would limit interest or dividends by mutual institutions whose reserves for losses do not come up to minimum standards. Stiffer requirements for allocation of earnings to reserves would serve this purpose.

While neither of these proposals may be politically feasible, they would, if strongly advocated, contribute to clearer thinking about the two types of savings institutions we have in our economy. With a better understanding of the two, we should be able to develop a public policy that would provide for the growth of both types, in an environment in which competition will occur between savings institutions in the market place, where it belongs, rather than between trade associations in the political arena, where it does not belong.

PUBLIC POLICY AND TIME DEPOSITS

Now for the second part of our main question: Should banks as a matter of public policy be encouraged to accept savings deposits? My answer to this part of the question also is "yes." The reason is simple. Unless banks do grow, and grow steadily and substantially, credit needs will not be met as fully or as efficiently as required for economic growth. Unless bank growth comes largely in savings deposits, it will not occur.

Although I am prepared to argue that commercial banks are efficient allocators of financial resources, in the interest of time I merely call attention to their widespread distribution, their broad lending and investment powers, and their competent although frequently conservative management. With adequate time, I would present the case for a system of financial institutions in which the specialized intermediaries supplement and perhaps stimulate the more generalized and more adequately financed banks. A financial system in which the banks play a minor role among specialized giants would, in my opinion, be less efficient, less responsive to public needs, more unstable in the short run and less conducive to economic growth. I hope you agree.

As to the impossibility of banks growing very rapidly if they depend solely on demand deposits, I hope I have made that point in dealing with banks as individual firms. I do want to add, however, that the ability of banks to grow in demand deposits depends on monetary policy, and that an easy money policy such as would permit substantial growth in demand deposits would quickly become inflationary and unsustainable except in time of war—or perhaps severe depression. Why? Because we do not want—and our economy does not need—a rapidly growing money supply. But the economy does need a rapidly growing volume of savings.

Professor Pritchard showed very clearly that current savings transferred to nonbanking intermediaries do become invested and that no expansion in the banking system is necessary to accommodate this saving. He also demonstrated that without expansion of the banking system, current saving cannot be accommodated if savers choose bank savings deposits as their savings medium. He then concluded that the bank system will not expand or cannot expand, hence that savings deposits are lost to investment; and he stated that "the burden of proof is upon those who would contend that a shift from demand to time deposits will induce the Reserve authorities to follow an easier (or less restrictive) monetary policy." I accept this burden.

Let us see what would happen if people chose to let their "money" savings accumulate in savings deposits in the banks. Would the deposits become stagnant, as Professor Pritchard suggested? Or would they be "activated" by monetary policy that permitted banks to expand, hence to "accommodate" the savings generated by their depositors? There is no question in my mind. I cannot conceive of a monetary authority that paid no attention to whether savings are accumulating in banks or in nonbanking intermediaries.

This point can best be answered, perhaps, by asking ourselves what we would do if we were the monetary authority and were faced with a return—or attempted return—of savings from nonbanking intermediaries back to the banks. For example, suppose for some reason people decided they would rather have their savings in banks than in savings associations. As associations began losing their cash balances, stopped making new loans, and increased their borrowing from the Federal Home Loan Banks, would we not begin to make reserves available to the banking system so that banks could buy some Home Loan Bank obligations, make some mortgage loans, or buy some bonds so that insurance companies could make some mortgage loans? And would the doing of these things not increase deposits so that the banking system could accommodate the attempted transfer of funds from associations to banks? The answer would have to be "yes" unless we were blind to the financial needs of our economy.

Savings deposits in banks are not stagnant, nor are they lost to investment. Our banking system can invest any amount of savings its depositors wish to accumulate, and monetary policy will make certain that this is so.

But monetary policy will also see to it that in prosperity the banking system does not grow beyond its depositors' desire to hold bank deposits. If banks are to grow, they must increase the demand for their special types of financial assets and decrease the demand for the types offered by nonbank intermediaries. At the moment, savings deposits are the only type banks have to offer for which the demand seems subject to very much increase. Therefore, banks should promote savings as a matter of self-interest, and banks should be encouraged to promote savings as a matter of public policy.

Selection 17

SHOULD COMMERCIAL BANKS ACCEPT SAVINGS DEPOSITS?

LESTER V. CHANDLER

In this final selection on the subject of the competition for time deposits, Professor Chandler attempts to evaluate the major arguments. He shows that key questions relate to the extent to which the monetary authorities change their monetary policy when there is a shift from demand deposits to time deposits, the extent to which an increase in velocity of demand deposits may offset any decline in demand deposits, and the probable behavior of the public in the event that commercial banks did not, or were not permitted to, accept time deposits—would the public simply hold more demand deposits, or would it reduce its demand deposit holdings and hold shares in savings and loan associations and other money substitutes?

• From Lester V. Chandler, "Should Commercial Banks Accept Savings Deposits?" Part III, *Proceedings of the 1961 Conference on Savings and Residential Financing,* May 11 and 12, 1961, pp. 40–48. Reprinted by permission of the United States Savings and Loan League and the author.

Both speakers have raised three principal questions: First, are savings deposits profitable for the banking system as a whole? Second, are savings deposits profitable for the individual bank? And third, is it in the public interest for commercial banks to accept savings deposits? We have had something less than unanimous agreement here. I shall not pretend that I know the truth, but I can perhaps spotlight some of the reasons for the differences in judgment that you have heard.

I shall spend most of my time on the first question, namely: Are savings deposits profitable for the commercial banking system as a whole? I am going to take a fairly long view, allowing enough time for changes in institutional structure, changes in attitudes, advertising and that sort of thing, which seems to me appropriate in view of the nature of the debate.

Professor Pritchard's argument, as I understand it, is that the commercial banking system is not enabled to increase its earnings assets at all when the public decreases its holdings of demand deposits and holds savings deposits instead. He believes that if all the banks refused to accept savings deposits, the public would merely shift its holdings to demand deposits, that the banking system in the final outcome would not suffer a decrease in its total earning assets and that banks would be more profitable because they would escape the payment of interest on savings accounts.

THE CASE WITH A NEUTRAL MONETARY POLICY

I shall analyze this argument in several easy stages. To do so I shall use a highly simplified model in order to reduce the number of variables to be considered. Specifically, I shall assume that there is no net currency drain from the banking system and no net inflow of currency to the banking system, that legal reserve requirements against demand deposits average 15 per cent and that reserve requirements against savings deposits are 5 per cent.

Suppose, now, that the public shifts $1,000 from demand deposits to savings deposits. The immediate results will of course be to increase excess reserves by $100. Required reserves against demand deposits are reduced by $150 and required reserves against savings deposits are increased by $50. This can be stated as follows:

$$E = \$1,000 \ (r_d - r_s),$$

where E is the change in excess reserves, r_d is the required ratio against demand deposits, and r_s the required ratio against savings deposits. Endowed with $100 of new excess reserves, the banking system can proceed to expand its loans. If all the proceeds of the loans give rise to demand deposits, the amount of expansion will be $100/0.15 or $666.67. Summarizing the effects of all these operations, we find that the balance sheet of the banking system has been changed as follows:

Assets	Liabilities
	D — $1,000
	T + $1,000
Loans + $666.67	D + $ 666.67

Thus, the net change in bank liabilities will be an increase of $1,000 in savings deposits and net decrease of $333.33 in demand deposits. On the asset side there will be a net loan increase of $666.67.

I am sure that Professor Pritchard and Professor Edwards would agree that this would be the outcome if the central bank followed a "neutral" policy. Instead, it will note the rise of net free reserves of the banking system and the easing of money market conditions, owing to the new loans that flow into it, and will mop up the newly created excess reserves to prevent a change in the credit situation. In this case, the banking system will not be permitted to expand its loans at all and the net outcome will be merely a $1,000 decrease in demand deposits and a $1,000 increase in savings deposits, on which the banks will now have to pay interest.

LONG-RUN OBJECTIVE OF FEDERAL RESERVE POLICY

I approach the matter in a somewhat different way. I agree that in the short run the Federal Reserve often looks to such things as the status of excess reserves, member bank borrowings and the degree of tightness or ease in the money markets. But surely a more basic and, over a longer run, a far more important objective is to secure some desired behavior of the level of spending for output—to achieve a certain level of GNP, or to cause the level of GNP to increase at some desired rate. Let us suppose the Fed's objective is to achieve a certain level of spending for GNP which I shall designate as y_o.

I measure the quantity of money on the horizontal axis and the level of GNP on the vertical axis. The amount of money that will be needed for this purpose will depend, of course, on the public's demand for money balances. This is illustrated by the line D_oD_o in the figure which follows. Let us assume that this is a demand for money balances on the part of the community. Now, if we are to maintan this level of GNP measured vertically, then the required money supply would of course be the line M_oM_o. Any larger amount of money would give us an unwanted expansionary force and a smaller amount would prevent us from achieving the desired level.

Suppose, now, that the $1,000 shift from demand to savings deposits reflects an equal decrease in the public's demand for money balances. This is shown on the illustration as a $1,000 leftward shift of the demand function. Assume that we simply shift this demand function to the left by $1,000, the new line being indicated by D_1D_1. It is perfectly obvious that with the decrease in demand for money balances, there will be created an excess supply of money at the y_o level of GNP, which will exert an upward pressure on the rate of spending for output. If an increase in spending is not to occur, then the money supply will have to mop up all the excess reserve created by the shift from demand to savings deposits so that the banks cannot expand their earning assets at all.

Thus, it appears that whether you accept Professor Pritchard's assumptions that the Federal Reserve will act to prevent an easing of the money market, or my assumption that it will act to prevent an unwanted rise of GNP, the

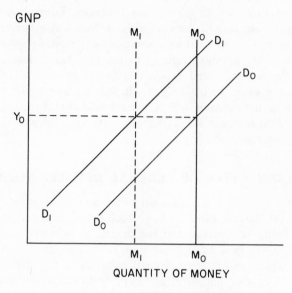

Figure 1

banking system will not be allowed to enjoy any increase in its earning assets simply because the public has shifted its holdings from demand to savings deposits. It would appear at this stage that it is Pritchard, and not Edwards who is right.

ALTERNATIVES TO TIME DEPOSIT BANKING

But the game is not over yet. Pritchard can claim to have established his conclusion that the banking system would be better off if it did not accept savings deposits at all, only if he can get favorable answers to at least two other questions. The first is this: What would the public elect to hold in place of the savings deposits that are no longer available; would it simply hold more demand deposits, or would it shift to holding other liquid claims, such as accounts at mutual savings banks, credit unions, or savings and loan associations? The second question is this: Are accounts at other financial intermediaries as good a substitute for money balances as savings deposits at commercial banks; will a shift by the public from demand deposits to, say, savings and loan shares decrease the demand for money balances as much as would an equal shift from demand deposits to savings deposits?

We can go along with Pritchard's conclusions only if we find at least one of these propositions to be true: (1) that the public, if deprived of savings deposits at banks, would shift most of these holdings to demand deposits; or (2) that accounts at other financial intermediaries are not nearly as good a substitute for money balances as are savings deposits at banks. If we grant Pritchard either of these propositions, we have probably granted him his case.

We do not, of course, know what would happen, but I gravely doubt that Pritchard is right on either count. My guess is that if savings deposits at banks were not available, the public would hold instead, not more demand deposits, but more liquid assets of other kinds. In this they would not be exactly discouraged by credit unions, savings banks, savings and loan associations, and others. Beguiling advertising, free pencils and pressure cookers, and perhaps new services would all play their part in the process. Moreover, I suspect that these other liquid assets are as good, or almost as good, a substitute for money balances as are savings deposits. I believe that the public can and does reduce its demand for money balances by shifting to holdings of, say, savings and loan shares just as it does by shifting to savings deposits.

SHIFT TO SAVINGS AND LOAN ACCOUNTS

Let us see what would happen if the banks refused to make savings deposits available and if the public decided to shift $1,000 from demand deposits to savings and loan shares. The immediate effects on the balance sheets of the banks and the savings and loan associations would be as follows:

Commercial Banks		Savings and Loan Associations	
Assets	Liabilities	Assets	Liabilities
	Deposits due public — $1,000	Deposits + $1,000	Shares + $1,000
	Deposits due savings and loans + $1,000		

At the banks, the only thing that would happen in the first instance would be that demand deposits owed to the public would go down by $1,000 and those owed to savings and loan associations would go up by $1,000. Then, the savings and loan associations would have plus $1,000 holdings of deposits and plus $1,000 liabilities in the form of shares. Thus far we see that the banks have experienced no change in their total deposits, their total reserves or their net reserve position, so their lending power remains unchanged. But the savings and loan associations have a $1,000 increase in their cash holdings. They can therefore increase their loans by that amount minus any amount they elect to retain as a reserve against the increase in their outstanding shares. Suppose they retain $50, or 5 per cent of the increase in their shares, and lend $950 to the public. When this is all over, the change in their balance sheets from their initial position will be as follows:

Commercial Banks		Savings and Loan Associations	
Assets	Liabilities	Assets	Liabilities
	Deposits due public — $50	Deposits + $ 50	Shares + $1,000
	Deposits due savings and loans + $50	Loans + $950	

For the commercial banks, deposits due to the public are down $50, deposits due to savings and loans are up $50 and, of course, the savings and loan associations will have increased their deposit holdings $50 and their loans $950. So at this stage we find that after the savings and loan associations have used the new funds, $50 has been used to increase their cash holdings and $950 to increase their loans. Still, the total deposits of the banking system remain unchanged.

But we are not yet through. The $950 increase of loans by the savings and loan associations is in addition to the supply of loanable funds and will presumably tend to lower interest rates and stimulate spending. If the Federal Reserve wishes to maintain the pre-existing degree of ease or tightness in credit markets, it will have to force the banks to reduce their deposits and their loans. In effect, the Federal Reserve will say to the banks, "Because the public has shifted its funds from you to the savings and loan associations, we are forcing you to reduce your loans."

Let me use here the same approach that I used earlier in connection with the public shift from demand deposits to savings deposits at banks. You will remember that I assumed that the $1,000 shift from demand to savings deposits reflected an equal decrease, a leftward shift, of the public's demand for money balances. Professor Pritchard did not, I believe, object to this assumption. I shall now assume that the $1,000 shift from demand deposits to savings and loan shares reflects an equal decrease in the public's demand for money balances. This creates an excess supply of money at the y_0 level of GNP and generates an upward pressure on the rate of spending. To prevent any rise of spending, the Federal Reserve will have to reduce the money supply by an amount equal to the decrease in the public's demand for money balances, that is, by $1,000. The banks will be forced to decrease both their deposits and their loans by $1,000.

Let us now compare the two cases. In the first case, where the public shifted from demand deposits to savings deposits at commercial banks, the final outcome was that the banks were not permitted to increase their earning assets at all. The banks now had to pay interest on the $1,000 of new savings deposits but were permitted no increase in their lending power. In the second case, where the public shifted from demand deposits to savings and loan accounts, the final outcome was that the commercial banks had to reduce their loans by $1,000. Thus the moral would seem to be that if banks accept savings deposits they may not increase their total lending power, but if they do not accept savings deposits they will have to reduce their loans.

In short, I contend that it may indeed have been an unhappy day for the commercial banks when highly liquid assets were invented to compete with demand deposits. These other forms of liquid holdings tend to decrease the public's demand for demand deposits, or at least to slow their rate of secular increase, and thus to hold down the amount of earning assets that commercial banks can acquire by issuing this form of liability. Professor Pritchard is quite right, of course, in pointing out that commercial banks tend to compete with themselves when they issue savings deposits. I contend that highly liquid earning assets will be made available to the public anyway, and will be demanded by the public whether or not banks accept savings deposits. I have noticed no marked reluctance on the part of savings and loan associations, savings banks, credit unions and others to manufacture these liquid claims. My guess is that over a period of time—and I want to emphasize that this may not happen immediately—a refusal by commercial banks to accept savings deposits would bring about, not an increase in the public's demand for money balances, but a shift of funds from savings deposits to claims against these other institutions. Thus, the existence of other liquid claims may indeed reduce the profitability of commercial banking, but my point is that the profits of banking may be less adversely affected if banks continue to accept savings deposits, so that they, and not other types of institutions, hold the earning assets back of the various types of savings accounts.

THE CASE FOR INDIVIDUAL BANKS

This brings us to one of the other major questions: Is it profitable for the individual commercial bank to accept savings deposits?

Here again the answer is greatly affected by one's assumptions concerning the source of savings deposits at the individual bank. One possibility is that savings deposits at the banks represent merely a shift from demand deposits at that bank, and that the demand deposits would have continued to be held at that bank even if it refused to accept savings deposits. In such cases a bank would almost certainly reduce its profits by allowing its own customers to shift from demand to savings accounts. But I doubt the quantitative importance of such cases over a longer period. My guess is that most savings deposits represent funds that would be shifted to other institutions or other liquid earning assets if the individual bank refused to pay interest on them. The individual bank would not have the funds for free; it would not have them at all. In other words, in determining its revenues and costs from savings accounts, a bank is in much the same situation as a savings and loan association.

But even assuming that a bank would otherwise lose the funds represented by its savings deposits, is it profitable for the bank to accept savings deposits? I must confess that I have little to contribute on this subject except to deplore our lack of relevant information. I find it impossible to interpret the various statistics that show lower percentage profits on net worth for banks as the percentage of their savings deposits to total deposits rises. These may indeed reflect faithfully the rates of profits actually enjoyed on the over-all business of the banks. But they cannot, of course, get directly to the crucial question: Would the bank's profits be higher or lower if the bank divorced itself completely from all savings deposit business? To answer this crucial question we need some sort of accounting on the basis of marginal revenues and marginal costs. I find it hard to believe that many banks, already equipped to do a demand deposit business with all that it entails, would find that adding on savings deposits would increase their costs more than it would increase their revenues.

I do not see why a commercial bank should decrease its profits by adding savings deposits to its demand deposit business, while mutual savings banks operate profitably on the basis of savings accounts alone. If this is the case, there must be something wrong about the portfolio composition of commercial banks, or savings banks, or both. And the appropriate remedy would be, not to take commercial banks out of the savings business, but to review both government regulation and managerial policies relative to portfolios.

TIME DEPOSITS AND THE PUBLIC INTEREST

I turn now to the third question: Is it in the public interest for the commercial banks to accept savings deposits? This involves several issues. I confess that I cannot accept Professor Pritchard's argument that the existence of savings deposits arrests the flow of savings into investment. I do agree that savings deposits are "stagnant" in the sense that they are not used as a medium of payment and have a velocity of zero. But exactly the same thing is true of savings deposits of mutual savings banks, accounts at credit unions, and shares of savings associations. They also have a velocity of zero. What Pritchard should add is that the existence of these near-money substitutes decreases the demand for money balances proper and frees money for spending. In effect, it increases the income velocity of money.

Professor Pritchard emphasized his belief that if the banks refuse to accept savings deposits, the demand function for money balances would be larger; that is, the public would demand larger balances of demand deposits and other money relative to the level of GNP. I have already expressed my doubts about this. But suppose he is right; suppose that the public would indeed hold much larger money balances relative to GNP. I fail to see that this would be in the public interest. It might be profitable for the banks, which the monetary authorities would have to allow to create a larger volume of checking deposits and to acquire a larger volume of earning assets. But why be so solicitous about the banks rather than other financial institutions? Why try to deprive the public of attractive liquid assets that yield no income? I see no resulting public benefit that would justify depriving the public of such an attractive alternative.

In fact, such a policy, if it were successful, might well accentuate economic fluctuations by permitting an increase in the amplitude of fluctuations in the income velocity of money. The greater the holdings of money itself, in excess of the minimum amounts needed for current transactions, the greater the scope for activating these "idle balances" under boom conditions.

Let me make one final point. I believe that it is in the public interest for banks to accept savings deposits in order to increase the mobility of loan funds among their various possible uses, especially in local markets. Some of the banks' closest competitors for savings tend to restrict their loans to a narrow range of purposes; funds gathered by savings and loan associations, for example, are channeled principally into home mortgages. But banks lend for a much wider range of purposes; their loans range all the way from consumer credit and short-term and medium-term business loans to mortgages. I believe, therefore, that a larger volume of lending power in the hands of the banks would increase the fluidity of credit within local markets. Perhaps this situation will be remedied in the future by a broader diversification of the types of loans made by savings and loan associations and mutual savings banks. But, at least until that time comes, it will be useful to maintain a large lending power by commercial banks in the interest of the fluidity of credit among uses.

Part Three

FINANCIAL INSTITUTIONS AND THE MONEY MARKET

5

Money Markets

THE TERM "MONEY MARKET" IS SOMEWHAT MISLEADING. There is no single, homogeneous market for funds in the United States. Rather, there are numerous overlapping markets, each subject to partially separate forces of supply and demand. There are markets for long-term and short-term funds; for federal, state and local, and business borrowers; and for loans distinguished by the specific provisions of the debt agreement and by the collateral offered. All of these markets are interrelated; for each there are borrowers and lenders who participate in that particular market and also in others. Nevertheless, the specialization of financial functions—the financial counterpart to the minute division of labor that characterizes productive activity in the United States—does draw identifiable lines between them.

The selections in Chapter 5 are not intended, however, to provide exhaustive coverage of all types of financial institutions and their activities in the many markets in which financial claims are treated. Instead, we are concerned primarily with a highly specialized type of operation in short-term liquid assets which has come to be called "the" money market in common usage. This market has no physical location, no geographic boundaries; it is national in scope and the hundreds of thousands of actual or potential buyers and sellers are linked by telephone, wire, and mail. The primary functions of the money market, defined in this way, are (1) to provide an outlet for the surplus funds of financial institutions in highly liquid short-term securities; (2) to facilitate adjustment of the liquidity positions of both financial and non-financial business firms; (3) to facilitate short-term financing by government and corporate borrowers. In performing these essential functions the money market also makes it possible to carry out monetary, debt management and related governmental policies in an orderly and efficient manner.

To some extent, of course, a market for short-term funds has existed in the United States for many years. It has become a true money market, however, only with the huge expansion in the volume of government securities and the rise of specialized government security dealers on whom the forces affecting the supply of and demand for liquid assests is focused. The readings in Chapter 5 concentrate on the postwar development of the money market and the increasingly important role that it plays in the allocation of loanable funds and the implementation of government credit policies.

The major money market instruments are United States treasury bills and sometimes other government securities, commercial paper, either directly placed by sales finance companies or "dealer paper" handled through dealers, bankers' acceptances, and short-term tax-exempt securities issued by local public housing agencies and certain state and local government units. A relatively new money market instrument is the negotiable time certificate of deposit. These certificates have increased in volume very rapidly; at the end of 1963 it is estimated that there were $9.6 billion of time certificates of deposit, as compared with somewhat over $50 billion of treasury bills, $6.7 billion of commercial paper, $4.9 billion of short-term municipal securities and $2.9 billion of bankers' acceptances. A secondary market for time certificates of deposit has developed and market yields on certificates approximate those on prime commercial paper and bankers' acceptances. Thus the time deposit activities of commercial banks, discussed in the preceding chapter, have resulted in the last few years in an important change in the money market. Time certificates of deposit are not discussed in the selections in this chapter; for a brief review see "CDs As a Money Market Instrument," Federal Reserve Bank of Chicago, *Business Conditions,* August, 1964, pp. 11–16, and Morgan Guaranty Trust Company, *Money-Market Investments: The Risk and the Return* (New York: Morgan Guaranty Trust Company, 1964), esp. pp. 18–21.

Selection 18

THE FEDERAL FUNDS MARKET

A STUDY BY A FEDERAL RESERVE SYSTEM COMMITTEE

This selection describes the nature of the "Federal funds" market—the market for deposit balances at the Federal Reserve Banks. Since

• From *The Federal Funds Market,* May, 1959, pp. 1–12. Published in 1959 by the Board of Governors of the Federal Reserve System, Washington, D. C. Reprinted by permission of the Board of Governors of the Federal Reserve System.

some banks have excess reserves while other banks have reserve deficiencies, it is possible for banks having excess reserves to earn a small return on such funds by lending them, for a short time, to banks that need additional reserves. No additional reserves are supplied to the banking system by this process, but it makes possible more effective utilization of available reserves. Since checks drawn on deposit balances held in Federal Reserve Banks are payable immediately, banks that need funds can obtain them without delay. Interaction of demand and supply determines the rate paid for Federal funds; the rate tends to fluctuate rather widely, as demand shifts and supply changes. Thus it is a sensitive indicator of money market conditions.

The *Federal funds market* refers to the borrowing and lending of a special kind of money—deposit balances in the Federal Reserve Banks—at a specified rate of interest. Such transactions are commonly referred to in the financial markets as purchases and sales of Federal funds. As ordinarily used, the term does not include borrowing from the Reserve Banks.

The need for readily available media for adjusting cash and reserve positions is especially important for commercial banks which are required by law to maintain certain minimum reserves against their deposits. A multitude of business and financial transactions are constantly shifting funds among the upwards of 13,000 independent banks, so that some have excess reserves and others have deficiencies. The larger banks in financial centers are especially subject to wide day-to-day swings in their reserve positions. For these larger banks particularly, the Federal funds market is an important method of making adjustments for these daily changes.

ORIGIN AND GROWTH OF FEDERAL FUNDS MARKET

The Federal funds market is not a recent development. It originated in New York City in the early twenties. Several conditions contributed to the emergence of the market at that time. The post-World War I depression resulted in sharp disparities in the reserve positions of New York City banks, some having substantial excesses and others having to borrow at the Reserve Bank. At times the discount rate was above some short-term market rates, providing an additional incentive for deficit banks to borrow excess reserves of other banks. Officials of some of the New York City banks talked things over and began buying and selling excess reserves to adjust their reserve positions. The transfer was usually accomplished by an exchange of checks—the lender's check being drawn on its reserve balance at the Federal Reserve Bank and presented for clearance the same day, that of the borrower being drawn on itself and payable through the clearing house the next day.

Although member banks were the first to buy and sell Federal funds, New York City acceptance houses, in their dealings with the Federal Reserve Bank of New York as well as in other transactions, received and paid out Federal funds in the normal course of their operations. Dealers with more Federal funds than needed in settling their own transactions began selling them in the market. Gradually, the acceptance dealers began to shop among the banks for funds, getting daily information about the demand and the available supply. Soon the dealers began to buy and sell Federal funds at a ¼ per cent spread and later, as interdistrict transactions developed, the spread sometimes reached 1 per cent because of discount rate differentials among the Reserve Banks. Usually, only small amounts were purchased outright, large amounts being acquired on an option basis.

New York City dominated the early Federal funds market, both in terms of volume of transactions and number of institutions participating. Local markets also developed in other financial centers, such as Chicago, Boston, Philadelphia, and San Francisco, but the volume of trading was much smaller than in New York City. There were some interdistrict transactions in Federal funds, but the volume was relatively small. New York City acceptance houses with branches in the principal cities, discount rate differentials which were common among the Reserve Banks, and the differences in time between East and West all contributed to the development of interdistrict trading in Federal funds.

There was little activity in the Federal funds market in the thirties. In the early thirties, doubt about the financial position of borrowing banks was a limiting factor. Later there was little need to borrow because of the large volume of excess reserves. During World War II and immediately following, member banks had ready access to Reserve Bank credit through sales of government securities at pegged rates, and banks held such large amounts of these securities that there was little demand for Federal funds.

Several developments set the stage for a revival of the Federal funds market following World War II. As a result of a change in character, the call-loan market no longer served as a significant medium for adjusting bank reserve positions. Growth of the Treasury bill market provided a suitable means for most temporary adjustments but not for those expected to last for only one day or a few days. Activity in Federal funds was limited, however, as long as banks had ready access to reserves at low cost under the System's policy of supporting the prices of government securities.

Following the Federal Reserve-Treasury "accord," monetary policy became more flexible. In periods of credit restraint, member banks were forced to rely more frequently on borrowing to obtain needed reserves. The tendency was to increase the demand for Federal funds, and the rise in market rates made it more profitable to sell such funds. Dealers in government securities often found it both expensive and difficult in periods of tight money to meet their financing needs by borrowing from New York City banks. In seeking outside financing, dealers extended their contacts in the Federal funds market.

Several technical factors also contributed to the growth of the Federal funds market. The reduction in the deferred availability schedule in the collection of checks resulted in a substantial rise in float. Even though the impact of float on total reserves could be largely offset by System action, periodic fluctuations in the reserve positions of individual banks tended to encourage adjustments in the Federal funds market. Other factors that encouraged the use of Federal funds were an improvement in wire-transfer facilities and bank competition, particularly with respect to accommodating correspondent banks.

STRUCTURE OF THE MARKET

The Federal funds market, although national in scope, is loosely organized. Unlike the securities market, there are no dealers who maintain a position in Federal funds and stand ready to buy or sell at quoted prices.

The Federal funds market is predominantly a bank market. This was clearly revealed by interviews and daily reports of Federal funds transactions received from a sample of banks and dealers during November 1956. At that time, about 150 banks—mostly the larger ones in financial centers—were active participants in the market. In addition, a number of smaller though still sizable banks occasionally entered the market—usually as sellers of funds. Banks accounted for approximately 80 to 90 per cent of the total dollar volume of Federal funds transactions reported in the November survey.

Government securities dealers have become active participants in the Federal funds market in recent years. Dealers have been drawn into the market by the practice, which has grown rather rapidly in recent years, of settling government securities transactions in Federal funds. The bulk of the transactions in short-term issues and some of those in long-term issues are settled in Federal funds. As a result of this practice, dealers receive and pay out Federal funds in the ordinary course of their operations.

In recent years, dealers have also developed out-of-town sources of financing, both advances and repayments usually being made by wire transfer and consequently in Federal funds. Dealers, however, account for only a small part of total transactions—well below 10 per cent in the November 1956 survey. Other participants include foreign banks and their agencies in New York City, which are usually suppliers of Federal funds; and a few savings banks which occasionally participate in the market indirectly by asking their commercial banks to buy or sell Federal funds for them. This "other" group is relatively unimportant, supplying less than 8 per cent of the banks' purchases and accounting for less than 1 per cent of their sales of Federal funds in the November survey.

A stock brokerage firm in New York City, which is a member of the New York Stock Exchange, and the correspondent banking system play leading roles in bringing buyers and sellers of Federal funds together. The stock exchange firm operates purely as a broker, mostly with banks and on a national scale.[1]

Beginning early and continuing through most of the day, banks report their needs and offers of Federal funds to this brokerage firm, which attempts to put the two sides together as quickly as possible. The firm is often given considerable discretion, particularly by potential buyers, in arranging transactions. Sellers of funds are typically more discriminating, the most important limitation placed on the broker being a list of approved banks to which they

---

[1] Two other New York institutions recently instituted a brokerage service in Federal funds; however, the description of the activities of the broker who has been in this business for several years continues to be typical of the brokerage function in the Federal funds market.

are willing to sell Federal funds. The brokerage firm does not make a specific charge for its services. Most banks compensate the firm by giving it some of their stock brokerage business. A small percentage of the banks prefer to pay a flat fee, usually a commission of 1/16 of 1 per cent.

Correspondent banks also play a significant role in facilitating funds transactions. A large part of the total volume of transactions is among these banks. A few of the large city banks "accommodate" their correspondents—by buying from and selling Federal funds to them—even when the transactions run against their own reserve positions. A larger number buy and sell with correspondents only as needed in adjusting their own reserve positions. The large city correspondents are also sources of information on potential buyers and sellers of Federal funds, and the "going" rate; and the correspondent account is an important medium for handling interest payments on funds transactions.

MECHANICS OF OPERATION

The daily volume of bank purchases of Federal funds in November 1956 ranged from a low of $600 million to a high of $1.1 billion. Transactions in Federal funds fall into two general categories. About three-fourths of the dollar volume in November was in the form of overnight, unsecured loans. The remainder involved the transfer of securities either in the form of repurchase agreements or buybacks, the securities usually being run through a bank's books as an outright purchase or sale.

Under a repurchase agreement, the lender of funds buys securities, mostly short-term government securities, and the seller agrees to repurchase them within a stated time at an agreed price and rate of interest. In the case of a buyback, the lender enters into two contracts at the same time: one, to buy securities, usually Treasury bills, for delivery and payment the same day; the other, to sell the same issue of securities for delivery and payment the following day. In both contracts, settlement is in Federal funds. The securities are bought and sold at agreed prices, or rates of discount in the case of Treasury bills. The difference in prices or rates of discount represents the interest cost to the borrower of the Federal funds. It is significant that in both repurchase agreements and buybacks the risk of price change is eliminated. In this respect, repurchase agreements and buybacks differ from outright purchases and sales of securities. . . .

Transactions in Federal funds are typically negotiated by telephone and later confirmed by wire or letter. In transactions between banks in different Federal Reserve districts, the funds are advanced and repaid by wire transfer. The payment of interest, however, is usually by credit to a correspondent bank account. The mechanics of handling intracity transactions vary. Transactions among New York City banks are still settled by an exchange of checks—the lender giving a check on its reserve balance, and the borrowing bank giving its own check payable through the clearing house the next day. In cities other than New York, local transactions are usually negotiated by telephone and, upon instructions by draft or letter, settlement is by debits and credits to the reserve accounts.

Federal funds are typically traded in units of $1 million or more, but transactions for smaller amounts frequently occur. Some of the larger banks, as a matter of policy, buy and sell smaller amounts to accommodate their correspondents. When reserve positions are tight, banks may also be willing to deal in smaller units in order to meet their needs. . . .

USE OF MARKET BY BANKS

In recent years, most of the larger banks, in order to keep fully invested, have followed a policy of daily or at least very short-term adjustments in their reserve positions. Such a policy frequently requires quick turnarounds in the market; a bank may be a lender of excess reserves one day, a borrower to meet a deficiency the next. The Federal funds market is more suitable than the short-term securities market for these adjustments. A bank can lend excess reserves in the Federal funds market without incurring any risk of loss from a price change or without absorbing any cost from a spread between buying and selling prices. Call loans formerly had the same advantages, but in recent years they have taken on more of the characteristics of customer loans. Consequently, banks rarely ask immediate payment of call loans. . . .

Interviews with officials of banks active in the Federal funds market revealed rather wide variation in attitudes toward this method of adjusting reserve positions. On the basis of motives for using the market, banks may be classified into two broad groups—adjusting and accommodating banks. These groupings, however, are not mutually exclusive.

Most of the bank participants use the Federal funds market only in adjusting their own reserve positions—to dispose of an excess or to meet a deficiency. These banks seldom lend and borrow on the same day. They may do so occasionally when the morning estimates of their reserve positions prove to be inaccurate.

"Adjusting banks" may be subdivided into three groups. The largest consists of banks trying to balance out the reserve week without either an excess or a deficiency. These banks shift between lending and borrowing, as necessary, to dispose of an excess or to cover a deficiency in reserves. Another group, consisting mostly of the smaller banks active in the Federal funds market, follows a policy of keeping a cushion of excess reserves. These banks are typically sellers, rarely buyers. A third but small group of banks appears to use the Federal funds market, in part at least, to meet persistent reserve deficiencies. These banks are typically buyers of funds or, if both buyers and sellers, net buyers on balance.

Federal funds data for selected banks were available at the Reserve Banks of New York and Chicago for longer periods than at other Reserve Banks, and afforded a comparison of borrowing from the Reserve Banks with Federal funds transactions by the same banks. It appeared that the more or less continuous borrowers preferred the Federal funds market. Few of the banks, however, were able to meet all of their needs in the Federal funds market, and most of them had to resort occasionally to the discount window as well.

"Accommodating" banks use the Federal funds market for two purposes:

to adjust their own reserve positions, and to accommodate their correspondents and other customers. These banks, relatively few in number, commonly buy and sell Federal funds the same day. They are two-way traders, often engaging in accommodation transactions which are contrary to their own reserve positions.

The attitude of the larger banks toward buying and selling Federal funds to accommodate correspondents varies widely. A few banks pursue a policy of accommodation purchases and sales as a service to correspondents and as a means of broadening their contacts so that Federal funds will become a more reliable source of reserves. Other larger banks are opposed to such a policy. Important reasons given were the expense and inconvenience of handling a growing volume of small transactions, the dilemma of making unsecured loans to all correspondents or of incurring the ill will likely to be provoked by selectivity, and apprehension that in the long run accommodation purchases and sales might tend to reduce correspondent balances. Even though opposed in principle to accommodation purchases and sales, some large correspondent banks engage in such transactions when necessary to meet competition.

The extent to which banks use the Federal funds market in adjusting their reserve positions depends on several factors. Relative cost of alternative sources is an important but not necessarily a dominant consideration. The fact that the prevailing Federal funds rate does not rise above the discount rate, however, is evidence that preferences for the Federal funds market are normally not strong enough to induce banks to pay more than the cost of borrowing from a Reserve Bank.

Expectation as to the length of time a reserve excess or deficiency is likely to continue is another factor having a significant influence on choice of a reserve adjustment medium. The spread between bid and asked quotations and the risk of price change make the Treasury bill and other short-term securities unsuitable for very short-term reserve adjustments. On the other hand, short-dated securities are more suitable than Federal funds as a medium of adjustment for an excess or a deficiency expected to persist over a period of time. Inasmuch as Federal funds and the Treasury bill are used for largely different types of reserve adjustment, the Federal funds rate is not tied so closely to the bill rate as to the discount rate.

A third important influence on use of the Federal funds market is the attitude of bank officials toward borrowing from the Reserve Bank. Traditional reluctance toward borrowing from a Reserve Bank manifests itself in different ways. Some banks have a strong preference for the Federal funds market, using the Reserve Bank as a source of last resort. The majority of banks participating in the Federal funds market appear, however, to be willing to borrow at the Reserve Banks as well as in the market. Some prefer to borrow from a Reserve Bank to meet deficiencies, and to use the Federal funds market only to dispose of excess reserves.

Bank use of the Federal funds market is influenced by the attitude of officials toward such things as the convenience of using the Federal funds market and its reliability as a source of funds as compared to alternative adjusting media. Availability of Federal funds also affects the use of the market by banks. The supply available may be quite limited at times because excess reserves are held largely by banks which do not participate in the market.

DETERMINATION AND SIGNIFICANCE OF THE RATE

A New York City brokerage firm and correspondent banks play significant roles in bringing buyers and sellers together. As bids and offers begin coming in early in the morning, the broker attempts to match them and establish an opening rate. This opening rate is widely quoted as large banks and dealers call in to check on the rate. Some banks call their correspondent bank and government securities dealers to check on the rate.

The New York City rate tends to set a pattern for the rest of the country. The November, 1956, survey revealed only minor regional variations in the Federal funds rate. Such differences become more significant, however, during periods when the discount rates of the Reserve Banks are not uniform.

The Federal funds rate is inherently a sensitive indicator of bank reserve positions. Banks use the market primarily to adjust their reserve positions, and they account for the bulk of all transactions. The rate's significance as a money market indicator, however, is limited in three important respects. First, it reflects conditions in only a segment of the money market—the ebb and flow of reserve funds among the larger banks, government securities dealers, and a few other institutions. Second, the Federal funds market is used primarily for very short-term reserve adjustments. It does not directly reflect the impact of longer term adjustments made through the securities market. Third, in periods of credit restraint the Federal funds rate tends to move up to the discount rate and remain there for extended periods. Under these circumstances, the Federal funds rate fails to register any intensification—or possibly any moderate easing —of pressures on bank reserve positions. In periods of credit ease, the large supply of excess reserves relative to the demand for them may push the Federal funds rate well below the discount rate. In this event, the Federal funds rate tends to reflect day-to-day changes in the availability of reserves in the Federal funds market.

FUNCTIONS OF THE MARKET

The Federal funds market has become a significant means of adjusting the reserve positions of the large banks in financial centers. The market is particularly suited to day-to-day reserve adjustments because it does not involve the risk of price change or the cost of a spread between bid and asked prices as does the securities market.

Directly, the Federal funds market increases the mobility but not the total volume of reserve balances. Through the market's facilities, banks with deficiencies purchase the excess reserves of other banks. The effect, therefore, is to make the excess reserves of one area or group of banks available to meet the reserve pressures which may converge on others. Indirectly, the operation of the Federal funds market, by increasing the availability of excess reserves, probably results in a somewhat lower level of total reserves than would exist otherwise. In borrowing Federal funds, banks draw on existing reserves to meet their deficiencies. In the absence of a Federal funds market, it is unlikely that deficiencies would be met without some addition to total reserves. Borrowing from a Reserve Bank would result in a corresponding increase in total reserves. Selling securities, unless purchased by banks with excess reserves or by nonbank buyers drawing checks on banks with excess reserves, would pass along the reserve deficiencies to other banks. In the subsequent process of adjusting reserves, banks with deficiencies would probably borrow from the Reserve Banks, thereby adding to the total volume of reserves. Thus the Federal funds market, by facilitating use of existing reserves, tends to reduce the level of reserves which otherwise would be outstanding under a given set of circumstances and to minimize repercussions from the temporary shifting of reserve funds among banks.

Selection 19

TECHNIQUES OF TREASURY DEBT MANAGEMENT

—The Dealer Market

TILFORD C. GAINES

The growth of a substantial public debt made government securities the most important money market instrument. The market for government securities is almost wholly an "over-the-counter" market, in contrast to the greater importance of trading on the organized securities exchanges for corporate stocks. The major traders in government securities are a small number of dealers and banks that specialize in this activity. Because the government securities market is a dealer market rather than an auction market (like that for many corporate stocks), dealers absorbing securities into their inventories and selling securities from their portfolios can have some stabilizing influence on interest rates. The following selection describes the market organization and market mechanics of this important segment of the money market.

In discussing the organization of the government securities market, it is useful to draw a clear distinction between the great number of brokers, commercial banks and other intermediaries throughout the coutry who may, from time to time or fairly regularly, execute orders in government securities for a customer, and the dealers who specialize in making broad, continuous markets for government securities. Most of the more than 3,000 brokers and dealers registered with the Securities and Exhange Commission will execute orders in government securities, and there are more than 80 commercial banks which main-

—————
• From Tilford C. Gaines, *Techniques of Treasury Debt Management*, pp. 205–221. Copyright 1962, as a joint publication of the Graduate School of Business, Columbia University, and the Free Press of Glencoe, New York. Reprinted by permission of the Graduate School of Business, Columbia University, the Free Press of Glencoe, and the author.

tain trading facilities with whom government securities might be bought or sold.[1] However, the total trading in United States government securities by all of these concerns probably amounts to only a very small fraction of the volume handled by the dealer firms specializing in this market. The trades outside the primary dealer market would, in nearly all cases, be reflected in the dealer market in any event, since the intermediary presumably would be acting in the capacity of agent and would turn to a dealer to execute the order.

NUMBER OF DEALERS

Currently (end of 1961), there are thirteen nonbank dealer firms specializing in making markets for United States government securities, and six large commercial banks (four in New York and two in Chicago) maintain separate dealer departments specializing in government issues. Among the nonbank firms, six are substantially more important in the market than the remainder; three of these six are corporations, the other three are partnerships. All of the nonbank dealers maintain their trading offices in the financial district in New York City, although the home office of one of the firms is in Chicago and the nonbank dealers, as a group, maintain a total of 34 branch offices in 14 separate cities. These nineteen firms during the first six months of 1961 handled a daily average of $1.5 billion in transactions, representing an annual volume rate of some $375 billion.[2] Most dealers during this period complained that the market was inactive, so it may be assumed that this figure does not overestimate the typical volume of trading.

PRICING

Many of the dealers (both bank and nonbank) publish daily quotation sheets, showing bid and offer prices and yields on all outstanding marketable United States government and government agency issues as of the close of business on the previous day. These quotation sheets, however, are not effective bids or offers at which the dealer will transact business as of the opening of business the next day. Prices and yields change constantly, in response to developing supply and demand conditions and the myriad of influences—some real, some "psychological"—that affect the market outlook. Virtually all trading in the government securities market is conducted over the telephone, and dealers stand ready at all times to quote their current prices on any securities in which a customer (or another dealer) might be interested. Dealers employ salesmen who visit customers throughout the country, as well as call them by telephone, but these salesmen do not take the initiative in quoting bid or offered prices. Because of the constantly changing influences in the market, responsibility for quoting prices rests with the senior traders, who are continuously in touch with the flows

[1] Irwin Friend, *et al., The Over-the-Counter Securities Markets* (New York: McGraw-Hill Book Company, 1958), p. 113; estimate of banks maintaining trading departments is for 1949.

[2] The Federal Reserve System began publishing statistics for dealer positions and trading volume on a consistent and continuous basis in 1961.

of orders through the market and thus are able to judge the technical strength or weakness of individual issues.

The bid and offer prices quoted over the telephone by a dealer are usually the "outside" prices at which the dealer will buy or sell; they are not necessarily the actual prices at which a trade will be effected. If the customer actually has an order to execute and is not just checking prices, the dealer usually will shade his prices in order to compete for the business; the "inside" market on which large transactions are executed usually reflects a smaller price spread between bid and offer quotations than the dealer quotes on a routine request. In other words, each large transaction is a negotiated deal and will not necessarily be at either the bid or offer price currently quoted by most dealers in the market.

Treasury bonds, notes, and certificates are currently quoted on a price basis, with fractions in $\frac{1}{32}$ of a point (although prices on the "inside" market frequently are refined to $\frac{1}{64}$, and occasionally to $\frac{1}{128}$), and Treasury bills are quoted on a yield basis, with quotations reading to two decimal points. Dealers' quotations usually contain a spread of $\frac{4}{32}$ to $\frac{8}{32}$ between bid and offer prices on longer-term securities, $\frac{2}{32}$ to $\frac{4}{32}$ on intermediate obligations, and $\frac{1}{32}$ to $\frac{2}{32}$ on certificates or short-term notes and bonds; yield spreads on three-month Treasury bills customarily are 4 to 5 basis points (.04 to .05 per cent). Inside quotations, at which most large orders are executed, would reduce these spreads by perhaps one-half. The efficiency of the market organization is suggested by the fact that even if the "outside" quotations are used, the margin between bid and offered prices is no more than $\frac{1}{4}$ point on long-term bonds, $\frac{1}{16}$ on one-year certificates, and only $\frac{1}{100}$ point on three-month bills; per $100 transaction, these figures reduce to 25 cents, 6 cents, and 1 cent.

SIZE OF TRANSACTIONS

The volume of securities which a dealer will buy or sell at the prices he quotes over the telephone depends upon a good many factors. Obviously, the most important conditioning factor is the dealer's judgment of the breadth of the market for the issue involved, and thus of his ability to reverse the transaction at a profit. If prices are declining and a supply of securities is overhanging the market, a dealer will be reluctant to buy more than a relatively small amount of the issue at his original quotation, although he might negotiate to take larger amounts on a declining price scale; alternatively, he might arrange to take the order on an agency basis rather than for his own account. Even in a declining market, however, a particular dealer might have a short position to cover or might know of a buyer for the securities (perhaps involving a succession of "swaps" in several issues) and be a willing buyer on a rather large scale. Moreover, individual judgments as to the likely course of prices frequently vary, and certain dealers might well be buying for position at the same time that other dealers are retrenching and reducing the size in which they will trade.

In short, the scale in which an investor may buy or sell a particular issue at a price close to prevailing market quotations depends upon the current supply-demand balance in the market, dealers' technical positions in the particular issue, and the general set of expectations as to the outlook for prices and interest rates currently shaping market attitudes. At most times, an investor may feel confident of being able to execute an order for $1 million or more long-term bonds, $3-5 million intermediate obligations, and $10 million or more short-term securities, without difficulty. In a strong and rising market, sell orders several times this size may be effected with ease but buy orders might take time to execute; in a falling market, even sell orders of this size might encounter some problems, but much larger purchase orders could be handled quickly.[3]

DEALER POSITIONS

An important characteristic of the government securities market is the fact that the bulk of the vast volume of trading is executed on a dealer basis, with dealers buying and selling for their own accounts and at their own risk. Depending upon their evaluation of the outlook, therefore, dealers are able to absorb temporary imbalances in the supply of and demand for particular issues, or in the total of all issues, in their own positions. For example, a net supply of short-term securities customarily comes into the market in the closing weeks of each year as corporate investors and others liquidate to pay taxes or dividends or to improve their cash positions in preparation for their year-end financial statements. Similar seasonal movements in aggregate demand or supply of government securities occur at the other corporate tax and dividend dates, and for other reasons, throughout the year.

Dealers are able to minimize the impact upon interest rates of these purely seasonal movements by absorbing securities into position or by net sales from position. A similar stabilizing influence is exerted at times of Treasury financing. Direct allotments of new issues to dealers do not ordinarily bulk large in the total of any Treasury financing operation, but dealers play an important role in the redistribution through the market of "rights" or "when-issued" securities. Whether the operation involves the refunding of an outstanding issue or the sale of new securities for cash, there is likely to be a temporary over-supply of the new securities until there has been time for investment demand to materialize in sufficient volume to absorb the issue. During this period, dealers' positions will be temporarily swollen. On balance, the fact that dealers buy for and sell from position means that price and yield movements are more orderly and less subject to seasonal or random influences than they would be in an auction market serviced by brokers. . . .

In summary, the development of the government securities market as an over-the-counter dealer market rather than as an exchange auction market makes it necessary for the professional dealers in United States government securities to carry inventories in order to facilitate the servicing of customer orders. Reliance upon corresponding investor sales and purchases in the market to balance

---

[3] The latter statement requires some qualification. At some times when prices are moving rapidly in one direction or another, the actual trading market becomes quite thin. Particularly when prices are falling sharply, dealer positions are likely to be quite limited, and problems might be encountered in filling a large purchase order—even though the market generally continues to fall.

out fortuitously from day to day, the only alternative to dealer inventories, probably would not allow for orderly execution of the volume of trades currently passing through the market. These inventories customarily are fairly large, but their size, per se, is not particularly important. The important elements in dealers' management of their positions are:

1. Seasonal imbalances in the supply of and demand for short-term government securities are absorbed, in large part, in dealer positions, thus smoothing out short-term rate movements and providing continuity to the trading market.
2. Wide cyclical swings in dealer positions accelerate the rapidity of interest rate adjustments at times of fundamental shifts in expectations as to prospective rate movements and, presumably, increase the amplitude of rate movement over the business cycle.
3. Procedures developed by dealers to finance their positions have contributed to the development of a sensitive national money market.

MARKET MECHANICS

The volume of trading in the United States government securities market since World War II and the development of that market as the key institution in the national money market have required highly refined market machinery, trading techniques, and market procedures. The important services performed by the market for the Treasury, for the Federal Reserve System, and for the national economy have been made possible, in a significant sense, by the intelligent origination of the proper mechanical procedures for the job that was to be done. . . .

Probably the greatest volume of transactions, both in number and in dollar value, result from more or less routine requests for bids or offers that are executed on the initial call or after a brief check of the market; dealers are reluctant to hold a firm bid or offer open for more than a few minutes for fear the market will move while the customer is hesitating. Execution of the order may call for "regular" delivery, i.e., delivery of the securities and payment the following business day, or it may call for "cash" delivery, i.e., delivery and settlement on the same day. . . . In addition, the contract may call for settlement in clearing house funds or Federal funds; all settlements made in funds located outside of New York are automatically in Federal funds, since settlement will be over Federal Reserve wires. There has been a tendency in recent years for more and more transactions in short-term securities to be for cash delivery and for settlement in Federal funds, and much the largest part of all transactions in such issues is now in this form.

Nearly all of the nonbank dealers use a single New York bank as clearing agent; the bank dealers use their own messengers and clearing facilities for transferring securities and making settlements. The clearing bank extends day-loans to the dealers to finance changes in their positions within a given day, and supplies Federal funds (in effect an overnight loan) where a dealer's payments in Federal funds have exceeded his receipts in this form during the day. The clearing agent bank does not ordinarily, however, extend regular financing to dealers. The clearing bank acts as custodian for the securities the dealers have in position, and upon receipt of instructions from a dealer, in reflection of a trade the dealer has executed, will deliver securities to their new owner or his agent and receive payment for the dealer's account or will receive securities the dealer has purchased and settle for them with its own check (either clearing-house or Federal funds). A small clearing charge is made by the bank each time it delivers securities, but not for receiving securities. In the event the transaction involves transfers of ownership to or from a customer located outside the Second Federal Reserve District, the transfer is effected over the wires of the Commissioner of the Public Debt. For example, if a dealer instructs his clearing bank to transfer specified securities to *Bank X* in Chicago, the clearing bank will deliver these securities to the Federal Reserve Bank of New York subject to receipt of payment for account of the dealer. The New York Reserve Bank, as agent for the Treasury, cancels the securities and wires instructions to the Federal Reserve Bank of Chicago to issue and deliver identical securities to *Bank X* upon receipt of payment to order of the dealer. No charge is made by the Treasury for wire transfers of any United States government securities within one year of maturity, and a nominal charge is made for bonds or notes more than one year from maturity.

In addition to net purchase and sale transactions between a dealer and a customer, two other types of trades are important in the over-the-counter market for United States government securities. These are professional transactions between dealers and swap transactions that involve two or more Treasury issues and, perhaps, more than one customer. The new Federal Reserve data suggest that typically about 30 per cent by value of all dealer trades are with other dealers. Dealers are in constant telephone communication with one another, checking market quotations and attempting to locate a supply of a particular issue (or issues) for which they have a potential buyer or a demand for an issue (or issues) which they have in position in unwanted size or which they have an opportunity to purchase but do not wish to add to position. All inter-dealer contacts of this sort are at arms-length, and every precaution is taken to avoid revealing information that might be advantageous to the other dealer. At the same time, the stream of inquiries from "the street" provide a trader with clues as to potential buyers or sellers of particular issues if he should have occasion to trade these issues.

Inter-dealer contacts and trading of this sort give the market an additional dimension and a fluidity that it would not have if all contacts were only between dealers and customers. . . .

A large but indeterminate proportion of all trading in the over-the-counter market for government securities involves swaps of one issue for another rather than net purchases or sales. In its simplest form, an investor acting on his own initiative or on a dealer's recommendation will sell one issue and simultaneously purchase another of similar maturity. His purpose may have been to readjust the maturity structure of his portfolio to fit his cash requirements (for example, by selling near-maturity bills and buying longer bills), to establish a capital loss or gain for tax purposes, or to take advantage of a yield differential that appears to promise an arbitrage profit.

Swap transactions are identical in all technical details to outright trades, but their significance, as in the case of inter-dealer trading, is the greater fluidity and depth they impart to the market. Activity in swaps may be particularly pronounced immediately after the Treasury has placed a new issue with investors. The new securities ordinarily will carry a somewhat higher effective yield for a period after they are issued, and this higher yield provides the inducement for investors to sell other issues—usually shorter maturities—to buy the new securities. In the process of shifting about, the new Treasury security is gradually placed in firm hands with a minimum of disturbance to the market. From the point of view of a dealer, the swapping procedures that have been developed enable him to take into position larger amounts of a single issue than he might wish to assume if it were then necessary for him to find outright purchasers of that single issue. By arranging the necessary swaps, the dealer can substitute in his position a variety of issues for the single issue he had purchased in size, and by so doing he is in a better position to find net buyers to reduce his overall position to its size prior to the original large transaction. The ability to work off large blocks in this fashion is particularly important, as noted above, in maintaining continuity in the market following a large Treasury financing.

Trading arrangements and practices are substantially uniform for government issues of all types, i.e., bills, certificates, notes, and bonds. Perhaps the most important exception to this generalization is the tendency for the market to become thinner the longer the maturity of the obligation. Ordinarily, regular Treasury bills can be traded in large amounts with less difficulty than other types of Treasury issues, even though they are of similar maturity, because of the position that Treasury bills have come to occupy as the prime financial asset for liquidity investment and money-market adjustment. The constant flow of bills through the market in both directions gives to the Treasury bill market a depth and breadth not found, to the same degree, in the rest of the market. Although bills accounted for less than one-fourth of the publicly-held marketable debt at the end of 1960, it is likely that these instruments account for much the largest part of all trading in marketable United States government securities.

The thinnest and least active portion of the government securities market is in longer-term bonds, although this market can be characterized as thin and inactive only by comparision with the volume of trading in shorter-term governments, certainly not by comparison with market depth or trading activity in any other capital market. In part, the limited activity and relative lack of depth in longer-term bonds is due to the relatively small and declining volume of longer-term securities outstanding. More importantly, it may be traced to the fact that funds ordinarily accumulate only slowly in the hands of institutions interested in investment in long-term government securities. It is in the nature of longer-term securities, of course, that prices and trading activity should be more sensitive to interest rate movements and expectations of rate movements than prices and activity in shorter-term obligations. The potential price change, and thus potential profit or loss on an investment position, increases with the maturity of the instrument. Therefore, dealer positions in longer maturities vary relatively more than in other maturities. During prolonged periods of tight money and credit restraint dealers frequently comment that the limited "street" supply of long-term bonds is, in itself, a positive factor tending to limit trading volume. At the same time, when interest rates are rising or are expected to rise, dealers would be unwise to carry other than a minimum or carefully hedged position in long-term issues.

Selection 20

TREASURY OPERATIONS AND BANK RESERVES

THOMAS G. GIES

Banks adjust their reserve positions by borrowing from Federal Reserve Banks, by buying and selling Federal funds, by buying and selling government securities, and through other means. At the same time, their reserve balances are significantly affected by operations of the Treasury, which result in changes in Treasury balances held in ordinary commercial banks and in the Federal Reserve Banks. The Treasury affects the money market through collection of tax and other revenues, through expenditures for government activities, through issuance and redemption of government securities, and through purchase and sale of gold and silver. Unless the effects of these transactions are understood, the significance of many developments in the money markets may not be appreciated. The following selection indicates some of the factors that must be considered in analyzing effects of Treasury operations.

Treasury operations—the collection and disbursement of tax revenues, the issuance and redemption of debt, and the purchase and sale of gold and silver—have always been an important influence on commercial bank reserve positions. At certain earlier times, the Treasury gave little recognition to these effects, and banks experienced strong fluctuations in reserve balances in consequence of periodic and irregular Treasury financial operations. Today, these operations are carried out on a far larger scale. Consequently, their potential effect on bank reserves is far greater. Questions have been raised, therefore, as to the over-all effect of Treasury operations on bank reserves. Do present large government budgets, with accompanying heavy tax collections, tend to drain commercial bank reserves? Does the sale of Treasury securities to private investors—individuals and corporations—reduce deposits and tend to reduce the capacity of banks to purchase these securities or to extend credit to private borrowers? Do Government transactions in the monetary metals tend to alter bank reserves? These fundamental questions concerning the relationship of Treasury operations to commercial bank reserves are discussed below.

ADMINISTRATION OF TREASURY BALANCES

The very high level of expenditures by the federal government requires the maintenance of a very sizable volume of funds to make payments as they

---

• From Thomas G. Gies, "Treasury Operations and Bank Reserves," *Monthly Review,* Federal Reserve Bank of Kansas City, March, 1954, pp. 9–14. Reprinted by permission of the Federal Reserve Bank of Kansas City.

come due.* For this reason, the Treasury normally maintains deposit balances ranging from 3 to 7 billion dollars. The major portion of these balances is held in some 11,000 commercial banks throughout the country, with the remainder held at the twelve Federal Reserve banks, except for a small amount in foreign and territorial depositaries.

Initially, tax and loan proceeds are channeled largely into commercial bank depositaries. Funds derived from withheld individual income and payroll taxes are eligible for placement in these accounts, as are most excise tax payments. On certain quarterly tax dates, large income payments by corporations and individuals also are placed in these accounts. In addition, a majority of the proceeds from the sale of savings bonds, savings notes, and other public debt obligations issued for cash are credited to Treasury balances at commercial banks. Payments for Treasury bills, which are credited directly to Reserve bank accounts, are the principal exception to this practice in regard to debt transactions.

Because virtually all disbursements of Treasury funds are made by drawing on balances at the Reserve banks, transfers to the Reserve banks of funds on deposit at commercial banks are made as the need arises. Changes in rate of disbursement from Reserve banks require changes in rate of withdrawals from commercial bank depositaries.

When the Treasury presents checks received from the public for credit to its accounts at commercial banks, there is no net loss of deposits by the commercial banking system and hence no loss in reserves. Not until these funds are shifted to the Reserve banks do commercial bank depositaries experience a loss of deposits and, consequently, an equal loss of reserves. On the other hand, when funds are disbursed from Treasury balances at Reserve banks, commercial banks gain an equivalent amount of deposits and reserves. Thus, it is clear that the coincidence of disbursements from the Reserve bank accounts of the Treasury and calls on commercial bank depositaries is of major importance in damping fluctuations in commercial bank reserve balances. The greater the stability in Treasury balances at the Reserve banks, the smaller the resulting changes in aggregate reserves of commercial banks.

In addition to possible effects on commercial bank reserves in the aggregate, Treasury operations also present a problem of shifts in the volume of funds held by particular banks or groups of banks. Even though withdrawals may be approximately offset for the commercial banking system as a whole, government collections and outlays may result in expansion or contraction of deposits and reserves in particular areas. To some degree, sharp drains on the funds of individual banks can be temporarily alleviated by redepositing with a bank large checks drawn by its own depositors for certain tax payments. However, the movement of Treasury funds from one area to another is determined necessarily by the geographic pattern of tax and loan receipts, together with the regional pattern of disbursements. Although recognizing the importance of such movements, this discussion is restricted to the aggregate problem.

* _Editor's note:_ This requirement results from the fact that Treasury receipts and expenditures are subject to entirely different influences, and consequently the Treasury's balances fluctuate widely over the course of a year.

EFFECT OF TREASURY BORROWING ON BANK RESERVES

Apart from the effects which arise from movements of funds through Treasury accounts, it may be of interest to consider what distinctive results are associated with Treasury sale of securities to individuals and businesses, as opposed to sale of securities to banks. For example, does sale of tax anticipation issues to corporations reduce the capacity of the banking system to acquire securities, or does liquidation of Treasury issues by depositors enable banks to enlarge their holdings?

Confusion on this question has led to assertions that increased bank demand for government bonds in the latter months of 1953 was generated in part by smaller security purchases by corporations. Declining yields on short-term governments were said to have increased bank deposits, since corporations tended to drop out of the market as security buyers. This was thought to have added to the pressure on banks to find suitable outlets for "excess" funds. Such misunderstanding apparently is based on the assumption that sale of securities by the Treasury to nonbank investors not only reduces deposits of those buyers but also necessarily reduces both deposits and reserves of the commercial banking system. While sale of securities to such investors by the Treasury clearly depletes their deposits, the transaction actually reduces neither total deposits nor reserves of the commercial banks. The proceeds of the sale of securities, as described earlier, usually are redeposited by the Treasury in commercial banks. Thereby, the transaction results only in a change in ownership of the deposits. . . .*

The volume of funds which may be offered by the banking system is quite independent of offers by nonbank investors, and vice versa. Bank purchases are controlled by the volume of excess reserves, while purchases by individuals and businesses are conditioned by the amount of deposits held beyond expected needs for transactions and other purposes. These two sources of demand for Treasury securities thus are supplementary and not mutually limiting. There is one important difference between bank and nonbank acquisitions, however. Net purchases by commercial banks tend to expand deposits, and thus total money supply, by an equal amount, and since the new deposits raise the level of required reserves, excess reserves are thereby reduced. . . . Occasionally, the Treasury sells securities—very short-term issues—to the Federal Reserve banks. Such sales have distinctive results for commercial bank reserves. In these instances, the securities are paid for by crediting the Treasurer's deposit at the Reserve banks. In other words, a deposit is created in favor of the Treasury. As the proceeds of this sale are spent, the funds move into the commercial banking system and tend to increase reserves by an equal amount. . . .

Thus, the marketing of Treasury securities—whether sold to bank or nonbank investors—in no case reduces total commercial bank reserves. Sale to the

* *Editor's note:* This and other transactions referred to in the remainder of this selection may be clearly shown in "skeleton" balance sheets for the Treasury, Federal Reserve Banks, and commercial banks. In this case the liability side of the balance sheet of commercial banks would show a reduction in deposits of individuals, partnerships, and corporations, and an increase in Treasury deposits.

Reserve banks, furthermore, serves to increase bank reserves and the ability of banks to acquire assets.

If Treasury tax collections exceed expenditures and the resulting surplus were employed to retire outstanding debt, the effect upon reserves would be essentially the reverse of events described in connection with issuance. Reduction of nonbank-held debt could be expected to leave total bank deposits and reserves unchanged. The initial collection of taxes would result in a shift in ownership of deposits at commercial banks from the nonbanking public to the government. When the obligations were redeemed, individuals and businesses would receive checks on Treasury balances at the Reserve banks, which they would deposit in commercial banks. Replenishment of Treasury deposits at Reserve banks by transfers from commercial bank depositaries, however, would offset this gain. In the event debt held by commercial banks were returned, a net reduction in commercial bank deposits would take place, but there would be no loss in reserves. The extinction of deposits would reduce required reserves and increase excess reserves in equivalent amount.

If a Treasury surplus were used to retire securities held by Reserve banks, government deposits would be extinguished in an amount equal to the value of securities redeemed. The replenishment of Treasury balances at the Reserve banks through transfer of funds from commercial bank depositaries, in this instance, would not be offsetting an increase in these depositaries. Hence, the transaction would result in a net reduction in deposit balances and reserves of the commercial banks.

The role of the Treasury investment funds in determining bank reserves can be described readily.* These funds represent a bookkeeping account of the net accumulation of contributions by employees, employers, veterans, and so forth, and are held in trust by the Treasury. Contributions to the funds are received into the commercial bank depositaries initially, along with other tax collections. While the investment fund accounts are credited with the receipts collected, the Treasury, at its discretion, may either issue special obligations to the funds or purchase outstanding government securities from the market. Purchase of securities from the market, like any other disbursement to the public, tends to increase deposits and reserves of the commercial banks only to the extent that such withdrawal of Treasury funds at the Reserve banks is not offset by calls on commercial bank depositaries. The issuance of special obligations to the investment accounts is merely an intra-governmental transaction and results in no movements of deposits or reserves.

EFFECT OF TRANSACTIONS IN GOLD AND SILVER

Treasury operations outside the area of the budget, the trust accounts, or the debt accounts, also are capable of exerting strong influence over bank reserves. Movements of gold into the banking system—whether imports, domestic production, recovery from industrial use, or release from earmark for foreign

---

* *Editor's note:* The role of these funds in the money market is discussed in more detail in "Federal Investment Funds in the Money Market," Federal Reserve Bank of Kansas City, *Monthly Review,* November 1956, pp. 9–15.

account—directly increase commercial bank reserves. Similarly, increments in the monetary stock of silver may serve to expand reserves.

An import of gold, for example, arising in connection with international trade, would be sold to the Treasury for storage in its vaults. The Treasury would pay for the gold by drawing on its balance at a Reserve bank. The transfer of this balance to the seller's account at a commercial bank would be accompanied by an increase in that bank's reserve balance at the Federal Reserve bank of its district. So far, the transaction is no different from any other purchase made by the Treasury. In this case, however, the Treasury is permitted by law to issue gold certificates against the newly-aquired gold. These certificates are issued to the Federal Reserve banks in return for a deposit balance. Thus the Treasury balance at the Reserve bank is restored to its former level, while the commercial banking system has received a net increase in reserve as well as deposit balances. This is a distinctive quality of transactions in the monetary metals, as compared with Treasury purchases of other goods and services. In the cases previously described, depletion of Treasury balances at the Reserve banks was offset by transfer of funds from the commercial bank depositaries, the latter counterbalancing the gain from receipt of checks drawn on Treasury balances at the Reserve banks. In this case, there has been a net gain of reserves to the commercial banks and Reserve banks, considered as a system. Treasury purchases of silver from either domestic producers or importers result, similarly, in expansion of bank reserves and the money supply. . . .

The expansion in holdings of monetary metals described above is reversible. Gold may be exported to meet foreign payment requirements, placed under earmark for foreign account, or withdrawn from the Treasury for use in the arts. Likewise, stocks of silver may be drawn down. In such instances, sale of the metal by the Treasury would involve redemption of outstanding certificates and a reduction of bank reserves.

The foregoing description of the significance which major Treasury operations have for commercial bank reserves ignores possible modifying actions which may occur. Additional reserves may be made available or existing reserves withdrawn through Federal Reserve action which compensates for Treasury operations and other influences. While comprehensive analysis of changes in bank reserves would require consideration of these additional factors, this discussion has been focused on the results of the movement through Treasury accounts of funds arising from tax collection and debt financing, as well as the functioning of the monetary accounts.

Selection 21

THE FUNCTIONS OF A FOREIGN-EXCHANGE MARKET

JEROME L. STEIN

> *One part of the money market, sometimes not given the attention it merits, is the foreign-exchange market. Just as domestic transactions may be accounted for in national income accounting (for income transactions) or flow of funds transactions (for both income*

*and other transactions which constitute sources and uses of funds),
international transactions may be analyzed through the use of an
accounting statement known as the balance of payments (a type of
source and use of funds statement). Although some transactions,
such as certain military aid shipments, may involve no payment,
a large proportion of the transactions recorded in the balance of
payments involve purchases and sales of foreign exchange (financial
assets denominated in foreign currencies), in one country or another.*

*Transactions involving purchases of goods and services and
investment income are recorded in what is termed the "current
account" section of the balance of payments. These transactions
constitute the portion of national income and expenditure arising
from international transactions. When these transactions balance
over a period of time, the current account section is said to be in
equilibrium—there is no tendency for demand to exceed supply at
a given exchange rate, or vice versa, and hence no tendency for the
exchange rate to rise or fall, or for other adjustments to be required
if a fixed exchange rate is in effect. Loans and other transfers of
claims are recorded in the capital account section of the balance of
payments. The foreign-exchange market is the mechanism through
which exchange rates (prices for foreign currencies, or foreign exchange) are determined, and changes in exchange rates are the
mechanism that forces countries to settle balances in gold or reserve
currencies, unless they wish to permit exchange rates to fluctuate.
The international payments system agreed upon in the Bretton
Woods Conference (1944) is essentially one of fixed exchange rates,
only limited exchange rate fluctuations being permitted.*

*In addition to those who purchase and sell foreign exchange as
a result of their need to make payments for commercial transactions
or to receive such payments, there are individuals and institutions
that engage in foreign-exchange transactions for investment and
speculative purposes. The following selection explains the roles
of some of these participants in the foreign-exchange market, and
shows how the foreign-exchange market is related to the domestic
money market through investment activities.*

A. THE EFFICIENCY OF A FOREIGN-EXCHANGE MARKET

Although the basic balance of payments may be in equilibrium [1] over the
year as a whole, at a given exchange rate, it is unlikely that the balance will be
in equilibrium every day, week or month. The balance on current account varies
during the year from a surplus to a deficit, particularly in countries producing primary products. In the United States, for example, the balance on current account
during 1959 was $172 million; but there were surpluses in the first and last

---

[1] The basic balance of payments is the sum of the current-account balance plus the
long-term capital account plus unilateral transfers. The term equilibrium has many meanings, especially in the balance-of-payments literature. In the present discussion it is used to
mean that the sum of surpluses and deficits over a given period of time is equal to zero.

• From Jerome L. Stein, *The Nature and Efficiency of the Foreign-Exchange Market,*
Essays in International Finance, No. 40, "II. The Functions of a Foreign-Exchange Market," pp. 7–14. Copyright 1962 by Princeton University, Princeton, New Jersey. Reprinted
by permission of Princeton University and the author.

quarters, and deficits in the second and third quarters, of the year. A foreign-exchange market which results in a situation whereby the basic balance is in equilibrium at every quarter, month, week, or day is an inefficient market. An analogy can be made between the fluctuations in the net supply of wheat and in the net supply of foreign exchange. Wheat is harvested a few times during the year. It is socially desirable that the consumption of wheat, or foreign exchange which is simply a command over imports, be spread out over the year. This spreading (or smoothing) out can only occur if there are institutions willing to sell foreign exchange during periods of shortage and buy foreign exchange during periods of surplus. A period of shortage occurs when our basic balance tends to be negative; and a period of surplus occurs when our basic balance tends to be positive. An efficient market exists if there are institutions willing to buy and sell foreign exchange for, and from, inventory during these periods. In effect, these institutions invest in foreign exchange during periods of surplus and disinvest during periods of shortage. Through variations in the inventories of these private institutions, i.e., the short-term capital account,[2] the supply and demand for foreign exchange will be equal every day, although the basic balance may be in equilibrium only over the year as a whole.

A year is an arbitrary period of time. At a given exchange rate, the basic balance may be in equilibrium over the current year. Suppose that a shortage or a surplus of foreign exchange is anticipated for the following year. An efficient exchange market should induce the economy to prepare for future shortages or surpluses. If a shortage is anticipated, the economy should be induced to accumulate foreign exchange at present: i.e., to export short-term capital. On the other hand, if a surplus is foreseen, the economy should be induced to borrow (import) short-term capital during the current period. Again, an analogy can be made with wheat production. If a wheat shortage is expected, the economy should be induced to accumulate wheat inventories. That is, current production should exceed current consumption. On the other hand, if a surplus of wheat is expected, current consumption should exceed current production and wheat inventories (if they exist) should be reduced.

An efficient foreign-exchange market cannot exist unless there are institutions which can be induced to accumulate foreign exchange during periods when there is a surplus in our basic balance, and decumulate stocks of foreign exchange during periods when there is a shortage in our basic balance. The terms "surplus period" and "shortage period" refer to a longer period of time, over which the basic balance is zero.

The institutions which can be induced to import or export short-term capital occupy a crucial role in determining the efficiency of the foreign-exchange market. A general and simplified discussion of the variables which influence

---

[2] The short-term capital account refers to the private sector's net change in short-term claims against foreigners. The sum of the short-term capital account plus the net change in official claims against foreigners is identically equal to the basic balance. Since the analysis here is devoted exclusively to the private sectors, variations in the official or government claims against foreigners are excluded from the present analysis of how the foreign-exchange market operates.

their behavior is the subject of this discussion. The phenomena of interest arbitrage, the switching of finance with the exchange risk covered, speculation in foreign exchange and the necessity of a set of professional risk-bearers are explained.

B. SHORT-TERM INVESTMENT AND BORROWING

1. Risk-avoiding short-term investors

Many institutions which invest in domestic Treasury bills and other domestic short-term securities can be induced to invest in foreign Treasury bills and other foreign short-term securities, and vice versa. A comparison of the relative rates of return on domestic and foreign assets is one of the key considerations involved in the selection of an efficient portfolio. Suppose that the investor firmly expects to hold the bill until its maturity three months later. The expected return on an investment of $1 in United States Treasury bills is $1 multiplied by the Treasury-bill rate. The expected return on $1 invested in United Kingdom Treasury bills is not necessarily $1 multiplied by the United Kingdom Treasury-bill rate. There is no certainty that the American investor will be able to sell his sterling for the same price at which it was purchased. Whenever there is uncertainty concerning the rate of exchange, the expected return on foreign investment is not necessarily the same as the foreign-interest rate.

Whenever forward markets exist, the risks of exchange-rate fluctuations can be reduced by shifting them to the professional risk-bearers. The investor in United Kingdom Treasury bills can get a quotation on a *swap* from a professional risk-bearer. The *swap* is a simultaneous purchase and sale of foreign exchange of different maturities, entered into with a given party. Thus the investor may be told, on March 28, 1962, that he can buy pounds for $2.81¾ and that he can sell his pounds three months later for $2.80⅛. The investor could contract a current (spot) purchase and a forward sale of pounds, on that date, at a cost of 2.307 per cent per annum. A potential short-term investor would compare the Treasury-bill rates in the two countries with the cost of the swap, to determine relative returns on comparable assets. His expected return on a United Kingdom Treasury bill held to maturity would be equal to the United Kingdom Treasury-bill rate less the cost of the swap (2.307 per cent). It is this rate of return, with the exchange risk covered, that can properly be compared with the rate of return on a United States Treasury bill. Whenever the foreign-interest differential (i.e., the foreign rate less the United States rate) exceeds the cost of the swap, the rate of return on a foreign asset held to maturity exceeds the rate of return on a domestic asset held to maturity. Thereby an outflow of short-term capital is induced; that is, Americans are induced to accumulate interest-yielding foreign exchange.

On the other hand, when the foreign-interest differential is less than the cost of the swap, an inflow of short-term capital is induced. For example, if on March 28, 1962, the United Kingdom Treasury-bill rate was 4.5 per cent and the United States Treasury-bill rate was 2.7 per cent, the expected return on a United States Treasury bill to maturity exceeded the return on a United Kingdom Treasury bill held to maturity, with the exchange risk covered. An institution which owns, or has access to, pounds could do the following on March 28, 1962: (1) buy dollars for pounds; (2) invest in United States Treasury bills; and (3) sell the dollars forward for pounds, to be delivered in three months. It would earn 2.7 per cent on the Treasury bills and 2.307 per cent on the swap, for a total of 5.007 per cent. This exceeds the 4.5 per cent return that it could earn on United Kingdom Treasury bills held to maturity; and it would have pounds at the end of three months for use in its main business. In this situation, an English branch of the American concern is induced to de-cumulate pounds, and an English concern is induced to supply pounds in the present.

Interest arbitrage is the phenomenon whereby firms tend to invest abroad with the exchange risk covered with a forward sale of the currency. The institutions engaged in this form of investment, the interest-arbitrageurs, are risk-avoiders.

2. Risk-avoiding short-term borrowers

The same variables which induce short-term investors to invest in (say) New York, rather than in London, induce certain firms to borrow short-term funds in London rather than in New York. The choice among alternative sources of finance, with the exchange risk covered, is the counterpart of interest arbitrage discussed above. Its effects are exactly the same as those of interest arbitrage.

An American concern in need of funds for (say) three months may command such an outstanding international reputation that it can borrow as easily in London as it can in New York. Most likely, it will have branches in all major money markets. The prime-commercial-paper rate in New York may be 3.25 per cent per annum, and in London it may be 4.63 per cent per annum. If the concern in question borrows in London, its expected cost in dollars is uncertain if it sells the borrowed sterling for dollars, and fails to protect itself against the exchange risk. When the loan has to be repaid, the price of sterling may have risen above, or have fallen below, the price at which the borrowed sterling was originally purchased. The borrowing concern, if it chooses, can reduce the exchange risk by comparing the costs of borrowing in London and in New York with the exchange risks covered.

To borrow in London the firm must pay 4.63 per cent annum. If the sterling is sold for dollars and simultaneously repurchased for delivery in three months, the firm will make 2.307 per cent per annum (given the rates quoted in section B above). Its net borrowing cost would be 2.323 per cent (4.63-2.307 per cent) per annum. On the other hand, if it borrowed in New York its cost would be 3.25 per cent per annum. The foreign-interest differential of 1.38 per cent (4.63-3.25 per cent) is less than the discount on the forward pound of 2.307 per cent. Hence, if the debt will be repaid at maturity, it is cheaper to borrow abroad with the exchange risk covered than it is to borrow at home. Thereby a supply of pounds is produced in the foreign-exchange market.

Whenever an inflow of funds into the United States is induced as a result of interest arbitrage, American firms are induced to borrow abroad rather than at home. This increases the supply of (spot) foreign exchange offered in the market. Foreign firms are discouraged from borrowing in New York and, as a result, the demand for foreign exchange is reduced. Conversely, whenever an outflow of funds from the United States is induced by interest arbitrage, foreign firms are induced to borrow in New York rather than in their own countries and, as a result, the demand for (spot) foreign exchange is increased. American firms are discouraged from borrowing abroad, and the supply of foreign exchange is reduced.

3. Uncovered positions

Institutions may invest in foreign short-term securities, or incur liabilities denominated in foreign currency, without protecting themselves against exchange-rate fluctuations. Suppose that the maximum decline in the price of foreign exchange, within its stabilization limits, is less than the foreign-interest-rate differential. Then an institution which thinks that devaluation is improbable within three months may not bother to sell forward exchange at a discount, when it purchases a foreign Treasury bill or Bank bill. Thereby it saves the cost of the swap, which is the cost of an insurance premium, on an asset which will be held to maturity. Similarly the firm which borrows in the low-interest-rate money market need not purchase forward exchange, if it is at a premium, provided that the maximum rise in the price of foreign exchange is expected to be less than the interest differential. An institution which fails to secure forward cover (i.e., to offset its foreign-exchange asset with a forward sale, or to offset its foreign-exchange liability with a forward purchase) is not necessarily speculating. In the pre-1914 gold-standard era, short-term capital flowed among countries without forward covering, because the spread between the gold points was often narrower than the interest differentials and devaluation was considered most improbable. Speculation was not responsible for the failure to cover. The investors or borrowers did not consider the insurance worth the cost.

C. RISK-BEARING

1. Professional risk-bearers

The risk-avoiders are the investors in foreign assets who want to protect themselves against the decline in the price of foreign exchange, and the institutions which have incurred liabilities in foreign currency and want to protect themselves against a rise in the price of foreign exchange. If there were no institutions willing to buy and sell forward exchange, then the risks of exchange-rate fluctuations would deter many from investing or borrowing abroad. An efficient foreign-exchange market requires that there be short-term capital exports when our basic balance *tends* to be in deficit. Over the entire period the basic balance should be in equilibrium; but as already noted, it is inefficient to restrict monthly or quarterly imports to be exactly equal to the corresponding value of exports. If the risks of foreign investment and borrowing are great, there will be few institutions willing to accumulate foreign exchange during periods of surplus and sell foreign exchange during periods of shortage. The market would then be forced to restrict its imports of goods and services to the value of exports of goods and services. For primary-products producers, imports would be cheap and lavishly consumed shortly after the harvests, and imports would be scarce during the rest of the year.

Insofar as investors and borrowers can shift the exchange risks onto a set of professional risk-bearers, there will be a more abundant flow of short-term capital among countries. The professional risk-bearers quote prices for forward exchange and for spot exchange. Sometimes the forward exchange is at a premium and at other times it is at a discount relative to the spot exchange. In the example cited above, the forward pound was at a discount (or the forward dollar was at a premium) of 2.307 per cent per annum. An investor in sterling short-term assets who protects himself against the exchange risk pays an insurance premium of 2.307 per cent per annum to the risk-bearer. On the other hand, the firm which borrows in London and protects itself against the exchange risk by selling forward dollars to (i.e., by purchasing forward pounds from) the professional risk-bearers, finds that it will gain 2.307 per cent per annum by "purchasing" this insurance. The insurance cost, in a sense, is negative. (Cost here is defined to mean the difference between the forward price at which the foreign exchange is purchased and the spot price at which the borrowed foreign exchange is initially sold.)

In a world of exchange-rate uncertainty, the professional risk-bearers facilitate the international flows of short-term capital. In so doing they contribute to the efficiency of the foreign-exchange market.

Moreover, their willingness to bear risk stimulates international trade and leads to more efficient international distribution and production of goods and services. Exporters may quote prices either in terms of domestic currency or in terms of the currency of the importers. In either case, one of the parties to the transaction incurs an exchange risk. By shifting the exchange risk to professional risk-bearers, the volume of trade can be increased. A vivid example of how the existence of risk-bearers can stimulate trade concerns German-Russian trade in the last quarter of the nineteenth century. The British exporters "never quoted in terms of a fluctuating currency," and Russian importers would have had to bear the entire exchange risk. German exporters were willing to quote in terms of rubles since a well developed forward market existed in Berlin. The German exporters were able to shift the exchange risks to the professional risk-bearers who purchased forward rubles. I think that partly as a result of this ability, of German exporters and importers to shift the risks to a group specializing in risk-bearing, one-third of Russia's foreign trade was with Germany. The inducement to engage in international trade and profit from international differences in price, is increased by the presence of professional risk-bearers who make markets in forward exchange.

2. Speculators

Theoretically, the exchange market could be efficient if speculators were willing to purchase foreign exchange when the basic balance tended to be in surplus, and were willing to sell foreign exchange when the basic balance tended to be in deficit. Then the existence of the forward market would not be necessary to induce inflows and outflows of short-term capital. The speculators would perform the functions of foreign investors, borrowers, and risk-bearers. To revert to the wheat analogy, the speculators would be the purchasers and storers of wheat in the post-harvest season, and the sellers of wheat out of stocks during the pre-harvest season.

The main body of speculators in foreign exchange are the exporters and importers who have claims or liabilities denominated in foreign currencies. Their main method of speculation is via the leads and lags in international payments. When there is an excess supply of foreign exchange the price tends to fall. If the speculators think that this decline is temporary, the importers who must make payments in foreign currency accelerate their purchases of foreign exchange. Thereby, they accumulate foreign-exchange inventories in anticipation of a rise in price. They are both foreign investors and speculators. Similarly, the exporters who have received payment in foreign currency may lag their sales of foreign-exchange receipts. They will continue to hold these foreign assets in anticipation of a price rise. The net effect of the leads and lags is to produce a short-term capital outflow, when a period of shortage is expected to follow the current period of surplus. The economy thereby stores foreign exchange for the anticipated period of shortage.

When a surplus in the basic balance is anticipated, the leads and lags operate in reverse and produce a capital inflow. Importers who have incurred liabilities in foreign currency speculate by lagging, or delaying, their payments. An attempt is made to maintain their foreign-exchange liabilities in the anticipation of a decline in the price of foreign currency. This lag reduces the demand for foreign exchange. Importers who lag their payments are similar to the firms which borrow abroad and expect to repurchase the foreign exchange at a lower price than it was sold originally. Exporters speculate against a currency by accelerating the sales of their export receipts before the price falls. This increases the supply of foreign exchange prior to the appearance of the surplus. The net effect of the leads and lags, in this example, is to produce a capital inflow in anticipation of a surplus in our basic balance. Thereby the economy is induced to increase its present rate of import consumption in view of an expected increase in foreign-exchange receipts.

Although speculators are substitutes for interest-arbitrageurs, for borrowers who cover themselves against exchange risks, and for professional risk-bearers who make (inter alia) markets in forward exchange, they are imperfect substitutes. First, the total supply of international short-term capital would be reduced if potential investors could not shift the exchange risks to the professional risk-bearers. On the other hand, the existence of forward markets and professional risk-bearers does not reduce the supply of speculative capital. Second, when there is exchange-rate uncertainty, the existence of a forward market increases the volume of international trade. A contraction of international trade, which would occur if forward markets were reduced in scope by official restrictions and therefore made more risky, would reduce world national income and welfare. Hence speculators are not perfect substitutes for professional risk-bearers.

6

Interest Rates

THE READINGS IN CHAPTER 6 INTRODUCE THE STUDENT TO
one of the most important areas of monetary economics—the
determination of interest rates. They provide a summary of
modern theories dealing with the question of what determines
the level of the complex of interest rates. Another important
area considered is the analysis of alternative explanations for
the structure of interest rates: the relations among short-, in-
termediate-, and long-term interest rates and the spreads among
rates paid by different types of borrowers.

Attention is also directed to the importance of interest
rates as indications of changes in the composition of investor
preferences and in the general level of economic activity.

Selection 22

THE CURRENT STATE OF THE THEORY OF INTEREST RATES,
WITH SPECIAL REFERENCE TO MORTGAGE RATES

PAUL A. SAMUELSON

*Modern theories of interest are often classified as "real" theories,
which emphasize the supply and demand of real capital—saving and
real investment in capital assets—and monetary theories, which emphasize the supply and demand for money. Professor Samuelson*

*points out that the productivity of capital is apparently a techno-
logical fact; this fact gives rise to a demand for capital. At the
same time, fears of risk and preference for current consumption
limit the supply of saving. The rate of interest is determined, like
other prices, by supply and demand. But interest rates are also
influenced by changes in the supply and demand for money, as
Samuelson goes on to show in a thumbnail review of monetary
theories of interest. If the demand for capital increases, real money
income rises (via the multiplier); and with a higher level of real
money income, more money is demanded for transactions purposes,
leaving less for precautionary and speculative purposes. Hence, interest rates (being in one respect the return on credit instruments,
money yielding no interest return) should rise, because money should
have a greater value—there should be a greater differential between
the yield on money (zero) and the yield on bonds or other credit
instruments (assuming no change in the supply of money).*

*Although Professor Samuelson's presentation in this selection
is very brief, it touches upon so many of the pertinent points that
the editors believe it is well worth reading—and perhaps rereading.
The importance of interest lies in the fact that it is both the price of
funds for real investment and the price of funds for financial investment. Demand for funds for real investment (investment spending
not financed by available funds) and demand for funds for financial
investment (acquisition of financial assets, or claims on wealth) both
affect market interest rates; similarly, the supply of real capital
(saving) and the supply of financial assets (money and credit) both
affect interest rates. Interest rates are thus the link between money
and spending (flows) and between stocks of money and other financial assets (commonly referred to as credit)—a key position in
influencing economic activity. Interest rates affect spending flow
decisions because they relate present to future; they also are determined by demands for and supplies of assets and securities—
existing stocks as well as newly created assets and securities.*

MODERN THEORIES OF INTEREST RATES

Now let me turn to a catalogue of modern theories of interest rates. This
will have to be brutally brief. I believe it is fair to put theories into two major
headings.

First, real theories of the interest rate. Such theories generally could almost
be formulated in terms of a barter economy. They put very little emphasis on
the crucial factor of uncertainty about the future to explain the "basic minimal
rate" of interest. Only in the final pages of such theories will there be discussions about uncertainty, primarily to explain the spread of uncertain interest
rates and to raise risky interest rates above the so-called pure rate of interest.
(Incidentally, such theories seem usually to assume implicitly the full employment conditions of traditional classical economics.)

A second category of theories of interest rates might be called "monetary

---

• From Paul A. Samuelson, "The Current State of the Theory of Interest Rates with
Special Reference to Mortgage Rates," *Proceedings of the 1960 Conference on Savings and
Residential Financing*, May, 1960, pp. 20–25. Reprinted by permission of the United
States Savings and Loan League and the author.

theories of interest rates." Notice that I have changed "interest rate" to the plural, to "interest rates." Monetary theories used to be associated with monetary cranks generally but, what is perhaps not quite the same thing, in recent decades they have been associated with the name of Keynes. Here uncertainty plays a dominant role, not simply as afterthoughts in explaining the spread of risky rates, but from the very beginning in determining the whole structure of interest yields on a wide array of assets, which range from money to various near-money substitutes, close-money substitutes—such as government bills and so on—to the other extreme of assets involving a great deal of market risk, illiquidity and uncertainty phenomena generally. Changes in the level of unemployment and in the degree of effective demand are often made part and parcel of this analysis.

Let me express very briefly my own opinion that a useful synthesis of these notions can be made and that this gives a superior theory for understanding what happens in the real world, better than the two polar cases which are its components.

It is dull to be eclectic; but as my old teacher, Gottfried Haberler, used to say, "How do you know nature isn't eclectic?"

THE CONTRIBUTION OF BÖHM-BAWERK

Let me return to modern real theories of interest. I could give a long list of seemingly different theories of interest, but this is not the place for that. I need only refer you to the massive historical researches of Böhm-Bawerk. These have just come out in a very attractive three-volume new translation. As a prelude to putting forward his own theory of interest, Böhm-Bawerk felt it his duty to review all previous theories and to point out where they went wrong. (Of this last fact he seems never to have had any doubt.)

The catalogue is a long one. Turgot had a "fructification" theory of interest, and it was faulty. Ricardo had a "colorless" theory of interest; in addition to being colorless it, too, was faulty. J. B. Say had a "naive productivity" theory, and need I mention what Böhm thought of that? Nor do I have to go on to Senior's abstinence theory or Marx's exploitation theory of interest.

I must own up to mixed feelings about Böhm-Bawerk. He was an expert expositor and a tireless worker. He managed to fulfill the duties of Austrian finance minister well, and yet to give detailed answers to each and every criticism of his book. Until Alfred Marshall came along after 1890 to dominate the scene, Böhm-Bawerk was the best-known economist in the world. But if I go back to read the excellent three-volume translation of his work, a feeling of boredom creeps in. Is not the master over-differentiating his own product? Is there not a great deal of rabbinical casuistry and splitting of logical hairs? If this is indeed literary economics at its best, has not the law of diminishing returns long since set in? And is not the discipline of economics in need of the new tools of statistics and mathematics, and of a fresh impetus to study the problems of actual history and experience rather than to rehash the problems of historical doctrine?

But still let me illustrate the kind of discussion—and I should like to cite the case of housing—which has some concern to us. The really stupid man in the street might not see that housing involves a problem of interest at all. To him, a dollar today and a dollar twenty years from now seem like the same thing—unless, of course, you give him a choice and let him reveal by his eagerness how different his own preferences are.

But the more sophisticated economist—and this is the fellow who is the target for Böhm's polemics—is able to recognize in housing something akin to a machine. It is a durable good, rendering useful services for its owner over a long period of time; to make it easier to quantify, let it render services that can be rented out for a competitively determined rental. Hence, it is said that housing capital is productive and its fruits are interest.

"How naive," says Böhm. "Of course, there may be a gross productivity of a house as determined by its gross rentals. But how do you know that when these are accumulated over the whole life of the structure they will not exactly equal the original cost of labor and other primary factors needed to build the house? In that case the fruit of a house is not interest; its rent fruits are just enough to replace the house or give you back your original principal."

Of course, you may defend yourself by saying, "The lifetime rentals will most certainly add up to more than depreciation charges; for otherwise, only a fool would have built the house. Because of the returns he could have made elsewhere, any sensible person would have preferred to tie up his money elsewhere than in such a project."

I need not worry you with the details of the rebuttal to this. "Aha!" says Böhm. "I've caught you begging the question. You have already been implicitly assuming interest, and that is precisely what it was for you to prove. It remains for me in the 1880s to give the positive or definitive answer to the question."

Without belittling Böhm-Bawerk's achievement, his own theory boils down to one of supply and demand. On the one hand, the existing supply of physical capital goods of all types—shoe tongues and other goods in process; seed corn and the corn that will keep farm producers alive while they work to bring in the next harvest; machinery that can be used over and over while it ages and becomes obsolete, and residential structures and other durable consumer goods —all this comes to us as a heritage of previous capital formation. Such capital formation, and the rate of capital formation that is now going on and which will be the inheritance of future periods, imply the giving up of current consumption by someone in the community. Therefore, the habits and motives (time preference, risk fears and all that) which keep people and nations from devoting more or less of their resources to capital formation have a strong bearing on the time behavior of the supplies of the various components of physical goods.

On the demand side, Böhm-Bawerk follows Jevons in talking much about the extra productiveness of more "roundabout" methods of production. But this says no more than the following: If you look at two countries which have labor forces of the same size and natural abilities, which have the same land and natural resource endowments, which have the same knowledge of technology and which started out even, the country which has in the past consumed less and used more of its resources for producing various physical capital goods will end up capable of producing more consumption and/or capital goods than the other country. And the betting odds are that it also will be found to have land selling at longer purchase terms, consumption loans that bear a lower "rate of interest" and generally to be using productive methods that look more "long-lived" to the casual observer.

It is in this sense that "capital," whatever that may be, can be said to have a "net productivity." And no modern bickering about textbook quantification of the capital concept should blind us to this apparent technological fact of nature, as true for a Soviet system as for a complete laissez-faire system. In the end, as Wicksell pointed out, Böhm-Bawerk must, like any productivity theorist, accept this technological fact and it involves no begging of the question to make it a strand in an eclectic theory of interest.

Irving Fisher's 1930 *Theory of Interest* gives perhaps the best exposition of modern real theories of interest. Although Böhm-Bawerk would not admit this, Fisher's analysis comes to much the same thing as his. Fisher's is a modern, graphical, verbal and mathematical exposition of the equilibrium; and precisely this, Böhm-Bawerk felt, was not enough, for methodological reasons that a modern like myself finds difficult to follow. Such equilibrium analysis, Böhm felt, does not really get to the true "causation," to the "why" of interest. This question of "why" was apparently not the same thing as the ethical observers search for. Except for an occasional slip, Böhm-Bawerk claims not to be interested in the normative aspects of the subject but only in its positive aspects.

I think I can barely understand this. My own teacher, Schumpeter, was an Austrian economist much influenced by Böhm, even though he put forward the heretical theory that in the long run the equilibrium interest would, in the absence of technological change ("development"), have to be zero. For Schumpeter it was a meaningful procedure to split the problem up into two stages: First, what is the essence of interest and why should a (positive) interest rate exist? Then, after having settled the qualitative problem of essence, one could go on to a quantitative theory of actual interest rates.[1]

MONETARY THEORIES OF INTEREST RATES

I must go on to give a brutally brief review of monetary theories. Just over a quarter of a century ago, undergraduates like myself were taught that the interest rate is determined by the intersection of productivity of capital schedules and supply of capital schedules (as determined by past and present full-employment thriftiness).

Let me just mention that the theory of interest rate expounded by Keynes—

---

[1] As I have shown in a somewhat controversial article in the 1958 *Journal of Political Economy*, it is not hard to conjure up a negative equilibrium rate if one concentrates upon the fact that the desire to eat during old age retirement creates a reverse time preference from that thought normal by Böhm, in which one would gladly give up a unit of consumption today for less than a unit of future consumption if there were no alternative physically possible (such as storing goods costlessly or investing in "fruitful" production processes). I might also mention that Carl Menger wrote a letter to Walras more than 75 years ago in which he claims as a superiority for his literary method over that of the mathematical method that he alone can get at the "essence" of things!

and I would say it is slightly overstated by him in the 1936 *General Theory*—put a great deal of emphasis on the fact that interest is the difference between the zero yield on money and the yield on various impacts of money. It sounds a little like the old version of the differential land rent theory that rent must disappear if land were all alike. It sounds almost as if, were all uncertainties in the world and all transaction frictions removed, the differential between money and bond yields would disappear; it would disappear by interest coming down to the zero yield on money!

Keynes himself, in the 1937 Irving Fisher *Festschrift* called "Lessons in Monetary Experience," I think, said here is a crucial test to separate the sheep from the goats. If you think that upward shifts in investment opporunities, or the marginal efficiency schedule, will raise the interest rate, then you are a goat and you belong in the classical pen. But if you think that an upward shift in the marginal efficiency schedule will increase employment and production rather than interest, then you are of the annointed: you are a sheep and you belong in the Keynesian pen.

It is a nice attitude, but of course it is all wrong in terms of Keynes' own economics, except in an extreme liquidity-trap version, which Keynes did not, so far as I know, ever fully accept. What happens if there is an increase in the marginal efficiency of capital schedule? This raises the level of investment, and by the multiplier this raises the level of real money income. This increases the need for money, the transaction demand for money out of a fixed total of money. This leaves less to be held for speculative and precautionary purposes, and thus we run up the liquidity preference schedule and get a higher rate of interest. So this crucial test really does not separate out sheep from goats or anyone else.

I shall mention another respect in which our views in the 1930s may have been overstated. I used to quote with approval something like the following: Interest is too unimportant for short-lived projects to affect their rate of investment; for long-lived projects the factor of uncertainty becomes so important as to swamp the effects of interest, so that such investments are also interest-inelastic. Since interest affects neither short- nor long-run investment, its influence is, so to speak, confined only to the semicolon in between. The Oxford prewar questionnaires, the Ebersole Harvard Business School case studies, the Tinbergen failure to identify significant regression coefficients for investment against interest—all these seemed to confirm the notion of extreme interest-inelasticity of investment.

Whether this was or was not a legitimate hypothesis for the late 1930's, I now doubt that it is a useful assumption to understand the 1950's and 1960's.

Without regard to ancient rationing effects, take out your sharp pencil and verify the difference it makes for a long-term decision between being able to get money, let us say, at 5 per cent rather than 7 per cent. That may mean all the difference between making a profit of $2 million or a profit of $350,000 on a project; and maybe, in view of the risk, a $350,000 return is not suitable.

A recent *Wall Street Journal* alleged that a prominent corporaton was paying 20 per cent for its money now. This is not perfectly safe interest money, but it shows that we should not just go on talking about a variation of discount rate between 4 per cent and 3½ per cent, but should think beyond to the lever-aged effects on risk capital involved in such a change.

I am sorry I have used up my time and have not covered all I wanted to cover. But let me just ask a final question which, knowing I would come here to talk, I have been presenting to various of my colleagues.

If, as an American citizen today, I want to get the highest possible safe return on my money, even though I have no interest in housing I must indirectly invest my money in twenty-, thirty-, and forty-year old structures. I say this be-cause I can presumably get 4½ per cent in an insured savings and loan asso-ciation, with a guarantee by an agency of the federal government; and although in point of law I might be required to wait thirty days to take out my money, it is almost certain that upon short notice I can receive the money. Is this a fact that anybody from Mars could have predicted? Is this a rational conse-quence of the nature of the world or of economic theory? And if it is not, is it true, as I heard at a similar meeting of savings bankers not long ago, that mort-gage financing is unable to get its fair share of the capital that accrues in our modern society?

Selection 23

THE MATURITY STRUCTURE OF INTEREST RATES

WARREN L. SMITH

> *Having considered some of the factors that determine the level of "the" rate of interest, we may now turn to some of the complexities of an interest rate structure in which there are many interest rates on debt contracts of varying maturities. Why are rates on long-term instruments different from rates on short-term instruments? Do short-term rates and long-term rates always have the same relation-ships? If not, what factors affect the "yield curves" that graphically illustrate the various levels of rates on instruments of varying maturities at a given moment of time?*
>
> *Asset preferences of lenders and investors are influenced by a number of factors—their wealth, expectations concerning changes in interest rates and in prices of commodities and services, and others. The question to which Professor Warren Smith addresses himself in this selection is how these factors influence demand for various debt instruments, having various maturities—given certain assump-tions about the supply of such debt instruments.*

The interest rate structure at any particular time is determined by a com-bination of factors, of which the most important are the expectations of borrow-ers and lenders concerning future interest rates. As the economy moves from prosperity to recession and back again, the rate structure moves in a way which is at least roughly predictable.

• From Warren L. Smith, *Debt Management in the United States,* Study Paper 19, materials prepared in connection with the study of employment, growth, and price levels for the Joint Economic Committee, 86th Cong., 2nd Sess., Jan. 28, 1960, Chap. IV, "The Maturity Structure of Interest Rates," pp. 81–88. Reprinted by permission of the Joint Economic Committee, Congress of the United States, and the author.

Generally, interest rates on debt contracts of all maturities move up and down together.[1] This is simply because demand schedules for credit in all sectors tend to move up and down together as credit conditions change and because both lenders and borrowers commonly have some flexibility with respect to the maturity sector in which they will operate, so that if rates in a particular maturity range get out of line with other rates, corrective forces are set in motion.

Thus, in a boom period interest rates in all maturity sectors ordinarily rise, while in recession periods they fall. However, the changes in interest rates are ordinarily different for different maturities. In particular, as the level of interest rates rises and falls, short-term interest rates usually move over a considerably wider range than do long-term interest rates. These differential movements of rates in different maturity ranges can be explained, at least approximately, by reference to patterns of interest rate expectations.

To illustrate how interest rate expectations influence the interest rate structure, let us consider a situation in which the consensus of expectations on the part of borrowers and lenders is that interest rates are going to rise in the near future. Before these expectations developed, for whatever reason, suppose that short-term and long-term interest rates were approximately equal. As a result of the change in expectations, lenders would have a tendency to eschew long-term securities, because they would expect to suffer capital losses on investments in such securities when interest rates rose and because they would feel that it was preferable to hold back and wait until prices of longer term securities fell before investing in them. Investors with this kind of expectations would tend to shift their flow of funds toward shorter term loans and securities. In fact, some investors might even sell out their existing holdings of long-term securities in advance of the expected price decline and put their funds into short-term securities. Thus, there would be a shift in the supply of funds from the long- to the short-term market. Borrowers, on the other hand, would tend to make a reverse shift. To the extent that they felt that interest rates were going to rise, they would feel that the present was an auspicious time to borrow at long-term in order to take maximum advantage of the existing relatively low rates. As a consequence of the shift of supply from the long- to the short-term market and the shift of demand from the short- to the long-term market, the long-term rate would tend to rise relative to the short-term rate, thus producing an upward-sloping yield curve. Under circumstances in which interest rates were expected to fall, precisely the opposite kinds of shifts would tend to occur. Supply would shift from the short- to the long-term market and demand from the long- to the short-term market, thus producing a rise in the short-term rate relative to the long-term rate and a downward-sloping yield curve.

If investors or speculators are prepared to move funds between the various maturity sectors on a carefully calculated basis, the determination of the rate structure becomes somewhat more precise than the above discussion suggests.

---

[1] This is not always the case—occasionally short-term and long-term interest rates move in opposite directions. However, this is usually a transition phenomenon which lasts only a short time. See footnote 6 below.

If investors held identical expectations with complete certainty, the long-term rate for any specified period would become equal to the average of the expected short-term rates over that period. That is, neglecting compounding of interest, if the present rate for six-month loans were 3 per cent and this rate were expected to rise continuously to 4 per cent, 5 per cent, and 6 per cent, respectively, for the next six-month periods, the current rate for a two-year loan would be about 4.5 per cent, the average of these rates.[2] The reason for this is that the investor would have to be able to get the same return for investing for two years as he could obtain for investing now for six months and successively reinvesting in similar six-month contracts over the next two years. If this relationship did not hold, shifts of demand and supply similar to those discussed above would occur until it did prevail.

When allowance is made for the fact that the expectations of investors are uncertain and that expectations differ from one investor to another, the precision of the expectational theory is destroyed. Nevertheless, the expectational theory seems to explain, at least in broad outline, the typical pattern of movement of the interest-rate structure. To complete the explanation, however, it is necessary to add one further element. It appears that, at least as regards movements of interest rates associated with short-run fluctuations of business conditions, investors' expectations are determined in relation to some level of interest rates which they regard as "normal" or "conventional." Thus, as interest rates rise to "high" (at least by recent standards) levels during a period of inflation, the expectation that they are going to decline in the near future becomes more and more widespread, and as a consequence, short-term rates rise relative to long-term rates. In such circumstances, short-term rates may actually rise above long-term rates. On the other hand, when interest rates fall to "low" levels during recession periods, the expectation becomes increasingly widespread that they are going to rise, and, accordingly, short-term rates fall substantially below long-term rates. At times when rates are not expected to change or when an increase or a decrease seems approximately equally likely, short-term and long-term rates may be approximately equal, although this statement is subject to an important qualification to be pointed out shortly.

It is a commonly observed phenomenon that, as interest rates and security prices move up and down, short-term interest rates ordinarily fluctuate over a wider range than long-term interest rates, while long-term security prices fluctuate over a wider range than short-term security prices. This typical pattern of movement constitutes a fairly impressive piece of indirect evidence in support of the expectational theory as outlined above. It can be shown that if investors' elasticities of interest rate expectations are between zero and unity—that is, if a rise in current interest rates causes investors to revise upward their expectations of future interest rates over their planning horizon but by an amount less than

[2] The "expectational" theory of the interest-rate structure is expounded in J. R. Hicks, *Value and Capital* (2d ed.; Oxford: the Clarendon Press, 1946), Chap. XI; F. A. Lutz, "The Structure of Interest Rates," *Quarterly Journal of Economics,* LV (November, 1940), pp. 36–63, reprinted in W. Fellner and B. F. Haley (eds.), *Readings in the Theory of Income Distribution* (Philadelphia: Blakiston Co., 1946), pp. 499–529. See also R. A. Musgrave, *The Theory of Public Finance* (New York: McGraw-Hill Book Co., 1959), Chap. XXIV.

the rise in current interest rates—the expectational theory will produce the patterns of movement in interest rates and security prices that are typically observed.[3]

Lenders may have a preference for liquidity—that is, price stability—because of the possibility that an unforeseen contingency may require them to sell securities on short notice. At the same time, borrowers, particularly those who are borrowing for long-term purposes such as investment in fixed plant and equipment, clearly have a distinct preference for long-term debt contracts, since with such contracts they avoid the necessity for frequent renewal of their loans perhaps at inconvenient times. Thus, lenders have an inherent preference for short debt and borrowers for long debt, and this tends to bias the short-term interest rate in a downward direction compared to the long-term rate. For this reason, even when interest rates are not expected to change, the short-term rate is likely to be somewhat below the long-term rate. Also, of course, there are limitations on the mobility of funds from one maturity sector to another, and some lenders and borrowers have conventional preferences for debt of certain maturities, which interfere with the full realization of the rate pattern that would be produced by the free reign of expectations.[4] Nevertheless, the actual movements of the interest rate structure seem to be broadly consistent with the expectational theory.

Figure 1 presents a somewhat idealized picture of the way in which the term structure of interest rates might be expected to behave according to the expectational theory as outlined above. Yield curve I is the kind of pattern that would tend to prevail in recession periods when interest rates were low and most investors expected them to rise in the future. Curve III is the type that would prevail in boom periods when interest rates were high and most investors

[3] To illustrate, suppose we have two securities, a $1,000 3-per cent "bill" having a maturity of 1 year and a $1,000 3 per cent consol. Suppose the typical investor has a planning horizon of 1 year and his elasticity of expectations is 0.5. To begin with, both securities are selling at par, to yield 3 per cent. Suppose now that, for whatever reason, the yield on consols rises to 3.1 per cent so that the price of consols falls to $967.74. With an elasticity of yield expectations of 0.5, the investor will expect that the yield on consols at the end of his 1-year horizon will have fallen halfway back to its original level, or will be 3.05 per cent so that the price of consols will be $983.61. If he invests $967.74 in a consol and holds it for 1 year, his expected return will be $30 interest plus a capital gain of $15.87, or a total of $45.87, giving a yield (for 1 year) of 4.74 per cent. In order to equalize the returns for holding consols and "bills," the interest rate on bills will have to rise to 4.74 per cent, and the price of outstanding 3-per cent bills will have to fall to $983.39. Thus, the yield on bills will rise more than the yield on consols, while the price of consols will fall more than the price of bills. This pattern of behavior will be obtained only if the elasticity of expectations lies between zero and unity—which is a technical translation of the idea that investors' expectations are dominated by convention or the concept of a normal yield level. It may be noted that in this illustration it was assumed that the short-term yields adjust to become consistent with current and expected long-term yields rather than the other way around. In fact, however, the two approaches are equivalent. This extension and adaptation of the expectational theory is developed by Tibor Scitovsky in "A Study of Interest and Capital," *Economica*, VII, n.s. (August, 1940), pp. 304–306. See also Musgrave, *op. cit.*, p. 596.

[4] These factors are stressed in J. M. Culbertson, "The Term Structure of Interest Rates," *Quarterly Journal of Economics*, LXXI (November, 1957), pp. 485–517. We shall also make use of them below to explain certain peculiarities that have appeared in the rate structure recently.

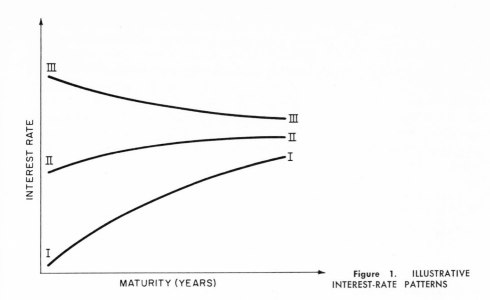

Figure 1.   ILLUSTRATIVE
INTEREST-RATE PATTERNS

expected them to fall. Curve II is the type that would prevail in periods in which most investors expected rates to remain unchanged for some time in the future or when expectations of increases were about as common as expectations of decreases.[5] As business conditions change, the rate structure would move continuously from one position to another—for example, during a period of recovery from recession, the structure would gradually change from type I to III.[6] Thus interest rates would tend to rise together, but with short-term rates moving over a considerably wider range than long-term interest rates.

For many years up until rather recently, the term structure of interest rates in the United States was of type I variety, with short-term interest rates substantially lower than long-term rates. During the depression of the 1930's, interest rates fell to low levels, as is characteristic of such periods, and investors, judging the rate level by the conventional standards established in the 1920's, felt that rates were abnormally low and could be expected to rise. Accordingly, short-term rates fell to very low levels and the yield curve took on a sharply

[5] Curve II has a gentle upward slope due to the inherent preferences of lenders for short-term debt and of borrowers for long-term debt, referred to above.

[6] There may be times when short- and long-term rates move in opposite directions. For example, during the early stages of a recovery period when interest rates begin to rise and investors expect the rise to continue for some time as the recovery develops, lenders may hold funds back from the long-term market to wait until rates begin to stabilize, putting these funds temporarily into the short-term market, while borrowers may anticipate their needs for long-term funds and accelerate their long-term borrowing in order to meet their requirements before rates rise further. In these circumstances, long-term rates may rise sharply while short-term rates are rising only slightly or perhaps even declining. In terms of our earlier analysis, this is a circumstance in which market participants have elastic expectations rather than the inelastic expectations which normally seem to prevail. This is likely to be a transition phenomenon, however, which accelerates the rise in long-term interest rates to a point where inelastic expectations again prevail and short-term rates rise sharply to produce a type III curve.

upward-sloping shape. During World War II, the Federal Reserve System, in coordination with the Treasury, decided to peg the interest rate structure in order to assist the Treasury in financing the war. The rate structure selected for pegging was approximately the one then prevailing, which reflected the effects of the prolonged depression. The Treasury bill rate was fixed at ⅜ per cent and the certificate rate at ⅞ per cent, with rates rising to 2½ per cent for long-term Treasury bonds.[7] Although the bill and certificate rates were freed in July and August 1947, and somewhat greater flexibility was introduced into the short-term end of the rate structure, the fixing of the long-term rate and control over the rate structure was maintained until the accord of March, 1951. Even after the accord, flexibility was introduced only gradually. Since the "bills-only" policy was put into effect in 1953 by the Federal Reserve System, the rate structure (as distinct from the rate level) has been determined almost entirely by market forces with very little intervention by the authorities other than the incidental effects caused by the open market operations in bills.

The combined result of the depression, war finance, and the policies of the early postwar period was to produce a situation in which the short-term rate was below the long-term rate—and frequently very much below it—continuously for approximately a quarter of a century. As a result of this experience, the notion came to be widely accepted that a rate curve sloping steeply upward was the normal thing. In accordance with the expectational theory, the existence of this view in itself tended to inhibit movements of the rate structure away from the upward-sloping position. Historically, however, during the period prior to 1930, short-term rates appear to have been above long-term a good deal of the time.[8] And the basic forces of the market appear to be reasserting themselves as the implications of a flexible interest rate policy come to be more widely understood. Thus, we seem to be witnessing a reappearance of the classic pattern in which the short-term rate is above the long-term rate during prosperous times, while the opposite relation holds during recession periods.

In one respect, however, the interest rate structure during recent periods when monetary policy has been restrictive and the level of interest rates has risen has departed from the pattern described above. As interest rates have risen recently, a bulge has appeared in the yield curve in the intermediate maturity range. This is illustrated in Figure 2, which shows the yield curves for

[7] For a discussion of the decision to fix the rate structure, see H. C. Murphy, *The National Debt in War and Transition* (New York: McGraw-Hill Book Company, 1950), pp. 92–103. The fixing of this rate structure created some problems for the Treasury and the Federal Reserve, because the structure itself contradicted the expectations created in the minds of investors. The upward slope of the yield curve corresponded with expectations of rising rates, while the decision to fix rates created expectations that rates would not change. Under these circumstances, it became increasingly difficult to get investors to hold short-term securities. If the rate structure is to be pegged, the structure selected should be one in which short- and long-term rates are approximately equal—that is, a curve of the type II variety as shown in Figure 1.

[8] See David Durand, *Basic Yields of Corporate Bonds, 1900–1942,* National Bureau of Economic Research, Technical Paper 3 (New York: National Bureau of Economic Research, 1942), especially charts showing yield curves for individual years from 1900 to 1942.

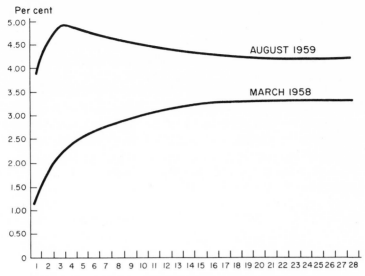

Figure 2. TERM STRUCTURE OF INTEREST RATES—MARCH 1958 AND AUGUST 1959

Treasury securities in March, 1958, and in August, 1959. The March, 1958, curve is a typical yield curve for a recession period, with the short-term rate very low relative to the long-term rate. By August, 1959, the forces of recovery which increased credit demands, combined with a rather restrictive Federal Reserve policy, had caused a considerable rise in interest rates generally. Short-term rates had risen sharply from their recession lows. However, the rate structure in August, 1959, rose quite sharply from about 3.80 per cent for the shortest term securities to about 4.85 per cent at a maturity of about 2½ years and declined steadily thereafter to a level of slightly over 4 per cent for the longest term securities.[9]

It seems likely that the tendency for the shortest term interest rates to remain below the rates on intermediate-term securities, even when rates rise to relatively high levels, is due to the existence of important groups of investors who are strongly interested in liquidity. For example, nonfinancial corporations have become an important factor in the government securities market in recent years. Corporate treasurers have become increasingly sophisticated in managing their cash positions so as to economize on cash balances and earn interest by investing in Treasury bills and other short-term government securities.[10] These investors seldom invest in anything but quite short-term securities because of their aversion to price variability, since the funds invested are, in effect, trans-

[9] A similar pattern made its appearance in 1956 when monetary policy became restrictive and persisted through most of 1957 until the trend of monetary policy was reversed to counter the recession late in that year.

[10] Corporations also invest their surplus funds in open market commercial paper and in repurchase agreements with government security dealers. However, short-term governments are by far the most important outlet for their funds. See C. E. Silberman, "The Big Corporate Lenders," *Fortune* (August, 1956).

actions balances which may be needed on short notice to make payments.[11] Commercial banks are also interested in short-term governments, which constitute the bulk of their secondary reserves. Foreign accounts and state and local governments have become increasingly important investors in governments. Like nonfinancial corporations, these groups of investors, being interested chiefly in liquidity, do not ordinarily speculate on changes in security prices and therefore concentrate their holdings in the short-term sector regardless of interest rate expectations.[12] The fact that all of these investor groups added substantially to their holdings of government securities between mid-1958 and mid-1959 suggests that their activities may have served to moderate the rise in interest rates in the shortest maturity range and thus have been mainly responsible for the failure for short-term interest rates to rise more than they did.[13] If a restrictive monetary policy continues to be applied, it may become necessary at a later time for some of these investor groups to liquidate their holdings of short-term governments in order to finance expenditures or to meet loan demands (in the case of commercial banks). If and when this happens, short-term rates may rise sharply, thus producing the sort of downward-sloping yield curve which characterized prosperous periods in earlier times.[14]

[11] On the theoretical aspects of the management of transactions balances, see James Tobin, "The Interest-Elasticity of Transactions Demand for Cash," *Review of Economics and Statistics,* XXXVIII (August, 1956), pp. 241–47, and W. J. Baumol, "The Transactions Demand for Cash: An Inventory Theoretic Approach," *Quarterly Journal of Economics,* LXVI (November, 1952), pp. 545–556.

[12] Of course, commercial banks do shift the composition of their portfolios of government securities in accordance with changing interest rate expectations. But, as far as their secondary reserves are concerned, they tend to maintain large holdings in the short-term sector under most circumstances.

[13] Between June 30, 1958, and June 30, 1959, nonfinancial corporations increased their holdings of government securities by $6.1 billion (from $13.9 billion to $20 billion). While no data on maturities are available, it can be assumed that these increased holdings were heavily concentrated in short maturities. Foreign accounts increased their holdings by $3.4 billion (from $6.2 billion to $9.6 billion); most of this increase was in bills and certificates. State and local governments added $1.3 billion to their holdings. Commercial banks increased their investments in government securities within 5 years of maturity by $3.4 billion (data from *Federal Reserve Bulletin*).

[14] This explanation of the bulge in the rate structure in the intermediate maturity range emphasizes compartmentalization of the market. Such factors are stressed by Culbertson, *op. cit.,* as an important factor in determining the rate structure generally. It may be noted that a bulge would be produced by the expectational theory if investors expected rates to rise for a time and then fall. However, compartmentalization appears to be a more plausible explanation for this particular phenomenon.

Part Four

CENTRAL BANKING
AND
MONETARY MANAGEMENT

7

The Structure and Practice
of Central Banking in the United States

IN TERMS OF BOTH ORGANIZATIONAL STRUCTURE AND operating technique, the Federal Reserve System is unique among central banks. Some of the peculiarities of its organization reflect the traditional American reluctance to vest strong economic power in central government agencies; to a very considerable extent in its initial form and in some degree today the decentralization of the operating units of the Federal Reserve System in twelve district banks reflects this political attitude. The repercussions of this are felt even in its current methods of formulating and carrying out policy. The readings in this section are designed to supplement the usual textbook discussion of Federal Reserve operations by providing some insight into the decision-making processes and sources of power in the Federal System today. The central bank, perhaps more than any other government institution, must be judged on the basis of the accuracy of its decisions and the timeliness of its actions. The effectiveness with which the Federal Reserve System mobilizes data and acts on it is of real significance in appraising the potential and limitations of monetary management.

Selection 24

THE CENTRAL BANK IN A MARKET ECONOMY

ROBERT V. ROOSA

No central bank can lay down with complete candor its objectives and the precise methods it will normally use to achieve those objectives. To do so would invite a deluge of speculative action by the private sector in anticipation of Federal Reserve actions. By the same token, however, no central bank can act in a vacuum; it must have before it a basic theoretical structure of the operation of the economy of which it is a part, and of the relations among money, credit, and the aggregate performance of that economy. In this selection, one of the former distinguished economists of the Federal Reserve staff, who is now (1964) Under Secretary of the Treasury, presents an admirable summary of the general economic philosophy of the Federal Reserve System and of the role of central banking in the American economy.

There is a vast body of experience and understanding that most of the central banks of the world share in common. There are also some pervasive and persistent differences. The clearest of these distinctions emerges between the performance of central banks in the totalitarian countries and in the democracies. In general, the central banks of the dictatorships or the regimented economies are subordinate instruments, providing payment facilities in the national currency and a kind of accounting audit for the implementation of a national plan, while the central banks of the democracies exercise a wider influence and have a greater degree of autonomy. Even the central banks of the advanced "Western style" economies, however, are only independent *within,* and not independent *from,* their governments.

This paper attempts to generalize from observation and study of central-banking policy and practice in a number of the market economies, particularly over the years since World War II. Much that is said in the first part of this article may, in the attempt to generalize, have been reduced to a simplicity that seems naive, but later on it will be argued that much of the opposition and many of the impediments confronting central banking today could have arisen only because some of these simple first principles of a market economy have been neglected.

With growth reportedly proceeding at rapid rates in some of the totalitarian countries, voices are being raised within the democracies—out of rivalry, or fear, or considerations of prestige or national defense—demanding faster growth and admonishing central banks to hold interest rates at low levels in order to encourage more investment as an inducement to growth. Others claim

---

• From Robert V. Roosa, "The Central Bank in a Market Economy," *Fortune,* March, 1961, pp. 124–127, 168–181. This article was adapted from "Monetary and Credit Policy" by Robert V. Roosa in *Economics and the Policy Maker,* copyright 1959 by the Brookings Institution, and is reprinted by permission of the Brookings Institution and the author.

that the new circumstances of the postwar period inherently generate an inexorable upward push of costs, rendering futile any efforts of the central bank that are directed against rising prices. Thus in resisting inflation, these critics argue, central banks only choke off needed investment and demand, causing unemployment and stifling growth.

Though usually quite unconscious of their further implications, proponents of these views are, in fact, striking at the very fundamentals of a market economy; in actual effect, they would dissipate the energy and weaken the stamina that the free economies will need over the years ahead. For, as will appear on fitting these various "new" conditions into the simple framework of the market economy soon to be outlined here, the unequaled vitality and expansion of the "Western" economies can be sustained only if, along with many other things, flexible and effective central banking can be preserved. . . .

MONEY IN A MARKET ECONOMY

Any growing, diversified economy needs a flexible money supply. To provide it, each economy, whether guided by a plan or by the action of markets, must have some kind of accepted apparatus for monetizing credit. Characteristically the market economies have met that need by evolving a fractional reserve, deposit banking system, in which each marginal change in the money supply is inseparably connected with a marginal change in the actual extension of credit. Such an apparatus for money creation thus makes possible a flexible variation in the total of credit availability, because the changeable margin added by created bank credit is superimposed on whatever underlying total of credit has been provided by past savings. This flexible variation at the margin can, in turn, be responsive to the shifting credit needs of a dynamic economy and be reasonably well apportioned among the thousands upon thousands of different centers of initiative within the economy, because the banks that monetize credit are in competition with each other.

It is the automatic linkage between money creation and credit creation, and the desirability of assuring productive use of the new credit which appears as a joint product whenever money is created, that makes fractional reserve banking such a crucial part of the mechanism of a market economy. Yet the mere existence of facilities for furnishing this flexibility embodies a latent potentiality for abuse. This power to create credit, and to decide where it will go, is not in a market economy all concentrated in the central bank but is divided among a number of competing banks, no one of which can be guided by over-all views of what the changes in the grand total ought to be. Thus if everything depended only on the cumulative result of the individual actions of each of the commercial banks, more credit might be created than a nation's physical resources could support, and more money might be created than orderly procedures in making payments and holding cash balances would require at current levels of prices. For any other kind of commodity or service, competition might be relied upon to bring over-all production eventually in line with demand, even though no single firm could know or judge what the total ought to be.

But this is not true of money, the common denominator for everything else. There is no longer any need to demonstrate that "money will not manage itself." The inherent risk of creating too much, or too little, makes essential some kind of general control by a public body in the public interest. That is the principal reason for the existence of central banks.

Within the market economies, the central bank is generally regarded in some sense as the conscience or the guardian of a nation's financial responsibility, so that a unique position is found for it within each governmental structure. Perhaps that helps to explain why central bankers everywhere, almost without exception, feel that they have much in common and tend to see their ultimate objectives in the same terms. They must use what powers they have, within the framework of each country's financial markets, to keep the flow of money and credit adequate for the productive use and expansion of resources, capacity, and employment opportunities. They must also give full practicable assistance to the necessitous financing of government. But they must keep the total of money and credit generated for all of these purposes within limits. They may differ somewhat in the weights given to various criteria in setting the limits, but they all consider the same array of criteria; they all realize the necessity of demonstrating that they can and will actually set limits; and they all act through a process of successive approximation, setting limits by changing marginal increments, and not by meeting a target for the total (or its many parts) that has been set in advance by a national plan. They all know, too, that theirs is only a partial role within the whole of governmental economic policy, and that they cannot expect to produce alone the results toward which they aim; but they also know that unless they take aim on the basis of a full view of the ultimate objectives any constructive force which they might exert will be scattered and wasted.

UNEMPLOYMENT AND PRICE STABILITY

The ultimate objectives of a central bank include, of course, the stimulation and expansion of real output and real income—in keeping with the broad aim of maximum growth with minimum fluctuation. More often than not, the difficult problems become translated into immediate significance in terms of employment and prices. It is through a closer look at the supposed conflict between optimum employment and reasonably stable prices that the key issues confronting any central bank, in deciding where to set the limits on money and credit, are most readily clarified.

The starting point must be to recognize that some unemployment is virtually inevitable in any growing economy—so long as successive innovation adds new products and new methods, so long as the users of products are free to change their preferences, and so long as there is neither direction of labor nor commandeering of plant and materials by some higher authority. Statistics may seem to show that some countries usually keep unemployment down to a vanishing point, while others regularly run with unemployment percentages of 2, or 3, or even 4 per cent of the labor force. But on inspection these differences usually disappear into the limbo of differences in concepts as to what is being measured or differences in the way in which the measuring is actually done. The essential point for this analysis is simply to recognize that some unemployment is inherent in change, that it occurs everywhere, in the free and planned economies alike, and that its magnitude (apart from periods of "recession" in the free economies and "reorientation" in the planned economies) is usually relatively small. To state this fact is not to deny the personal hardships often wrought by change and unemployment, but it is to suggest that transitional assistance is always going to be a part of the social charge that any dynamic economy must bear.

Despite the fact that there will always be some unemployment, it is also paradoxically the case that a vigorous market economy will usually have within it more individually worthy ventures (all reaching out for more credit and resources) than could possibly be satisfied, in total, by its presently existing mix of immediately available facilities and labor skills. That is because the new projects or the possibilities for expansion that continually arise do not necessarily need just the manpower, or plant, or materials that may currently be available. Moreover, much of the time the aggregate of all new ventures would simply exceed the bounds of what could physically be undertaken at once—at least without abruptly dislodging many other existing uses of the same resources. That is why, even though reliable statistical measures show that there is some unemployment of men, or capacity, or materials, central banks may often have to decide that they cannot open wide the valves for releasing more money and credit.

GROWTH AND FLEXIBILITY

Surely one of the conditions for diversification and expansion of production and the optimum fulfillment of consumer preference is that there must also continually be some shifting about of capital, as well as labor. In a market economy that redistribution is accomplished through market processes. Thus any attempt to flush out more money and credit, in the hope of re-employing idle men or materials right where they are, may only prevent or impede the kinds of shifts upon which further growth depends. And simply to put funds at the disposal of every venture would lead to a run-up of prices and costs that would jeopardize the new ventures themselves and generate speculative distortions for all. That is why no central bank can take responsibility for assuring *full* employment.

Some of these same considerations may, however, in other circumstances clearly call for a further release of money and credit, in order to help expand useful employment and production, even though average prices might have been rising—perhaps because of bottleneck situations or seasonal shortages in particular sectors. That is why no central bank is likely to assert that constant prices, or even price stability, will always be its overriding objective. To be sure, if a market economy worked without frictions, movements in employment and prices might never seem in conflict. The unemployed would consist only of people en route from one job to another, or en route into or out of the labor force.

Individual prices would move up or down as guides to the flow of resources,

but there would be no persistent pull or push upon the averages in an upward
direction, and repeated rounds of innovation and quickened productivity might
over time generate a gradually declining level of prices as a whole. But it is because these ideal conditions are never fulfilled that any policy which is related to
the performance of the economy as a whole must instead work within a "band
of compromise"—where there are no absolutes, and each objective is weighed
against the others, in the existing circumstances, to find a balance of optimum
utility for the kinds of influences that marginal changes in the availability of
money and credit can exert.

Though the historical result may not be price stability, the essential condition would seem to be that the central bank should be influential enough to
maintain genuine uncertainty, at any given time, as to the path of over-all price
changes that may lie ahead. Perhaps that can best be illustrated by going to an
extreme. Any effort through general measures to stimulate complete employment
of men and resources, in an economy characterized by dynamic change and
flexibility, inevitably creates strains that produce continued increases in prices.
There must, if demand is to be kept large enough to assure the employment of
everyone all the time, be sellers' markets everywhere, with a resulting deterioration of efficiency and loss of cost discipline. Confronted with the resulting evidence of steadily rising prices, the members of a market economy will certainly
make use of their basic freedoms—the same freedoms that they must have to
assure the dynamic flexibility of the system—in order to protect themselves
against the implied erosion in the value of the monetary unit. They will hoard
materials, step up capital programs, and delay payments.

TO MAKE UNCERTAINTY CERTAIN

Thus it is inescapable, given the essential conditions of a market economy,
that inflation, even of the "creeping" variety, once it has persisted long enough to
become fixed in the expectations of individuals and business firms, distorts
further and further the orderly procedures upon which the continuous performance and growth of a market economy depend. To break the circle before
it becomes vicious, public policy must exert sufficient resistance against the chain
reaction of expectations to succeed in creating genuine and widespread uncertainty as to the path the general level of prices may follow in the particular
months or years that lie just ahead. Without the "certainty of uncertainty," the
freedom that is essential to a market economy will be utilized by businesses
and individuals to find ways of protecting themselves against the price increases
confidently expected on the products they buy. Exercising the same freedom,
they will also be strongly tempted to speculate on expected price increases for
the products they sell. The result soon becomes a fusion of mass expectations
that seriously impairs the usefulness of the national currency as a standard of
value.

Thus it seems to be inherent in a market economy that price objectives must
be given a leading place alongside employment objectives. That is why policy

aims with respect to employment, as well as prices, must be viewed in terms of variability within a band, with the degree of relative emphasis between them continually reappraised.

THE DEGREES OF PRESSURE

There is a unifying concept running through the actual performance of most of the central banks of the Western economies—a concept of "pressure." Within the special institutional arrangements of each country, central banks everywhere are using, or looking for, those techniques that make it possible to alter the degree of pressure, either expansive or restrictive, being exerted upon the performance of the economy as a whole by changes in the quantity of money and in the credit creation related to it.

The central bank controls the supply of reserves and thereby determines whether or not there can be marginal increases—or whether or not there shall be marginal decreases—in the total supply of credit and in the volume of money available for the transactions and balance needs of a money-using economy. Having gauged and interpreted the prevailing pressure for additional bank credit, the central bank must relate this to its appraisal of the economic situation as a whole. If aggregate output and employment are declining, for example, does it appear that general credit pressure is one of the causes? Should that seem to be a contributing factor, clearly some easing would be indicated. Or even if restrictive credit pressure is not aggravating a decline, but the decline persists, might a general easing of credit availability be of some help in offsetting the downward thrust of other forces? How much easing? May the money-supply side of the shield impose some limit on how far to go in expanding the base for bank credit? Does liquidity already seem redundant, so that little more stimulus might be expected from further easing on the credit side, while there might be a risk that further additions to liquidity would only create a source of potential speculative pressures once a turnaround is reached and strong expansion begins?

Conversely, if expansion is proceeding rapidly, while liquidity is shrinking and velocity is rising to high levels, and if all sources of credit are being fully tapped and demand for more credit at the banks is insistent, the central bank must decide whether to relieve that pressure somewhat by releasing more reserves, or to hold steady and let demand intensify the pressure, or possibly add further to the pressure by actually absorbing reserves.

IS IT ALL USELESS?

There are today a number of problems being posed for most of the central banks of the market economies. Growth has become not merely a universal slogan but a central theme of public policy throughout the world. It is regrettable, though perhaps unavoidable, that much of the "growth economics" seems to suggest that tonnages and kilowatts are the only meaningful units of measure for comparing the relative attainments of nations and civilizations. In any event, however, without contesting the relevance of different ways of measuring a nation's growth in total welfare, the market economies have no reason to shy away from physical comparisons—even though they also have and enjoy in addition, superimposed upon mere physical production per capita, the immeasurable richness of personal freedom that permeates all aspects of their culture. And when measurement is undertaken in the physical sense, surely the levels or magnitudes attained are of first importance, although there is indeed significance, too, in rates of change. Yet it is only in the latter sense, that of current rate of increase, that any basis can be contrived for a comparison between the regimented and the market economies that is unfavorable to the latter.

Even so, whether contrasts of that kind are merely invidious or really meaningful, it is also true that any nation wants to have its economy producing more next year than last, and wants that growth to be large, sustainable, and widely distributed. The questions now being asked, against that general background of common aspirations, center upon a number of changes that are supposed to have occurred, or to have become much more prominent, in recent years. Upward pressures on wages and other labor costs are said to be stronger; effective resistance by managements to downward adjustments of prices and their ability to "administer" increases (almost regardless of changes in volume) are said to be greater; costs of government and the need for public services are said to be expanding inexorably. The climate now, in the "free" economies is therefore said to be one of continually increasing costs, prices, and taxes.

In the face of these pressures, the critics ask what useful purpose can be served by central banks attempting to maintain monetary stability, or even a reasonable steadiness in average prices? What other purpose does a restrictive monetary policy accomplish besides that of raising interest rates? And when interest rates rise for everyone, does not the allocation of credit remain the same as it would have been if all rates had been allowed to remain lower—and is not the only real effect that of giving larger returns to the moneylenders at the expense of the borrowers? In turn, because of tight money and high interest rates, some borrowing and investing may simply not get done at all; in that event, what happens to the capital formation that is needed for growth?

Much of the answer to this series of questions has already been provided over the past five to ten years by the actual performance of the economies and the central banks in one country after another—though not yet, to be sure, in all. Without referring to individual countries, a considerable part of what has emerged from these various forceful demonstrations may be summarized briefly here under three headings: "cost push" and price rigidities, flexible interest rates, and the essential requirements for sustained growth in a market economy.

"COST PUSH" AND PRICE RIGIDITIES

There is always an understandable tendency in a market economy, where changes work themselves out through a sequence of give-and-take adjustments, for observers, in attempting to discern patterns in what is going on, to confuse corrective processes with new trends. It may be confusion of just that kind which underlies much of what has been said, on the basis of observations in a few countries for a very few years, concerning the inexorability of the "cost push"—in terms not only of wages but perhaps also even of taxes. The problem is not with rising labor costs as such, nor with higher taxes, but with increases that outrun gains in average productivity.

So far, in one way or another, the genuine market economies have, often with the aid of governmental action in some form, always evolved a workable solution. Individual industries rise and fall, areas change their character, labor gains mobility, international influences come into play, and competition becomes effective.

Any alternative approach (depending upon clear-cut and decisive, but arbitrary and calculated, authoritative action) necessarily carries many other implications. To impose independently determined wage rates for large sectors of the country, or to enforce uniform increases in wages or other labor benefits, would seem to be as disruptive of the conditions essential for the functioning of a market economy as would decrees setting rigid prices or fixing rigid profit margins. Moreover, there is a powerful compulsion in logic and events that leads from any one of these forms of rigidity, once imposed, into a mantle of controls that includes them all.

To all of this the current critics of monetary policy might well agree, only pointing out further that this still means there will be periods when wages can for some time be pushed up faster than the average gains in productivity over the years can support. But what they fail to see is that any relaxation of monetary discipline, while these other influences are in the disruptive phase of an evolutionary change, would gravely reduce the chances that the corrective processes could be carried through. For the very sound principle that anything priced out of its market will find its own correction holds true only so long as no artificial props are erected to support or perpetuate a distorted situation.

Monetary and credit policy has a definite and clear responsibility to avoid being used as such a prop. Can it, should it, when unemployment seems large but labor costs are rising, add to the supply of money and credit in the hope of providing quick employment opportunities? If existing credit is already fully used, what are the chances that new increments will finance new employment opportunities? Or instead will the new increments result mainly in general price increases, in an accentuation of cyclical instability, and in stunting longer-range projects that could otherwise provide part of the basis for sustained growth? These are the kinds of questions that a responsible central bank, when confronted by a "cost-push" situation, must try to resolve.

FLEXIBLE INTEREST RATES

It is an inescapable by-product of all that has just been said that interest rates must remain flexible. Expectations tend to jell even faster in the financial markets than they do in the community as a whole. That is why it is essential to maintain some uncertainty concerning the probable future path (and the level) of interest rates. Without that uncertainty, trading in financial markets tends to move all to one side. If it appears certain, for example, that interest rates (particularly long-term rates) will rise and remain high, a stalemate, or conditions of outright disorder, may ensue very swiftly as rate quotations are moved up, and traders try to sell in order to become liquid and thus able to take advantage of the highest rates that may be reached. If the certainty is for declining rates that will remain low, most traders want to buy in order to hold securities as the rates decline because that means the prices of these securities will be higher. The price increase is viewed as a sure thing, and the yield earned currently is, moreover, higher than anything likely to be available later on. Thus expectations tend to push the market quickly toward wherever the "certainty" of views thought it would go.

The greatest risk, both to effective central banking and to the maintenance of the general flexibility and uncertainty a market economy needs, lies in the formulation of mandates that put interest rate objectives, as such, ahead of the broader requirements of monetary stability. For in a market economy neither prices nor interest rates are ends in themselves.

The experience of most leading central banks since World War II confirms the view that flexibility of interest rates, under the play of shifting competitive pressures, has been essential to the performance of the market economies. There were many that attempted, as did the U.S., to peg, or stabilize, or support some or all segments of the maturity range. In the end, every country that chose to preserve the essence of a market economy gave up the effort to maintain interest rates at what were thought to be "socially tolerable" levels when these proved in practice to be sustainable only by inflating the rest of the economy with increasing quantities of central-bank credit. Some, instead, forthrightly turned to the full apparatus of a planned economy, and began a proliferation of special devices for insulating parts of the markets and sheltering others. But even these efforts, in democratic economies that were extensively "planned," have now largely broken down because a national plan could not build effective barricades against the forces of competition at work in international trade. The evidence would seem persuasive that so long as a country is heavily dependent upon international trade, or if not, so long as it chooses to have a market economy (which is necessarily responsive to many of the same forces that are conspicuously revealed in international trade), interest rates must be flexible.

WHAT SUSTAINED GROWTH REQUIRES

Those who challenge restrictive monetary policies as arbitrary deterrents to growth have two lines of argument. One is that more bank credit would assure more aggregate demand; more demand necessarily evokes more investment; more investment generates more demand, and that represents more growth. Either way, the underlying assumption is that there are any number of productive projects standing by, just awaiting the release of more credit, or credit at lower rates of interest, in order to get started. And there is a further assumption that the added income and production which result from taking off credit restraints will shortly absorb any undue inflationary pressures that may have been initially set off by the stimulus of easier money.

This argument does not reckon with the damage done by inflation to the market's function of allocating resources. No economy, planned or free, can avoid shortages or bottlenecks in some manpower skills, or some material resources, as change and growth occur. The planned economy may break recurrent bottlenecks by crude and abrupt shifts of people or things. The market economy works out its adjustments through the guidance provided by the price mechanism. The central bank, in a market economy, cannot presume to replace the mechanism of the market; it cannot masquerade as the totalitarian planner by judging which particular uses should receive credit, which should not.

The classic problem of growth economics has always been that of rationing investment. For in any economy with an immediate growth potential there will always be more desirable and useful projects, being pressed by various interested parties, than could physically be undertaken at once. All, or virtually all, would promise to be productive. Each proponent singly might believe that the needed resources in skills or materials were available, provided credit could be obtained to put the project in motion. Yet the one absolute certainty would be that if enough credit were suddenly created, over and above that arising from current gross savings, to satisfy all at once, the collision among them all would create havoc. There would not be enough of the basic essentials to go around. Some projects might, nonetheless, be completed and get into production; but for each of those there would be many abandoned part way to completion. Some resources would have been irretrievably lost, others made useless for a long time; and the flow of production expected as an offset to the price rises set off in the initial scramble would never fully materialize. It is for such simple reasons that central banks must, in the interest of optimum growth and sustained employment of all resources, limit carefully the total expansion of created bank credit. And it also follows, inevitably, that there will always be an unsatisfied fringe of users of credit, protesting that growth—their own and that of the economy—is being thwarted by the limits presently being imposed by the central bank.

The government's role is to help assure the functioning of the checks and balances in a market economy; it helps to adjust imbalances by taking action at the margins, but it never dictates the composition of the whole nor does it actually operate many of the parts. The conditions for full realization of the possibilities for growth and for full enjoyment of the fruits of growth in a market economy require a reasonably settled environment, but there must be a modicum, too, of uncertainty. The role of the central bank is to direct the power of money creation toward three inextricably intertwined aims: the fostering of growth, the moderation of cyclical fluctuations, and the maintenance of a reasonably stable value for the monetary unit.

IMPLEMENTATION OF THE POLICIES OF THE FEDERAL OPEN MARKET COMMITTEE

ROBERT G. ROUSE

Open market operations are the very core of the Federal Reserve System's monetary control powers. The impact of open market operations on bank reserves and the money supply is easily explained. Most students, however, do not realize the magnitude of the tasks involved in formulating open market policy, implementing that policy in day-to-day operations by the Federal Reserve Bank of New York, and assembling and analyzing daily the mass of financial information needed. This article summarizes the full range of activities that lie behind the phrase "the Fed is in the market."

Open market policy is determined by the Federal Open Market Committee, which meets regularly at approximately three-week intervals in Washington. These determinations are based on a broad and careful analysis of all aspects of the current state of business, credit conditions, international developments, and related matters. The Federal Reserve Bank of New York has been designated by the Committee as the institution in the System that conducts actual operations, on behalf of all twelve Federal Reserve Banks, to put the Federal Open Market Committee's policy into operation.

As Manager of the System Open Market Account, it is my responsibility to supervise the execution of all open market transactions carried on in accordance with the Committee's policy decisions. In view of my position as Manager of the System Account, I attend the meetings of the Open Market Committee. At each of these meetings, I make a report of System operations and stand prepared to answer any questions that any member of the Committee may care to raise on the manner in which the Committee's directions have been carried out. My attendance at the meetings gives me an opportunity to hear at first hand what the Federal Open Market Committee has in mind as to policy for the succeeding period as developed in the meeting. As you know from the record of policy actions contained in the *Annual Report* of the Board of Governors, the Federal Open Market Committee at each meeting issues a directive to the Federal Reserve Bank of New York setting forth the Committee's policy in broad terms. In addition, the Committee arrives at a consensus during the course of each meeting, which tends to specify in somewhat more concrete terms, but still in a relatively general way, a series of guidelines for the Manager of the Account. It is my duty as Manager of the Account to make sure that

• From Robert Rouse, "Implementation of the Policies of the Federal Open Market Committee," *Monthly Review*, July, 1961, Federal Reserve Bank of New York. Statement before the Joint Economic Committee of the Congress of the United States (Patman Committee), June 1, 1961. Reprinted by permission of the Federal Reserve Bank of New York and the author.

the intentions of the Federal Open Market Committee as to the management of the Account during the period between meetings of the Federal Open Market Committee are clear to me. My presence at those meetings affords me an opportunity of raising any questions that I have at that time. In addition to the directive and the consensus laid down by the Committee, I have the benefit of hearing all the detailed statements by the several members of the Committee and by the other Presidents of the Reserve Banks who are not currently serving on the Committee. The views expressed in these statements serve as an important supplement to the more formal statement of the directive and the consensus, and furnish a number of additional guideposts for day-to-day operations.

A great deal remains to be said about the process by which day-to-day decisions to buy or sell government securities are made on the basis of the Committee's policy intentions, and about the process by which the day-to-day activity of the Account is reviewed by the Committee on a current basis.

First of all, it should be remembered that the Committee's decisions do not take place in a vacuum, but are made against the background of recent experience in the money and credit markets. I should like to emphasize this ever-present element of continuity. Quite often policy can be summarized in terms of creating somewhat more or somewhat less pressure in the money market and on member bank reserve positions, or in terms of maintaining about the same conditions that prevailed in an earlier period. In moving from a policy decision to day-to-day operations, the first question for determination is the effect of the natural influences in the market on bank reserves and on the degree of tightness or ease in the money markets. It may be, for example, that in the period immediately ahead, float, or a return flow of currency from circulation, or an inflow of gold, may be reasonably counted on to supply reserves to the market. If the Committee has decided upon a policy of ease, this natural flow of funds through the market may do a great part of the Manager's job for him. If, on the other hand, the Committee is pursuing a policy of restraint, an increase in bank reserves through such natural factors will require offsetting operations and thus will tend to make the Manager's problem more complicated.

In order to keep abreast of the very latest developments in all the factors affecting member bank reserve positions and the money market, the Federal Reserve has developed an elaborate system for collecting information, designed to feed into the Manager's hands all the latest data pertaining to bank reserve positions and the various factors that may be affecting these positions. On each morning, for example, we have on hand a complete nation-wide picture of the reserve positions of member banks as of the close of business the night before, including full information on the distribution of reserves as between the money market banks, reserve city banks, and country banks. In addition to up-to-the-minute information on past developments, we have a number of specialists who forecast changes in factors affecting bank reserves for the period immediately ahead. These estimates are revised each day for the next succeeding three- or four-week period.

But it is clear that cold statistics do not provide sufficient basis for the conduct of day-to-day operations. We also rely heavily on the specialists who work on our Trading Desk, which serves as the listening post of the Federal Reserve System on the nation's money and securities markets. Located as we are in the heart of the country's financial center, and with direct communication with the government securities dealers and the money market banks, we have a unique opportunity to follow developments in the market as they are occurring.

Part of our job is to disseminate this information on current developments throughout the System, and to the Treasury for which we execute transactions as fiscal agent of the United States. But in addition, hour-by-hour developments, particularly those in the Federal funds market, in the government securities market, in the progress of government securities dealers in finding the financing required to carry their portfolios of government securities, provide the Manager of the Account with information which gives him an informed judgment of the degree of ease or tightness in the market—sometimes referred to as the "feel" of the market. The Federal funds rate tells us something about the availability of excess reserves in the banking system, with a rising rate indicative of somewhat greater pressure and a falling rate indicative of declining pressure on bank reserve positions. Similarly, if government securities dealers—who scour the country each day in search of funds from banks, corporations, and state and municipal bodies—are having an easy time finding funds to finance their portfolios at relatively low rates, we know that there is a ready availability of short-term funds throughout the country. Movements in Treasury bills rates, too, may at times be indicative of nonbank liquidity as well as bank liquidity, and may be an important part of the information we use in reaching decisions on operations. Current trends in the capital markets are also taken into consideration in viewing the mix of pertinent factors.

The Manager of the Account is also directly concerned with activity by foreign central banks, monetary authorities, and international institutions in our money market. Developments in our balance of payments and in the international position of the dollar are, of course, taken into consideration by the Federal Open Market Committee in its policy deliberations. But as Vice President in charge of the Securities Department of the New York Bank, I have a direct and immediate technical interest in these operations, since foreign central banks hold and invest so large a part of their dollar reserves through the Federal Reserve Bank of New York. Transactions for foreign accounts affect member bank reserves and thus must be taken into account when operations for System Account are being considered. The gold outflow in 1960, for example, was one of the major factors affecting member bank reserves with which we had to deal. The fact that the Federal Reserve Bank of New York has close institutional relationship with foreign central banks and performs so large a percentage of transactions for their account in the money market enables us to have first-hand information concerning the timing and the potential market impact of these transactions. At times the coordination of these foreign operations in the government securities market with Federal Reserve open market operations can become a particularly important undertaking. Transactions for foreign accounts in the market on occasion may make the job of the Manager of the System Account somewhat easier; on other occasions, they may complicate it. At times, for example, it is possible for us to avoid an undesirable market impact of foreign account transactions by arranging transactions among these accounts or directly with the System Open Market Account. In any event, the fact that we have knowledge of such foreign transactions permits us to integrate them with System operations.

To sum up, then, we start from a policy decision of the Committee as to the degree of pressure or ease desired, and on the basis of our knowledge of the present and prospective influences on bank reserves as a result of the operation of natural factors, together with the information that is fed to us on a current basis by the money and securities markets themselves, a decision whether to supply reserves to the market or absorb reserves through open market operations is arrived at. This is a decision that has to be reached each day in light of all the factors that I have mentioned before. Our estimates and forecasts of bank reserve positions are subject to wide fluctuations as a result of any number of factors that can only be imperfectly predicted, and I might add that a decision not to undertake open market operations is as difficult as a decision to buy or sell. I should emphasize here that, while the management of the System Open Market Account is in constant touch with the market, the Account does not necessarily operate in the market every minute, every hour, or even every day or week.

I think it is obvious that a considerable amount of judgment is required as to the nature, the timing, and the exact amount of any given open market operation. The very nature of open market operations means that they must be approximate and directional in nature, rather than precise, and it is only by a constant review of the impact of our operations on the money market and on bank reserve positions that we can answer the question of how much we should do and when we should do it.

Although the Federal Open Market Committee meets periodically, open market operations must be conducted on a day-to-day basis. While the Open Market Committee lays down a number of guidelines for the Manager of the Account, the nature and complexity of our financial structure precludes the Committee from setting forth a precise schedule of purchases and sales of government securities that the Manager should follow on each day. This should not be taken to indicate, however, that the Manager operates solely on his own initiative between meetings of the Committee, and hence has an opportunity to determine policy on his own account. I shall not attempt to go into the many advantages that stem from the regional character of the Federal Reserve System. The fact that we do have a regional system, however, and the fact that the Board of Governors is located in Washington while operations are, of necessity, conducted in New York, does require a highly developed system of communications within the System to insure that each member of the Board of Governors and each President of a Federal Reserve Bank is kept fully informed of the Manager's operation of the System Account on a day-to-day basis.

To start with, each morning there is a conference call at 11 o'clock, at which time the Account Management talks by telephone with a representative of the Board of Governors and one of the Presidents of a Reserve Bank who is currently serving on the Committee. Quite often, Mr. Hayes, the Vice Chairman of the Committee, and his alternate on the Committee, Mr. Treiber, the

First Vice President of the New York Bank, sit in with my associates and myself on this call, and one or more of the Governors of the Board may sit in at the Washington end. After a summary of conditions in the money and capital markets as they have developed during the first hour of trading in the morning, a summary of the reports received from dealers as to the volume of trading in government securities and their positions at the close of business on the preceding day, a review of the country-wide reserve positions, with special attention to the reserve position of the New York and Chicago money market banks, a review of developments expected for the day in the Treasury balance and other information that may appear pertinent, the Account Management outlines the approach it proposes to take with respect to operations during that day. (This review of our intentions is, of course, based on our assessment of conditions as they exist at 11 o'clock or thereabouts, and is subject to change should there be a significant change in the market atmosphere.) The other participants in the call may choose to comment on the course of action outlined by the Manager and may review any other developments that appear to them to be pertinent in this respect. A rather detailed summary of this call is prepared at the Board of Governors and placed before each member of the Board within a short time after the completion of the call. The same information is transmitted by telegram to the Presidents of all the other Reserve Banks, so that within a very short time the entire System has been alerted to the morning's developments and to the course of action that the Manager deems appropriate to implement the policy laid down by the Committee. This rapid dissemination of this information permits each member of the Committee to assess the desirability of the action contemplated by the Manager, and to make comments and suggestions if he believes it desirable to do so.

I might add that, while the final responsibility for determining day-to-day operations rests with me, I rely heavily upon the staff work of specialists, traders, statisticians, economists, and others who devote so much of their time to the conduct of our System operations. I am, of course, able to discuss at any time problems that may arise with the Vice Chairman of the Committee or his alternate on the Committee, and if there are particularly troublesome problems, I may consult directly with Chairman Martin or request a telephone conference of the full Open Market Committee.

In addition to this daily call, a written report is submitted daily to the Board of Governors and to interested officers of other Reserve Banks, and at the end of each statement week, a full written report of Account operations as well as developments in bank reserve positions, the money, government securities, and capital markets is submitted by me to the members of the Open Market Committee and to the other Presidents. Similar reports are prepared to cover developments between meetings of the Open Market Committee, including a report which covers developments and Account operations up to the close of business on the Monday night preceding a meeting. Thus, when the Committee convenes on a Tuesday morning, it has a full written record of all the activity conducted for the Account, as well as a description of the background against which these operations were conducted.

And this is not all. During the course of the day, we submit hourly reports
to the Board of Governors on prices and interest rates on government securities,
and indicate, on an hourly basis, the operations that have been undertaken by
the Account Management. In addition, a summary of the day's developments
is also transmitted by telephone to a member of the staff of the Board of
Governors by the Trading Desk after the close of the market at 3:30 p.m., and
a summary of this information is prepared for distribution to members of the
Board.

In addition to these informational activities, the System has devised, as part
of its Emergency Planning Procedures, a program whereby certain officers and
staff members of the other Reserve Banks and of the Board of Governors spend
two to three weeks with us at the Trading Desk in New York. While this program was devised mainly to provide some measure of continuity in System
operations in case of a national emergency, it has served to provide key people
in the System with a broad understanding of the scope of, and the problems
involved in, day-to-day open market operations.

All in all, while this program of information and training takes great time
and effort, we feel that it is absolutely essential and that it has been quite
effective in keeping the entire System up-to-date on operations undertaken on
behalf of the Open Market Committee. The completeness of the information
provided, and its current nature, permits each member of the Committee to be
fully informed of the operations undertaken, and provides members of the
Committee an opportunity for continuous review of, and comment concerning,
the manner in which the Manager is carrying out the instructions he received
at the meeting of the full Committee.

Selection 26

THE POLITICAL STRUCTURE OF THE FEDERAL RESERVE SYSTEM

MICHAEL D. REAGAN

*The Federal Reserve System, like any central bank, must develop
and change in ways that are appropriate to the structure of the
economy and over-all government activities. In this article, the
Federal Reserve System is weighed and found wanting in this
respect. The author argues that vitally important shifts in the "Fed's"
functions, generally in the direction of a more powerful role in
national economic stabilization, have not been matched by appropriate changes in its organizational structure. Not all economists
would share the author's dissatisfaction with the present structure
of the Federal Reserve System; but few would deny that each of
the points he considers should be given careful public consideration
to assure the most effective performance by an agency as important
as the central bank.*

• From Michael D. Reagan, "The Political Structure of the Federal Reserve System,"
American Political Science Review, Vol. LV, No. 1, March, 1961, pp. 64–76; American
Political Science Association, Princeton University, Princeton, New Jersey. Reprinted by
permission of the *American Political Science Review* and the author.

Public policy is not self-generating; it emerges from institutions. Foremost among the institutions charged with monetary and credit policy formation—an area, like fiscal policy, that has not received from political scientists the attention accorded to micro-economic regulation of particular firms or industries—is the Federal Reserve System. The purpose of this paper is to examine the "fit" of the System's formal structure to (1) the policy functions and the informal policy-forming mechanisms of the "Fed," and (2) the pattern of interests and values affected by monetary policy. Its thesis is that a substantial gap has developed between these elements.

A brief sketch of the formal structure of authority and the historical development of System functions is needed to begin with; this is followed by analysis of the formal and the effective roles of each component of the System along with the internalized interest representation at each level. Then the linkage between the Federal Reserve System and general economic policy is explored. Finally, the conclusion summarizes the finding and suggests briefly how formal structure and policy functions might be brought into closer, more effective alignment.

I. STRUCTURE AND FUNCTIONAL DEVELOPMENT

The pyramid

The Federal Reserve System [1] can be described as a pyramid having a private base, a mixed middle level and a public apex. At the apex stands the Board of Governors (frequently referred to as the Federal Reserve Board or FRB). Its seven members are appointed by the President, with the consent of the Senate, for fourteen-year, overlapping terms, one term expiring at the end of January in each even-numbered year. Members are removable for cause, but the removal power has not been exercised. In making appointments, the President must give due regard to "fair representation of financial, agricultural, and commercial interests, and geographical divisions of the country," and not more than one member can be appointed from a single Federal Reserve District. The Chairman is selected by the President for a renewable four-year term. The Board is independent of the appropriations process, for its operating funds come from semi-annual assessments upon the twelve Reserve Banks.

At a level of equivalent authority to the Board itself, but in the "middle" of the public-private pyramid, stands the statutory Federal Open Market Committee. It is composed of all FRB Members plus five of the twelve Reserve Bank Presidents, with the President of the New York Reserve Bank always one of the five and the others serving in rotation. The Chairman of the Board of Governors is, by custom, the Chairman of the Committee.

The Reserve Banks are quasi-public institutions: their capital stock is subscribed by the member banks—all national banks and about one-third of the

---

[1] For more detailed description of the formal organization, see Board of Governors, *The Federal Reserve System* (Washington, D. C., 1961) and G. L. Bach, *Federal Reserve Policy Making* (New York: Alfred A. Knopf, Inc., 1950).

state-chartered banks, at the statutory rate of six per cent (one-half paid in) of their capital and surplus—but their role is public as a part of the central banking system. While a six per cent cumulative dividend is paid to the member-bank stockholders, and a surplus equal to twice the paid-in capital has been accumulated, the remainder of the Reserve Banks' now sizable earnings is surrendered to the national Treasury. Their annual contribution to the Treasury currently amounts to about a tenth of the annual interest cost of carrying the public debt. In contrast with their paid-in capital of $387 million (as of December 31, 1959), their assets include some $27 billion in Treasury securities, and their earnings derived chiefly from the interest paid on these holdings.

The Reserve Bank Presidents are not government appointees; they are elected by the boards of directors of their respective banks, subject to FRB veto; and their compensation—far above civil service levels—is fixed in the same way. Thus their selection is initially private, but with public supervision. The Board of Directors of each Reserve Bank consists of nine persons, six of whom are elected by the member commercial banks of that District (these banks, the "owners" of the Reserve Banks, constituting the private base of the pyramid), while three (including the Chairman and Deputy Chairman) are appointed by the FRB in Washington.

Off to the side stands the final element of statutory organization, the Federal Advisory Council (FAC). This group of twelve men is composed of one commercial-banker representative from each district, annually elected by the respective regional Boards. The FAC meets quarterly with the FRB to discuss general business conditions and may make recommendations to the Board on matters of policy. The twelve Reserve Bank Presidents constitute a non-statutory Conference of Presidents that meets three times a year; a Conference of Reserve Bank Chairmen meets annually with the FRB.

The location of policy powers

The three major tools of monetary policy are the rediscount rate charged by Reserve Banks of member bank borrowers on their loans from the System; the setting of reserve requirement levels for the member banks; and—most important today—open market operations in securities of the federal government. Decision regarding each of these instruments is formally located in a different organ of the System, although (as will be developed below) channels for advice and influence cause a mingling of the decisional powers in fact. The levels of reserve requirements are set by the FRB; open market policy is a function of the Open Market Committee (OMC), thus providing the regional and quasi-private elements of the System with formal access to the heart of monetary policy formation; and the Reserve Bank Boards of Directors share with the FRB formal authority over the discount rate. The rate is "established" every fourteen days by each regional Bank, but "subject to the review and determination" of the Board of Governors. In addition the FRB shares with the Comptroller of the Currency, the FDIC, and state authorities a very considerable list of regulatory and supervisory powers over member banks and their officers.

Functional change since 1913

When established, the Federal Reserve System was thought of as exercising only the technical function of quasi-automatic adjustment of an elastic currency supply to the fluctuating needs of commerce and industry. The System was pictured as a "cooperative enterprise" among bankers for the purpose of increasing the security of banks and providing them with a reservoir of emergency resources.[2] To this day the Federal Reserve Act mandate reflects this view: it instructs that the discount rate and open market policy shall be operated with a "view of accommodating commerce and business," and that reserve requirements shall be handled so as to prevent "excessive use of credit for the purchase or carrying of securities." Nothing in the Act relates the monetary authority to the function of national economic stabilization; yet this is its prime task today.

In 1913, it was not foreseen that the techniques of monetary policy would become instruments of economic stabilization with their consequences for employment, growth and price stability overtaking their specific banking objectives in importance. Yet this is what has happened, beginning in the Twenties but more strongly and with more explicit recognition in the policy process since the Great Crash.[3] With this shift, the operation of the Federal Reserve System necessarily moved into the political mainstream, for the goal of stabilization requires making choices among alternatives that have important and visible consequences for substantial interests and community values. Once macroeconomic policy had become the primary *raison d'etre* of the System, the breadth of interests involved became coterminous with the nation, not just with the bankers; and monetary policy, as well as depositors' safety, became a public concern rather than a private convenience.

A corollary of the rise of stabilization to stage center is that the scope of FRB action has become essentially national, belying the assumption of relative regional independence that underlay the original legislation. Divergent policies for each region become undesirable—even impossible—if national stabilization is to be achieved in an increasingly interdependent national economy.

II. ROLES AND INTERESTS OF THE COMPONENTS

We turn now to a comparison of formal roles and interest composition with the informal roles and interest-impact of each level of the System's structure.

[2] E. A. Goldenweiser, *American Monetary Policy* (New York: McGraw-Hill Book Company, 1951), p. 295.

[3] In the mid-1920's it dawned on the Reserve Banks—sooner than on the Treasury or the FRB—that open market purchases, first undertaken to improve Reserve Bank earnings, could be managed to offset declines in member banks' outstanding loans; see L. V. Chandler, *Benjamin Strong, Central Banker* (Washington: The Brookings Institution, 1958). The Banking Act of 1935, reorganizing the FRB and the System, ratified emergency improvisations in 1932–33 to restore bank liquidity by enabling advances to be made to member banks on the security of any of their assets deemed acceptable, and not just on "eligible" commercial paper as before. Federal deposit insurance was introduced in 1934, in recognition of the fact that more public policy objectives than the rescue of depositors in failing banks were at stake in the maintenance of confidence in the safety of bank deposits. The architects of the 1913 Act supposed they had, by and large, provided for the safety of deposits by establishing the rediscount privilege and strengthening bank examination powers.

The commercial bank base

The formal role of the member banks is that of an electoral constituency in the selection of six of the nine directors for each Reserve Bank. While the member banks have no direct policy voice, this electoral role originally gave them an indirect one, on the assumption that the regional boards would be policy-making bodies through their authority over the discount rate. That authority is negligible today. Furthermore, the "ownership" of the Reserve Banks by the commercial banks is symbolic; they do not exercise the proprietary control associated with the concept of ownership nor share, beyond the statutory dividend, in Reserve Bank "profits." As in the large, publicly held corporation, ownership and control have been divorced. No doubt the FRB, for example in the adjustment of reserve requirements, has been solicitous for the maintenance and improvement of commercial bank earnings. But if the record of the other "independent" regulatory commissions is any guide, this would have been true regardless of their stockholdings in the Reserve Banks.

Bank ownership and election at the base are therefore devoid of substantive significance, despite the superficial appearance of private bank control that the formal arrangement creates.

Reserve Bank Boards of Directors

The Reserve Bank Boards' authority to set rediscount rates, subject to "review and determination" by the FRB, is considerably diminished by the ultimate formal authority of the latter, for "determination" includes final decision and even initiation of rate changes. It is further reduced by informal practice: to avoid the embarrassments of public disputes, discount rate policy is discussed at OMC meetings and the determinations settled upon therein are usually followed through uniformly at the next meetings of the respective regional Boards of Directors.[4] The special formalities are "of little significance; rediscount policy is made in much the same way and on essentially the same considerations as in reserve and open-market policy." [5] The nationalization of function has thus removed the basis for the assumption of regional autonomy that underlay the original grant of authority to the Reserve Banks. The major tasks of the Directors now are to provide information on regional conditions for OMC and the FRB to take into account, and to serve as a communications and public relations link between the System and local communities—both the general community and the specific "communities" of commercial banking, industry, merchants and other financial institutions. They do not exercise important substantive authority.

This may be fortunate in view of the structure of interests that prevails at this level. For the range of interests, reflecting the banker-business orientation of 1913, is narrow by legal specification and narrower still in fact. By statute,

---

[4] Joint (Patman) Committee on the Economic Report, *Monetary Policy and the Management of the Public Debt, Replies to Questions,* Sen. Doc. 123, 82d Cong., 2d sess., 1952, pp. 278–79. Cited hereafter as Sen. Doc. 123.

[5] Bach, *op. cit.,* pp. 81–82.

each regional Board has three classes of membership: Class A consists of three commercial bankers; Class B of three men active in commerce, agriculture or "some other industrial pursuit"; and Class C, without occupational restriction. Class C members are appointed by the FRB; the others are elected by the member banks of each region.

Class A directors are elected by a method that groups the member-bank stockholders into size categories for voting purposes and assures the selection of one director from a large bank, one from a middle-sized bank and one from a small bank within the District. Informally, Classes B and C tend to be quite similar. Both are dominated by executives of manufacturing firms, utilities, oil and chemical firms, and large distributors—although Class C also includes an occasional academic economist or publisher. Very large firms predominate; very small firms, "family farmers," and labor are not represented. The list of Directors reads like a *Who's Who* of American industry.[6]

The propriety of excluding other segments of the economy from these Boards is not a substantively important question at present because of the decline in the Boards' authority, though the appearances could themselves become a political issue. But it is worth asking what functional value this elaborate structure possesses and whether the Boards would be missed if they were simply abandoned. The informational role of the Directors could be as well—perhaps better—performed by the Reserve Bank Presidents, who are full-time officials in close daily contact with their districts.

The Reserve Bank Presidents

The Presidents, by virtue of the membership of five of their number on the OMC (and the participation of all twelve in OMC discussions) are more significantly related to the policy process than are their nominal superiors, the regional Boards.

Selection of the Presidents is by the respective Boards, but subject to FRB veto: initially private but finally public. Increasingly, they are men with substantial Reserve System experience. Two-thirds of the incumbents have had such experience; one-third have come to their posts from careers in commercial banking. Their daily contacts are with private bankers and one observer suggests that they have been "inclined to favor more cautious, mild policies that would be less disturbing to the normal courses of banking and the money markets" than has the FRB.[7] Yet another writer, granting a "commercial banker mentality" in the early days of the System, argues that a public, central banking view is coming to prevail as a majority come up through the System.[8] In one respect the Presidents have clearly differed from the FRB: in their support of a change urged by commercial bankers that would place authority for all monetary actions in the OMC—a change the FRB has opposed.

[6] See, for example, the *Forty-Sixth Annual Report of the Board of Governors of the Federal Reserve System* (Washington, 1960), pp. 134–48, for the list of names and affiliations as of December 31, 1959.

[7] Bach, *op. cit.,* pp. 57–58.

[8] Goldenweiser, *op. cit.,* p. 296.

As a statutory minority on the OMC, the views of the Presidents cannot be controlling in themselves. In the apparently unlikely event of a split within the FRB segment of the Committee, however, a solid front by the five President-members would enable them to determine public policy. Since they are not appointed by the President, nor removable for policy differences with either the President or the FRB within their five-year terms, the present structure allows the possibility that policy with a highly-charged political potential may be made by men who lack even indirect accountability to the national public affected. Former FRB Chairman Marriner Eccles has pointed out the uniqueness of the arrangement in these words: "There is no other major governmental power entrusted to a Federal agency composed in part of representatives of the organizations which are the subject of regulation by that agency." [9]

The situation of the Reserve Presidents reverses that of the regional Boards: while the latter's structurally important place has been downgraded by loss of function, the former's structurally inferior position has been upgraded by increased authority.

The Board of Governors and the Board Chairman

The gap between formal and informal roles in the Federal Reserve is readily apparent at the FRB level. By statute, it controls by itself only one of the major monetary instruments, the setting of reserve requirements. In fact, it is in a position to, and does, exercise authority in varying degree over all three instruments of policy—and is popularly recognized as *the* monetary policy authority. Further, the effective voice within the Board is that of the Chairman, despite the formal equality of all seven Members—and this too is popularly recognized. William McChesney Martin's name may not be a household word, but it is far better known than those of his colleagues. Over the years, the Board has seldom contained, besides the Chairman, more than one or two members at a time whose stature commanded independent respect.

The Board has final authority over discount rates through its power to "review and determine" the decisions of the Reserve Directors. The Members of the FRB constitute a seven-to-five majority in the OMC and thus—barring defections—control the most important of monetary tools. In fact, decisions on all three instruments of policy are taken on the basis of discussion within OMC. Since 1955 the Committee has been used as a "forum, a clearinghouse for all of the aspects of policy determination in the System." [10] Thus the formal distribution of authority is belied in practice by unified consideration. Unified control seems inevitable, since the types of decision are logically related and it would be unthinkable to have them operating in contradictory directions. Because of the political importance of monetary policy, however, and the desirability of fiscal-monetary coordination, it is questionable whether a twelve-man,

[9] Joint (Douglas) Committee on the Economic Report, *Hearings, Monetary, Credit and Fiscal Policies,* 81st Cong., 1st sess., 1949, p. 221.

[10] Chairman Martin in Senate Committee on Finance, *Hearings, Investigation of the Financial Condition of the United States,* 85th Cong., 1st sess., 1957, p. 1260. Cited hereafter as Senate Finance Committee *Hearings.*

quasi-private body provides an adequate or appropriate locus for policy determination; of this, more presently.

The size, length of term and interest composition of the FRB have been the subject of considerable Congressional attention and have undergone some change over the years. The Board began with five appointed Members with staggered ten-year terms and two *ex officio*—the Secretary of the Treasury and the Comptroller of the Currency. Both the latter were removed in the 1935 revision of the Banking Act, at the insistence of Senator Carter Glass, then chairman of the Banking and Currency Committee. Now there are seven Presidential appointees, and the term is fourteen years. No Member, incidentally, has yet served a full fourteen-year term, but a few have served *more than* fourteen years through successive appointments to unexpired terms.

The Chairman is selected by the President for a four-year, renewable term. This definite term was adopted in 1935, apparently with the intent that an incoming President should have a free hand. Resignations and new appointments have not coincided with presidential inaugurations, however, with the result that the incumbent's appointment, for example, expired in 1963.

The Federal Reserve Act has from the beginning stipulated group-interest qualifications for FRB Members. Originally, two had to be experienced in banking or finance, and the total membership had to provide "fair representation" of industrial, commercial and financial interests—as well as a regional balance designed to avoid eastern "domination." In 1922 the requirement of financial experience was dropped and agriculture was added to the list of represented interests. The actual composition for the 1914–50 period was as follows: thirteen from banking, five each from business and agriculture, and four from law.[11] Those appointed since 1950 have included one from private banking, two from business, two from agriculture and one each from the deanship of a business school and from a government career. Two of the post-1950 group also had experience of several years each on a Reserve Bank Board and one appointee's major experience has been as a Reserve Bank officer. "Promotion from within" is the trend. Among the major organized interests, labor is conspicuous by its absence. Business has been represented, but by substantial independents (ranchers, lumbermen, realtors) rather than by executives of large industrial corporations.

The size, length of term, interest composition and geographic distribution are all of questionable value to the System's policy functions and administrative effectiveness. It has been argued that fourteen-year terms provide an opportunity for Members to develop a knowledge of monetary economics and that they insulate the Board from partisan considerations. But many posts of equal technical complexity in other agencies are adequately staffed on a much shorter basis and, more importantly, insulation from politics is as impossible as it is democratically undesirable for an agency functioning so near the center of national economic policy. I shall return to this point later.

Although replacement of the Board by a single executive has been suggested only rarely, many observers, including Chairman Martin, are on record

[11] Bach, *op. cit.,* p. 119.

as favoring a smaller group than seven, on the ground that more capable men might be attracted to the Board.[12] Clearly a seven-man board cannot collectively negotiate effectively with the President, the Secretary of the Treasury, the Chairman of the Council of Economic Advisers, or the lending agencies whose programs impinge on economic stability; yet coherent policy requires negotiation, consultation and a program coordination constantly. Nor would a five-man board be notably better in this respect.

As it is now, the Chairman *is* the Federal Reserve Board for purposes of negotiation. In recent years he has lunched with the Secretary of the Treasury weekly,[13] and has sat in with the President's informal inner council on economic policy.[14] Congressional committees rely upon the Chairman to speak for the Board and rarely bother to interrogate other Board members. These arrangements apparently work because none of the other members is strong enough, personally or politically, to challenge the Chairman; and also, it seems reasonable to suggest, because there is no alternative save chaos. It is supported too by the tradition of secrecy that attends the actions of central banks, and that is defended as necessary to prevent the exploitation of leaks to private advantage: the fewer the negotiators, the less the likelihood of leaks. The gap between formal structure and the necessities of action reflected in the informal but decisive accretion of power to the Chairman (not only to the incumbent, but to McCabe and Eccles before him) is too great to be bridged by a minor adjustment in the size of the group.

Because of the importance of the Chairmanship, and the necessity for cordial relations between the head of the FRB and the President, Martin and McCabe have both suggested that the four-year term of the Chairman should end on March 31 of the year in which a President begins his term of office. Simpler still is the suggestion that the Chairman's term should be at the President's pleasure, as with most other national regulatory commissions. Whichever way the matter is handled, the need is for a relationship of mutual trust between President and Chairman, both for the sake of consistent economic policy and for democratic accountability through the President as chief elected representative of the public.[15] The present system of a fixed four-year term that (accidentally) does not coincide with Presidential inaugurations is unfortunate on both counts. Moreover, since the staggered 14-year terms of members expire in January of even-numbered years, a new President—even if the Chairman stepped aside—would be confined to the membership he inherits, in choosing a new Chairman, unless some member resigned to create a vacancy.

The policy suitability of geographic and interest qualifications for membership on the Board is a question that would become moot if the Board were replaced by a single head. If not, the answer must be that such qualifications are unsuitable because they are irrelevant and, in their present form, inequitable as well. They are irrelevant because the function of the Board is no longer

---

[12] Sen. Doc. 123, p. 30.
[13] Senate Finance Committee *Hearings,* 1959, p. 2180.
[14] Conversation with staff members, Council of Economic Advisers.
[15] Bach, *op. cit.,* pp. 227–28.

simply to accommodate business, but to stabilize the national economy. The Board is not engaged in mediating group conflicts where the direct representation of parties-in-interest may be an irresistible political demand, but in a task of economic analysis and political judgment affecting the interests and values of *all* groups and individuals. Given the agency's function, independence of mind and familiarity with government finance and money markets, and with macroeconomic analysis, are far more desirable qualifications than group representation.[16] Sensitivity to basic political currents—a quite different kind of "expertise"—is also pertinent, but not sensitivity only to the needs of a few special segments of the economy. The geographic qualification is equally irrelevant because of the nationalization of economic forces; five of the twelve districts must go unrepresented at any given time, as it is. And some geographic spread would be secured in any event, although without the severely restrictive effects of the current requirement upon the availability of capable men, simply because presidential politics would work in this direction in the FRB as it does in cabinet and Supreme Court appointments.

The inequity of existing group representation requirements lies in the exclusion of interests as much affected by monetary policy as those that are included by statute. The present range reflects the original, restricted concept of the System. Today, if groups are to be represented as such, labor has as strong a claim as the farmers or industrialists, because employment levels are dependent on monetary policy to a significant extent; fixed-income receivers, whether corporate bond-clippers or Social Security pensioners, are directly and adversely affected if the tools of the FRB are not used with sufficient vigor to combat inflationary tendencies. Chairman Martin has even defined the objectives of monetary policy as providing job opportunities for wage earners and protection of those who depend upon savings or fixed incomes.[17]

One political consequence of the existing interest exclusions is to lessen the acceptability of monetary policies in the eyes of organized labor—or, at least, in the eyes of its leadership. The AFL-CIO Executive Council launched an attack in February, 1959, on banker and corporate-executive "domination" of the Fed, drawing a direct connection between the pattern of representation at both national and regional levels and what it called "misguided anti-inflation measures" that stifle growth while increasing bank profits.[18] At we have seen, the regional Boards lack the power to determine policy independently and the labor complaint is misdirected to that extent. Yet the *appearance* of the System may be as important as the substance in determining reactions to policy, and the appearance leaves the System open to this type of charge. As regards the national Board, the charge *could* have relevance: a labor representative might be more hesitant than other members in espousing "hard" policies that could dampen employment; but it is equally possible that he would in time adopt the coloration of his surroundings, which in the case of the Federal Reserve would apparently

---

[16] See Chairman Martin's remarks, Sen. Doc. 123, p. 300, and Bach, p. 121.

[17] Senate Finance Committee *Hearings*, p. 1262.

[18] Statement (mimeograph) of the AFL-CIO Executive Council on *Monetary Policy,* San Juan, Puerto Rico, February 24, 1959. See also, *New York Times,* February 26, 1959, p. 30, and March 6, 1959, p. 24.

mean an institutional bias for "sound money" and a priority for anti-inflation goals.

Even if labor and pensioner representation were added, however, the list of affected interests would be far from exhausted. As Emmette Redford has written of interest representation in regulatory agencies generally, "It is difficult, if not impossible, to include representation of all the interests which might legitimately make a claim for some representation." [19] A non-interest or "general interest" criterion for appointments would be the simplest way to avoid the problem entirely if a multi-member Board is retained. A statement expressing the views of the House Committee on Banking and Currency in 1935 sums up the matter nicely:

> It is important to emphasize in the law that Board action should reflect, not the opinion of a majority of special interests, but rather the well considered judgment of a body that takes into consideration all phases of the national economic life.[20]

The Open Market Committee and policy unification

In origin and development, the OMC represents the leading structural response of the Federal Reserve System to its change in function. But the response has not been entirely adequate and further modifications in the structure and scope of authority of the Committee have been advanced from a number of quarters.

When the System began operations, the discount rate and the levels of reserves were thought to be the major tools of policy. As the public debt grew, and as the macro-economic function of stabilization developed, open market operations by the Reserve Banks increased in importance. The initial structural response came in 1922 when an Open Market Committee was established informally, more under the leadership of President Benjamin Strong of the New York Reserve Bank than of the FRB. The Banking Act of 1933 gave the OMC statutory recognition as a twelve-man group, selected by the Reserve Banks, to carry on open market operations under rules laid down by the FRB, thus substantially increasing the power of the national, public component. The Banking Act of 1935, largely written by then-Chairman Eccles as an effort to enhance the centralized, public character of the monetary authority, reorganized the Committee into its present form: the seven FRB members and five Reserve Presidents.[21] (The House version—not enacted—of the 1935 Act would have gone further with the centralizing process by transferring authority for open market operations to the Board alone, with a requirement of consultation with an advisory committee of the regional Banks.) In short, change in economic circumstance, i.e., the growth of a large federal debt as an inescapable component of the nation's financial structure, and the development of a new function

[19] *Administration of National Economic Control* (New York: The Macmillan Co., 1952), p. 270; and see Ch. 9 generally.

[20] House Report No. 742, 74th Cong., 1st sess. (April 19, 1935), p. 6.

[21] Marriner S. Eccles, *Beckoning Frontiers* (New York: Alfred A. Knopf, Inc., 1951), pp. 167–71. These pages contain an excellent capsule summary of OMC development.

led to an institutional addition to the System. Informally, the change has gone one step further: as mentioned earlier, the OMC is used as a forum for discussion of the entire range of monetary actions, not just for decisions regarding the tool that lies formally within its jurisdiction.

There is widespread agreement among participants and observers that unified handling of the three major techniques is essential for coherence; but there is sharp disagreement over the appropriate composition of the OMC and over the division of labor between OMC and FRB. The disagreements involve in a politically sensitive way the central-regional and public-private balances in the policy process. The range of specific proposals is as follows:

(1) Consolidate all instruments in a publicly appointed Board, either the present FRB or a smaller one, abolishing the OMC but requiring consultation with the Reserve Bank Presidents. Variants of this have been suggested by the Hoover Commission Task Force, Eccles, and Bach, who see this approach as the proper way to secure the advantages of both public responsibility and "grass roots" information.[22]

(2) Consolidate by merging the OMC and FRB into a single Board constituted of three Members appointed by the President and two Reserve Bank Presidents, each of the latter group serving full time for a year on a rotating basis. This was proposed by former Chairman McCabe in 1949 as the proper change if any were to be made at all;[23] it would have the effect of displacing the New York Bank President from his present permanent seat on the OMC.

(3) Consolidate in the OMC as presently constituted. This is the position once favored by the regional Presidents.[24]

(4) Consolidate reserve requirements and open market policy in a reconstituted OMC consisting of the present five Reserve Bank representatives and a smaller FRB of five Members—thus creating an even balance between central and regional, publicly and semiprivately appointed elements. This proposal was advanced by the New York Clearing House Association, which also urged that in case of a disagreement between a Reserve Bank and the FRB over the rediscount rate, either party should be allowed to refer the question to the OMC for final decision.[25] The Association apparently felt that commercial bank influence was greater with the Presidents than with the national Board.

Those preferring no change at all include Martin, who has defended the existing arrangement as consistent with the "basic concept of a regional" System and as a way of promoting close relations between the Presidents and the Board.[26] The Patman subcommittee saw no reason, as of 1952, to disturb the

[22] Commission on Organization of the Executive Branch of the Government, *Task Force Report on Regulatory Commissions*, Appendix N, January, 1949, pp. 113–14; Eccles, pp. 224–26; Bach, pp. 234–35.

[23] Joint Committee on the Economic Report, *Monetary, Credit, and Fiscal Policies, A Collection of Statements*, 81st Cong., 1st sess., 1949, pp. 68-69.

[24] *Ibid.*, p. 162. By 1952, the Presidents were less enthusiastic for change (see Sen. Doc. 123, p. 673). They perhaps feared that the unified control might go to the FRB rather than to the OMC if the subject were opened up at all.

[25] New York Clearing House Association, *The Federal Reserve Reexamined* (New York, 1953), pp. 138–39.

[26] Sen. Doc. 123, p. 294.

status quo, but Representative Patman has more recently proposed consolidation in an enlarged FRB of twelve Presidential appointees.[27]

The rationale underlying the all-powers-to-the-Board approach can be summarized in the principle that public functions should be lodged in public bodies, and the assertion that open market operations are in no sense regional in character. Eccles has pointed out that the Reserve Presidents are not appointed by or accountable to either the President or Congress, and for this reason argues that their participation in national, public policy formation is inappropriate.[28] Bach has emphasized the national character of open market policy,[29] and he is joined in this view by Jacob Viner, who has said that:

> The regional emphasis in central banking is an obsolete relic of the past. No country, not even Canada, which is much more a collection of distinct economic regions than is the United States, has thought it expedient to follow our initial example of introducing regionalism into central banking.[30]

The argument for OMC as the top body derives from the importance attributed to regionalism and (inferentially at least) from a belief in the financial community that the Committee is more sympathetic than the FRB to the felt needs of bankers. The regional case has been most strongly stated by President Delos C. Johns of the St. Louis Reserve Bank:

> Each Reserve Bank President is in a position to judge possible alternatives of national monetary policy with due regard to the particular characteristics of his region. This makes for adoption of national monetary policy that squares realistically with actual conditions in the regions. . . .[31]

Macro-stabilization as the major function of the System clearly forecloses regional devolution in the making of policy, yet regional circumstances should be considered. The valid claims of regionalism, however, require only a consultative voice, not a decisional one. And public policy, I would agree with Eccles, should not be made by a body containing men who are not accountable to the national public whose welfare is affected by the decisions made.

In *operations,* as distinct from policy determination, regionalism may well possess continued utility; and centralization of policy is entirely compatible

[27] Subcommittee on General Credit Control and Debt Management, Joint Committee on the Economic Report, *Monetary Policy and the Management of the Public Debt,* Sen. Doc. 163, 82d Cong., 2d sess. (1952), p. 54; H. R. 2790, 86th Cong., 1st sess. (1959).

[28] Joint Committee on the Economic Report, *Hearings, Monetary, Credit and Fiscal Policies,* 81st Cong., 1st sess. (1949), p. 221.

[29] Bach, *op. cit.,* p. 234.

[30] Subcommittee on General Credit Control and Debt Management, Joint Committee on the Economic Report, *Hearings, Monetary Policy and the Management of the Public Debt,* 82d Cong., 2d sess. (1952), p. 756, cited hereinafter as General Credit Control Subcommittee *Hearings,* 1952. Regionalism in the Federal Reserve—or at least its modern defense—perhaps owes more to an unexamined bias in favor of "federalism" as a matter of political ideology than to an empirical examination of the national economic structure.

[31] Sen. Doc. 123, pp. 677–79.

with a considerable degree of regional diversification in operations. The point of greatest overlap between national policy and Reserve Bank operations appears to be in the handling of the "discount window," that is, the ease or difficulty with which a member bank may avail itself of the rediscount privilege. A uniform national policy could, for example, suggest "easier" loan conditions in any District whose area rate of unemployment was "x" percentage points above the national average, and thus provide for regional differentiation while maintaining central policy control.

Federal Advisory Council

The Federal Advisory Council began as a compensation to the commercial bankers for their failure to obtain direct representation on the FRB.[32] Its function today has been described as providing "firsthand advice and counsel from people who are closely in touch with the banking activities of their particular district," [33] although available information does not explain how these bank representatives are able to contribute something that the Reserve Bank Presidents with their extensive staff aids, could not supply as well or better. Assuming that their advice is not redundant, however, it is questionable whether the FRB should accord *statutory* advisory status to commercial bankers only, now that the System's policy may affect many other social groups just as significantly as the bankers; e.g., nonbank financial institutions, home builders, state and local governments, Golden Age Clubs, wage-earners, and so on. The Board has at times used formal consultants from outside the commercial banking sphere, as when consumer credit regulations were being formulated,[34] but this is apparently infrequent. Once again, we see that the System's structure has become outmoded by the change in scope of function.

III. THE FEDERAL RESERVE AND NATIONAL ECONOMIC POLICY

The analysis to this point has focused upon internal factors. We come now to the question: What is the source of the Federal Reserve's policy goals? Does existing structure adequately relate the monetary authority to the President and to the monetary management operations of the Treasury, to lending agency decisions, and to the Council of Economic Advisers? Does an adequate mechanism exist for resolving disputes that threaten the coherence of an Administration's over-all economic policy? These can only be answered by going beyond the internal organization of the Fed to a consideration of its external relationships.

The first place to look for the mandate of an agency is in its organic statute; but the Federal Reserve Act deals sparsely with the matter of goals, and has in any case, as already noted, been outpaced by events. Since the law does

---

[32] Robert E. Cushman, *The Independent Regulatory Commissions* (New York: Oxford University Press, Inc., 1941), p. 160.

[33] Martin, in Senate Finance Committee *Hearings,* 1957, p. 1261.

[34] Letter, Kenneth A. Kenyon, Assistant Secretary, Board of Governors, to the author, August 17, 1960.

not provide a mandate fitted to the modern concerns of the System,[35] it is to the Employment Act of 1946 that one must look for goals written in macro-economic language: "it is the continuing policy and responsibility of the Federal Government to use all practicable means . . . to promote maximum employment, production, and purchasing power." This declaration applies to the Federal Reserve as to all other agencies of the national government, and is often mentioned in FRB descriptions of the System's role. But as a policy guide it is less than complete. For one thing, it does not mention price stability, although it has been widely interpreted as including this goal by logical extrapolation from those explicitly specified. For another, it leaves open such questions as, should employment be maximized today by measures that may bring on unemployment tomorrow by over-stimulating a "boom," or conversely, contribute to unemployment today lest inflation come tomorrow?

Thus the Employment Act mandate shares the imprecision of most such statements. While it could perhaps be sharpened, a need for interpretive subsidiary definition probably cannot be eliminated because any language tight enough to do this would inevitably place too inflexible a strait-jacket on agency operation.[36] Elaboration of goals at later stages of the policy process may be expected to continue. The President, who enters office with a vague mandate that is partly personal, partly party doctrine, commonly sets at least the tone for the specific interpretation of statutory directives, by the nature of his appointees. But the President's authority over the Federal Reserve is restricted, unless vacancies occur, to one appointment of a member (for fourteen years) every other year starting a year after his own term begins; and to appointment of the Chairman for a fixed four-year term. The independence of the agency conflicts with the President's responsibilities for over-all economic policy.

In support of the position that independence should prevail—i.e., that the FRB should not take its mandate from the President—the argument is advanced that anti-inflationary measures are unpopular though necessary; that "hard" decisions are more acceptable "if they are decided by public officials who, like the members of the judiciary, are removed from immediate pressures," [37] and that the accountability of the System to the electorate is adequately achieved

[35] Had Eccles been successful in writing his ideas into the 1935 amendments to the Federal Reserve Act, the Act would have anticipated by eleven years the declaration of national economic policy adopted in the Employment Act. The Eccles mandate would have directed the FRB "to exercise such powers as it possesses in such manner as to promote conditions conducive to business stability and to mitigate by its influence unstabilizing fluctuations in the general level of production, trade, prices, and employment so far as may be possible within the scope of monetary and credit administration." H. Rept. No. 742, 74th Cong., 1st sess. (1935), p. 9.

[36] An attempt to clarify the Federal Reserve's role by means of a clearer mandate has been urged by Senator Paul Douglas and by Jacob Viner, see Sen. Doc. 163, p. 74; General Credit Control Subcommittee *Hearings, 1952*, pp. 771–72. It has been opposed by Goldenweiser and the Reserve Bank Presidents: *ibid.,* p. 765, Joint Committee on the Economic Report, *Monetary, Credit, and Fiscal Policies, A Collection of Statements,* 81st Cong., 1st sess. (1949), p. 101. The absence of any mandate legislation since the Employment Act suggests insufficient Congressional consensus upon its substantive content. Organized labor has opposed amendments to add price stability to the goals of that Act, as intended to water down its emphasis on "maximum employment."

[37] Martin, in Sen. Doc. 123, p. 242.

through its responsibility to Congress.[38] On the other side, the President is required by the Employment Act to submit a program for achieving the Act's goals; such a program must include recommendations on monetary policy to be meaningful; and thus the President must be "the coordinating agent for the whole national economic program." [39] Men on both sides agree on one point: there should be a strong advocate within the government for the monetary stability viewpoint, and the central bank is the logical home for such advocacy. The major disagreements are whether a substantial degree of insulation from other agencies engaged in economic policy determination helps or hinders the expression of that viewpoint, and whether a clear locus of authority is required for settlement of disputes between the institutions variously responsible for monetary and fiscal policies.

The issue of FRB accountability to Congress is a false one and should be exposed as such. Contrary to a myth strongly held by System spokesmen—and many Congressmen—the FRB, even more than the other regulatory commissions, is *less* accountable to Congress than are the line departments in the Presidential hierarchy. The Federal Reserve does not depend on appropriations and thus is freed from the most frequently used tool of Congressional administrative supervision. And Congress has exercised an unusual degree of restraint in even suggesting its policy views to the Board. All executive agencies that have statutory basis may be said to be "creatures of Congress," and those with single heads are more easily held accountable than those with boards that diffuse responsibility.[40] For agencies with substantive powers, the price of accountability to Congress is accountability to the President.

On the need for a coordinating authority, Martin's position has been to grant the need for coordination but to argue that it can be achieved adequately through informal consultation.[41] The Advisory Board on Economic Growth and Stability established by President Eisenhower in 1953 would appear to be in line with his thinking: ABEGS (under leadership of the then CEA Chairman Arthur Burns) could bring about full exchange of information and full discussion, but could not *commit* the participating agencies to a unified course, even before it fell into desuetude after Burns' departure. The same was true of the Treasury Secretary-FRB Chairman luncheons and the President's informal economic policy discussions with agency heads during the Eisenhower Administration. Thus the problem of a possible stalemate or contradiction between Presidential and FRB policy is not resolved by these consultative arrangements.[42] A stronger incentive toward reaching consensus would be provided by the Clark-Reuss

[38] See, for example, FRB Research Director Ralph A. Young's remarks, Antitrust Subcommittee, Senate Committee on the Judiciary, *Hearings, Administered Prices*, 86th Cong., 1st sess. (1959), Part 10, pp. 4887–91.

[39] See H. Christian Sonne's comments, from which the quotation is taken, in General Credit Control Subcommittee *Hearings*, 1952, pp. 848–50.

[40] For discussion of this and other pertinent administrative myths, see Harold Stein's remarks in General Credit Control Subcommittee *Hearings*, 1952, pp. 758–59.

[41] Sen. Doc. 123, pp. 263–73.

[42] See the remarks of Leon H. Keyserling and Roy Blough in Sen. Doc. 123, pp. 848–51.

bill.[43] This would make it the "sense of Congress" that the President's Economic Reports under the Employment Act should include "monetary and credit policies to the same extent as all other policies affecting employment, production and purchasing power," with provision for inclusion of an FRB dissent, if necessary, in the Reports.[44] But again, unity would not be assured and accountability would remain obscure. Only if the FRB Chairman served at the will of the President, and a centralized authority directed the use of all credit instruments, would a formal basis for cohesion and accountability be laid.

Would a proposal of this kind mean the subordination of monetary stability to a frequently assumed low-interest, easy money predilection in the Treasury Department and the White House? While an unambiguous "No" cannot be given in reply, the weight of argument is in the negative direction. Independence may mean isolation rather than strength, for independent agencies lack the power of Presidential protection and Presidential involvement. Paradoxically, the real ability of the Fed to influence national economic policy might very well be increased if its formal independence were diminished. Have not the informal steps taken in the past seven or eight years toward closer liaison between the FRB and Presidential policy makers already made the Board (i.e., the Chairman) somewhat stronger than was the case during the Truman Administration?

In addition to Presidential elaboration of Congressional policy statements, further interpretation is invariably made at the agency level. When the FRB or OMC decides to change, or not change, the degree of restraint or ease in credit policy it is deciding—*necessarily*—whether to place emphasis for the short-run on the price stability or the maximum-employment-and-growth side of its imprecise mandate. The question of internal interpretation, therefore, is whether the policy preferences of the monetary authority are likely to coincide with those of the politically accountable originators and interpreters of the mandate. The probability is that the central banking agency will be to some extent more conscious of the monetary than of the employment-and-growth aspects of stabilization, the major reasons being (1) the role of the institution, (2) the inevitably close relationships of the policy makers to their commercial banking "clientele" as the focal point of immediate policy impact, and (3) the social backgrounds of the policy makers. The Administration (of whichever party) and Congress, however, are likely to give greater weight to employment than are the central bankers, simply because the political consequences of unemployment are likely to be—and **are** even more likely to be perceived as—more unfortunate for elected office **holders** than those of price inflation. This difference may be pronounced or slight, depending on the personal emphasis and understandings of the men involved; but that they will continue to exist even when the general orientation of both sides is similar was shown by the occasional disputes

[43] Its most recent form, at the time of writing, was embodied in S. 2382, 86th Cong., 1st sess.

[44] For extended discussion of the Clark-Reuss proposal, see: Executive and Legislative Reorganization subcommittee, House Government Operations Committee, *Hearings, Amending the Employment Act of 1946*, 86th Cong., 1st sess., 1959, and Subcommittee on Production and Stabilization, Senate Committee on Banking and Currency, Hearings, *Employment Act Amendments*, 86th Cong., 2d sess., 1960.

between the President's economic advisers and the FRB during the Eisenhower Administrations.[45]

The internal structure of authority affects FRB policy in one other respect pertinent to the mandate question. This is the absence of an instrument for dealing with what has come to be known as "administered price" or "market power" inflation; i.e., inflation caused, not by excessive demand, but by the ability of unions and companies in situations of diminished competition to raise wages and prices even in periods of unutilized manpower or productive capacity. Such inflation can only be dealt with effectively by monetary or fiscal techniques if employment and growth are depressed beyond the political limits of public acceptability. A policy dilemma results. The Fed does not have (and probably does not want to have) authority to take direct action against this type of inflation. Nor, since the tools for such action would be non-monetary in nature,[46] is it appropriate that the central banking agency take on such a task. Yet in the absence of any but the traditional instruments the FRB is faced with a cruel choice: its own rationale calls for it to fight inflation, but doing so would create rising unemployment. If it refrains from acting, in order to preserve high employment, it may fail to stop inflation. Does it have a mandate to make such a choice? One could be extrapolated from the general stabilization directive, but not with any clear political sanction. As economist Gardiner C. Means has said, "there is a good deal of question whether such a momentous decision should rest with the Federal Reserve Board." [47]

IV. CONCLUSION

The basic finding of the analysis presented above is that the formal structure of the Federal Reserve System is inappropriate to its functions and out of line with informal arrangements that have the logic of necessity behind them. These gaps flow from changes in the monetary authority's function and in the structure of the economy. Devised as a service agency for banking and commerce—to achieve a semi-automatic adjustment of the money supply—the Federal Reserve has become as well a policy-making institution with major responsibility for national economic stabilization. Ancillary arrangements for interest representation based on an assumption that monetary actions were of important concern only to bankers and businessmen now have the appearance of unjustified special access because the range of affected interests and values is seen to be as broad as the nation itself.

Informal developments—most notably the unified handling of major monetary techniques and the preeminence of the Chairman's position—and the formal changes of 1935 that in a degree public-ized and nationalized the Open Market

[45] E.g., in the spring of 1956; see discussion in Senate Finance Committee *Hearings,* 1957, pp. 1361–63.

[46] See Emmette S. Redford, *Potential Public Policies to Deal with Inflation Caused by Market Power,* Joint Economic Committee, Study Paper No. 10 for Study of Employment, Growth and Price Levels, 1959.

[47] Antitrust Subcommittee, Senate Committee on the Judiciary, *Hearings, Administered Prices,* 86th Cong., 1st sess. (1959), Part 10, p. 4917.

Committee did something to improve the fit of form to function. But these alterations have not been sufficient to ensure adequate accountability for what is today an authority of first-rank political importance; they have not brought the quasi-private "face" of the System into line with its public responsibilities; and they do not provide a sufficient organizational base for coherent integration of the fiscal and monetary components of national economic policy. A more complete face-lifting is in order.

The Chairmanship is the key both to accountability and to effective performance. The four-year fixed term, having produced a result contradictory to the one intended, should be repealed in favor of service at the pleasure of the President. The informal preeminence of the Chairman should be recognized formally by abolishing the Board and the OMC and centralizing authority over the discount rate, reserve requirements and open market operations in the hands of the Chairman, who might be re-titled the Governor of the Federal Reserve System. The need for information from below could be handled through regularized reporting from the Reserve Bank Presidents on regional conditions, and by strengthened staff analysis in the Office of the Governor. By these alterations, the public, i.e., political quality of monetary policy, would be accorded appropriate recognition; responsibility would be clearly located; a means of settling possible disputes between fiscal policy under the President and monetary under the Fed would be created; and the process of consultation and negotiation by the Fed with the Treasury, the CEA, and the lending agencies would be made more effective. In short, a single head, enjoying the confidence of the President, would be able to speak with vigor for the central banking viewpoint in the formation of economic policy; yet once the deliberations had been completed an assurance would exist that the Fed would be at one with the rest of the government in executing the policy determined upon.

A second, lesser category of structural change would have the object of revising the Fed's appearance to fit the public nature of its responsibilities. Election of two-thirds of the Reserve Bank Directors by commercial banks, and "ownership" of the Reserve Banks by commercial banks, are admittedly matters of no great substantive importance today. But since they are functionless elements, and their appearance of special interest access is harmful to the legitimacy of monetary actions, the Reserve Boards should be eliminated (or, at least, all of their members should be publicly appointed) and the commercial banks' shares in the Reserve Banks should be bought out by the government—thus making the Reserve Banks in form what they largely are in fact: field offices of the national, public monetary authority.

Adoption of this series of proposals—or others, perhaps milder in form but having the same essential consequences—would significantly improve the economic policy machinery of the national government. These changes represent a logical extension of the premises of the Employment Act:

> In no major country of the world today, except in the United States, is there a central bank that can legally, if it wishes, tell the head of its own government to go fly a kite. It seems to me that if we are to hold government responsible for carrying out the new doctrine of economic stabilization, there must be a

chain of responsibility reaching through the Presidency to all the instrumental-ities that do the stabilizing.[48]

Selection 27

THE MYSTERIOUS WORLD OF THE FED

DELBERT C. HASTINGS AND ROSS M. ROBERTSON

> *In any organization as complex as the Federal Reserve System there will always be a substantial gap between authority as laid down in the organizational structure and authority as actually exercised by the people who man key positions. This selection presents an un-usually thorough view of the inside workings of Federal Reserve policy formation and decision making, with emphasis on the sources of power within the organization, written by men who have been a part of the team.*

First-time visitors to the lovely Washington building that houses the Board of Governors of the Federal Reserve System are invariably struck by its lofty tone. Federal Reserve personnel and guests alike move decorously through marble halls and amber-lit, carpeted rooms that epitomize the vast dignity of the monetary authority. Highly placed staff members approach the offices of Board members with deference; lesser functionaries enter with an obsequious respect that makes onlookers uncomfortable. Indeed, an almost religious aura pervades the place, and the uninitiated expect momentarily to catch a whiff of incense or the chant of choirboys not far off.

The physical atmosphere is simply an extension of a carefully nurtured public image of trustworthiness and high morality. Because of the technicality of its operations and the obscurity of its statements of purpose, the Federal Reserve has avoided evaluation and criticism of its actions by the public at large. Instead, explicit comment has been left to academicians, highly placed financial managers, and a few members of Congress. Thus, the public trusts the Fed without fully understanding it; with the possible exception of the Federal Bureau of Investigation, no other government agency enjoys such high repute and splendid public relations.

To be sure, much of the System's prestige is merited. It performs its vast service roles—collector of checks, fiscal agent for the United States government, and issuer of currency—with accuracy and dispatch. At both board and bank levels, the Federal Reserve can boast a research organization second to none. Yet it is by no means certain that the Fed has managed the money supply

---

[48] Elliott V. Bell, "Who Should Manage Our Managed Money?" An address before the American Bankers Association Convention, Los Angeles, California, October 22, 1956.

• From Delbert C. Hastings and Ross M. Robertson, "The Mysterious World of the Fed," *Business Horizons,* Spring, 1962, pp. 97–104, Graduate School of Business, Indiana University. Copyright 1962 by the Foundation for Economics and Business Statistics, Indiana University, Bloomington, Indiana. Reprinted by permission of *Business Horizons* and the authors.

better than the money supply would have managed itself, nor is it clear that Federal Reserve influence on growth, stability, and price levels has been as beneficial as the Fed's reputation would suggest.

In a word, the Federal Reserve System has nobly performed its service functions. On the other hand, it is by no means certain that the control functions have been discharged with the imagination and vigor that modern central-bank action requires. Painfully sensitive to criticism, which invariably evokes defense reactions, the monetary authority gives continual evidence of an eroding self-consciousness. Indeed, System acceptance of responsibility for stability of prices and output seems to vary from time to time. The Fed certainly wants no competitors; whenever it has been suggested that an Administration economic policy group be formed, there is immediate central-bank resistance to the proposal. Yet System authorities occasionally come close to admitting their inability to stabilize the economy, and, whenever the Congressional heat is on, central-bank spokesmen are at pains to explain that they can only nudge the economy in one direction or another, that there are too many variables to be controlled by any one institution. System attitude seems to be, "We will use the tools we choose in the way we choose, and if they don't do the job, we deny responsibility in the matter. But we don't want anyone else interfering." To understand the Fed, we must apprehend this deep-rooted instinct for self-preservation that manifests itself in insistence upon insulation from "political" interference.

The mysterious world of the Fed is really known only to its employees and its alumni—the insiders, as it were. No amount of examination, no amount of Congressional testimony, no amount of study by scholars temporarily connected with the System can reveal the inner workings of Fed mentality. Only years of participation in the charismatic effort of central-bank policy provide the sense of System motivation so essential to an interpretation of Fed dogma, facetiously referred to, internally, as the "party line." As alumni, now a decent interval away from System activity, we herewith set forth our observations about (1) the nodes of power in the System and (2) the tenuous lines of communication that carry power impulses from one node to another.

THE NODES OF POWER

Although its major structural outlines were laid down by the original Federal Reserve Act, the Federal Reserve System has evolved in a way clearly not foreseen by its founders. As in every organization that must act, there are important nodes of power within the System; the relative standing of these power centers depends somewhat on law, somewhat on custom, and somewhat on the economic facts of life, such as the size and wealth of the different Federal Reserve districts. In roughly descending order of power, the major nodes are as follows: 1. the Chairman of the Board of Governors; 2. the other Governors; 3. the staff of the Board, in particular the senior Advisers; 4. the Federal Open Market Committee; 5. the trading desk of the New York Federal Reserve Bank; 6. the President of the New York Federal Reserve Bank; 7. other Federal

Reserve Bank Presidents; 8. boards of directors of the twelve banks; 9. System-wide committees, standing and ad hoc; and 10. the Federal Advisory Council.

This listing will doubtless raise eyebrows inside and outside the System, but we consider it, nonetheless, a fair appraisal of the current order of power loci in the System. It is impossible to understand the operations of today's central bank without knowing the relative importance of these power centers.

It is common knowledge, of course, that the Banking Act of 1935 made a drastic switch in the seat of System power. Under the aegis of Benjamin Strong, fair-haired boy of J. Pierpont Morgan and the 1913 New York banking community, real authority in the System lodged in the hands of the chief executive officers of the several Reserve Banks. Indeed, the quick seizure of the term "governor" by the executive heads of the twelve banks revealed their own assessment of their authority. Until Strong's death in 1928, the Federal Reserve Board made nearly futile efforts to seize the power it never had, and the terrible failure of the Federal Reserve to arrest the deflation of 1929–32 gave positive proof, if proof were needed, that board authority had been emasculated in practice. The designation in the Banking Act of 1935 of the "Board of Governors" signified the intent of Congress to make it the "board of bosses."

Even so, no one could have foreseen a generation ago the gradual settling of vast power in the person of the Chairman of the board. The tradition of chairman domination was, of course, started during the reign of Marriner S. Eccles, but it has reached a new high under Chairman William McChesney Martin, Jr., able son of one-time Governor Martin of the St. Louis Reserve Bank.

This is not to say that other board members are without authority. Yet the position of each one depends upon his intellectual quality and personal force. A board member not deemed a contributor to the welfare of the System is likely to be shunted aside and given assignments that keep him away from inner councils. On the other hand, a particularly knowledgeable governor may be given heavy responsibilities, especially if he has a bent for economic or legal analysis.

The fact remains that the Chairman of the board is in a position to exercise a great measure of control over the board and thus over the entire System. His is the final word on appointments at both board and bank levels. He is the System spokesman in its relationships with Congress, other executive branches of the government, the President, and even with foreign governments. Within the law, his powers are circumscribed only by the personal qualities of the other governors and by the four-year term of his appointment to the chair. When, as in the case of Martin, the Chairman possesses an uncommon singleness of purpose and great political ability, he will work by persuasion rather than by ukase. He nevertheless operates as a dominant political figure in the best and highest sense of the word.

The staff of the Board of Governors, particularly the senior Advisers, are a frequently overlooked power center. To be sure, their influence is derived from that of the Governors. But their proximity to the Governors, their long service, and their familiarity with Fed history give them a more than considerable influence on policy matters. Old pros like Woodlief Thomas [who retired in June, 1962] and Ralph A. Young command enormous prestige. Younger men like Guy

E. Noyes, Director of Research and Statistics [now Adviser to the Board of Governors], exert their influence through control of research activities at both board and bank levels; all publications of the several banks as well as reports of System-wide committees must receive the approval of the board staff before release, and directives sent by staff members to the banks are accepted as bearing the authority of the Board of Governors.

Because it nominally determines the magnitude and direction of the most important monetary weapon—purchases and sales of government securities— the Federal Open Market Committee is the next most powerful organization within the System. Since it is the official forum as well as the administrative body for monetary policy actions, the FOMC has a key place in System councils. As late as 1953, the Open Market Committee met only quarterly, with an executive committee meeting more frequently to perform the significant policy-making functions. Since that time, however, the full committee has met at intervals of approximately three weeks. Although the official membership consists of the seven Governors and five of the twelve Federal Reserve Bank Presidents, all the Presidents try to attend regularly.[1]

Resisting the inexorable erosion of authority at the bank level, the Federal Reserve Bank of New York always poses something of a threat to Board authority in Washington. The trading desk, which administers the open market account upon receipt of FOMC directives, is the very nerve center of the System. Since, as we shall see, orders of the Open Market Committee are always ambiguous and often nebulous, the account manager, a vice-president of the New York Reserve Bank, must have great latitude in making judgments. And though he may have many masters, not excluding the senior staff member of the board who advises with him each day, it goes without saying that the account manager's immediate boss, the President of the New York Reserve Bank, will not be without influence. Indeed, a strong New York President can be a source of great annoyance and even friction in Federal Reserve councils. It is no secret that many officers in the System heaved a collective sigh of relief when Allan Sproul, one-time chief officer of the New York bank and in some respects the most artistic of all American central bankers, went into retirement. But no matter what the attitude of a New York President toward Washington may be, the counsels of that officer are bound to have weight as they reflect the opinions of the New York financial community.

It is no deprecation of the abilities and prestige of the other eleven bank Presidents to say that they rank well down the list of System power centers. The Presidents are in general gifted and articulate men, and their views will always be weighed by the Board and its Chairman. Nevertheless, the last remaining power of the banks vanished when the original tool of monetary management— changes in the discount rate—lost its money-market effectiveness. And since the appointments of Presidents and First Vice Presidents are subject to Board

---

[1] The President of the Federal Reserve Bank of New York is a permanent member and vice-chairman of the committee. Membership rotates among the other bank Presidents as follows: Boston, Philadelphia, and Richmond; Chicago and Cleveland; St. Louis, Atlanta, Dallas; and Minneapolis, Kansas City, and San Francisco.

approval, really serious resistance to Board decisions is not to be expected at bank, to say nothing of branch, levels. It is probably not unfair to say that the boards of directors of the twelve banks have had their power reduced to that of nominating committees, which on occasion submit to the Board of Governors the names of possible President and First Vice President candidates. Like the boards of directors of the Reserve Bank branches, their positions are largely honorific; and though the Board expresses public gratitude for the "economic intelligence" furnished by bank and branch directors, the plain fact is that their monthly meetings are simply genteel bull sessions.[2]

Indeed, it is probably a fair generalization that the Reserve Banks, at least outside New York City, exert their remaining vestiges of influence by placing their talented officers and economists on System committees. Thus, a System Committee to Study Consumer Credit unquestionably affected Board and Administration thinking with its multivolume 1957 report; more recently, a System committee has produced an influential report on the Federal funds market. Furthermore, articulate individuals like Robert V. Roosa and George Garvy of New York, Clay J. Anderson of Philadelphia, and Homer Jones of St. Louis, through their writings and oral presentations, are likely to have an earnest and respectful hearing by the policy makers in Washington. They are nevertheless a long way from the seat of power.[3]

The Conference of Presidents, once the vehicle of dominance over System policy, is now regarded largely as a forum for administrative and operating problems of the several banks. The Presidents advise with each other on such matters as check collection, currency and coin issue, agency functions for the Treasury, and personnel classifications. The Federal Advisory Council, never even ostensibly a part of the formal power structure, is clearly an honorific group. Although their advice is presumably weighed by the Board of Governors, council members, like directors of banks and branches, bring personal prestige and orthodox witness as their chief contribution.

TRANSMISSION LINES OF POWER

Few Federal insiders would make a major rearrangement of the order in which we have listed the nodes of power, but many would express the honest conviction that we have underestimated the democratic processes by which System decisions are made. A look at these procedures may be helpful to a clear comprehension of them.

As a prerequisite to understanding, we must divest ourselves of a good bit of textbook foolishness about how monetary policy is effected. Although it is customary to speak of the instruments of monetary control, there is really only one—the extension and absorption of central-bank credit. The *means* by which central-bank credit is manipulated are irrelevant. Changes in reserve require-

[2] Branches of Federal Reserve Banks are a historic anomaly, originally established to salve the feelings of citizens disappointed at their failure to get a Reserve Bank in their city. For this story see Ross M. Robertson, "Branches of Federal Reserve Banks," *Monthly Review,* Federal Reserve Bank of St. Louis, XXXVIII (August, 1956), pp. 90–97.

[3] Mr. Roosa is presently Under Secretary of the Treasury for Monetary Affairs.

ments, though still employed, are an anachronistic inheritance from the excess-reserve problem of the 1930's; any sensible person knows that required reserve ratios can be set at any level with consequent central-bank and commercial-bank adjustment to them. Changing the discount rate, though originally conceived to be the *only* weapon of monetary control, has long since lost its effectiveness; the discount rate is no longer a true money-market rate but serves simply as a Fed signal of reaffirmation of a policy in being or a change in monetary policy. In practice, the only demonstrable effect of the discount rate is to set an upper limit to the Federal funds rate—that is, the rate charged one bank by another for the short-term loan of deposits with a Reserve bank. So we are left with one important instrument of monetary control—open market operations. System intervention in the government securities market is a day-to-day, hour-to-hour, minute-to-minute activity that intimately affects the lives of us all.

We have suggested that the Chairman of the Board of Governors is by all odds the most powerful person in the System. But power is synonymous with substantial control over Federal Reserve credit. How, then, does the Chairman exercise his great influence? Largely by being the mouthpiece and deciding vote of the Federal Open Market Committee.

In the conduct of FOMC meetings, a formality is observed that requires each Governor and President in attendance, whether currently a member of the committee or not, to give a brief economic analysis and state his policy recommendations. By custom each member, together with the Board Secretary, the senior Advisers, and the Manager of the Open Market Account, occupies a fixed position around the great oval table in the committee room. After a brief business and financial analysis by the senior staff members, the Account Manager reports on his activities since the last meeting. Next, the Governors and Presidents take turns in order of their seating at the table, the circuit being made in one direction at one meeting and in the opposite direction at the next. The chairman speaks last, customarily framing his closing remarks in the form of a consensus of the preceding recommendations. Often, however, there is less than complete agreement among committee members; less often, but not infrequently, the Chairman may wish to give stronger than usual direction to current policy. In such circumstances, the "Martin consensus" has emerged, this consensus being largely the view of the Chairman himself, whether or not it coincides with that of the majority. Rarely—if then—are policy recommendations put into a motion and voted upon.

The Account Manager listens to the discussion and at its conclusion is asked by the Chairman if he comprehends the wishes of the committee. He almost always answers in the affirmative. But though the account manager listens with great care, even tabulating the recommendations of each speaker, FOMC members frequently complain that they cannot communicate precisely with the manager. This problem has several dimensions. First, each committee member, being a rugged individualist, would probably be satisfied with little less than complete direction of current policy. Second, because the FOMC does not make a precise statement of its wishes, the Account Manager must consider nineteen sets of recommendations, some of them rambling discourses on the state of the union. Third, the three-week interval between meetings is long enough to require adaptations on the part of the Manager, and these cannot possibly coincide with all nineteen committee opinions. Fourth, policy recommendations of FOMC members are stated in terms that are at best ambiguous—"a little tighter," or "about the same degree of ease," or "shoot for net free reserves between $500 million and $600 million." Committee members frequently disavow the free reserves target, pointing out that it lacks sufficient connection with the complex of economic variables to be useful as a measure of the effectiveness of policy. It is little wonder then that communication between the FOMC and the trading desk is poor. Nor is it any wonder that Chairman Martin, for better or worse, must determine a consensus that would lead only to endless argument if it were brought to a vote.

A more basic difficulty of communication arises from the unwillingness of the committee to state its economic outlook in precise terms. There exists in the Federal Reserve System an unwritten rule against explicit forecasting of business conditions; even modest attempts at prognosis are blue-penciled if written and ignored if expressed verbally. Members of the FOMC often remark that "we are making policy only for the next three weeks," the implication being that inaction or wrong action can be reviewed or corrected at the next meeting. Now it is manifestly impossible to frame an intelligent monetary policy without at least implicit forecasting; and since a major objective of monetary policy is cyclical amelioration, the forecast period must be a major portion of a cycle. Fortunately, many FOMC members have their own unstated projections. But the emphasis on the short term, the avoidance of a solid, common forecast, and the frequency of FOMC meetings all lead to erratic action, lagged responses, and policy more often than not based on correction of past errors rather than on anticipation of future events.

But whatever the difficulties and ambiguities of communicating with the trading desk, transmissions *are* made and received. However, the man in charge of the desk, no matter how dedicated, has a rough, tough job. If, as is frequently true, the FOMC has set some range of free reserves as its most precise measure of policy direction, the Account Manager ideally tries to achieve this goal in his day-to-day operations. But the goal is elusive, simply because some of the money-market factors affecting reserves cannot be predicted at all and others can be estimated only with difficulty. (Actual figures may become available only two or three weeks later.) Actions taken by the desk on the basis of the daily predictions of the money-market factors frequently turn out to have been perverse—in the wrong direction. The chief upsetting factor, of course, is Federal Reserve float, which is extremely volatile and almost completely unpredictable on a daily basis. Float could be safely ignored on a daily basis and dealt with only on a weekly average basis, Federal Reserve studies having shown that commercial banks do not alter their short-term investment positions on the basis of changing float levels. Yet fear of commercial-bank response ostensibly forms the basis for the frequency of a Fed's float-offsetting action, with consequent uncertainty in the money markets when desk action is in the wrong direction.

Another major influence on the administration of the trading desk is the solicitude of the Fed for the government security dealers, particularly for the nonbank dealers. The basic premises of this solicitude are that a "broad, deep, and resilient" market for government securities is necessary for successful Federal Reserve action and that such a market can be made only by financially impregnable dealers who can obtain financing on favorable terms. A "negative carry"—that is, a yield on any security held in inventory smaller than the rate paid on funds borrowed by the dealer—is taken as conclusive evidence that financing terms for the dealers are not favorable. The same concern is not felt for bank dealers, since they are assumed to have a ready internal source of funds to finance their positions.

Solicitude for the dealers is expressed in several ways. For example, the FOMC has approved and the desk has made frequent use of the repurchase agreement. Although this instrument is a means by which the desk can make bank reserves available for a short time with automatic withdrawal, it is also a means by which short-term credit is extended to a dealer.[4] The timing is usually to the advantage of the dealer, because the desk makes the privilege available when there is a real pinch in the money market. The repurchase agreement is in reality a fully secured loan, the desk purchases securities (bills) from the dealer, who agrees to repurchase them within a definite period (maximum, fifteen days). Interest is computed on the basis of amount and term of loan rather than by reckoning the difference between purchase and sale price of the bills, as would be true in the case of a true purchase and repurchase.

Fed concern for the government securities dealer is further demonstrated by the expressed opinion that the money-market banks ought to favor the securities dealers in financing arrangements, particularly during tight-money periods. The money-market banks have protested that no group ought to be favored merely because of its function. Although the interest of the Fed authorities in maintaining a facilitating market organization is understandable, it is doubtful that financing favoritism is essential to a strong dealer organization. A hands-off attitude, requiring dealers to stand the market test of services rendered, charges made, and competition for custom, seems more likely to achieve ultimate Federal Reserve aims.

Nor is arranging Fed intervention in the government securities market to suit the convenience of nonbank dealers likely to inspire public confidence. Federal Reserve acceptance of the notion that System entry into the government securities market should be in short issues, preferably bills, had its philosophical basis in a weird principle of "minimum effective interference," a mystical idea that the limitless authority of the central bank could somehow be softened by dealing in securities "closest to money" in the spectrum of financial assets. But

---

[4] Compare Robert V. Roosa, *Federal Reserve Operations in the Money and Government Securities Markets* (New York: Federal Reserve Bank of New York, 1956), esp. pp. 25–26 and 83–87.

a careful reading of the famed *Ad Hoc Subcommittee Report* of 1952 makes it clear that strong support for the "bills only" dogma came from the dealers, who would avoid, for obvious reasons, "capricious" System purchases and sales throughout the maturity range of the Treasury list. Dealers with positions in bonds naturally want to be warned of fluctuations in bond prices by preliminary changes in the prices of bills.

RETURN TO REGIONALISM?

Knowledgeable men know perfectly well that the informal power structure of an institution—whether a Christian denomination, a great corporation, or a university—may well be more important than its formal one. So long as the distinction is clear, so long as people are aware of what is really going on, it makes little difference whether the formal or informal power centers are operative. But it makes a great deal of difference if the people in a democracy, unaware of the arbitrary nature of the actual decision making, go on believing that the money power, like all other sovereign power, is responsive to democratic processes. For plainly it is not.

We do not for one moment question either the integrity or the sincerity of the money managers. If government at all levels were staffed by men of the competence and dedication of those found in the Federal Reserve System, the American political system would be upgraded tremendously.

We do believe, however, that a realistic appraisal of System structure in terms of its genuine power centers leads to only one conclusion—that the regional structure, adopted by the framers of the Federal Reserve Act two generations ago, is presently outmoded and has become an expensive anachronism. We may as well face up to the fact that Federal Reserve Banks have become only operating offices with responsibility for service functions and not, in any real sense, for monetary policy.

In our view a workable regional system *could* be devised. A return to regional structure would require, as a very minimum, restoration of the discount rate as an instrument of monetary control. Such a restoration implies the rescinding of Regulation A, the complex and meddlesome set of rules by which the twelve discount windows are presently administered. It further implies free access to discount windows at whatever rates the regional banks prescribe.

Ostensibly, the discount rates of the several banks are set by their boards of directors. In practice, they are raised and lowered at the wish of the Board of Governors. When Chairman Martin senses the strategic moment has arrived for a discount-rate change, he initiates action via a discreet telephone call to one or more bank Presidents out in the provinces. Once a Reserve Bank President (at St. Louis, Kansas City, Atlanta, or Dallas, for example) has the word, it is up to him to get his board of directors, or the executive committee of his board, to do what the Reserve Board wants. When the change is made, the business press ordinarily announces it as the simultaneous decision of two or more banks. Within ten days or so, all the other banks fall in line—not by mere chance, you may be sure.

There is much to be said for operating the discount window on a rate basis rather than on an administered basis. To be sure, Federal Reserve credit must be injected partly with regard to grand strategic considerations, as determined by the board and the New York Bank. But much of the hour-to-hour and day-to-day intervention by the trading desk could be avoided by letting the commercial banks tell the Fed when they need reserves. It sounds a little old-fashioned to suggest that the private banking community may on occasion know what's best for it, but we'd like to return some of the reserve-injection initiative to the commercial banks.

There are reasons why it may be impossible to go back to a regional system. For one thing, the American economy has lost most of the provincial character-istics that marked it as late as the eve of World War II. For another, our understanding of monetary (stabilization) theory has changed since the forma-tion of a geographically decentralized central bank, placing emphasis on unified control of the economy rather than on patchwork assistance to parts of it.

Yet there would be a demonstrable gain from making central-bank control less authoritarian. Moreover, continued centralization of the money power leads logically to the ultimate in a centralized power structure—combination of the central bank and the Treasury under a single head. Those who feel that such an arrangement bodes no good would do well to reflect on the possibility of greater reliance on markets in the implementation of central-bank policy.

8

Instruments
of Monetary Management

THE FEDERAL RESERVE SYSTEM NOW HAS AVAILABLE techniques of monetary control that bear little resemblance to those provided in the original Federal Reserve Act. It has acquired significant new powers at various times—particularly during the depression of the 1930's—and the environment within which its management techniques are employed was drastically changed by the financial aftermath of World War II. This chapter presents a critical evaluation of the instruments of monetary management now available to the Fed and of the ways in which they are used, singly and in combination. Particular attention is focused on postwar developments, since both commercial banks and the Federal Reserve System have had to undergo a process of re-education in appropriate use of member bank borrowing privileges, the Federal funds market, the market for short-term government securities, and the integration of monetary and debt management policies.

Selection 28

TOOLS AND PROCESSES OF MONETARY POLICY

RALPH A. YOUNG

> *This selection outlines the use of the major tools of monetary policy —open market operations, discount operations, changes in reserve requirements, regulation of stock market credit, and other special-purpose instruments—and explains some interrelationships of the tools. The author is Adviser to the Board of Governors of the Federal Reserve System.*

INSTRUMENTS OF FEDERAL RESERVE POLICY

In regulating the reserve base of the commercial banking system, the Federal Reserve System relies on three interrelated instruments: open market operations, discount operations, and changes in reserve requirements. System policy has one objective—to promote maximum economic growth over the longer run, while preserving the purchasing power of the dollar. In carrying out its policy, the System uses these three instruments in a complementary fashion to affect the supply of reserves and their cost to member banks.

Besides these general instruments, the System has one selective authority for influence on credit markets—the regulation of stock market credit. This is a special-purpose instrument, designed to prevent the excessive use of credit in the stock market.

OPEN MARKET OPERATIONS

Open market operations generally consist of Federal Reserve purchases or sales of securities in the open market. Regardless of who may sell the securities purchased or who may buy the securities sold by the Federal Reserve, these transactions have a direct impact on the volume of member bank reserves. The distinctive aspect of open market operations is that they are undertaken at the initiative of the Federal Reserve System and, therefore, are an active reflection of prevailing monetary policy.

Explanation of operations

Open market purchases or sales of securities are made by the manager of the System's open market account under instruction of the Federal Open Market Committee, the System's central policy-setting body. These transactions are in United States government securities primarily, but they may include bankers' acceptances in relatively small amounts. The purchase or sale orders are placed

---

• From Ralph A. Young, "Tools and Processes of Monetary Policy," *United States Monetary Policy,* pp. 18–37. Copyright 1958 by The American Assembly, Columbia University, New York. Reprinted by permission of the American Assembly and the author.

with dealers who buy and sell government securities or acceptances on their own account as well as for others, and who are prepared to permit the execution of orders to affect their own inventory of securities. The established dealers number about a score. Placement of orders by the System's open market account is usually preceded by competitive bidding among the dealers and is always on the basis of the best price offered or bid by them.

When the Federal Reserve, through the manager of the open market account, places an order with a dealer for a given amount of government securities, the dealer either buys the securities in the open market or sells them from his own portfolio. In payment the dealer receives a check on a Reserve Bank, which he deposits in his own account with a member bank. The member bank then deposits the check in its reserve account with a Reserve Bank. Federal Reserve purchases of government securities thus add to the reserve balances of member banks. Conversely, sales of securities reduce reserve balances. The resulting changes in reserve positions affect the ability of member banks to make loans and to acquire investments.

System open market operations are conducted ordinarily on a cash basis. Sometimes, however, purchases are made under agreement that the selling dealer will repurchase the securities within a specified period of fifteen days or less. These arrangements provide reserves on a temporary basis—put out reserves with a string on them, as it were. This type of operation also pro-

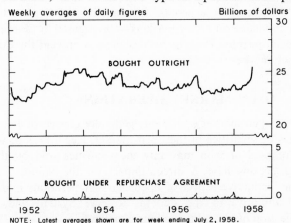

Weekly averages of daily figures   Billions of dollars

BOUGHT OUTRIGHT

BOUGHT UNDER REPURCHASE AGREEMENT

Figure 1. SYSTEM HOLD-INGS OF U. S. GOVERNMENT SECURITIES

1952   1954   1956   1958

NOTE: Latest averages shown are for week ending July 2, 1958.

vides dealers in government securities with temporary financing of their inventories when funds are not freely available in the market except at interest rates significantly higher than yields on their inventories. Repurchase agreements may at times be renewed.

Evolving practices

Federal Reserve open market operations since 1953 have been confined to short-term government securities, primarily to Treasury bills maturing within 90 days.* These securities are the closest to cash of any money market instrument,

---

Editor's note: The manner in which this policy has been modified since 1960, largely because of balance of payments problems, is discussed in later selections—e.g., Selection 44.

and the most active and continuous trading is in the short-term sector of the market. Federal Reserve operations in this part of the market have the desired impact on bank reserves with a minimum of direct effect on the supply of and demand for securities and, therefore, on the prices and yields of specific securities purchased or sold.

The short-term end of the government securities market is the area of most active and continuous trading for various reasons. Foremost among them is the fact that all commercial banks, as well as other financial institutions, invest the bulk of their operating or secondary reserves in short-term government securities. Likewise, large commercial and industrial corporations invest in them any excess cash balances and funds accumulating for large payments, such as taxes and dividends. Short-term government securities are, in effect, a haven in which liquid funds of the financial and business community can earn an interest return until they are needed for operating purposes. The sales and purchases made daily by thousands of financial institutions and businesses in adjusting their operating positions make for a steady stream of trading in short-term securities.

The relationship of open market operations to Treasury debt management operations was also modified early in 1953. During World War II, the Reserve System used its open market instrument to facilitate Treasury borrowing operations. These activities, which continued after the war, involved System open market account transactions in maturing issues, in when-issued securities, and in outstanding issues of maturities comparable to those being offered by the Treasury in a particular refinancing. One effect of such operations was that the System, with its virtually unlimited resources, competed against the market in such transactions. Market traders, in consequence, tended to limit their own trading during the period of the refinancing. The risk to System policy stemming from these operations was the undesired release of more Federal Reserve credit than was consistent with basic objectives of monetary management at the time. Accordingly, in the interests of furthering a more self-reliant government securities market and of limiting open market operations to purely monetary objectives this kind of operation was discontinued.

An additional change in System open market methods was made in early 1953. Since 1937, the System had stated officially that maintenance of orderly conditions in the money and securities markets was an aim of its open market operations. This objective sanctioned, if it did not make necessary, operations in all sectors of the government securities market. Since System postwar experience had shown that open market operations conducted for bond market stability ran the risk of adding to or subtracting from bank reserves in amounts inconsistent with a stable purchasing power for the dollar, an alternative basis for open market operations was adopted. Intervention in the bond market for purposes of coping with its instability was limited to the correction of disorderly situations in the market, if such situations were encountered.[1]

[1] In connection with these and other actions referred to in this section, see the Open Market Policy Record for 1953 in the *Annual Report* of the Board of Governors for that year.

Operations in short-term vs. longer-term securities [2]

The System's general practice of recent years of confining open market operations to the short-term sector of the market, primarily to Treasury bills, has been criticized on the grounds that it prevents the System from fostering economic stability by directly influencing long-term interest rates. Interest rates on government securities are pivotal rates in the United States capital market. Because there is no risk of default on United States government securities, their market yields run lower than yields on other securities, but by a systematic margin that reflects the constant appraisal by investors of the worth to them of the risk differential. Thus, according to critics, System transactions in long-term government securities will affect all prices and yields in the long-term market and in the process the volume of funds available to that market. By affecting market prices, yields, and supply in this way, the argument runs, the System can influence significantly the volume of long-term financing and thereby the volume of the economy's investment activity.

This criticism appears plausible at first glance, but in reality it confuses the issue. The important impact of System open market operations on the credit and capital markets is through its impact on bank reserve positions. Under our percentage reserve system, additions to or subtractions from commercial bank reserves have a multiple expansive or contractive effect on bank lending and investing power. This means that any given change in System holdings of securities will be accompanied by a change in commercial bank portfolios of loans and investments several times as large. Thus, the major effect of System open market operations on market prices and interest rates will be the one that results from commercial bank transactions in securities to expand or contract their loan and investment portfolios. The effect on market prices and interest rates as a result of an increase or decrease in Federal Reserve holdings of particular securities and a corresponding decrease or increase in their market supply will be relatively minor. In evaluating this latter effect, it needs to be kept in mind that the size of System open market operations is ordinarily small in relation to the volume of any category of securities outstanding in the market.

Combining monetary and savings functions, commercial banks are unique financial institutions. In this dual role, they carry both demand and time liabilities and so can acquire assets having maturities distributed throughout the range of the market. Thus, changes in the level of their combined reserve balances give rise to bank portfolio transactions in all sectors of the market, and so have an impact on long-term interest rates as well as on short-term interest rates.

Other investors in government securities, especially savings institutions, also try to maintain a distribution of maturities of their portfolio holdings adapted to their needs. The professional managers of these portfolios are on the alert for changes in the various supply and demand factors in the market, including the

---

[2] This subject is treated more fully in an article by W. W. Riefler, "Open Market Operations in Long-term Securities," *Federal Reserve Bulletin,* November, 1958, pp. 1260–1274.

changing reserve and asset position of the commercial banks. Their alacrity in adapting their portfolios to changes in market factors helps to spread the effect of changes in bank reserve positions on interest rates through the entire market.

An important objection to Federal Reserve open market operations in long-term securities is their potential effect on market professionals and portfolio managers. Long-term securities are normally subject to wider price fluctuations than are short-term issues and, therefore, trading or portfolio positions in them incur the greater price risk. Furthermore, the System holds the largest single portfolio of government securities in the United States economy, and it is the only investor of virtually unlimited means. If the System conducts open market operations in longer-term securities, professional investors and portfolio managers may either step to the sidelines or endeavor to operate on the same side of the market as they believe—perhaps from rumor—the System to be operating.

In the former case, the Federal Reserve would become in fact the price and yield administrator of the long-term government securities market. In the latter event, the operations might encourage either artificially bullish or bearish expectations as to prices and yields on long-term securities, and lead to unsustainable price and yield levels that do not reflect basic supply and demand forces. Either of these effects would permeate and disturb the whole capital market. Consequently, instead of working as a stabilizing force for the economy, open market operations in long-term securities could have the opposite result.

The function of the long-term capital markets is to transmute the money savings of the economy, as supplemented by bank credit, into real investment. Tendencies in security prices and yields in these markets are vital and sensitive indicators of the relative pressures of the supply of money savings and bank credit and the demand for funds to finance real investment. If the Federal Reserve were to intervene in the functioning of supply and demand in order directly to administer prices and yields on long-term securities or in a way that resulted in unsustainable prices and yields, it would impair the usefulness of an important guide to monetary policy.

DISCOUNT OPERATIONS

Provision of facilities for lending to commercial banks is a traditional function of central banks. In the United States, lending by the Federal Reserve Banks to member banks has come to take the form chiefly of advances secured by United States government securities. While commercial and other business paper of prime quality and short maturity is eligible for discounting, borrowing against government securities as collateral is more convenient and timesaving for the borrowing bank, since the collateral is riskless and instantly appraisable.

From the viewpoint of the individual member bank, a decision to borrow is usually prompted by the desire to avoid a deficiency in its legal reserve. Such a deficiency is likely to result from a drain of deposits and therefore of reserves to another bank. In adjusting to such a reserve drain, the individual bank has the alternative of selling an asset or borrowing at the Federal Reserve or from another bank.

When a member bank borrows or discounts at a Reserve Bank, the proceeds of the loan are added to its reserve balance on deposit at the Reserve Bank. Conversely, when the indebtedness is repaid, the amount of repayment is charged against the indebted bank's reserve balance. Federal Reserve advances to or discounts for member banks are usually of short maturity—up to fifteen days. The interest rate paid by member banks for this accommodation is known as the discount rate.

Described in this way, the discount facilities of the Reserve Banks appear as little more than a convenience to member banks, enabling them to adjust their reserve positions to shifts in deposits. The fact is, however, that use of the discount facilities, as will be explained later, puts member banks under pressure to limit their loan expansion.

Discount administration

Federal Reserve Bank discounts of member bank paper are not automatic; the discount facilities are made available to member banks as a privilege of membership in the System and not as a right. Under Regulation *A* of the Board of Governors, applicable to the discount process, all of the Federal Reserve Banks in accommodating member bank applications for discount credit adhere to the following guiding principles set forth in the Regulation:

> Federal Reserve credit is generally extended on a short-term basis to a member bank in order to enable it to adjust its asset position when necessary because of developments such as a sudden withdrawal of deposits or seasonal requirements for credit beyond those which can reasonably be met by use of the bank's own resources. Federal Reserve credit is also available for longer periods when necessary in order to assist member banks in meeting unusual situations, such as may result from national, regional, or local difficulties or from exceptional circumstances involving only particular member banks. Under ordinary conditions, the continuous use of Federal Reserve credit by a member bank over a considerable period of time is not regarded as appropriate.

> In considering a request for credit accommodation, each Federal Reserve Bank gives due regard to the purpose of the credit and to its probable effects upon the maintenance of sound credit conditions, both as to the individual institution and the economy generally. It keeps informed of and takes into account the general character and amount of the loans and investments of the member banks. It considers whether the bank is borrowing principally for the purpose of obtaining a tax advantage or profiting from rate differentials and whether the bank is extending an undue amount of credit for the speculative carrying of or trading in securities, real estate, or commodities, or otherwise.

Member bank reluctance to borrow

Federal Reserve Bank discount standards are in practice reinforced by a tradition among this country's banks against operating on the basis of borrowed reserves—at least, for any extended period. This tradition does not mean that member banks feel reluctant to rely on Federal Reserve lending facilities to meet temporary or unusual cash drains. But it does mean that under normal conditions member banks will make a practice of limiting their resort to Reserve Bank borrowing to necessary contingencies, and that, once in debt, they will seek to repay promptly. Continuing pressures on their reserve positions and other special developments may, at times, weaken this reluctance, but it nonetheless persists as a factor affecting member bank borrowing.

Member bank attitudes toward operating with borrowed funds vary from bank to bank. Many banks never borrow from a Federal Reserve Bank, preferring to make reserve adjustments in other ways. Reluctance to borrow, as well as incentive to repay promptly, results from the disposition of depositors, especially business and financial depositors, to be critical of the liabilities assumed by borrowing, since, in case of insolvency, they take precedence over the claims of depositors. Another consideration is that borrowed funds are generally more expensive than funds obtained through deposits.

Federal funds market

In a banking system made up of as many independent units as that of this country, and with as widely varying banking conditions, individual banks will at times be deficient in reserves and at other times have excess reserves. Since total reserve funds are limited in supply, a fairly well-organized market has developed, known as the Federal funds market, in which banks with balances in excess of needs offer to lend them on a day-to-day basis to banks deficient in reserves. Such transactions, when they are arranged, rarely occur at rates above the Reserve Bank discount rates.

Conditions of supply and demand in the Federal funds market, and also the proximity of the Federal funds rate to the discount rate, necessarily vary directly with general credit conditions and influence member bank borrowing from the Reserve Banks. When funds are readily available in this market, use of the discount facility by member banks is reduced, largely because fewer banks are experiencing reserve deficiencies, but also because the Federal funds market is a cheaper source of temporary funds.

The discount rate

Technically, the discount rate is the publicly announced charge applied by the Federal Reserve Banks on discounts or advances to member banks. As such, it measures for the member banks the cost of reserve funds obtained by such borrowing. Because there is a close interrelationship between the level of Reserve Bank discount rates and short-term money rates in the market, and because the establishment of the rate entails a Federal Reserve judgment as to whether the current flow of bank credit and money is consistent with the country's transactions and liquidity needs, discount rate changes are commonly viewed as an important index of the direction of Federal Reserve policy. Each Federal Reserve Bank must establish its discount rate, subject to review and determination by the Board of Governors in Washington, every fourteen days.

From the viewpoint of the individual member bank, reserve adjustments can be made either by borrowing at the Federal Reserve (or from other banks) or by selling short-term assets in the market. The margin of preference as between one form of reserve adjustment and another is in part affected by relative cost.

The cost of adjusting a reserve position by selling securities is measured by the interest earnings forgone. Thus, the margin of preference as between discounting and selling securities is influenced by the relationship between the discount rate and the market yields on types of securities that are likely to be held by banks as liquid assets or a second line of reserves. Prominent among these are United States Treasury bills and other short-term government obligations.

Tendency to uniform discount rates

The founders of the Federal Reserve System contemplated that Reserve Bank discount rates would be set in accordance with regional financial conditions. They expected that variations in regional conditions would lead to variations in discount rates among the twelve Banks. In recent decades, the tendency has been for rates to be uniform, although there have been temporary periods in which different rates have obtained. Basically, this modern tendency toward uniformity reflects improvement in the facilities and speed of communication and transport as well as further industrial, commercial, and financial integration.

Credit is the most fluid of resources and flows promptly to the market of highest yield. Growth in the number and assets of regional and national enterprises that are capable of meeting their financing needs readily in the cheapest market has increased the mobility of demand for funds. The highly sensitive markets for Treasury bills and other government securities and for Federal funds provide a mechanism through which these forces of fluid supply and mobile demand ultimately converge, giving rise to pressure for equality of discount rates among the Reserve Banks. Thus over the years, it has become increasingly appropriate to think of System discount rate policy in terms of "the discount rate" rather than in terms of twelve Reserve Bank rates.

Relation of discount rate to market rates

The Federal Reserve discount rate and market rates on prime short-term paper are interdependent. In a period of monetary restraint, short-term market rates tend to rise in response to demand for funds and also as a result of bank

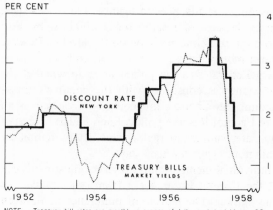

NOTE: Treasury bill rates are monthly averages of daily market yields on 90-day bills. Discount rate is that charged by the Federal Reserve Bank of New York. Data plotted through June, 1958.

Figure 2. DISCOUNT AND BILL RATES

sales of Treasury bills and other liquid assets. As short-term market rates rise above the discount rate, the Reserve Banks are likely to raise the discount rate in order to maintain the discipline of the discount mechanism as a deterrent to bank loan expansion.

On the other hand, as the discount rate rises above market rates, banks are likely to shift away from discounting toward selling government securities as a means of reserve adjustment, in view of its lower cost. But this in itself, by increasing the market supply of short-term securities relative to the demand, tends to drive up short-term interest rates toward or above the discount rate. Thus, in a period of credit restraint, short-term market rates tend to cluster around the discount rate, and they are likely to rise together in a series of upward adjustments, until the need for restrictive monetary policy has passed.

No simple rules govern the interpretation of changes in the discount rate. In some circumstances, a change in the discount rate may express a shift in direction of Federal Reserve policy toward restraint or ease. In other instances, it may reflect a further step in the same direction. In still other cases, a change may represent merely a technical adjustment to market rates designed to maintain the existing degree of credit restraint or ease.

CHANGES IN RESERVE REQUIREMENTS

Federal Reserve authority to vary the required reserve percentages for commercial banks is a relatively new instrument of reserve banking; it was first made available through banking legislation in 1933 and 1935. Under the provisions of the Banking Act of 1935, the Federal Reserve System may vary within specified limits the required reserve percentages for each of the three classes of banks—central reserve city banks, reserve city banks, and country banks.* The permitted changes in requirements may be applied to one or more classes of banks at the same time, but they must be kept within the limits set for each class and must be uniform for all banks within a class. . . .

Action to change the level of reserve requirements does not affect the amount of member bank reserve balances, but it does affect the amount of deposits and, therefore, of loans and investments that member banks can legally maintain on the basis of a given amount of reserves. A given amount of member bank reserves, in other words, can be made to do more or less bank credit and monetary work according to the level of reserve percentages. . . .

Two things happen when the required reserve percentages are changed. First, there is an immediate change in the liquid asset or secondary reserve position of member banks. If reserve percentages are raised, banks that have no excess reserves must find additional reserve funds by selling liquid assets in the market or by borrowing from other banks or from the Reserve Banks. If reserve percentages are lowered, individual banks find themselves with a margin of excess reserves available for investment in earning assets and for debt repayment. Since banks maximize their earnings by keeping debt free and their own resources as fully invested as possible, their usual response to a lowering of reserve require-

* *Editor's note:* Since 1962, there are only two classes—reserve city banks and "country" banks.

ments, after retiring indebtedness, is to acquire earning assets. Initially they are likely to purchase short-term market instruments of high liquidity as assets for temporary holding.

Second, there is a change in the rate of multiple expansion of deposits for the entire banking system. If the required reserve percentage is 20 per cent, $1 of reserves will support about $5 of deposits. If the percentage requirement is reduced to 15 per cent, $1 of reserves will support about $6.67 of deposits. The 15 per cent requirement, thus, will support one-third more of deposits than the 20 per cent requirement.

The authority to make changes in required reserve percentages is sometimes described as a clumsy and blunt instrument of monetary control. For one thing, such changes affect at the same time and to the same extent all member banks subject to the action, regardless of their individual reserve needs on the occasion. For another, even small changes in reserve requirements, say of one-half of one percentage point, result in relatively large changes in the total available reserves and in the liquidity positions of member banks as a group. If, to avoid a large reserve effect, a change is limited to a particular class of banks, a difficult and perplexing problem of equity as between classes of banks is presented.

Moreover, changes to a new level of reserve requirements cannot be spread over a period of time, but must become effective on some selected preannounced date. The credit market is forewarned that on this date either demand or supply pressures will be accentuated, with the risk of disturbance and instability in the prices and yields on securities at the time.

Finally, there is the consideration that a bank's reserve percentage serves as an anchor for current and forward management decisions. Abrupt change in the weight of this anchor can have an upsetting influence in the portfolio programs of individual banks.

For these reasons, the reserve requirement instrument of monetary policy is not readily adaptable to day-to-day and short-run operations. Since the authority to change reserve requirements became available in 1935, its use has been restricted to situations calling for reserve changes of more than temporary import. . . .

REGULATION OF STOCK MARKET CREDIT

Since 1933, the Federal Reserve System has been enjoined by law to restrain the use of bank credit for speculation in securities, real estate, or commodities. Since 1934, the System has been specifically directed to curb the excessive use of credit for purchasing or carrying securities by regulation limiting the amount that brokers and dealers in securities, banks, and others may lend on securities for that purpose. At brokers and dealers the regulatory limitation applies to any type of security; at banks, it applies only to securities registered on national security exchanges. The regulatory limitation does not apply to any loan for other purposes, even though the loan may be secured by stocks.

The mechanism of stock market credit regulation is not widely understood. The amount that lenders will loan against securities will always be less than the current market value of the securities to be pledged as collateral. The lender calls the difference between the two the customer's margin. For example, if a

loan of $7,500 is secured by stock worth $10,000, the customer's margin is
$2,500 or 25 per cent. Thus, by prescribing the customer's margin, the loan
value of the securities may be controlled; the greater the margin required, the
less the amount that can be lent. Currently, the margin required by Federal
Reserve regulation is 70 per cent. The lower limit of the required margin during
postwar years has been 50 per cent.

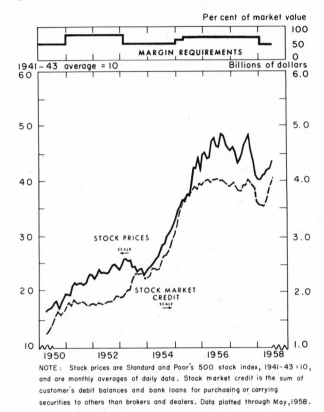

NOTE: Stock prices are Standard and Poor's 500 stock index, 1941-43 =10,
and are monthly averages of daily data. Stock market credit is the sum of
customer's debit balances and bank loans for purchasing or carrying
securities to others than brokers and dealers. Data plotted through May, 1958.

Figure 3. STOCK MARKET

Federal Reserve regulation requires the lender to obtain the specified margin in connection with the purchase of the security. If the collateral security for
the indebtedness subsequently declines in value, regulation does not make it
necessary for the borrower either to put up additional collateral or to reduce the
indebtedness. However, the banker or broker making a loan may require additional collateral if he deems it necessary.

Regulation of stock market credit by the margin requirement, though bearing directly on the lender, puts restraint on the borrower and thus dampens
demand. A very important aspect of this restraint is the limitation it places on
the amount of pyramiding of borrowing that can take place in a rising market
as higher prices create higher collateral values and permit more borrowing on
the same collateral. An increase in the required margin in periods of rising stock
prices may be indicated to limit acceleration of stock market credit expansion
resulting from tendencies toward pyramiding.

The purposes of regulation through margin requirements are to minimize the danger of excessive use of credit in financing stock market speculation, and to prevent the recurrence of speculative stock market booms based on credit financing, such as culminated in the price collapse of 1929 and the subsequent severe credit liquidation. A stock market boom followed by collapse is always possible, but without excessive feeding by credit it is not likely to assume the proportions or to have the effects that it had in earlier periods.

OTHER SPECIAL-PURPOSE INSTRUMENTS

Under special conditions of national emergency, or exceptionally strong inflationary pressures, the bank reserve instruments have been temporarily supplemented by two other selective tools—regulation of consumer credit and regulation of real estate credit. Consumer credit was subject to regulation during World War II and for two years following, and again in two later periods of strong inflationary tendencies, including the post-Korean period. Regulation of real estate credit was specially authorized during the post-Korean period. The authority for this regulation was divided between the Housing and Home Finance Administrator with respect to governmentally aided lending and the Federal Reserve System with respect to other construction lending.

These types of regulation, though effectuated through the lender, accomplished their purposes by making the conditions of borrowing more restrictive to the borrower, thereby dampening his demand for credit. They limited the amount of credit that might initially be granted by a lender in relation to the value of the property being financed, or they limited the time that might be agreed upon by borrowers and lenders for the repayment of obligations, or they did both. All grantors of credit of the types specified under these regulations were subject to them, were required to register under them, and could be penalized for their violation.

In postwar years, these two regulations have been imposed under special and temporary authority provided by the Congress. Although statutory authority for their application has not been available in recent years, public discussion of the desirability of such authority has continued, especially with regard to regulation of consumer credit. In 1956 and 1957, the Board of Governors of the Federal Reserve System, at the request of the President and the interested Committees of the Congress, undertook a comprehensive investigation of consumer installment credit with a view to the advisability of a continuing authority for its regulation, when appropriate, in periods of inflationary pressures. The evidence assembled through this study concerning the desirability of such a continuing regulatory authority was inconclusive, and, consequently, no statutory enactment was either recommended or provided.

The regulation of consumer credit and of real estate credit presents much more difficult problems of administration, compliance, and enforcement than arise in the regulation of stock market credit. These problems partly grow out of the large numbers of lenders, in addition to banks, that are affected by regulation. They also stem, however, from the diversity of financing practices and circumstances that characterize these credit fields. These instruments, consequently, are less flexible and adaptable selective tools than is the margin requirement instrument.

COORDINATION OF MONETARY POLICY INSTRUMENTS

In its monetary management operations—seasonal, cyclical, and growth—the Federal Reserve System's major tools are those affecting the reserve position of member banks. Open market operations are the most flexible and constantly used instrument, and hence the principal means of coping with short-term forces influencing member bank reserves, including those associated with seasonal variations in the public's uses of currency, in Federal Reserve float, and in business, farmer, and consumer use of bank credit. Discount operations, while they play some part in cushioning seasonal pressures on individual banks or on groups of banks in communities subject to special seasonal fluctuations, perform their main role as a complement to open market operations in dealing with cyclical swings in credit demand and money balances.

Provision of bank reserves for meeting the economy's need for growth in the supply of money is accomplished in part by open market operations and in part by changes in reserve requirements. Use of the latter instrument for growth purposes may be made in times of economic recession, in order to gain whatever stimulative effects on the economy that monetary expansion may have at that time. Reserve requirement levels may also be changed in special situations where large changes in the volume of reserves, such as result from sizable international movements of gold, need to be offset or cushioned.

Regulation of stock market credit, a special-purpose instrument as mentioned earlier, functions as a supplement to the bank reserve instruments. By providing a means of dealing directly and selectively with a highly volatile type of credit, it serves to moderate the strength of general credit action that otherwise might need to be taken as a result of stock market speculation and credit use. Since these aspects of stock market activity fluctuate with general business conditions, changes in the margin requirement are similarly correlated.

The main cyclical work of monetary management is carried out by complementary reliance on open market and discount operations. The ultimate effect of the joint use of these instruments in a growing economy is on the rate of expansion of member bank deposits and assets. When monetary policy is operating restrictively in a period of boom, there will be a retardation in the rate of expansion of total bank deposits and assets and of the active money supply—demand deposits and currency. Under a stimulative monetary policy in periods of recession, sooner or later there will be an increase in the rate of expansion of these magnitudes. Situations that require monetary action to induce an actual contraction in these strategic quantities will seldom arise.

INTERRELATIONSHIP OF TOOLS
IN PERIODS OF MONETARY RESTRAINT

The interplay of open market operations and discount operations in regulating the rate of expansion of bank deposits, bank assets, and active money balances needs brief explanation. When the volume of the economy's transactions is expanding rapidly and inflationary pressures develop as active spending financed by credit, especially bank credit, presses against the capacity to produce, restraint on monetary expansion will be called for. On the basis of historical patterns in these circumstances, the Federal Reserve undertakes open market operations that provide a smaller amount of reserves than the banks are seeking as they attempt to satisfy the many and varied demands for credit.

As a result of this action by monetary management, individual banks will find it necessary to sell government securities in the market in order to obtain funds with which to meet demands for loans by their customers. Although such sales of securities provide additional reserves to individual banks, they do not add to over-all bank reserves unless the Federal Reserve purchases the securities. As each bank sells securities, it draws reserves from other banks, whether the securities are purchased by other banks, by businesses or individuals, or by other financial institutions.

As a policy of monetary restraint continues or is accentuated, there will be more frequent and more widespread reserve drains among member banks. This will lead an increasing number of banks to borrow temporarily at the discount window of the Reserve Banks in order to maintain their legal reserve positions. For each bank, the borrowing will be temporary, but the repayment by one bank draws reserves from other banks, which in turn will have need to borrow at a Reserve Bank. Thus, restrictive monetary action leads to a larger volume of member bank borrowings, as more banks find their reserve positions under pressure more often.

It can be said that a Federal Reserve decision to limit the volume of member bank reserves is, in a sense, a decision to put member banks as a group under pressure to borrow reserve funds. A higher level of member bank borrowings, representing increasing frequency, amount, and duration of discountings by a growing number of banks, is a normal and an expected reaction to a restrictive monetary policy.

Since borrowing at the Reserve Banks adds to member bank reserves, it may seem that use of the discount facility is more an offset than a supplement to restrictive monetary action. The discount mechanism in these circumstances serves, it is true, as a safety valve, providing banks with a temporary means of reserve adjustment. Use of the safety valve, however, does not afford an escape from monetary restraint.

In the first place, an increase in member bank discounts does not necessarily increase on balance the total of member bank reserves. Federal Reserve open market operations (sales of government securities) will be an offset, at least in part, to the increase in discounts; the rise in discounts, in fact, will be a result of restrictive open market operations. Second, the cost of using the safety valve is likely to be increased as Reserve Bank discount rates are raised. Third, individual banks that are in debt to the Reserve Banks use any free reserves that come into their possession to repay their debts rather than to make additional loans and investments, and thus restrict their own credit expansion. Meanwhile, continued Federal Reserve restriction of the supply of reserve funds requires member banks in the aggregate to maintain a large volume of borrowings.

In summary, in periods of monetary restraint member banks find it necessary or desirable to borrow to avoid reserve deficiencies. After they have borrowed, their lending policies tend to become more stringent because they are under pressure to repay their indebtedness. Yet, efforts of the individual banks to free themselves of debt to the Reserve Banks cannot free member banks as a group from indebtedness as long as the Federal Reserve maintains pressure on reserve positions. Hence, member bank attitudes toward lending and investing will remain conservative and even become cautious.

INTERRELATIONSHIPS IN PERIODS OF MONETARY EASE

When an inflationary boom in economic activity has slackened off, correction of the excesses and distortions of the boom period may set in motion contractive forces, with the result that a period of downswing in economic activity ensues. As recession symptoms appear, the objectives of monetary management will shift from restraint to ease. The Federal Reserve will supply reserves more actively through open market operations and, if such action is deemed consistent with longer term monetary needs, the System may supplement open market action by reducing the level of member bank reserve requirements.

The first response of the banking system to these actions, experience shows, will be a reduction in member bank indebtedness to the Reserve Banks; that is to say, the initial quantity of reserve funds supplied will be absorbed by the efforts of indebted banks to pay off their borrowing. When this phase has passed —and its duration will depend in part on Federal Reserve action—the reserve funds supplied will flow into bank loans and investments, with an accompanying expansion of bank deposits.

NET RESERVE POSITION

The immediate focus of the Federal Reserve's policy instruments is such that the credit market partly gauges the direction of System monetary policy by observing closely the net reserve position of banks—the difference between the aggregate of member bank reserves in excess of requirements and member bank borrowing at Reserve Banks. While the amount of reserves held in excess of requirements by member banks as a group will fall or rise to some extent with monetary restraint or ease, the movement of excess reserves is generally rather small. The volume of member bank borrowing, on the other hand, moves with greater amplitude in response to changes in monetary policy.

As an index of monetary policy, the net reserve position of member banks has various defects. For one thing, it is subject to fairly wide day-to-day and week-to-week fluctuations resulting from unpredictable changes in the various monetary factors discussed earlier in this chapter. For another, a static reserve position may not be fully revelatory of monetary action. Just as a constant temperature reading in a house in winter may reflect a varying flow of heat from the furnace, so a constant reserve position may be the result of varying monetary actions to make reserves available. Finally, a change in average level of net

Billions of dollars

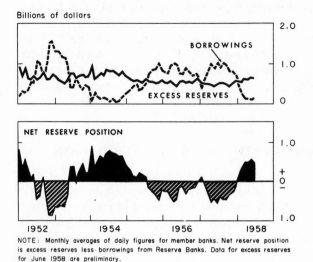

NOTE: Monthly averages of daily figures for member banks. Net reserve position is excess reserves less borrowings from Reserve Banks. Data for excess reserves for June 1958 are preliminary.

Figure 4. RESERVES AND BORROWINGS

reserves may not represent a basic shift in emphasis of monetary policy but may merely reflect an adaptation in the use of instruments to current credit and economic developments. When, for instance, reserve pressure or ease is greater than is consistent with appropriate growth in the economy's supply of bank credit and money, it is, of course, desirable that such pressure or ease be moderated. While the immediate focus of monetary management is on the net bank reserve position, its ultimate focus is on the expansion of money balances in relation to expansion of real output and this ultimate focus needs constantly to be kept in mind.

Selection 29

TOOLS OF MONETARY POLICY

MILTON FRIEDMAN

> *Dr. Friedman, the leading figure in the modern quantity theory school of monetary economists, has long been an outspoken critic of discretionary monetary policy in general, and of the Federal Reserve System in particular. In this article he presents a thoughtful critique of Federal Reserve policy and proposes significant changes in both central bank powers and discretionary authority in their use.*

I turn now to the major powers of the Reserve System, the tools of monetary policy—open market operations, rediscounting, and variable reserve requirements. With respect to these, I shall argue that open market operations alone are a sufficient and efficient tool for monetary policy. Rediscounting is an anachronistic survival of an earlier day and an earlier need. Its original function has disappeared. Variation in reserve requirements, though a more recent innovation, shares with rediscounting the property of being a technically poor instrument for controlling the stock of money. Both should be eliminated or greatly altered. In presenting this view, I shall first demonstrate that open market operations are a sufficient tool and then examine rediscounting and variable reserve requirements.

THE SUFFICIENCY OF OPEN MARKET OPERATIONS

The total stock of money in existence at any time, by which I shall mean currency plus commercial bank deposits adjusted to exclude interbank deposits, United States government deposits, and items in process of collection, can be expressed as a function of three variables: (1) the amount of currency outside the Treasury and the Federal Reserve available for use by the public and as vault cash plus bank deposits with Federal Reserve Banks—the amount of high-powered money, as it is generally termed; (2) the ratio of the public's currency holdings to its deposits, or the currency-deposit ratio; and (3) the ratio of commercial banks' holdings of high-powered money (including both vault cash and deposits with Reserve Banks) to their deposit liabilities or the reserve-deposit ratio.[1] Given the value of the two ratios, the stock of money is directly proportional to the amount of high-powered money. Given the amount of high-powered money, the stock of money is higher, the lower the currency-deposit ratio, and also the lower the reserve-deposit ratio.

Currently, the Federal Reserve can affect the amount of high-powered money in two ways: by buying or selling securities and by altering discount

[1] Algebraically, let

$$C = \text{currency held by the public}$$
$$D = \text{deposits held by the public}$$
$$R = \text{vault cash plus commercial bank deposits with Reserve Banks}$$
$$M = \text{money supply}$$
$$H = \text{high-powered money}$$

Then

$$M = C + D$$
$$H = C + R$$

$$\frac{M}{H} = \frac{C + D}{C + R} = \frac{\dfrac{C}{D} + 1}{\dfrac{C}{D} + \dfrac{R}{D}}$$

Hence

$$M = H \frac{\dfrac{C}{D} + 1}{\dfrac{C}{D} + \dfrac{R}{D}}$$

Note that the various terms must be defined consistently. For example, if D includes deposits in mutual savings banks, then their vault cash must be included in R; if D excludes deposits in mutual savings banks, their vault cash must be included in C. If D includes all deposits in commercial banks, as we shall suppose throughout, then R includes all high-powered money held by commercial banks. If D is restricted to demand deposits, then either R must still be defined to include all high-powered money held by commercial banks, in which case $\dfrac{D}{R}$ is not a very meaningful ratio, or the high-powered money held by commercial banks must be regarded as composed of two parts, one held in connection with demand deposits, the other in connection with time deposits; only the first included in R, and the second included in C.

rates and thereby giving member banks a greater or lesser incentive to rediscount with, or borrow from, the System. In addition, the amount of high-powered money is affected by factors outside the direct control of the System. The most important of these are changes in the amount of member-bank rediscounting or borrowing occurring for reasons other than alterations in the discount rate, changes in the amount of Federal Reserve "float" arising out of its check-clearing operations, gold flows, and changes in Treasury balances in cash or at Reserve Banks.

The Federal Reserve cannot currently affect the currency-deposit ratio directly. Its actions may have indirect effects, for example, by altering interest rates or the level of prices which in their turn may influence the currency-deposit ratio that the public seeks to maintain. A historical example of a rather different kind of indirect effort occurred in the early 1930's when the failure of the Federal Reserve to expand the amount of high-powered money sufficiently to prevent widespread bank failures arising out of initial attempts by the public to convert deposits into currency helped to intensify the loss of confidence in banks. In the main, however, the Reserve System must regard the currency-deposit ratio as determined by forces outside its control which shape the preferences of the public about the form in which it wants to hold its cash balances.

The Federal Reserve System can currently affect the reserve-deposit ratio by altering reserve requirements and thereby the amount of high-powered money that banks seek to hold relative to their deposits, although there is, of course, no fixed mechanical relation between reserve requirements and the actual reserve-deposit ratio. In addition, the reserve-deposit ratio may change for a variety of other reasons, such as shifts in deposits between demand and time accounts and among banks which hold different ratios of high-powered money to deposits, or changes in the rates of interest banks can earn on assets or must pay to borrow or in anticipated demands for conversion of deposits, which alter the amount of high-powered money banks wish to hold.

To demonstrate that open market operations alone would be sufficient for the conduct of monetary policy, almost regardless of the objectives toward which that policy is directed, let us assume for the moment that the Reserve System cannot make loans to its member banks or discount paper for them and that reserve requirements are frozen at their present level, with the Reserve System having no power to raise or lower them. In all other respects, we may suppose the Reserve System to operate just as it does now, and its deposit liabilities to remain the only medium of exchange satisfying the reserve requirements of member banks.[2] Member banks would meet any needs for additional reserve

---

[2] The complete avoidance of all loans to member banks would require a change in methods of clearing checks, since present methods involve a loan at zero interest to member banks in the form of Federal Reserve "float." For simplicity, I shall ignore this problem. Float is a source of considerable day-to-day and week-to-week variability in Federal Reserve credit outstanding, so that a full reform along the line I am suggesting would require some attention to it. At the same time, it is an automatic resultant of the method of clearing checks, not a source of credit that is manipulated either by the System or member banks, or could easily be.

funds by borrowing from other banks, through the Federal funds market or otherwise, or by disposing of assets, as they do mostly now and as they did almost exclusively for a long period in the 1930's.

Under these hypothetical arrangements, the Reserve System could influence the stock of money only by changing the amount of high-powered money, and it could change the amount of high-powered money only by buying and selling securities.[3] But these techniques would not only be adequate to produce any changes deemed desirable, they would in fact enable such changes to be made through open market operations more smoothly than at present and with less slippage between the desired change and the actual change.

Let us suppose, for example, that it were desired to expand the stock of money at a specified rate. The Federal Reserve would then purchase securities in order to increase the volume of high-powered money. The amount it purchased would depend on two factors: first, the amount by which it wanted to increase high-powered money; second, its estimate of likely changes in other factors affecting high-powered money.

To determine the first would, as now, require allowance for possible changes in the currency-deposit and the reserve-deposit ratios, that is, it would require an estimate of the rate at which high-powered money would have to increase to produce the desired rate of increase in the stock of money. With respect to this step, the one difference between the hypothetical and the present arrangements is in the factors affecting the reserve-deposit ratio. At present, this ratio is affected by the availability of rediscount facilities and the possibility that reserve requirements may be changed. The significance of these factors varies considerably over time and hence they render the reserve-deposit ratio more unstable than it would be in their absence. In consequence, it would be possible to estimate the change in high-powered money required to produce the desired change in the stock of money somewhat more accurately than now. However the difference in this respect would not be large.

A more important difference is in the second step, the likely changes in other factors affecting high-powered money. Currently, these other factors include the amount of member bank borrowing at the Federal Reserve. This sum is not only variable for other reasons but, more important, is affected in a highly variable fashion by Federal Reserve open market purchases. Member banks are likely to use some part of the increased high-powered money they obtain as a result of such purchases to pay off indebtedness at the Reserve System. If the part they used were fixed, it would simply mean that a dollar of Federal Reserve purchases would add, not a dollar to high-powered money, but a stable fraction of a dollar, say 80 cents, so that the System would have to buy a dollar and a quarter's worth of securities to increase high-powered money by a dollar. In fact, the part used is not fixed but varies widely depending on a host of circumstances affecting both the amount of member bank borrowing outstanding and the desire of member banks to increase or reduce

[3] For simplicity, I am assuming that Treasury balances with the Federal Reserve are not subject to Reserve control. In practice, of course, through cooperation with the Treasury, the amount of high-powered money in the hands of the public could also be changed by a shift of Treasury deposits between commercial banks and the Federal Reserve.

borrowing. Under the hypothetical arrangements, member bank borrowing would be non-existent and a dollar of Reserve purchases would add a dollar to high-powered money. Though allowance would still have to be made for other factors such as gold flows and changes in Treasury balances, the problem of doing so would be no different than at present. Hence, there would be a decidedly closer and more predictable relation between Reserve System purchases and changes in high-powered money under the hypothetical arrangements than at present.

The same conclusions are valid if it is desired to reduce rather than increase the stock of money at a specified rate. The System would then sell securities to reduce the volume of high-powered money. Again, the amount by which it would want to reduce high-powered money would depend on the anticipated behavior of the currency-deposit and reserve-deposit ratios, and the second ratio could be estimated somewhat more accurately under the hypothetical than under the present arrangements. The amount of securities it would have to sell to achieve the desired reduction in high-powered money would again depend on the anticipated behavior of other factors affecting high-powered money and again, one of the most variable of these, member bank borrowing, would be absent under the hypothetical arrangements, so that it would be possible to estimate more accurately the amount that needed to be sold.

The greater ease in producing desired changes in the stock of money also implies that it would be easier to avoid undesired changes, and this for the same reasons. Some existing sources of such changes would be eliminated under the hypothetical arrangements and no new ones introduced.

The limit to the expansion in the stock of money that could be produced by open market operations alone is set by the amount of securities available for the System to buy—though its gold reserve requirements might as now set a narrower limit; the limit to the contraction in the stock of money, by the amount of securities available for the System to sell. At present, these limits are so wide as to be largely irrelevant: Federal Reserve purchase of all outstanding marketable United States government securities would involve something like a quadrupling of the stock of money under the hypothetical arrangements; Federal Reserve sale of all securities in its portfolio, more than a halving of the stock of money. Within these limits, the System could produce any change in the stock of money it wished through open-market operations alone. The only time, historically, when these limits clearly hampered Federal Reserve operations was shortly after its establishment. Large inflows of gold after the outbreak of the European War in 1914 added to the stock of high-powered money and the Reserve System was powerless to offset this inflow because it had no earning assets to sell. The Reserve System regarded itself as hampered also in 1935–37, when excess reserves were larger than the System's security holdings, an episode to which I shall return. As a practical matter, such situations are not likely to arise again. In principle, however, it would be desirable to give the Reserve System power to issue its own securities, as has frequently been proposed, in order to assure that such situations could not arise.

I have expressed this analysis in terms of changes in the stock of money because the stock of money seems to me the desirable variable in terms of which to express Federal Reserve policy, whatever may be the particular pattern of change in the stock of money that it is desired to produce. However, the conclusions do not depend on this proposition. Let us suppose policy were expressed in some other terms—say, to take the alternative that would perhaps command widest support, "the" interest rate, to which we may give operational content by interpreting it to mean a weighted average of market interest rates on a specified list of securities. Under the hypothetical arrangements, the System can affect this average rate directly by buying or selling the securities in question, if they are of a kind it is authorized to buy and sell, and, indirectly, by altering the high-powered money in the hands of the public and thereby the willingness of banks and the nonbank public to purchase the securities in question. If the desired change in the interest rate can be achieved under present arrangements, then it can also be achieved under the hypothetical arrangements, subject only to the limitation that it not require changes in high-powered money greater than the available stock of securities the Reserve System can buy or sell, a limit of no practical significance. It is rather more difficult to establish that open market operations would be a more effective tool for this purpose in the absence of rediscounting and variable reserve requirements than it is now. The reason for this is that we know too little about the connection between changes in particular interest rates and in the money supply to be at all specific. But since persons who favor the use of interest rate changes as a guide or criterion for monetary policy generally regard changes in the stock of money as a major channel through which interest rates are affected, a more stable and predictable relation between open market operations and resultant changes in the money supply would presumably also imply a more stable and predictable relation between open market operations and changes in particular interest rates.

The sufficiency of open market operations as a tool for monetary policy is not, of course, a decisive reason for relying on this tool alone. Under some circumstances, discounting alone or variable reserve requirements alone might be sufficient; and under these or other circumstances, these other tools might achieve other desirable objectives that would justify rendering open market operations less effective. Let us therefore examine these other tools.

REDISCOUNTING

The Federal Reserve System was created by men whose outlook on the goals of central banking was shaped by the money panics during the national banking era. The main problem requiring solution seemed to them to be banking crises produced by, or resulting in, a widespread desire on the part of the public to shift from deposits to currency, generally because of a loss of confidence in banks arising out of a few notable bank or commercial failures. Under a fractional reserve banking system, widespread conversion of deposits into currency requires either an increase in high-powered money or a drastic shrinkage in the total amount of money. Prior to the Federal Reserve System, a sizable increase in high-powered money generally could come only from gold imports. This took time and required a fairly drastic incentive. In consequence, a serious liquidity crisis could seldom be met in this way in the first instance. An individual bank might be able to convert its assets into currency; the system as a whole could not do so. The attempt by many individual banks to do so produced pressure for wholesale liquidation that led to contraction of the total money supply. Unless the process were halted fairly early, the attempted liquidation would drive down the prices of bank assets and render most banks technically insolvent.

As already noted, the therapeutic device that developed was the so-called suspension of payments—an agreement among banks, generally through their clearing house associations, that they would honor all requests to transfer deposits "through the clearing house," but would refuse to convert deposits into currency on demand, though continuing to do so for some purposes and for some customers. The suspension of payments in this sense did not involve even the temporary closing of the banks on any large scale or the cessation of their financial operations—as occurred during the much more drastic Banking Holiday of 1933. It meant rather the creation of two only partly convertible media of payments, currency and deposits, with deposits only imperfectly convertible into currency and hence with currency at a premium in terms of deposits. Once adjustment was made to the use of two such media of payments convertible into one another at a flexible rather than a fixed rate, the suspension could continue for months on end, as it did at times, without producing an economic breakdown and indeed in conjunction with economic revival.

The solution to the problem of panics embodied in the Federal Reserve Act was, in the words of its title, "to provide an elastic currency." Federal Reserve money was designed to differ from other forms of money by being subject to substantial change in quantity over short periods of time for reasons other than the immediate profitability of either the issuer or, as with specie, the importer or exporter. In this way, when depositors wished to convert deposits into currency, additional high-powered money could be made available in the form of Federal Reserve notes. Fundamentally, "elasticity" was aimed not at changes in the total amount of money but in the amount of one kind of money—currency—relative to another—deposits—though there was of course much confusion then as now between these two kinds of elasticity. Rediscounting was designed as the means whereby additional high-powered money could be put into circulation and subsequently retired. By rediscounting their assets, banks could convert them into the currency which their customers were demanding without reducing the reserves of other banks. The Reserve System was to be a "lender of last resort," ready to provide liquidity in a time of crisis to satisfy a widespread demand for currency that otherwise would produce either suspension of payments or a substantial decline in the total stock of money.

Rediscounting was therefore not originally intended to be used continuously to determine or alter the total stock of money. When the Act became law, the gold standard ruled supreme. It was taken for granted that it would continue to do so and that it would dominate the longer-term movements in the total stock of money. This view is reflected in the gold reserve ratios that were incorporated in the Federal Reserve Act. During and after World War I, the gold standard changed its character and the gold reserve ratio became a largely irrelevant guide for short-term movements. Rediscounting then developed into one of the two blades of the scissors continuously controlling the stock of money, open market operations being the other. In the 1929–33 contraction, the kind of situation developed that had been contemplated when the System was established and that an elastic currency issued through rediscounting had been designed to handle. In the event, these tools did not enable the System to cope with the crisis. Whether they need have been inadequate if differently managed is a moot question.

One result of the banking collapse was the enactment of federal insurance of bank deposits. Its purpose was to protect depositors against the kind of cruel losses they had experienced during the preceding years, not primarily to solve the problem of bank panics. It has, however, succeeded in doing so where rediscounting failed. Although deposits are technically insured only up to $10,000, bank failures involving losses to depositors have become almost a thing of the past. Banks still become insolvent, but they no longer fail. Instead, they tend to be merged with other banks or to be reorganized, with the Federal Deposit Insurance Corporation assuming responsibility for the bad assets. An indirect result has been to prevent any chain reaction such as used to occur. Even if a bank fails or is reorganized, there is no reason for depositors in other banks to become concerned. Changes in the ratio of deposits to currency still occur as a result of changed preferences. Such changes, however, even if sizable, tend to be gradual and do not involve runs on individual banks. A liquidity crisis involving such runs on a widespread scale is now almost inconceivable. The need for rediscounting in order for the Reserve System to serve as "a lender of last resort" has therefore become obsolete, not because the function has been taken over by someone else but because it no longer needs to be performed. . . .

Having lost its initial function, rediscounting has acquired three very different and less critical roles. In the first place, it is a means whereby member banks can obtain funds from time to time at a lower cost than by alternative devices. In this respect, it involves special governmental assistance to a particular group of financial institutions. It is hard to see why it is appropriate or necessary for government to render such assistance or why commercial banks should be singled out to receive it. The capital market is a well-functioning and sensitive market, and banks can readily manage to provide for special needs in other ways—as for example they did throughout the later 1930's when, for reasons I shall mention shortly, rediscounting was hardly resorted to.

In the second place, rediscounting is a means whereby member banks can readily adjust their reserve balances to conform to reserve requirements when they unexpectedly discover that they are likely to be in deficit. Other means are however available and widely used for this purpose, the most notable among them in recent years being the Federal funds market. In consequence this function, like the preceding, is solely a convenience offered to member banks.

In the third place, as already noted, rediscounting is a means whereby the Reserve System can influence the total amount of high-powered money in existence and thereby the total stock of money. This is its major current function and the function in terms of which it must basically be judged. And it so happens that rediscounting is a technically defective tool for this purpose.

The distinctive feature of rediscounting is that the initiative to rediscount is in the hands of the member banks. In consequence, the Reserve System cannot itself determine the amount of money it creates through the discount window or, for that matter, by a combination of the discount window and the open market. It can affect the amount of discounting by exercising discretion with respect to the banks for whom it will discount and the amount of discounting it will do for individual banks, or by changing the discount rate and thus the incentive on the part of banks to discount. The exercise of discretion is an undesirable kind of specific credit control that involves detailed intervention into the affairs of individual banks and arbitrary decisions by governmental officials. Moreover, it is incapable of being applied in a sufficiently sensitive way to produce predictable results over short periods. Hence, it is not even an efficient tool for controlling the amount of rediscounting. Most of the time, it has been held in abeyance. It has been brought into play generally only when the System has wished to avoid using its major weapons of discount rates or open market operations; notably in 1919, when the rediscount rate was being kept unchanged under Treasury pressure; in 1928 and 1929, in connection with the use of direct pressure to discourage so-called speculative loans; and in 1950–51, when the bond-support program was in effect. Whatever else is done about rediscounting, this feature should be changed. If rediscounting is retained, it should be a right, not a privilege, freely available to all member banks on specified terms.

The discount rate is the primary means used to influence the amount of discounting, so much so that "discount policy" is generally regarded as concerned exclusively with setting the discount rate. In practice, the discount rate has been used as a discontinuous instrument, changes being made only at substantial intervals and by sizable amounts. This operation by fits and starts introduces unnecessary instability into the economy. It also means that changes in the discount rate are newsworthy and attract attention. There is speculation about what they will be and much significance is read into them when they occur. If the System could predict accurately the future course of events and could establish an unambiguous connection between changes in the discount rate and its predictions, these "announcement effects" might be highly desirable, since individuals would then be led to behave in a way that would reinforce the System's actions—though in that case, the same result could almost surely be attained simply by publishing the System's predictions. As it is, the "announcement effects" are an additional source of uncertainty in the economy.

A second defect of the discount rate is the extreme difficulty of predicting the effect of a change in the rate on the amount of discounting, let alone on the stock of money. The effect on the willingness of member banks to borrow is very different under different circumstances, depending on such factors as the level of other rates of interest, the state of the demand for loans and the supply of funds from other sources, the investment opportunities available, and so on.

A closely related defect is, in my view, much the most important. The discount rate is something that the Federal Reserve System must continually change in order to keep the effect of its monetary policy unchanged. But changes in the rate are interpreted as if they meant changes in policy. Consequently both the System and outsiders are led to misinterpret the System's actions and the System is led to follow policies different from those it intends to follow.

The key point underlying these perhaps cryptic statements is one that became familiar in the course of the discussion of the post-World War II bond support program: a constant absolute rate of interest, whether it be the yield on government securities or a discount rate, does not in any relevant sense mean a constant monetary policy. If market rates rise, while discount rates do not, the incentive to discount is increased. This will tend to produce an increase in the amount of credit extended through discounting, an increase in the total amount of Federal Reserve credit outstanding, and a faster rate of growth of the stock of money than would otherwise have occurred. Conversely, if market rates fall, while discount rates do not, the incentive to discount is reduced, which will tend to reduce discounting and the amount of Federal Reserve credit outstanding, and to reduce the rate of growth of the stock of money. The same discount rate can thus correspond to "easy" money or "tight" money, however those ambiguous terms are defined, depending on the level of market rates; and maintaining the discount rate constant may imply a shift from "easy" money to "tight" money or conversely. In order to keep the degree of "ease" or "tightness" constant, the discount rate must be continuously changed.

Failure to recognize this point, and a tendency to regard the absolute level of the discount rate—or its level relative to some earlier date—as a measure of "tightness" or "ease" has been perhaps the single most pervasive source of confusion and error in the System's experience. In 1920, this fallacy was one reason why the System followed an unduly tight policy and maintained it too long. The discount rate of 6 per cent imposed by all the Reserve Banks in January-February of 1920 and perhaps even the 7 per cent imposed by the New York and three other Reserve Banks in June, 1920, would probably not have been high enough to have prevented the money stock from rising if they had been imposed in 1919. By late 1920, these rates were forcing a drastic monetary contraction, yet they were maintained, becoming increasingly "tight" in their effects, until May, 1921. The mild reduction at that time still meant a relatively "tight" policy.

From 1929 to 1933, the System kept repeating that it was following an "easy money" policy, pointing to the successive declines in discount rates—aside from the disastrous rise in the fall of 1931. Yet market rates were falling so much more rapidly that by any relevant test the System's policy must be adjudged exceedingly tight—certainly if either the behavior of the money supply or the condition of financial institutions is taken as the guide.

The System has been widely regarded as following a very "easy" money policy in the later 1930's. In fact, the discount rate, though low in an absolute sense by historical standards, exceeded market rates on short-term funds by a wider margin than at any previous time, with the exception only of a few months before the 1933 Banking Holiday, when the discount rate was even farther above short-term market rates. As a result, discounting fell into almost complete disuse in the later 1930's. The substantial and relatively rapid increase in the money stock from 1934 to 1936 and again from 1938 to 1940 owed nothing to easy money policy: it reflected entirely a large gold inflow. The gold inflow in its turn was produced at first mostly by the Treasury's gold and silver purchase programs reinforced by the flight of capital from Europe after Hitler's accession to power, then mostly by the flight of capital to the United States as the threat of war increased, reinforced by the gold and silver purchase programs.

The ill-fated bond support program of World War II and the postwar years is the most widely recognized example of the fallacy in question.

A more recent and more sophisticated version of the fallacy is the emphasis that was placed for a time on "free reserves" as a criterion of the "ease" or "tightness" of monetary policy, and to some extent still is. "Free reserves" are defined as the difference between the reserve balances of member banks and the sum of their required reserves and their borrowings from the System, or, equivalently, the difference between "excess reserves" and "borrowings." Arithmetically, it is clear that any given level of free reserves is consistent with either a rapid increase in the money supply or a rapid decrease. Both excess reserves and borrowings can remain constant, yet total and required reserves rise or fall at any rate, and excess reserves and borrowings can both change, yet their differences remain the same. Economically, there is presumably some level of free reserves that banks desire to maintain at any given time, a level that they try neither to increase by liquidating assets nor to decrease by acquiring assets. I shall call this level "desired free reserves." If the Reserve System tries to maintain a higher level by open market operations, the banks will seek to use the excess to add to their assets and in the process will increase the money supply and required reserves, and so reduce free reserves. The System can frustrate the banks by creating still more high-powered money, which will produce a continued increase in the money supply. Conversely, if the System tries to maintain a lower level of free reserves than desired, it can do so only by forcing a decline in the money stock. At any given time, therefore—and this is the element of validity in the free reserves doctrine—there is a level of free reserves consistent with no change in the money supply; higher levels imply an increase in the money supply and the higher the level, the more rapid the increase; and conversely for lower levels. But the levels corresponding to constant, increasing, or decreasing money supply do not remain the same over time. What matters is the size of free reserves relative to desired free reserves, not their absolute size. And the level of free reserves that banks desire is not itself a constant. It depends on the conditions of demand and supply for funds, or market rates of interest and their relation to the discount rate. Let the discount rate be unchanged, but market rates fall, and banks will desire to maintain larger free reserves. A level of free reserves that formerly was consistent with, let us say, a rate of rise in the stock of money of 3 per cent a year, may now imply a rate of rise of zero per cent—this is the way in which the crude fallacy about discount rates enters in this more sophisticated analysis. I rather suspect that something like this is what happened in 1957 and accounts for the System being as tight as it was in the final months of that year.

As the 1957 example suggests, the fact that the same discount rate or the same level of free reserves implies different rates of monetary expansion, is particularly unfortunate at cyclical peaks. The System like the rest of us is unlikely to recognize that a decline is under way until some time after it has begun. In the meantime, the maintenance of the same discount rate or the same level of free reserves implies deflationary monetary pressure. In this way, there is an automatic tendency for a peak in business to produce a reduction in the rate of increase in the stock of money, just the opposite of the automatic reaction that most students would regard as desirable.

A final disadvantage of the use of the discount rate to control the amount of rediscounting is that it tends to promote confusion between what might be called the "monetary" effects of monetary policy—the effects on the stock of money—and the "credit" effects—the effects on recorded rates of interest and other conditions in the credit market. It is easy to see why these two should be confused. In modern financial systems, the creation of money is linked with lending and investing activity and changes in the stock of money generally take place through the credit markets. There is, however, no necessary connection. In an economy with a pure commodity money, for example, changes in the stock of money would take place through the purchase and sale of a commodity and not through credit markets at all. In practice, the actual link between the stock of money and credit conditions has varied widely. But the fact that there is a link has tended to lead to undue emphasis on the means whereby the money stock is changed rather than on the change itself. An ancient example of the confusion is the "real bills" fallacy already referred to. More recently, the change in economic ideas associated with the name of John Maynard Keynes led to an almost complete neglect of the "monetary" effects of monetary policy and concentration on the "credit" effects. Changes in the stock of money were treated as if they had no effect except insofar as they led to changes in a limited range of recorded market interest rates and thereby to changes in flows of spending. Analysis of the effects of monetary policy, both inside and outside the System, have therefore tended to be restricted to the level of recorded interest rates and movements in them to the complete neglect of changes in the quantity of money.[4]

It is analytically possible to treat all effects of changes in the quantity of money as taking place via changes in interest rates and their effects in turn on flows of spending. But to do so in a comprehensive way requires taking account of a much broader range of rates of interest than "recorded market" rates, for example, implicit rates entering into consumer decisions about stocks of durable goods to hold.

The confusion between the "monetary" and the "credit" effects of Reserve policy is an evil almost regardless of the views one may hold about the economic importance of changes in the stock of money or the channels through which

[4] A striking example is Roose's exhaustive, and otherwise excellent, analysis of the 1937–38 contraction. Though Roose is highly eclectic in his approach, he devotes no attention whatsoever to the effects of the Reserve System's policy on the stock of money, considering only its effects on market interest rates. Kenneth D. Roose, *The Economics of Recession and Revival* (New Haven: Yale University Press, 1954), pp. 101–02.

such changes exert their influence. The Federal Reserve System occupies a commanding role under present circumstances in determining the stock of money—it can make the stock of money whatever it wants within very wide limits and to a high degree of precision. By contrast, it is one of many institutions in the capital market. It may be able to fix the yield on a few securities but only by sacrificing its control over the stock of money and even then only within fairly narrow limits. It cannot for long determine the whole structure of yields on capital assets. These propositions have surely been adequately demonstrated by postwar experience in this and other countries. Hence even if one were to believe —as I do not—that changes in the stock of money are relatively unimportant in their economic effect compared to changes in the capital market, and exert their influence predominantly by affecting recorded rates, the Reserve System's role is to control the stock of money. Its tools should be judged by their efficiency in enabling it to do so, though one might then wish to determine what changes it should make in the stock of money on the basis of the changes it was desired to produce in recorded interest rates. The fact that discounting means the setting of a specific interest rate fosters the belief that the System is directly controlling rates of interest and that its aim is to do so. This leads both the System and outsiders to misjudge its policy. It also inhibits Reserve policy because the Reserve System is attributed credit or blame for matters that are in fact outside of its control. It is described as aiming at a "higher" or "lower" level of interest rates when in practice any effects on interest rates may be entirely incidental to its purpose. It may, and I would say should, be raising or lowering discount rates not in order to affect interest rates but to affect the rate of change in the stock of money.

To avoid these disadvantages, rediscounting should be eliminated. The Federal Reserve would then no longer have to announce a discount rate or to change it; it would then have direct control over the amount of high-powered money it created; it would not be a source of instability alike by its occasional changes in the discount rate and by the unintended changes in the "tightness" or "ease" of policy associated with an unchanged rate, nor would it be misled by these unintended changes; and it would be less subject to being diverted from its main task by the attention devoted to the "credit" effects of its policy.

If rediscounting were eliminated, one minor function now performed by the discount rate would need to be provided for in some other way. Since required reserves are calculated after the event and need to be estimated in advance, some discrepancies between required and actual reserves are unavoidable, yet some penalty must be imposed on such discrepancies to enforce the reserve requirements. Currently the penalty is generally a charge equal to interest on the deficit at a rate equal to the discount rate plus 2 percentage points. The simplest alternative would be a fixed rate of "fine." To avoid discrepancies becoming an indirect form of discounting, the "fine" should be large enough to make it well above likely market rates of interest. The fine would then become the equivalent of a truly "penalty" discount rate—to use the language that was the source of so much discussion in the early days of the System—except that no collateral, or eligibility requirements, or the like would be involved.

An alternative to the complete abolition of discounting is to follow the Canadian precedent of tying the discount rate automatically to a market rate—currently the Canadian rate is set each week at ¼ of 1 per cent above the latest average tender rate for Treasury bills. If the differential were sufficiently high, this would be equivalent to abolishing discounting. Otherwise, while such a device would eliminate some of the disadvantages I have enumerated, it would be decidedly inferior to the abolition of rediscounting, and would leave much room for the authorities to affect the discount rate through the amount of bills offered for sale, or similar devices if some other rate were used.

VARIATION IN RESERVE REQUIREMENTS

The power to vary reserve requirements is the most recent of the major monetary powers of the System. It was granted as an emergency power to be exercised only with the permission of the President in the Thomas Amendment to the Agricultural Adjustment Act of 1933 and then made a permanent power not dependent on Presidential permission in the Banking Act of 1935.

The initial use of the power, in 1936 and 1937 to double reserve requirements in three steps, was drastic and most unfortunate. The mistake arose from a misinterpretation of the large amount of reserves in excess of legal requirements accumulated during the 1930's. The System regarded these excess reserves as a largely unintentional and passive accumulation by member banks arising out of a shortage of demand for loans or a short supply of acceptable bank investments. In consequence, it believed that raising legal reserve requirements would involve simply a relabelling of reserve balances and have no other current effect. In fact, it seems fairly clear, at least in retrospect, that the accumulation of excess reserves was largely motivated by a shift in liquidity preferences on the part of the banks. Bitter experience during the years from 1929 to 1933 had taught banks that it was not enough to keep in the form of high-powered money only the minimum amount required by law; legally required reserves could not be drawn on to meet emergency demands without the banks' being liable to closure; and the ability to rediscount had proved an inadequate recourse for all too many banks. Little wonder that the survivors of the holocaust felt it necessary to provide their own protection against unexpected demands. Deposits in excess of required legal reserves were essentially uncovered liabilities for which only the excess of high-powered money over required reserves provided an effective reserve. True, the enactment of federal deposit insurance was to render unnecessary the maintenance of such a reserve, as was later the conversion of government securities into the equivalent of cash by the support program of the Federal Reserve. But at the time, deposit insurance was new and its effects unclear, and bond support still in the future. Doubling of required reserves was therefore much more than a change in labels; it reduced drastically the cushion of effective reserves, as the banks viewed them, available against these liabilities needing protection. As is strikingly clear from the detailed figures, the result was to induce banks to seek to rebuild their so-called excess reserves, thereby producing downward pressure on the money supply. The effects of the second and third steps in the rise in requirements were further intensified by the contemporaneous sterilization of gold by the Treasury. . . .

A mistake of this kind is not likely to occur again. Excess reserves are now very small. The Reserve System now interprets changes in reserve requirements as more than a relabelling, acting as if an increase or decrease in excess reserves would tend to promote or retard expansion of earning assets by banks. It now recognizes their discontinuous effects, so that all reserve requirement changes since the end of the war have been accompanied by open market operations designed to offset the initial effect on reserve positions. Since 1951, all reserve requirement changes have been reductions, made when the System wished to promote ease. Nonetheless, variable reserve requirements are a technically defective instrument for controlling the stock of money and should be eliminated. If fractional reserves are to be retained, they should be set at a fixed level and kept there.

Variable reserve requirements share some of the same technical defects as discounting, and have additional defects of their own. A major one, as is clear from the discussion of the 1936–37 episode, is the fact that changes in reserve requirements are discontinuous in time and in practice have also been discontinuous in amount. The smallest change ever made is one-half of one percentage point. Applied to all member banks, this is a change of more than 4 per cent of total required reserves—an amount that is larger than typical year-to-year changes in the absence of changes in requirements. It seems dubious that a policy instrument that proceeds by such large doses is desirable. There is no chance to see its effect or to adjust by small steps to effects different from those expected. Moreover, this defect is intensified by the difficulty of predicting how banks will react to changes in reserve requirements. The reaction of banks depends on many attendant circumstances, including their anticipation about whether the change in reserve requirements will be reversed or is a harbinger of further changes in the same direction.

Recognition of this defect of reserve requirement changes accounts, as mentioned above, for the Reserve System's postwar policy of accompanying reserve requirement changes with offsetting open market operations. Insofar as the open market operations initially offset the reserve requirement change fully, this would mean that changes in reserve requirements were being used not to affect the stock of money but simply to change the ratio of earning assets of banks to their total assets, that is, to alter the profitability of commercial banking. In practice, for reasons just noted, it is impossible to know what open market operations are required to fully offset a change in reserve requirements. The 1936 interpretation that a shift between excess reserves and required reserves has no effect is one extreme; it would call for no open market operations. The interpretation, now widely current, that a change in excess reserves has the same effect whether it arises out of a shift between required and excess reserves or out of change in total reserves, is another extreme; it would call for open market sales or purchases equal in dollar amount to the amount of excess reserves released or absorbed. The correct interpretation is presumably between these two, its precise position depending on circumstances and varying from time to time. In consequence, the combination of a reserve requirement change and a supposedly off-setting open market operation is not "neutral" but introduces an expansionary or contractionary stimulus of uncertain and varying amount.

Changes in reserve requirements, like discount rate changes, are public and newsworthy, which means that they, too, have disturbing announcement effects and that there is strong resistance to reversing a change shortly after it is made if it does not have the expected effects or if economic conditions develop in an unexpected way. Further, it is not only difficult to predict the effect on the stock of money of changes in reserve requirements themselves but in addition such changes enhance the difficulty of predicting the effects of other factors such as gold movements, open market operations, and the like. Finally, changes in reserve requirements alter the profitability of commercial banking, which makes for a kind of pressure on the System that has nothing to do with its central function.

Aside from their variability, there are other features of reserve requirements that have monetary effects and need reform. . . . Differences in reserve requirements among different classes of cities, as well as failure [before 1960] to count vault cash as part of reserves, mean that changes in the distribution of deposits among cities tend to alter the total amount of money that is consistent with a given total of high-powered money. In consequence, here again the System must keep doing something in order to stay in the same place. It would simplify the System's task if these extraneous sources of changes in the money supply could be eliminated. As it happens, the two defects have tended partly to offset one another, since vault cash has tended to be higher for country than for reserve city banks and for reserve city than for central reserve city banks, whereas reserve requirements have differed in the opposite direction. It is therefore desirable that the two defects be removed simultaneously. The recently enacted authority to permit vault cash to be counted as reserves should be exercised,* with offsetting changes in reserve requirements to avoid any net expansion or contraction in the stock of money. The recently enacted elimination of the differences between central reserve and reserve city banks in minimum and maximum reserve requirements is a step in the right direction and should be followed by a complete elimination of differences in actual requirements both between these two classes of banks and between them and country banks, again with offsetting changes designed to prevent any net effect on the stock of money. The differentiation in requirements among cities is a relic of the National Banking Act which made some sense at the time because deposits with banks in reserve and central reserve cities could be counted as reserves by other banks. It now has no such justification.

The different reserve requirements for demand and time deposits are another source of extraneous influences on the volume of money. This distinction was first introduced by the Federal Reserve Act. Prior to that time, reserve requirements were imposed on all deposits alike, whether demand or time. Evidence since then suggests that shifts between these categories have from time to time had their origin in pressures on reserves. Time deposits are of course

* *Editor's note:* This was done.

different from demand deposits and by some definitions of "money" would not be treated as money but as a near-money. But this difference does not justify a difference in reserve requirements. The greater rate of use of demand than of time deposits may lead a bank holding both to expect greater variability in net withdrawals of demand than of time deposits and hence lead it to hold more liquid assets as the counterpart of its demand than of its time deposit liabilities. But, as we have seen earlier, required reserves do not perform this "banking" or "liquidity" function. Their function is very different. It is to enable the monetary authorities to control the stock of money. For this purpose, the differential requirements only complicate the task of the authorities. I would therefore urge that the present differentiation in the reserves required for time and demand deposits be eliminated, again, of course, with offsetting changes to avoid any net expansion or contraction in the stock of money.

CONCLUSION

The elimination of discounting and of variable reserve requirements would leave open market operations as the instrument of monetary policy proper. This is by all odds the most efficient instrument and has few of the defects of the others. It can be used continuously, from day to day, and in amounts varying by fine gradations. It need involve no public announcement, and thus there are neither announcement effects nor any obstacles to reversal of policy within a brief compass of time. It need involve no setting of rates of return or yields on securities, and does not directly affect the profitability of the banking business. It is highly impersonal and its effects are diffused over the banking community. The amount of purchases and sales can be at the option of the Federal Reserve System and hence the amount of high-powered money to be created thereby determined precisely. Of course, the ultimate effect of the purchases or sales on the final stock of money involves several additional links—what is happening to such other factors affecting high-powered money as the gold stock and Treasury balances; what is happening to the ratio between deposits and currency that the public is seeking to maintain; and what is happening to the ratio between deposits and reserves that banks are seeking to maintain. But the difficulty of predicting these links would be much less if rediscounting and variable reserve requirements were eliminated, and if reserve requirements were modified as I have suggested. The suggested reforms would therefore render the connection between Federal Reserve action and the changes in the money supply more direct and more predictable and eliminate extraneous influences on Reserve policy.

It has been said that open market operations are not themselves a fully general and impersonal tool because their effects depend on the kinds of securities purchased or sold. The restriction of purchases or sales to "bills only" since 1953 has been the most recent source of controversy. This range of problems is intimately connected with debt policy.*

* *Editor's note:* For discussion of these problems and the shift from the "bills only" policy, see later selections, esp. selections 42 and 44.

One likely criticism of the proposals made in this chapter is that the streamlining of tools suggested involves reducing the "power" of the Federal Reserve System. Nothing could be farther from the truth. Retaining defective instruments of control which interfere with the operation of more efficient instruments does not mean retaining power any more than a marksman's ability to hit a distant target with a rifle would be enhanced by requiring him to shoot a blunderbuss at the same time with his left hand. On the contrary, by simplifying the System's instruments and making them better suited to the System's major functions, the reforms would increase its ability to achieve its objectives.

A frequent excuse for inadequacy of performance has been that the System lacked "power." So far as I can see there is only one episode on record for which this excuse is fully justified—the inflation resulting from large inflows of gold after the outbreak of the European War in 1914. On every other occasion, the inadequacy of performance has reflected either the adoption of an irrelevant or inappropriate objective or the failure to use power that was available. Except for the incident at the outbreak of World War I, there is no occasion since when the System lacked the technical power, or would have done so under the proposals I have made, to achieve any movements in the money supply that one might retrospectively have desired.

Selection 30

CREDIT POLICY AT THE DISCOUNT WINDOW*
CHARLES R. WHITTLESEY

For nearly twenty years, from 1932 to 1951, the importance of the authority of the Federal Reserve System to lend reserves to member banks was virtually extinguished—first by the Great Depression, with its plethora of bank reserves, and later by subordination of central banking activities to the financing of World War II. Since 1951, however, bank reserves have been so close to required levels that the mechanics and economic significance of the discount operation have come under renewed scrutiny. The Federal Reserve System and the commercial banks have been feeling their way toward a new set of relationships at the discount window, partly because of the significant changes in the American money market after World War II and partly because of new powers and objectives of the Federal Reserve System. The following discussions by Dr. Charles Whittlesey and Dr. Robert Roosa indicate some major issues in the analysis of discount operations and their impact on Federal Reserve stabilization policies.

Limitations of space prevented the inclusion in these readings of a number of selections that provided information and viewpoints of significance; a good description of the discounting process, not included herein, is provided in "Borrowing from the Fed," Federal Reserve Bank of New York, Monthly Review, September, 1959, pp. 138–142, in which major reasons for such borrowing are commented upon. These include miscalculation of the need for reserves (but this should not occur more than infrequently), an unexpectedly large seasonal loss of reserves, or an inability of local public bodies to sell bond issues already scheduled, necessitating borrowing from local banks. This article attempted to indicate that borrowing for the purpose of obtaining reserves to enable an increase in loans to be made is inappropriate, because such borrowing, if permitted by the Federal Reserve Banks, could result in an increase in the money supply contrary to the desire of the Federal Reserve System authorities. The task of the Federal Reserve System is to provide the appropriate amount of money and credit for the economy as a whole, not to provide an increase in money and credit for fast-growing areas of the country.

The purpose of this article is to correct certain prevailing misconceptions with respect to discounting by the Federal Reserve Banks.[1] The justification for attempting to do so is that the terms in which discount operations are customarily described give a false impression of what actually takes place: the idea is simply not correct that the discount window is the locus of a selective process where, in the interest of economic stabilization, some banks asking to borrow are accepted and others refused.

MISCONCEPTIONS CONCERNING DISCOUNT PRACTICES

The view that member banks are, in fact, subject to refusal of requests for loans is well-grounded in the words of the Federal Reserve Act:

> The Board of Governors of the Federal Reserve System may prescribe regulations further defining within the limitations of this Act the conditions upon which discounts, advancements, and the accommodations may be extended to member banks. Each Federal Reserve bank shall keep itself informed . . . in determining *whether to grant or refuse* advances, rediscounts or other credit accommodations.[2]

The idea is carried forward in the Board's familiar little handbook describing the Federal Reserve System:

> When a member bank applies for accommodation, the Federal Reserve Bank is under no automatic obligation to grant the credit.[3]

In these examples and elsewhere, although the language seems to suggest that member banks are sometimes refused credit, it does not specifically state that this is the case.

[1] As distinguished, that is, from changes in the discount rate, see fn. 14.

[2] Section 4, Paragraph 8. Italics supplied. The subsequent provision of this paragraph with respect to suspending a member bank "from the use of the credit facilities of the Federal Reserve System" is likewise one that is not actually put into effect and, so far as has been determined, never has been.

[3] *The Federal Reserve System: Purposes and Functions,* Board of Governors, (3d ed.; Washington, 1954), p. 33.

• From Charles R. Whittlesey, "Credit Policy at the Discount Window," *Quarterly Journal of Economics,* May, 1959, pp. 207–216. Copyright 1959 by the President and Fellows of Harvard College. This article was written during tenure of a Faculty Research fellowship granted by the Ford Foundation. Reprinted by permission of the *Quarterly Journal of Economics* and the author.

Similar statements are to be found in publications by the various Federal Reserve Banks. In a recent annual report of the Federal Reserve Bank of Cleveland the steps in borrowing by member banks are listed in detail:

    1. Request is made. . . .
    2. A note is executed. . . .
    3. Consideration is given. . . .
    4. If the loan is approved. . . .[4]

Statements abound elsewhere in the literature on the Federal Reserve and recur in current discussion of monetary policy indicating that applications for loans by member banks are, in practice, subject to refusal by the Reserve Banks. Such views are expressed alike by practicing bankers and by academic students of banking and monetary policy. They proceed also from highly placed officials of the Federal Reserve System.

Close examination of such statements will usually show that they are not technically incorrect inasmuch as they do not explicitly state that the selection occurs at the discount window itself rather than earlier, e.g., prior to the Step 1 referred to in the preceding paragraph. It would appear, however, that only the very sophisticated reader would fail to infer that refusals occur at the discount window, i.e., at Step 4. Examples of such statements are:

> The authority of each Federal Reserve Bank to grant or refuse requests for discounts is of considerable significance in the operation of the discount mechanism in that it tends to strengthen the mechanism as a restrictive device.[5]

> Banks have been forced to turn to borrowing. . . . But bank reserves supplied in this way represent a privilege, not a right; discounts may be refused.[6]

A clear illustration of erroneous inferences being drawn from statements such as these is to be found in a colloquy between the President of the New York Federal Reserve Bank and a Congressman from the state of New York at Congressional Hearings late in 1957.

> Mr. Hayes: We hope that our *administration at the discount window* prevents a bank from abusing the opportunity to make a substantial spread. . . .

> Mr. Multer: By the control of the discount window, making discounts or refusing to make discounts, you can control the amount of credit the bank can get, and no matter what the rate is, if they want the money, you can make it available to them or not, in your discretion, regardless of the interest rates? Is that it?

[4] Federal Reserve Bank of Cleveland, Annual Report, 1956, p. 14.

[5] Charls Walker, "Discount Policy in the Light of Recent Experience," *Journal of Finance,* March, 1957, p. 225. Comment: The authority exists but the exercise of it does not. It may be, of course, that the statutory power to refuse has the effect stated, even though it has always remained in abeyance.

[6] Robert D. Roosa, "Monetary Policy Again," *Bulletin of the Oxford University Institute of Statistics,* August, 1952, p. 258. Comment: It is true that refusal is legally possible. So far, however, as it has been possible to discover, no member bank is ever refused a loan request actually made.

Mr. Hayes: I am sure that the level of rates would not have too much influence on that.[7]

The impression conveyed by Mr. Hayes that loan requests are refused at the discount window was quickly corrected by the head of the Federal Reserve Bank of Richmond: [8]

Mr. Leach: The window is always open for appropriate purposes, and it is not closed in the sense that any one bank cannot come there and get funds through a loan on that day. . . . We in our bank have not actually turned down any bank on a loan.[9]

Other Reserve Bank presidents concurred, including Mr. Hayes who, despite the impression previously left with Congressman Multer, remarked that the Reserve Banks could by statute refuse to make loans as requested by member banks but in fact never do refuse.[10]

Another common misconception is that lending policy is adjusted to changing business conditions. The fact is that neither the way in which the discount window is administered nor the standards by which member bank borrowing is judged are modified to conform to over-all monetary policy.[11] In the words of Mr. Leach, "Our discount window doesn't vary when money is tight or money is easy." [12] Lending policies of the Reserve Banks are governed by the provisions of Regulation A as laid down by the Board of Governors. These provisions are designed to prevent individual banks from borrowing too long, too continuously, too much or for speculative purposes. Nor does the Board ever declare that it is an appropriate time for the Reserve Banks to lend; it takes the position, rather, that the purposes laid down in Regulation *A* remain the same regardless of conditions of tightness or ease.[13]

In short, the administration of Reserve Bank lending to member banks is directed toward the avoidance of undesirable operating practices on the part of the individual bank and not at all toward controlling the volume of credit. Nevertheless, it works out that the pressure on banks to refrain from borrowing ordinarily operates in a cyclical manner. For obvious reasons, the amount of borrowing tends to be greatest in periods of credit tightness and least in periods of credit ease. Consequently, the situations of "undue use of bank credit" contemplated in Regulation A are likely to arise in the former but not in the

---

[7] Italics supplied. "Problems of Small-Business Financing," *Hearings,* Select Committee on Small Business, House of Representatives, 85th Congress, 1st Session, Nov., 1957, p. 17. (Hereinafter referred to as *Hearings.*)

[8] Confusion on this point is by no means of recent origin. A writer in the late 1920's referred to the refusal of loans by the Federal Reserve Banks as "the most drastic example of direct action" (Joseph Stagg Lawrence, *Wall Street and Washington,* Princeton University Press, 1929, p. 237). He then went on (p. 240) to show, however, that the limitation of borrowing was effected not by the rejection of actual loan requests but by conferring with the officers of banks which were inclined to borrow more than they should.

[9] *Hearings,* pp. 18–19.

[10] *Ibid.*

[11] *Ibid.,* pp. 7–8.

[12] *Ibid,* p. 18.

[13] *Ibid.,* pp. 18, 20.

latter periods. Such variation as occurs, however, in the pressure exerted on member bank borrowing by the Reserve Banks is automatic. It does not represent, as in the case of open market operations or changes in the discount rate, the conscious adaptation of Federal Reserve policy to changing economic conditions.

HOW LIMITATION OF DISCOUNTING IS EFFECTED [14]

Although requests for loans are never refused, significant restraint may be brought upon member bank borrowing by inducing banks to refrain from further requests. This is accomplished through direct negotiation of Reserve Bank officials with the officers of member banks. Where the borrowing privilege seems to be in danger of being abused the loan asked for will be granted but officials of the Reserve Bank will then suggest to officers of the member bank that it is advisable for them to take steps to reduce their dependence on borrowing at the Federal Reserve. In the words of Mr. Hayes, "They always do." [15]

The description given by President Hayes of the process whereby Reserve officials restrain member banks from borrowing without ever actually refusing to lend is very similar to that outlined by his predecessor, Benjamin Strong, over thirty-five years earlier. Governor Strong described the technique as "educational," "to point out that certain kinds of loans should not be made." [16] The expression used by Robert Roosa, Vice President of the Federal Reserve Bank of New York, is similar but somewhat more grim, "we help a bank decide not to borrow from us." [17] It would appear that this phase of discount policy should best be regarded as a form of moral suasion.[18] The initiative in such a situation is with the Federal Reserve officials; i.e., the officers of the member bank do not obtain advance clearance as to whether or not they will be allowed to borrow.[19]

[14] Apart, that is, from changes in the discount rate. The judgment of the presidents of the Federal Reserve Banks at the Hearings referred to above (esp. pp. 20–22, 29) was that minor changes, e.g., from 3 per cent to 3½ per cent, have no significant effect on borrowing. An increase from 3 per cent to 6 per cent, however, was presumed to be quite influential. Due acknowledgment was, of course, made to possible psychological effects and Mr. Hayes ascribed importance to the discount rate, somewhat obscurely, as "part of a total program" (p. 27). The question of the effect of changes in the discount rate lies outside the scope of the present paper which is concerned solely with administration of the discount window.

[15] *Hearings,* p. 19.

[16] Joint Commission of Agricultural Inquiry, *Hearings,* Part 13, 67th Congress, 1st Session, 1921, pp. 704–8.

[17] *Hearings,* p. 37.

[18] The Board of Governors has expressly included this aspect of discount policy under the broad definition of moral suasion. Cf. "United States Monetary Policy: Recent Thinking and Experience," *Hearings,* Subcommittee on Economic Stabilization, 83d Congress, 2d Session, 1954, p. 13. It is to be noted, however, that in this case the moral suasion is determined on the basis not of general credit conditions but of the operating practices of individual banks.

[19] *Hearings,* p. 23.

In the absence of prior warning by Reserve officials, the member bank can assume that its request for a loan will not be refused. There is the possibility, of course, that this request, though granted, will be a factor in causing the Reserve authorities to intervene to discourage further loan requests. In such a situation it is fairly customary to indicate that reborrowing is not in order within a period of one or, preferably, more periods after existing notes mature or are paid off.

Some Federal Reserve Banks have the reputation throughout the system of being stricter than others in their enforcement of the provisions of Regulation A. Such differences appear, however, to have grown less in the past few years. On such major points as applying the same tests in periods of monetary ease or tightness and never refusing requests for loans there is uniformity throughout the System. Variations among Federal Reserve Banks may reflect differences in the personal attitude of discount officers. In one district a bank might be expected to sell long governments even in a falling market, if necessary in order to pay off an advance, while at another Reserve Bank more time might be allowed. Differences may exist with respect to interpretation of what constitutes "continuous" borrowing. Some discount officers may be more lenient than others with respect to allowing a gradual scaling down of indebtedness over a series of dates as compared with an immediate pay-out.

The general impression one gets is that, by and large, the Reserve Banks are disposed to be tolerant toward borrowing by banks whose resources are temporarily strained because of some understandable emergency or economic misfortune, such as a crop failure or period of drought. On the other hand, they are strongly opposed to allowing the resources of the Federal Reserve Banks to be drawn upon to facilitate a member bank's speculating in government bonds. The chief offenders appear to have been good-sized banks which bought governments in the expectation of an appreciation in their price, and then turned to the Federal Reserve for advances rather than dispose of their holdings at a loss or without profit when a rise failed to materialize as had been anticipated.[20]

Precise data with respect to the administration of the discount window are closely guarded. Inquiries at a number of Federal Reserve Banks, however, elicited information which suggests the general order of magnitudes involved. It seems that in a recent fairly active year approximately 20 per cent of the member banks of the districts concerned had borrowed at one time or another during the year. The maximum number borrowing at any one time was a little less than half that figure. Banks discouraged from further borrowing amounted to somewhat less than 1 per cent of total membership in the districts. In at least one district a higher proportion of banks, roughly 2 per cent, was admonished.

---

[20] In such cases borrowing is resorted to not in order to invest but in order to avoid disinvesting. The immediate need for additional reserves may be in order to accommodate rising loan demands by established customers of the bank. It may reflect a lack of adequate secondary reserves in the form of Treasury bills or other short-term assets (even where this means hanging on to such assets merely to preserve some ratio which the bank administration has come to look upon as sacrosanct). If the reserve deficiency is expected to be short, borrowing is a means of avoiding in-and-out expense.

INTERACTION WITH THE TRADITION AGAINST BORROWING

The view is persistently maintained by certain of the Federal Reserve officials that administration of the discount window is a significant feature of over-all credit control and not, as the foregoing description suggests, an adjunct to the supervisory function. In support of such a contention, Mr. Hayes has spoken of an "interaction" between open market operations and the use of the discount window.[21] The words in which the alleged interaction was described, however, seemed to put open market operations in the active role and to make discounting wholly passive, if not, indeed, something that may at times interfere with them:

> If you sell securities in the open market, other things being equal, you tend to put more pressure on the bank(s) and force them into the discount window to adjust their positions to come out evenly, and that per se, tends to put the banks under greater pressure.[22]

It seems clear from this description that the deterrent which makes it possible for open market sales to put pressure on banks is the tradition against borrowing and not the "use of the discount window." To the extent that borrowing takes place in spite of the tradition—which, as noted above, is freely open to member banks as long as they have not violated the standards laid down in Regulation *A*—resort to the discount window interacts with open market operations not to support them but to provide an escape, i.e., to offset them! [23] It is extremely difficult to conjure out of this particular set of "interactions" a significant role for administration of the discount window as a positive element in the control of credit by the Federal Reserve.

It might be argued that the tradition against borrowing is sustained in a passive way by the language of Regulation *A*. The law is broad enough, apparently, to enable the authorities to withdraw the privilege of discounting in the interest of stabilization if they should choose to do so. And it might perhaps be inferred that the feeling that this could be done is a deterrent to greater resort to the discounting privilege, lest this should lead to outright refusals of loan requests by the Reserve authorities. But any such inference would be no more than conjecture, and rather farfetched conjecture at that.

A more significant possibility is that administration of the discount window, in the admonitory, moral suasion sense, has a tendency to strengthen the attitude of mind among bankers, "the instinct against borrowing," which is at the basis of the tradition. The tradition against borrowing presumably derives ultimately from a belief that continued borrowing may be interpreted as a confession either of

[21] *Hearings,* p. 19.

[22] *Ibid.*

[23] In some instances a better figure is that of a safety valve. Borrowing may appropriately occur as a means of cushioning the uneven impact of such general instruments as open market sales and increases in reserve requirements. It is a means whereby banks which have been squeezed by the reduction in reserves can obtain temporary relief. Cf. Board of Governors, *Annual Report for 1957,* pp. 12–13.

weakened condition or of poor management.[24] In any case, the experience of being cautioned against undue borrowing is one which a commercial banker does not relish. In such a relationship he is accustomed to appearing in the opposite role. To be admonished is likely to seem embarrassing and even humiliating. Thus the mere fact that the borrowing activities of bankers are occasionally called into question by officials of the Federal Reserve may help to keep the tradition against borrowing alive and at times to strengthen it.

An example of a refurbishing of the tradition against borrowing is to be found in the recent experience of one of the midwest Federal Reserve Banks. For some years this district had been conspicuous for the relatively high proportion of borrowing by its member banks. The conclusion was reached that this continuing feature was not sufficiently accounted for by agricultural difficulties or other economic characteristics of the area. It was decided that the question of undue borrowing had not been brought sufficiently to the attention of the bankers of the district. Accordingly, a deliberate educational program was undertaken by the Reserve Bank officials to explain the system's attitude toward member bank borrowing.[25] An effort was made to differentiate between desirable and undesirable borrowing. An added note of formality was introduced into the borrowing procedure by the use of application forms and by requiring banks to submit condition statements at each reserve period when they found themselves in debt to the Federal Reserve. So successful was the campaign to rehabilitate the tradition that the ratio of borrowing in the district fell to one of the lowest in the system.[26]

CONCLUSION

For the overwhelming majority of member banks, those which are not in contravention of the relatively narrow provisions (as applied) of Regulation A governing discounts, the privilege of borrowing, despite conventional statements

[24] Large banks are said to be less reluctant than smaller banks to borrow from the Federal Reserve. A possible explanation of this difference is that large banks are likely to feel sufficiently sure of themselves not to fear such an invidious interpretation of their action in borrowing. It may, perhaps, be conjectured that the growing strength of banks, carrying with it heightened self-confidence of bankers, will have a tendency over the years to weaken the force of the tradition against borrowing.

[25] A senior officer of one of the Federal Reserve Banks listed the following as justifiable reasons for borrowing from the "Fed."
(a) Reserve adjustment, as where a city bank experiences a sudden short-period drain of reserves.
(b) Seasonal need, beyond what can reasonably be anticipated and prepared for.
(c) Economic distress, as in the case of crop failure or work stoppage in a one-industry community.
Another officer gave as the usual reason for undue borrowing the attempt of the particular banker to "run a bigger bank than he has got." The aim of the Federal Reserve was described b yone discount officer as being to "get them out, not keep them out." Cf. also Karl R. Bopp, "Some Basic Principles," *Business Review,* Federal Reserve Bank of Philadelphia, June, 1958, pp. 6–7.

[26] Because bankers are great traditionalists, practices to which they are accustomed tend to be perpetuated. The tradition against borrowing when once re-established is not readily reversed. This fact would interfere with use of discount policy as an anticyclical instrument.

to the contrary, is, in practice, tantamount to a right. At a time of general overexpansion of credit, an increasing number of banks would doubtless cross the line of clearance at which borrowing is frowned upon as being excessive in amount or too continuous. In any situation that can realistically be imagined, however, there would still be a great many banks whose record was clear. Under long standing practice, these banks could count on being able to obtain credit by borrowing at the Reserve Banks whenever they so desired.

During the business boom of 1955–57 the *Economic Report of the President* declared that, "the pressure on reserves induced member banks, despite an increased discount rate, to borrow more heavily from the Federal Reserve." [27] Despite such testimony as this, there is no significant evidence that resort to discounting, whether it is called a privilege or a right, has been on such a scale as to weaken appreciably the efforts of the Reserve authorities to tighten credit. That this has not occurred is apparently strongly influenced by the tradition against borrowing.[28] Thus the Federal Reserve has been able, mainly by open market sales or by refraining from purchases in the face of growing demands, to tighten reserves without having their efforts seriously hampered by undue resort to member bank borrowing. It is not, however, the refusal of loans at the discount window that makes this possible but the forbearance of member banks from requesting advances, even though they are perfectly free to do so.

The discount window as presently administered is perhaps no more than a paper threat to the power of the Federal Reserve to control credit. Potentially, however, the discount window is an avenue of escape from the limitations of Federal Reserve credit policy because of the ability of the vast majority of member banks to obtain reserves on their own initiative if they should choose to do so.

Under one interpretation, the discount window may be looked upon as an "engine of inflation" which remains stalled not because of the control exercised by the Reserve Banks but because of the complaisance of the member banks. Under a different interpretation, it could be viewed in the light of a very efficient police system which is seldom called upon to make an arrest. The truth may lie somewhere between these two interpretations. Fortunately, there is nothing to indicate that the present situation cannot go on indefinitely.

Whether or not the discount window is to be viewed as a potential threat to Federal Reserve credit control, it surely does not deserve, as presently administered, to be regarded as a direct factor in the exercise of such control. The chief influence of the administration of Federal Reserve loan operations may well be indirect, viz., that of helping to keep alive and reinforce the tradition against borrowing, without which discount policy as presently conducted could quickly break down.

[27] Jan. 1956, p. 6.

[28] The fact that a rise in member bank borrowing generally occurs when an increase in the financial inducement is provided by significantly higher market rates suggests that the tradition is far from binding. It may be that what we have is a tradition against borrowing except when the spread between discount and market rates is sufficiently attractive to make them want to do so! Certainly a significant widening of the spread greatly increases the attraction of borrowing from the Federal Reserve Banks.

There was a time during and after World War I when member bank borrowing at the Federal Reserve exceeded total reserve balances, part of the time by a substantial amount. It could then be said that member banks operated entirely on borrowed reserves. Various developments have tended to reduce the importance of borrowing as a source of reserve balances. The longer reserve averaging period has made banks somewhat less dependent on the discount window. [29]

The rise of the Federal funds market has provided individual banks with a convenient means of obtaining additional reserves when needed. So also have the large holdings of short-term Treasury obligations. It is still true, no doubt, that discounting offers a number of not inconsiderable advantages.[30] But for the time being, at least, discounting and the direct control exercised through the discount window possess little of the strategic importance still customarily ascribed to them.

Selection 31

CREDIT POLICY AT THE DISCOUNT WINDOW: COMMENT

ROBERT V. ROOSA

Robert V. Roosa's comments on Professor Whittlesey's article, in this selection, give some flavor of the shadings of viewpoint among experts. Roosa admits that "any bank with a good record can be virtually certain that it will get a loan," but he emphasizes some other aspects of borrowing from the Fed. Because the United States has a banking system composed of thousands of unit banks, rather than a few large branch banking systems, Roosa believes that there is a need for borrowing from Federal Reserve Banks, as a mechanical facility intended to aid the smooth functioning of the process of control of the money supply, and that this may be somewhat obscured in Professor Whittlesey's discussion. Borrowing might be used to obtain funds to lend or invest at a higher rate of return, if it were not for a traditional reluctance to borrow on the part of the banks and surveillance by the Federal Reserve System. Roosa views the discount window as a safety valve, but of course one which should not become an important escape route for avoidance of Federal Reserve control. Readers may wish to compare this view with the views of Milton Friedman in selection 29.

At the inception of the Federal Reserve System, it was expected that the discount rate would be an important tool of control. With the growth of the national debt and the resulting dominance of open market operations as the means of control of the money supply, attention turned from early concern with rediscounting as a possible means of obtaining funds to lend at a profit to concern with rediscounting as one means among several for banks to obtain reserves. As the money and capital markets evolved, banks could obtain reserves in the Federal funds market (see selection 18), by selling

---

[29] Federal Reserve Bank of Boston, *The Federal Funds Market* (Boston, 1957), pp. 15–16.

[30] Cf. Federal Reserve Bank of Kansas City, *Monthly Review*, Feb., 1958, p. 5. Also Walker, *op. cit.*, pp. 225–30.

> *Treasury bills, and by other means, as well as through rediscounting. Since banks could obtain reserves by such means if not by rediscounting, at rates generally lower than interest rates on loans, attention shifted from the idea of some older economists that the rediscount rate should be higher than the prime rate on loans to the question whether the rediscount rate should be higher than other rates at which banks might obtain reserves—should the rediscount rate be a "penalty" rate in the sense of being higher than other rates which banks might pay in order to obtain reserves? Mr. Roosa comments on some aspects of these and other questions in his brief but stimulating discussion.*

Professor Whittlesey's "Credit Policy at the Discount Window" is concerned with the arrangements through which member banks borrow from Federal Reserve Banks. He is not concerned with the discount rate, nor with the traditional aspects of the reluctance to borrow. But he thinks there are some serious misconceptions abroad to the effect that Federal Reserve Banks, on their own initiative, ration credit at the discount window, refusing one bank or accommodating another as a sort of selective credit control. That is not done, and Whittlesey is quite right in saying so. Yet in his determination to root out such misconceptions, he may partly have obscured the use that the discount window does have in reinforcing general credit controls, while perhaps overlooking the significant contribution that discounting makes to the smooth daily performance of the American deposit-money system.

Why is it that Federal Reserve sources have themselves stressed the discretionary nature of Reserve Bank lending? It has certainly not been for the purpose of nourishing such misconceptions as those Whittlesey has described. Indeed it ought to be as clear to those engaged in the daily review of individual borrowing banks as it is to Whittlesey that the criteria used, in fact, closely resemble some of those used by the bank supervisory authorities in appraising bank examinations. The stress is on good banking practices; no attempt is made to orient each borrowing bank's position into the broader policy aims of current Federal Reserve credit control. Moreover, any bank with a good record can be virtually certain, as Whittlesey says, that it will get a loan.

Perhaps part of the confusion, and it exists in some banking circles as well as in the world outside, comes from the compulsion many of us feel to classify decisions rigidly into two categories—the "yes" and the "no." From that often follows the arbitrary determination that whatever is not unequivocally "no" must be "yes." Without returning to the philosophy classroom, one might hope to find agreement that it is no more arbitrary to turn this quite around, so that whatever is not unequivocally "yes" must be considered "no." And on this equally dubious scale, Whittlesey would have no difficulty in finding scores, if not thousands, of rejections. A bank that would not hesitate to present a note (supported by ample collateral) for a sum equal to, say, 10 per cent of its reserve balances, or perhaps 20 per cent of its capital accounts, would be

• From Robert V. Roosa, "Credit Policy at the Discount Window: Comment," *Quarterly Journal of Economics,* May, 1959, pp. 333–337. Copyright 1959 by the President and Fellows of Harvard College. Reprinted by permission of the *Quarterly Journal of Economics* and the author.

most apprehensive in asking for a sum several times larger than this, regardless of the collateral, and would expect to provide an explanation in an effort to justify the amount on a very temporary basis. A bank that wanted to borrow for more than a few days, even in relatively small amounts, would know that no note can run for more than fifteen days, that a renewal request would be scrutinized closely to judge the adequacy of the provision being made to pay off shortly with funds obtained in other ways, and that its chances of full accommodation would be particularly slim if it had been borrowing in several other reserve-computation periods during recent months.

The truth is, of course, that Whittlesey is neither all wrong nor all right, and that in the same way the discount window is never either wide open or tightly closed. Insofar as human frailties permit, it is always the same window, open in the same way at all times for borrowers of the same circumstances. What makes the impact of these continuous standards seem to vary is that the circumstances of the banks themselves change. In some part, nearly all of the time, the changes reflect what has been done to the reserve base, as a whole, by the open market operations or other actions of the Federal Reserve. Hence the continuous interest, at the policy level within the Federal Reserve System, in the interactions between the degree of general pressure exerted through open market operations and the reinforcement of that pressure as individual banks find themselves, more often or less often, in need of temporary borrowing assistance to average out their required reserves.

The crucial point is that the central bank should not give up the ultimate initiative for control over the creation of bank reserves. In the American setting, the fact that banks borrow only as a privilege means that even though any individual bank can temporarily, in effect, cause the creation of reserves by borrowing at the discount window, that same bank simultaneously takes on an obligation to find ways of extinguishing those reserves—the more promptly the better, in order to preserve its privilege for use again when unexpected reserve drains occur. Thus, as a general rule, the larger the aggregate volume of bank borrowing from the Federal Reserve, the greater will be the effort then going on, through the banking system, to limit credits and bring reserves into balance with the requirements against deposits. But the pressure exerted on credit extension is gradual and not precipitate. Time is allowed for any one bank to shift some of its burden of adjustment to others, rather than undergo the full shock alone, if an unexpected reserve drain has left it far short of requirements in a single reserve-computation period.

There are sharp contrasts, of course, between the role of discount operations in the American unit banking system and the purposes served by discounting in most other countries. In many, the absence of an active trading market in the instruments of short-term liquidity (Treasury bills, bankers acceptances, and the like) prevents the central bank from relying upon open market operations, and discounting becomes the principal means of supplying central bank credit (i.e., bank reserves) to the banking system. In such countries, there must be a substantial amount of discounting in existence all of the time, and effective variations are induced by changes in the borrowing ceilings established for individual banks, by changes in the margin applied in valuing some kinds of collateral, by changes in the discount rate, or by other means. Within rather wide limits, borrowing at the central bank becomes a right; not, as in this country, a privilege—carrying an implication that early repayment is necessary in order to preserve the widest latitude for later use of the borrowing facility at times of large and sudden reserve strains.

In other countries, fortunate enough to have a money market, the banking structure usually consists of only a few, large branch banks. There, the reserve losses of one branch office may be netted against the gains of another, as deposits move about the country, without any net strain visible in the total reserve position of the parent bank as a whole. In the United States these inescapable physical by-products of a check-payment mechanism are all brought out into the open. No individual bank can feel assured that it will get back from others, each day or each week, a volume of deposits equal to those withdrawn. There may be an evening out over time, or through seasons, but the short swings for any single bank can be very wide indeed. So long as there are frictions in redistributing reserves, with some banks always ending their reserve-computation periods in a deficient position, and unable to tap promptly all of the excesses lodged in other banks elsewhere, there will be need for borrowing at the Federal Reserve. And because this is, within reasonable limits, merely a mechanical facility, aiding the smooth functioning of the deposit-money process, no purpose would be served by trying to fend off borrowing by using a stiff "penalty rate" concept of the discount rate in this country. On the contrary, banks faced with unexpected withdrawals might, if the discount rate were set well above going money market rates, be induced to make abrupt curtailments of other loans or investments, in an effort to meet their reserve requirements, with upsetting, or at least capriciously disturbing, effects in their local communities.

Yet the same facility which many banks may need in meeting the unavoidable exigencies of deposit shifts, as money moves about from day to day in doing the nation's business, might also be tapped, if there were no frictions imposed upon access to the discount window, for the more obvious purpose of borrowing at a lower rate in order to lend (or invest) at a higher rate of return. That is why, in the administration of the discount window, and in the exercise of bank supervision, banks are continually reminded that they cannot rely upon any funds borrowed from the Federal Reserve as a permanent, or quasi-permanent, addition to their own resources. It is to make certain that the discount window is used, and only used, to meet actual needs for temporary assistance in maintaining reserves at the required levels that surveillance becomes necessary. It is very difficult, as Whittlesey has found, to say where the influence of surveillance begins and the influence of the traditional reluctance to borrow runs out. But there is really no need to try. Both are certainly present; and whenever the check imposed by tradition might begin to falter, the limits imposed by surveillance would begin to take hold. Quite understandably, moreover, at times when Federal Reserve policy is aimed at limiting the over-all growth of bank credit and the money supply, more banks will be running their reserve positions very close to the margin, and deficiencies in these positions will occur more frequently, and in a larger aggregate total for the country as a whole, as deposit shifts continue to work their uneven incidence among individual banks from day to day. It is for that reason, and not because there is any wholesale breakdown in the reluctance to borrow, or in the surveillance, that the volume of borrowing tends to rise when Federal Reserve policy is restrictive.

When an increase in borrowing is going on, the policy arm of the Federal Reserve will be attempting to judge, very broadly, whether the total volume of borrowing that has emerged is exerting too much pressure toward the limitation of bank credit, or not enough, or perhaps is about right. If the general diffusion of pressure seems too great, in the light of over-all credit policy objectives, then, without any need to decide that one bank should have more reserves at the discount window, or another less, the Federal Reserve can make a change that will result in some of the banks, somewhere, borrowing less. It can release new reserves into the banking system, and would ordinarily do so through open market operations. As these funds begin to flow from bank to bank, some banks will find themselves able to repay borrowings without having to sell other investments or reduce other credits, and there will be fewer banks (or at any rate a smaller aggregate of borrowing requests) stepping in to take their place in the next round of borrowings at the discount window.

With no changes in the criteria used at the discount window, an additional release of reserves through open market operations, while other conditions remain the same, will bring about a reduction in the volume of borrowing. The "pressure component" in the total volume of bank reserves will have been reduced. But at no time, either when total borrowing was high, or after it had been reduced, would the Federal Reserve have been in any danger of losing control over the creation of bank reserves. It is, in effect, the decisions made with respect to open market operations that determine, within rough limits, the volume of borrowing that will emerge within the unchanging framework of lending criteria applied at the discount window. And it will normally be the combined influence of the forces released by open market operations and those generated by the persistent urge to repay borrowings, that together determine the degree of pressure toward further expansion of credit, or toward a limitation upon such expansion, that may exist in the commercial banking system at any given time.

Selection 32

CREDIT POLICY AT THE DISCOUNT WINDOW: REPLY

CHARLES R. WHITTLESEY

> *This selection gives, for completeness, Professor Whittlesey's "reply"
> to Mr. Roosa's comments (selection 31) on Whittlesey's views on
> the discount window (selection 30). It should be read in connection
> with those selections, and readers may draw their own conclusions
> after consideration of the three comments on the discount window.*

• From Charles R. Whittlesey, "Reply," *Quarterly Journal of Economics,* May, 1959, pp. 337–338. Copyright 1959 by the President and Fellows of Harvard College. Reprinted by permission of the *Quarterly Journal of Economics,* and the author.

Few students inside or outside the Federal Reserve System have a more intimate knowledge of its workings than Dr. Roosa and few have been more generous in sharing that knowledge with others. The present interesting comment accepts my essential point, namely, that at any given moment, whether in boom or depression, the discount window is indubitably open for the vast majority of member banks. It may leave the impression, however, that the whole discount business is nevertheless just about as we have been led to believe all along.

Perhaps the most important observation is the old one that open market and discount operations are complementary instruments. It is the cushioning effect of member bank borrowing, however, rather than the reinforcing effect that stands out most clearly, even in Roosa's explanation. That it may provide an important escape route as well is, I fully agree, no more than a paper threat.

The term "refusal" may, perhaps, be interpreted to apply to the difference between what a bank asks for and an amount "several times as large" which it might somehow have liked to borrow. The same is true of any other borrower. But surely no ordinary mortal could be expected to place this construction on the casual references by Federal Reserve authorities to refusal of loans to member banks. While one may be free to attach whatever meanings he wishes to words as familiar as "privilege" and "right" or even "yes" and "no," public enlightenment will be increased if those in a position to know will bear in mind that the words they use may leave uncorrected, if they do not in fact nourish, misunderstanding on matters as central as the discount-window part of the discount function.

9

Money, Prices, and Output

CONTROVERSY OVER THE RELATIONSHIPS BETWEEN THE
stock of money on the one hand and the level of output and
prices on the other has raged for decades. Until the Great
Depression, American and English economists, working largely
within the framework of the so-called quantity theory of money,
tended to stress the relative stability of payment habits and
therefore the velocity of money, and thus assigned a major role
to changes in the stock of money as a determinant of changes
in total spending. Because classical economic theory was based
on assumptions that involved full employment of economic
resources, little consideration was given to the determination of
the level of output and employment in the short run, and money
was regarded as an important determinant of the price level,
but not of the level of real output. The depression of the
1930's caused much attention to be given to short-run problems
and especially to factors determining the level of income and
employment. The virtual revolution in monetary theory touched
off by the work of John Maynard Keynes moved to an opposite
extreme; money was regarded as only one of many factors—
and certainly not the most important—determining the level
of aggregate spending and therefore of output, employment,
and prices.

The more dogmatic versions of both points of view have

tended to disappear in recent years. The modern quantity theorists and the modern income expenditure theorists both recognized that changes in the stock of money exert significant influence on aggregate behavior of the economy. They differ primarily in the relative weight assigned to the quantity of money as a causal element in economic fluctuations and in the analytical framework through which the impact of changes in the quantity of money is traced out. Readings in this chapter present excellent summaries of the two major approaches to the influence of money on output and prices by leading members of the opposing schools of thought. It will be evident that the issues are far from resolved, but that both groups are moving toward a broader and more useful analysis of the monetary aspects of economic behavior, with the areas of broad agreement expanding steadily. The current need appears to be for more thorough study of the transmission process through which changes in the supply of money and demand for, supply of, and prices of other financial assets and of real assets are interrelated.

Selection 33

A PROGRAM FOR MONETARY STABILITY—PART I

MILTON FRIEDMAN

> *Professor Friedman, as indicated previously, is one of a small but influential group of economists who regard the activities of the Federal Reserve System as more likely to destabilize than to stabilize prices, output, and employment in the American economy. In the continuing controversy, evident in all aspects of a political democracy, over "rules versus authorities," Dr. Friedman is uncompromisingly on the side of rules. In the following selection, he outlines a series of drastic proposals consistent with his thesis that money is too important to the economy to be left to the decisions of central bankers and fractional reserve private banks.*

As you all know, the unduly high hopes which were placed in the Reserve System in the 1920's as a means of promoting a permanent new era and a high level of stability were disappointed by the Great Depression of 1929 to 1933.

The profession of economics as a whole then shifted very radically from one course to another. From a general belief that the stock of money and the changes in it are tremendously important in controlling economic affairs, the profession shifted toward the view that money has little importance and does not matter except in rather trivial ways. It shifted toward the belief that the important things to look at are the flows of investment expenditures, on the one hand, and consumer expenditures, on the other. It was said that if these are taken

• From Milton Friedman, "A Program for Monetary Stability, Part I," *Proceedings of the 1962 Conference on Savings and Residential Financing,* 1962, pp. 12–32. Reprinted by permission of the United States Savings and Loan League and the author.

into account, it really does not make much difference what happens to the stock of money.

In the last five or ten years or so, there has been something of a counter-revolution with respect to these ideas, both in this country and abroad. This has been partly a result of the experience which countries had after the war with the policies which seemed to follow from the neglect of money. Those policies called for easy money, for trying to keep interest rates low. Their adoption was very widely accompanied by problems of inflation. These problems of inflation, in turn, caused renewed attention to and emphasis upon money.

At the same time, there have been developments in the world of ideas and theories which also led to a reincorporation of monetary factors into economic thought, so that by now economists are again putting a great deal of emphasis on monetary matters. They are once again concerned about the problems of how money ought to be managed, although the reasons they now give for these concerns may be somewhat different from what they were thirty or forty years ago.

It is surprising that economists, even for so short a period as several decades, should have adopted so extreme a position as they did about the unimportance of money. This is particularly surprising in the United States, it seems to me. In looking over our own historical background, it is clear that the problems of controlling the stock of money have played a major role in both political and economic affairs ever since the founding of this nation. The problem of money probably has been of greater importance in American experience than in that of many another country. . . .

EXPERIENCE UNDER THE RESERVE SYSTEM

The period since 1914, under the Federal Reserve System, is well known, but it is interesting nonetheless to contrast it with the prior period. The interesting thing to ask, I think, is: Comparing the period from 1914 to the present date with the preceding forty to fifty years, in which case did we have a greater degree of monetary stability?

There is no doubt about the answer. There was a greater degree of monetary stability in the period before the establishment of the Federal Reserve System than in the period after, whether measured by changes in interest rates, instability in the stock of money, instability in prices or instability in economic activity. By any measure I know of, the period after has been more unstable than the one before.

One obvious reason is that there were two world wars after 1914. Those wars would have caused instability under any system. But omit the wars and the answer is still the same. The period since 1914 has been more unstable, in the peacetime years alone, than the period before 1914.

I hasten to add that this is an oversimplification. The great period of instability was the twenty years between the wars, 1919 to 1939. There is no other twenty-year period in our history that comes anywhere close to having such great instability. That period contained three major contractions. First, there was an inflation from 1919 to 1920, then a severe contraction, then the 1929 to 1933 episode and then the 1937 to 1938 contraction. The period since the end of World War II has not been more unstable than earlier periods, but rather more stable than most.

GREATER INSTABILITY SINCE 1914

Yet, taking as a whole the period since 1914, there is no question that it has been more unstable. Moreover, that period contains the worst banking panic in our history. The 1933 banking panic with its bank holiday, when banks were closed for a week, was incomparably severer and more sweeping than any earlier panic. Whereas the earlier panics came before banks failed and prevented them from failing, the 1933 panic came after the banks had failed and indeed closed the doors of many good banks that were open the day before the panic. The number of banks that opened their doors after the banking holiday in March, 1933, was decidedly less than the number that had been open before, and a large fraction of the banks that did not reopen ultimately paid out 100 per cent to their depositors.

So here was a system, established in 1914 for the purpose of preventing banking panics and providing monetary stability, which in practice was associated with the greatest banking panic in United States history and a great deal of instability of money.

Is the reason simply that the problems the System had to cope with were severer after the war, so that the earlier system, too, would have had the same problems? I cannot hope to indicate here the reasons I think the answer is in the negative, but if you were to examine in detail the successive episodes in the period after 1918, I think you would agree that that is the only conclusion justified by the evidence.

Under the earlier monetary and banking system, imperfect though it was, we would have had less of an inflation in World War I. The wartime inflation would have been there anyway, but the postwar inflation from 1918 to 1920 would not have occurred, which would have eliminated a third of the total inflation. We would not have had the drastic fall in prices in 1920 and 1921, the sharpest fall within a brief period in the whole history of the United States and perhaps of any other country. Prices fell nearly 50 per cent, and two-thirds of the decline came in the six months from August, 1920 to February, 1921.

THE GREAT DEPRESSION

Most important of all, under the earlier system we would not have had the Great Depression of 1929 to 1933. This depression had a traumatic effect upon the thinking of people and their attitude with respect to money and many other matters. It was this event that led to a shift from the belief that money is of the greatest importance to the belief that it is a minor matter which can be left to one side. It was the major event that led to a shift of emphasis from monetary policy to fiscal policy and that produced a widespread expansion in the role of government in the economy after 1933.

It has been widely taken for granted that 1929 to 1933 demonstrated the impotence of monetary control. It has been said that here we had a system which was established to prevent such a depression and which had the power, but which in fact did not prevent it. Therefore it was concluded that it must be that money is not very important. I myself think that the episode suggests just the opposite. It suggests that money is so powerful that it needs to be controlled more closely than it was then. If you examine the 1929 to 1933 episode, you will conclude that it was a needless episode. There is no doubt that with the powers then existing in the hands of the System, a very large part of the decline could have been prevented.

I do not mean to be casting blame or suggesting incompetence or lack of will or anything like that. It may be that the ablest, the most intelligent, the most public-spirited men would have made the mistakes that were made at that time.

Economists as a whole have no reason for feeling proud of their own record during that period. A year ago I read over the volumes of the Proceedings of the American Economic Association from 1929 to 1933. They are not something to make you feel proud of your profession. While the world was tumbling around the economists' ears on the outside, there was hardly a sign of it in the papers presented at those annual meetings. They dealt with strictly academic matters, even monetary and long-term banking matters. I remember one study, in 1932, of the failure of banks. It was concerned primarily with what had happened during the '20's and stressed the fact that country banks which failed had made poor mortgage loans, whereas in fact the important thing happening at the time was the widespread failure of city banks.

GREAT POWER IN A FEW HANDS

So I am not trying to say that the mistakes made were not understandable. What I am trying to say is that a system which could produce mistakes of that magnitude is a bad system by its very nature. It is like the cartoon in the New Yorker a couple of weeks ago, in which one man is sitting at a table in front of a big computer and another man is looking over his shoulder and saying, "Four thousand mathematicians in four thousand years couldn't have made a mistake like that." That is exactly the point. A mistake like that could not have been made under our earlier system or under a system which did not concentrate so much power in a few hands.

Let me spend a few minutes more in discussing the details of that episode, because it was so important in forming people's ideas. I think it is very important, in judging the episode, to distinguish the first year, from mid-1929 to the fall of 1930, from the subsequent years. We have had business recessions for several hundreds of years and we will have them for hundreds of years more. I have no doubt about that. Economic affairs move in fluctuations. The most we can hope for is that we can keep them relatively mild.

It may be that, monetary policy or no monetary policy, there would have been a recession from 1929 to 1930. There were signs of monetary tightness in that period as a result of the undue concern of the System with the stock market. In point of fact, the expansion of 1927 to 1929 is the only one I know of on record in which prices did not rise during a period of business expansion and in which the stock of money was lower at the end than it was at the beginning of the expansion. From 1929 to 1930, the stock of money fell about 3 per cent. This was more than it had fallen in all except the severest previous depressions. Nevertheless, 1929 to 1930 can be described as an ordinary garden variety of recession—somewhat severer than most recessions, but not out of line. There were, in particular, no aspects of monetary weakness and no bank failures on any substantial scale, and no sign of any weakening of public confidence in the banking system. The ratio of deposits to currency prior to the Federal Deposit Insurance Corporation was an infallible sign of public attitude. This ratio stayed up or went up a little over that period, so that up to September or October of 1930 there was no sign of a liquidity crisis or a banking problem.

That period must be distinguished sharply from the one that followed. It is the later period, from late 1930 to 1933, for which, it seems to me, the Reserve System or the monetary authorities bear responsibility of a real kind.

In October and November of 1930, a series of bank failures started out here in the west and spread, culminating on December 11, 1930, with the failure of the Bank of the United States in New York. That was a large bank with something like $200 million of deposits. Its name made its failure more important than it otherwise would have been. Although it was an ordinary commercial bank, it was widely interpreted by people abroad, and also by immigrants in New York and throughout the United States, as being a government bank. Indeed, this may be one reason that it was permitted to fail. The banks in New York were very unhappy about having a bank with the name "Bank of the United States" in New York, as well as being unhappy about some of the irrelevant characteristics of the owners and managers of the bank. As a result, there was less sympathy for this bank than there would have been for many another bank. It was allowed to fail, and it precipitated a real liquidity crisis.

From this point on, the character of the contraction changed. The ratio of deposits to currency started to fall. Time and again, depositors sought to withdraw deposits; this caused a stream of bank failures, with one bank failure bringing on another. The crisis would taper off for a while and then start again.

FAILURE TO PROVIDE LIQUIDITY

What did the Federal Reserve System do during this period? It behaved as impassively and inactively as you can conceive of its doing. In 1931, after six months of this kind of behavior, Federal Reserve credit outstanding was less than it had been two years earlier in the middle of 1929. There is not a single sign that the Federal Reserve engaged in extensive open-market operations or in any other way tried on its own initiative to provide banks with the liquidity which would enable them to withstand a run, although this is what it had been set up to do. Every time there is a sequence of runs, discounts rise, but only as a necessity of the banks and not because of any encouragement from the Federal Reserve System.

I may say that there were voices within the System arguing for a more appropriate policy. George Harrison, the Governor of the Federal Reserve Bank of New York, pleaded for the System to engage in open-market operations, but he was vetoed as a result of an administrative change that had occurred in the Open Market Committee. It had been changed from a five-man to a twelve-man committee—hardly a change likely to facilitate vigorous action. The twelve-man committee of bank presidents continuously vetoed Harrison's proposals for open-market operations, and the Reserve System did nothing and allowed banks to fail by the score.

The next important date is September 1931, when Britain went off the gold standard. This time the Reserve System reacted to the external threat as it had not to the internal threat. Within two weeks it raised discount rates more than it had before or has since, and there was a sudden increase in bank failures. There was a decline in the stock of money and, in the course of six months following this episode, something like 10 per cent of the banks in the United States went out of business and deposits fell by something like 15 per cent. But there is no sign at all of any autonomous easing action on the part of the Reserve System until the spring of 1932, when, faced by great congressional pressure and threats of congressional investigation, the System engaged in open-market operations to the tune of a billion dollars. It stopped two weeks after Congress adjourned. The final episode was the last series of bank failures ending with the banking panic of 1933.

CAUSE OF DECLINE IN THE STOCK OF MONEY

The main lesson I want to drive home is that the 1929–1933 period was not one in which the economic depression forced a decline in the stock of money. The decline in the stock of money was a direct consequence of the sequence of bank failures. The banking failures were not important primarily because they involved the failures of financial institutions. They were important because they forced a decline in the stock of money. They forced a decline in the stock of money because the therapeutic device that was earlier available, the device of concerted restriction of convertibility of deposits into currency, was not available because the Reserve System had been established as a lender of last resort. However, the lender of last resort did not perform the function of providing the liquidity in the market that would have enabled the banks to meet their obligations.

At all times the Reserve System had ample power to keep the stock of money from declining. It is literally inconceivable that if the stock of money had stayed constant instead of falling by a third, money income could have fallen by a half or that prices could have fallen by a third. I do not mean to say there would not have been a recession or contraction. It might have been a severe one, but it would have been of a wholly different order of magnitude, and not a catastrophe.

We come to the very important step that was taken: the establishment of the FDIC in 1934, which did prevent banking panics by insuring depositors, thus preventing contagion from spreading as a result of bank failures. In the latter 1930's the Federal Reserve System was almost entirely passive. The Treasury took over the role of being the money manager.

THE FED'S POSTWAR PERFORMANCE

The Federal Reserve did not assume an active role in monetary policy again until after the Treasury-Federal Reserve accord in 1951. This postwar period is one with which you are all familiar in great detail; but nonetheless, let me comment very briefly on the last few episodes in order to suggest that the capacity to make mistakes has not been eliminated. The actual performance in the postwar period has been vastly better. This is because the performance has been within a narrower range. We have not moved very vigorously in either direction.

When we had a contraction in 1957 to 1958, the Federal Reserve System was severely criticized for having maintained what was regarded as a tight money policy for too long, for not reversing itself until late in 1957. It was widely feared that the contraction would be sharp and that the Reserve's hesitancy in reacting to it would make it sharper still. So in early 1958 the System turned around, and in late 1958 there was a very rapid expansion in the stock of money. The increase in the rate of expansion in the stock of money coincided with economic expansion. The recession turned out to be milder than many people expected it to be. The Reserve System, in consequence, must have felt that its own position was rather supported by contrast with that of its critics. It felt that the reason it had had to be so tight from 1956 to 1957 was that it had maintained ease for a very long time before 1955.

This time it decided to have a different policy. The expansion had been under way barely six months when the Reserve System tightened up, early in 1959. The rate of change in the stock of money reached a peak during the summer of that year, and then started going down. I think this clearly was one of the major factors that produced a business cycle peak in 1960 after a very short and brief expansion. That expansion did not run its natural course; it was choked to death early. The steel strike which came at the end of 1959 made it a little difficult to see what was going on, but I think the fact of the matter was that money was tightened up unduly early and that the effect was not felt for something like a year or a year and a half. When it was felt, there was a contraction from 1960 to 1961.

Once again the Reserve System turned around and started to put on a great deal of steam, and again the contraction turned out to be relatively mild, reaching its trough in the spring of 1961. Since then we have been in an expansion, and already there are signs that exactly the same policy is being repeated.

Once again we are taking monetary measures, it seems to me, that are likely to spell an early end to this expansion. In this latest episode there is more excuse because of the so-called gold problem, which if I have time I will come to for a moment at the end. Nonetheless, the main point I want to make is that we again have a series of erratic changes.

In retrospect, it seems perfectly clear that we would have been better off if we had avoided the tightening and the easing and had kept the policy on a steady, even keel instead of shoving one way and then shoving too far the other way.

The lesson I draw from this brief survey of history is that the major problem is how to avoid major mistakes, how to prevent such a concentration of power in a small number of hands that that group can make a major mistake. The great virtue of a decentralized system is that mistakes average out. If one unit does something wrong, it does not have a wide effect. If the power is centralized, there is a great deal of power to do good but, along with it, a great deal of power to do harm. The problem is how to erect a system which will have the effect of reducing the power for harm without unduly reducing the power for good, and which will provide a background of monetary stability.

THE PROBLEMS OF MONETARY REFORM

That brings me to the problems of monetary reform. These can be classified under three headings: institutional organization of the private banking system; monetary powers of the Federal Reserve and the Treasury; and criteria for controlling the stock of money.

With respect to the institutional organization of the private banking system, we have had extension of governmental control over the private banking system largely because of the intimate relation of banks to the stock of money. Banks have been controlled more closely than other financial institutions for this reason primarily. It recently has been argued extensively, as you know, that the commercial banking system has been declining relative to financial intermediaries such as savings and loan associations, mutual savings banks and so on, that in some way or other the expansion of these intermediaries limits the effectiveness of monetary management and that it would be desirable to extend control by the Federal Reserve to them.

I think this whole argument reflects a fundamental misconception of wherein the power of the Federal Reserve System lies. The detailed control of banks has almost nothing to do with the essential power of the System. The essential power of the System is the power to determine the total stock of what we call high-powered money—pieces of paper we carry around in our pockets and the reserve balances which the banks hold at the Federal Reserve Banks.

Conceive for a moment a system in which no commercial banks are members of anything called the Federal Reserve System and in which no government agency has any direct control of banks. Let there be no legal reserve requirements for banks at all. Let there be, however, an agency which has an exclusive monopoly of the printing of pieces of paper that can be used for hand-to-hand currency or for vault cash by banks to meet their obligations.

I submit to you that such a system retains all the essential power which the Federal Reserve System now has and that all the rest is trimming. Legal reserve requirements of banks, the ability of the Federal Reserve System to alter these requirements, the requirements that banks keep their reserves as deposits with the Federal Reserve System, the supervision by the Federal Reserve System over day-to-day operations of banks, the clearing of checks by the System —these are all trimmings. You could strip them away and you would not destroy the Reserve System's power.

On the other hand, set up an alternate agency that can print the green paper stuff available for hand-to-hand currency or for vault cash by banks, and the power of the System is destroyed. In consequence, I really think that there is no justification for extending control to financial intermediaries.

CONTROLLING INTEREST ON DEPOSITS

What we want to do along these lines is to reduce the degree of control which the System exercises over commercial banks. The most obvious way in which the degree of control could be reduced is in minor respects. The present ceilings on interest rates and the present law that makes it illegal to pay interest on demand deposits could and should both be abolished. Their potential for harm has been demonstrated very clearly in recent months.

The prohibition of interest on demand deposits makes for a greater degree of instability in the relationship between demand deposits and time deposits than would otherwise prevail. When interest rates in general go up, the interest rate that commercial banks pay on time deposits tends to go up also, and this tends to increase time deposits in relation to demand deposits. If interest were paid on demand deposits, it could go up, too, and offset the rise in interest on time deposits. Because of the interest ceiling on time deposits, every now and then a still greater degree of instability is introduced into the banking situation because of the arbitrary movement in the fixed price.

In December, 1956, the price that banks could pay on time deposits was raised. There was a period, prior to that, of a very slow rise in commercial bank time deposits, and then a very rapid rise. In December, 1961, the rate of interest that could be paid by banks was raised again. There has been an extraordinarily rapid rise in time deposits since then, which has made it very difficult to read the monetary figures and to know what they are saying and what is going on.

This instability has nothing to do with the nature of the system. It is introduced entirely by arbitrary regulations of prices; and a very minor, but not negligible, reform would be obtained by either of two devices. The Reserve System could inaugurate one of these on its own. It could set the maximum that the commercial banks could pay on time deposits at 20 per cent; that would keep the regulation from being a source of difficulty. Or, preferably, Congress could pass a law repealing the provision that the banks may not pay interest on demand deposits and repealing any price fixing on time deposits. Either of these would be a minor reform, but worth while.

BANKING UNDER 100 PER CENT RESERVES

To go much further in reforming the institutional organization of the banking system, it would be necessary to go in the radical direction of eliminating controls over individual banks, in the direction of 100 per cent reserve banking. This move would tend to eliminate all control over the lending and investing activities of banks and would separate out the two functions of banking. On the one hand, we would have banks as depository institutions, safe-keeping money and arranging for the services of transferring liabilities by check. They would be 100 per cent reserve banks, pure depository institutions. Their assets would be government liabilities—either pieces of paper or deposits to the credit of the bank on the books of a reserve bank or its equivalent. I would favor the government's paying interest on those liabilities just as it now pays interest on its general government debts. Under a 100 per cent reserve bank, it would be desirable to do this in part because it would provide such banks with an appropriate source of income to enable them to compete on the right level with other banks for funds. Even if we did not go this far, it would be desirable, under present law, to have the government pay interest on its liabilities to commercial banks, namely, on commercial bank demand deposits with the reserve system.

If 100 per cent banking were established, our present banks would be sliced off into other branches operating like small-scale investment trusts. They would be lending and investment agencies in which private individuals would invest funds as they now do in investment trust and other firms, and these funds would be used to make loans. Such organizations could be completely exempt from the kind of detailed control over financial activities that banks now are subject to.

So much for the institutional organization of the private banking system, which I am skipping over very hastily because I want to turn to matters that perhaps are more important, namely, the monetary powers of the Federal Reserve System and the Treasury.

SUPERVISORY AND MONETARY POWERS

In addition to its monetary powers, the Federal Reserve System currently has supervisory and examination responsibilities with respect to member banks. In practice, the actual examination is done by an examiner employed by the Comptroller of Currency, by the FDIC or by a state banking commission, so that each bank is not in fact examined by the three agencies that technically have supervisory responsibilities. It seems to me that it would be desirable to go further along these lines. Even if nothing more is done now in the way of extensive reform, supervisory power should be concentrated in one of the other agencies, such as the FDIC, rather than in the Reserve System; and the Reserve System should be relieved of any technical supervisory responsibility and its role legally concentrated on exercising monetary powers.

The more important problem is these monetary powers of the Reserve System. As you know, they consist primarily of three items: (1) the power to change reserve requirements of member banks; (2) the power to rediscount for member banks; and (3) the power to engage in open-market operations.

Of these three powers, the first two are, I think, inefficient and poorly designed tools of monetary management. In making this judgment, I am assuming that our present system is in all respects unchanged, that the institutional organization of the banking system is what it is and that the criteria for controlling the stock of money are whatever they now are. My purpose in doing this is to separate issues: Whatever the criteria are, there remains the question whether present powers are efficient tools for achieving them.

What changes in the present powers of the System would make it more efficient? There seems to be a very strong case for streamlining these powers by eliminating the power of the System to change reserve requirements and to rediscount, and by requiring it to limit its activities to open-market operations. It really is not true that three tools are necessarily better than one, if they can go in opposite directions or if they get in one another's way. That is the case here. To change the metaphor, it is easier to juggle one ball than three.

SUGGESTED CHANGES IN PRESENT POWERS

The power to change reserve requirements is a poor tool because it is discontinuous. Changes in reserve requirements tend to be by one percentage point or half a percentage point. If they were by 1/100 of a percentage point it might not be so bad, but a change of 1 per cent in reserves is a very large change. In order to offset the effect, the Reserve System does two things at once. If it makes a one percentage point decrease in reserve requirements with the one hand, with the other hand it pulls out the reserves released; similarly, if it increases the required reserve ratio, it provides additional reserves by open-market operations. This is what it must do if it is going to smooth the effect of reserve requirement changes and prevent them from becoming a serious source of difficulty. But because it is hard to predict the effect of a reserve requirement change, the offset is never accurate and the whole operation becomes simply an unnecessary source of disturbance. Anything that can be done with reserve requirement changes can be done with open-market operations. Hence, the power to vary reserve requirements ought to be abolished.

So far as rediscounting is concerned, it no longer serves the function of providing a lender of last resort. It was introduced originally for the purpose of enabling banks to have an additional source of liquidity in time of need. That function is now performed indirectly by the FDIC, whose existence helps to prevent banks from getting into a position where there may be a run on them or, if there is a run on one bank, prevents that run from spreading to other banks.

As a tool of monetary management, rediscounting is unsatisfactory. It tends to lead the Reserve System to do things at times that it has no intention of doing. How tight a particular discount rate is depends on market conditions. Suppose market rates are falling, for whatever reason, as in late 1959, while the Federal Reserve rediscount rate is stable. The same rate then becomes tighter than it was before. The willingness of banks to borrow depends upon the relation between the discount rate and the market rate. If the market rate is high compared to the discount rate, banks have an incentive to borrow. If it is low, they have an incentive to get out of debt to the Reserve Banks, which is the situation now.

The fall of 1959 is a good example. The discount rate was held stable. Market rates moved from a level above the discount rate to below. I am oversimplifying, but the result was that Federal Reserve credit outstanding declined, but not because of any desire on the part of the System to make it decline. The stock of money fell, but not because of any explicit design on the part of the System to make it fall. The System did not deliberately intend to produce a decline in the stock of money from 1959 to 1960; this happened in spite of the System's behavior and, in that particular case, largely because the rediscount rate, being fixed, led to this result. I could give many other examples, but I think this one illustrates my point that the rediscount rate gets the System into trouble.

One way to prevent the discount rate from being a source of trouble would be to fix it at 20 per cent. That would solve the problem. As an alternative, the power of the System to engage in rediscounting could be abolished by law. That would leave available only open-market operations, which are by all odds the most effective way to control the stock of money.

With respect to open-market operations, I should add, however, that there are two agencies now operating. The Federal Reserve and the Treasury both engage in open-market operations.

ROLE OF TREASURY IN OPEN MARKET

The Treasury's operations illustrate the general principle that the problem is to keep people from making mistakes. The Treasury's debt operations could promote stability, but in fact they have been highly irregular and a source of uncertainty in the market. The best thing to do would be to eliminate that effect. Technically, the best way to do it would be to put all debt management in the hands of the Federal Reserve; it does not make any sense to have two independent agencies in debt management. There would, however, be great political objections to consolidating debt management in the Federal Reserve System.

An alternative that would be just about as good would be to have the Treasury Department adopt a policy that would be stable and predictable. One component of such a policy would be for it to sell no further securities except by auction. To do so it would have to alter the present system of auctioning, which cannot be used in this way for long-term bonds because it is a system in which people pay the price they bid. It is a discriminatory pricing system.

The Treasury ought to sell all securities by a method of auction under which all actual purchases are made at the same price. A second component of such a policy would be to reduce the sale of securities to only two kinds or at most a small number of securities, perhaps a very short-term bill and a long-term bond. A third component would be that it should offer them for sale at regular intervals and in stated amounts, so that the public would know six months or a year ahead of time that every week, say, there is going to be an auction for a specified amount of bills and every month for a specified amount of the longer bonds. Further manipulations of the amounts outstanding could be left to the Federal Reserve in connection with its policy for open-market operations.

These changes would provide a streamlined system in which, on the one hand, the Federal Reserve has a simple and efficient tool—open-market operations—and, on the other hand, the Treasury no longer messes up the monetary situation by its erratic debt issues—by its experiments first with one long-term bond and then another, first with advance refunding and then some other "gimmick."

CRITERIA FOR CONTROLLING THE STOCK OF MONEY

What should this streamlined machinery be used for? What should be the criteria for deciding how to change the stock of money? With an old professorial habit, I have let myself talk so long that all I can do on this subject is to make a few dogmatic remarks. I apologize for the dogmatism, but exigencies of the clock leave me no alternative.

As I see it, there are only three kinds of criteria for controlling the stock of money.

One is the kind of automatic criterion that is provided by a commodity standard, a gold standard in which we do not have discretionary management of the system but in which the amount of money in the system is determined entirely by external affairs.

I think such a system is neither desirable nor feasible in the United States today. It is not desirable because of the cost involved in getting people to dig up the gold in one part of the world in order to bury it in another part of the world. It is not feasible because we cannot do it on our own; it depends on the willingness of nations all over the world to engage in an international gold standard, and this, I believe, they are not willing to do. It also is not feasible because we are not willing at home to obey its discipline; we are not willing to subordinate domestic stability to the necessities of the external balance of payments.

I should qualify this last statement. Nobody will say he is willing to sacrifice domestic stability to the balance of payments, yet our present policy is one in which we are doing it. Precisely because we are not willing to face the issue clearly, I think we are doing in practice what nobody will say explicitly he is willing to do. Mr. Lerner will have more to say on that, I suspect, in his talk.

So I do not believe that a "real" gold standard is feasible or possible.

The second alternative is to have discretionary management of money on the part of a group of managers. I have gone at great lengths into our historical record to show the kinds of results discretionary management yields. I do not believe that we have learned so much more than our predecessors that it now is safe to trust these powerful tools in the hands of discretionary managers. The conclusion I have reached on the basis of both the past and recent records is that money is too important to be left to central bankers, if you will permit me to paraphrase Clemenceau.

I come to the conclusion that there is only one other alternative. That is to adopt some kind of rule which will guide our monetary managers, the Reserve System or anybody that controls the stock of money. Many economists have been in favor of the rule that the System be instructed to keep a price level stable. I myself think it is not a good rule. I think the relation between the stock of money and the price level, while close, is too loose, in short intervals and over short periods, for that rule to specify precisely what the Federal Reserve System or any other governmental authorities should do. It still leaves a dispersal of responsibility and the possibility of major mistakes being made.

STEADY RATE OF GROWTH DESIRABLE

So I am led to suggest as a rule the simple rule of a steady rate of growth in the stock of money: that the Reserve System be instructed to keep the stock of money growing at a fixed rate, $\frac{1}{3}$ of 1 per cent per month or $\frac{1}{12}$ of 1 per cent per week, or such and such a percentage per day. We instruct it that day after day and week after week it has one thing, and one thing only, to do and that is to keep the stock of money moving at a steady, predictable, defined rate in time.

This is not, under our present system, an easy thing to do. It involves a great many technical difficulties and there will be some deviations from it. If the other changes I suggested were made in the system, it would make the task easier; but even without those changes, it could be done under the present system. While this is by no means necessarily an ideal gadget, it seems, in looking at the record, that it would work pretty well. It would have worked far better, as far as I can see, over the last fifty years than what we actually had, and I think it would continue to work well in the future. I think we do not really know enough under present circumstances to do much better—and this has nothing to do with the particular people who are in control.

I do not believe anybody here, including myself, knows enough to do any better. Almost everyone is in favor of countercyclical monetary policy. However, when you ask each one what he means by that policy, you find that Mr. Jones's policy is anathema to Mr. Smith, and Mr. Smith's to Mr. Robinson. In point of fact, there is agreement only on the glittering generalities that the Reserve System should do the right thing in the right way at the right time. There is no agreement on how you know the right time and the right thing to do. The appearance of agreement dissolves, once you put it to the test. Thank you.

Selection 34

A PROGRAM FOR MONETARY STABILITY—PART II
ABBA P. LERNER

Dr. Abba Lerner presents a spirited rebuttal to Dr. Friedman's position, but elaborates his own explanation—again, shared by many influential economists—of the weakness of monetary policy in dealing with situations characterized by rising prices and substantial unemployment. Like Dr. Friedman, he proposes remedies that appear extreme; but, extreme or not, they warrant serious consideration by careful students, since they deal with some of the critical economic problems of our time.

I find myself 95 per cent in agreement with what Milton has said; in fact, I find myself 105 per cent in agreement with some of it. Unfortunately, this does not add up to 100 per cent agreement with everything he said. I like many of his suggestions for streamlining and improving the efficiency of the monetary control mechanism—I would even go a little further with some of them—and that is why I say I am 105 per cent in agreement. I do not, however, agree that, having improved and strengthened the mechanism, we should decide not to use it. I think we would then be able to do many things with it much better than we have done in the past.

What Friedman has shown is that if we set up a system for providing money in the last resort and it does not provide money in the last resort, we get into a mess. The moral, to my mind, is that we should have people running the system who will in fact provide the money in the last resort. Essentially, the difference between Friedman and me is one of temperament. I do not believe that we are quite incapable of getting intelligent and informed action. I am quite sure, although Friedman is modest about this, that if people like him had been in charge, many of the big mistakes would not have been made. With the better mechanism which Friedman has shown us we can have, we can really go about doing what we want to do, which is not merely to minimize cycles but to obtain a satisfactory level of employment and economic activity all the time.

I would like also to put a somewhat different emphasis on the importance or unimportance of money in the Keynesian revolution and in the so-called anti-Keynesian counterrevolution in economic thought.

In discussing the way in which thought has developed in the area, I am really leading up to something which is outside this question altogether. We may have a discretionary monetary and fiscal policy for maintaining economic stability, as I think we should have, or we may depend on nondiscretionary monetary policy following rigid rules, as suggested by Friedman, but we will

• From Abba P. Lerner, "A Program for Monetary Stability, Part II," *Proceedings of the 1962 Conference on Savings and Residential Financing,* 1962, pp. 34–47. Reprinted by permission of the United States Savings and Loan League and the author.

get into serious difficulties in either case. This is because we live in a society where the price mechanism does not work in the way in which we economists have been in the habit of assuming. In the real world, prices do not adjust themselves to supply and demand the way they do in theoretical economic systems of perfect competition.

Since the same problem remains, whether we have rules or whether we permit discretion in our policy for economic stability, much of our debate becomes somewhat beside the point. I will therefore try to go quickly through the trend in economic thought on inflation and depression.

Looking over my notes reminds me of the first lecture I gave at the London School of Economics when I first began teaching economics. I wrote my lecture out in full and then found that it lasted me the whole semester. I will try not to keep you as long as that.

THE DEVIL THEORY AND THE CRUDE THEORY

Much older than any kind of economics is the "devil theory" of inflation and depression, the theory that inflation is due to wicked profiteers and that depression is due to heartless capitalist employers. This semisocialist or sentimental approach says that to stop inflation we must pass laws against rising prices and punish the profiteers, and that to prevent depression we must get rid of the capitalists.

It was such a great advance on this, when economists connected inflation and depression with the quantity of money, that one should not be surprised at the development of an *overemphasis* on the quantity of money. I think Mr. Friedman provides the latest example of this.

The first economic theory of inflation and depression is what I call the "crude monetary theory." It attributes inflation to the creation of too much money, deflation to the creation of too little money, and depression to the rigidity of wages. This theory of depression is very natural for businessmen. Each businessman looks at his own experience and knows that if he were only able to lower his prices he would be able to sell much more and to employ many more people, and that that would cure the depression. However, he cannot reduce his prices because his costs are high. Since wages are the most important item in his costs, he declares that a cut in wages would solve the problem. If labor unions were not obstinate and the laborers were not stupid, they would agree to the wage cut and the depression would be cured!

It is the sad task of the economist to show that this argument is no good because it does not consider the economy as a whole. The economist has to point out that the businessman is forgetting that what he is proposing would also have to be done by his competitors, and that if their wages and their costs and their prices fall, too, the wage-cut cure does not work.

LESS-CRUDE AND KEYNESIAN THEORIES

When this is pointed out, what happens is not that the remedy is given up. What happens is that other reasons are dreamed up for keeping on proposing the same cure. The second or "not quite so crude monetary theory" recognizes that if everybody cuts wages and costs and prices, this changes the picture. However, it argues that the same income will still be able to buy more goods. A 5 per cent cut leading to a 5 per cent reduction in prices would enable people with the same income to purchase about 5 per cent more goods, and this would cure a 5 per cent depression.

Then the economist has to come along and earn his name as a practitioner of the dismal science by showing that this argument is no good either, because it cannot be assumed that incomes would remain the same. If we cut wages, costs and prices (and the profit margin between them), we also cut wage incomes (and profit incomes). Income goes down together with prices, so that we are just about where we were before.

We then get a third argument for the same remedy of cutting the wage. This argument is usually put forward as a criticism of Keynes, but a very large part of it is pure Keynesian theory. Notice that the first monetary argument proposed reducing money wages relative to prices. The second monetary argument proposed reducing money wages *and prices* relative to incomes. The third argument proposes reducing wages and prices *and incomes* relative to the money stock, as illustrated in the following Keynesian set of equations:

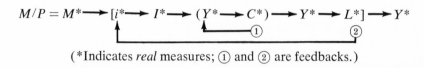

(*Indicates *real* measures; ① and ② are feedbacks.)

What this says is that to cure a depression we must increase M/P, the quantity of money in real terms (or money relative to prices). One way of doing that is to reduce P, or prices (by reducing wages and prices and incomes). We will then get an increase in the real quantity of money (M^*), people will find themselves more liquid, and this will result in a reduction in the rate of interest (i). The reduction in the rate of interest will result in more investment (I). Extra investment will result in people earning more income (Y), and people who earn more will spend more on consumption (C). We then get feedback (1): the expenditure on consumption (C) again creates more income (Y), this again creates more consumption, and so on, and we have a multiplier effect on income (Y). By this long series of steps the increase in the real quantity of money (M/P *or* M^*) results in an increase in income, in expenditures and in employment, and so cures the depression.

Now all this is Keynesian analysis. It is nothing but a summary of the monetary theory that takes up the greater part of Keynes's great book, *The General Theory of Employment Interest and Money*. This hardly fits in with the notion that Keynesian theory plays down the importance of money.

It is, however, unquestionable that there is a widespread impression that Keynes did say that money was unimportant. This impression is due to the fact that there was a depression in America at the time Keynes wrote and that American economists, while trying to listen to Keynes, were really thinking about the depression. The result was that they absorbed only the part that was immediately relevant to the severe depression going on in the United States.

SEVERE DEPRESSION A SPECIAL CASE

A severe depression is a special case, which Keynes does discuss, when the mechanism sketched above does not work. In a severe depression the difficulty is not that people cannot get hold of money but that investment does not look profitable. An increase in the quantity of money does not make the rate of interest go down, because it is already at the lowest point it can reach. This is called the liquidity trap. If the rate of interest does go down, we still do not get more investment. People are afraid they will lose money if they invest, and they are not eager to lose money if they can borrow it at 2 per cent instead of 4 per cent. This is called the collapse of confidence.

In such cases monetary policy, with which the greater part of Keynesian analysis is concerned, does not work and something else is needed to cure the depression. This is where fiscal policy comes in. Fiscal policy can cure depression by increasing expenditure and incomes *directly* instead of by way of an increase in the stock of money in real terms. The government can increase its own expenditure or it can reduce taxes, leaving more money for the taxpayers to spend.

KEYNESIAN VS. CLASSICAL APPROACH

The Keynesian general approach differs from the classical approach only in the method by which the ratio of money to prices (M/P) is increased. The classical approach calls for increasing the real value of the money stock by reducing the denominator P of the fraction M/P. If prices fall, the real value of the money stock increases (unless M decreases as much as P). The Keynesian approach stresses the difficulties and delays in waiting for P to fall enough. This takes too long. But we can achieve the same increase in M/P by increasing M, the *nominal* quantity of money, instead of waiting for P to fall. The rest of the process is exactly the same.

Incidentally, I want to point out that in this connection Friedman shows himself more Keynesian than classical because, in his rule, he calls for the required increase in the real quantity of money (M/P or M^*), not by waiting for prices to fall, but by increasing the quantity of nominal money. Like Keynes, he recognizes that to wait for the required fall in prices is not practical; that we do not have a system in which the market makes prices fall rapidly as soon as we have any depression, i.e., a level of employment that is less than satisfactory.

Where the process of curing the depression by increasing the real quantity of money does not work, either because a liquidity trap prevents the reduction in the rate of interest, or because a collapse of confidence prevents an increase in investment even if the rate of interest does fall, monetary policy does not work. Only fiscal policy works. This is the Keynesian special case.

There also is the opposite special case when, instead of a very low response of the rate of interest to the quantity of money or of investment to the rate of interest, there are very high responses of interest to money and of investment to interest. This is the classical special case when fiscal policy does not work. Only monetary policy works.

The Keynesian general theory includes both of these extremes and the whole range in between when both monetary and fiscal policy work and we can make use of whichever one seems more convenient. That, of course, involves a certain amount of discretion.

THE NEOCLASSICAL THEORY

I have gone through a series of monetary theories, from the very crude through the more refined up to the Keynesian general theory which reaches from the Keynesian special case to the classical special case. I want to mention one more, which I call neoclassical, usually put forward by people who call themselves anti-Keynesian.

These people bring up a fourth argument for the same cure for depression, namely, to let wages and prices fall. They say that Keynes is "all wet." Even in the Keynesian special case with the liquidity trap and the collapse of confidence, the authorities should still hold firm and wait for falling wages to bring the automatic cure. If only the authorities will let everybody know that they will not be bullied or bluffed into undertaking dangerous increases in the quantity of money, they say, wages and prices will have to fall. If wages and prices keep on falling, ultimately this will cure the situation. Even with the liquidity trap and the collapse of confidence, if prices fall enough, people are bound to buy more goods, thus curing the depression. If prices fall enough, everybody who has a dollar will become a millionaire, and before that happens he will decide to buy a yacht, as befits his new situation. Without going to such extreme cases, one can say that as prices keep on falling, the result is a *wealth effect* which bypasses even the Keynesian special case.

The wealth effect is most closely associated with Professor Pigou of Cambridge, England, and Professor Patinkin of Jerusalem, Israel. But they developed this theory not because they were thinking of any practical policy. They just wanted to round out an ideal abstract theoretical system, and I sympathize very much with them because I am prone to this kind of aesthetics myself.

The wealth effect does complete the picture. But one must be careful, as Pigou and Patinkin were careful, to point out that it is of no practical significance as an automatic cure for depression because it calls for a degree of price flexibility which does not exist and which could not possibly exist. Its aesthetic purpose is to show that there is no internal contradiction in the classical system of economics. If we had perfect flexibility of prices, full employment *would* be automatic and none of the problems we are talking about could arise. There are some careless expressions in Keynes where he says that depression does not depend on price inflexibility, but what he means is that it does not depend on such price inflexibilities as we could hope to remove.

ADMINISTERED DEPRESSION

Let me go on to discuss what I have called administered depression. This is one place where I think Keynes "missed the boat." He spoke about the prob-

lems arising because of the *downward stickiness* of wages and prices. It is because wages and prices do not fall quickly and easily enough to cure or prevent
depression that we have to increase the quantity of money instead of waiting for
wages and prices to fall.

Friedman recognizes this, too. In his rule he has the quantity of money
increasing only because of the downward stickiness of wages and prices.
But why are wages and prices sticky downward? What does this mean? I think
this is a much more serious matter than is recognized by either Keynes or
Friedman. It means that the market mechanism is not working. If the market
mechanism did work, anyone who was unemployed would offer to work for
less and instantaneously all those who are employed would have to offer to work
for still less if they did not want to lose their jobs to the unemployed. Wages
and prices would fall instantaneously, thus increasing M/P, the real stock of
money, setting in motion the Keynesian, and if necessary the neo-classical,
process for restoring or maintaining full employment.

STICKINESS IN WAGES AND PRICES

The downward stickiness of wages and prices means that it is not *the
market* which is determining wages and prices but some *people*, or organizations
of people in *institutions*, who have the power to tell wages and prices to dis-
obey the market. If there is an excess of supply, the market says that the price
should fall. But monopolies, trade unions, cartels, government controls or other
institutions say, "No, prices should not fall," and wages and prices obey them
and do not fall.

Once it is recognized that the downward stickiness of prices is something
about people and organizations who make these decisions and give these orders,
and not about prices (which cannot really make decisions themselves), the
greater seriousness of the situation becomes apparent. The same people who can
stop prices from falling when the market says they should fall, can make the
prices rise when the market says they should remain steady or should fall.

And this is exactly our situation. There is a continuing pressure for wages
and prices to go up. Even at less than full employment, i.e., if there is more
than the 2 per cent unemployment that is needed for the efficient operation of
the economy, the upward pressure on wages and prices regularly causes inflation.

What can be done to stop this kind of inflation? One way is to introduce enough depression to cause some prices—those which are governed by
the market—to go down enough to offset the increase in those prices which
are being pushed up, so that the general or average price level will stay where
it is. This is the nature of the administered depression which we are now
enjoying.

FROM KEYNES TO ADAM SMITH

Our situation can be described in the following way: Keynes has been
victorious. The monetary and fiscal authorities all have a copy of Keynes's

General Theory hidden away in the closet because they are all officially anti-Keynesian. When there is a depression, they secretly go to their closets and look up their Keynes. It says there that if we have unemployment, what they must do is to increase the quantity of money or decrease taxes or increase government spending. They do this faithfully in an attempt to diminish the unemployment. Many of them do it with very bad consciences because they feel it is wicked. On the other hand, they want to be re-elected and they do not like to have a depression; so they take this action and, sure enough, it does have the effect of decreasing the unemployment.

But what happens then is that prices go up. There is no longer sufficient depression to cancel the upward pressure on prices, and there are bitter outcries of inflation. So the authorities go back to the closet, pull out Keynes again, and read that if we have rising prices, what they must do is to increase taxes, reduce government spending and make money tighter. This will check the inflation. So they do that, and the inflation is indeed checked.

But then again there are complaints about an increase in unemployment. After several such ups and downs, the authorities lose patience with Keynes and say: "The hell with Keynes! Let's go back to Adam Smith."

I think this is part of the reason for the growing concern in the last year or two about the national debt, and for the recent ingenious attempts by several economists to appear to support the belief of the man in the street that the national debt is a burden on our grandchildren. (This is done by giving the terms "burden" and "generation" unusual meanings so that while not saying anything that is *really* incorrect, they appear to the man in the street, who misses the redefinitions, to be supporting his superstitions.)

COST OF ADMINISTERED DEPRESSION

It seems to me that we need something like 6 per cent or 7 per cent unemployment in order to maintain price stability, and this is about what we have been getting. At the present moment we have a little less than 6 per cent or 7 per cent unemployment and we are suffering from pressures to raise prices, such as the recent business about steel. This average level of unemployment—about 7 per cent—would come about automatically if we followed a rule like Friedman's for keeping the amount of money increasing at a constant rate. If Friedman's rule kept the money stock increasing at a constant rate, and there was less than 7 per cent unemployment (I hesitate to use the number "seven" because it looks like a very special or magic number; perhaps it is 6¾ per cent and may vary from time to time), prices would rise and the real volume of money would not increase as much or would actually decrease. Unemployment would then increase until it reached that equilibrium level (about 7 per cent) which keeps the price level stable. If there was more than 7 per cent unemployment, prices would fall and the real value of the money stock would increase by more than the 3 per cent or 4 per cent automatic increase in nominal money supply, so that unemployment would fall to the 7 per cent equilibrium level of unemployment which keeps the price level stable.

Exactly the same thing would happen with a discretionary monetary and fiscal policy that concentrated on stabilizing the price level. Whenever there was more than 7 per cent unemployment, prices would fall. The authorities would then undertake expansionary policies. Whenever there was less than 7 per cent unemployment, prices would rise. The authorities would then undertake restrictionary policies, bringing unemployment up again to the 7 per cent price stability level.

Friedman's rule and discretionary price stabilization both would give the same average general result—administered depression on the average at the level that stabilizes prices. The difference between the two different stabilization methods becomes secondary, because that is only a question of whether one or the other would give greater fluctuations around the average 7 per cent unemployment level—a far less important matter than the average level of depression which would automatically be established by either of these policies.

Now, what do we do about it? Here, I come to the second half of the semester.

AUTOMATIC PRICE MECHANISM UNRELIABLE

A recognition of the nature of the situation, if my analysis is sound, means that we do not and cannot depend on the automatic price mechanism as it now works to achieve both of the objectives we are interested in, namely, a satisfactory level of employment *and* price stability. The reason for this is that the market is not working in important parts of the economy. Prices do not fall whenever there is an excess of supply or of potential supply over demand. They rise unless there is a certain minimum of depression. This level of depression is what is achieved and maintained if we concentrate monetary and fiscal policy on the maintenance of price stability.

We could, instead, have a policy directed at the maintenance of full employment (i.e., with something like the 2 per cent unemployment which is sufficient for the economy to operate efficiently and which would consist of relatively painless short rests between jobs). But this would result in rising prices in an inflation that might become cumulative if it continued for some time. Thus, as long as we limit ourselves to the automatic price mechanism as it now works, we are faced with a choice between the two objectives. We can have either price stability or full employment, but not both. We also can choose some intermediate position, with some inflation and with less than 7 per cent unemployment, remembering that the smaller the unemployment rate below the 7 per cent, the more rapidly will prices rise. The question, then, is what to do in such a case.

TRADING INFLATION AGAINST DEPRESSION

An economist tends to say that we should equalize the marginal disutilities. We should trade inflation against depression at the margin until we have just so much inflation that a little more depression would be worse than the little bit of extra inflation it would displace, and a little more inflation would be worse than the little bit of extra depression it would prevent. At that point the marginal disutilities of the two are just equal, and we will have minimized the total amount of damage from both inflation and depression.

In making a calculation of that kind, we must compare the quantities of harm done by the incremental, marginal, extra bits of inflation and depression that are the alternatives between which we can choose. If we try to make a rough calculation of this kind, it appears that inflation is much less damaging than depression, for equal per cent rates. A 5 per cent inflation has the effect of redistributing considerably less than 5 per cent of the national output from creditors to debtors (including in "creditors" all receivers of relatively fixed incomes and including in "debtors" all whose incomes rise more than the prices of what they buy). The redistribution would amount to 5 per cent only if the economy were strictly divided into pure debtors and pure creditors. But this is not the case. Most people are on both sides of this account, and a large part of the redistribution cancels out. Although the redistribution is an ethically unwarranted one, some of it may even be desirable; i.e., it will be from people we do not like, to people we do like. But a significant part of the redistribution will hurt people we think ought not to be hurt.

It would be possible to compensate all the people that on balance would be hurt by a 5 per cent inflation if we allocated not more than 2 per cent of the national income for this purpose, and this 2 per cent would not be an absolute loss but only a redistribution (by taxation and compensatory payments) from those who have gained to those who have lost by the inflation. Such a redistribution is a nuisance, but it is certainly not more so than a 1 per cent loss of national income would be. Comparing this with the 5 per cent absolute loss which comes from a 5 per cent depression, a 5 per cent inflation certainly looks like a much smaller evil. One would therefore think it rational to choose more inflation than more depression, at least up to some point where inflation became cumulative and the alternative to each 1 per cent of depression was at least five percentage points of inflation.

If my figures are good guesses, we could have either no inflation with 7 per cent unemployment, or full employment with 5 per cent inflation, at least to begin with. Depression begins only with more than 2 per cent unemployment, but on the other hand each 1 per cent of extra unemployment cuts national output by about 2 per cent. So our choice is between 10 per cent depression $[2 \times (7 - 2)]$ and 5 per cent inflation. It would therefore seem rational to choose full employment (i.e., 2 per cent unemployment) with 5 per cent inflation or at most, say, 2 per cent depression (i.e., 3 per cent unemployment) with 4 per cent inflation.

THE PRICE OF ZERO INFLATION

This is not what we are in fact doing. What we are doing is buying zero inflation by paying all the depression that is necessary for this, namely, 7 per cent unemployment, which means a 10 per cent depression—a loss of potential output of about 10 per cent of national income, or about $50 billion worth of depression!

This is nicely illustrated by the President's annoyance at the recent attempt to raise the price of steel. He thought he had bought price stability at the bargain price of only 5 per cent or 6 per cent unemployment—i.e., only 3 per cent or 4 per cent of the national income, a mere $30 billion or $40 billion —and nothing annoys a politician more than someone who does not stay bought.

The choice of price stability at even this bargain price does not seem to me to be wise; but that is a matter of judgment or taste, and I cannot be dogmatic about the choice. It is probable that the actuality of depression bothers only the minority who suffer severely from it, while the thought of inflation bothers more voters, and our government recognizes and responds to this. But could we not avoid the necessity for the choice by modifying the way the automatic price mechanism now works so as to eliminate or reduce the upward pressure of prices at less than full employment?

There are those who say we are rich enough to pay the 7 per cent unemployment or 10 per cent depression for price stability. We are still very well off. Why bother to get involved in dangerous and new-fangled devices which involve some kind of price regulation and wage regulation? We can afford the price. We can even compensate the unemployed more generously and still come out very well.

If I were to think only of what goes on in the United States, I might agree with a proposal of this kind, like that of Galbraith. It really is not very important to raise the average standard of living in the United States. I do not think we can produce much more without people finding more ways of wasting money. As it is, we have to spend about $10 billion yearly to persuade people to buy some $100 billion worth of things they do not need. But we cannot think about the United States alone.

We have great obligations abroad, not only for defense but for the development of the rest of the world. No future can be secure, even if we should escape nuclear annihilation, with the world divided into very rich countries and very poor countries, especially if the rich countries are mostly white and the poor countries are mostly colored. The problem takes on a racial complexion, justified or not, which we cannot afford. We have to do something to cure the cruel poverty of two-thirds of the world. The remedy requires a great deal of money—but only a fraction of the $50 billion worth of stuff which we could produce but which we do not produce each year because we are feeding it to the depression that keeps inflation at bay—and its appetite is increasing more rapidly than our growing economy.

REMEDY: NEW TYPE OF PRICE
AND WAGE REGULATION

Now, I have asked several times what we can do to avoid the choice between depression and inflation without giving the answer. That is because

I am a little shy. The answer is very unpalatable because it means some kind of wage and price regulation which I think the people of this country are not ready to undertake. This is largely due to a verbal confusion. There is a powerful tendency to identify wage and price regulation with price control, and price control is a terrifying term. I am myself a violent opponent of price control, and I was able to use this terror some years ago when I was an economic adviser to the government of Israel. While everybody was debating whether wages should be increased by 10 per cent or 15 per cent, I proposed that they be cut by 25 per cent. I was able to survive this outrageous proposal because I pointed out to my opponents that the alternative was price control. This term made them pale. They were mostly politicians, and they knew their constituents were violently against price control. They would not even use the term in Israel. They called it "under the counter" and "queuing up" and other expressions descriptive of what happens when there is price control.

But this is a confusion which in time may be clarified, because the kind of regulation which is needed is the *direct opposite* of price control. What we need is a regulation which would prevent prices (including wages) from being raised only in situations where they could not be raised if there were competition, and which would force prices down only in situations where they would have been forced down by competitive market forces. In short, the regulation would make prices behave the way they would if they were governed by competitive markets and not by *price administrators*—by monopolies, cartels, trade unions or indeed government price controllers. "You cannot raise the price of steel," the regulation would say, "unless there is a shortage of steel, and you cannot claim that there is a shortage of steel if you are working at less than 80 per cent of capacity; and you must reduce the price of steel if you are working at less than say 60 per cent of capacity."

HOW REGULATION WOULD WORK

Price control tries to keep the price of a commodity down when the price should go up because there is not enough of it to go around at the low price. It is when the price is held low so that there is not enough to go around that we naturally get black markets, "under the counter" transactions and all the evils of price control. Regulation would stop the price administrators from raising prices only when there *is* enough to go around at the lower price so that the *market* would not have told the price to rise; and it would force prices down only when there is much more than enough to go around at the current price.

In the case of wages, the regulation would be slightly different. It would have wages in general rising at a constant, regular rate, following a rule which is remarkably similar to Friedman's rule for controlling the quantity of money, namely, that wages in general must rise by $\frac{1}{4}$ of 1 per cent per month or 3 per cent per annum. This is necessary for price stability, given that degree of increasing productivity. But in an industry or area where labor is much scarcer than in general, wages would have to rise more; and in industries or areas where the opposite is the case, where there is an excess supply of labor much greater than in the economy as a whole, wages should not rise as fast or even should not rise at all.

Coming back to steel, many people are disturbed—I would say confused—about the President's action. They say it was probably a good thing to stop the price increase in steel. It would have led to wage increases and other price increases and inflation. But it was a bad thing for the President to have mobilized so many parts of the whole executive branch to threaten, bully and intimidate the companies into a withdrawal of the price increase. At the same time, they are violently against regulation.

That leaves them in an untenable position. They say that the end was good, that the means were bad because arbitrary, yet they are *against* the use of means that are not arbitrary because that is regulation, which they identify with the hated price control. But the only alternative to arbitrary or discretionary acts of the President and the Attorney General is to apply rules like those I have just described, which set out when prices and wages may rise and when they must fall, in those cases where this is not determined by competitive markets. If the natural market does not work, we need an artificial market which will make prices do the same thing. That is the regulation that would make it possible to have full employment without inflation.

Regulation is not going to be activated for some time. It is very unpopular. But it leads me to a suggestion for a policy which perhaps is slightly Machiavellian. As long as we do not have the regulation and must choose some combination of depression and inflation, we should lean a little toward the inflation side because it seems pretty clear that inflation arouses much more political passion than does depression. Such a policy, while very close to minimizing the combined damage from inflation and depression, might build up the political pressure necessary to establish the regulation of prices and wages that would make possible a policy for maintaining both full employment and price stability.

If this were to happen, then we ought to have the debate between Friedman and me all over again, because then the issue between discretionary monetary and fiscal policy, on the one hand, and nondiscretionary monetary policy by fixed rules, on the other hand, would not be overshadowed by the more important problem of administered depression.

Selection 35

REFLECTIONS ON CENTRAL BANKING

PAUL A. SAMUELSON

> *This selection is based on the testimony in 1962 by Dr. Paul A. Samuelson before the Canadian Royal Commission on Banking and Finance; this selection is a fragment of his testimony. Dr. Samuelson, among the most distinguished of American economists, presents a third view of the art of central banking, with special emphasis on the potential and the limitations in the use of monetary controls to achieve stable economic growth. His views lie between the ex-*

tremes presented in the two previous selections, and probably rep-
resent quite closely the prevailing opinions of a majority of
American economists. Testimony of several other experts was pub-
lished in the Essays in International Finance series, published by the
International Finance Section, Department of Economics, Princeton
University. Essays published in that series include those of the late
Sir Dennis Robertson, Marius W. Holtrop, Harry G. Johnson, and
Jacob Viner. All merit careful reading.

Professor Samuelson points out that those who prefer "rules versus
men" or "automaticity versus discretionary action" must believe that
at least the men who formulated the rules or established the auto-
matic system were wise, and then analyzes the nature of discre-
tionary management of monetary policy as a complex process in
which both the channels through which an increase in the money
supply is effected and the amount of such increase are important.
If "money will not manage itself," and if the formulation of rules
itself involves discretion, the alternative seems to Professor Samuel-
son to be to "get the best guidance possible from experience itself"
and to formulate stabilization policy so as to "vary with the prob-
ability pattern of the system to be stabilized." In this process both
the goals and the methods of central banking will inevitably change,
in a historical process of development of economic institutions.

Contrary to the opinions of many contemporary economists (and to some of my own earlier views), I believe that monetary and credit policies have great potency to stimulate, stabilize, or depress a modern economy. This belief is based on my evaluation of the tremendous amount of empirical data given by (1) history, (2) current statistics, and (3) case studies of business behavior. These data are diverse, conflicting, and often inconclusive, and therefore have to be interpreted with the help of all the tools of economic analysis inherited from the past and developed by the present generation of scholars.

In thus differing from the pessimists, I want to make clear that I am *not* agreeing with that much smaller group of older economists who think that monetary policy by itself is the sole or principal mechanism for controlling the aggregative behavior of a modern economy. I believe such a view to be factually wrong or irrelevant; and would add that, even if monetary policies truly had this exaggerated degree of potency, I would not deem it optimal social policy to rely exclusively or primarily upon that weapon alone.

Today all experts dismiss the ancient view that *laissez-faire* can properly hold in the field of money and banking. "Money will not manage itself." Banking institutions are not perfectly-competitive self-regulating enterprises that can be free from strict governmental regulations and controls. They are "public utilities vested with public interest" and the same is true in equal or lesser degree of various financial intermediaries, such as savings institutions, finance companies, and insurance concerns. Let me make clear that all this is stated from the standpoint of one who philosophically values individual freedoms. A person

• From Paul A. Samuelson, "Reflections on Central Banking," *The National Banking Review,* September, 1963, pp. 15–28, The Comptroller of the Currency, United States Treasury. Reprinted by permission of the office of the Comptroller of the Currency and the author.

who cheerfully accepts the idea of direct price, wage, and production controls can afford to give a relatively large measure of freedom to credit institutions; but one who wishes to minimize (except in emergency periods) the use of such direct controls will realize that we maximize total freedom in a society by limiting it in the areas which crucially determine the aggregate of effective demand.

I must firmly disassociate myself from the small but important group of writers who, agreeing that money will not run itself, go on to argue that it ought to be determined permanently by certain automatic formulas. Sometimes this is put in the fancy language of "rules versus authorities," or "laws versus men," or "automaticity versus discretionary action." Of course, no one, myself included, will admit to favoring arbitrary caprice of bungling rulers over the even-handed justice of well-formulated rules. If every form of explicit cooperative action set up by men is bound to be completely nearsighted, venal, and blundering, then recourse to astrological rules might pragmatically be defended —although no wise man could have any secure belief that such bungling human beings would ever bind themselves and stay bound to such arbitrary mechanisms. The vicissitudes of ancient coin standards—which were at the mercy of the accidental discovery of precious metals in Latin America, Australia, California, Alaska, South Africa, and now Soviet Russia—would certainly be preferable to some forms of "managed money."

In practice, however, there have always been—for both good and evil— substantial departures from any automatic coin, bullion or other kind of gold standard. In principle, the choice has never been between discretionary and non-discretionary action: for when men set up a definitive mechanism which is to run forever afterward by itself, that involves a single act of discretion which transcends, in both its arrogance and its capacity for potential harm, any repeated acts of foolish discretion that can be imagined. Since I have argued elsewhere the philosophical principles involved in this choice and have never seen any written refutation of these arguments by adherents of the "automaticity" school, I shall merely state here that the relevant choices have to be made pragmatically in terms of the goodness or badness of behavior patterns that result from various kinds of discretionary action.

Specifically, consider the suggestion of a money supply which is to grow at exactly 3 per cent per year, a policy advocated by some who think no other actions would then be required. Suppose this had been enacted in the United States in a random recent year, without knowledge of the balance-of-payments problems just ahead, and without knowledge of the massive shift to time deposits such as we have been experiencing as a result of both raised interest-rate ceilings on such deposits and the natural shift to such deposits as interest rates generally rise. The results could have been quite bad in comparison with what actually happened; and if the balance-of-payments situation had, for unpredictable reasons, been a great deal worse, the results could have been disastrous. I realize the adherents of such proposals will argue that such dire results might have been avoided if there had been floating exchange rates, perfectly flexible wage rates, and never, never any interest-rate or other ceilings. But since we do not and shall not live in such a never-never land, legislating part of the package would surely do more harm than good.

I. THE QUANTITY THEORY AND MONETARY POLICY

There are many reasons why any automatic gadget can be improved upon by decision-makers, even by fallible decision makers. This statement will be denied by those who are firm believers in the ancient quantity theory of money. If it were true *in a causal sense* that there is an invariant relationship between, on the one hand, total dollar income and spending, and on the other, the supply of money defined in such a way as to be capable of predetermination by the central bank, then an autogyro which kept total money supply growing smoothly would, by hypothesis, keep total money income growing smoothly. While I know that some modern scholars have tried by historical studies to establish an empirical concomitance between money supply and aggregate income, let me simply state here that I find the implied proof of a simple, controllable, causal proportionality relationship unconvincing.

It is the easiest sport in the world to shoot down any crude formulation of the quantity theory. But I think it quite illegitimate to conclude from this what the Radcliffe Committee and many modern scholars have stated: namely, if total money supply, M, does not invariably create an exactly proportional total income and product because the income velocity of circulation of money, V, is not a constant—it follows that we should turn our attention away from conventional central bank controls and rely instead upon some global concept of "liquidity." As will become evident, I attach considerable importance to various concepts of liquidity.

But I think it wrong to believe that recognizing such concepts should undermine the belief that conventional central bank operations of open-market purchase and sale of securities, discount lending, and reserve-ratio changing are likely to have important effects upon the total of investment and consumption spending. Emphasizing "liquidity" quite properly serves to debunk a crude quantity theory, and it thereby scores a fatal point against advocates of simple automaticity gadgets. But it leaves the position I am here expounding unscathed, and it is for this reason that a number of reviewers have criticized the Radcliffe Report.[1]

Because of the human temptation to deify any concept that has been defined and to tend to regard, as approximately constant, the last variable that one has defined, I do not find the velocity variable, V, a very useful one. But older economists did, and some younger ones are beginning to again. So I shall restate the heart of the matter in such terms.

If the requisite V were a strict constant, $P \times Q$ would, by hypothesis, be exactly proportional to the requisite definition of money, M. Experience shows that V is not a constant: it shows certain historical trends in the long run; in

---

[1] See John Gurley, "The Radcliffe Report and Evidence," *American Economic Review* (September, 1960).

the course of the business cycle itself, rising in good times and falling in bad. After more studies have been made, I believe V will also show certain fluctuations with interest rate and other conditions, tending, other things equal, to rise when interest rates are high and the opportunity cost of cash balances is great, and tending to fall when short term investment opportunities all have a very low yield.

The behavior of V will also be quite sensitively affected by the particular concept of the money supply that is adopted, being quite different if currency alone is considered (as with the nineteenth-century Currency School and Edwin Cannan in the 1920's) than if demand deposits are included and various categories of time deposits and close money substitutes are, or are not, included in the definition of money. Some of the movements of V will be erratic and relatively unpredictable; others will be in some measure predictable. In particular, although they are operationally hard to identify in the empirical record, certain changes can always be expected in V that are themselves induced by the change in M itself and, certain other things being held constant, are part and parcel of such a change in M. Some sensible probability statements can be made about these induced changes in V at various phases of the business cycle and at various time points in history.

Now, if it were the case that recognition of the importance of money substitutes and various concepts of liquidity were to imply that changes of M in one direction could be expected to be followed systematically by opposite changes in V just large enough to offset any resulting induced changes in $MV = PQ$, then the casual reader of the Radcliffe Report would be right in thinking that central banks are unable to affect significantly aggregate spending by conventional open-market and lending operations. But none of the testimony or arguments in connection with the Radcliffe Committee succeed, in my judgment, in establishing a presumption in favor of this doctrine of induced-velocity-changes-that-just-offset-money changes.

Not only is this not demonstrated in the historical record, but, in addition, such a finding is not in accordance with that type of analysis which is thought to have displaced the old quantity theory. For, in the various Keynesian models, there is generally a presumption that an increase in M engineered by the central bank will cause such a reduction in interest rates and such increases in credit availability as to generate an increase in investment and total spending just large enough to create an extra level of income which would absorb in transaction balances the new increment of money created. While the mechanism just described holds for the most primitive Keynesian model, the same conclusion is found to be valid for more sophisticated models, which pay explicit attention to wealth and other stock effects and which distinguish a long chain of assets that range from being very near to money (like short-term government bonds) to being very illiquid and difficult to sell or evaluate (like built-in machinery that is highly specific to a particular location and owner). And the qualitative nature of the conclusion—that the central bank can expand spending by expansive open-market, lending, and reserve-ratio fixing operations—will still hold, even after we have admitted the existence of relatively-less-controlled financial intermediaries such as savings banks, finance companies, insurance companies, mutual or unit-trust funds, and various forms of equity and loan participants.

With his permission, I will refer briefly to an interesting demonstration by Professor James Tobin of Yale in an unpublished manuscript [2] privately circulated several years ago. Suppose that we have a chain of substitutes, which instead of being called tea, coffee and cocoa are called bank money, short-term bonds, long-term bonds, insurance assets, and so forth; call them M_1, M_2,—and suppose that their respective prices are N_1, N_2, . . . If the central bank could decrease all of the M totals together by operations and fiats that apply to insurance companies as well as to banks and to all financial intermediaries, then no one doubts that the total of "liquidity," however measured, would go down and that this would, other things equal, tend to have a depressing effect on aggregate spending and general inflationary pressures. Specifically, with every M_1 decreasing because of direct central bank action, the unweighted or weighted sum of the M's and every other recommended measure of "liquidity" would also go down. But now suppose that the central bank can only decrease directly M_1, having no direct controls on the reserve-ratios or totals of any other sectoral M_1. A reader of the whole of the Radcliffe Report and Hearings might be forgiven for inferring that in this case nothing positive could be said about the ability of the central bank to affect total liquidity, as measured by some kind of total of the M's or weighted-sum of the M's or other measure of liquidity; and hence, that we should abandon the simple notion that a modern central bank can by its conventional operations push aggregate spending in a desired direction. Tobin, however, in his unpublished memo, has shown that, provided the M's are all *substitutes* (in the sense that the excess demand for each M_1 decreases when its own N_1 price rises but increases when some other M_j's N_j goes up—as, for example, that an isolated increase in the price of short-term bonds should cause less of them to be demanded and more of long-term bonds to be substituted for them), then the central bank can cause *every* M_1 to go down by simply depressing M_1! . . . This important Tobin result accords well with intuition. One should not push it beyond its actual statement: each indirect effect is, generally speaking, weaker than each direct effect, *and* the central bank may have to push undesirably harder on M_1 to get the same change in over-all M's than it would have to do if it were given direct powers to affect financial intermediaries.[3] Later I shall have to point out some important limiting cases where the potency of central bank action becomes quantitatively zero or almost zero.

It has often been said that monetary policy is more effective in contracting an economy than in getting it to expand. There is an important grain of truth in this observation. Thus, when the bank rate or the discount rate is 6 or 7 per cent, and the commercial banks' excess reserves are at a minimum and the

[2] Cowles Commission Study Paper #63.

[3] This corresponds to a theorem that, in appropriate units, $\partial N_i/\partial M_i > \partial N_j/\partial M_i > 0$ for certain systems of Leontief, Metzler, and Mosak-Hicks type, as has been recognized by diverse writers, such as Hicks, H. Johnson, Morishima, and others. It does not deny that in certain limiting cases of perfect substitution these effects will be equal, or that in certain limiting cases one or both may be zero.

business community is heavily dependent upon bank borrowings for its current investments in inventories and other items, then further restrictive action by the central bank can, by a variety of channels, cut deeply into the aggregate of investment and total spending.

On the other hand, in a period like the 1930's, when the market yield on short-term government securities has already been driven down to a fraction of one per cent, and when banks have copious excess reserves and business firms are regretting their past investing and regarding the marginal profitability rate on all further investments as negative, there would be little potency indeed in conventional central bank operations. (Buying short-term bonds in the open market would then merely take from the community a very close money substitute and replace it by money itself.) This would not have much further depressing influence on the interest rate structure and would not make credit more readily available to borrowers (who are in any case virtually non-existent and automatically regarded as suspiciously risky chaps, if they should come forward with a loan application).

From the technical fact that monetary policy works more effectively at high than low rates, no one should make the mistake of concluding that the goal of policy should be to avoid low rates. Forks must be made to fit fingers, not fingers, forks: when an economy will suffer from tight markets and the technician will benefit, it is of course the technician who must properly give way.

This last case then is one where an induced change in velocity can be expected to wipe out almost completely any contrived change in money narrowly defined. It is the case often referred to as the Depression-Keynes model, where (1) there is a liquidity trap near to a zero rate of pure interest, at which the Keynesian liquidity preference schedule is practically infinite in elasticity so that the system will absorb great amounts of M at practically the same interest rate and credit-availability; and/or where (2) the rate of investment spending is almost completely inelastic with respect to changes in the interest cost and availability of credit.

I believe, in the face of some doubters, that such a depression model has occasional empirical validity—certainly in the short run and possibly for a vexingly long time. Moreover, bitter experience in the United States of the last few years leads one to suspect that it is not always so easy to engineer a deepening of capital by conventional central bank operations, even when one is not in a deep-depression liquidity trap: for, even when gilt-edge rates are lowered farther and farther, the effective profit rates that businessmen must anticipate to get them to make somewhat risky investments may remain quite high—say 15 per cent before corporate taxes or 8 per cent after taxes. Thus, even massive open-market purchase of government bonds may not be able to push the system down through a high-profit floor that acts rather like the older Keynes liquidity trap interest floor in keeping investment resistant to expansion.

I know it can be argued that the central bank, provided it is ready to abandon notions of feasibility and force the market rates of interest up to 40 per cent in boom times and down to zero or, for that matter, down to negative rates of interest, can control the amount of total money and spending activity to any desired levels, regardless of adverse fiscal policies and adverse behavior propensities on the part of business and the public. Personally, I consider it irrelevant to talk about 40 per cent bank rates, and in any case undesirable to put the burden of such extreme adjustments on the narrow sectors most affected by monetary actions. And as far as forcing extremely low interest rates is concerned, it is simply not true that lending money to people at negative interest rates is guaranteed to result in any desired expansion in spending: making gifts might, but if these are loans that have to be paid back, it would be rational for people to borrow at negative interest rates and just hold the proceeds in safety lock boxes, thereby earning a handsome yield. The total of something called M might rise, but that does not mean that the requisite MV can be achieved in any short period by *conventional* central bank operations.

My purpose here is not to score a point against some extreme quantity theory formulation, but to call attention to the fact that in many social situations a well-running democracy will want its central bank to engage in *unconventional* activities. (Examples: in the 1930's Federal Reserve Banks made loans directly to certain small businesses: in a future balance of payments crisis, the central bank might want to provide certain guarantees and investment insurance to desired domestic investments, while keeping up the yields on short-term government bills; and the day could come when the central bank would want to make loans at negative interest rates to applicants who satisfied certain requirements, such as a guaranteeing that the proceeds would go into resource-using investment; if *laissez-faire* conditions should prove to choke off deepening of capital when profits rates are still as high as 10 per cent and conventional credit operations proved not able to overcome this, the intrinsic logic of central banking requires recourse to new unconventional programs.)

Finally, I once felt it necessary to point out a minor flaw in certain descriptions of the asymmetry of monetary policy's potency. It is not correct to say that monetary policy can contract an economy more easily than it can expand it. In buoyant times when interest rates are already high and credit already tight, monetary policy is quite potent enough to *both* expand and contract the system from its previous situation; in slack times when interest rates are near the floor and the system is swimming in liquidity, monetary policy is quite impotent with respect to contraction and expansion of the system from its previous level. Thus, the true symmetry is not that depicted by a corner in the schedule relating general activity and central bank activity, with the slope for an up movement being greatly different from the slope for a down movement; the asymmetry merely refers to the putative difference in slope at any given point in a slack as against a tight credit market.

Central bankers abhor a situation which they feel is not closely responsive to their control. So they naturally dislike being so expansive as to create a "sloppy market." As shown above, the consequences of this abhorrence may not be too costly in the short run; yet they should often brave the displeasure of commercial bankers (who abhor sloppy markets for the good commercial reason that such markets are hard on bank earnings) and flood the market with a view to the longer-run stimulus in investment that may come from gradual penetration of alleged liquidity-trap floors. One has no right to assume away such longer-run benefits from a policy of "over-ease." The central banker will tend to feel that the cost of such a policy will be the danger that in the subsequent recovery period the redundant credit, which had previously done no harm and precious little good, will come to life and create the possibility of an over-fast expansion and of undue inflationary pressures. This is just another aspect of his reluctance to let the money market get out of his immediate control.

While recognizing some merit in this view, I would point out that the goal of policy is not to minimize the unease of central bankers; they are supposed to suffer psychic pain when that is in a good cause. Moreover, some quickening in their contractionary actions early in the recovery may serve to undo much of the harm to be expected from an earlier policy of over-ease, and such a quickening would in many cases be a worthwhile price to pay for improving the slump situation. What I am saying here would not be so important if the only thing to fear were a regular cycle involving a recession known to be short-lived. But when an economy moves into an epoch when profit rates are sluggish (having been competed down by the plentifulness of capital stock relative to labor, and the nature and speed of contemporaneous technical change) and investment is hard to coax out at still lower profit rates, the best policy for conventional central banking operations is to keep the money market flooded with reserves, with a view to eroding gradually resistant long-term interest rates and the profit-rate floors that businessmen insist upon getting, if they are to make resources-employing investments. Specifically, in the United States environment of the 1930's, it was right to have great excess reserves and minimal short-term rates: the slow, too-slow, drop in long-term interest rates was thereby encouraged. With due regard to future international payments considerations, the same strategy will be needed in certain future times; and American central bankers are wrong to reproach themselves for over-ease in the 1953-54 and 1957-58 recessions.

Zealots for monetary policy are, somewhat pardonably, infuriated by a related asymmetry that used to be argued by critics. These critics would say in one breath, "Monetary action is practically impotent," and in the next breath they would add, "But using monetary policy determinedly will plunge the system into a crisis and major depression." This argument is thought to involve almost a self-contradiction. How can a thing be simultaneously both weak and strong? Formally, this can be saved from being utter nonsense by modifying it to say, "For a small exercise of monetary policy, the results will be not only small but disappointingly small; for a really large exercise, the results will be disastrously large." To this, defenders of the view that M can take care of everything will naturally reply, "Aha then, it is really only a matter of using the right (intermediate) dosage."

On the whole, I have to agree with this defense of monetary policy, particularly in the historical context of the postwar United States debates as to whether letting War Bonds fall below par would entail uncontrollable disaster. But in terms of the logic of all the situations that could possibly arise, two qualifications ought to be made. (1) If the response to a control lever satisfies a function that changes suddenly from a low slope to a high one, and at an unknown spot, then a correct dosage is extremely hard to reckon or to work out experimentally, so in some, perhaps rare and unrealistic, situations the asymmetry arguments of the pessimists might have a measure of validity. (2) There is a second complication of this asymmetry argument; namely, the possibility that in certain situations market expectations are important, with investment demand depending on the bond prices that the central bank engineers and also on the *rate of change of prices*. . . . An example would be the case where shovelling a little snow up hill may, at an unknown and quite unpredictable point, set off an avalanche of snow. To say in such a situation, "It is only a question of the right intermediate dosage," is to miss the point.

II. EFFECTS OF MONETARY POLICY ON PRICE AND OUTPUT

It was once widely believed, and some central bank authorities still believe it, that the central bank operates to control money, or M, and that M operates directly to control the price level, P. In the old days the quantity of output, Q, was not thought to need determining by any particular agency, since something like full employment was more or less taken for granted. In more recent decades, holders of the present view have been prone to think of government *fiscal* policy as somehow having the ability to control Q, with monetary policy controlling P. The point I want to make is a purely mechanical one and has nothing to do with subjective value judgments. It is simply untrue that money and credit programs have any way of peculiarly affecting the P or price factor: successful monetary expansion will, as I have shown above, have some favorable effect on the dollar value of total output $P \times Q$, and so will expansionary fiscal policy. The resulting change in $P \times Q$ will get distributed between expansion in Q as against expansion in P, depending upon how much or how little labor and capital remains unused to be drawn on, and upon how strong or weak are the cost-push upward pressures that come from the institutional supply conditions of organized and unorganized labor, of oligopolistic price administrators and more perfectly-competitive enterprises.

No one has been able to establish any presumption that either monetary policy or fiscal policy has some special impact upon the price as against the output factor. Indeed, one cannot too often correct the view widespread among non-economists, that a "natural" upswing in consumption or investment spending is less inflationary than an equivalent upswing in aggregate spending, $P \times Q$, brought about by deliberate public policies. (It is true that one expects a somewhat different mix of expenditures to result from new investment spending induced by credit policy than from new consumption spending induced by tax rate reduction. Likewise, a private inventory boom will encounter price rises from bottleneck pressures different from those of a private equipment boom or those of a defense boom. But there is no differential price-level presumption associated in general with deficit, credit, or private stimulation.)

I have been careful to state the quantity theory of money in terms of proportionality between M and $P \times Q$, rather than in the older terms of proportionality between M and P. The first of these formulations has the advantage that it allows real output to increase considerably from an underemployment situation without there having to be much price rise up to the time that bottlenecks and resource scarcities appear. It allows also for the occurrence of "sellers' inflation," in which there may be an upward push on prices from the wage, profit, and raw material cost side. Since V and Q both tend to rise with the business cycle, Irving Fisher and older writers thought that the ratio of P to M might be approximately constant; however, the facts of the last forty years do not accord well with such an hypothesis. . . .

III. PRICE CHANGES AND DISTRIBUTION EFFECTS

Simple models do great good in clarifying issues. They can also do great harm if carelessly applied to real life in all its complexity. History does not record nicely balanced changes in all prices that are as neutral with respect to real effects as would be a dimensional transformation in which one chooses to reckon in terms of cents rather than dollars, or in terms of dozens of eggs rather than single ones. And what is more relevant, when the central bank increases one or another measure of the money supply by 10 per cent, this will not, and cannot, result in a nicely balanced change in all prices and values. It literally cannot do so because all past contracts and past prices are already determined: as a debtor your real position is altered by this new change in M, just as my position as a creditor is altered. Nor is there the slightest guarantee that what I gain you will lose, since there is no law of conservation of total well-being under such a change. Indeed, since the time of David Hume, it has been generally thought that mild *unexpected* price rises tend to expand the degree of utilization of resources and to channel resources into the hands of the more active entrepreneurial elements at the expense of more inert classes. During periods of mild or severe inflations, certain *changes in relative* prices have been considered to be characteristic.

While the conditions for a strict quantity theory to be valid are unrealistic, they probably become somewhat less so in the long run. I suspect that after more research has been done we shall learn that many of the systematic changes in *relative* prices induced by transitional inflations are not so great as has been believed; for it seems odd that continuing price rises should keep coming as a surprise to people. Moreover, the longer the run, the less important will be the effects of past contracts and remembrance of lower levels of past prices. The past is, one supposes, as long as the future. But well-behaved and stable price systems tend to have the property of gradually "forgetting" the past. If that were not so, the way that the War of the Roses was financed would be as important for 1962 behavior as the sliding-scale wage contracts of 1961. So a once-and-for-all doubling of money will eventually imply that the distortion inherent in the fact that past prices certainly have not doubled will become less and less relevant. The simpler minded quantity theory is thus seen to have its greatest measure of empirical validity in the longest run.

Having emphasized this kernel of truth, I must quickly add the warning that it is precisely in the long run that other things will not have remained equal: exogenous and endogenous shifts in the relations determining equilibrium will certainly have taken place, thereby vitiating any simple price-scale change as an interpretation of the empirical facts. Even if one could rule out purely exogenous disturbances, real economic life does not consist of a return to the same predetermined real equilibrium after a transient change in money supply. I live but once and, if an inflation wipes out my real net worth, that is an irreversible fact. The distribution of income and corporate power was never . . . quite the same after the 1920-23 German inflation: even if a Lorenz curve depicting the inequality of distribution of income or wealth begins to revert toward its earlier form, the class ownership of wealth could be permanently different. Even the same Lorenz curve will not imply the same people in the background and the same behavior propensities. Capitalism, as we know it today, probably would have been systematically different if Columbus had never discovered the New World with its vast areas of gold and silver. All that I have just been saying is rather hypothetical. But there can be no doubt that if Canada and the United States had followed policies which prevented the Great Depression of the 1930's today we would have an entirely different stock of capital goods. And it is wrong to argue that this means merely that we arrive today at the state we would have otherwise reached in 1953 or 1945: to have arrived at our present "capital abundance" prior to knowing the discoveries of *recent* science would imply a qualitatively and quantitatively different pattern of economic history. . . .

While my examples have been primarily taken from price rises, the hysteresis effects from price declines are greater still because of price and wage rigidities which persist even in the long run. The attempt after World War I to roll back the price rises by reverting to 1913 gold parities has aptly been compared to the act of running over a man and then backing up over him a second time to undo the first effects. The corpse would recognize hysteresis effects even if many of the best economists of that day did not.

All this may seem abstract, and admittedly it is expressed in technical language. Yet it does have fundamental economic implications. Simple believers in M as the determinant of total effective demand do not feel the need to distinguish between, say, an increase in M that comes from the Treasury's (or central bank's) printing new dollar bills and (1) sending them to all family heads, or (2) lending them at interest to investors, or (3) spending them on subsidies to investors, or (4) buying back Treasury bills with them. The same increase in M leads, they allege, to the same change in $P \times Q$ (and by strict "homogeneity" reasoning to the same real magnitude). This is, of course, patent nonsense in the short run, as they concede when challenged. Under (1) consumption is presumably stimulated and interest rates, if anything, raised; under (2) interest rate falls, and presumably V too, depending upon how much investment rises. Only in the longest run, if then, can one assume that the new M gets distributed "ergodically" (i.e., independently of its original point of entry): I say, *if* then, because, at best, the stock of capital is permanently different.

Note that (4) is without direct Pigou effects and hence is presumably permanently different.

Gustav Cassel's famous purchasing-power-parity theory of war-dislocated foreign exchange rates was, prior to its reformulation by Keynes and others as a mere condition of spatial price equilibrium, based originally upon precisely the homogeneity assumption I have just described. It could be precisely applied only to balanced inflation—a situation which did not exist around the time of World War I. As a matter of fact, in such an hypothetical balanced inflation resulting from a mere change in the absolute amount of an essentially neutral money, we would not get any predictive power from the purchasing-power-parity formulation, since in such a world of perfect flexibility the exchange rates would already be at their equilibrium; but to this Cassel would no doubt reply that his theory would have predictive powers in cases where there are only short-term transient departures from balanced inflation and deflation, and during such times his theory would point to the longer-run equilibrium. Eclectic defenders of the usefulness of the reasoning that underlies the strict quantity theory and purchasing-power-parity doctrines will gladly jettison the notion that a trillion-fold increase in 1920 German marks will result in an exactly trillion-fold change in domestic prices and foreign exchange rates: it is enough for their purpose, and mine, to stress that such massive changes in M and related magnitudes will inevitably be associated with massive changes in price levels; and that such massive changes in price levels cannot take place if the total of currency, bank deposits, and related magnitudes are kept fairly constant.

IV. THE TIMING OF MONETARY POLICY

The effects of monetary policy are not instantaneous. This is not surprising, since there are no effects in nature that are secured instantaneously. Even when I turn my key in the lock, the fact that there are no perfectly rigid metals means that a slight twisting and delay is inevitably involved. But the intrinsic delays involved in effectuating monetary policy are much longer than this. It is widely believed that monetary policy delays are considerably less than those involved in fiscal policy actions—such as public works. And this is considered to be one of the great advantages of monetary policy. Actually, however, not a great deal is known in this area, and the empirical researches performed so far are only a beginning. . . . I merely want to point out that the inevitable lags both underscore the lack of perfection to be expected from monetary control and condition the procedures to be followed in making optimal decisions.

If monetary policy acted almost instantaneously and were subject to easy cancellations,[4] the central bank would find its task a much easier one: thus it might not have to take anticipatory action prior to a turn down of business activity from a full-employment level; for many purposes it would be sufficient

---

[4] This inability to cancel out previous action without delay is the one valid argument, which I referred to in an earlier section, for not relying upon the flooding of the money market in time of presumably short recession; note, however, the need to be able to forecast correctly the shortness of the recession.

to recognize a turn after it had already happened, which would be a procedure relatively immune from the false forecasts of turns which always plague practical forecasters. But once we recognize that lags of some considerable number of months are involved in securing the effect of new actions, there may be grave harm in a policy which tries to offset a new movement only after enough months have passed to make the direction of that movement terribly obvious. "Don't try to look over hills or beyond valleys" is the sage advice often given by those leery of our ability to forecast. This can be very bad advice, and, in fact, one has to be very arrogant concerning his understanding of the exact degree of a government's ability to forecast, in order to be able to set down this rule or any other specific rule concerning the sluggishness with which an adapting mechanism is to adjust and react to the information input available. . . .

So, few *a priori* rules can be stipulated in advance and certainly none by those who profess to be nihilistic about man's ability to forecast at all. We must get the best guidance possible from experience itself. I'm quite sure that economic historians will feel that the Federal Reserve System was not premature in taking anticipatory action to ease the money market in the spring of 1960, which was prior to the May turning point and which definitely involved looking over hills and not waiting to find out exactly which way the wind was blowing in order to lean against it. It is precisely the consideration that optimal stabilization policy must vary with the probability pattern of the system to be stabilized, which makes it rather ridiculous to specify in advance and for all times that some particular gadget like three-per-cent-money-increase-per-year should be adhered to, in season and out of season. Were the cold war suddenly to end, imagine the avoidable evil consequences that would follow from such a predetermined policy.

V. EVOLUTION OF CENTRAL BANKING GOALS

Anyone who has studied carefully the evolution of central banking will have noted the steady broadening of its functions and goals. In the beginning, most central banks, being first among equals and merely endowed with certain special privileges and duties, were hardly distinguishable from a commercial bank. Long-run profit maximization was their proper criterion of action. Gradually the profit motive became subordinate, and today it should be of no consequence at all. (The various money creation privileges given by the government to the central bank usually have implied more than enough profits anyway; and in a modern economy the accumulated earnings beyond a nominal minimum must be thought of as reverting, eventually or continuously, to the government —and note that I did not write the Treasury, since that is merely an administrative subdivision.) Profit maximizing is at least a definite task and its disappearance makes the job of decision-making all the more ambiguous and difficult.

After central banks had been recognized as quasi-public institutions, there continued to be an evolutionary broadening of their functions and goals. And I ought to say that these purely factual trends are regarded by most economic experts as desirable developments. The same cannot always be said about the attitude of bankers. And even central bankers are not to be regarded as reliable authorities on the proper role of the modern central bank. Governor Strong of the New York Federal Reserve Bank and Montagu Norman of the Bank of England agreed on many things; from beyond the grave they undoubtedly would disapprove of most changes in central banking which are not even matters of controversy today. If Canada appoints another Royal Commission to look into this matter 25 years from now, the witnesses before it will take for granted many changes that would shock the present generation of central bankers. I suspect that the direction of many such changes can be fairly confidently predicted today. I should add that these developments impress me as being, for the most part, salutary moves in the battle to improve the performance of nontotalitarian mixed-enterprise systems.

Part Five

ON THE EFFECTIVENESS AND LIMITATIONS OF MONETARY, FISCAL, AND DEBT MANAGEMENT POLICIES

10

Current Issues
in Monetary Policy

IT MUST BE REMEMBERED THAT FEDERAL RESERVE POLICY
has operated in its present setting only since 1951. Throughout
the period 1930-1940 the Federal Reserve System was virtually inoperative as a regulatory agency. In the depths of the
Great Depression the overriding problem was to stimulate
expenditure, not control it, and the banking system was so
saturated with reserves that the Federal Reserve System had
literally exhausted its stimulating powers. Thereafter it could
play only a passive role in recovery efforts. With the onset of
World War II monetary policy was, of necessity, subordinated
to the prime objective of winning the war. In effect, the Federal Reserve System became a money factory, with the basic
responsibility for preventing inflation shifted to agencies with
direct controls over prices and wages. Not until a decision in
1951 freed the Federal Reserve System of the responsibility
for maintaining prices of government securities did it emerge
again as a regulatory agency prepared to deal with the inflationary pressures that persisted in the postwar period.

The readings in Chapter 10 bring out the striking differences between the financial environment in which the Fed op-

erates now and that of the 1920's, the last period in which it retained full freedom of action. Both the banking system and the Federal Reserve System itself
had to be re-educated to the operations of the market in government securities
and to new techniques and criteria for member bank borrowing. In a broader
sense, the objectives of monetary management, the nature of the stabilization
problem in general, and the appropriate role of monetary policy in economic
stabilization remain matters of vigorous argument.

Selection 36

SOME UNSETTLED ISSUES IN MONETARY POLICY

WARREN L. SMITH

*The years following the accord of 1951 between the Treasury and
the Federal Reserve System were characterized by considerable uncertainty as to the proper scope of monetary policy in an over-all
program of economic stabilization. Professor Warren Smith has
singled out for analysis some of the principal issues that arose during
this period. Though he concludes that the high hopes of the proponents of monetary management were not realized in full, the
elements of weakness in monetary stabilization policies are not
entirely insurmountable. This article draws a highly useful distinction between those limitations that are inherent in monetary policy
and those that stemmed from specific debt management policies
and the effects of the growth of nonbank financial intermediaries,
neither of which is exempt from further change.*

It is now just eight years since the Treasury and the Federal Reserve System arrived at the famous Accord of March, 1951. During that time, we have
had considerable experience with flexible monetary policy, and I believe it is
fair to say that it has not fully lived up to the expectations that some of its
enthusiastic supporters had for it at the time of the Accord. New research,
stimulated by the revitalization of monetary policy and based largely upon our
recent experience, has turned up a number of perplexing questions and knotty
problems, and the whole subject is still the center of considerable controversy
among economists as well as government officials and the public.

Without in any way attempting to be exhaustive in my coverage, I have
selected for discussion a few of the important issues that have come to the fore
as a result of our experience with and our study of monetary controls. While
there are many other problems related to monetary policy, the ones discussed
here seem to me to be central to the controversy and to pose serious questions
for the monetary authorities.

  • From Warren L. Smith, "Some Unsettled Issues in Monetary Policy," *United States
Monetary Policy,* pp. 14–30. Copyright 1959 by Duke University and the American
Assembly of Columbia University, Durham, North Carolina. Reprinted by permission of
Duke University, the American Assembly, and the author.

THE PROBLEM OF FINANCIAL INTERMEDIARIES

One controversy has to do with the effects of the rapid growth of financial intermediaries other than commercial banks. Some have argued that the presence of such a large sector of the financial system outside the reach of Federal Reserve authority has seriously reduced the effectiveness of the traditional monetary controls.[1]

There can be no doubt that financial intermediaries have been growing more rapidly than commercial banks in recent years. This is clearly disclosed for the period from 1900 to 1952 by Raymond Goldsmith's studies.[2] That this disparity in growth rates has continued in the last few years is shown by the fact that total financial assets of commercial banks increased by 16.7 per cent from the end of 1952 to the end of 1957, while the combined assets of all financial intermediaries increased by 58.8 per cent during the same period.[3]

It has been argued that financial intermediaries are really very much like commercial banks since, being subject to fractional reserve requirements (largely self-imposed), they can engage in multiple credit expansion. It is true that they cannot create means of payment as can commercial banks, but some of them issue claims to the public which are very close substitutes for money—such as time deposits, savings and loan shares, etc. Not being subject to the controls of the Federal Reserve System, it is said, these institutions may be able to go on expanding credit or even increase the tempo of their credit-creating activities when the Federal Reserve applies restrictive controls to the commercial banking system. In this way, the operations of such intermediaries may represent a very important "leakage" in monetary controls. This line of reasoning can easily lead one to the conclusion that effective monetary policy requires the extension of the controls of the Federal Reserve to such intermediaries.

I believe the line of reasoning suggested above is a considerable oversimplification which exaggerates the similarities between commercial banks and nonbank financial intermediaries and can easily result in incorrect conclusions about policy. It is true that financial intermediaries, such as savings and loan associations, can *in principle* create credit and engage in multiple expansion of their claims in very much the same way as commercial banks do. For example, a savings and loan association which received a $100 cash deposit from a customer can lend out nearly all of the $100. If the recipient of the loan or the

---

[1] The pioneering article on this subject is: J. G. Gurley and E. S. Shaw, "Financial Aspects of Economic Development," *American Economic Review,* XLV (Sept., 1955), pp. 515–38.

[2] R. W. Goldsmith, *Financial Intermediaries in the American Economy Since 1900* (Princeton, 1958).

[3] These calculations are based on mimeographed tables prepared in connection with the Federal Reserve flow-of-funds study and obtained from the Board of Governors. The term "financial intermediaries," as used above, includes mutual savings banks, savings and loan associations, credit unions, insurance companies (life and nonlife), self-administered pension and retirement plans, insurance activities of fraternal orders, security and commodity-exchange brokers and dealers, finance companies, open-end investment companies, banks in United States possessions, and agencies of foreign banks in the United States.

person to whom he pays the money then deposits the proceeds in a savings and loan association, another round of lending is possible, and the process can continue in this fashion until a very large amount of credit (and savings and loan shares) has been created. However, I submit that this is not a very realistic way to view the operations of savings and loan associations.

I believe that commercial banks really do have a unique ability to expand credit for a reason that is simple but often overlooked. What is truly unique about commercial banks is the speed with which the reserves lost by one bank when it makes loans are restored to the banking system. It makes no difference what disposition is made of the funds paid out by the borrower—whether the recipient decides to spend the money, save it and use the savings to buy a claim in a nonbank financial intermediary or to buy a primary security, or hold it in the form of an idle demand deposit, the reserves lost by the bank making the loan are normally restored to the banking system quite promptly and mechanically due to the virtually universal practice of depositing a check in a commercial bank promptly after receipt.[4] That is, the restoration of reserves to the commercial banking system within a few days of the time they are lost through lending is a built-in feature of our *payments* mechanism, and it is for this reason that their distinctive role as the issuers of means of payment gives commercial banks a peculiar ability to expand credit.

Credit expansion by financial intermediaries, to the extent that it occurs, follows an entirely different pattern and has an entirely different significance. When a person deposits a check in a commercial bank, there is absolutely no presumption that he has performed an act of saving, whereas, subject to certain qualifications to be taken up shortly, I believe the deposit of funds in a financial intermediary, such as a savings and loan association, does involve such a presumption.

Consequently, to the extent that something called credit expansion takes place through the operation of financial intermediaries, its time path is likely to be entirely different from similar expansion by commercial banks. As a first approximation at least, I believe we can say that only to the extent that the process of credit expansion results in the creation of additional income, a portion of which is saved and a smaller portion (a portion of the portion that is saved) deposited in financial intermediaries, can such institutions be said to engage in credit expansion. Moreover, if at each round the deposit of funds in an intermediary results from an act of saving, "credit expansion" by these institutions is merely a by-product of their function of channeling this saving into investment. Thus, to the extent that their operations are those here indicated, financial intermediaries *really are* intermediaries. In contrast, it is interesting to note that, since savings out of income when held in the form of demand deposits makes no more funds available to the capital market than would an equivalent amount of spending and merely restores to the banking system the reserves that were

---

[4] Cash drains complicate things a little due to the fact that, in effect, currency is subject to 100 per cent rather than fractional reserve requirements. However, this is an unimportant institutional detail which we shall overlook.

lost when the income payment was made, commercial banks are *not* intermediaries!

If this were the whole story, I believe there would be very little to the recent furor about financial intermediaries. However, it needs to be modified a little, and the modifications serve to bestow upon intermediaries a modest power to contribute to instability. There are two important ways in which the operations of intermediaries can help to supply funds to finance income-generating expenditures other than out of current savings.

1. Intermediaries may liquidate a portion of their holdings of securities—particularly government securities—and use the proceeds for current lending. To the extent that the securities are purchased by holders of idle cash balances and the proceeds of the new loans are spent on current output, the intermediary serves as an agent to facilitate dishoarding, and the process is inflationary. In fact, it can be said that there is an inflationary effect unless the rise in interest rates caused by the security sales results in a reduction in expenditures somewhere in the economy which is as large as the new expenditures financed out of the loan proceeds. An inflationary effect equal to a substantial proportion of such operations seems very likely.

2. When credit tightens and interest rates rise during inflationary periods, those intermediaries—such as savings banks and savings and loan associations—which issue claims that are close substitutes for money, may raise the interest rates or other incentives they offer to holders of their claims. To the extent that this induces members of the public to substitute intermediary claims for their holdings of demand deposits, the supply of credit is expanded, since reserve requirements on such intermediary claims are much smaller than reserve requirements applicable to demand deposits. The effect of this process is to activate idle balances to finance income-generating expenditures.

How important are these destabilizing elements in the behavior of financial intermediaries? Sales of government securities from the portfolios of intermediaries have not been a very important source of funds in the last few years and do not appear to have been a serious destabilizing influence. Intermediaries have been net sellers of government securities in most years but since 1953 the sales have consistently been less than $1 billion a year. The relatively slight importance of this factor is strikingly illustrated by the fact that during the period of inflation and credit restriction from the end of 1954 to the middle of 1957, when financial intermediaries extended $47.9 billion of credit to the private sector, they obtained only $0.8 billion, or 1.7 per cent of the total, through sales of government securities. The portfolio policies of most intermediaries are relatively stable, and they engage in comparatively little switching between government securities and private debt under reasonably normal circumstances.

The other destabilizing element discussed above, shifts of funds by the public between demand deposits and claims against financial intermediaries, appears to have been more important. During the entire postwar period, interest rates have shown a notable upward trend, interrupted by brief and moderate declines during recession periods. The stock of fixed value redeemable claims issued by intermediaries has increased substantially more rapidly than demand deposits during this period as a whole, and there is some evidence that destabilizing shifts between demand deposits and such claims have occurred at times. The most striking example of this was in 1957, when there was an unprecedentedly large increase in time deposits at commercial banks at a time when the amount of publicly-held demand deposits and currency actually declined. This suggests that depositors withdrew funds from checking accounts and put them in savings accounts, the reason for this behavior probably being the easing of regulations by the Federal Reserve and the Federal Deposit Insurance Corporation to permit commercial banks to pay higher interest rates on time deposits.

Are the destabilizing effects of intermediaries sufficiently serious to justify the extension of Federal Reserve controls to these institutions, and, if so, what form should these new controls take? My own opinion is that, in general, intermediaries have not constituted a major breach in the armor of Federal Reserve policy—in fact, as I shall indicate, I think there are other far more serious problems. However, I believe a case could be made for equalizing—or at least substantially narrowing the difference between—reserve requirements on demand deposits and reserve requirements on intermediary claims in order to eliminate or reduce the destabilizing effects of shifts between the two. This could be accomplished partly by reducing reserve requirements for demand deposits as the opportunity arises during recession periods or when additional reserves need to be supplied. There are good arguments for this on other grounds as well, and, as we all know, the Federal Reserve has been moving modestly in this direction. In addition, I think a case could be made for increasing the reserve requirements applicable to time deposits at commercial banks and, on grounds of equity as well as to strengthen monetary controls, for extending the requirements to nonbank financial intermediaries as well. We should forget the fiction—which never did have a very logical foundation—that legal reserves are designed to preserve liquidity, and recognize them for what they are—the fulcrum of monetary policy.

THE RESILIENCY OF THE FINANCIAL SYSTEM

The financial structure and institutions of the United States have undergone a number of notable changes in recent years. The most important of these is the great expansion of the public debt and the accompanying development of the government securities market. It has been argued that the growth of the government securities market and the increased participation in it by nearly all types of investors, together with the increased importance of financial institutions, referred to earlier, has increased the influence of monetary policy. The widely-held public debt is said to have linked up the financial markets of the country and provided channels by which the effects of Federal Reserve action are rapidly communicated from one sector of the economy to another. Moreover, it is said that the new institutional investors are very sophisticated in their portfolio policies and that the volume of funds they are willing to make available may be greatly influenced by even small changes in rates of interest.

I believe the experience we have had during the last few years has cast grave doubts upon this thesis. The widely-held public debt has indeed served to spread the effects of monetary policy throughout the economy, but, more important, it has constituted a means of mobilizing the existing supply of funds more effectively in support of economic activity at times when the supply of new bank credit was being restricted by Federal Reserve policies. Transactions in government securities have served as a vehicle for transferring funds from holders of idle cash balances to spending units in need of funds. Thus, the development of a highly efficient government security market has increased considerably the mobility of funds and has helped to create a situation in which credit-tightening measures by the Federal Reserve tend to induce offsetting reactions in the financial system which, in turn, result in a more intensive utilization of the available supply of loanable funds.

Although there are several ways in which transactions in government securities may serve the function of mobilizing loanable funds, there is one type of operation of this kind which seems to be especially important. I refer to the tendency of commercial banks to build up their liquidity by accumulating large quantities of short-term government securities during periods of recession and easy money, as they did in 1953-54, and later to liquidate these securities and shift into loans in times of inflation and monetary restriction, as happened in 1955-57. The importance of this factor is indicated by an examination of the latter period. From the end of 1954 to the middle of 1957, when the System was following a restrictive policy, commercial banks expanded their loans and holdings of private and state and local government securities by $22.5 billion. The money supply (demand deposits and currency) actually *declined* over this period by $1.2 billion. The funds to finance this tremendous expansion of private loans and securities were obtained from two sources for the most part. Banks obtained $14.5 billion by selling off Treasury securities to other investor groups, and they obtained another $7.0 billion from an expansion of their time deposits. The time deposit aspect of the problem has already been discussed. With respect to the sales of government securities, I believe that the deflationary effects of the liquidation of these securities were much less powerful than the inflationary effects of the increased lending to the private sector so that the process was, on balance, strongly inflationary and took a good deal of the steam out of the System's restrictive policy.

These shifts in the composition of bank portfolios have been a systematic destabilizer, and we can probably expect them to continue in the future. This suggests the desirability of considering methods of controlling—or at least exerting some direct influence over—the composition of bank portfolios. There are various methods that might be considered for accomplishing this purpose, but the subject is too specialized to be taken up at this time. I do believe that the destabilizing effects of such portfolio shifting by commercial banks are much more serious than any of the activities of financial intermediaries referred to earlier. If I am right, it suggests that the lack of direct controls over intermediaries has been a less serious defect of Federal Reserve policy than in its inability to exercise effective control over commercial banks. Since the commercial banking system is the Federal Reserve's traditional area of responsibility, it should be possible to do something to correct this situation. I might add, however, that little can be done about it as long as the Federal Reserve adheres to its traditional attitude that its only proper function is to control the money supply. If the above discussion brings out anything, it is that control over the effective supply of credit is what is needed and that this is by no means synonymous with control of the money supply.[5]

In addition to the increased importance and improved efficiency of the government securities market, just referred to, a number of other means of economizing loanable funds have been developed under the impact of tightening credit conditions in recent years. For example, there has been a notable increase in participation in the Federal funds market by banks; this has economized the use of reserves and permitted a given amount of reserves to support a larger supply of credit. Sales finance companies have perfected techniques for marketing commercial paper, and, in particular, have succeeded in developing a market for such paper among nonfinancial corporations having surplus funds. Government security dealers have likewise devised methods of tapping corporate surplus funds. Both of these latter developments signalize the appearance of a more alert attitude on the part of corporate treasurers toward the management of their liquid reserves. As a result of the increased participation of life insurance companies operating on a national scale as well as the easing of geographical restrictions on the investment of funds by savings and loan associations and the establishment through the Federal National Mortgage Association of a secondary market for FHA-insured and VA-guaranteed mortgages, considerable progress has been made in broadening the market for mortgages and increasing the mobility of mortgage funds.

More examples of this kind could be given, but the point is sufficiently clear. Under the pressure of credit restriction and rising interest rates, the managers of our financial system have demonstrated great ingenuity in devising means of getting more financial mileage out of the existing supply of funds. Moreover, changes of this kind, once wrought, become a permanent part of the financial system—we will certainly never return to the simpler and less sophisticated arrangements that formerly prevailed. In future periods of credit restriction, these methods of economizing funds are likely to be used even more widely than in the past, and we can trust the ingenuity of our financial managers to uncover still further economizing techniques.

There is not much that the Federal Reserve can do about this propensity of our financial system to be ingenious; it is simply a cross that the System has to bear and one that makes the implementation of effective monetary policy somewhat more difficult. Moreover, I do not, in general, think it would be wise

---

[5] Analytically, the problem can be stated as follows. Sales of government securities to holders of idle cash balances result in the destruction of such balances, while the ensuing loans to private spending units create balances which promptly become active. Thus, the banks act as agents in the process of dishoarding. Since both new money creation and dishoarding are means of financing potentially destablizing excesses of *ex ante* investment over *ex ante* saving, it is just as legitimate for the central bank to control dishoarding as to control money creation, particularly when the commercial banking system, which is the central bank's traditional province of responsibility, is involved in the process.

to interfere with these developments even if it were possible to do so. These new techniques have served to increase the mobility of funds, reduced interest rate differentials, and caused our financial system to perform more efficiently its basic function of allocating capital. Most of these developments have probably not been quantitatively very significant in their impact on monetary policy; moreover, the fact that many of them seem to be irreversible means that they probably do not have an important systematic destabilizing effect. Some slight reduction in the effectiveness of monetary policy is perhaps not too high a price to pay for these improvements.

PROBLEMS OF INSENSITIVITY AND LAGS

We turn now to a group of problems which, in my opinion, constitutes a more serious obstacle to effective monetary policy than anything we have discussed up to now. I refer to the apparent lack of sensitivity of most types of income-generating expenditures to moderate variations in interest rates and credit conditions, together with the long lags that seem to characterize such effects as are present.

This is not an appropriate place to undertake an extensive survey of the evidence bearing on the probable interest-elasticity of various income-generating expenditure schedules. The basic source of insensitivity seems to be the uncertainty about the future which is an inherent feature of business investment decisions. This uncertainty requires compensation and probably causes businessmen, in general, to undertake only those projects which promise a fairly high rate of return. As the matter has sometimes been put, if a project is so marginal that the prospective profit on it would be imperiled by a 1 or 2 per cent rise in the rate of interest, it probably would not have been considered in the first place. The insensitivity attributable to uncertainty is reinforced by institutional factors, including the fact that today a very high proportion of investment is financed out of retained earnings and depreciation allowances and is therefore not directly subject to the discipline of the market, and the fact that in very many cases such increases in interest costs as may occur can be passed on to customers through increases in prices. There is a fairly impressive body of empirical evidence to support the insensitivity thesis.

In response to the accumulation of evidence that expenditures are insensitive to interest rates, the supporters of monetary policy have shifted their position somewhat. They have in recent years stressed the effects that Federal Reserve policy may have on the availability of funds and de-emphasized the effects of interest rates on borrowers. For reasons indicated earlier, however, it has proved to be rather difficult to control the availability of credit because of the offsetting reactions of the financial system.

If methods could in fact be devised which would permit really effective control of the supply of credit the availability doctrine might come into its own. But it is by no means certain that the fluctuations in interest rates that would be a by-product of really effective control of credit availability would not turn out to be so large as to put an unbearable strain on financial markets and complicate the Treasury's debt management problems to an undue degree. While availability may be an independent factor in the very short run, it is hard to believe that in the course of time changes in the supply of funds relative to demand will not come to be reflected in interest rate adjustments.

However, in addition to the problems just discussed, although not entirely independent of them, as we shall see, another serious difficulty presents itself. Considerable evidence has accumulated in the last few years that whatever effects monetary policy may have are likely to be realized only after relatively long time lags. A recent study by Professor Milton Friedman covering nineteen business cycles from 1879 to 1954 has uncovered consistent and rather long lags between turning points in the time rate of change in the money supply and turning points in general business conditions.[6] At upper turning points, the lag averaged 16 months and ranged between 13 and 24 months for specific cycles. The average lag at lower turning points was 12 months with a range of 5 to 21 months. Although I find such purely historical studies, unaccompanied by any effort to explain the nature and source of the phenomena somewhat less than 100 per cent convincing, I think these findings are suggestive, particularly in light of the results of other recent studies.

Actually, the problem of lags is interrelated in a very complex fashion with the question of sensitivity and also with the resiliency of the financial system referred to earlier. The lag in monetary policy can be broken into three additive components: the time it takes for the authorities to recognize that action is needed, the time required to initiate the necessary action, and the time required for the action to exert its effect on the economy. For convenience, we shall refer to these as the *recognition lag,* the *administrative lag,* and the *operational lag,* respectively. The recognition lag has undoubtedly been growing shorter as the Federal Reserve's speed in collecting and skill in interpreting statistics has increased; it could, in principle, be negative if economic forecasting were a sufficiently dependable instrument so that the authorities dared base significant policy actions upon it. However, even though the Federal Reserve may recognize quite promptly the need to begin, let us say, a restrictive policy, it is rarely possible to visualize with much clarity at the beginning how powerful are the forces it must combat. In consequence, it is likely to proceed cautiously and tentatively at first.

The administrative lag for monetary policy is usually acknowledged to be quite short, since the Federal Reserve has a great deal of policy discretion and a very flexible administrative organization. In a sense this is true, but I believe it needs to be qualified considerably. This is where the degree of sensitivity of expenditures to credit conditions, as well as the resiliency of the financial system, comes into the picture. To the extent that the effects of monetary policy work through interest rates, if expenditure schedules are very interest-inelastic, it will take large changes in interest rates to accomplish the desired effects. And, if the financial system is strongly resilient as discussed earlier in this paper, it may

---

[6] Milton Friedman, "The Supply of Money and Changes in Prices and Output," in *The Relationship of Prices to Economic Stability and Growth.* Compendium of Papers Submitted by Panelists Appearing before the Joint Economic Committee (Washington, 1958), pp. 241–56.

well take operations—say, in the open market—on a very large scale to produce the necessary effects, not only on interest rates, but on the availability of credit from the commercial banks. In practice, it may be necessary to proceed slowly in conducting such operations, partly because of the danger of accentuating the Treasury's debt management problems, but also—and more important, in my opinion—to prevent serious disruption of financial markets generally. In other words, even if the System knew from the outset precisely the position it needed to get to in terms of interest rates and credit conditions, it might take considerable time to get there without disrupting the security markets.

Finally, we come to the operational lag. This is the lag between the effects on interest rates and credit availability and the effects on income-generating expenditures. For example, for a construction project financed by borrowing, it would consist of the time elapsing between the raising of funds and the initiation of the project plus the average time elapsing between the initiation of the project and the actual expenditures. This lag undoubtedly varies a great deal from one type of expenditure to another and, in general, depends upon the circumstances existing at the time. A recent study by Professor Thomas Mayer suggests that this lag is perhaps roughly six months for residential construction, something over a year for other types of construction, about six months for manufacturing equipment outlays, two months for consumer credit, and three months for inventories.[7]

When all these factors are taken into account, it seems to me that the picture we get of monetary policy as a device for maintaining economic stability is not very reassuring. It is not at all difficult to imagine a situation in which it would require two or three years for a monetary policy as strong as the authorities dared to put into effect to come to grips with a serious inflationary situation. In fact, I believe something of this sort occurred in the 1955–57 period—and I am not sure monetary policy had much effect on the economy as a whole even at the end of this period. Moreover, if a restrictive policy does eventually take hold, its effects may very well carry over for a considerable time after the inflationary situation has ended and a recession is under way. In fact, in a situation of this kind, it is perfectly possible for monetary policy to do more harm than good—that is, due to the lags involved, a policy ostensibly designed to stabilize the economy might actually accentuate instability.[*] I do not believe the situation is actually as bad as this, but it is certainly not impossible. The situation is partly saved by the existence of some sectors that are affected rather strongly and reasonably promptly by monetary controls—the main instance of this being residential construction, the sensitivity of which is mainly due to the existence of ceilings on the interest rates that may be charged on FHA-insured and VA-guaranteed mortgages.

What can be done to overcome the problems just referred to? In the first place, I believe it would help considerably if we could tighten Federal Reserve control over the supply of bank credit by instituting some kind of controls over bank portfolios in order to prevent the destabilizing portfolio shifts

[7] Thomas Mayer, "The Inflexibility of Monetary Policy," *Review of Economics and Statistics,* XL (Nov., 1958), pp. 358–74.

[*] *Editor's note:* See also, however, the different view of William H. White in Selection 38.

referred to earlier. This would increase the speed with which the effective supply of bank credit could be brought under control. More generally, the length of the administrative lag is probably dependent to a considerable degree upon the types of credit instruments employed, and this suggests the desirability of trying to find or devise controls involving shorter lags than those now in use.

Another possibility, of course, would be so to improve our methods of forecasting that action could be initiated sufficiently in advance of the need for it to overcome the remaining lags. This may well be the eventual solution, but for the near future it is not a very promising possibility, since forecasting would have to be very good indeed—vastly better than it is now—before official policy actions could be based upon it.

If the lags are long and intractible in nature, there is something to be said for placing most of our reliance on automatic stabilizers, together with an effort to create inelastic expectations so that the automatic reactions of the private sector would help to maintain stability. This approach already has important support, including Professor Friedman, the Committee for Economic Development to some extent at least, and now, apparently, Professor Shaw. We could give up discretionary monetary policy entirely, as Friedman and Shaw suggest, and simply establish some arbitrary rule, such as that the money supply should be increased by x per cent per year. I think it is too early to say that all is lost as far as discretionary monetary policy is concerned and go over to such an "automatic" system; moreover, to be realistic about it, I do not believe such an arrangement has a ghost of a chance politically. Political realities, including an increasing public insistence on a degree of stability that may perhaps be virtually unattainable, mean that discretionary policy is here to stay.

Another possibility is that we might be able to design complicated policy prescriptions which take the lags into account. This could perhaps be done if we had a pretty good idea what the lags involved in our policy weapons were, but it would also require a considerable knowledge of the structure of the economy including the lags in its reactions. For the near future, this approach, like reliance on forecasting, is wholly impracticable.

I do not pretend to know what the answer to this problem is. For one thing, the evidence on lags is still rather meager and the problem may not be as serious as recent studies seem to suggest. But I do not think it is a matter that can properly be brushed aside and wished out of existence, and I urge all who are interested in monetary policy to give it the respectful study and attention it deserves.

CONCLUDING COMMENTS

Before closing, I want to say a word about the question of cost-push inflation arising from wage pressures. If this problem is really a serious one, it cannot be dealt with by means of policies which work on aggregate demand without producing an intolerably high level of unemployment and underutilization of capacity. We must recognize that the problem is a by-product of a contest over the distribution of the national income and should set up procedures for the orderly adjudication of this contest. However, I believe that an important part of the inflation we have experienced in the last few years has been due to excessive demand. Furthermore, when aggregate demand is as plastic as it has been during recent inflationary periods, it does not provide a very firm framework within which to conduct wage negotiations and arrive at price decisions. When demand adapts itself readily to changes in the level of costs, employers have little incentive to resist excessive wage demands and unions have little incentive not to make such demands, since both parties feel that, if necessary, any rise in costs which results can be passed on through price increases.

Thus, it is still very important to perfect our controls over aggregate demand and its major subdivisions so that they will take effect quickly and in a predictable fashion. As I have indicated, I believe the most serious difficulties with monetary policy are the excessive resiliency of the financial system which causes it to resist Federal Reserve actions and thus slow down the achievement of the desired effect, and, related to this, the existence of insensitivity and rather lengthy lags in the mechanism by which monetary controls make themselves felt. Although there are doubtless ways of overcoming these difficulties, at least in part, I believe we cannot hope for complete success in this regard. Monetary policy is bound to fall considerably short of the perfect instrument of economic stabilization.

This suggests that efforts to resuscitate monetary policy should be combined with attempts to strengthen fiscal policy by improving its unnecessarily cumbersome administration. The lags in fiscal policy are at least as long as those involved in monetary policy, but they are of a different nature and seem to be more amenable to correction. Fiscal policy involves longer lags in the initiation of the necessary action than does monetary policy, but the lag between the time action is taken and the time the economy is affected is probably shorter for fiscal than for monetary policy. Thus, the lag in monetary policy is largely inherent in the structure of the economy and is therefore extremely difficult to deal with, while the lag in fiscal policy, being more dependent on administrative arrangements, should be easier to correct.

In fact, even in the absence of autonomous pressures from the cost side, to stay on the narrow path between inflation and unemployment and at the same time to achieve a reasonably satisfactory balance in the distribution of resources among private consumption, private investment, and the provision of government services will surely tax the resources of the best instruments, both monetary and fiscal, that we can hope to devise.

Selection 37

MONETARY POLICY AND ITS CRITICS

JAMES R. SCHLESINGER

An abiding mystery of economics is the emotion that centers on the effectiveness of monetary policy as a device for economic stabilization. Probably no other field of public policy (with the possible exception of conservation) has been so characterized by deft manipulation of statistical data and slogans. This article stresses the im-

portance of distinguishing weaknesses that are inherent from those that arise from poor conception or poor execution. Of special interest is the extent to which current criticisms of monetary policy are mutually inconsistent and, in some cases, associated with a general unwillingness to rely on the operation of the market price system.

In assessing the import of the criticisms of monetary policy which seemingly have flowed in an unending stream during the last three decades, it is wise to recognize at the outset that some people simply do not *like* monetary policy. This antipathy rises from nonlogical policy judgments concerning the *suitability* of monetary restraints, but it is reflected in a continuously evolving set of charges concerning the *operation* of monetary policy. Whenever one argument appears defective, these critics readily turn to another—one which may or may not be consistent with what was previously espoused. It is this underlying emotional response which helps to explain the quality of changeableness that has characterized the debate over monetary policy.

Much of the antagonism to monetary policy stems from its reliance on the price mechanism. A rationing process that operates through the market seems inhuman to many people, and the results are regarded as unfair or harmful. In addition, the impact of monetary policy on spending decisions is so subtle that many doubt that it is there at all. Influencing total spending by bringing about changes in the value, the volume, or the composition of the financial assets of the community strikes some observers as a mechanism too weak or too indirect to be relied upon. Thus there are doubts about the effectiveness of monetary policy as well as about its appropriateness, and, of course, legitimate doubts along these lines inevitably are seized upon by self-interested groups to attain monetary conditions more satisfactory from their point of view. Still, the genuine misgivings do raise certain issues of public policy which ought to be considered explicitly.

A substantial portion of the recent debate has been concerned not with the monetary mechanism itself but with a particular monetary policy. For example, it has been argued that the level of demand consistent with a stable price level is somewhat lower than that necessary to achieve full employment. Much of the present criticism of Federal Reserve policies consists of assertions that the System has chosen the wrong monetary goal—preventing cost inflation —and that its attempt to influence aggregate supply conditions through its control over the money stock is foolhardy. Such criticisms do not imply that the critic necessarily distrusts or disapproves of the use of monetary controls; they are simply disagreements over details of monetary policy. To cite one prominent example, Sumner Slichter was a vigorous critic of Federal Reserve policies, yet nowhere in his writings is there any indication that he felt any doubt that some degree of monetary restraint is necessary for the proper functioning of the economy. Other observers, especially quantity theorists, have argued that the

• From James R. Schlesinger, "Monetary Policy and Its Critics," *Journal of Political Economy,* December, 1960, pp. 601–616. Copyright 1960 by University of Chicago. Reprinted by permission of the *Journal of Political Economy* and the author.

Federal Reserve is at fault for permitting rises in the price level. By the very nature of their position, such critics cannot be taken to believe that monetary controls are either unnecessary or inappropriate.

In this paper we shall not be concerned with such surface disputes over goals but with the much more fundamental criticisms of those who argue that monetary policy is, for one reason or another, *inherently defective*. Put into three general categories, these charges maintain that monetary policy is (1) ineffective, (2) discriminatory, and (3) contrary to sound social policy. Each will be considered in turn.

I. THE QUESTION OF EFFECTIVENESS

Although it is almost a truism that to question the effectiveness of monetary policy is potentially the most devastating of the criticisms, the neoclassical economists never appeared to entertain such doubts. From Wicksell to Keynes (of the *Treatise*) it was generally believed that monetary policy, by lowering interest rates and, concurrently, the supply prices of capital goods, could induce investment demand sufficient to maintain the constancy of the price level or, to stress a more modern consideration, sufficient to achieve the utilization of all factors of production. Conversely, it was believed that a rise in interest rates would serve to deter enough marginal borrowers to contain total spending within the limits of total supply at the prevailing price level. The investment-demand schedule was assumed to be sufficiently elastic so that correct monetary policy, in the long run if not in the business cycle, would insure the absorption of full-employment savings. Yet this Age of Faith was soon to be followed by an Age of Despair.

a) The 1930's

The deep and seemingly unshakable depression of the thirties simultane-ously dragged monetary policy down from the position of honor that it had occupied and raised doubts as to whether it had any influence on spending at all. Skeptics questioned whether so minor an item in the total cost picture as a small rise in the interest rate was sufficient to alter the spending decisions of borrowers. For short-lived investments such as those in machinery and equipment, the period of investment was too brief for changes in the interest rate to have any substantial influence on costs. (Such considerations were reinforced by corporate rules of thumb which required every piece of machinery to pay for itself in some arbitrary time period.) On the other hand, it was argued that, for long-lived investments, where it is obvious that even a small change in the rate of interest will have a substantial impact on costs, the risk allowance was so large that variations in the cost of borrowing would be swallowed up by the allowance for risk. Consequently, investment demand could be considered insensitive to interest-rate variation. Of course, the abler critics, such as the late Sir Hubert Henderson, who was the guiding figure in the iconoclastic Oxford studies of the price mechanism, did recognize that there were certain long-lived, relatively riskless investments—in housing, public utilities, and public investments—

which were extremely sensitive to interest-rate changes. They argued, however, that population growth in most Western nations had either slowed down or ceased entirely and that it was toward population growth that the interest-sensitive categories of long-lived investment were oriented.[1] The fact that this area of investment activity had shrunk further reduced the impact of interest-rate changes.

Empirical studies during the period tended to confirm this skeptical appraisal of monetary policy. Investigators,[2] using either questionaires or case studies, reached the conclusion that perhaps half the firms studied paid no attention whatsoever to interest rates and that only a small minority considered them to be significant. Of course, it is necessary to make allowance for the period in which these studies were made; nevertheless, the number of relevant issues which the investigators *failed* to consider is noteworthy:

1. Since the bulk of investment activity is concentrated in the largest firms, is not the percentage-of-firms criterion misleading? Were the minority of firms that borrowed heavily and invested heavily the ones that were sensitive to interest-rate changes, as seems likely?

2. Does not the responsiveness of firms to monetary policy vary with the time and the economic climate? Consequently, will conclusions drawn in a depressed period characterized by excess capacity be applicable under other conditions—particularly periods of expansion?

3. If interest rates do not control the investment decision, do they influence the *timing* of the expenditures which follow from that decision?

4. Do interest rates affect corporate dividend policy (that is, corporate savings), thus providing non-credit sources of expenditures?

5. Are expenditures influenced by credit conditions other than interest rates or by the general tone of the money market of which the interest rate is simply a symptom?

6. Are businessmen actually able to appraise the determinants of their own decisions; is it not likely that they are constitutionally far more alert to positive inducements such as sales than to (negative) inhibitors like interest rates?

7. Finally—and perhaps most important of all—do not investigations of this sort, which make inquiries of individual businessmen and then argue from the specific to the general, ignore the *indirect* influence of interest rates on spending decisions? Cannot an all-round process of expansion be generated from slender beginnings? If even a few businesses are induced by cheaper credit to expand outlays, may not other concerns also be persuaded to increase expenditures as their sales rise?

To raise questions of this sort is to underscore the conceptual defects of the empirical investigations. Nevertheless, at the time, these studies did tend to confirm the new analytical presupposition that investment decisions were insensitive to changes in the interest rate. Moreover, difficulties posed by the

---

[1] H. D. Henderson, "The Significances of the Rate of Interest," *Oxford Economic Papers*, No. 1 (January, 1938), reprinted in *Oxford Studies in the Price Mechanism*, ed. T. Wilson and P. W. S. Andrews (New York: Oxford University Press, 1951), pp. 20–22.

[2] See the articles by J. E. Meade and P. W. S. Andrews reprinted in *Oxford Studies in the Price Mechanism*, pp. 27–30, 51–66; also J. F. Ebersole, "The Influence of Interest Rates upon Entrepreneurial Decisions in Business—a Case Study," *Harvard Business Review*, XVII, No. 1 (Autumn, 1938), pp. 35–39.

inelasticity of the investment-demand schedule were compounded by the Keynesian view of liquidity preference, which hinted that monetary policy had little effect on interest rates anyway. Even with limited demand for investment funds, the long-term interest rate, it was believed, would not fall below some positive level, say 2 per cent, because the threat of capital loss at lower interest rates was so great that the public would absorb in cash balances more and more money without bidding up bond prices or lowering interest rates. Buttressed by such conceptions, dominant opinion in the late thirties and in academic circles held that monetary policy was ineffective.

Nevertheless, it remains a distinct possibility that the sensitivity of investment to interest-rate changes and the strength of liquidity preference may vary substantially with changes in the over-all economic climate. If we recall the influences bearing on the effectiveness of monetary policy, it seems plausible to argue that the observers of the thirties erred in generalizing from conditions prevailing in the deepest depression ever experienced. When national income has at one point fallen by almost 50 per cent, when many industries are operating at 20–30 per cent of capacity, when new investment is deterred by excess capacity, when no new markets are foreseen and business confidence has ebbed, low interest rates are unlikely to have much stimulative effect, no matter how low they fall. Such conditions may well be described by an inelastic investment-demand schedule.

In addition, consider the strong desire for liquidity then prevailing, the willingness of the public and the banks to hoard rather than to commit funds (the theory of credit expansion precludes excess reserves). In the period after 1929 there was a run to liquidity. By 1933 the banking system had reached a state of collapse. Many banks were forced to shut their doors because of illiquidity at the same time that the financial community was still being blamed for the speculative excesses of the twenties. Is it surprising that both the public and the banking community exhibited under these conditions a strong liquidity preference, reflected in excess reserves and in the astonishing gap between long-term and short-term interest rates?

Moreover, the economic difficulties were reinforced by political conditions that were hardly conducive to business confidence. Monetary policy attempts to influence business decisions at the margin; yet such considerations become insignificant when the social system appears to be in chaos. Labor conditions were unsettled. Businessmen, who were widely used as scapegoats, were apprehensive. Neither the path to an effective monetary policy nor the path to recovery lies in the direction of alarming those who make investment decisions. Plainly, it would be unwise to regard monetary policy as *generally ineffective* on the basis either of the analysis or of the conditions of the thirties.

b) The 1940's

Financial developments of the forties provided an institutional rationalization for the skepticism concerning monetary policy, yet at the same time gave rise to the inflationary pressures which eventually were to strike the wartime chains from monetary policy. At the end of World War II, however, the heritage of control, associated with fear of the consequences of the use of the traditional weapons provoked by the enormously expanded public debt, reinforced the anti-monetary attitudes of the thirties.[3] Rising interest rates, it was argued, would not inhibit spending, yet would increase the cost of debt service to the taxpayer—failure to reckon the costs of inflation, of course, tended to lead to undue stress on the cost of debt service. Perhaps more important was the belief that the bulk of the debt was infirmly held and that rising interest rates would provoke a panic, in the course of which a substantial part of the debt, perhaps including even savings bonds, would be jettisoned. If, eventually, the Federal Reserve were forced to intervene to pick up the pieces, why not prevent such a cataclysm by an initial policy of support to the government securities market? Periodic Treasury refunding operations which would require Federal Reserve support were held to reinforce such considerations. These arguments were so widely accepted that for a time even the Federal Reserve System readily acquiesced in its own Babylonian captivity.[4]

In view of the excess liquidity which characterized the postwar period, it is certainly arguable that monetary controls would have had little immediate effect, even though, as a general proposition, monetary policy is more effective in coping with inflationary pressures than with depression. There may always be an interest high enough or monetary pressure severe enough to check invest-ment demand, but, in conditions already characterized by monetary redundancy, it may not be practicable to bring this about. When anything that is bought can be sold, when inflation will justifiy any investment, when markets appear over-whelmingly promising, money expenditures will rise as the circulation of money increases, even though the supply be held constant. Some inflation is inevitable as a phase of the process of reducing excess liquidity. Yet, even if monetary restraint could not have dissipated the inflation potential in 1945–46, there is clearly no long-run case against monetary control. Moreover, events have demonstrated that fears of the collapse of the government securities market, understandable as they may have been in light of our lack of experience in handling so large a debt, have been excessive. The market for governments is normally stable in the sense that when some holders wish to sell securities, purchasers other than the central bank stand ready to buy. There is no *cumula-tive unloading* of securities but rather a *transfer* of securities among holders without the intervention of the Federal Reserve system. Nevertheless, the "loose-cargo" argument did cling curiously to life. As the years passed, the Federal Reserve System became increasingly restive under conditions such that its open-

[3] Cf. Lawrence H. Seltzer, "Is a Rise in Interest Rates Desirable or Inevitable?" *American Eonomic Review,* Vol. XXXV, No. 5 (December, 1945). One interesting aspect of Seltzer's article is that it contains an early expression of the belief that monetary policy remains utterly useless up to the point that it becomes potentially disastrous and that there are no intermediate effects. This view has been modified by more recent writers, but (for other reasons) it is still with us. Today it is argued that sizable interest-rate changes may precipitate a depression, but that, up to the point that it becomes danger-ous, monetary policy is ineffective. Based on the presupposition that even a small rise in the interest rate would provoke a panic in the government securities market, Seltzer's formulation was far more coherent than the more recent one.

[4] See the 32d, 33d, 34th, 35th, and 36th *Annual Report of the Board of Governors of the Federal Reserve System* (1945–49).

market operations accentuated, first, the inflation of 1946–48, then the recession of 1949, and then the renewed inflation of 1950–51. Yet down to the Accord of 1951 and later, a substantial body of academic opinion regarded monetary restraint as unnecessary, monetary policy as ineffective, and general credit controls as obsolete.[5]

c) The 1950's

With the revival of monetary policy, far greater stress was placed upon the *availability* of credit as opposed to its *cost* than would have been deemed appropriate in neoclassical thought. But interest rates move sluggishly. Debt instruments are imperfect substitutes for each other. Save in the open market, lenders are subject to a sense of restraint. Consequently, it seems clear that it is more than the price of credit itself that limits borrowing. The willingness of lenders to lend is an important consideration; lenders may prefer to curtail requests for credit without increasing rates.[6] Borrowers themselves may become reluctant to borrow when they do not feel assured about their long-run liquidity position, even if they are undeterred by the cost of borrowing per se. It is the availability of credit that is most important, and rising interest rates may merely be symptomatic of the several forces at work during periods of monetary stringency.

In response to the renewed emphasis upon monetary policy, a third type of criticism has developed, drawing on the older arguments, yet transposing or inverting the elements contained therein.[7] Basically, it is contented that the na-

[5] Consider the comments of the various contributors to the "Symposium on Monetary Policy," *Review of Economics and Statistics,* Vol. XXXIII, No. 3 (August, 1951), at the time of the revival of monetary policy in this country and also those of the contributors to "Monetary Policy: A Symposium," *Bulletin of the Oxford University Institute of Statistics,* Vol. XIV, Nos. 4, 5, and 8 (April, May, and August, 1952), when British monetary policy was revived.

[6] The new emphasis on the lender as opposed to the borrower was stressed by Robert V. Roosa as a part of what came to be called "the availability doctrine" (see "Interest Rates and the Central Bank," in *Money, Trade, and Economic Growth: In Honor of John Henry Williams* [New York: Macmillan Co., 1951]; also I. O. Scott, Jr., "The Availability Doctrine: Development and Implications," *Canadian Journal of Economics and Political Science,* Vol. XXIII, No. 4 [November, 1957]). One aspect of the doctrine upon which Roosa laid some stress was the belief that a small rise in the rate of interest might bring about a curtailment of lending on the part of conservative financial institutions. Such a rise might generate caution in disposing of liquid assets like bills and at the same time lock these institutions into their portfolios of long-term governments on account of the reluctance to take capital losses. From the vantage point of the late fifties, it appears that this restraining influence was a phase of the transition from the kept markets of the forties to the free markets of the fifties. In recent years, financial institutions have not been at all reluctant to dispose of government securities in the face of rising interest rates.

[7] The most vigorous exponent is W. L. Smith. See his "On the Effectiveness of Monetary Policy," *American Economic Review,* Vol. XLVI, No. 4 (September, 1956); his "Monetary Policy and the Structure of Markets," in *The Relationship of Prices to Economic Stability and Growth: Compendium of Papers Submitted by Panelists Appearing before the Joint Economic Committee* (Washington, D.C., 1958), pp. 493–98; and his "Some Unsettled Issues in Monetary Policy," in *United States Monetary Policy* (Durham, N.C.: American Assembly, Duke University, 1959), pp. 14–30; see also W. W. Heller, "CED's Stabilizing Budget Policy after Ten Years," *American Economic Review,* XLVII, No. 3 (September, 1957), pp. 646–49; and L. S. Ritter, "Income Velocity and Monetary Policy," *American Economic Review,* Vol. XLIX, No. 1 (March, 1959).

tion's financial machinery, through the lubricating medium of the government debt, can effectively and automatically mobilize idle balances to maintain monetary expenditures whenever pressure is applied. Rising interest rates, which are a consequence of monetary restraint, supply the incentive and the mechanism through which such idle balances are mobilized. During boom periods, banks are subjected to pressure to expand business loans. As they attempt to sell bonds, interest rates rise, and this increase induces those who held idle or excessive balances at lower interest rates to purchase securities. The sale of securities by the banks frees reserves and permits the expansion of business loans. This process of replacing investments by business loans is considered to be inflationary, even though the liabilities side of the banks' balance sheets is left unaffected. The exchange of assets permits the activation of the money supply. As velocity increases, so do monetary expenditures, even though the money stock is held constant. Thus "mere" control of the money supply will not seriously limit expenditures in the short run; monetary policy is ineffective.

It is interesting to compare the ingredients of the current critique with those of the older arguments. First, it is believed that rising interest rates in themselves have little deterrent effect on expenditures—this is, of course, a necessary element in any questioning of the effectiveness of monetary policy. Second, Keynes's notion of liquidity preference has, more or less, been turned on its head. Initially designed to demonstrate that increases in the money stock would not serve to lower interest rates in depression and therefore were an ineffective stimulus, it is now used to demonstrate that rising interest rates are the means through which monetary hoards are mobilized and consequently that control over the monetary stock in inflation is an ineffective restraint. Third, the government debt is seen not as an incubus making interest-rate variation risky but as the lubricating element structure. It is a point of historical irony that some of those who support the new criticism previously held the "loose-cargo" view of the government debt. Nevertheless, it would be folly—despite some rather abrupt changes in the positions of the critics—not to recognize that the new indictment is the most profound criticism of monetary policy yet devised, not at all dependent on the peculiarities of deep depression or the vagaries of wartime finance. There is, no doubt, some element of truth in the argument. Increasing velocity, by activating idle balances, does reduce the *immediate* effectiveness of monetary policy. But there is some limit to the increase of velocity, so that in the intermediate period,[8] at least, monetary restraint does imply the ability to limit money expenditures. The problem is how rapidly. If there is a *substantial* lag before monetary restraints take hold, then, by their nature, monetary controls may be a weak tool to *rely* upon in dealing with *short-run* fluctuations.

Even in the short run, one should recognize the limits of the argument.

[8] In the short run, velocity might rise because of the activation of idle balances. In the long run, in principle at least, velocity might rise because of an adjustment in the community's methods of completing financial transactions (frequently of receipts and expenditures, etc.); this is particularly pertinent in the age of the credit card. It is in an intermediate period that monetary controls can take hold, that is, after idle balances have been exhausted but before the habits of the community have time to change.

First, investment demand is probably more sensitive to interest rates than the critics admit, and the declining liquidity associated with the growing pressure for bank loans undoubtedly plays some role in deterring expenditures. Second, the possibility of *substantial* loan expansion through the sales of securities may have been in part a temporary manifestation associated with the high proportion of governments in commercial bank portfolios after the war. The higher the ratio of loans to total bank credit becomes, the more limited is the possibility of further expansion through exchange. Third, the effect of the long-term decline in the securities ratio on the willingness of banks to dispose of investments may be reinforced by a debt-management policy which during recession (unlike the Treasury policy in 1954) prevents the excessive accumulation of highly liquid, short-term items which serve as the basis of loan expansion on the return of prosperity. Finally, it can be argued that increasing velocity is a part of the mechanism of restraint.[9] The Federal Reserve does not wish to close off spending from borrowed sums but merely to encourage reconsideration of spending decisions. Unless velocity is perfectly elastic in its response to monetary pressure, some restraint will occur. Although the argument based on loan expansion and variable velocity is the most reasonable of the criticisms of the effectiveness of monetary policy, it should be emphasized that the argument does not imply any doubt concerning the necessity for monetary control; it asserts only that monetary policy should not be *exclusively* relied upon for dealing with short-term fluctuations. This position is perfectly consistent with advocating monetary restraint in boom times for the purpose of alarming potential spenders about their future liquidity positions. Monetary policy, although it should be employed, may not be *sufficiently* effective by itself; therefore, it should be strengthened and supplemented by other devices.

II. THE QUESTION OF DISCRIMINATION

The broad charge of discrimination implies that monetary restraint is unfair because of its disproportionate impact on certain categories of borrowers who either lose access to funds or else become subject to *exceptionally* onerous terms of borrowing.[10] The ordinary indictment implies that monetary restraint

[9] Since velocity is regarded as a constant, increases in velocity could not be expected to be *part* of the mechanism of restraint in a rudimentary quantity theory such as the one based on the Fisherine equation. Milton Friedman has argued, however, that in a more sophisticated version of the quantity theory one would not expect velocity to be a constant but rather to vary with interest rates (*Studies in the Quantity Theory of Money* [Chicago: University of Chicago Press, 1956], pp. 12–13). Without considering one's self a quantity theorist, one can surely accept this position with regard to the effect of restraint on velocity.

[10] The most prominent proponent of this position is Leon H. Keyserling, see, *inter alia,* his statement, *January 1957 Economic Report of the President: Hearings before the Joint Economic Committee* (Washington: Government Printing Office, 1957). It has also been indorsed by J. K. Galbraith and S. E. Harris; see Galbraith's statement, *January 1958 Economic Report of the President: Hearings before the Joint Economic Committee* (Washington: Government Printing Office, 1958), and the joint communication, "The Failure of Monetary Policy," which is included. This position has also been reiterated perennially by countless representatives of affected groups.

affects the *allocation of resources* in a way that drastically and inappropriately affects the interests of certain categories of borrowers and at the the the same time is potentially damaging to the national economy. Plainly, this charge is wholly inconsistent with the preceding argument, for if monetary policy can affect the allocation of resources and the volume of expenditures, it cannot at the same time be *ineffective.* Yet resource allocation is inextricably meshed with the *distribution of income,* so that sometimes the charge becomes the assertion that monetary restraint unfairly alters the income distribution. This is a traditional political refrain among legislators whose constituents include large numbers of farmers or small businessmen—the charge having overtones of "the people" versus "the interests." It is essentially a protest against higher interest rates which ignores both the change in the demand for borrowed funds and the possible costs of inflation. To be valid, it has to be assumed that those who need borrowed funds are somehow more deserving than those who supply them. Some of the current cries of discrimination do involve such a notion—consumer credit is almost a pure case in point—yet, for the most part, charges of discrimination are concerned with the effect on resource allocation.

It must be recognized at the outset that monetary policy cannot fail to affect different citizens differently. Since it affects the availability of credit, the impact of monetary policy must be "disproportionate" in that it is asymmetrical in its consequences. Such inherent asymmetry may be traced to two causes: (1) Some institutions are more dependent on borrowed funds than are others; of those dependent on borrowed funds, some are especially dependent on bank credit, whereas others have access to other sources—that is, security markets. (2) Within the camp of borrowers, the strength of the demand will vary among the several groups. Those whose demand is not so inelastic will be unwilling to pay as high a price as will others, and consequently, as interest rates rise, their share of the funds will fall. Now surely it would be trivial if those who charge discrimination had these kinds of disparities in mind. It is hardly logical to charge discrimination simply because the cost of borrowing has risen, even though those who are forced to pay higher rates are likely to be resentful. Nor would it appear logical to charge discrimination because those who use borrowed funds more than others are more damaged by increased competition (that is, demand) for such funds or a reduction in supply. (Is it contended that the available funds be allotted by some sort of parity system based on historical norms?) Nor would it appear logical to charge discrimination when those whose demand is less intense receive a smaller share of the available funds.[11] (Would it then be fairer or less discriminatory for those whose demand is less intense to share equally with those whose demand is more intense?)

Plainly, those who argue that monetary policy is discriminatory must have something more than these banalities in mind. After all, in a market *not character-*

---

[11] If this were not so, the charge of discrimination could be raised in behalf of any and all borrowers. When money becomes tight, some borrowers will pay substantially higher rates; all others will discover substantial reductions in their volume of borrowings. Since all pay higher rates or suffer from a reduction in funds, all may charge discrimination, according to the above logic.

ized by discrimination, one may anticipate that, with the tightening of credit, interest rates will rise most and borrowings fall least in money submarkets in which demand is most inelastic and that interest rates will rise least but borrowings will fall most in money submarkets in which demand is most elastic.[12] Any results other than these would constitute a prima facie case of discrimination. Critics of monetary policy, however, must have in mind situations in which the market does not behave in this normal way—that is, situations in which some borrowers are faced with a more-than-to-be-anticipated increase in rates or decrease in funds. Complaints of this type are put forward by, or on behalf of, five categories of borrowers—homebuilders, municipalities and state governments, small businesses, consumer borrowers, and affected industries. Each type of complaint will be examined in turn.[13]

a) Homebuilding

In periods of tight money, new housing starts sometimes show an extraordinarily rapid decline. For example, from 1955 to 1957—years of intensifying boom and rising interest rates—housing starts actually dropped from 1.3 million to 1.0 million per year, although housing starts had risen by some 20 per cent in the preceding period of recession. Such changes may in large degree reflect the elasticity of demand for housing credit—housing is a long-lived asset, so that a small rise in the interest rate means a sharp rise in the supply price. Nevertheless, other factors may help to account for the decline—in particular, the entire fall may be attributed to the decrease in Veterans Administration and Federal Housing Authority mortgages. While government-underwritten new housing starts fell by 400 thousand units, those with conventional mortgages rose moderately by some 70 thousand.[14] Congress has set a maximum rate on mortgages, beyond which the Veterans Administration and Federal Housing Authority cannot insure. Is the sharp drop in government-underwritten mortgages a type of discrimination attributable to monetary policy? When credit grows tight, what other result could be expected than that those who are restrained by legal restrictions from bidding emphatically will be eliminated from the market? Clearly, it is the law that discriminates, implying that homebuilders should not be encouraged in an unwise inclination to sign a mortgage bearing (at that time) more than 4¾ per cent

---

[12] Those categories of borrowers who are unwilling to pay higher rates will probably not have their borrowings fall to zero because of the desire for the diversification of holdings on the part of lenders.

[13] In the discussion which follows I am very much indebted to the investigations of Harmon H. Haymes ("An Investigation of the Alleged Discriminatory Impact of General Credit Controls in Periods of Monetary Stringency" [unpublished Ph.D. dissertation, University of Virginia, 1959]).

[14] The *Federal Reserve Bulletin* provides the following data on new housing starts:

	New housing	*Mortgages*	
	starts	*Gov't*	
Year	*(Thousands)*	*underwritten*	*Conventional*
1955	1,329	670	659
1957	1,042	313	729

Since the value of construction as opposed to the number of starts fell relatively little, it may be argued that the effect of the law was to encourage the building of fewer but bigger houses.

interest. In any event, the charge that it is monetary restraint which is discriminatory should be dropped.

b) Local government borrowing

During the boom, 1955–57, complaints were heard from both municipalities and state governments that they were unable to raise the funds that they needed. Despite rising demand for funds, new-security issues of state and municipal governments fell from $7.0 billion in 1954 to $5.4 billion in 1956. Yet, during the mid-fifties, interest rates rose proportionately more rapidly for municipal bonds than for corporate bonds or for United States government bonds. To put the issue another way, the premium which municipals had previously enjoyed over competing bonds disappeared during the same period. Is this not a case of discrimination, with both volume falling and interest rates rising sharply? The fall in volume is largely explicable in terms of the attitudes of local governments. Many municipalities have ordinances prohibiting the paying of more than, say, 4 per cent on debt issues; when market rates rise, they are unable to borrow and are eliminated from the market. The same results follow in other municipalities because of the unwillingness of officials to pay more than some stipulated rate. Apparently, the citizens in the localities have examined the intensity of their demand for local improvements and their willingness to pay taxes and have correspondingly limited their bids for funds. Consequently, during periods of tight money, the volume of borrowing falls. The reluctance to pay higher taxes may be shortsighted, to be sure, but the fall in volume cannot be charged to the discriminatory impact of monetary policy.[15]

The proportionally more rapid rise of interest rates on municipal bonds may be attributed to another structural characteristic of the market—the response to the tax-exemption privilege. As long as demand is small enough to be satisfied by the supply of funds from those who benefit sufficiently to pay a premium for tax-exempt returns, interest rates will remain low. When, however, the demand rises (as it has in the fifties) or the supply of funds from those willing to pay a premium drops, interest rates will rise suddenly to a competitive level, since the municipalities will have to pay enough at the margin to fulfill their requirements. Such results can hardly be charged to the discriminatory impact of monetary policy but rather to the evaporation of a tax feature designed to aid (discriminate in favor of) local governments.[16]

c) Small business

During periods of credit restraint the accusation is invariably made that tight

---

[15] The niggardliness of local governments has come in for considerable criticism lately. The underlying notion that the citizen-consumer is foolish or misguided, although difficult to express publicly, is really somewhat different from the charge that there has been discrimination.

[16] This does not eliminate the equity problem posed by the fact that certain well-to-do people have been obtaining high tax-free returns while the municipalities have not been obtaining any compensating advantage in the terms of borrowing. The justification that municipalities could get cheaper financing without dispensing much in the way of ill-gotten gains seems to have worn thin in recent years.

money discriminates against small business vis-à-vis large business. Of all the charges of discrimination, it is here that the evidence seems best to substantiate the charge. "True" discrimination—a failure of ordinary market forces—occurs when certain categories of borrowers lose access to credit, although they are willing to pay competitive rates. Large business concerns usually maintain substantial lines of credit which may normally be unused. In boom periods they will draw upon these lines of credit; so that banks may be forced to reject loan requests by small businesses willing to pay market rates or higher. In the main this appears to be a problem of small businesses located in larger communities where banks are likely to have "big business" customers. Of course, during boom periods small businesses can and do turn to other sources of credit—open book accounts, factors, etc. Such substitutes are inferior to bank credit and frequently far more costly. Much bank credit is siphoned to small business through the accounts receivable of large business borrowers. Small businesses do get by, but this does not solve the problem posed by the fact that our financial system discourages small business, while it is public policy to encourage it. Action by the Small Business Administration and the recently formed investment companies under the Small Business Investment Act seems desirable in counteracting such tendencies.

d) Consumer credit

Sometimes it is argued that tight money discriminates against users of consumer credit. In fact, consumer credit rises rapidly during periods of boom (tight money) and tends to contract mildly in periods of recession, so that the charge of discrimination must relate to its allegedly unfair impact on income distribution rather than resource allocation. A leading congressional critic is fond of rhetorically informing Federal Reserve officials that they are forcing the ordinary man to pay more for his house, for his car, and for any other purchase on time. With respect to consumer credit, at least, this charge seems to be inaccurate. Interest rates on consumer credit are normally very high and rigid, some of them pressing against state maximums; the demand for this credit is highly inelastic. Thus, during prosperity, rates rise little, if at all. Because of the relatively high rates, lenders, including banks, are always ready to satisfy any demand for consumer credit. In prosperity the rise of other rates reduces the relative attractiveness of consumer credit, but not enough to divert funds to other uses. In a market in which tight money barely affects the volume of funds lent and has only a slight effect on interest rates, the charge of discrimination would appear to be at its wildest.

e) Affected industries

As might easily be anticipated, industries especially sensitive to monetary restraint are likely to see themselves as victims of discrimination. This is especially true of the construction and railroad industries. The late Robert R. Young, for example, was one of industry's most persistent, if not most perceptive, critics of tight money, ready to explain to interested congressional committees how many more boxcars the New York Central could have bought, had interest rates not been so unwarrantedly high.[17] On occasion similar criticisms are heard from the electric-power, natural-gas-transmission, and automobile industries as—for other reasons—from the farming and small-business sectors of the economy. Most of such complaints use the word "discrimination" in the sense that a general control bears down more heavily on those sectors of the economy which are sensitive to it than on those sectors which are not, rather than that there are discriminatory standards for the several industries. It should be understood that such complaints do bring to the surface grave policy issues. How fair is it, for example, to help stabilize the general economy by forcing a particular industry like housing through wider fluctuations, using monetary policy reinforced by Veterans Administration and Federal Housing Authority controls? But, for the most part, the policy issues raised by the affected industries verge upon the third general criticism of monetary policy—that its results are contrary to sound social policy.

III. THE QUESTION OF SOCIAL POLICY

Even if monetary policy is effective, even if it is non-discriminatory, it may be argued that its consequences are in conflict with either long-run welfare considerations or the national interest. In particular, restrictive monetary policy operates by cutting down on investment activity and thus militates against economic growth.[18] Monetary policy may be all too effective in reducing what may be referred to as "social investment" and for this reason may be less attractive than certain forms of fiscal policy. By its nature, monetary policy is particularly effective in deterring the long-lived, relatively riskless investment that can be considered especially conducive to progress (business investment in plant, electric-power production, transportation, including pipelines, and educational facilities) or conducive to social health (housing, municipal and other public services). Even if monetary policy is not discriminatory in the technical sense, it works by curtailing those expenditures which are in the public interest. The affected categories of borrowers (in effect, those charging discrimination) do not have to be protected against discrimination; they should nevertheless be encouraged in the long-run interests of the society.

Reliance on monetary policy, so the argument runs, means that national re-

[17] In his statement (*Monetary Policy: 1955–56: Hearings before the Subcommittee on Economic Stabilization of the Joint Economic Committee* [Washington: Government Printing Office, 1957], p. 54), he comments: "We have slowed down the scheduling of our building of boxcars just because we cannot afford to pay 5½ per cent for money when the Interstate Commerce Commission gives us a 3 per cent return. It is just that simple. . . . If the figures were reversed, we would start building; if we paid 3 per cent for money and we were allowed to earn 5 per cent, we would cure the boxcar shortage overnight."

Young was, no doubt, correct in his last assessment. The problems of the regulated industries, in which investment tends to be long-lived and riskless, cannot simply be laid at the door of monetary policy, however.

[18] Keyserling and others have argued in these terms but have failed to recognize the implications of the argument, in that some alternative restraint on spending must be employed. Of those economists concerned with the growth issue, Arthur Smithies has been most forthright and consistent in urging not only fiscal restraints but the use of selective controls to restrict consumption (see his "Uses of Selective Credit Controls," *United States Monetary Policy* [New York: American Assembly, Columbia University, 1958], esp. pp. 73–81).

sources are wasted on additional consumption goods or on "silly" investment in neon lighting and amusement parks rather than being devoted to "worthwhile" purposes. This view of consumer expenditures as superfluous is plainly at the opposite pole from the one maintaining that the defect of monetary policy is that it discriminates against the poor man who must use consumer credit to lift his standard of living, since the chief defect alleged in this case is that credit resources are "wasted" on consumption goods and other fripperies. It may readily be understood how the appeal of an argument stating that our social values are wrong and that we are not sacrificing enough for economic growth has been reinforced by concern over the menacing posture of the Soviet Union.

It is difficult not to have some immediate sympathy for this position. Our scale of social priorities may indeed be askew. Many are affronted by the current "boom psychology" and its accompanying orgy of materialism. Surely we ought not to permit credit to be wasted on consumer goods when it might be used to create additional productive capacity. Still, if this orgy of materialism is so vicious, what is the purpose of additional economic progress? Why should consumers not buy automobiles now, so that plants may be built to produce more automobiles in the future? Why should resources be diverted from washing machines to electric-power facilities at the present time, so that future generations of consumers have electric power for their washing machines? Viewed in this way, the criterion of more investment for more rapid growth becomes somewhat less compelling. Even in regard to social services, particularly those provided by municipalities, it seems perfectly apparent that the higher interest costs of new schools, new sewerage systems, and the like could be met without inducing a lower interest rate, if citizens saw a compelling social reason. The taxpayers have decided, rightly or wrongly, that they do not wish to bear the cost. Stern Galbraithian denunciations of "the unseemly economics of opulence" notwithstanding, the American people seem to like more, shiny, tasteless consumer goods. In monetary policy as elsewhere, responsibility for unsound social standards should be placed where it belongs and not attributed to the conventional wisdom of economists.[19]

Still, it may be that our scale of social priorities is distorted and that reliance on monetary policy tends to aggravate such perversions. Assuming that the American people could be converted to this way of thinking, what kinds of alternative policies seem appropriate? What remedies can be suggested by those who argue that restrictive monetary policy is inconsistent with a desirable level of social investment? Disregarding those who explicitly or implicity argue that there are no limits to the nation's resources and all that need be done to increase production is to increase demand, it seems plain that if restrictive monetary policies are de-emphasized, some substitute method of restricting total expenditures must be employed. The likeliest choice is a more restrictive fiscal policy. If the protests

---

[19] Economists as a group can no more be accused of discouraging the public from paying for public services than they can of urging the public to litter the national parks. (Despite the entreaties of billboards and broadcasts, the public seems to regard littering as a constitutional right, not to be compromised by the penalty of paying for the picking-up of the beer cans they have been unwilling to refrain from discarding. "The fault, dear Brutus, lies not in our stars but in ourselves that we are underlings.") Cf. J. K. Galbraith, *The Affluent Society* (New York: Houghton Mifflin Co., 1958), p. 253.

against the social implications of restrictive monetary policy are to be any-thing more than the futile whine that it is unpleasant to have the nation's aspira-tions limited by its resources, those who make such criticisms must in all consistency demand more rigorous fiscal restraints, particularly those which bear down heavily on consumption. Failing in this, if the argument is to make any sense at all, it represents a plea for direct controls over investment activities (and other activities?), and, until now, the American people have given no indication that they would permit such powers to be exercised in peacetime. If one abandons general controls, there is no alternative save direct controls to rapid inflation. Selective controls, particularly on consumer spending, may ease the problem some-what, but selective controls have in the past revealed administrative, political, and economic weaknesses that have inevitably led to their breakdown. If the argu-ment that monetary restraint leads to undesirable social consequences is accepted, the nation must be assured that some alternative form of control will, in fact, be substituted for such restraint before it can be abandoned.

IV. IMPLICATIONS FOR MONETARY CONTROL

It should be clear that the various strands of criticism cannot be woven to-gether to form a well-meshed case against monetary policy. Each line of argu-ment is discrete, and sometimes inconsistent with other lines. Plainly, if monetary policy is ineffective, if it has no impact on total expenditures and resource allo-cation, then it cannot be undesirable because it brings about an allocation of resources which is contrary to sound social policy or because it squeezes particular sectors of the economy in a discriminatory manner. Monetary policy can hardly be defective *both* because it discriminates against consumer credit *and* because it permits credit that could be used "productively" to be diverted into frivolous consumption. Much of the criticism of monetary policy reflects the desire of the critic to substitute his own judgment for what he regards to be the defective results of the market process. Since individual judgments vary widely, clearly the critics are likely to disapprove as vehemently of each other's diagnoses and prescriptions as they are of monetary restraint itself.

Any single criticism may quite reasonably be defended. Most of the more perceptive critics do confine themselves to one line of attack—that is, ineffective-ness or discrimination. Others, with much less logic, attempt simultaneously to maintain several contradictory lines of criticism. Such attitudes can only be ascribed to the emotional, rather than the critical, faculties. Some of the incon-sistencies may be attributed to the fact that the defects of monetary policy have varied with economic circumstances over the last three decades. Since the argu-ments have emerged fortuitously, they could not be expected to form a logical whole.[20] At one time monetary policy might be ineffective, at another it might be

---

[20] The views of Seymour E. Harris, who has frequently been a penetrating critic of monetary policy, may be one example. Over the years they have undergone various metamorphoses. In *Twenty Years of Federal Reserve Policy* (Cambridge, Mass.: Harvard University Press, 1933), he argued that monetary policy failed in the twenties because the Federal Reserve officials invariably were timid in the face of political pressure. To this theme he returned after a Keynesian interlude (*The New Economics* [New York: Alfred A.

effective but discriminatory, etc. Nevertheless, the simultaneous employment of contradictory arguments can hardly be defended, and the rapidity with which new arguments emerged as the debate shifted over the years can be attributed to the antagonism felt by many professional and lay observers toward monetary policy.

Monetary policy is surviving the debate, albeit somewhat scarred in places. Plainly, the Arcadian view of monetary policy of the twenties has departed. Various institutional changes—the rise of liquidity, the declining importance of bank credit in the spending decisions of large corporations, the problems of debt management, and the removal of certain spending decisions from the market— have reduced somewhat the immediate effectiveness of monetary policy. But the major attacks on monetary policy have also been blunted. The technical charge of discrimination is, for the most part, fallacious, save in the case of small versus large businesses, and even here the importance should not be exaggerated. With regard to effectiveness, the extreme, depression-born doubts that monetary policy could have little influence on spending decisions have disappeared, along with the war-born refusal to use credit policy for any purpose other than mainte- nance of the interest-rate pattern on the government debt. What remains is a reasoned critique of monetary restraint, not so much a case *against* monetary control as a case *for* recognizing its limitations and its defects and for searching for alternative policies and tools. This critique consists of two parts:

1. In boom periods, monetary controls may "take hold" only after an operational lag of substantial duration. The integration of the financial community in association with the widespread holding of government securities permits rapid mobilization of idle balances during periods of pressure. A restructuring of the assets of the banking system may permit rising money expenditures through rising velocity, though the money supply is held constant. But this *does not imply that monetary control is unnecessary.* Control over the money stock is essential in the long run. Even in the short run, rising interest rates, rising velocity, and falling liquidity are all parts of the mechanism of restraint. Even if it operates slowly, monetary control operates in the right direction. At worst, all that this argument implies is that the nation should not rely upon monetary restraint as its sole

Knopf, 1948], pp. 50–51) in his comments in the "Symposium on Monetary Policy" (*op. cit.,* pp. 179–84, 198–200), arguing that it is the lack of courage on the part of the central bank rather than the weakness of its weapons that frustrates monetary policy. At various points in the argument he makes the following observations: "The problem [of monetary policy] has certainly not been one of impotency of weapons. . . . The Federal Reserve . . . is surely in a position to deny the economy the money without which a large inflation could not be carried on" (p. 183), and "monetary restraints are the easiest approach to inflation control—much less painful than more taxes or less public expenditures. . . . [T]heir atrophy is the result not of ignorance, but of the determination not to fight inflation which prevails in the country" (p. 180). In the *January 1959 Economic Report of the President: Hearings before the Joint Economic Committee* (Washington: Government Printing Office, 1959), he readily admits, though with mixed feelings, that this generation of Federal Reserve officials has not yielded to political pressure and has in his view been altogether too courageous in defending its convictions. All this is understandable. But in the communication with Galbraith ("The Failure of Monetary Policy," *loc. cit.*), he argues that monetary policy simultaneously is ineffective, discriminatory, and dangerous. How the view that tight money is ineffective can be reconciled with his views of 1951 is not made clear, nor is it explained to the reader how monetary policy can be so ineffective in dealing with in- flationary pressure, yet curtail demand sufficiently to bring on a depression.

instrument for combating short-term fluctuations. Monetary control cannot be dispensed with, but the search should continue for other instruments of general control.

2. Monetary restraint, as it becomes effective, may lead to results which we would not prefer on other grounds—national interests, economic progress, welfare considerations, etc. But this does not imply that monetary restraint in itself is undesirable, it merely hints that the results of alternative policies might be better. It imposes upon the critics the obligation of proposing and of obtaining public acceptance of alternative instruments of control. The use of alternative instruments may permit the alleviation of monetary restraint; it will never permit dispensing with monetary control.

From the standpoint of the more dramatic charges, the above critique is very modest indeed, representing a plea for de-emphasizing monetary policy, while accepting the necessity of monetary control. Needless to say, it would not be accepted by all economists, particularly those who feel that maximum welfare is invariably obtained through the market process. For the latter, monetary policy has additional advantages in that it reflects the current savings decisions by individuals in a way that fiscal restraints cannot. Yet, supposing the critique is accepted, it is clear even then that there is a residue of monetary policy which must be used. Until such time that fiscal restraints and other alternative controls have been perfected to the point that over-all demand can be precisely controlled, there will be minimal need for monetary policy at the fringes. To argue to the contrary is to imply that fiscal policy is more flexible, less crude, than we have experienced it to be in fact—a Beveridge Plan type of utopianism. In democracies, particularly those in which authority is divided, fiscal controls have proved to be incapable of achieving a delicate adjustment of demand. Since a free economy is prone to periodic surges of spending, inevitably, in the quest for stability, a minimal use of monetary policy cannot be avoided.

Much of the public criticism of monetary policy arises from restlessness under any form of restraint, a restlessness that reflects a natural and inevitable human distress at the fact that resources are limited. Economists should try to counteract such tendencies. In order to achieve maximum impact on public policy, it is necessary that economists occasionally coalesce on fundamentals. With the exception of a few ultra-moderns,[21] virutally all economists do agree that monetary policy must be used to some extent in the attempt to stabilize the economy. True, under some

---

[21] It is somewhat ironical that the recent arguments that monetary policy is ineffective in the short run but potentially dangerous in the long run *because of the existence of lags* (as in the Galbraith-Harris communication cited in nn. 10 and 20) run exactly parallel to criticisms directed against discretionary fiscal policy (see Milton Friedman, "A Monetary and Fiscal Framework for Economic Stability," *American Economic Review*, XXXVIII, No. 3 [June, 1948], esp. pp. 254–58). Friedman has consistently adhered to the logically impeccable position that lags constitute an argument against all forms of discretionary authority. But many of those who currently criticize monetary policy on the basis of lags can hardly be described as skeptics about discretionary *fiscal* policy. To me, it appears true that lags do complicate the work of using either the fiscal or the monetary instrument and place limits on the effectiveness of both. This represents, however, an argument for greater flexibility rather than the abandonment of either instrument. That is tantamount to throwing out the baby with the bath water.

conditions monetary policy may not be effective, particularly in the short run; in any given case, however, the only way to learn how effective it is, is to use it. In discussing the need for coordinating monetary policy and fiscal policy, economists have come to recognize that neither of these instruments is necessarily either immediately or precisely effective; that is the nature of instruments which seek to influence *voluntary* spending decisions on the part of the public. But both instruments have their roles to play; neither can be disregarded.

Selection 38

THE FLEXIBILITY OF ANTICYCLICAL MONETARY POLICY

WILLIAM H. WHITE*

Of all the charges leveled against discretionary central bank policy as a stabilization device, none is more serious than the argument that the effects of such action lag so far behind recognition of the need for change as to make Federal Reserve action neutral or even destabilizing. Thomas Mayer, in an article entitled "The Inflexibility of Monetary Policy" (Review of Economics and Statistics, *November, 1958, pp. 358-374), attempted to test statistically the timing of reactions to monetary policy actions. After examination of effects on many types of spending believed to be sensitive to monetary policy, Mayer concluded that the lag in effect is sufficiently great to cast serious doubt on the usefulness of discretionary monetary policy. Professor Mayer's article was too lengthy for inclusion in this book of readings, but advanced students will wish to read it for insight into the statistical problems of testing the lag in reaction to monetary policy changes.*

In this selection, William H. White examines the same question and arrives at a very different conclusion. After reviewing Mayer's major findings, White considers some of the problems related to the measurement of lag. The importance of speedy effect of monetary policy on inventory holdings, the length of time necessary for construction, and the sensitivity of spending for machinery and equipment to monetary policy changes are important considerations. Another important consideration is the question whether use of monetary policy in restraining a boom may aggravate the subsequent recession by preventing the starting of investment projects that would continue during the downturn. White points out that if monetary policy achieves its objective of restraining excess demand that would result in price increases but might not result in much additional real investment, this would not be a significant objection to the use of monetary policy.

Neither Mayer nor White claims to have resolved the issues; the interested reader may wish to refer to a subsequent article that adds a few refinements—Thomas Mayer, "Dr. White on the Inflexibility of Monetary Policy," Review of Economics and Statistics, *XLV (May, 1963), pp. 209-211. Obviously, a great deal of sophisticated*

* This paper was prepared in the course of a research project for the Brookings Institution. The views expressed are the writer's own and do not represent those of the Brookings Institution or of the writer's employer, the International Monetary Fund.

work remains to be done before we can be sure of the length and determinants of the time periods between a need for action, recognition of such need, action taken, and the achievement of significant effects on total spending. The work of both authors deserves careful attention, since the stakes are very high indeed; if Mayer's conclusions are correct, the very grounds for an active central bank policy are removed. Before such drastic conclusions can be accepted, however, it is clear—as Dr. White stresses—that we must be on much more solid ground, statistically and analytically. Analysis of the process through which effects of changes in the money supply are transmitted to changes in portfolio holdings of other assets, and to spending for consumer goods and services, is clearly the next task in monetary economics. Whether there may be feedbacks from consumer and investment spending to changes in the money supply— in fact, the whole question of the relative importance of influences in the two directions—is a key question for theory and for policy decisions. If the major influence runs from money supply to spending, the quantity theory approach is more nearly correct; if the major influence runs from spending to the money supply, the income-expenditure approach is more important. In any event, however, both must be supplemented by analysis of the transmission mechanism.

The penultimate paragraph of the article and related footnotes were added by Dr. White in this printing, and were not included in the original version.

Anticyclical monetary (and fiscal) measures achieve their effects on total money demand only after a lag. There has been growing concern about the length of this lag among economists, and this may have been a consideration deterring the authorities from administering full-strength doses of anticyclical medicine. These lags are said to be so great that anticyclical measures would have to be reversed far in advance of reversals in current movements in economic activity. Building on the model presented in one of the most important sources of this skepticism about anticyclical measures—Professor Milton Friedman's well-known *a priori* arguments for expecting aggravation more often than moderation of the cycle,[1]—an important recent study by Professor Thomas Mayer has now provided a set of empirically-determined reaction lags and multiplier lags in the realization of anticyclical effects.[2] This valuable, almost encyclopedic, contribution to knowledge about the potentialities of monetary policy makes possible an approach to quantification of the actual lag and of the limits to the stabilizing effects of monetary measures. As published, the findings confirm suspicions at least about the

[1] Milton Friedman, "The Effects of a Full-Employment Policy on Economic Stability: A Formal Analysis," reprinted in his *Essays in Positive Economics* (Chicago: University of Chicago Press, 1953), pp. 117–32.

[2] Thomas Mayer, "The Inflexibility of Monetary Policy," *Review of Economics and Statistics,* XL (November, 1958), pp. 358–74.

feebleness of the results that can be expected: the probable reduction in the amplitude of the typical short cycle is merely 5 to 10 per cent.[3]

The present article proposes modification of Mayer's empirical evidence and of his model, modifications which may yield the conclusion that the lag problem in anticyclical policy is too small to require hesitancy in using, or abandonment of, cycle stabilizing measures.

Professor Mayer finds that under the most plausible assumptions (aside from some gift of benefit of doubt to monetary policy when evidence for a single quantitative value was lacking), the effects of a new monetary policy on the current income level would require eleven months to grow to the point where they could outweigh the persisting opposite effects of the opposite monetary measures applied in the previous cycle phase (expansion or contraction).[4] This lag is the resultant of several underlying lags: the lag from change in monetary conditions to effects on investment decisions, the lag from investment decision to start of investment project plus the lag from start to completion of project (projects already under way or close to initiation being assumed immune to the effects of change in monetary conditions), the lag in working out the multiplier effects of such investment changes, and the resulting persistence of the effects of prior investment changes on current GNP levels even after the prior monetary measures have been reversed.

In addition to these structural lags, Mayer found a two-month delay after cycle turning points for cancellation of the old monetary policy and eight more months for gradual intensification of the new measures (which could be treated as equivalent to half-strength measures adopted four months after the new policy's actual introduction). Allowance for these led to a finding that anti-recession measures would start to raise current income after seventeen months after the cycle peak and that anti-inflationary measures would start to restrain income seventeen months after the cycle trough.[5] Given the National Bureau average contraction and expansion periods of 23 months, anticyclical measures would therefore begin to work only six months before the trough or peak of the cycle. This starting date of anticyclical benefits was considered rather late for important effects in cycle stabilization; applied to the six National Bureau cycles starting in the years 1919 through 1945, it yielded a median reduction in cycle amplitude of perhaps ten to fifteen per cent. This result is achieved only if measures of the optimum strength for the given reaction lags and impending cyclical movements are applied. Allowance for inability to determine the optimum leads Mayer to conclude that only 5 to 10 per cent of the cycle amplitude could have been

[3] Mayer, *loc. cit.*, p. 374.

[4] Mayer, *loc. cit.*, p. 371.

[5] Mayer also gives attention to another lag that is eleven months longer than this one —the lag until the perverse effect on income levels first experienced is compensated by later net beneficial effects—called the lag to the "compensation point" (*loc. cit.*, pp. 371–72). The "perverse" effect is merely a symptom of change in the cycle's timing, and the lag in "compensation" for it is therefore of no concern and will not be discussed here. Even in the absence of a timing shift, only the small segment of the compensation that took place toward the extreme of the next contraction or expansion phase, if .any, could constitute unfavorable evidence against monetary measures, and such evidence would not be conclusive.

expected to be cancelled by anticyclical monetary policy. He mentions similar results (not yet published) for anticyclical fiscal policy also.[6]

1. *Anticyclical monetary measures have two objectives: smoothing the cycle by transferring demand from the vicinity of the peak to the vicinity of the trough, and preventing the excess, in-real-terms unsatisfiable part of demand from expressing itself in pushing up prices.* The multiplier model employed in the derivation of Mayer's results makes provision only for the former effect and disregards the fact that some of the frustrated investment demand (and, via the multiplier, consumption demand) could not have been realized even in the absence of tight money. Because such investments would not have been made in any case, their absence as a sustaining force in the earlier stages of the recession should not be treated as an offset to the early effects of the easy money measures adopted after the beginning of the downturn. (Specifically, these forestalled investment demands could not have led to the starting of plant construction projects, spending on which would have had to go on after the recession began until completion of the plants.)

Thus, given strong prosperity movements wherein a major part of the forestalled spending would have led to price increases, the anticyclical program achieves net effects on current (real) income levels much earlier in the recession than appears from a model that ignores the major, anti-inflationary function of restrictive monetary policy.[7]

2. *That part of inventory investment which is subject to monetary influences (and is not provided for elsewhere in Mayer's very thorough model) is primarily a stock variable which can undergo fairly rapid, once-and-for-all adjustment fairly early in the life of the newly-adopted monetary program.* It should not be treated as a flow variable (like fixed investment) on which the current monetary policy exerts pressure for as long as it continues.[8] Concentration of the inventory reaction in the earlier stages of a new monetary program leads to an important amount of shock treatment which rapidly cancels persisting effects of the old monetary policy and therefore yields attainment of the appropriate net effects of GNP in appreciably less than seventeen months.

Because stocks of inventory holdings are so large relative to the annual flow of gross fixed investment (including housing and state and local investment), plausible inventory reactions to monetary conditions must be large relative to what the total plausible fixed investment reaction of a one-year period would be (even after fixed investment reactions had grown to their maximum level). Because the inventory reaction is concentrated toward, say, the first half of the first year in which a new monetary policy begins affecting expenditure, we find that the lag

[6] *Loc. cit.,* pp. 370, 371, 374. The benefit was, of course, increased by the contribution of monetary measures toward avoidance of "speculative fever" in boom and liquidity crisis in recession (page 374).

[7] This discussion is not much affected by introduction of wage (profit) inflation that is accepted as a necessary price for the prime objective of full employment. In a full employment investment boom there will exist demand for loanable funds beyond what is necessary to handle the wage-induced rise in prices. Money then is "tight" when it tends to deny financing to this surplus amount of excess demand.

[8] That inventory is treated, like fixed investment, as a flow variable is shown by the mimeographed appendix supplied by Mayer, Table 3, pp. 17–18.

in the building up of the total investment response to monetary measures is much shorter than was estimated with Mayer's model. Important reductions of the seventeen-month lag in achieving net monetary effects of proper sign are therefore to be expected.

3. *A major factor in the finding of a lag as long as seventeen months appears to be the use of a very long period of construction (fifteen months) for construction expenditures by manufacturers.*[9] With this much time required for completion of factories (more than) fifteen months of tight money must elapse before the old, pre-tight-money projects have been completed and all of the current plant investment spending can have been subjected to tight money measures. The fifteen-month period is the weighted average found by a survey (covering firms reported as undertaking construction projects), which all but excluded the less-ambitious plant repair, modernization, and expansion projects in favor of expenditures for complete new plants.[10] The former projects presumably have shorter construction periods than complete new plants; and the construction periods for projects costing under about $90,000, which could not be given any representation in the survey sample at all,[11] should be particularly short. Strong evidence of the unimportance of complete plant projects in manufacturers' total construction investment is provided in the annual reports to the Census Bureau by manufacturers doing the greater part of manufacturers' fixed investment: these firms' total investment in entire new plants that were not completed during the report year were only 7-10 per cent of their total construction outlays for the year.[12] Now even with plant construction periods shorter than Mayer's fifteen months, the year's spending on entire new plants that *are* completed during the year should not be greater than the amount spent on entire new plants that are not completed during the year.[13] It follows, therefore, that on the average complete new plant spending should be only 14-20 per cent of total construction outlays, so that over 80 per cent of manufacturers' construction expenditures should be on less ambitious projects, which presumably have construction periods well under fifteen months. In fact, the 1954 *Census of Manufactures* provides some evidence that the greater part of building investment is made up of the very-small-scale and presumably rapidly-completed projects costing under $90,000, which were not covered at all in the survey of plant construction periods. For plants with 100-200, 200-500, and 500-1,000 employees, the data yield average total

[9] *Loc. cit.,* p. 363. Plant construction and the associated equipment investment is the slowest to respond of all the sectors analyzed by Mayer.

[10] Mayer, mimeographed appendix, Table 1, p. 8, shows that 70 per cent of the cases in the survey sample were new plants, 20 per cent were "plant additions so large they took as long to plan or construct as a new plant," and 10 per cent were more rapidly completed "plant additions."

[11] Mayer, Appendix, p. 5.

[12] U. S. Bureau of the Census, *Annual Survey of Manufactures 1952, 1953, 1955, 1956 and 1957,* pp. 105, 114, 118, 119, and 112, respectively; and *Census of Manufactures 1954,* Vol. 1, p. 206–2. In the first *Annual Survey* to carry such information, the ratio was 13 per cent (*Annual Survey of Manufactures, 1951,* p. 117).

[13] Thus, given certain reasonable simplifying assumptions of stable expenditure rates, even a twelve-month construction period would raise the year's spending on plants completed during the year only to equality with the amount of spending on plants that were not completed during the year.

capital spending per plant of $71,000, $160,000, and $390,000, respectively.[14] In view of the fact that the plants involved made 40 per cent of total capital expenditure, it is clear that the exclusion of separate construction projects costing under $90,000 seriously distorted the results.

Evidence that large firms' smaller projects have short construction periods is provided by the chairman of the Board of Directors of General Electric. He reported a lag of two or more years from investment decision to completion of project in the case of "a large project such as the turbine building." This is similar to the 21-month time lags used by Mayer for all kinds of construction projects: six months from final decision to start of construction, and fifteen more months to completion of construction.[15] But General Electric has much shorter construction periods for less ambitious projects: "In other instances a project may be planned, approved, and completed within the same calendar year." "A facility for the manufacture of small appliances may be in production within a matter of a few months from the date on which the commitment is made for the capital expenditure." [16]

Mayer provides some breakdown of his survey findings on plant construction periods. Comparison of the separate average periods found for complete new plants (70 per cent of the cases) and plant "additions" (30 per cent) suggests that perhaps only a one-month reduction in the plant construction period might be justifiable if complete new plants were reduced from their over-70 per cent weight in the weighted average to the appropriate under-20 per cent weight. Even that shortening of lag could increase the prospects of sufficiently prompt anti-cyclical effects. And introduction of a suitably large proportion of the disregarded group of projects costing under $90,000 would doubtless shorten the average construction period, and hence the lag, still more. Moreover, the Mayer survey evidence that only a one-month reduction in construction period would be justified is questionable; that evidence is based on the several unweighted average construction periods presented for various components of the sample, all of which are close to eleven (rather than fifteen) months. The weighted average period for the entire sample of fifteen months used in the lag estimates presumably diverges

[14] *Op. cit.,* p. 203–1. The data exaggerate the amount of plant spending per project in existing plants because they combine plant and equipment (plant being for the aggregate only one third of the total—page 206–2), and because they combine a single plant's separate projects into one total; on the other hand, because of the inclusion of all plants, many of which did no plant spending in a recession year, they understate the average expenditure per project. In this connection it may be noted, however, that 1954 plant expenditures were not smaller than in the prosperous year 1955 and only ⅕th smaller in real terms than in the investment boom years 1956–57 (cf. *Survey of Current Business,* July, 1959, p. 31).

Mayer notes that the $90,000 minimum for the sample led to some bias from under-sampling of small *plants* but evidently set this bias off against other biases of opposite direction that he also noted. With the demonstration above that most spending was for plant repairs and additions rather than for new plants, and that most construction probably involved projects of whatever sort costing under $90,000, it becomes clear that plants of all sizes, as well as large companies who own plants of all sizes, are involved. The bias thus must be assumed to outweigh greatly the counterbiases set off against it.

[15] Mayer, *loc. cit.,* p. 364, Table 4.

[16] See statements by Philip D. Reed in Joint Committee on the Economic Report, *Volume and Stability of Private Investment, Hearings, Pt. 2* (Washington, 1950), p. 531.

from the eleven-month figure primarily because the cases of complete new plants —which presumably have longer than average construction periods and cost much more than the average of other construction projects—are given much greater influence than their 70 per cent numerical share by the introduction of weighting. (In particular as Mayer notes, "Bias may have resulted . . . from the heavy weight given the two large observations in Table 4.") [17]

From these considerations, it seems safe to assume that the actual weighted average time taken to complete manufacturers' building projects should be markedly reduced below the fifteen-month period built into the Mayer model. This shortening of the plant construction period has two and one-half times as much effect on the aggregate monetary policy lag as the volume of manufacturers' building investment might suggest, for the equipment outlays linked to (the later stage of) a plant construction project are assumed to cost 50 per cent more than the plants themselves.

The same bias from overweighting complete new plants (and large plants) appears to be present in the estimate of the cut-off point after which introduction of tight money cannot prevent subsequent start of construction projects. The cut-off point leads the start of construction by the average between the lead of final decision to invest and the lead of completion of financing for the investment. In the case of manufacturing investment, the weighted average for the former lead is six months.[18] No unweighted average is presented, but for the lead of start of drawing plans over start of construction, the weighted average is seven months, whereas the unweighted average is six months. More important, the unweighted averages for three components of plant investment are: seven months for complete new plants, five months for large additions to existing plants, and three months for small additions.[19] Given the dominance of the latter types of project in total plant expenditure, an additional reduction of at least one month in the reported lag in achievement of full effects on plant spending seems justified.

The other of the two leads over start of construction used as cut-off point is also open to question. It is now reported that in addition to the twelve companies having a three-month weighted average lead of completion of financing over start of construction, there were seven companies that had negative values for this lead.[20] These seem properly included in the average, with zero leads assigned, since the project is presumably started on the assumption that the fi-

---

[17] Appendix 6, note 1. [*Editor's note:* Table 4 refers to a table in Mayer's article, showing the numbers of months in various measures of time involved in financing and constructing factories.] The direction of the possible bias is not given, but it is hardly likely that weighting could raise the average from eleven to fifteen months if these two influential cases had construction periods as short as fifteen months. The closeness of cluster of the unweighted averages for two sets of four subcategories presented by Mayer makes it even more likely that additional overweighting of complete new plants was the cause of the rise from an unweighted figure of eleven months to the weighted average figure of fifteen months.

[18] *Loc. cit.,* p. 363.

[19] *Loc. cit.,* Table 4, p. 364 and Appendix 8.

The order-placing and plans-drawing leads, which are also presented in both weighted and unweighted form, show similar biases from improper weighting.

[20] T. Mayer, "Plant and Equipment Lead Times." *Journal of Business of the University of Chicago,* April, 1960, p. 128.

nancing problems to be met will be roughly the same as those existing at the start of construction.[21] This should justify a further one-month reduction of the plant-spending effect's lag.

4. *A further basis for shortening the lag seems to exist in Mayer's assumption that the estimated third of machinery and equipment that is not associated with plant investment—the fastest-responding investment category after inventory —is only half as vulnerable to monetary measures as are plant and associated equipment.* The reasons given—relatively more self-financing of independent equipment; its relatively greater role in routine, mechanical replacement outlays; its lesser sensitivity to interest rate changes because of relatively short economic life [22]—seems far from sufficient to demonstrate the halved sensitivity. The probable extent of greater external financing of plant investments shrinks when it is recognized that eighty per cent or more of plant spending is *not* for complete new plants; in any case the frequent statements that plant investments are made "to meet demand," whereas independent equipment investments are relatively more likely to be made on the basis of profit calculations, should make it likely that those using external finance for plant outlays would often consider their independent equipment outlays the ones that would have to justify themselves against the cost of outside funds (see, for example, J. Duesenberry, *Business Cycles and Economic Growth*, pp. 62–63). Mayer himself must give little weight to the lesser interest-rate sensitivity argument, since his study apparently assumed that monetary measures operate primarily through money availability rather than money cost,[23] and in any case, as the writer intends to show elsewhere, shortening economic life reduces interest sensitivity far less than customarily supposed.

Professor Friedman's reasoning that the impossibility of sufficiently good forecasting of the next cycle turning point and cycle shape made cycle aggravation likely on the average was subjected to a partial test by Professor Mayer's dry runs with the six actual cycles starting during 1919-45. Mayer's results contradict Friedman's expectations in two respects: (a) benefits could be secured on the average even though the monetary policy change was assumed to have occurred (and then to have been made strong only gradually) *after* the turn in the business cycle,[24] and (b) in no instance was the *aggravation* of particular cycles foreseen by Friedman found. Even lengthening the "normal" seventeen-month lag in

[21] These negative financing leads should perhaps be counted at their actual negative values (rather than being valued at zero leads), for projects are sometimes slowed or scaled down when tight money is introduced *after* their financing has been obtained; the tight money conditions may justify diversion of part of the funds obtained to later, more lucrative projects which the necessity of financing in tight money conditions would otherwise restrict.

[22] Appendix, p. 20.

[23] Anticyclical monetary measures are identified throughout the study as "easy money" and "tight money," except in Table 3 of the Appendix, p. 17: "Per Cent of Full Effectiveness Reached by Monetary Policy in Various Months. . . ." The first column of this table is labeled "Number of months after change in credit availability." Interest rates are also mentioned (note 20, p. 361), in the same deprecatory way as used for independent equipment, in connection with housing repair loans.

[24] The two-month delay after the cycle turning point used might still be too brief to permit confidence that the turning point really had occurred. The assumption of gradualness in intensification of the new monetary measures makes this reservation of limited importance, however.

achievement of effects on income of the proper sign to nineteen months[25] did not lead to a finding of increase in cycle amplitude for any of the six cycles (although for two of them the maximum reduction in amplitude was cut to 1 per cent and 2 per cent). It is true that avoidance of any instance of cycle aggravation is conditioned on the employment of anticyclical measures that are not too much stronger than the optimum levels; and in the two extreme instances just cited, and in some of the other cases of little scope for cycle stabilization, excessively strong anticyclical measures might be expected. However, the danger that the anticyclical efforts may occasionally prove excessively strong seems less than Mayer's results for the seventeen-month lag would indicate: the more recent of the observed cycles tested may already reflect the application of anticyclical measures which were already achieving a portion of the reduction in cycle amplitude that optimum measures could produce. In that situation the achievements found for Mayer's *additional* anticyclical measures must have under-represented the true potentialities for anticyclical policy.[26]

Important further enlargement of the potentialities is provided by the various reasons offered above for expecting less of a lag in achieving GNP effects of proper sign than Mayer's seventeen months: freedom from deflationary hangovers into the recession insofar as restrictive measures merely prevent price inflation; concentration of inventory effects into a period shortly after the monetary policy change begins to be felt rather than even distribution of inventory effects over the policy's existence; marked reduction in the reaction lag of Mayer's slowest-responding sector—manufacturers' plant and associated equipment investment; and an increase in the role assigned the fast-reacting independent equipment sector. These adjustments seem sufficient both to compensate for whatever (unjustified) benefit of doubt was given to monetary policy in instances where quantitative lag information was lacking and to produce an important reduction in the seventeen-month monetary effects lag. With a twelve-month lag the ideal one (given the 23-month cycle expansions and contractions used by Mayer), these adjustments should yield a close to ideal timing for changes in monetary policies first begun two months after the cycle turning point and cautiously intensified over a period of eight months more; there is no logical barrier under these conditions to (almost) complete smoothing out of the business cycle. The fact that anticipatory and/or rapid changes in anticyclical monetary (or fiscal) policy are not necessary for success in management of the cycle means that the dangers of making a (strong) change in policy that is later proved unjustified by erratic cycle behavior need not be serious.

If the 23-month contraction phase should be displaced by the twelve-month or shorter contractions recently experienced (and assuming that the shortening of the observed contractions would prove *not* to be simply the consequence of anticyclical policies), the chances for leveling up the trough of the cycle would be

[25] The points where benefit of doubt was given to monetary policy aside, Mayer considers this an extreme limit for the lag (*loc. cit.*, p. 370).

[26] This assumes that the actual lags were not much larger than those used by Mayer and that the actual anticyclical policies were not misconceived. Mayer notes that the test should ideally have been applied to the policy-free, pure cycles but only in a way indicating that merely a loss of realism rather than that a systematic bias could have resulted (note 89, p. 374).

reduced. The shortening of the seventeen-month lag proposed above might be insufficient to prevent a slight deepening of the trough. Even here anticyclical measures seem worthwhile, for substantial additions to the depressed income levels still experienced after the trough had been passed could be expected, and the long recovery and boom period would provide ample time for appropriate anticyclical effects in the prosperous stages of the cycle. . . .

The preceding has been concerned with the nonaccelerator elements in the business cycle. Insofar as the accelerator is important, the problems of timing become much more complex; in fact they are commonly thought to be insoluble.[27] However, a major part of the complexity is illusory: the long and variable distributed lags in the carrying out of decisions to invest can be (almost) disregarded; all that is necessary for reducing the amplitude of the accelerator cycle is that anticyclical policy be flexible enough to moderate the effects on a given period's investment *decisions* produced by prior changes in GNP (or in utilization of capacity). Moreover, the final decision may not be affected by *current* monetary conditions, as Mayer assumes, but by *earlier* changes in GNP (because of both a recognition lag and the uncertainty whether very short-term changes in GNP are more than just random variations). This would probably make monetary policy having the flexibility reported by Mayer adequate to serve as an antiaccelerator. Finally, the problem of nonlinearity in the accelerator (investment being more strongly affectable by changes in GNP, the closer industry is to full capacity) may also be unimportant in the case of stabilizing monetary policy because the cyclical variations in strength of accelerator effects on investment decisions are paralleled by variations in dependence on external financing and hence in degree of susceptibility to monetary policy.[28]

Subject to confirmation of Professor Mayer's important empirical findings[29] and of the validity of the various modifications in details of these findings here proposed—and subject to whatever modifications are required by the counteracting influences of the accelerator and the lead of the income-stimulating effects of new orders over production of the ordered goods—the arguments for aggressive use of anticyclical measures must now be considered persuasive.[30]

[27] See, for example, W. J. Baumol, "Pitfalls in Countercyclical Policies: Some Tools and Results," *Review of Economics and Statistics,* XLIII (February, 1961), pp. 21–26.

[28] See W. H. White, "Inventory Investment and the Rate of Interest," *Banca Nazionale del Lavoro Quart. Review,* No. 57 (June, 1961), pp. 147–148 (Brookings Institution Reprint No. 57, pp. 9–10).

[29] Tentative evidence found by the writer that financing in advance of need in anticipation of the tightening of money is not important suggests that the financing lead Mayer derived from a recession-time survey would require only minor adjustment.

[30] Professor Friedman recently presented a new kind of argument against anticyclical monetary policy: from statistics showing that the peak in the rate of change of the money supply leads by a large but variable number of months the cyclical peak in industrial production, he has inferred that the decline in the rate of money expansion causes (after an unpredictable delay) the subsequent decline in production (Joint Economic Committee, *Hearings, Employment Growth and Price Levels,* Pt. 4—"The Influence on Prices of Changes in the Effective Supply of Money," Washington, 1959, Chart 2, p. 639; pp. 661, 615–16). With the rate of change in industrial production itself reaching a peak before the peak in industrial production and with rising velocity of circulation in cyclical expansions elsewhere explained by Professor Friedman as a consequence of cyclical expansion rather than a cause of later contractions (*The Demand for Money, Some Theoretical and Empirical Results,* National Bureau of Economic Research, Occasional Paper 68, New York, 1959), publication of a fuller description of the relationships inferred must be awaited.

Selection 39

TOWARDS IMPROVING THE EFFICIENCY OF THE MONETARY MECHANISM

JAMES TOBIN

The theme of the preceding selections is carried further in this article. At issue is the efficiency of the monetary control mechanism, as distinguished from the skill with which it is manipulated. Dr. Tobin's central theme is a simple one: a major source of "sloppiness" in the effects of Federal Reserve actions is traceable to the variability of commercial bank reserve positions. To the extent that the banks maintain excess reserves during periods of monetary ease and cut them back sharply during periods of tight money, the lag in effect of central bank policy is accentuated. He offers two structural changes in the mechanics of Federal Reserve control over bank reserves designed to shorten the response time of the banking system to a change in Federal Reserve policy. Both proposals are radical in nature, though surprisingly simple in operation. They warrant careful attention for the reasons outlined in previous sections—unless the Federal Reserve System can bring its weight to bear against excessive or deficient aggregate demand within a fairly short period of time, its usefulness as a flexible instrument of economic stabilization dwindles to the vanishing point. Professor Tobin's proposals should also be compared with those of Professor Friedman presented in Selection 33.

Appraisal of the operation of a machine may focus on (1) the purpose for which the operator is using it, (2) the skill of the operator, or (3) the efficiency of the machine itself. The machinery of American monetary control has been abundantly discussed from the first two points of view, and scarcely at all from the third. The objectives, timing, and techniques of Federal Reserve control are criticized and defended daily. The adequacy of the machinery of control is seldom questioned. This is not because the machinery is of a new design clearly appropriate to its current uses. On the contrary, the mechanism was designed for quite different purposes in 1913. Neither then nor at the time of emergency repairs in 1933-35 was the design related to what is now regarded as the overriding task of monetary control—accelerating, damping, or reversing short-run changes in aggregate demand for goods and services. The original objectives were to prevent financial crises and panics by providing a "lender of last resort," and to meet the "needs of trade." The remodeling twenty years later had as its principal purpose the prevention of bank failures. Perhaps the only important innovation adopted to improve the efficiency of monetary control is the power to vary reserve requirements, obtained by the authorities in 1935.

Our relevant experience of monetary control is surprisingly short, perhaps no longer than the past decade. Most of the Federal Reserve's half of a century has been dominated by the special circumstances of two wars and a great depression. Monetary control of a sort was emerging in the 1920's. But the consciousness of the authorities that economic stabilization was their objective and responsibility was far from fully developed, and the environment was very different from today's, especially with respect to the size and role of the public debt. For its pioneering efforts of the past decade, the Federal Reserve inherited machinery designed for different purposes in a different economic environment under the spell of different economic ideas.

Yet there is no evidence that the drivers at the wheel during this first decade of modern monetary control have longed for a new or improved machine. Their complacency leaves it up to outsiders to ask whether the monetary mechanism can be made a more efficient engine for accomplishing the goals of the authorities. The best way to encourage thinking in this direction is to make concrete suggestions. The two proposals below are advanced, somewhat tentatively, in this spirit. They are of course not exhaustive. It should not be, but perhaps is, necessary to repeat that efficiency is a technical question, distinct from the more important issue of objectives. Whether the goals of economic policy should be those of Martin, Roosa, Douglas, or Keyserling is not the topic here. Whatever the goals, it is a good idea to have efficient instruments to pursue them.

1. *The Federal Reserve Banks should pay interest at the discount rate on member bank reserve balances in excess of requirements.* At present a bank earns no interest on positive excess reserves, funds it is lending to the Fed, but must pay the discount rate on negative excess reserves, its borrowings from the Fed.[1] The proposal is motivated by more than a simple passion for symmetry. Its purpose is to strengthen the Federal Reserve's control over the tightness of bank credit. The willingness of banks to make loans and the terms which they will offer to borrowers depend on the opportunity cost of loan funds to the banks. This cost is the return the bank can earn by investing in Treasury securities of Federal funds or by reducing its indebtedness to the Fed. The various instruments of monetary control all exert their influence by changing this opportunity cost. But they add up to a loose, uncertain, and possibly quite slow control. The proposed reform would make the discount rate much more effective as the measure of the cost of loan funds. The discount rate would be effective, not only as at present for a bank in debt to the Fed, but equally for a bank with excess reserves. By raising the discount rate, the Federal Reserve would clearly, directly, and quickly make lending less attractive—to all banks, regardless of their net free reserve positions.

It is true that the present Federal funds market tends to accomplish this same generalization of the discount rate. But the market is quite imperfect, and lending in it is not an effective alternative for many banks. Moreover, the Federal funds rate can fall below the discount rate when net free reserves are large, or even rise above it when borrowing is heavy. Under the proposal, the Federal Reserve itself would make a perfect Federal funds market at the discount rate.

---

[1]On a reserve deficiency not covered by borrowing a bank pays a penalty rate two points above the discount rate.

The discount rate would also become a floor to the rate on Treasury bills and similar short-term paper that banks might hold as secondary reserves. The differential of the bill rate above the discount rate would be related to the relative shares of excess reserves and secondary reserves in the liquidity position of the banks. Open-market operations in bills would influence this differential, as at present. But open-market operations would not be essential to "make the discount rate effective." It would never be possible for the money market and the discount rate to lose touch.

Readers who are rightly concerned to avoid techniques of monetary stabilization that unduly enrich bank shareholders should hold their fire at least until they read the second proposal. But the first proposal even by itself is not such a bonanza for the banks as may at first appear. It is true that gains would accrue to banks which now choose, because of imperfections in the money market and Federal funds market, to hold excess reserves at zero interest. Although bank holdings of excess reserves would increase, their holdings of short-term Treasury securities, which banks now use as secondary reserves, would be diminished. These securities and the interest they bear would be absorbed by the Fed. Since excess reserves are a perfectly liquid demand obligation, banks will hold them at a somewhat lower rate than they require of Treasury securities. An ultimate corrective to excessive enrichment of banks at the expense of the Treasury is an increase in reserve requirements; under the proposal, required reserves would remain barren of interest.

2. *Banks should be released from the prohibition of interest payments on demand deposits and from the ceilings on interest rates on time and savings deposits.* The second proposal is the logical extension of the first. The purpose of the first is to tighten the control of the Federal Reserve over the marginal cost of bank lending. The purpose of the second is to tighten the Federal Reserve's control over the opportunity cost that bank depositors charge against any alternative investment of funds. Under existing arrangements the advantages of holding bank deposits are the convenience and economy of avoiding frequent transactions between deposits and other assets. The "cost" of a reduction in average bank balances in order to increase investment elsewhere is an imputed and unobservable one, differing widely among depositors. The monetary authority affects this cost indirectly, increasing it by making deposits relatively scarce in supply and diminishing it by making deposits relatively abundant. But they are operating very much in the dark. They cannot know how, and how soon, a given monetary action will affect the supply of funds by bank depositors to other financial intermediaries or the terms on which depositors will be prepared to make direct investments.

If interest on bank deposits is competitively determined and if the discount rate is generalized as suggested above, the Federal Reserve will have a very tangible control over the attractiveness of deposits. The rate that banks pay depositors will be closely geared to the discount rate, since a bank will always be able to earn a fraction of the discount rate (one minus the required reserve ratio) on a new deposit. By changing the discount rate the central bank will affect both the calculations of banks concerning the relative attractiveness of excess reserves and other assets and the calculations of the public concerning the relative attractiveness of deposits and other investments.

The proposal has several important additional advantages. First, it would largely eliminate what is now a real cost of restrictive monetary policy, namely the unproductive efforts devoted to economizing cash in periods of high interest rates. Second, it would replace with price competition some of the existing wasteful and imperfect nonprice competition for deposits. Better to pay depositors interest than to seek their patronage by organ music, free silverware, and plush surroundings. Better to attract deposits by interest than to seek them by the threat and promise of preferred loan treatment to faithful depositors.[2] The allocative efficiency of the banking system, and indeed of the entire financial system, in channeling the funds of the ultimate lenders to productive borrowers would be improved. Third, it would reduce the connection between bank profits and the tightness of monetary policy; measures can be appraised for their effects on the economy rather than for their effects on bank stocks.

The circumstances that led to prohibition of interest rate competition for bank deposits in 1933 no longer apply. The principal argument for this prohibition as a measure of social policy was that excessive competition for deposits led to insolvency and bank failure. Other measures adopted at the same time, especially of course deposit insurance, give the public ample protection. No doubt commercial bankers have the usual reasons for desiring protection from competition within the industry, although many would welcome the chance to compete for funds that now go to other financial institutions. Small banks would be the main gainers from the first proposal, but perhaps also the main losers from the second. There may be some banks that are able to remain in business only because present federal legislation enables them to capture rents that would otherwise go to their depositors. Should they remain in business? Needless to say, the proper role of the government is to oppose rather than to compel collusive price conventions.

An incidental result of the two proposals would be to simplify the week-to-week operating problems of the Treasury in debt management. Much of the short-term debt would be transferred from corporations and banks to the Federal Reserve, and these holders would instead lend to the government via the media of member bank and Federal Reserve Bank deposits. The headaches the Treasury now suffers from the weekly maturities of its bill issues would be largely transferred to the Fed and amalgamated with their general headaches concerning monetary policy, in particular the appropriate basic interest rate.

These two proposals would make the discount rate, which it would then be more appropriate to call the Federal Reserve rate, the most powerful tool in the central banker's kit, and a very powerful tool indeed. The reform would be of no avail unless the authorities were prepared to use this tool. To counter the inventory cycle they would have to be ready to change the rate promptly and drastically; counter-cyclical monetary control may well require much wider fluctuations in short-term interest rates than we have yet had the courage to try.

[2] This consequence of the prohibition of interest on deposits has been emphasized by Donald Hodgman.

Those who do not have faith in the values, judgment, or capacity of monetary managers in general or in particular will not wish to entrust them with more efficient instruments. But those who believe that a democratic society should seek to control its own economic destiny will wish the government to have the means to carry out its will.

11

Monetary, Fiscal, and Debt Management Policies

THE UNITED STATES EMERGED FROM WORLD WAR II WITH a national debt of unprecedented size. The problem of debt management—that is, replacing maturing issues with others of appropriate maturity and yield—is itself an exacting task if orderly borrowing procedures and minimal interest burden are to be achieved. On many occasions in the last ten or fifteen years, policies that would have been most desirable from the standpoint of debt management, which aimed at an optimum debt distribution and a low interest cost, were in direct conflict with those that would best implement Federal Reserve policies aimed at control of aggregate spending. The resolution of these conflicts and the alternative methods of integrating monetary and debt management policy are explored in this chapter.

Attention is also focused on the interrelationship of monetary and fiscal policies. Whenever the federal government runs a deficit or surplus it affects the over-all liquidity position of the household and business sectors of the economy. The way in which this impact is distributed and its strength are both affected by monetary policies that accompany the budgetary decisions. In effect, the Treasury has to some extent the functions of a central bank, and the Federal Reserve System, through its open market operations, participates in debt management. During periods of general inflationary or deflationary pressure it is obviously essential that the policies of the two agencies be directed toward the same objectives and that their interrelationships be thoroughly understood.

Developments of recent years have allayed fears that the huge federal debt incurred in World War II would cause serious economic instability. Nevertheless, its very existence presents problems. All of the debt must be held by someone, and each year decisions must be made as to the types of new securities to be offered to replace maturing issues. Any deficit or surplus in the federal budget calls for additional decisions affecting the composition and average maturity of the debt. Open market operations of the Federal Reserve System also involve some measure of debt management.

The three selections of this chapter examine objectives and techniques of debt management.

Selection 40

INTERRELATIONSHIP OF MONETARY AND FISCAL POLICIES

SAMUEL B. CHASE, JR.

> *In this selection, the use of fiscal policy to reinforce monetary policy is analyzed in terms of their effects on private demand. Use of fiscal policy as a tool to help achieve economic stabilization has been accepted by many; but questions still arise, even among those who accept this use of fiscal policy, concerning the length of the period over which the budget may be unbalanced for this purpose. Moreover, use of fiscal policy has important effects on the composition of private demand, as is pointed out toward the end of the following selection.*

In recent decades, attitudes toward government finance have undergone a gradual but striking change. As the growing importance of government budgets in the national economy has created a heightened public awareness of their significance, concurrent advances in economic analysis have demonstrated that budget policy can make a positive contribution to the over-all performance of the economy. Whereas at one time the financial operations of government were judged in terms of what were held to be inflexible laws, present thought is more nearly characterized by its consideration of the appropriateness of budget policy in terms of prevailing national economic objectives.

Perhaps the outstanding example of this change in attitudes has been the rather general agreement that budgetary policy should be designed to contribute to the over-all stability of the economy, rather than to maintain an annual balance. Thus the stimulus to economic activity provided by the reduction of tax liabilities during the economic decline of 1957-58 was widely held to be felicitous

• From Samuel B. Chase, Jr., "Interrelationship of Monetary and Fiscal Policies," Federal Reserve Bank of Kansas City, *Monthly Review,* February, 1960, pp. 3–9. Reprinted by permission of the Federal Reserve Bank of Kansas City.

under the circumstances, and fiscal policies during the decline were made with a recognition that attempts to increase tax revenues might tend to reinforce recessionary developments. Similarly, the increase of tax liabilities that has accompanied economic recovery is generally regarded as appropriate to a period when total demands for goods and services are rising in relation to productive capacity. The conscious approbation of year-to-year instability in the net financial position of the Treasury is striking evidence of the widespread recognition that budget policy has a vital bearing on the performance of the economy.

THE BASIC BUDGET POSITION

However, the cyclical behavior of the budget is only one aspect of budgetary policy, and the abandonment of the principle of annual balance in favor of a flexible budget designed to modify economic fluctuations leaves open the question of what might be referred to as the underlying or long-run budgetary position of the federal government. The federal budget might tend toward more or less continual deficit or surplus over the course of an entire business cycle, or it might tend toward balance, with the surpluses accumulated in years of prosperity tending to match the deficits resulting from recession. Compensatory fluctuations in the Treasury's budget position can take place under any of the three alternative underlying budgetary trends.

It might seem at first glance that the long-run budgetary position of the federal government should be permitted to evolve out of short-run considerations of economic stabilization. For example, it has been argued that, given prevailing economic and financial conditions, the federal deficit or surplus each year should be of a magnitude which provides for high levels of employment and production without inflation. But this argument overlooks the fact that there are alternative economic policies, particularly monetary policies, that are presently employed as tools of economic stabilization, and that different mixtures of monetary and fiscal policies may each be consistent with economic stability. While there are various alternatives that may lead to economic stabilization, the choice of a particular blend of monetary and fiscal policies is significant with respect to the achievement of other social objectives, since monetary and fiscal policies tend to produce differing effects on the distribution of the economy's productive resources among their various possible uses.

This article deals with the effects on resource allocation that may stem from alternative mixtures of monetary and fiscal policies. Following the general discussion of these effects, a brief review of past trends in the federal budget is followed by some consideration of possible trends in the federal budgetary position during the years ahead.

GOALS OF FISCAL AND MONETARY POLICIES

The underlying trend of the federal budget plays an important role in determining the strength of private demands for goods and services through its influence on the finances of the businesses, households, and other spending units that comprise the private sector of the economy. Aside from federal fiscal influence, the other major area of control over private demands is monetary and credit policy. Primarily through its control over the lending power of the banking system, monetary and credit policy affects the cost and availability of borrowed funds for use in financing private spending. A paramount objective of credit and fiscal policies taken together is to regulate the strength of private demands for goods and services so as to achieve the full utilization of the productive capacity of the economy without generating excessive demands that would create inflationary pressures. Stated more specifically, the goal of credit and fiscal policies combined is to foster a "target" level of demand for goods and services that is appropriate to the realization of the national economic goals of full employment and stable prices.

Although the ultimate level of private demand is affected both by fiscal and by monetary and credit policies, a given target level of spending can be achieved with a wide variety of combinations of the two types of influence. The possible influences of the budget on private spending range, by continuous gradations, from the very expansive effects of a large deficit to the very restrictive effects of a large surplus. Regardless of the phase of the business cycle, the more permissive is fiscal policy with respect to private spending, the more restrictive must be monetary and credit policy if a given target level of private demands is not to be exceeded. Conversely, the more restrictive is fiscal policy, the more permissive may be monetary and credit policies.

THE GOVERNMENT BUDGET AND PRIVATE INCOMES

The significance of the state of the budget lies mainly in its effects on the level of disposable income available for private spending. When the budget is balanced, the fiscal actions of the Treasury leave private disposable incomes unaffected in the aggregate. Federal outlays, which are sources of private income, are precisely matched by federal revenues, which reduce the disposable incomes of those who pay them. Thus a balanced budget subjects the aggregate disposable income of the private sector of the economy to two opposing influences of equal strength. This accounting truism has led economists to the preliminary working proposition that a balanced budget has no impact on private demands for goods and services. The conclusion is correct only under strictly limited conditions not likely to be realized in practice, mainly because almost any combination of spending and taxes has important effects on the distribution of private wealth and income that will invariably influence both the amount and the kinds of private demands for goods and services. For example, corporation income taxes bear more heavily on incomes otherwise destined for investment spending than do personal income taxes, and the relative importance of the two taxes has an important influence on the composition of private demands as between investment goods and consumer goods and services.

However, even though such considerations weigh heavily against the probability that a balanced budget is actually neutral with respect to private demands for new output, an unbalanced budget can exert a profound influence of a different nature because it directly affects the level of disposable income in the private sector. If the budget shows a deficit, disposable private incomes are raised as the government outlays add more to them than is being taken out by current taxation. This increased income is available for disposition in the form of both larger consumption outlays and greater private savings which are potential sources of demand for investment goods. Conversely, a budgetary surplus lowers private disposable incomes as the government takes more funds from the private sector than it provides through its current outlays. This influence operates to reduce private consumption spending and the amount of private savings being made available for investment.

In the light of the influence of the budget on the ability of the private sector to finance consumption and investment out of current income, it is clear that the credit conditions appropriate to the achievement of a given target level of private spending are not independent of the state of the budget. The higher the level of private disposable income (that is, the smaller the budget surplus or the greater the deficit), the greater must be the restriction on the ability of the private sector to finance demands through borrowing if the target level of spending is not to be exceeded.

OFFSETS TO UNBALANCED BUDGETS

To a certain extent, the Treasury debt operations that normally accompany an unbalanced budget provide a credit market offset to the effects of the imbalance on private disposable incomes. A deficit is usually accompanied by a roughly equal amount of government borrowing which involves an absorption of funds from the money and capital markets that might otherwise be used to finance private spending. The superimposition of government demands for borrowed funds on private demands creates upward pressures on interest rates which discourage private borrowing, and fosters more restrictive bank lending policies. In effect, then, the deficit leads to a channeling of funds away from private borrowers to finance the gap between government receipts and expenditures.

However, the upward pressure on interest rates may attract new supplies of loan funds into the credit markets as it becomes profitable for individuals and businesses to cut down working cash balances to take advantage of the higher level of interest rates. To the extent that this happens, the government demand for borrowed funds tends to create its own supply without reducing the amount of funds available to private borrowers. Additional restraint in the credit markets may be required to compensate fully for the stimulus to private spending arising out of the deficit. Thus, in the achievement of a given target level of demand for goods and services, a deficit implies a greater stringency in the credit markets than would be appropriate if the budget were balanced.

Conversely, when a Treasury surplus is devoted to the retirement of outstanding government debt, the holders of the repaid government obligations are in a position to buy private securities or invest the money directly, thus augmenting the sources of private demands for new output. The reduction of private disposable incomes that goes with a surplus is thus at least partly offset by an expansion in the availability of credit funds. Interest rates tend to be lower, and bank credit accommodation easier, than they would be if the budget were balanced. However, the augmentation of the supply of loan funds that accompanies the surplus may work, through its downward pressure on interest rates, to discourage the economizing of working cash balances because it lowers the cost of holding cash in terms of foregone interest income. To the extent that the debt retirement merely leads to an increase in private cash balances, it must be reinforced by a further easing of credit if the desired level of spending is to be achieved.

CYCLICAL DEVELOPMENTS OBSCURE FISCAL INFLUENCE

The foregoing line of reasoning as to the influence of the state of the federal budget on credit conditions might lead to the supposition that Treasury deficits are typically accompanied by tight money, while Treasury surpluses normally produce conditions of credit ease. More often than not, the pattern has been just the opposite because other financial developments have tended to obscure the influence of federal debt operations on credit conditions. Wartime experiences aside, Treasury deficits are generally expected to occur during periods of recession and recovery when tax revenues are low. These are precisely the times when private demands for borrowed funds are weak.

Conversely, Treasury surpluses are usually expected during periods of general economic prosperity when tax yields are high; during these periods, private demands for loan funds are very active and tend to overpower the influence of debt retirement on the supply of loanable funds.

It is nonetheless true that the state of the federal budget has an important bearing on the credit conditions existing at any time because the influence of the budget on the private sector's ability to finance demands out of disposable income operates at all points in the economic cycle. At any given point smaller deficits or larger surpluses would make appropriate easier credit conditions; looked at the other way, larger deficits and smaller surpluses make necessary greater credit restrictions throughout the course of the business cycle if a given target level of spending is to be achieved.

Thus, the more or less continual use of debt rather than taxes to finance government spending implies the development of substantially greater restraints on private credit financing than would be necessary if the budget were basically in balance. On the other hand, an underlying surplus in the federal budget makes possible an augmentation of the supply of funds available for private borrowing while still holding spending down to the appropriate target level.

THE UNDERLYING TREND OF THE BUDGET AND THE COMPOSITION OF PRIVATE DEMANDS

The significance of the choice of a particular blend of budget and credit policies to achieve a given target level of private demands derives importantly from its influence on the character of private demands. Although compensations in monetary and credit conditions can allow for a wide range of alternative budgetary policies while preserving the target level of demand for goods and services, the particular mixture of fiscal and monetary influences that is used has an important influence in shaping the kinds of demands that make up the total. Since the greater part of private disposable income is used to finance household expenditures on current consumption, while the greater part of private borrowing is used to finance spending on producer and consumer durable goods, a fiscal policy that is permissive with respect to private spending is generally looked upon as exerting upward pressures on consumer demand in particular, while restrictive credit policies are thought to hold down the demand for durable goods that add to the wealth and productive capacity of the economy. To the degree that this is true, the choice of a particular blend of fiscal and monetary policies influences the allocation of the economy's productive resources between producing for current consumption and producing durables that add to wealth and future capacity.

An awareness of this aspect of the implications of federal budgetary policy is highly useful in making intelligent policy decisions. Those who favor the promotion of economic growth at the expense of current standards of consumption are prone to argue that the monetary and credit restrictions necessitated by an underlying budgetary deficit are in general prejudicial to capital formation. It is widely recognized, however, that the present state of empirical knowledge can offer only limited information concerning the precise effects of fiscal and credit policies. While it is true that credit is extended primarily for the purchase of producer and consumer durable goods, and that credit restrictions tend to hold down these outlays, just which kinds of spending on durables are most sensitive to credit restrictions is problematical.

On the consumer side, the rate of spending for residential housing appears to be much more sensitive to interest rate changes than does the demand for the shorter-lived consumer durable goods, such as automobiles, furniture, and home appliances, that are often financed by consumer instalment loans. In part this is because the ceiling rates of interest on government-insured mortgages discourage investment in them as the general level of interest rates rises, although the practice of discounting these mortgages has, to some extent, made it possible for lenders to realize more than the legal maximum rate. In addition, since the interest component of the total payments on long-term mortgages bulks much larger than does the interest component of payments for shorter-term consumer instalment loans, the demand for mortgage funds is apt to be the more sensitive to interest rate changes.

The same kind of logic is used to argue that long-term capital investment is generally more susceptible to influence through changing interest rates than is shorter-term business spending on such items as inventories and short-lived machinery. There is some empirical evidence that may be used to buttress the logic of this point, but the analyst must be wary of trying to push too far his reasoning as to the effects of credit conditions on particular kinds of business investment. Many who favor government policies designed to promote long-term capital investment therefore argue for the use of other devices, such as tax incen-

tives for capital outlays, or reduced corporation income taxes to increase the
amount of corporate earnings retained for investment. . . .

Selection 41

MANAGING THE FEDERAL DEBT

HERBERT STEIN

> *This selection presents one viewpoint on debt management. Al-
> though it is recognized that debt management may affect spending,
> and thus affect output and prices, it is argued that monetary policy
> also can do this, and that there is no valid reason, except in special
> circumstances, to use debt management instead of monetary policy
> —partly because use of debt management may be costly in terms
> of interest payments. Long-term borrowing in periods of prosperity
> forces the Treasury to engage in long-term borrowing when inter-
> est rates are high. Mr. Stein regards economic stability as the major
> policy goal, and assumes that monetary policy is or can be used to
> achieve that goal.*

From the end of World War II until 1951 federal debt management was
shackled by adherence to a fixed long-term interest rate. During that period the
federal government issued no marketable securities with a maturity in excess
of five years. Abandonment of the bond-price peg opened the way to more
flexible debt management. In 1952 the Treasury issued $5.2 billion of over-five-
year debt. The amount of such debt issued rose to $6.2 billion in 1953 and
soared to $21.7 billion in 1954. After that, however, offerings of longer-term
debt declined sharply to $2.7 billion in 1955 and zero in 1956. In 1957 no debt
with maturity in excess of five years was issued until the last quarter of the year,
after the recession had started. The debt issues after 1952 were long enough to
arrest the decline in the average maturity of the privately held marketable debt,
which had fallen from eleven years at the end of 1946 to about six years, but
did not lengthen the average maturity significantly by the end of 1957.

This record has been a source of disappointment to many observers on
two grounds. First, the big sale of long-term debt in the 1954 recession and the
decline in such issues during the subsequent boom is considered to be contrary
to the requirements of a stabilizing counter-cyclical debt policy. Second, failure
to lengthen the average maturity of the debt is considered, not necessarily by
the same people, to be contrary to the long-run requirements of a sound debt
structure.

It is not my purpose here to analyze or defend this record. Rather I want
to consider two questions that are raised by this experience:

1. What should be the cyclical behavior of debt management? Should it
take advantage of the easier credit conditions of recession to issue longer-dated

---

● From Herbert Stein, "Managing the Federal Debt," *Journal of Law and Economics,*
October, 1958. Copyright 1958 by the University of Chicago. Reprinted by permission of
the *Journal of Law and Economics* and the author.

securities, as we did in 1954, and stay out of the long market when credit is tight, as we did in 1956? Or does debt management have a function in stabilizing the economy which calls for issuing long securities in booms and short ones in recessions?

Should debt management seek to achieve a longer maturity distribution of the debt than we now have, even though cyclical considerations may at certain times prevent movement in that direction or even require movement towards a shorter debt?

I define debt management as policy with respect to the composition of the federal debt held outside the government and Federal Reserve Banks. The size of the federal debt held outside the government is a matter of budget policy, and the amount of federal debt held by the Federal Reserve Banks is an aspect of monetary policy.

Also, I shall concentrate this discussion on the question of the maturity of marketable debt. The debt has, of course, many features other than its maturity distribution—such as taxability, callability, eligibility for purchase by specified classes of investors, and marketability. However, maturity distribution is the main and most general problem. And in fact, the debt is becoming more homogeneous in respects other than maturity.

THE THEORY OF DEBT MANAGEMENT FOR STABILIZATION

The belief that debt management can and should be used counter-cyclically as an instrument of economic stabilization rests basically upon one proposition. It is that a lengthening of the maturity of the debt will tend to restrain private expenditure and that a shortening will tend to stimulate private expenditure. What is essentially involved is that the shorter debt is more like money, and that its ownership is a closer substitute for ownership of money, than is the longer debt. If short-term debt is retired as it comes due, and long debt is issued in its stead, the former holders of the short debt will not want the long debt, or at least they will not regard it as a good substitute for the short debt. They will still want to hold short dated, safe securities, and since the supply of these has been reduced their prices will rise, their yields decline and the former holders will try to increase their ownership of cash. The new offerings of long debt, on the other hand, will not induce their purchasers to reduce the amount of cash they want to hold. The long debt is closely competitive with private and municipal debt. The long debt will have to be offered on terms that induce investors to reduce their holdings, or rates of acquisition of nonfederal debt. Interest rates will rise, discouraging private and municipal investment. Also the value of assets will decline, further discouraging private expenditure.

It seems *a priori* likely that this process should work. A ranking of federal securities from *A* to *Z* in the order of their nearness to money should be possible, and it seems reasonable that this ranking should correspond to ranking according to maturity dates. Then a shift from *A* to *Z* would be a deflationary, or restrictive move, and a shift from *Z* to *A* would be expansive. Such shifting could be used as an instrument of economic stabilization.

There is nothing in the argument to imply that the shifts should always be between A and Z rather than between A and M or G and S. Presumably a shift between A and Z has more effect per dollar of shift than a shift between any other pair. But unless the total dollar amount of shifting is limited, this is not a sufficient reason for choosing the shift from A to Z. Suppose a certain, desired, antiinflationary effect can be achieved by a $1 billion shift from A to Z or by a $2 billion shift from A to M. If the interest rates on A, M, and Z are one, one and one-half, and two and one-half per cent, respectively, the $2 billion shift from A to M costs less than the $1 billion shift from A to Z.

Supposing that a policy of lengthening the debt in inflation and shortening it in recession would be stabilizing, is this sufficient reason to follow such a policy? It seems obvious, at first glance, that we want to do everything we can to achieve stability. But we do not really mean this. We want to do *enough* to achieve stability. We have several instruments that can be used for achieving stability. The question about debt management is not whether it can also be used but whether a combination of instruments that includes debt management would be more likely to achieve stability than a combination that does not.

In fact, the question can be put more specifically. A counter-cyclical debt management policy would operate in much the same way as flexible monetary policy—upon the public's supply of liquid assets and upon credit conditions. Can debt management do anything that monetary policy cannot? Unless it can, there are two good reasons for not including counter-cyclical debt management in the arsenal of stabilization weapons. One is that division of responsibility among different instruments, especially if they are managed by different agencies, permits evasion of responsibility. The other is that counter-cyclical use of debt management may have costs in terms of other objectives, notably minimizing the interest burden.

Denial that counter-cyclical debt management can add anything to monetary policy as an instrument of stability does not imply the absence of limits to the effectiveness of monetary policy. For example, the success of monetary policy may be limited by the difficulty of estimating when and how strongly to act. Or there may be political limits set by the reluctance of the government to accept the tight credit conditions that antiinflationary monetary policy may impose. But a combination of money and debt policy would not be less subject to these limits than monetary policy alone.

There is, at least on paper, one kind of limit to monetary policy that debt management might help to overcome. Suppose that the monetary authority wishes to impose monetary restriction to combat inflation. It tightens the reserve position of the banks by selling short-term securities and perhaps also by raising reserve requirements. The banks respond to this by selling short-term government securities which they own. With a small increase in the yields of these securities individuals and businesses are willing to hold more of them instead of holding cash. But the small rise in short-term interest rates does not restrain borrowing or expenditure. The monetary contraction automatically produces an offsetting reduction in the demand for money and *no* antiinflationary effect. It is essential for this argument to say "no" effect, rather than "only a little." "Only a little" would mean "only a little per dollar of monetary contraction" and would imply that there is some amount of monetary contraction that would be enough to produce the desired antiinflationary effect.

In these circumstances a policy of issuing long-term debt and retiring short-term may be able to achieve what monetary policy cannot. It is only necessary to postulate that the offering of more long-term securities will raise long-term interest rates and that an increase of long-term rates will cut private expenditures, while the offering of more short-term securities does not raise short-term interest rates or a rise in short-term rates does not reduce private expenditures.

Similar conditions can be described that would limit the effectiveness of monetary policy in stimulating the economy but still leave debt management capable of producing a result.

Our ability to postulate such conditions is not evidence that they ever actually exist. In fact, there seems to me an inherent implausibility about propositions whose validity depends upon some elasticity being either infinity or zero. But formulating a debt management policy does not require us to decide whether such conditions *ever* exist. Unless we can assume that these conditions always exist we have the problem of how to manage the debt in periods when they do not exist, when debt management cannot add to the stabilizing effectiveness of monetary policy and when stabilization alone cannot be a sufficient guide to debt management. The only way we are going to know whether we are in such a period will be by trying—that is, by trying monetary policy and finding whether it works or not. I think that the periods in which monetary policy encounters a limit that can be overcome by debt management will be rare. I doubt that we have had any such period since the end of the war.

What difference will it make whether we use counter-cyclical monetary policy alone or counter-cyclical monetary policy in combination with counter-cyclical debt management, in circumstances where either course can yield the desired stabilization effect? One difference will be in the fluctuations in the supply of funds and in interest rates in long-term credit markets and short-term credit markets. With counter-cyclical debt management more long-term debt would be issued in booms, more short-term debt in recessions. Long-term rates would rise more in booms, when interest rates are rising anyway, and fall more in recessions. Is there any affirmative reason for preferring this? I think not. On the contrary, if stabilization does not require it there are equity considerations against government policy that requires borrowers at one time to commit themselves to much higher interest rates than borrowers at another time. Also, subject to the same reservation, that stabilization does not require it, wide fluctuations of long-term interest rates are undesirable as introducing an unnecessary uncertainty into investment planning.

Another consequence of counter-cyclical debt management is a higher interest burden on the debt. The Treasury would do its long-term borrowing when interest rates are high and would get only a short-term advantage when interest rates are low. And it is an advantage, simply in terms of the tax-transfer problem, to hold down the interest of the debt insofar as that is consistent with economic stability.

My conclusion from the above considerations is that the proper guide to the cyclical management of the debt should not be economic stabilization. More long-term debt should be issued in recessions, more short-term debt in booms. This would hold down the federal interest burden, reduce fluctuations in long-term interest rates and leave to monetary policy the responsibility for helping to stabilize total money expenditure through influencing the supply of money, supply of liquid assets, asset values and interest rates. This conclusion is subject to the qualification that debt management should stand by to help if it can in situations where monetary policy is unable to discharge this responsibility, situations that I would expect to be rare.

THE STRUCTURE OF THE DEBT

A policy of lengthening the debt in one phase of the business cycle and shortening it in another phase is consistent with either lengthening or shortening the debt in the long run. The debt can be lengthened in the long run, even though it is shortened in some cyclical phases, if it is lengthened even more in other phases. Of course, we must start with the debt we have. And if debt policy is uniquely determined by short run considerations at every moment, these considerations will also determine the structure of the debt for all future time. But short run debt policy is not so uniquely determined. If we accept the lengthening of the debt in the long run as a goal we can do more lengthening when lengthening is appropriate, and less shortening when that is appropriate, than we would otherwise do. It is therefore necessary to ask whether we should be seeking to achieve, in the long run, a different structure of debt than we now have.

The main current criticism of the present structure of the debt is that it necessitates frequent refundings which inhibit the execution of a restrictive monetary policy. On January 1, 1957 there was $45 billion of privately held marketable debt coming due during 1957. About $23 billion of this was in thirteen-week bills which roll over fairly regularly and in tax anticipation bills that would be returned at tax dates. The remaining $22 billion would, in the ordinary course of events, be refunded by new issues of one-year maturity or longer. In six months during the year the Treasury would be involved in large refunding operations. This is a typical pattern with the present composition of the debt.

For a period of several weks surrounding each of these refundings the Federal Reserve feels severely limited in carrying out a restrictive monetary policy. It cannot tighten credit conditions, or allow them to tighten, to a point at which the Treasury offering would be substantially undersubscribed. Credit conditions must be maintained in a state at which the terms of the Treasury offering are attractive. We may thus end up the period of the subscription with looser monetary conditions than the Federal Reserve would have preferred on grounds of stabilization alone. But once this has been allowed to happen, it is difficult to correct in the interval before the next Treasury issue. Once credit expansion has occurred, loans made, commitments undertaken and investment begun, it is more "disruptive" to cut back than it would have been to prevent the expansion in the first place.

This argument raises a number of questions. If an issue is undersubscribed, could not the Treasury raise the cash it needs, quickly, by raising its weekly offering of bills, at least temporarily, without Federal Reserve support? Since there are always some new loans being made, some new investment projects being started, need a roll-back of total credit involve a roll-back of individual plans or commitments? In the six years since the end of the fixed support under government bonds have monetary conditions ever been looser, for more than a few weeks at a time, than the Federal Reserve would have liked? For example, is there any reason to think that if less federal debt had to be refunded monetary policy would have been more restrictive in 1956 than it was?

Despite these questions the reality and universality of money-managers' feelings about government refunding operations must be recognized. Even if monetary policy could be adequately restrictive in the presence of large and frequent refundings, the chances of adequate policy would be increased if refundings were smaller and fewer. Therefore holding down the refundings that have to be done during a period of monetary restriction is an appropriate goal for the structure of the debt.

Three things should be noted about this goal:

1. It does not require lengthening the average maturity of the debt. Of course the ideal debt from this standpoint would consist entirely of consols. But much can be accomplished short of this. On January 1, 1957, as already noted, $22 billion privately held debt other than bills and tax anticipation certificates came due within one year. At the same date the average maturity of all such debt was about seven years. If the average maturity had been the same but with equal amounts of debt coming due each year, only about $7 billion of debt would have come due each year. The main problem is not the average maturity of the debt but the great unevenness of the distribution with the concentration in the first year. Even if only the debt due in the next five years were evenly distributed over that period, the amount coming due in the first year would be $12 billion rather than $22 billion.

2. This goal does not require that especially long-maturity debt be issued during a boom when monetary restriction is in order. The important thing is the amount of debt coming due during the boom, which will be as much influenced by the debt issued during recessions as by the debt issued during booms.

3. This goal is not inconsistent with concentrating long-term borrowing in recessions in order to reduce the interest burden. In fact, both goals call for reducing the amount of debt that comes due in booms.

The two objectives for the debt discussed up to this point may be summarized as:

1. The proportion of the debt outstanding at any time that was issued at the low interest rates of recession should be high.

2. The maximum proportion of the debt coming due in any year should be low.

Substantial progress toward both objectives could be made without increasing the present average length of the debt. But still more could be done with a longer debt. At the extreme we could eventually get the debt to consist entirely of consols that had been issued during recessions. Would it be desirable to lengthen the maturity of the debt beyond its present level?

It seems to me that this is almost entirely a matter of cost. In other words, considerations other than cost seem so uncertain, on balance, as not to justify lengthening the debt if substantially more interest cost would be required. A longer debt would have the advantage that its market value would fluctuate more with rises and falls of interest rates, which would increase its effectiveness as a built-in economic stabilizer. On the other hand, a longer federal debt may mean shorter private debt, which would be undesirable from several standpoints. And once the concentration of maturities that now embarrasses monetary policy has been reduced as far as the present average length of the debt allows, further spreading may not be urgent.

A decision that lengthening the debt does or does not involve additional interest costs necessarily requires an estimate of future interest rates. This means that a guess must be made, and this guess will sometimes prove to be wrong. However, it is important to make sure that a succession of wrong guesses does not lead to excessive concentration of maturities. For example, if the debt-managers persistently estimated that interest rates would be lower in the next year, and re-funded all maturing debt into new debt due within one year, the proportion of the debt coming due annually would soon be enormous. Therefore, judgments about the policy that will minimize the interest burden should be exercised subject to some limit, such as that the debt (excluding bills) coming due in any one year should not exceed a given proportion, say 10 or 15 per cent of the total debt (excluding bills). With such a safeguard the consequences of possible errors in forecasting interest rates should not be serious.

Anyone who argues for giving substantial weight to holding down the interest burden as an objective of debt management must protect himself against one misinterpretation. I am not arguing for a policy of easy money as a means of holding down interest burdens. I am assuming that monetary policy will do what it can do to promote economic stability. Only because I assume this can I argue that the interest burden should be a major guide to debt management. If monetary policy fulfills its proper function with respect to the important objective, stability, debt management can pay attention to the interest burden.

Selection 42

THE ECONOMICS OF TREASURY DEBT MANAGEMENT
TILFORD C. GAINES

This selection presents the general theory of debt management as it is now practiced. The view expressed in this selection is that debt management is a useful supplement to monetary and fiscal policy, because the size of the debt gives the Treasury power to influence the amount of debt instruments of various maturities. An increase in short-term debt creates a financial atmosphere conducive to an easy availability of credit and the encouragement of spending. If the increase in short-term debt is accompanied by a reduction in out-standing long-term debt, the supply of long-term debt is reduced, and financial institutions and other purchasers of long-term debt are encouraged to buy other securities—thus facilitating investment.

Debt management is a necessity with a large federal debt. The wise use of debt management is desirable because several objectives are being sought at the same time: because business activity was increasing, monetary ease was not required; at the same time, a relatively high rate of unemployment made it desirable to make long-term capital funds available at relatively low rates to finance new investment; and, at the same time also, an outflow of funds that added to the balance of payments problem made it desirable to finance through short-term and medium-term securities and yet to prevent the banks from becoming unduly liquid by preventing expansion of bank reserves, through use of monetary controls. The fact that there were several target variables made it desirable to use several instrument variables to achieve the desired goals.

The view presented by Mr. Gaines recognizes the importance of the fact that particular financial and other economic institutions typically channel funds into particular types of loans and investments. Analysis simply in terms of changes in the money supply, or in terms simply of the role of investment and consumption spending, is oversimplified; money supply, general liquidity of various sectors of the economy, and consumer and investment spending all have significant effects on aggregate demand, output, employment, and prices—including interest rates.

Attitudes toward the United States public debt range from regarding it as an unmitigated evil to seeing in the debt the beneficial foundation of our money and financial mechanism. Good or bad, the debt is with us and, if it is not to be a disturbing influence in the economy, it must be managed wisely and with understanding of the economic consequences that may result from debt management decisions.

The total of new securities issued by the Treasury each year to meet its cash needs and to refund existing debt runs to many tens of billions of dollars. Treasury financing no doubt exceeds the total of all other debt issues year by year. Given its ability to shift vast amounts of debt from shorter to intermediate or long term, or the reverse, the Treasury may have profound influence upon the supply of credit available to other borrowers in any particular sector of the market or upon the supply of liquid, spendable assets in the economy. If it lengthens its debt, corporate, municipal, and mortgage borrowers may find the available supply of long-term credit sharply reduced. If it allows the public debt to shorten, the supply of inflation-feeding, near-money liquid assets may be dangerously increased.

The power inherent in the management of the public debt may advance

• From Tilford C. Gaines, "The Economics of Treasury Debt Management," *Banking,* May, 1964, pp. 42–44, 146. Reprinted from *Banking,* Journal of The American Bankers Association, with the permission of the journal and of the author.

important public policy objectives and help promote a more viable financial market when it is used wisely. Used unwisely, public debt management may seriously disrupt financial markets and the economy generally.

COMPOSITION AND OWNERSHIP OF THE DEBT

At the end of 1963, the gross public debt amounted to some $310 billion, $6 billion greater than a year earlier and up nearly $20 billion since December 1960. As Table 1 shows, however, purchases by the Federal Reserve System in

Table 1
U.S. GOVERNMENT DEBT
(Billions of dollars)

End of year	Gross public debt	Owned by FRS and Treasury	Owned by the Public		
			Total	Marketable	Nonmarketable
1945	278.7	51.3	227.4	171.0	56.4
1955	280.8	76.5	204.3	134.1	70.2
1960	290.4	82.5	207.9	154.5	53.4
1961	296.5	83.4	213.1	160.5	52.6
1962	304.0	86.4	217.6	165.7	51.9
1963	310.1	91.7	218.4	165.9	52.5

SOURCE: United States Treasury Department

Table 2
PUBLIC OWNERSHIP OF MARKETABLE GOVERNMENT SECURITIES
(Billions of dollars)

End of year	Total [1]	Comm'l banks	Saving banks and insurance companies	Other corporations	State and local governments	Individuals and others
1960	160.7	62.1	18.1	20.1	18.7	41.7
1961	165.6	67.2	17.5	19.7	18.7	42.5
1962	170.1	67.2	17.5	20.1	19.5	45.7
1963	169.6	63.5	16.7	20.8	20.6	48.1

[1] Includes investment series bonds

SOURCE: United States Treasury Department

its open market operations during the three years 1961 through 1963 and by the Treasury for its trust accounts absorbed more than $9 billion of the total increase in debt. As a result the Treasury found it necessary to place only $10.5 billion with other investors. The public took some $11.4 billion of marketable securities while reducing its holdings of nonmarketable bonds by almost $1 billion (see Table 1).

For purposes of this discussion of Treasury debt management, the relevant portion of the debt is that owned by the public and, more particularly, the marketable debt owned by the public. Investments of the Federal Reserve System and the Treasury trust accounts are determined by monetary policy objectives and by net inflows to the trust funds, and these investments must be in government securities. Therefore, this portion of the debt does not pose a financing problem for the Treasury. Nonmarketable public debt, principally Savings Bonds, has tended to be quite stable in recent years and, therefore, also has not created problems for the debt managers.

The portion of the debt with which we are particularly concerned, the publicly-owned marketable securities, has grown by more than $11 billion in the past three years, although it is still not back to the peak reached immediately after World War II. While this recent growth has constituted an important demand upon the supply of funds available in the capital markets, it should be recognized for purposes of perspective that the United States government was by no means as large a user of credit as other borrowers. During the same three years, *total* net debt in this country grew by $206 billion. Mortgage borrowers took $63 billion, business corporations borrowed $70 billion, and state and local governments increased their indebtedness by $22 billion.

Nonetheless, the United States Treasury through the management of the public debt is the most influential debtor in the credit markets. Decisions as to the timing and character of financing operations affect the availability of funds at various maturities to other borrowers and thus, in combination with Federal Reserve monetary policy, guide credit conditions. A good part of the power inherent in debt management derives from the fact that refunding of existing debt as well as new borrowing may be employed to achieve policy objectives. For example, marketable debt owned by the public increased by only $200 *million* in 1963, but the actual volume of new marketable securities issued to the public (exclusive of the weekly Treasury bills) was $50 *billion* [italics added by editor]. Debt owned by the public maturing within five years was reduced by $6 billion, while publicly-owned government bonds in the over-five-year maturity bracket were increased by roughly the same amount. The huge size of Treasury cash and refunding operations and the opportunity for massive reshuffling of maturities give Treasury debt management decisions a power to influence financial markets far out of proportion to the Treasury's importance as a net user of new credit.

Commercial banks are, by a rather wide margin, the largest holders of marketable United States government securities (see Table 2). At the end of 1963, commercial banks owned approximately $63 billion of the $166 billion of marketable Treasury securities held by the public. All types of investors and investing institutions own governments, however, and the wide distribution of ownership enables the Treasury, in its debt management decisions, to affect directly the full range of debt markets and investors. Industrial corporations, mutual savings institutions, insurance companies, and state and local governments are particularly sizable investors in United States government obligations.

DEBT MANAGEMENT AS AN INSTRUMENT OF POLICY

The decisions taken by Treasury officials in managing the debt have an influence upon the functioning of the economy principally through the effect they have upon the availability of credit funds to other borrowers and through their effect upon the liquidity of the economy. Debt management as an instrument of public policy, therefore, is similar to and inextricably entangled with the monetary policy of the Federal Reserve System. Of the two, monetary policy is no doubt the more powerful, but debt management policies at odds with monetary policies have at times created difficulties for the Federal Reserve and, to a degree, offset the effect of Federal Reserve policies.

One concern of monetary policy is to regulate the money supply or, more broadly, the total supply of highly liquid, near-money assets. To the extent that the Treasury increases or reduces its short-term debt it affects the liquidity of the economy—the supply of liquid assets—quite independently of Federal Reserve policy. Another concern of monetary policy is to regulate the total amount of credit of all types created in the economy and to influence the supply of credit available to borrowers in the various maturity brackets.

When the Treasury is a heavy net borrower in periods of restraint on credit, or repays debt when money is easy, it may have effects on credit creation just counter to what the Federal Reserve is seeking. Or when it lengthens or shortens the public debt, the effects upon the availability of different types of credit may be quite contrary to the results currently being sought by monetary policy. In a sense, monetary and debt management policies are opposite sides of the same coin. Effective economic policy demands that they be synchronized.

This description of the influence that Treasury debt management can have upon the effectiveness of Federal Reserve monetary policy contains at least two implicit assumptions. First, it assumes that inappropriate fiscal policy—resulting in deficits in prosperity or surpluses in recession—may cause the total usage of new credit in the economy to be more or less than the Federal Reserve would have intended. Second, it assumes that the total supply of available credit is not a single pool but a group of pools of long-term, intermediate-term, and short-term credit funds.

With respect to the first assumption, it should be mentioned that the Federal Reserve does not set a specific target for new credit creation. But behind Federal Reserve deliberations and policies is the desire to regulate credit in such a manner as to avoid either inflation or deflation. Theoretically, the Federal Reserve can ignore the Treasury's financing needs in the execution of its credit-regulating policies, requiring the Treasury to compete for its share of the available supply of credit. But realistically this may not be possible. For example, if the Treasury has a sizable deficit to finance in a period of prosperity, when other credit demands are heavy, the result might be the creation of a total amount of new credit greater than the Federal Reserve might have wished. To force the Treasury to cover its needs out of a limited total supply might deprive private borrowers of the credit needed in the private economy to sustain prosperity.

SECOND ASSUMPTION

The second assumption is an everyday fact of life to bankers and bond market specialists, although it has been a matter of some dispute among economists. Stated simply, the new credit funds generated by certain types of savings and investing institutions, such as insurance companies and savings and loan associations, are directed principally into long-term investments; banks typically give first priority to business credit in the allocation of their resources; corporate cash typically is invested in short-term instruments; and so forth. Since, in our highly complex financial system, the flows of funds through these various institutions are subject to different influences and since the demands for credit of different types also are subject to their own influences, it is possible to have differing degrees of ease or tightness in different sectors of the maturity range or for different types of credit. Given the vast size of Treasury financing and the discretion the Treasury has as to the terms and maturity at which it finances, it is understandable that Treasury finance is capable of having a strong influence upon the relative availability of credit of different types.

An instance of collision between Treasury financing requirements and Federal Reserve policy occurred in 1959. The $12 billion budget deficit in fiscal 1959, a period of strong and expanding business activity, had to be financed at a time when other demands for credit were unusually strong and when the Federal Reserve, fearing a renewed outbreak of inflation, was attempting to maintain strict limits upon credit growth. Because of the Treasury deficit, the actual credit growth in calendar 1959 was by far the greatest in any peacetime year to that time. Moreover, in spite of strenuous efforts by the Treasury debt managers to finance the deficit in a way that would harmonize with Federal Reserve policies, it simply was not possible to avoid financing at shorter term. The long-term funds were not available to the Treasury short of critically starving other users of long-term credit. And an important technical limitation upon the Treasury was the fact that market rates of interest were at a level that made it impossible for the Treasury to sell bonds within the statutory 4¼ per cent ceiling on Treasury bonds. In fiscal 1959, the public marketable debt more than five years from maturity declined by $9.5 billion while shorter debt increased by $21 billion. The entire deficit, and much more, was financed at short term, adding to the supply of liquidity in the economy precisely at a time when the Federal Reserve System was attempting to reduce liquidity.

Within the limits set by the budgetary deficits to be financed or surpluses to be utilized, the public debt may be managed in such a manner as to promote the broad economic objectives of public policy. At times when the purpose is to encourage greater liquidity, to stimulate credit expansion, and to promote lower interest rates, the Treasury in both its cash and refunding operations may employ principally short-term securities. Simultaneously, the Federal Reserve would pursue a policy of easy bank credit.

The resulting growth in both money supply and short-term securities—money substitutes—would create a financial atmosphere most conducive to an easy availability of credit for all purposes and to the encouragement of spending. Meanwhile, the steady shortening of the public debt would tend to reduce the supply of longer-term governments and to encourage longer-term lenders to reach out for other types of investments, thus encouraging private investment.

Just the reverse of these policies would be followed in managing the debt in an economic boom, so as to achieve a restrictive influence.

At other times, the purpose of debt management policy might be simply to be "neutral," neither to supply nor to absorb longer-term funds and neither to add to nor reduce economic liquidity. Such purposes could not be served by offering no longer instruments, of course, since the outstanding debt moves steadily toward shorter maturities. The attempt might be made to issue approximately enough new securities in each maturity bracket to replace those moving into shorter brackets.

RECENT EXPERIENCE

The Treasury has had impressive results with a policy of this type in 1962 and 1963. Leaving aside for a moment the balance-of-payments situation, the problem to be dealt with was one of a good rate of economic expansion that did not require the stimulation of easy money and debt policies, side by side with a high unemployment rate which dictated that capital funds be available to finance new investment and even faster growth. Through a combination of cash, refunding, and advance refunding operations, debt of ten-year-and-longer maturity was issued in sufficient volume to offset those outstanding issues that moved to shorter maturities and to increase the total by only about $1.6 billion. Debt in the five-to-ten-year bracket was increased by $10.9 billion, the bulk taken by commercial banks that offset their purchases by sales of shorter governments. The net increase in intermediate debt and reduction in short debt was not restrictive since it was meshed with a Federal Reserve policy which permitted an adequate supply of reserves to provide for all new credit demand. At the same time, the resulting reduction of liquidity in commercial bank portfolios helped to create a setting in which more restrictive monetary policies could bite quickly if such policies were to be called for as economic expansion continued.

In short, the management of the public debt is a necessity which, in skillful hands, may truly become a virtue.

MANAGEMENT, LIQUIDITY, AND MONEY SUPPLY

The power that the government has to influence financial markets through changes in the maturity composition of its debt or through its selection of new issues to finance its cash requirements is, as mentioned earlier, very similar to the money management power vested in the Federal Reserve System. This similarity is seen most clearly in those cases where the Treasury finances a deficit in short-term securities or permits the structure of the outstanding debt to move toward shorter maturities. Since short governments are the very closest thing to money, in that investors holding them consider them virtually the equivalent of money, such an increase in short government debt has almost the same economic impact as an increase in the money supply itself.

It will be noted that this analysis has not referred directly to the question of whether or not a Treasury deficit should be financed through the sale of securities to commercial banks, and thus through an increase in the money supply. Much has been said on this matter over the years, particularly by those alarmed by the inflationary danger in such financing. It was omitted here because it is a question that is not relevant in a discussion of Treasury debt management.

The Federal Reserve System regulates commercial bank credit so as to provide for a growth in money supply and total credit consistent with its policies. If banks are among the net purchasers of part of any addition to the public debt it is because the Federal Reserve has supplied them with reserves sufficient to support this investment in addition to the other demands upon their resources. It is not because the Treasury has "financed through the banks." The Treasury finances in a competitive market and has no control over the ultimate purchasers of its securities, banks or otherwise.

As mentioned in the earlier discussion of the 1959 episode, however, a particularly inappropriate budget policy that results in a large deficit to be financed at a time of economic boom and of Federal Reserve policies aimed at restraining credit may force the Fed to permit more credit growth than it intended. The Treasury must be financed, and the remaining credit available to private borrowers cannot be held below some minimum level. But even in this case, the banking system may not be net buyers of governments. In 1959, for example, banks actually reduced their holdings of government securities by $7 billion while putting on $12 billion of loans.

BALANCE OF PAYMENTS

Management of the debt in recent years has been confronted with a new difficulty, new at least in modern United States history. The problem has arisen from our chronic international balance-of-payments deficits and from the freer international flow of investment funds that grew out of the adoption of currency convertibility by the major European countries some five years ago. As money and capital markets here and abroad have become more closely linked, there has been a growing tendency for investment funds to flow toward those markets that offer the best rate of return. Since interest rates in United States markets generally have been lower than rates abroad, this country has at most times been subject to an outflow of funds that has added to our balance-of-payments deficits.

This new difficulty created a dilemma for the Treasury's debt managers. Could management of the debt help check capital outflow while at the same time follow policies consistent with domestic economic needs? Since the greatest danger stemmed from outflows of short-term funds, the balance-of-payments portion of the answer appeared to be to concentrate financing in shorter securities so as to force short-term rates of interest upward to levels competitive with rates abroad. But this policy might conflict with Federal Reserve efforts to keep a close rein on the growth of liquidity as the economy expanded.

The resolution of the dilemma has been found through careful meshing of Treasury and Federal Reserve policies. Gradual tightening of bank reserves by the Federal Reserve has been supplemented by Treasury refunding operations which, through attractive rates, have encouraged banks to shift from shorter to intermediate-maturity governments. As a result, commercial banks have steadily become less liquid as business recovery has progressed. At the same time, the Treasury has concentrated its cash financing in short securities, which were purchased on balance by nonbank investors, and has timed its offering of these issues to achieve maximum effect in pushing short-term rates up to the levels sought by Federal Reserve and Treasury policy. And as mentioned earlier, this combination of polices in short and intermediate-term debt has been accompanied by a policy of issuing enough long-term debt to prevent the public debt structure from shortening while at the same time avoiding competition with private uses of long-term capital so as not to interfere with the achievement of a faster economic growth.

CONCLUSION

Recent experience with public debt management dramatically illustrates its usefulness as a supplement to fiscal and monetary policies. Stripped of all jargon, that usefulness derives from the fact that the size of the debt and the amount of financing it requires gives the Treasury considerable power to influence the supply of debt instruments outstanding at different maturities. The immediate objectives of debt management will change from one period to the next. But as a policy instrument, in concert with monetary policy, debt management is useful under a variety of circumstances to affect the availability of investment funds for different purposes and thus, in a broader context, to affect the composition of spending in the economy.

Part Six

INTERNATIONAL FINANCE

12

International
Financial Problems

MANY OF THE SAME PROBLEMS CONSIDERED IN EARLIER chapters arise in the field of international finance, which is often treated separately because of the fact that specialized institutions, assets, and markets are encountered. These institutional differences mean that a substantial amount of descriptive material is necessary to indicate the nature of the field of international finance, but the basic problems of liquidity, asset choice, and financial equilibrium are the same. The balance of payments is the social accounting framework for recording and analyzing international transactions, just as the national income accounts are a framework for recording domestic income and expenditure. (For a brief account of the nature of balance-of-payments statements, see Charles N. Henning, *International Finance,* New York, Harper & Brothers, 1958, Ch. 2.)

Selection 43

THE BALANCE OF PAYMENTS

HARRY G. JOHNSON

This selection shows the nature of the balance-of-payments adjustments as a policy problem. Classical theories viewed the balance of payments as economic phenomena in which an automatic ad-

*justment process tended toward equilibrium—either through gold
flows, interest rate changes, and price changes, or through exchange
rate changes. When it was recognized that these mechanisms might
not eliminate deficits or surpluses because of interferences with
the adjustment process, policies to correct disequilibrium became
the focus of attention. Professor Johnson analyzes the monetary
nature of the balance-of-payments problems, and considers the
policies which may be used to bring income and expenditures into
equality. He thus provides the general setting for consideration
of particular problems of recent years, and of some of the steps
which have been proposed to reform the international monetary
system. These problems and proposals are discussed in the four
remaining selections.*

In the past twenty years, there has been a great deal of change in the
theoretical approach to balance-of-payments problems and the mechanism of
adjustment. This has been associated, on the one hand, with the Keynesian revolution, which led to the formulation of theories in terms of disequilibrium rather
than equilibrium and, on the other hand, with the prevalence of balance-of-
payments problems particularly in the post-war period. Very briefly, the change
has been from the idea of a mechanism of adjustment to the idea of the balance of
payments as a policy problem.

In the classical theories, the analysis of balance-of-payments problems ran
in terms of automatic systems of adjustment towards balance-of-payments
equilibrium. The two cases considered were: one, the pure gold standard, where
adjustment came through automatic and free gold flows raising interest rates in
one country and lowering them in the other, thus reducing and increasing the
demand and price levels so as to bring about equilibrium; and, two, the other
extreme of an inconvertible paper currency, where adjustment came through
exchange rate changes which cleared the exchange market. In both systems, the
decisions and actions of monetary and economic authorities were treated as a
part of the system. The actions which monetary authorities took under the gold
standard, for example, were included in the automatic mechanism of adjustment.
In the past twenty years we have moved away from that view of an automatic
and free system of adjustment towards viewing the balance of payments as a policy
problem, and setting up an analysis in which we construct models designed to
display continuing disequilibrium, a circumstance which permits us to study
alternative ways of rectifying the balance-of-payments disequilibrium. These
models have been set up to promote and permit study of balance-of-payments
problems in both under-employment and full-employment conditions.

The change-over from the automatic system to the policy problem approach
was not an immediate result of the Keynesian revolution. The application of the
Keynesian ideas to international trade theory in the period immediately after the
Keynesian revolution was conducted largely within the old framework of

• Reprinted by permission of the publishers from Harry Gordon Johnson, *Money,
Trade, and Economic Growth: Survey Lectures in Economic Theory.* Cambridge, Mass.:
Harvard University Press. Copyright, 1963, by George Allen & Unwin, Ltd. Parts of the
book originally appeared in the Pakistan Economic Journal; this selection appeared in
VIII, no. 2, June, 1958, pp. 16–28.

the mechanism of adjustment. The theory of the foreign trade multiplier, for example, was developed in order to see how far the Keynesian mechanism of variations in income and employment would work to restore equilibrium in the balance of payments, once that equilibrium had been disturbed. Similarly, other extensive Keynesian analyses of the nineteen-thirties, such as that of Mrs. Robinson,[1] were concerned with the role of income and employment variations in the classical mechanism of adjustment framework.

The development of policy-oriented models has been a post-war development, a development which is due particularly to Professors Meade and Tinbergen. (I do not mean to imply that other writers have not contributed importantly to the subject; but these two writers have written books specifically concerned with this problem, whereas other writers have mainly confined themselves to articles.) Meade, in *The Balance of Payments*,[2] was primarily concerned with the conflict between the requirements of full employment and balance-of-payments equilibrium, and the means of reconciling them. Tinbergen, on the other hand, in his book *On the Theory of Economic Policy*,[3] was concerned with the more general problem of achieving a number of policy objectives with a variety of policy instruments. The general point of importance for economic policy which emerges from the work of both writers, incidentally, is that for each policy objective a separate policy instrument is required. For example, to achieve both full employment and balance-of-payments equilibrium—in Meade's terminology, to preserve *both* some means of control over its aggregate expenditure *and* some means of control (the exchange rate or trade restrictions) over its international trade. I shall develop this point later on; here I merely want to indicate the general theoretical point involved, that for each policy objective you need a policy instrument.

In the course of his analysis, Meade develops an approach to balance-of-payments problems which is much more suitable to postwar conditions of full employment than the Keynesian analysis previously available. Unfortunately, the most useful aspects of this approach tend to be hidden by Meade's habit of assuming the pursuit of appropriate internal control policies by the government, without investigating what happens if the government is not successful in maintaining knife-edge full employment with stable prices. The approach and its implications are more fully developed in Sidney's Alexander's article "The Effects of a Devaluation on a Trade Balance."[4] Alexander's method of analysis, which has come to be known as "the absorption approach," has recently been severely criticized by Professor Fritz Machlup, who defends the older "elasticity approach" to devaluation.[5] My own view of the matter is that the absorption approach is of

[1] Joan Robinson, "The Foreign Exchanges," in *Essays in the Theory of Employment* (London: Macmillan & Co., 1937), pp. 183–209.

[2] J. E. Meade, *The Theory of International Economic Policy, Volume I: The Balance of Payments* (London: Oxford University Press, 1951).

[3] J. Tinbergen, *On the Theory of Economic Policy* (Amsterdam: North-Holland Publishing Co., 1952).

[4] S. Alexander, "The Effects of a Devaluation on a Trade Balance," *International Monetary Fund Staff Papers*, II, No. 2, April, 1952, pp. 263–78.

[5] F. Machlup, "The Analysis of Devaluation," *American Economic Review*, XLV, No. 3, June, 1955, pp. 255–78.

much more general usefulness for balance-of-payments problems than appears from this particular debate—especially when Meade's work is looked at in the same context. In what follows I shall try to synthesize a general treatment of balance-of-payments problems in terms of this approach, laying particular emphasis on the policy problems.

To start with, it is useful to recall that the existence of a balance-of-payments problem assumes the presence of a monetary authority which intervenes in the foreign exchange market to peg the rate of exchange, using official reserves of gold or foreign exchange to do so. This permits a divergence to arise between the demands of the rest of the country (excluding the monetary authority) for foreign exchange to pay for purchases abroad, and the supply of foreign exchange in return for domestic currency to pay for sales abroad.

The usual approach to the balance of payments is to consider it as the difference between receipts from and payments to foreigners by the residents of the country, excluding the monetary authority. In symbols, the balance of payment is defined as $B = R_f - P_f$. But it is fruitful to define the balance in another way, by using the fact that receipts by residents from residents are identical with payments by residents to residents. By adding these receipts to and subtracting these payments from the balance of payments, the latter is transformed into the difference between total receipts by residents and total payments by residents (again excluding the monetary authorities). In symbols, $B = R - P$. This is the starting point of the absorption approach to balance-of-payments problems. In discussing these problems, I shall deal throughout with the case of a balance-of-payments deficit, that is, an excess of payments over receipts by residents.

Before I go on to discuss the policy problem, I think it is worth while to investigate briefly the monetary implications of a balance-of-payments deficit. A deficit means that payments by residents exceed receipts by residents, and this implies either one of two things. The first possibility is that residents are running down their cash balances, so that there is an increase in the velocity of circulation of money. With a deficit financed by running down of cash balances, the balance-of-payments deficit would obviously be self-correcting in time, because eventually residents would reduce their cash balances towards zero, and in the process of doing so the rate of interest will rise, demand will be restricted, possibly the supply of goods for export will increase and a variety of factors will set to work which will tend to correct the situation. But nowadays it is very unlikely that monetary authorities will be able to give the economy time to work out the correction of the disequilibrium, because the excess of payments over receipts has to be financed in foreign currency and the monetary authority may well have insufficient reserves to allow the balance-of-payments deficit to go on until it corrects itself. The second possibility is that the monetary authority replaces the cash which is being abstracted by the balance-of-payments deficit, through off-setting internal monetary operations. This will happen automatically if the monetary authority follows a policy of stabilizing interest rates. In this case, the deficit will not be self-correcting: it will be corrected only when the policy of the monetary authority is changed.

To sum up on this point, a balance-of-payments problem implies either that the domestic currency supply is insufficiently backed by a reserve of gold or foreign exchange or that the authorities of the country concerned are pursuing a policy which entails a balance-of-payments problem. In either case, it is evident that a balance-of-payments problem is monetary in nature and that it is fundamentally related to the fact that the banking system can create credit. Both where a country has insufficient international reserves to back its domestic currency and where the monetary authorities replace reserves by other internal assets, credit creation is involved.

That balance-of-payments problems are fundamentally monetary phenomena is an important proposition that must always be borne in mind; it is an obvious proposition, but one which is often overlooked. It has become a habit in writings on policy to discuss "structural" disequilibrium and other concepts as if exchange rates and other governmental policies had nothing to do with balance-of-payments difficulties. Such concepts may have some usefulness in sorting out primary causative factors or types of solution; but they cannot constitute rigidly separate classes of balance-of-payments problems. Balance-of-payments problems are always fundamentally monetary. This does not, however, mean either that they can always be ascribed to monetary mismanagement, or that monetary policy is either the most appropriate policy to employ or the policy instrument most likely to be effective in correcting a balance-of-payments problem. To put the same point another way, no matter what problems a country may have, their manifestation as a balance-of-payments problem is always a consequence of governmental policy; though it must be recognized that in many cases a balance-of-payments problem is easier to endure than the alternative problems the country could have.

Let me now turn to the policy problem posed by a balance-of-payments deficit. To simplify the argument, I shall exclude international capital transactions (other than those necessary for the financing of the deficit); this, together with the fact that intermediate transactions can be cancelled out, permits us to measure the balance of payments as the difference between total domestic output and domestic expenditure. In symbols, $B = Y - E$; to avoid certain difficulties, it is convenient to conceive output and expenditure in real rather than monetary terms.

A balance-of-payments deficit, on these various assumptions, entails an excess of expenditure over output or income. To correct it, expenditure and income must be brought into equality. The policies which may be employed to produce this result may be divided into two types: policies of expenditure reduction and polices of expenditure switching. A policy of expenditure reduction, or reduction of aggregate demand, implemented for example by higher taxes or interest rates, affects both expenditure and output. Expenditure is directly affected, and part of the reduction in expenditure falls on domestic production, in turn setting up multiplier effects which reduce expenditure and output still further. Thus an expenditure-reducing policy has two effects on the balance of payments, in terms of the equation: the first is the direct effect of the expenditure reduction, which is favourable; the second is the induced effect through lower output and consequently lower expenditure, which will be unfavourable so long as a reduction in income reduces expenditure by a smaller amount—that is, so long as the marginal propensity to spend is less than one. The unfavourable effect will be smaller, the more the initial reduction in expenditure falls on imports; and so long as the marginal propensity to spend is less than one, the net effect of an expenditure-reducing policy must be an improvement in the balance of payments.

Two further points should be made before we leave expenditure-reducing policies. One is that the reduction in expenditure and output may reduce the domestic price level, so giving rise to switches of expenditure between foreign and domestic goods; I shall discuss this type of effect in a moment. The second is that the reduction in expenditure, by reducing the country's imports, will bring about multiplier reductions in incomes abroad, which in turn will reduce foreign expenditure on this country's output. The analysis of these "foreign repercussions" is familiar,[6] and I shall not go into it here; so long as the marginal propensity to spend is less than one in all countries, the foreign repercussions will simply reduce the extent of the favourable effect of expenditure reduction, but will not make it unfavourable.

Let us now consider the other type of policy, that of switching expenditure towards home-produced and away from foreign-produced goods. Such switches of expenditure will increase domestic output, and so long as the marginal propensity to spend is less than one (so that expenditure rises less than income) will improve the country's balance of payments. Two types of expenditure-switching policies can be distinguished. One is devaluation, which by making the country's goods relatively cheaper compared with foreign goods will tend to switch both domestic and foreign expenditure towards domestically-produced goods. The other is the use of controls. These are usually applied to restrict imports, in which case there will be a tendency for frustrated domestic consumers to purchase domestic substitutes and for domestic expenditure towards domestic goods—though sometimes import restrictions are described very naively, as if preventing people from buying imports led them automatically to save the money they would have spent. Controls may also be applied in order to stimulate exports; in this case, the aim is to induce the foreigners to switch their expenditure towards domestic output.

In the case of both types of expenditure-switching policy, the aim is to increase the demand for domestic output. This raises the question of where the extra output required to meet this additional demand comes from. In this connection, we have to consider three possible cases for analysis.

The first is that in which there is widespread unemployment. In this case the switch of demand towards domestic output will give rise to increased domestic output and income by increasing the utilization of unemployed resources. The second case is that in which the country has conditions of full employment but the policy of switching expenditure is backed by a complementary policy of reducing domestic demand—a combination of an expenditure-switching and an expenditure-reducing policy. In this case the switch policy can be regarded as a trimming device designed to ensure that balance-of-payments equilibrium is attained without sacrificing full employment;[7] a policy of deflating demand by itself would tend to lead to unemployment because expenditure would have to be cut sufficiently to reduce demand for imports enough to rectify the deficit, imply-

[6] F. Machlup, *International Trade and the National Income Multiplier* (Philadelphia: The Blakiston Co., 1943).

[7] R. F. Harrod, "Currency Depreciation as an Anti-Inflationary Device: Comment," *Quarterly Journal of Economics,* LXVI, No. 1, February, 1952, pp. 102–16.

ing reduction in demand for domestic output; so the switch policy is used as a means of directing the reduction in expenditure entirely on to imports. In order to achieve the two objectives of policy, internal and external balance, it is necessary to use two policy instruments, control of aggregate demand and some sort of switch instrument. The third case is that in which a switch policy is employed under conditions of full employment, but is not reinforced by an expenditure-reducing policy. In this case the switch of demand to domestic output will tend to promote inflationary developments. This is the case analysed by Alexander, who has shown how the inflationary consequences may cure the initial excess of expenditure over income, by reducing effective demand in real terms. I am not going to discuss all the ways in which this may happen, only the more important ones, though I should mention that the argument was designed for European conditions and may be inapplicable to underdeveloped countries.

One possibility is that as income rises in monetary terms the real burden of taxation will become higher and higher. In so far as the government does not spend the extra tax revenue but accumulates it in a budget surplus, there is a deflationary effect through increased leakages into taxation. A second possibility is that price rises may lead to a redistribution of income to profits, and if we can assume—which may not always be reasonable—that businesses do not in consequence increase their investment, there will be an increase in real savings and a deflationary effect on expenditure. Because investment is influenced by the level of profits, it is debatable how far this factor will work in a favourable direction. A third possibility related to the second is that there may be a redistribution of income to wage-and-profit earners on the one hand from fixed-income groups on the other; this may or may not reduce aggregate consumption, depending on the relative sizes of the marginal propensities to consume of the groups concerned, and the way in which the redistribution is shared between wages and profits. Finally—a possibility to which Alexander devotes considerable attention—there is the effect of higher prices in reducing the real value of monetary assets and so inducing the public to spend less and save more. This effect depends on there being a stock of cash, or of government debt which is regarded as an asset by its holders but not, effectively, as a liability by the tax-paying public, so that a rise in the price level makes some asset-holders feel poorer without making anyone else feel richer. For ordinary private debts, nothing much can be deduced about the effects of rising prices, since while the creditor becomes poorer the debtor becomes richer in real terms, and the net effect on spending might go either way.

There is one further point I want to make at this stage of the argument, and that is that the use of import restrictions, in addition to a switching effect, may have a direct expenditure-reducing effect. For various reasons—the structure of the economy, or governmental controls—it may be difficult to provide domestic substitutes for imports, so that, instead of buying more remote substitutes, people simply save the money they are not allowed to spend on imports. I do not think, though, that this is a very important possibility, if we assume that the restrictions on imports are expected to last indefinitely; but it may be that people will save money temporarily, in the expectation that a little later domestic substitutes will become available at lower prices.

To summarize the argument so far: I have been dealing with the balance of payments, looked at as the difference between expenditure and income, and discussing two different types of policy for correcting a deficit, one aimed at reducing aggregate domestic expenditure and the other at switching domestic and foreign expenditure away from foreign towards domestic goods. I now want to discuss some special aspects of devaluation and the use of restrictions on trade, which I have glossed over in outlining the general framework of balance-of-payments theory.

To begin with the problems of devaluation, you are no doubt familiar with at least some of the analyses which have been made of the factors which determine whether or not devaluation will be successful in switching expenditure from foreign goods to home goods.[8] A great deal of effort has been expended on analysing the effect of devaluation on the trade balance, or, as it is sometimes called, the problem of exchange stability. There are in fact two different approaches to this problem. One is the Marshallian or partial equilibrium approach, which analyses the effects of devaluation in terms of the elasticities of demand and supply of exports and imports, The general formula is quite complicated, but the necessary condition for the balance of trade to be worsened by devaluation is that the sum of the elasticities of demand for imports be less than one. If supplies are inelastic, this has the general effect of restricting the responsiveness of trade to exchange-rate changes, thereby reducing the effects whether favourable or unfavourable; this is the reason why, if supplies are inelastic, devaluation may improve the balance even if the sum of the demand elasticities is less than one.

The Marshallian approach, however, depends upon two sorts of questionable assumptions. The first is that any cross-relations between exports and importable goods through demand and supply can be ignored, so that the export and import sectors of the economy can be dealt with in isolation from one another. The second is that international changes affect the country's aggregate expenditure only through altering its trade balance and hence its level of output. In recent years a considerable amount of work has been done in modifying these assumptions and approaching the problem in a more general way which includes the determination of the level of income along with the balance of payments, and takes into account both the interconnections between demands for different goods and the possible direct effects of changes in the terms of trade on the level of expenditure from a given income. The stability criterion that emerges from this work is that the sum of the elasticities of demand for imports should be greater, not than one, but than one plus the sum (for the domestic economy and the rest of the world) of certain complex factors embodying the direct effect of a change in the terms of trade on expenditure. These factors are each equal to the proportion of the change in real income due to the terms of trade which is reflected in a change in saving, multiplied by the ratio of the marginal propensity to import to the marginal propensity to save. Various approximations to these factors have

---

[8] Joan Robinson, *op. cit.,* and L. A. Metzler, "The Theory of International Trade," Chap. V in H. S. Ellis, ed., *A Survey of Contemporary Economics* (Philadelphia: The Blakiston Co., 1948), especially pp. 225–8.

been derived, which suggest that the elasticity requirement for stability is both higher than the Marshallian one and varies with the circumstances.[9]

The possibility of exchange instability, however, does not seem to me a very realistic problem, at least if one takes a sufficiently long-run view to ignore the problem of short-run speculation, and excludes cases of inflationary conditions in which devaluation is not an appropriate policy. In this connection, I should like to refer you to an article by E. V. Morgan in the June, 1955, issue of *The American Economic Review*, in which it is shown that exchange instability requires instability of the market for some commodity or group of commodities.[10] If you believe that the exchange market is unstable, you must believe that the market for some commodity or commodities is unstable. The point can be illustrated by means of our earlier formula, $B = Y - E$. Assuming E constant, B will improve if a reduction in the price of the country's output, relative to the price of the output of the rest of the world, will reduce the quantity of the country's output demanded.

The much more important practical problem concerns the possibility that devaluation will worsen the devaluing country's terms of trade. This raises the question of the effect of devaluation on the terms of trade; in theory, the effect may be either a worsening or an improvement, depending on the relative magnitudes of the elasticities of demand and supply for exports and imports. Some attempts have been made to deduce a general presumption that the term of trade will turn against the devaluing country from such considerations as that a country is likely to be more important in the market for its exports than in the market for its imports, but such arguments are obviously not very satisfactory.[11]

The proposition that devaluation will involve an adverse movement of the terms of trade underlies much of the argument that has been advanced for preferring controls of various kinds to devaluation. The argument about control versus devaluation I shall consider shortly; at this point, I should merely like to warn against two fallacies commonly perpetrated in putting the case for controls. In the first place, a deficit entails an excess of expenditure over income, and to correct it the country must forego the enjoyment of resources obtained on credit, either imported foreign goods, or domestic goods which must now be exported instead of consumed at home. This is true whether devaluation or controls are used, though exponents of controls sometimes imply that only devaluation entails this loss. Secondly, in circumstances in which the terms of trade are likely to turn adverse, controls also are likely to involve a substantial loss to the country through the inability of residents to obtain the goods they prefer. This is so because a severe adverse movement of the terms of trade implies that the country cannot readily do without imported goods or substitute exportable goods for them. It is

[9] See Harry G. Johnson, "The Transfer Problem and Exchange Stability," *Journal of Political Economy*, LXIV, No. 3, June 1956, pp. 212–25 [reprinted as Chap. VII of *ibid.*, *International Trade and Economic Growth* (London: Allen and Unwin, 1958)] especially Sec. III, for a survey of the literature.

[10] E. V. Morgan, "The Theory of Flexible Exchange Rates," *American Economic Review*, XLV, No. 3, June, 1955, pp. 279–95.

[11] See for example, Joan Robinson, *op. cit.*, pp. 197–8.

of course often argued in favour of controls that they permit a country to maintain the inflow of "essential" goods while keeping out "luxury" goods; but this is a "second best" argument, since there is no obvious reason why "unnecessary" consumption should not be tackled directly, and in any case control of such consumption through import controls may not in fact be effectively workable.

We now come to controls on trade. There are a great variety of such controls, but it is possible to classify them under two heads, financial controls and commercial controls.[12] Financial controls operate through control over the use of money, by restricting the freedom of use of domestic money either through regulation of certain uses or (as in the case of multiple exchange rates) by making some uses of money more expensive than others. Commercial controls, on the other hand, operate on the goods side of transactions by preventing people from buying certain goods or forcing them to buy others, or providing financial incentives (tariffs, subsidies) for certain kinds of sales or purchases. Whether financial or commercial, and whether applied to imports or exports, the effect of controls is to create a divergence between the internal and the external values of commodities: the restriction of exports makes the internal value of goods less than the external value; and the restriction of imports makes the external value of the goods less than the internal values. The divergence in turn implies an abnormal profit from foreign trade; this profit may be either absorbed by the state (through tariffs or export duties, state trading profits, or possibly the profits from the sale of trade control) or left to be reaped by private citizens (the consumer, the domestic trader, or the foreign trader, depending on the system of trade control). The existence of an abnormal profit on trade also creates an incentive to evade the controls, and a need for policing the controls to ensure that they are effective. Because controls of any form have the same effect of creating a divergence between the external and internal value of goods, they can all be treated as equivalent to a combination of export or import duties and a redistribution of income of some kind.

Controls on trade, as compared with the "price-system" method of devaluation, raise two important problems. The first is the effectiveness of controls, as against devaluation, in increasing net foreign exchange earnings. Roughly, we can think of devaluation as being the equivalent of an import duty and an export subsidy;[13] and an import duty is bound to save foreign exchange, whereas an export subsidy will save foreign exchange or not according to whether the elasticity

[12] For a more extended discussion, on which this brief account is based, see J. E. Meade, *op. cit.*, Chaps. XX and XXI.

[13] The equivalence is only rough because an import duty yields additional tax revenue and an export subsidy requires the imposition of taxes to finance it. These income effects can be assumed to cancel when the two are applied together (and the percentage rate is the same), but they should really be taken into account when comparing either alone with devaluation. The following argument ignores this complication; for a more accurate analysis, see J. E. Meade, *op. cit.,* Chap. XXIII, and Harry G. Johnson, *International Trade and Economic Growth* (London: Allen and Unwin, 1958), Chap. VII, Sec. IV, pp. 190–5.

of demand for the country's exports is greater or less than one. Thus an import duty by itself will only save foreign exchange to a lesser extent than devaluation if an export subsidy would actually reduce the country's earnings from exports, that is if the foreign elasticity of demand for exports were less than unity. If the elasticity of demand for exports were less than unity, the country should of course restrict rather than encourage exports. An export subsidy by itself would always be worse than a devaluation, since it would fail to obtain the necessarily favourable effect of devaluation in reducing the amount spent on imports. All of this argument, it should be noted, treats exports and imports as aggregates; for the maximum improvement in the balance of payments, it would obviously be desirable to distinguish between different export and import commodities according to their elasticities of demand or supply.

The second problem concerns the welfare aspects of the choice between trade controls and devaluation. Considering the welfare of the country concerned by itself, this choice depends on the relation between the existing degree of controls and the optimum degree of trade restriction, given the country's trading position. If the country possesses unexploited monopoly or monopsony power then it stands to gain by exploiting this power by further trade restriction; on the other hand, if its trade is restricted beyond the optimum level, it will benefit by relaxing its trade restrictions and devaluing still more than it would have to, if it left its trade restrictions at the existing level.[14]

Fundamentally, the optimum degree of trade restrictions depends on real considerations, and is not conditional on the state of the balance of payments. The balance-of-payments position provides only a second-best argument for trade restriction, that the optimum degree of restriction cannot be legislated without a balance-of-payments crisis. To this point there is one exception, which depends on confusion on the part of other nations—it may only be possible to get away with monopolistic trade restriction without invoking retaliation from other nations if a balance-of-payments deficit can be offered as an excuse for this behaviour.

There is one final point I should like to make about the optimum degree of trade restriction. The argument for seeking to achieve it assumes either that other countries will not retaliate, or that there is no possibility of reaching any international agreement on trade policy. Retaliation is too difficult a matter to discuss here; so far as agreement is concerned, it is obvious that it will never pay two countries to have trade barriers against each other. Such barriers could always be cleared down to a barrier on the part of one country only, to the benefit of both, and possibly they could be completely eliminated. If international income transfers were possible, freedom of trade could always be more beneficial than the preservation of barriers.[15]

---

[14] See S. Alexander, "Devaluation versus Import Restriction as an Instrument for Improving Foreign Trade Balance," *International Monetary Fund Staff Papers*, I, No. 3, April, 1951, pp. 379–96.

[15] See J. M. Fleming, "On Making the Best of Balance of Payments Restrictions on Imports," *Economic Journal*, LXI, No. 241, March, 1951, pp. 48–71, Meade, *op. cit.*, Chap. XXIV.

BALANCE OF PAYMENTS AND MONETARY POLICY

MAURICE MANN AND JOHN T. HACKETT

Much recent discussion has concerned the problem of the deficit in the United States balance of payments which existed during the 1950's and became alarmingly large beginning in 1958. This selection indicates the nature of the deficit in the United States balance of payments—which is unusual because there has been a surplus on current account (imports and exports of goods and services). This selection also shows the relationship between the factors which have created a balance-of-payments problem and monetary policies. The great importance of capital movements, and of financial policies aimed at modifying these flows, is evident. The selection concludes with discussion of a number of the measures taken in recent years to alleviate the adverse consequences of the balance-of-payments problem and to protect the international status of the dollar. Readers interested in further views concerning appropriate policies may wish to read the contributions by Arthur Smithies, John Kenneth Galbraith, and James Tobin in the Review of Economics and Statistics, XLVI *(May, 1964), pp. 111–126. The interest equalization tax referred to as "proposed" in this selection and by Professor Galbraith was enacted into law in August, 1964.*

Our discussion first reviews briefly the background of the United States balance of payments position. We then consider the major causes of the United States international payments problem, with emphasis on the outflow of funds from the United States and the influence that such flows have had on monetary policy. Because of the considerable importance of the flow of short- and long-term funds in the balance of payments, and because of the relationship of credit availability and interest rates to both the domestic economy and the balance of payments, monetary policy in recent years has had to perform a delicate balancing act at home, while performing new and complex operations in the international financial area.

Figure 1 shows, on an annual basis, the net results of United States transactions with the rest of the world during the postwar period. Although the chart conceals the relative strengths and weaknesses of the respective factors affecting the balance of payments, it does remind us that the United States has had payments deficits in twelve of the past thirteen years, and that the deficits became unsustainably large beginning in 1958. During 1950–56, the deficits averaged $1.5 billion annually; during 1958–62, they averaged $3.2 billion. In the earlier period, the deficits were a source of dollars for a world desperately in need of liquidity and were not accompanied by gold flows from the United States; in the

• From Maurice Mann and John T. Hackett, *Balance of Payments and Monetary Policy,* Federal Reserve Bank of Cleveland, October, 1963; 2nd printing, March, 1964. Reprinted by permission of the Federal Reserve Bank of Cleveland.

Billions of dollars

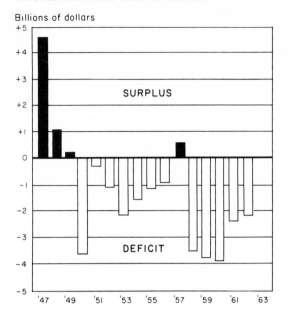

latter period, when the deficits became much larger, they were accompanied by
an outsurge of gold.

The impact of these developments is shown in Figure 2. For most of the
1950's, other nations primarily built up their dollar claims, increasing substantially
their holdings of deposits in United States banks and of United States short-term
securities. Beginning in 1958, however, the pattern shifted, with many foreign
creditors electing to take gold instead of adding to dollar claims. The drain on

Billions of dollars

Figure 2. GOLD STOCKS
AND LIABILITIES TO FOREIGN-
ERS—ANNUALLY, END OF
YEAR.

the United States gold stock in 1958–62 amounted to nearly $7 billion, and resulted in a decline in our holdings of about 30 per cent. The taking of gold did not prevent foreigners' dollar claims from continuing to increase, in fact from climbing even more rapidly than earlier; this was possible only because of the large-scale deficits incurred in our over-all payments accounts.

Some modest improvements were reported in the balance of payments in 1961 and 1962. Because the improvements reflected nonrecurring or special transactions, however, the fundamental fact still remained: the U.S. had not turned the tide of its international economic fortune. This was so despite considerable discussion and a larger number of suggestions for public policy, some of which had been implemented, some of which had not. The incompleteness of the U.S. approach is clearly revealed in the data for the first half of 1963. As Figure 3 shows, there was further deterioration in our payments position, with

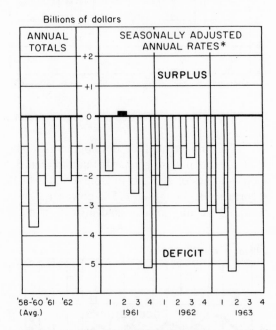

Figure 3. U.S. BALANCE OF PAYMENTS IN RECENT YEARS (Source: U.S. Department of Commerce).

* 2nd quarter 1963 estimated by the Federal Reserve Bank of Cleveland.

events reaching crisis proportions in the second quarter, when the deficit increased to $5.1 billion at a seasonally adjusted annual rate. The magnitude of the deterioration—and its impact—was reflected in the concern of national policy makers, and in a second round of discussions, proposals, and official actions that captured the front pages of the nation's press.

What are the various factors that have converged to create the balance of payments problem? Figure 4 separates out the major components of the United States balance of payments, placing each category on a net inflow or net outflow basis. The algebraic sum of the flows is equal to the total deficit in the over-all balance of payments. Transactions on current account (merchandise trade, serv-

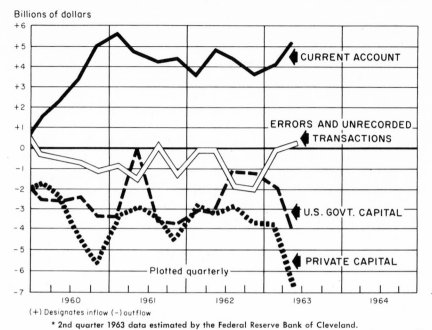

Billions of dollars

(+) Designates inflow (−) outflow

* 2nd quarter 1963 data estimated by the Federal Reserve Bank of Cleveland.
Figure 4. NET FLOWS—SEASONALLY ADJUSTED ANNUAL RATES (Sources: U.S. Department of Commerce).

ices, investment income) have been on balance our only consistent plus factors, with the net inflow averaging $4.2 billion at a seasonally adjusted annual rate in recent calendar quarters. In the second quarter of 1963 the inflow on current account is estimated to have improved substantially, rising to over $5 billion, the best showing since the first quarter of 1961.

Merchandise trade is the principal component of current account; our export surplus thus deserves much of the credit for the over-all current account surplus. Much official effort has been exerted to expand the current account contribution, in view of the fact that it is still insufficient to offset other outflows. Federal encouragement of private exports from the United States, the Trade Expansion Act, expanded export credit insurance, tying of foreign aid to purchases of United States goods, and a reduction in duty-free allowances granted to American tourists are a few examples. While such measures have produced some positive results, it is still an open question as to how much more assistance current account transactions will be able to provide. Near-term changes in the volume of merchandise exports and imports will of course be a crucial factor in the contribution of current account.

Turning to the categories that are on the minus side—the net outflows in the balance of payments—United States government payments to other nations through economic and military programs remain substantial. These payments on a net basis (not including the return flow due to exports tied under the aid program) have tended to stabilize at less than a $3 billion seasonally adjusted rate. The sharp deviations seen on the illustration for certain quarters reflect the incidence of special steps taken by the government to reduce the net outflow of funds. For example, in the second quarter of 1961 and the third quarter of 1962, large prepayments were made on long-term debts owed the United States by several European countries. Official efforts also have been exerted to reduce the net outflow on government account; United States military spending overseas has been reduced wherever possible, and other countries have been asked to share more of the foreign-aid burden. Concurrently, the Congress is taking a close look at our entire foreign aid program. As mentioned earlier, attempts are also being made to tie more of foreign aid to United States exports.

The net outflow of funds on private capital account and in the form of errors and unrecorded transactions are of special concern to the financial authorities. In the case of errors and omissions (a residual item), not only have they been showing up recently as minuses, but more importantly, prior to 1960 such transactions were on the plus side. Many observers associate part of the general reversal in this category, the second quarter of 1963 notwithstanding, with the movement of short-term funds overseas in the form of transactions that may be speculative in nature and do not get reported.

The final category shown on the chart is that of private capital flows. This grouping represents both short- and long-term funds and includes such diverse transactions as United States investments in short-term securities of foreign governments and in bank accounts, the establishment by United States firms of corporate subsidiaries overseas, and the purchase by United States residents of long-term securities floated by foreign firms and foreign governments. The net outflow on this account has been on balance the primary offender in our balance of payments in recent years. The deterioration in private capital outflows during the first half of 1963, particularly in the second quarter, was especially marked, and sparked renewed concern with the balance of payments problem.

During the past three years United States financial policy has been designed to deter short-term capital from moving abroad in response to higher interest rates, while at the same time encouraging private domestic investment. Largely as a result, the net outflow of short-term capital slowly subsided between mid-1960 and the first quarter of 1963, as shown in Figure 5. In fact, we experienced a small net inflow of short-term capital during the first quarter of 1963. However, a sharp redeterioration occurred in the second quarter, as the net outflow of short-term funds reached a seasonally adjusted annual rate of $2.2 billion—the largest outflow since the fourth quarter of 1960.

In addition to efforts to reduce the movement of short-term funds, there has been growing concern regarding the increasing volume of United States long-term private capital investment abroad. Since 1960 the outflow of long-term capital has increased markedly. For example, in the second quarter of 1963 long-term capital exports reached an estimated net annual rate of nearly $4.5 billion (seasonally adjusted), as compared with a rate of only $3 billion in the same period in 1962.

Thus, there appears to be increasing evidence that efforts to cure our balance of payments malady should include attempts to reduce exports of long-term

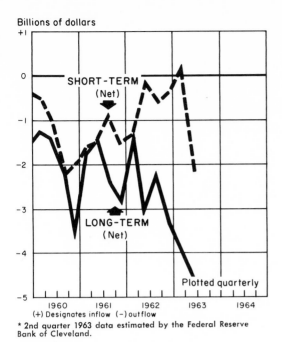

Billions of dollars

SHORT-TERM
(Net)

LONG-TERM
(Net)

Plotted quarterly

1960   1961   1962   1963   1964
(+) Designates inflow   (−)outflow
* 2nd quarter 1963 data estimated by the Federal Reserve
Bank of Cleveland.

Figure 5. PRIVATE CAPI-
TAL FLOWS — SEASONALLY
ADJUSTED ANNUAL RATES
(Source: U.S. Department of
Commerce).

capital as well as short-term outflows. In this connection, there is a substantial amount of confusion with respect to the nature and cause of these long-term capital flows, an understanding of which is essential to formulating effective policies.

In discussing long-term investment abroad it is important to distinguish between direct and indirect foreign investment. The first, and most important, of these two broad categories is direct investment. Direct investment represents United States business investment in foreign production and distribution facilities in the form of outright purchases of new or existing assets, or by the acquisition of the controlling interest in a foreign firm. The value of total foreign-based assets of United States business firms exceeded $37 billion at the close of 1962, as compared with only $7 billion at the beginning of the postwar period. By the close of 1962 the annual capital outflow associated with direct investments had become relatively stable at $1.3 billion, following a decline from the high of $2.4 billion in 1957.

The most recent increase in long-term capital outflows is more closely associated with increases in indirect investment, shown in Figure 6. Indirect investment is comprised largely of purchases of both foreign government and corporate securities by private investors in the United States, i.e., portfolio investment.

Evidence of increased indirect foreign investment by United States institutions and individuals began to appear in 1958 and again appeared in 1961, but it was not until 1962 that we really became concerned about the volume of foreign securities sold in the United States. In 1962 indirect foreign investment amounted to $1.2 billion, nearly 10 per cent more than in 1961 and nearly double the volume of 1960.

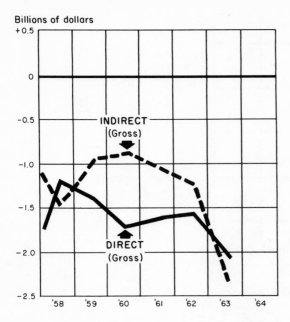

Billions of dollars

Figure 6. PRIVATE LONG-
TERM CAPITAL INVESTMENT—
ANNUALLY (Source: U.S. De-
partment of Commerce).

* 1963 based on first half data estimated by the Federal
Reserve Bank of Cleveland.

As mentioned earlier, figures for the first half of 1963 indicate a further
acceleration in the rate of long-term capital outflows. It is noteworthy that during
the first half of 1963 the amount of indirect investment exceeded direct investment for the first time in the postwar period. In the third quarter, however,
there were significant reductions in foreign security issues, as foreign borrowers
awaited the outcome of Congressional action on the proposed interest rate equalization tax.

Figure 7 shows those countries that have been responsible for large issues
of securities in United States capital markets since 1957. As the chart reveals,
Canada has accounted for a substantial amount of United States-held portfolio
investments in foreign issues. Western European countries and Japan, however,
have accounted for a growing proportion of the foreign securities issued in the
United States, particularly in the past five years. For example, in 1957 the
purchase of Canadian securities accounted for approximately one-half of our
net indirect foreign investment, while Western European and Japanese issues
accounted for less than 10 per cent. (The remaining 40 per cent were issues
of all other countries and international financial institutions such as the International Bank for Reconstruction and Development.) In contrast, in 1962 Canadian issues represented only one-quarter of the net outflow, while Western
Europe and Japan accounted for 40 per cent.

Proceeds of these indirect investments ultimately are used for a variety
of purposes, due to the wide assortment of borrowers. These borrowers include
foreign corporations and foreign governments, both national and local. We know,

Billions of dollars

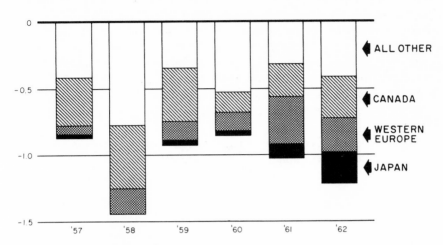

Figure 7. DESTINATION OF INDIRECT NET CAPITAL OUTFLOWS—ANNUALLY
(Source: U.S. Department of Commerce).

of course, that part of the dollars derived from the sales of these securities are used to buy American products, and therefore never leave the United States. On the other hand, no restrictions are placed on spending the dollars elsewhere; as a result, a part of the proceeds are converted to other currencies. Moreover, much foreign government borrowing is for the purpose of financing public works projects in the borrowing country and thus results in little spending in the United States.

The adoption of effective methods of countering these capital exports depends upon a clear understanding of the basic underlying causes of increased foreign investment. In the case of direct investment, it is difficult to assign any one factor as the predominant reason for the increased investment by United States business firms in foreign subsidiaries. In some instances the investment may have resulted from the need to develop new resources or new markets, or to increase the share of an existing market. In other instances direct investment abroad may have been triggered by a desire to establish production facilities to avoid the competitive handicap of particular tariffs. Nevertheless, the fundamental purpose for undertaking any business investment is the profit potential.

It is reasonable to assume, therefore, that the principal cause of increased direct investment is the opportunity to obtain more attractive rates of return than those available on alternative investment proposals in the United States. As a result, the most effective method of reducing the rate of direct foreign investment would be to adopt policies that lead to improved rates of return on domestic investments.

In this connection, recent actions liberalizing depreciation allowances, providing an investment tax credit, and curtailing the privilege of using "tax havens" to reduce United States tax liabilities on income from foreign investments should aid in encouraging investment in the United States rather than abroad. Indeed, adoption of the proposal for a reduced tax rate on corporate income would strengthen considerably the inducement to invest in the United States.

The causes of the recent acceleration in indirect investment are not as clear. Moreover, there is some doubt regarding the effectiveness of recently-proposed solutions. The underlying cause of the increase in indirect investment can be analyzed from two standpoints. First, what are those factors which have encouraged the expansion of foreign security offerings in United States capital markets? Second, what factors have attracted United States investors to these securities?

Figure 8 demonstrates one of two major reasons for the attraction of foreign borrowers to United States capital markets. Since 1957 the direct interest cost associated with issuing corporate bonds in the United States has remained below

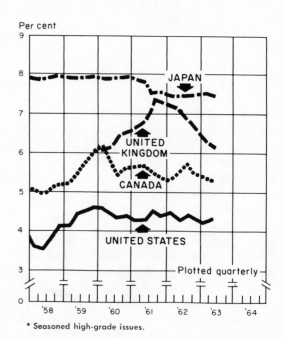

Figure 8. CORPORATE BOND YIELDS — SELECTED COUNTRIES (Sources: Bank of Japan, Actuaries' Investment Index, Bank of Canada, and Moody's Investment Service.)

the rates paid in Japan, the United Kingdom, and Canada. As a matter of fact, even with the recent downturn of rates in the United Kingdom and Canada, the latest data show that there is still a full 1 per cent differential between Canadian and United States rates, and nearly a 2 per cent differential between United States and United Kingdom rates. In the case of Japan, the differential exceeds 3 per cent. Thus, foreign borrowers have found the United States an attractive market in which to borrow even though they are often required to pay rates higher than those paid on similar quality United States issues, and usually have to pay a higher fee to investment bankers.

The same situation exists with respect to the sale of common stock in the United States. As Figure 9 shows, for example, the dividend yield is much lower on United States issues than on United Kingdom issues. Although corporate stock accounts for a very small proportion of total new foreign issues in the United States, the cost of equity capital, as well as borrowed capital, is lower in the United States than in other countries. It is this difference in capital costs that prompted the Administration's proposal for an interest equalization tax.

The second major reason for increased foreign borrowing reflects the abundance of funds in United States capital markets. Indeed, the availability of funds

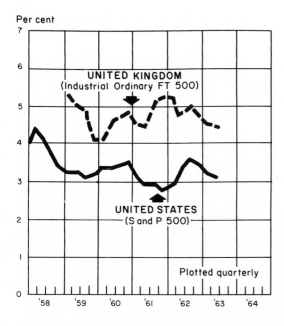

Figure 9. COMMON STOCK DIVIDEND YIELDS (Source: *Financial Times* and *Standard and Poor's*).

may be an even more important factor in the expanded use of United States capital markets by foreign borrowers than differentials in interest cost.

No other capital market is capable of satisfying large demands for funds as is the United States. The reason for this stems from the relative freedom, the organization, and current condition of our market, as well as from restrictions placed on foreign markets.

The United States market is characterized by a highly complex and efficient system of financial intermediaries that are free to channel large flows of savings to either domestic or foreign users. Obviously, the recent increase in the availability of funds in the United States, coupled with only moderate demands for capital by domestic users, has swelled the amount of capital available to foreign borrowers and encouraged them to issue securities in the United States. At the same time, the natural and legal restrictions imposed on the use of virtually all other world capital markets have prevented sufficient access to these markets by both domestic and foreign borrowers, and ultimately placed a greater reliance on the United States market.

The principal reasons for the increased interest in foreign securities by United States investors are similar to those cited for an increase in the volume of foreign security issues; namely, the surplus capital funds available for investment, recent high levels of liquidity in the United States, and the efforts of United States investors to acquire higher rates of return than those available on domestic investments. In addition, some of the suspicion of foreign securities which United States investors acquired from their experiences with foreign investments in the 1930's have been overcome. Thus, policies directed at reducing the rate of indirect investment would be most successful if they were aimed at shrinking the availability of capital funds and improving the rate of return on domestic investments.

The recent proposal to place a tax on the purchase of foreign securities by United States investors which, as mentioned earlier, is intended to offset differences in capital costs, fails to come to grips with two of the basic causes of increased foreign borrowing in this country; namely, the availability of capital and the inaccessibility of other capital markets. It is the opinion of many who are familiar with foreign borrowing patterns that the failure to deal with these two causes, together with the exceptions provided in the proposal, will seriously impair its effectiveness.

The United States balance-of-payments problem has created major difficulties for monetary policy. As indicated earlier, monetary policy has walked a

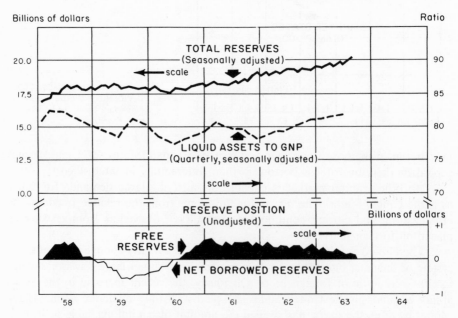

Figure 10. MEASURES OF MONETARY EXPANSION (Source: The Board of Governors of the Federal Reserve System).

particularly taut tightrope in recent years; it has tried to keep the economy well-stocked with the wherewithal to expand, but in a way that would minimize the damage to the balance of payments. Figure 10 shows that the Federal Reserve System has steadily increased the reserve base of the banking system in order to accommodate the credit needs of the economy. Adjustments have been made in the manner in which reserves have been supplied or made available, for example, through purchases of government securities other than Treasury bills and through changes in reserve requirements; but the primary point is that a high level of reserve availability has made possible substantial expansion of bank credit during the past three years.

Figure 10 also shows that the public's holdings of liquid assets—money, savings accounts, and the like—currently are at the highest relationship to the gross national product since 1958. Since late 1961 liquid assets have in fact increased at a faster rate than the GNP, a development which is completely contrary to what usually happens during periods of business recovery.

The banking system has been in free reserve status for a longer period of time than in any period since the rebirth of flexible monetary policy in the early 1950's. As the chart shows, there has been on balance a moderate downtrend in free reserves since the peak reached in early 1961; this partly represents the impact of the constraint imposed on monetary policy by the balance of payments problem. It may also represent evidence of recognition by the monetary authorities that the conduct of monetary policy should not be such as to attempt to solve problems that are clearly beyond its sphere of influence, for example, the problem of unemployed resources or manpower. The chart presents abundant evidence of the contribution made by monetary policy to the economy during recent years. It may even suggest that monetary policy has attempted to make too much of a contribution; that there has been too much ease.

Interest rates are influenced by levels of reserve availability and liquidity, as well as by the demand for funds. Interest rate movements in recent years have been dominated by both domestic and international considerations. During the 1960–61 recession, because of the international situation, the Federal Reserve System did not allow short-term interest rates to decline as they had previously; during the recovery, because of the domestic situation, short-term rates were prevented from rising as they had previously. As Figure 11 shows, short-term interest rates have been stable with a slight upward trend, in contrast to the wide movements usually associated with the ebb and flow of business activity.

Because of the international financial situation, interest rates here have generally been kept in rough alignment with those in major foreign financial markets to prevent excessive outflows of short-term funds. The net differentials between interest rates here and abroad are an important factor in the short-term capital flows portion of the balance of payments. When the differential moves above the zero line on the chart, it represents an advantage (in the form of higher returns) to shift funds from the United States. As the chart shows, differentials between rates on United States bills and those of other countries have more often than not been in favor of foreign nations, even after covering for exchange risks. This has been particularly true of the United States vis-à-vis

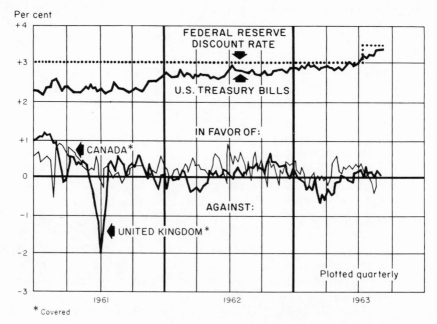

Figure 11. SHORT-TERM INTEREST RATE DIFFERENTIALS—ON THREE-MONTH TREASURY BILLS (Source: The Board of Governors of the Federal Reserve System).

Canada. In 1961, for example, there was an average weekly differential of 34 basis points in favor of Canada (on a covered basis), with a concurrent outflow of nearly $500 million of United States short-term funds to that country. In the second quarter of 1963 Canadian bills had an average yield advantage of 27 basis points, even after the purchasers "covered" their transactions by sales in the forward market. This failure to maintain the approximate alignment of rates between the United States and foreign markets resulted in substantial losses of short-term funds in the second quarter of 1963.

A number of monetary policy actions have been used in an effort to keep interest rate differentials as narrow as possible. The gradual upward drift in United States bill rates that has taken place since 1961 was achieved by the Federal Reserve, with help from the United States Treasury. For example, the Treasury added to the supply of bills in the market, while the Federal Reserve made bank reserves available in such a way as to reduce pressure on short-term interest rates. The recent increase in the discount rate was another step in this direction. (Such measures are effective so long as other nations cooperate by maintaining relatively steady interest rates.) In these operations, the objective of policy is not to prevent flows of short-term funds that arise normally from foreign trade, but mainly to prevent adverse effects on the dollar arising from shifts of funds in search of higher yields and speculative profits.

On a related front, the Federal Reserve System and the United States Treasury have been active in the area of international finance. Early in 1962 the Federal Reserve originated a series of currency swap agreements with central banks in other countries, with the System obtaining "mutual credit facilities on a stand-by basis." The purpose of these swaps is to help the System to keep watch over foreign exchange markets and to help defend the dollar. They work as follows: having drawn, say, $100 million worth of German marks, the System can enter the foreign exchange market and sell marks for dollars in order to prevent downward pressure on the dollar resulting from those who are selling dollars and demanding marks. Swap arrangements are meant to be short-term and reversible, that is, they are designed to counteract speculative and seasonal flows of funds that are expected to be reversed in a short time.

The System has available more than $1.5 billion in reciprocal currency arrangements, only a small amount of which is currently drawn. The Treasury has also entered the foreign exchange markets but to a more limited extent. In the broadest context, currency swap arrangements have helped to avert, or at least minimize, a number of developments that threatened to undermine or unhinge existing currency relationships in foreign exchange markets; these developments included the Canadian exchange crisis early in 1962, our stock market decline, and the Cuban crisis, among others. Notwithstanding the contribution of currency swap arrangements, it is clear that they will not solve our basic balance-of-payments problem; in fact, they were not intended to do that.

Still other innovations have been introduced to complement interest rate relationships and currency swap actions in maintaining order in foreign exchange markets and in maintaining foreign currency relationships. The United States has entered into agreement with nine other major nations to increase by $6 billion the lending resources of the International Monetary Fund. A "gold pool" has been established into which various nations are supplying gold for the London gold market to prevent speculative flare-ups in price such as occurred in late 1960. Beginning in late 1962, the United States Treasury issued securities denominated in foreign currencies to a number of countries that hold excess amounts of dollars in order to reduce the conversion of dollars into gold; in other words, to immobilize temporarily surplus dollars held by these countries. Finally, the Treasury recently arranged for a stand-by credit of $500 million from the International Monetary Fund, the first such arrangement this country has made.

These actions have unquestionably helped to alleviate the adverse consequences of the United States payments problem and protect the status of the dollar. In short, they have been successful in buying some time. But, even taken together, they can accomplish little in solving the basic problem of our balance of payments.

An improvement in the balance of payments was reported in the last half of 1963. This improvement occurred largely in private capital flows. Some reduction in short-term outflows reflects higher interest rates in this country, accomplished in part by the discount rate action in July, 1963. Also, the uncertainty accompanying the proposed interest equalization tax virtually eliminated the flotation of foreign bond and stock issues in this country, thus temporarily reducing our long-term capital outflow.

But the underlying problem still remains, demanding painful decisions about our present spending and investing habits overseas. It is now more crucial than ever that this country reevaluate its monetary and fiscal policy mix. We need to create more confidence and more incentive so as to get the economy expanding more vigorously. Monetary policy and fiscal policy must be used in combination to accomplish these objectives. In the opinion of many, this can be done through reduction in personal and corporate income taxes, increasing the returns on domestic investment. A stronger economy with better profit opportunities and a slightly firmer monetary policy would not only help to keep funds at home, but would attract funds from overseas. We might then achieve the best of all possible economic environments: high and sustainable levels of economic activity and an improved balance of payments.

ADDENDUM*

Information available since the publication of this booklet confirms that the balance of payments improved considerably in the third quarter of 1963, and that the improvement was maintained in the fourth quarter. The favorable turn of events after midyear reflected to a large extent both a closer alignment of interest rates here and abroad and a virtual moratorium on the use of United States capital markets by foreign borrowers as a result of the proposed interest equalization tax.

The marked improvement during the second half of 1963 brought the balance of payments to a more favorable situation at yearend than in any of the preceding five years; it also generated considerable optimism as to the near-term outlook for the balance of payments. For 1963 as a whole, the deficit in the balance of payments, including a number of special transactions, amounted to $1.9 billion, or less than the average deficit for the period from 1958 through 1962. It should be remembered, however, that the improvement in the over-all payments balance in 1963 was due in part to fortuitous developments, e.g., weather conditions abroad which stimulated larger United States exports of agricultural products and fuel, and transitory phenomena, e.g., uncertainty associated with the proposed interest equalization tax. Thus, it may be premature to conclude that our balance-of-payments problem is totally and permanently solved.

Selection 45

PLANS FOR REFORM OF THE INTERNATIONAL MONETARY SYSTEM—CHARGES AGAINST THE SYSTEM
FRITZ MACHLUP

> *The balance-of-payments problem of the United States, discussed in the preceding selection, is one example of a general problem in international finance—difficulties with the balance of payments of individual countries. As Fritz Machlup indicates in this selection, attention has also been given in recent years to the problem arising from the fact that there may be an inadequate growth of inter-*

---

* *Editor's note:* The addendum was included in the second printing, March, 1964. The "proposed" interest equalization tax was later (August, 1964) passed by Congress.

*national monetary reserves, and to the danger that there might be
an international financial collapse such as occurred in 1931. Machlup's discussion of present problems associated with the international
monetary system provides a useful background for analysis of
proposals for reform of that system.*

*Proposals for reform (in contrast to more limited proposals
related to particular balance-of-payments problems, such as that
of the United States) may be classified as (1) measures that make
fuller use of available international monetary reserves, (2) measures
that would increase the amount of such reserves, and (3) flexible
exchange rates, which would reduce the need for such reserves, since
adjustments would occur through fluctuations in exchange rates
rather than through transfer of reserves from deficit countries to
surplus countries.*

*Measures to make fuller use of available international monetary
reserves—such as cooperation among central banks in agreeing
upon swaps and other credits—cannot effectively meet the problem
of a long-run shortage in international monetary reserves, if such
arises. They can, however, be useful in offsetting short-run pressures
arising from temporary increases in balance-of-payments deficits.*

*Some of the measures that might increase the amount (or
value) of international monetary reserves, such as an increase in the
price of gold, are opposed by many central bankers and financial
experts, and have been explicitly ruled out of consideration in
studies made by two such groups.*

*Flexible exchange rates, although supported (at least in princi-
ple) by many economists, have also been ruled out of consideration
by the representatives of the group of ten nations sometimes referred to as the Paris Club (Belgium, Canada, France, Germany,
Italy, Japan, the Netherlands, Sweden, the United Kingdom, and
the United States), who have made one of the studies referred
to above. Thus it seems unlikely that such drastic measures will be
taken unless the situation should become much more serious than
it has been. The study made by the staff of the International
Monetary Fund itself led to the conclusion that quotas in the Fund
should be increased; see International Monetary Fund, 1964 Annual
Report, pp. 35–37. The report includes further discussion of the
adequacy of the growth of monetary reserves, discussed by Professor Machlup in this selection.*

Several experts, among them Per Jacobsson and Robert Triffin, have been
careful to distinguish three different problems connected with the present system.
To treat these problems separately is important not only for the sake of clarity
but also because not all the experts share all the misgivings concerning the
operation of the present system. Each of the three problems has at least two
aspects calling for our attention.

A. Difficulties with the balance of payments of individual countries

---

• From Fritz Machlup, *Plans for Reform of the International Monetary System,*
International Finance Section, Special Papers in International Economics, No. 3, pp. 5–11.
Copyright 1962 by Princeton University, Princeton, New Jersey. Reprinted by permission
of Princeton University and the author.

1. because of excessive deficits or insufficient surpluses[1] in the balance on current account;
2. because of massive international movements of speculative funds.

B. Inadequacy of the growth of monetary reserves
   1. relative to the demand for "domestic liquidity" or to the "desirable" supply of domestic money;
   2. relative to the growth of foreign trade.

C. Fragility of the gold-exchange standard
   1. dangerous to key-currency countries;
   2. dangerous to countries holding large exchange reserves.

A. DIFFICULTIES WITH THE BALANCE OF PAYMENTS

Problem A-1 should perhaps be stricken from the agenda since it cannot be regarded as a defect of the present system and since the balance-of-payments problem of particular countries could not be solved or eliminated by means of any of the reform plans. Yet, some of the plans are designed to institute a system of international payments that gives countries in difficulties much more time to wait for an improvement in their balance on current account without resort to the orthodox treatment with painful contractions of credit and effective demand. This tough remedy has become rather unpopular in a world more sensitive and less capable of adjusting to change. If the "old-fashioned" cure is at all accepted nowadays, one tries to postpone it as long as possible in the hope that things will get better without treatment.

There are, of course, other currency doctors, who find that such softheartedness toward patients suffering from current-account troubles is out of place and that postponement of the one reliable cure could only be harmful. As a matter of fact, some of the critics of the gold-exchange standard have stated, with a serious frown, that the acceptance of ever-increasing amounts of demand liabilities of the United States as parts of the monetary reserves of other countries postponed for almost eight years substantial gold outflows from the United States and thus postponed the warning signals which such outflows would have implied. Hence, the present system is blamed for having enabled the United States to continue a credit and fiscal policy that was basically incompatible with an appropriate balance on current account.

There is obviously a serious ambivalence in the views about this problem. Some find the present system deficient because it gives countries in difficulties with their balance of payments too much time, and others because it gives them too little time, to get over their troubles.[2]

No such ambivalence exists regarding problem A-2, that is, regarding difficulties with the balance of payments on capital account because of hot-money

---

[1] Surpluses on current account are regarded as "insufficient" when they fail to offset completely deficits in the balance of long-term capital movements and unilateral transfers. In this formulation the concept of "balance-of-payments difficulties" is confined to cases of gold and exchange outflows; some writers may prefer to extend the concept to include cases of heavy inflows of gold and foreign exchange.

[2] There can be a third point of view: that the present system operates unequally relative to different countries, particularly in that it provides inadequate discipline on key-currency countries but rather harsh discipline on other countries. Hence, it gives too much time for adjustment to some countries and too little to others. This seems to be Triffin's judgment.

movements. There is agreement on the desirability or need to improve present institutions to cope with speculative capital movements.[3] Massive movements of hot money are brought about either by sudden changes in international interest-rate differentials or by rumors of imminent changes in official exchange rates. The return to convertibility and the abolition of restrictions on capital transactions have undoubtedly increased the dimensions of international hot-money movements and have thereby created difficulties with the balances of payments which perhaps cannot be managed with foreign reserves of the size now at the disposal of the monetary authorities in the countries concerned.

One may ask why the gold standard before 1914 was not exposed to shocks of this sort and could work without any special shock absorbers. The answer is simple. In the old times there never were any rumors about impending devaluations, since no country ever seriously contemplated changing the gold par of its currency. In the old times, moreover, there were no disequilibrating differentials in interest rates or, at least, they were not allowed to last long, since the central banks were always trying to adjust their bank rates to the balance-of-payments situation. Under the rules of the gold-standard game, interest policy had to serve the equilibration of the balance of payments, and was not, as nowadays, subservient to employment and growth policies. Consequently, interest-rate differentials did not disturb but, on the contrary, helped maintain or restore international payments equilibrium.

This is in sharp contrast to present-day practice of some central banks, which insist on maintaining low interest rates (in order to fight unemployment) even if this leads to heavy outflows of funds.[4] A credit policy with so little regard for its external consequences is apt to aggravate widespread fears of devaluation. After all, so the apprehensive ones reason, a country which cares so little about a loss of reserves that it would not even put up with higher interest rates apparently does not care much about the maintenance of its gold parity. Under such circumstances, massive international movements of speculative funds must be expected. It may take special institutions to cope with them, chiefly by providing the means for "compensatory official financing," that is, the foreign funds needed to meet the speculative demand, without recourse to payments restrictions and without peril to the maintenance of the fixed foreign-exchange rates.

B. INADEQUACY OF INTERNATIONAL RESERVES

The question of the adequacy, or supposed inadequacy, of the growth of monetary reserves is controversial. It has been contended, for example by Sir Roy Harrod, that reserves have grown too slowly during the last ten or twelve

---

[3] This should not be confused with problems of long-term capital movements—portfolio investment, direct investment, and foreign aid—that is, outflows of investable funds that should be reflected in the balance on current account of the investing, lending, or aiding country. (This would be part of problem A-1, that is, difficulties due to a balance on current account that does not fully reflect the movements of long-term capital, including foreign aid.)

[4] The Federal Reserve Banks, in the summer of 1960, lowered discount rates in the face of payments deficits. The reverse side of the same practice is for a central bank to insist on high interest rates (in order to fight price inflation) even if this aggravates a heavy inflow of foreign funds. The German Bundesbank did precisely this until it learned the lesson.

years. Even as early as 1952 a group of experts appointed by the United Nations reported that the total stocks of international reserves were inadequate.[5] This view is opposed by Per Jacobsson, M. W. Holtrop, Karl Blessing, and several others, who deny that either the size of reserves or their rate of increase has been inadequate. Indeed, they hold that reserves have been excessive. Both factions seem willing to accept as a criterion of adequacy the influence which the reserves and their changes have upon the supply of money in the countries concerned. We have called this our problem B-1: the question of the adequacy of reserves relative to the needs of "domestic liquidity." According to Harrod this influence was deflationary and responsible for an unsatisfactory rate of economic growth. Jacobsson and the central bankers, on the other hand, regard the influence as inflationary since it permitted a general rise in the price levels of practically all countries. In view of these differences in judging the consequences of the operation of the international monetary system in the past, one cannot be very hopeful about reaching an agreement regarding the principles to be applied to the reform of the system.

The size and growth of foreign reserves relative to the needs of domestic liquidity and to the size and growth of the domestic money supply is only one of the possible criteria for judging the adequacy of the growth of gold and exchange reserves. Many experts prefer to rely on an indicator which "measures" the reserve position of the world as a whole, to wit, the numerical ratio between aggregate reserves and imports. This we have called our problem B-2. However, the difference between the two measures of adequacy is not simply one of statistical convenience, but reflects two separate functions of monetary reserves. They are used, on the one hand, as institutional determinants of the domestic money supply and, on the other hand, as international means of payments to finance temporary deficits in the balance of payments. Hence it is quite in line with this double function of international reserves that their adequacy is judged with reference to both national circulation and international payments.

Any reduction in the ratio between international reserves and total imports indicates to some observers that the growth of gold and exchange reserves has been inadequate. This, however, presupposes, even if it is not explicitly stated, that the ratio was "just right" at the outset, or was perhaps a barely tolerable minimum. Surely, if the reserves relative to foreign trade, or total imports, had been more than adequate in the beginning,[6] a decline in this numerical ratio need not imply that the reserves have become inadequate. The total value of imports of the countries of the free world did in fact increase from $59.6 billion in 1950 to $119.1 billion in 1960. Thus, the ratio of reserves to imports fell

---

[5] "Our examination of existing reserves has convinced us that they are not in general adequate." Economic and Social Commission, United Nations, *Measures for International Economic Stability*, 1952. Members of the group of experts were Angell, MacDougall, Marquez, Myint, and Swan.

[6] "Total international reserves immediately before the war were abnormally high in relation to the value of world trade." (Radcliffe) *Committee on the Working of the Monetary System* (London: H.M.'s Stationery Office, Cmnd. 827, 1959), p. 244, ¶671. The ratio of reserves to imports in 1938 was 117 per cent.

from 81 to 50 per cent. But who can say that the 81 per cent had been just right, or the bare minimum? Let us not forget that back in 1913 the ratio was only 21 per cent.

Apart from the question whether or not the ratio of reserves to imports was just right in the base year, and not unnecessarily high, there is absolutely no evidence for the contention that the need for reserves rises proportionately with foreign trade. It is true that in domestic circulation the need for cash balances on the part of householders is likely to increase approximately in proportion with consumption expenditures. On the other hand, the need for cash balances on the part of existing business firms does not usually increase proportionately with turnover. In all probability, the demand for cash balances in the economy as a whole will rise with the national product but the increase may be smaller if the share of investment in the income increase is greater. Even within the industrial circulation of money we may expect differences in the ratio of cash to turnover, depending on the different degrees of vertical integration of industries. Besides, one may say that with an increase in the volume of transactions the demand for cash balances will increase least in those sectors of the economy in which clearing systems have developed requiring only the payment of clearing balances. It seems to me that foreign trade falls into this group and that consequently there is no theoretical support for the assertion that the need for international reserves rises in proportion with imports.[7]

Even if, on this or other grounds, one refuses to admit that the growth of international reserves relative to the growth of international trade has been inadequate during the last ten or twelve years, one might still side with the inadequacy-theorists in their pessimism for the future. The prospects for the future growth of reserves would indeed be rather dim if one could not expect the pool of reserves to be fed during the next ten years or so through continuing increases in dollar claims; and indeed further increases in the demand liabilities of the United States at the fast rate of the past years might well be unacceptable to all parties concerned. If it is agreed that the short-term indebtedness of the two key-currency countries, the United States and the United Kingdom, must not be increased substantially in the coming years and if, as a result, international reserves can grow only by means of increased supplies of monetary gold, then it is quite plausible that a real, generally recognized scarcity of reserves will develop in the course of time. To prevent such a calamity, changes in the present system are favored even by some of those experts who do not consider the past growth of reserves inadequate.

C. DANGER OF COLLAPSE

The consideration that the fast increase of the share of dollar claims in the total reserves of the world may be deemed unbearable for the system has brought us to the third set of problems—the fragility of the gold-exchange standard.

---

[7] Cf. the comments on this point in my article, "Liquidite internationale et nationale," *Bulletin d'Information et de Documentation,* Banque Nationale de Belgique, Vol. XXXVII (Feb., 1962), pp. 105–116.

Ever since 1950, the United States, through its purchases, investments, loans, and aid, has put at the disposal of foreign countries more dollars than these countries have used for their purchases in the United States. In this fashion, foreign dollar claims, both of private holders and of central banks and other national monetary authorities, have increased at a fast rate. During the first seven or eight years this accumulation of the foreign-exchange reserves of various countries was welcomed by all; the demand for dollar balances was eager and the supply of dollars was therefore received with open arms. Later on, however, the accumulation of exchange reserves was continued only with formal politeness; the supply of dollars was received and added to currency reserves without great enthusiasm and merely in accordance with the customary etiquette practiced by central banks. (In other words, the same phenomenon from the point of view of the United States was elsewhere seen first as a symptom of "dollar shortage" and later as a symptom of "dollar glut.")

As the share of foreign exchange in the official reserves of the free world increased, more and more people began to doubt whether this steady excess supply of dollar liabilities could be absorbed without limit. With such doubts becoming more widespread, the willingness to accept further dollar supplies is further reduced and fears regarding the future value of dollar exchange become increasingly serious. If then, in addition, some experts raise their voices advancing—in support of the aims of gold producers and speculators—proposals for an increase in the price of gold, the position of the dollar and the preservation of the gold-exchange standard become precarious.

The strong demand for gold for speculative purposes and hedging, especially the impatience of holders of dollar deposits and other dollar claims to exchange them into gold, then leads to a further increase in the supply of dollars in the foreign-exchange markets. Since not all central banks stand ready to increase their exchange reserves at the expense of their gold stocks, it becomes necessary for the American monetary authorities to sell gold in order to safeguard the position of the dollar. Yet, these gold losses in turn aggravate the doubts concerning the ability of the United States to defend the gold parity of the dollar in the long run, and these doubts cause private banks and public authorities to be even less willing to offer shelter to increasing amounts of dollar exchange. Hence, the more serious the fears that the gold-exchange standard will break down once again (as it did in 1931, when Great Britain went off gold), the more real becomes the danger of its actual collapse.

The consequences of such a collapse may be manifold, but most probably they would include some of the following measures and repercussions: restrictions on or termination of all sales of gold by the monetary authorities of the United States; restrictions on international payments through the introduction of foreign-exchange controls and prohibitions of capital transfers; import restrictions of all sorts; blocking of deposits of foreign nationals; the end of convertibility of most currencies, including the present key-currencies; elimination of these key-currencies from the official reserves of central banks and consequently a drastic reduction in "liquidity" everywhere; severe losses incurred by those central banks which did not match the depreciation of the key-currencies with equal devaluations of their own currencies; [8] reductions in production and employment resulting from import restrictions and export reductions. It may, of course, be possible through skillful improvisations to avoid or mitigate some of the worst consequences of the collapse of the international payments system, but it would surely be wiser not to rely on improvisations and to avert a collapse of the system through appropriate reforms. It is on the basis of this kind of argument that monetary experts have offered their plans and urge their adoption.

Selection 46

GOLD IN THE WORLD'S MONETARY MACHINERY
FEDERAL RESERVE BANK OF CHICAGO

The last two selections in Part I of this book discussed the role of gold as a domestic monetary standard and the arguments for returning to a gold standard. This selection discusses the role of gold in international finance, in which it retains a substantial significance. Gold is primarily "international money," and continues to be important as a medium in which most countries carry at least part of their international reserves. Gold still "constitutes the hard core of international liquidity." Since gold is an important element in international monetary reserves, it is desirable that as much gold as possible be channeled into international monetary uses. Yet in the 1964 Annual Report of the International Monetary Fund it is estimated that in some recent years, such as 1962, nearly four-fifths of the supply of gold derived from gold production and from reported gold sales by the U.S.S.R. was absorbed into private holdings and industrial uses. Decreased uncertainty in international economic and political conditions might reduce private hoarding of gold and thus increase monetary gold reserves; at the same time demand for liquidity would probably decline, as expected payments deficits would be smaller. In an uncertain world, gold still has a place, in international finance if not as a determinant of the size of the money supply within a country.

The role that gold plays in the world's monetary arrangements gradually has become more specialized and probably less important over-all. Nevertheless, gold retains a position of prestige: many people automatically think of gold —and its erstwhile companion, silver—whenever the word "money" is mentioned.

Although important, these metals provide only a small part of the world's money; the proportion is especially small in countries where most payments are made by check. For example, probably no more than 2 per cent of all financial

---

[8] The losses which The Netherlands Bank suffered as a result of the depreciation of the pound sterling in 1931 exceeded the Bank's entire capital.

• From "Gold in the World's Monetary Machinery," Federal Reserve Bank of Chicago, *Business Conditions,* March, 1964, pp. 9–16. Reprinted by permission of the Federal Reserve Bank of Chicago.

transactions in the United States are made with coins—and gold is not included in these at all.

While gold and silver have a variety of uses in industry and arts, these are largely irrelevant to their use as money. Instead, these metals came into widespread use as money centuries ago because of their particular characteristics: durable, easily shaped and resistant to corrosion. But most important, these "noble" metals are relatively scarce and the total supply does not vary greatly from year to year as do supplies of many other commodities that might otherwise be satisfactory as monetary mediums. Because of these characteristics, they can serve as a combination "yardstick and warehouse"—that is, a measure of relative value and store of wealth.

In a country with a stable government and established customs, however, these functions can be provided better by "paper and ink." The weight is less; the flexibility is greater. Paper money, checks and various accounting arrangements that minimize actual transfers of money or in some instances avoid them altogether have gained popularity.

The supply of money in most of the industrially advanced countries has long been detached from, and largely unrelated to, the amount of available gold. Thus, it has been insulated against the effects of shifts in the stock of gold available for monetary use as well as shifts in private demand for gold to serve as a store of wealth. In the United States, for example, the private holding of monetary gold has been prohibited since 1933 and the holding of gold abroad by American citizens has been prohibited since 1961.

For international financial transactions, too, it is more convenient and efficient to use paper and ink and associated "promises to pay" than to incur the expense and nuisance of constantly moving monetary metals around the world and providing for their security against loss or theft. Thus in the international as well as the domestic financial arena, the allure of the yellow metal may be less strong than in some former periods.

Currently gold's major role is that of providing one form of linkage between the various national currencies and the economics of the countries that engage extensively in world commerce. It is largely because of this international linkage that developments such as the following attract widespread attention:

In 1963, the monetary gold stock of the United States declined an additional 461 million dollars—about half as much as in each of the two preceding years.

Soviet sales of gold in European markets rose to more than 400 million dollars—up from about 200 million in 1962.

Estimated free world production of gold in 1963 amounted to 1,365 million dollars, 75 million above 1962. The increase of production has been relatively large since about 1958 even though inflationary pressures have continued in evidence through much of the world.

The gold stocks held by central banks and governments in Western Europe and the International Monetary Fund rose between 700 and 800 million dollars in 1963, more than twice the increase in 1962. The relatively large rise reflects the lessened demand for private hoarding, increased sales of gold by Russia to obtain exchange used to purchase wheat and other commodities, and sales by the United States.*

GOLD IN THE U.S. MONETARY MECHANISM

The United States Treasury stands ready to purchase and sell gold at the official price of $35 an ounce, thereby fixing the value of the dollar in terms of gold. But since banks and the public in this country are not permitted to hold monetary gold or gold certificates, it is not possible for shifts in domestic private demands for gold to cause fluctuations in bank reserves and money supply.

The par values of most currencies that are not themselves defined by statute in terms of gold are stated to have par values relative to the United States dollar of 1944 gold content. In this way most of the world's currencies are anchored to gold.

So long as foreign monetary authorities have confidence that the United States will be willing and able to continue to maintain the official dollar price for gold, countries can treat dollars as the equivalent of gold. It is stipulated in the Bretton Woods Agreements Act of 1945, through which the United States became a member of the International Monetary Fund, that any change in the value of the dollar relative to gold shall require legislative action by Congress.

Federal Reserve Banks are required to maintain reserves in gold certificates (representing gold held by the United States Treasury) of not less than 25 per cent of their deposit liabilities and of their notes in circulation. This requirement can be changed by Congress, as it was in 1945, and it may be suspended by the Federal Reserve Board provided that the deficient Reserve Banks pay a tax graduated according to the amount of the deficiency.

There has been widespread discussion for some years whether the gold reserve requirement is obsolete since private holding of monetary gold is prohibited in this country. Moreover, the President has declared that this nation's entire stock of gold is available, if needed, to redeem foreign dollar claims. Many of the advocates of abolition of the gold reserve requirement believe that such action should only be taken at such time as the United States balance of payments deficit has been greatly reduced or eliminated.

While flows of gold into and out of United States monetary reserves still increase and decrease bank reserves, the effects on domestic money supply and credit conditions can be offset by appropriate action of the Federal Reserve System and is offset if this is deemed advisable from the standpoint of the System's over-all policy goals. Through purchases and sales of securities in the open market, changes in Federal Reserve Bank discount rates and changes in member bank reserve requirements, the Federal Reserve System can control the supply of reserves available to commercial banks and hence the amount of bank deposits and credit in the United States. The potentially inflationary or deflationary effects of gold inflows or outflows can thus be offset.

* *Editor's note:* for a graphic presentation of these changes, see International **Monetary** Fund, *1964 Annual Report,* Chart 24, p. 104.

GOLD IN OTHER COUNTRIES

The role of gold as a reserve currency and as a part of the domestic money supply varies widely among countries. There are only a few where the statutory reserves must be held exclusively in gold; elsewhere reserves consist of gold and foreign exchange. Nevertheless, the desire of monetary authorities to hold gold is still generally strong. This is true even of central banks whose statutory requirements have been suspended or which have never been subject to such requirements.

Most countries allow the private domestic holding of gold, but nowhere do the monetary authorities undertake to sell gold to their nationals at a fixed price or in unlimited quantity for this purpose. Practically all countries buy gold freely from individuals and banks at a fixed price, paying the seller in currency or check, but Switzerland also mints some gold coins. In some countries, for instance the United States, the buying rate is specified by law while in others it is set by administrative decision. Many permit private trading of gold, a smaller number permit free import and fewer still permit free export.

London is the world's most important bar gold market while coin markets are dominated by Paris and Zurich. Quoted prices in gold markets tend to reflect the public moods of optimism or pessimism about the economic or political future to the extent that they are not offset by official transactions. In addition to France and Switzerland, Germany, Italy, Belgium, the Netherlands, Greece, and Turkey have played a rather important role in European gold dealings.

On the Asiatic continent, Bombay despite prohibition against gold imports played a leading role as a gold importer until November, 1962, when the Indian government made gold transactions illegal and called in the metal. Since then, trading in black markets is reported to have developed. Bombay's decline allowed Beirut (Lebanon) to become Asia's ranking gold trading center, followed by Kuwait, Hong Kong, Macao, Bangkok, Singapore, Rangoon, Tokyo, Manila, Taipei, and Seoul. In Africa, Dakar, Djibouti and Casablanca are the leading centers, and in the Western Hemisphere, Mexico City, Toronto, Montevideo, Panama City and Rio de Janeiro are of some importance.

No precise measure of the amount of private dealings in gold in recent years is available but it probably totaled several billion dollars annually. When confidence in certain currencies declines, some wealthy persons may shift a portion of their asssets into gold bars while the "little man" under similar circumstances may seek refuge in gold coins.

Among the most popular coins are the French napoleon, once equal to 20 francs; the British sovereign, once equal to 20 shillings; and the United States double eagle, once equal to $20. These and other popular coins trade at a substantial premium above the value of their gold content, but premiums vary sharply from time to time reflecting changes in demand and the limited supply of these coins. Some of the popular gold coins are reported to command premiums about 25 per cent above the gold content.

Although Paris and Zurich are the chief centers for gold coin trading, there is no single marketplace for them in either city. Instead, the major commercial banks act as agents for buyers of gold coins and do much of the trading, storage and shipping.

Demand from collectors has come to play an increasingly important role in the gold-coin market. Another source of demand is from jewelers, who use gold coins to make pendants, cuff links, and other objects of personal adornment. The pre-Christmas demand from both of these sources causes a seasonal variation in gold-coin prices.

While gold continues to have a limited circulation throughout much of the world, its role in *national* money mechanisms clearly cannot be described as a dominant one and there is a growing tendency to consider gold as primarily, if not exclusively, an "international money."

GOLD IN THE INTERNATIONAL MECHANISM

Most international commercial transactions are "cleared" in the exchange markets through offsetting entries on the books of commercial banks and private traders. The balances remaining are for the most part settled by the use of United States dollars and British pounds sterling. Reflecting the importance of these currencies in international transactions, the central banks and treasuries of many countries keep a part of their monetary reserves in these so-called reserve currencies. Most or all of their remaining reserves are held in the form of gold bullion at home or abroad.

The nongold portion of international reserves is held largely in the form of dollar balances with American banks or in short-term investments, for example, Treasury bills. Second in importance as a supplement to gold holdings are balances in sterling in the London market.

There are wide variations between countries in the composition of the non-gold portions of their international reserves. The United States carries its reserves almost entirely in the form of gold. Western European nations generally hold much larger amounts in gold than in dollars while Japan has followed the opposite practice.

Since the end of 1958—the year of the largest gold outflow from the United States—foreign central banks and governments have maintained an almost constant ratio of gold to dollar reserves (about 2:1), using only a portion of newly acquired dollars to purchase gold from the United States Treasury. From December, 1957, to September, 1963, foreign gold reserves increased about $9.5 billion while the United States monetary gold stock decreased about $7.2 billion —from $22.8 to $15.6 billion. The remainder came from other sources—Russian gold sales and new production.

GOLD OUTFLOW REDUCED

Declines in the United States stock of monetary gold were smaller in 1961 and 1962 than in each of the preceding three years and the drain was reduced further in 1963. This welcome change reflects in part new forms of international cooperation, in particular the sale by the Treasury of special securities denominated in foreign currency.

The willingness of foreign central and commercial banks and individuals to increase monetary reserves and working balances in the form of dollars depends largely on confidence in the ability and determination of the United States to maintain the exchange value of the dollar in terms of their domestic currencies. This in turn is closely related to the success in achieving and maintaining an approximate balance in the United States international payments.

The United States in recent years has been more successful than most of its trading partners in arresting domestic inflation; there also is some indication that this country's merchandise export surplus is being further enlarged and will contribute even more to a reduction in the deficit in the international balance of payments than it has in the past.

Meanwhile, the dollar, as some of the other major currencies, is likely to be in large supply in the foreign exchange markets from time to time, with resulting pressures on the exchange rate. In order to moderate such temporary pressures, the Federal Reserve System since early 1962 has entered into a number of currency swap arrangements with foreign central banks and the Bank for International Settlements. It also expects to derive continuing benefit from the "gold pool," an arrangement closely connected with the operation of the London gold market.

LONDON GOLD MARKET

The London gold market was reopened in 1954 after being closed for about 15 years. There are two principal differences between the London market and the purchase and sale of gold by the United States Treasury: (1) any nonresident of the sterling area can buy gold in London from bullion dealers, but only monetary authorities can buy gold from the United States Treasury; (2) the London price is allowed to fluctuate in response to supply and demand while the United States Treasury's buying and selling prices do not change.

The arrangements for gold purchases and sales in London and New York are integral parts of the international payments mechanism, with central banks, treasuries and stabilization funds channeling their gold transactions mostly through London and New York. Gold traded in other places is related predominantly to private supply and demand, although Russia is known to have frequently sold gold in these markets in recent years.

Five men representing firms which together constitute the London bullion market meet every weekday morning in the offices of one of their members. The first order of business is to "marry," as far as possible, the buy and sell orders for gold previously received, and arrive at a "fixing price." These dealers are in telephone contact with the Bank of England, which largely controls the supply of newly offered gold.

While the fixing price is quoted as the official price for the day, business is often done later between banks and dealers at different prices. At the fixing the bullion dealers are normally acting as brokers (agents) only but later may be buying or selling also as principals.

During the first five years of operations after the reopening of the market in 1954, dealers were authorized to conduct only spot transactions (delivery and payment within two working days). The restriction on forward dealing was removed in 1959, but future prices may not be made public and thus forward deals are of minor importance.

South Africa, traditionally the world's largest gold producer, is a major factor in the market, but the basis on which the Bank of England sells South African gold and the amount it actually handles are not published. Important sources of demand in the London market are European commercial banks and Eastern dealers buying metal for resale in the Middle and Far East.

The basic trading unit is a gold bar of approximately 400 ounces, equivalent to something over $14,000 at recent prices. There may be a surplus of buy orders at the fixing, in which case the Bank of England will be informed of the excess demand. The Bank then decides whether to supply gold and in what amount and whether the dealers' bids are acceptable. In general, the bank's objective is to maintain a relatively stable price for gold, but if private supplies are large or private demand is exceptionally strong, the bank may permit sizable price swings. In order to maintain relatively stable prices, it may at times have to draw on its Exchange Equalization Account—in which all of Britain's gold and foreign exchange reserves are held—and purchase gold from the United States.

LONDON "GOLD POOL"

A gold pool was formed among the West's leading central bankers toward the end of 1961 for the purpose of providing joint action and support to the Bank of England in its efforts to stabilize the London gold market.

The pool is managed by the Bank of England and includes as additional members the United States, Germany, France, Italy, Switzerland, Belgium, and the Netherlands. Its monthly surpluses or deficits are settled at the close of the following month according to each member's quota, but activities are not publicized.

Relatively small fluctuations in the London market price of gold since the inception of the pool suggest that it has been quite successful in checking potentially large speculative price movements. The willingness of member central banks to channel their own demands through the pool and to refrain from buying in the market at certain times may also have helped to prevent wide swings in the market price of gold with resulting speculation against certain currencies.

CONCLUSION

The current international monetary arrangements are often described as the gold exchange standard. While their origin antedates World War I, their main features were set forth at the end of World War II in the Articles of Agreement of the International Monetary Fund.

Although the role of gold in the world's monetary machinery has gradually diminished, gold still appears to many people as the essence of wealth. This popular preference for a commodity that has tended to remain stable or to increase in value relative to the world's major currencies—though its purchasing power relative to goods and services has declined—is reflected in many of the world's markets in which gold in one form or another is still actively traded. As a determinant of the domestic money supply, however, gold plays a minor role at best in economically advanced countries.

On the other hand, there are few indications so far that gold will soon lose its importance as a medium in which most nations carry at least a portion of their international reserves. Although gold's share in total reserves has declined in the postwar period of rapidly expanding world trade, it still constitutes the hard core of international liquidity.

Whether it will continue to do so for a long time to come depends on many factors—gold production, the price at which gold is bought and sold by monetary authorities, the balanced (or unbalanced) growth of world trade and coordination of national economic policies, to name just a few. For years, private economists have offered proposals for reform of the international monetary system. Some of these envisage a freeing of the international payments mechanism from dependence on gold, while others would strengthen gold's position as an international reserve currency.

Selection 47

ASSURING THE FREE WORLD'S LIQUIDITY
ROBERT V. ROOSA

If a substantial increase in the price of gold and the adoption of flexible exchange rates both seem unlikely as reforms designed to make international monetary reserves more adequate, the alternatives of a "guarantee" of the present price of gold (so as to eliminate reluctance of countries to accumulate dollars to provide their necessary liquidity) and of establishment of an international central bank, or modification of the International Monetary Fund to transform it into a central bank, seem to merit further discussion. Robert V. Roosa, Under Secretary of the Treasury for Monetary Affairs, discusses these alternatives in the following selection.

Two important plans for creation of an international central bank merit comment: the Keynes plan for an International Clearing Union, advanced at the time of planning for the International Monetary Fund, and the Triffin plan for an expanded International Monetary Fund, advanced in 1959 and discussed extensively in recent years. The Keynes plan would have created a new international currency unit, Bancor, in which deposit liabilities of the Clearing Union would have been denominated, and central banks would have been permitted to obtain such deposits either by selling gold to the Clearing Union or by using overdraft (loan) facilities of the Clearing Union. Triffin's plan not only provides for overdraft (loan) facilities at the expanded International Monetary Fund, but would permit the IMF to initiate creation of monetary reserves through open market operations. Since an unwise excessive creation of such reserves might cause inflation, Triffin proposed that some upper limit might be set for annual increases in monetary reserves. (Those interested in the details of Triffin's plan should read his book, Gold and the Dollar Crisis. *New Haven: Yale University Press, 1960, esp. pp. 88–120.)*

In this selection Mr. Roosa argues that the existence of major differences in economic policies among countries would make it difficult to establish consistent policies for such an international central bank, and elaborates the general nature of the steps being taken to provide adequate world liquidity.

These steps include, Roosa indicates, measures to curb capricious raids on gold which serves as international monetary reserves, worked out through the London gold market with participation by the "Basle group"; reciprocal holdings of currencies, forward transactions in currencies, and borrowing of dollars or other currencies by the United States; additional standby resources for the International Monetary Fund provided by ten leading industrial countries (now coming to be known as the Ten); and other cooperative actions based upon a readiness of other leading industrial countries to begin to share some of the responsibilities until now carried by the United States and its dollar.

Mr. Roosa sees new possible arrangements which might be needed and desirable as and if the Common Market adopts a unified monetary system and as the volume of world trade grows. Evolution of the market for Eurodollars, which except for limitations of space might have merited inclusion of another article in this book of readings, is only one example of new developments which are changing the pattern of international finance, affecting velocity of money, and influencing the need for liquidity. Evolutionary development of a new system building directly upon existing payments procedures is what Mr. Roosa advocates, rather than drastic changes which might disturb expectations in unanticipated ways and affect uncertainty—the key phenomenon in monetary theory and policy— in unpredictable directions.

In the present international financial climate, three familiar proposals are being widely discussed again on the grounds that they can assure the international liquidity that is necessary to absorb the shocks of any spreading disturbances:

Devaluation of the dollar by doubling or trebling the dollar price of gold.

"Guaranteeing" the dollar's present price so that other countries can readily go on accumulating more dollars to provide their needed increases in liquidity.

Immediate launching of plans for pooling all the international reserves of the Western World's monetary systems in a new supranational bank—usually visualized as one empowered to create additional supplies of a new international reserve currency that all subscribing countries would bind themselves to accept.

• From Robert V. Roosa, "Assuring the Free World's Liquidity," Federal Reserve Bank of Philadelphia, *Business Review, Supplement,* September, 1962, pp. 3–12. Reprinted by permission of the Federal Reserve Bank of Philadelphia and the author.

The latest expressions of support for these revolutionary approaches come at a time, perhaps surprisingly, when the United States, in cooperation with most of the other free industrial countries, is completing the groundwork for the most comprehensive restructuring of international liquidity arrangements since the founding of the International Monetary Fund at the end of World War II.

The paradox is understandable, for while the nature of practical monetary operations demands that they be established with the knowledge and the confidence of responsible financial officials in other countries, it is equally necessary that progress of this kind must initially evolve within a framework of confidential discussions and limited, step-by-step operations. There are grave risks of setting off disruptive speculation if there should be haphazard or uncoordinated release of information on any negotiations in process, or if new steps should be initiated or announced without preparation for cooperation by other affected countries.

That is why—although Treasury and Federal Reserve officials have been negotiating and designing and installing parts of the new structure for the past year and a half—it has not been possible in public discussion to make more than a few hinting references to the over-all pattern as a whole.

That is why some alert critics have, quite understandably, charged that those bits and pieces of the new machinery which were actually installed and publicly announced seemed to be only a patchwork improvisation of minor devices.

And that is also why, during the recent unsettlement over economic conditions here—coming before the United States had achieved the fundamental correction of its balance-of-payments position upon which the real strength of the dollar in the world depends—responsible observers have turned to the better-known, widely discussed proposals of earlier periods of unrest, instead of joining in an appraisal of the potentialities of the new design.

Fortunately, enough has now been accomplished to be able to put together a sketch, if not a blueprint, of the structure as a whole. Each of the pieces already in place has been reviewed and approved by President Kennedy; those which involved interpretations of existing legislative authority have been discussed in advance with the Chairmen of the respective Congressional Committees; some have required legislation, whch has either been obtained or is now before the Congress. Other steps are ahead, but they will need to be shaped by critical public discussion, just as all of the measures already taken will be adapted on the basis of the experience now being gained.

Even the steps already taken would seem, however, to remove most of the premises on which cases have been built in the past for devaluation, or guarantees, or a heroic new supranational organization. Appraisals in the future will have to take into account all of the new developments, as well as the vast array of new dangers that any one of these three other approaches would create. But before turning to the sketch of what is new—a sketch that can be filled out more fully before the end of this year as other still-confidential efforts mature—it should be helpful to restate briefly the problem implied by the wide-ranging consideration of international liquidity and to take a look at the way devaluation, or guarantees, or a super-bank might be expected to cope with such problems.

I

International liquidity is needed to service the regular flow of payments among countries, to finance the shortfall when any particular country's out-payments temporarily exceed its in-payments, and to meet large withdrawals caused by outflows of capital. The responsible financial officials of virtually all countries are agreed that aggregate monetary reserves on hand or mobilizable in the world today are adequate for regular payments and for temporary swings in needs. The three debatable questions are: (1) whether particular countries, notably the less developed, have access to enough reserves for their regular needs, that is, whether the distribution of existing reserves should be improved; (2) whether the emergency sources of liquidity, particularly in the event of runs on any of the larger countries, are adequate; and (3) whether existing facilities assure an adequate growth of total reserves for the future needs of an expanding world economy.

Devaluation, guarantees, and a super-bank are all proposed to answer, in one way or another, these three questions. Yet each would, in providing its answers, gravely alter important parts of the monetary system on which the world depends, and which everyone takes for granted today. The new convertible gold-dollar arrangements, however, build upon existing currencies and payments facilities; recognize the limitations upon monetary devices as solutions for fundamental economic problems (including those underlying the recent United States balance of payments deficits); and avoid the hazards of despair and economic disruption so likely to result from the displacement of the dollar as the universally recognized supplement and alternative to gold in meeting the international liquidity reserve needs of the world.

II

Raising the price of gold by devaluing the dollar would certainly be followed by similar action on the part of other countries. An increase in the gold price would thus not help the United States balance of payments. It would, however, mean writing up the gold reserves now held by any country, presumably providing a "profit" which would permit all countries, large and small, to start afresh with a feeling that, by the stroke of a pen (or a legislative act), they had become richer. Any present maldistribution would presumably seem less constricting with everyone suddenly better off; the greatest gainers might feel better able to lend reserves to those still in some need; total reserves would be so much greater that concern over future liquidity requirements would disappear; and the larger totals would provide fresh supplies of liquidity to meet any capital flight likely to occur—or so the argument goes.

But, in fact, devaluation of the dollar would, for practical purposes in the future, virtually destroy as much reserve liquidity as it might seem to create. For every holder of dollars before devaluation would have been tricked into heavy losses, losses as large as the gains would seem to be to those who had held gold instead. The possibility that the dollar could again serve, in any meaningful volume, as a usable part of general monetary reserves would disappear. In effect, the dollar holdings of other countries would thereafter be consumed, and the large part of world liquidity now represented by dollars would be gone. The world would be left without a major currency, generally acceptable as a supplement to gold. That is why most serious consideration of international monetary reform has long since dismissed devaluation of the dollar as a practical possibility, and has turned instead toward "guarantees," or the founding of a super-bank, or both.

III

The appeal of a dollar "guarantee" is that it presumably assures the world that devaluation will not occur. For the key provision of any generalized guarantee must be that all dollars held as monetary reserves would receive full compensation for all losses in the event of devaluation. The aim of such contractual assurances is, of course, to persuade the other countries of the world that they can readily go on accumulating more dollars without any risk of loss. If guarantees were in this way able to assure all needed increases in liquidity without any offsetting consequences, it would seem that they could fit in very well as simply another feature of the new structure being erected for the convertible gold-dollar system.

In that event, so the argument goes, any existing maldistribution of liquidity could be met through assistance from the United States, with no risk that the further shifting about of such reserves, following their use by the needy countries, would bring them into the hands of unwilling holders. With everyone made absolutely certain that dollars held in monetary reserves would be revalued in the event of changes in the United States gold price, quick negotiations might ensue for effecting a uniformity in the ratio between gold and dollars in the reserve of other countries. Presumably there might even be a major move to turn in gold and acquire additional dollars, on which interest might be earned. There would seem to be no problem then of assuring ample liquidity for the indefinite future; an increasing supply of dollars would always be acceptable to fulfill such needs. Moreover, there would never be reason to fear the effects of any sustained balance of payments deficit, or to be concerned if domestic developments in the United States caused investors to move large blocks of capital out to other countries—in any such circumstances, the United States could simply take it for granted that the additional supplies of dollars thus created would end up in the monetary reserves of other countries, who would be content to hold them because of the guarantee.

But this recital of the gains to be expected from the use of guarantees itself suggests that perhaps the prescription is too good to be true. Those who have become enthusiastic proponents of guarantees seem sometimes to forget that the strength of the signature on any guarantee depends upon sustained confidence in the credit worthiness of the signer.

Moreover, the highest credit standing—and a currency capable of supplying the monetary reserves of the world should scarcely aim for less—is that of the debtor whose net worth is so great, and whose performance is so reassuring, that supporting guarantees would never be offered or required. What this means, translated into the position of the United States as supplier of reserves for the world, is that we cannot escape a fundamental interdependence between the strength of our economy, our balance of payments, and the dollar.

The case for guarantees rests upon a contradiction: in giving a guarantee, the United States would expect to release its domestic economic performance in some measure from the constraints imposed by the need for balance of payments equilibrium; in accepting a guarantee, other countries would expect the United States to maintain their confidence in its internal and external economic performance; otherwise, the guarantee would not be granted or renewed. Thus the United States would, in relying upon guarantees, incur an obligation initially or eventually to engage in recurrent negotiations with country after country. The end result would be either disciplines or constraints upon our own economic policy which, at the very best, could be no different from those already apparent, and which might at the worst, become a complicated straitjacket of additional obligations, or the guarantee would be found unacceptable and all its supposed advantages would be lost.

Many countries today object to our balance of payments deficit, on the grounds that we are financing an aid and military effort which they could not afford, or would not willingly undertake, by foisting on them dollar deposits which they have no need to hold. Why should they, simply because they are offered a contractual guarantee, become implicit partners in underwriting programs that they themselves would reject? On the contrary, how much more likely may it be that one country after another will interpose conditions on its readiness to accept a guarantee—conditions that will at the least interpose their judgments more specifically into the determination of our military, aid, or investment activities abroad, or perhaps be made dependent upon our adopting their own formulas for achieving the needed further shrinkage of our over-all balance of payments deficit? And where would we find ourselves when the demands of one of our guaranteed creditors conflicted with those of another? How close might our position then seem to be to that of the debtor approaching receivership, with tier upon tier of first, second, and third mortgage claimants to satisfy? Rather than negotiate the relative priorities of such contractual liens, the United States might be better advised (as Chairman Martin recently intimated when asked about guarantees by the Joint Economic Committee) to give up altogether the obligations of maintaining a reserve currency for the rest of the free world.

There are many of the industrial countries, too, which fear any further substantial diversion of the resources of the International Monetary Fund into the financing of recurrent distress situations in many of the underdeveloped countries —distress situations which the affected countries customarily view in simple terms as a shortage of liquidity available to them. Can we expect these same critical industrial countries to accept more dollars, just because they carry a guarantee, if the dollars arise from continued or additional American effort to supplement the contributions being made by the International Monetary Fund toward these frequent "liquidity" requirements of the less developed countries?

Some part of the current movement of capital from the United States toward Europe is apparently induced by interest rate differentials that are somewhat higher than normal relationships would otherwise bring about. Will the monetary authorities of our countries be content to go on acquiring more and more short-term dollar liabilities, as the by-product of these capital movements, simply because their gold value is underwritten by a contractual guarantee? Or will they take advantage of the negotiations relating to the introduction of guarantees to lay down their own conditions with an impact at least as severe, perhaps considerably more so, than that now exerted?

Surely any responsible financial official in this country would expect to negotiate in exactly that manner, and to exact much more precise and limiting conditions, if we were being expected to rely on a guarantee of the gold value of any one other currency to provide a major part of our own international reserve needs. The financial officials of the other countries are neither more modest nor reluctant to exact conditions than we would be.

There is, in fact, no real escape, certainly not so long as we maintain a reserve currency for the world, from the kinds of limits upon our complete freedom of action which these various illustrations suggest. The one way to be assured of greater freedom is to achieve balance of payments equilibrium and, from time to time, a surplus in our own balance of payments. The effect of guarantees is, indeed, instead of creating greater freedom for us, to center all responsibility upon us. For those in the position of accepting guarantees are able to dictate their terms. If, instead, there can be a sharing, in some increasing degree, of the responsibilities now borne so largely by the dollar alone, the leeway remaining to use for independent action on our own initiative should broaden rather than shrink as expanding liquidity needs are met over the years ahead.

And in all of these reservations concerning the possible role of guarantees, there is another pervading theme which cannot be obscured. The United States abrogated a gold clause in contracts once; the action was supported by the Supreme Court and approved by joint resolution of Congress. What assurance can a mere guarantee provide again? Is not the real basis for any confidence to be found in the strength, performance, and credibility of the American economic and financial system, and only there?

IV

One great attraction of a super-central bank, or "an International Federal Reserve System," is that it would clearly provide for a mutual sharing of responsibilities by all of the countries of the world. Whether created out of the existing International Monetary Fund, or established as a completely new institution, its role would be to pool the reserve balances held by all countries, or at any rate all countries of the Free World. The deposits held in the super-bank could be transferable on its books, so that the resulting differences between inflows and outflows of any given country could be settled through a central clearing house. The dollar would no longer have any special role to perform as a reserve currency; that role would instead be shifted to some newly christened monetary unit of account, representing the deposit balances held at the super-bank.

While gold might still hold some attraction, and could be used as an alternative means of settling differences of accounts among countries, there would presumably be no essential role for gold in the system. Much of it might find its way into the vaults of the super-bank itself, or gradually disappear in industrial uses.

On the assumption that the total supply of reserves available at the super-bank could grow, and grow at a controlled rate that would preclude world-wide inflation and a reluctance to hold the reserve balances on deposit there, any long-run growth needs could be readily satisfied. The liquidity requirements of under-developed countries might be met through advances or loans extended to such countries by the super-bank itself. And any serious pressures on a given country, because its balance of payments was in grave deficit on trade account, or because capital was leaving the country in heavy volume, could also be met through loans and overdrafts on the books of the super-bank.

There are many variations and nuances and combinations of these several features which have been suggested in the writings of various proponents. But all such elaboration would represent a fruitless exercise if the basic premises on which the establishment of such a super-bank rests should prove unsupportable. That, perhaps regrettably, is the inescapable conclusion dictated by the actual ways of the world—today and for any foreseeable future.

The money created by a super-bank would be the most high-powered ever generated by a man-made institution, yet it would have no supporting super-government to make good on its debts or claims. Even with all the underlying resources of the richest nation on earth, the performance of the United States in providing additional reserves has been at times rather conspicuously called into question. And in our case, the world has the basic assurance that our performance will continue broadly to meet the tests of economic requirements because otherwise pressures can be exerted upon us through our own balance of payments. There will be no comparable assurance, and no comparable underlying strength in the new body. Instead reliance must be placed upon the conflicting interests represented in a multi-national legislative body, to judge and resolve conflicting demands for larger or smaller increases in the supply of the new monetary unit, or for a greater or lesser shifting of its lending power toward one group of countries or another.

Even accomplishment of the first steps would be an heroic achievement. Simply to establish the super-bank would require all countries of the world to give up their present reserves and accept instead the first issue of a super-authority existing without a super-state. But assuming that could be done, what would happen when differences of view begin to exercise conflicting pulls upon the central organization? So long as monetary systems within individual countries continue to be managed by men who think and act as bankers, one after another will begin to hedge his country's own position either by acquiring gold or by acquiring increasing holdings of one or more currencies of other countries in which he has confidence. And so long as trade continues among sovereign nations the opportunity to convert holdings of the super-bank's monetary unit into holdings of one currency or another will be available.

Thus it would be inescapable, so long as major differences in economic policy arise among different countries, that those differences will prevent the systematic direction of the super-bank on uniform and consistent lines. The outcome, if it is not utter chaos and impairment of normal payments transactions among nations, is likely instead to be a drifting back toward systems of reliance upon clusters of currencies, and dependence on the strength given to them by the economies which underlie them. The drift, if it is in that direction will indeed be back toward a system of arrangements very similar to that now evolving as part of the structure of the new convertible gold-dollar system.

V

The claims for this evolving convertible gold-dollar system are necessarily modest. The experience gained as step-by-step innovations are being put in place is providing ample evidence that workable arrangements depend fundamentally upon confidence rather than upon binding compacts—and confidence in monetary affairs, as in political or business life, is not attained once-for-all in a single negotiation, or a single declaration or compact, but is gained through continuing performance. Moreover, it has become irrefutably clear, if there was ever any doubt, that major initiatives cannot succeed unless the leading countries are prepared to support them by working toward equilibrium in their balance of payments accounts, whenever internal disturbances, outside events, or ordinary economic developments create other pressures away from balance.

Nonetheless, it already seems reasonably certain that the new structure being erected around the established gold-dollar system can make possible important additions to the liquidity of underdeveloped countries; can provide ample resources for promptly meeting heavy drains or a run on the currency of any leading industrial country, including the United States; and can assure the flexibility and growth in total liquidity needed to serve the requirements of trade in an expanding world economy for some years ahead.

Further potentialities may come into view as and if the Common Market becomes a unified monetary system, and forward planning for that eventuality may soon introduce a new dimension into the consideration of arrangements for international liquidity. But at least until that greater fusion of the Common Market countries occurs, the essence of the monetary system of the free world will no doubt continue to be the fixed relationship between gold and the dollar, with the United States standing ready to buy or sell gold at its established price of $35 per ounce. The principal source of increases in liquidity will continue to be the annual increments of gold to the monetary reserves of the world, supplemented from time to time by controlled increases in the dollars held by other countries as a part of their monetary reserves.

Standing astride the gold and dollar reserves of most countries of the world will be the International Monetary Fund, into which all member countries have contributed working balances of gold and their own currencies, in amounts related to their own quotas (or conditional "drawing rights") in the Fund. Surrounding the dollar is a constellation of special bilateral relationships between the dollar and the separate currencies of most of the other leading industrial countries. Surrounding the gold reserves is a set of relationships now largely worked out through the London gold market, but representing participation by the leading European central banks, known colloquially as the "Basle group" which now also includes the United States.

The innovations of the past year and a half have centered upon the resources and usability of the International Monetary Fund, upon the direct relations between the dollar and other leading currencies highlighted by our initiation of activity in the foreign exchange markets, and upon the special arrangements for influencing the flow of gold into the world's monetary reserves. Virtually all of the changes have represented, and resulted from, a growing readiness on the part of the other leading industrial countries to begin to consider, and cautiously to undertake, some sharing of the responsibilities formerly carried so largely by the dollar.

Comprehending and reinforcing all of the new arrangements are the various activities of the OECD, and more particularly, its working party devoted to balance of payments and financial problems. Here, the opportunity for continuous interchange of information and criticism, among the leading industrial countries, provides the base of communications needed to carry forward operations that require mutual understanding of current developments and current policies. At the same time, it is conceivable that work can go forward through this and other organs of the OECD toward preparing the way for the next stage of practicable and foreseeable innovation in the area of international financial arrangements— the fusing of the United Kingdom into the Common Market; the evolution of a unified financial mechanism to serve the expanded Common Market; and the forging of appropriate operating and policy links between that organization, once it emerges, and our own financial institutions.

Meanwhile, it would be quixotic to hope, however, that the new arrangements will solve the liquidity needs of the underdeveloped countries; for in a full sense, nothing can. So long as these countries are energetically pursuing development programs, any international reserves not actually required as current working balances will be consumed in the purchase of more imports. Mere increases in reserves, therefore, will largely disappear. The need of these countries is for some greater assurance concerning the markets and prices of the raw materials they sell; for as much aid as can effectively be absorbed from whichever industrial countries are able to provide it; and for emergency facilities to provide needed foreign exchange to bridge unexpected seasonal or cyclical reverses. None of these needs can be met simply through broad global action; all are the object of energetic further effort by the United States and various international bodies at the present time.

So far as aid is concerned, the activities of already existing international institutions are being reinforced through the establishment of consortia to attract, into each of the underdeveloped countries as programs are developed, additional funds from the more prosperous countries of Western Europe. And with respect to emergency requirements, joint action by the International Monetary Fund and interested outside governments (often accompanied by leading commercial banks) provides practical possibilities for the kind of emergency assistance that can be used without abuse.

The most prominent question currently, however, is whether the new arrangements of the convertible gold-dollar system, once established and understood, can provide a mobilization of reserves to meet sudden and heavy drains upon the dollar itself. So far as the precipitation of a run through pressures on the London gold market may be concerned, the Basle group has already achieved important results. Price changes are occurring only over a range wide enough to make speculation costly, and there is now a close, participating interest on the part of the principal European countries, as well as the United Kingdom and the United States, in the maintenance of orderly conditions there. To be sure, so long as nations and individuals are free to exercise choices, and so long as changes occur in the degree of confidence in the dollar or in other currencies, it will be impossible to escape pressures. The gain has come in curbing capricious or mere follow-the-leader raids upon the gold which serves the world's monetary reserve needs, and in sharing the responsibility for required action. Perhaps in an ideal world the interrelated monetary systems would function even better if private individuals were not allowed to own gold in any country, and if no London gold market existed. But for the world that we have, the present arrangements represent a marked change and improvement—a change which necessarily rests upon mutual and voluntary action based upon confidence.

In a somewhat comparable way, through reciprocal holdings of currencies, through engaging in forward transactions in currencies, and through the outright borrowing of dollars or of other currencies from foreign countries, the United States has developed arrangements to cushion or offset a substantial part of any disruptive short-term capital outflows, or to minimize the impact on our central gold reserve caused by shifts of monetary reserves from countries whose gold ratios are low to those whose gold ratios are high. To be sure, these arrangements, too, could not be worked out if other countries felt that the credit risks were great; that is, if their confidence should weaken in our ability and determination to regain the initiative in controlling our own balance of payments, and to maintain the freedom of our capital markets as well as the ready interchangeability between dollars and gold. Nothing has been done which has not reflected the combined judgment of both countries involved in every set of bilateral relationships. Given that basic approach, and the mutual confidence it implies, however, a new pattern of arrangements can provide an increasing measure of protection for the dollar against incipient developments that might otherwise grow into serious runs.

But for the eventuality that a run might actually occur, new arrangements have also been made. By providing additional standby resources for the International Monetary Fund, the ten leading industrial countries, whose actions will become effective as soon as the necessary legislation passes through the appropriations process in the American Congress, have made certain that adequate supplies of other currencies will be available to meet any needs that we might expect to face. So far as other countries are concerned, the recent mobilization of more than $1 billion within a forty-eight hour period to stop a raid on the Canadian dollar provides striking evidence of the flexibility, the speed, and the magnitude of the facilities now available. And it is interesting evidence of the results that Canada has already, even before its longer range program has been announced or implemented, regained within two months roughly two-thirds of all the reserves it had lost over the first six months of the year.

Looking further ahead, the new arrangements also are capable of providing for a steady growth in the monetary reserves needed to service the trade requirements of an expanding world. Dollars are still the currency to which all countries turn for a substantial part, if not the entire amount, of their international payments. Our financial institutions and our markets are increasingly well equipped to service the payments requirements of the world. It is a role which naturally accompanies our leading economic and political position. The only reason that the usefulness of the dollar has come into doubt is that, for some time, dollars have been added to the "money supply," i.e., the monetary reserves, of other countries at too fast a pace. That is because our balance of payments deficit was, in effect, creating reserve dollars for others, at a rate which outran the current requirements for liquidity in the world's monetary reserves. In those circumstances, just as occurs when money is created too rapidly inside any single country, renewal of the ready acceptability of the currency depends upon limiting further increases until the uses for that liquidity should have caught up.

Once the United States has its balance of payments fully under control, the rate of increase in the supply of dollars available to serve the international liquidity requirements in the world can also be managed. Whether or not there is a corresponding proportionate increase in the underlying supply of gold in the world's monetary reserves, additional increases in the supply of dollars can rest upon an accumulation by the United States of incremental amounts of the currencies of other leading countries. These other currencies, while not equally capable of serving the multitude of functions required of a reserve currency, can, as the United States acquires holdings of them, be brought into a further mutual sharing of some of the responsibilities which the international reserve system must itself carry.

What this may mean in the future in the way of additional consultation and negotiation with respect to the particular currencies so used, and the manner in which such currencies may cushion drains upon the dollar at particular times —serving in that respect as a substitute for drains upon the gold reserve itself— all remain to be worked out in the tests of day-by-day experience. But the structure of the new relationship has already been established. Its potential capabilities for meeting the world's longer run liquidity requirements are clearly at least as promising as any of the more familiar proposals. And its possibilities or practicable operation in everyday affairs are clearly much enhanced by the fact that the new system builds directly upon the existing payments procedures to which governments and individuals are already well accustomed. This would seem to be not only the most promising, but also the most reliable, pattern for new developments to follow.